Advanced Studies in Theoretical and Applied Econometrics

Volume 48

More information about this series at
http://www.springer.com/series/5667

Jan Beran • Yuanhua Feng • Hartmut Hebbel
Editors

Empirical Economic and Financial Research

Theory, Methods and Practice

Springer

Editors
Jan Beran
Dept. of Mathematics and Statistics
University of Konstanz
Konstanz
Germany

Yuanhua Feng
Faculty of Business Administration
and Economics
University of Paderborn
Paderborn
Germany

Hartmut Hebbel
Helmut Schmidt University
Hamburg
Germany

ISSN 1570-5811 Advanced Studies in Theoretical and Applied Econometrics
ISBN 978-3-319-03121-7 ISBN 978-3-319-03122-4 (eBook)
DOI 10.1007/978-3-319-03122-4
Springer Cham Heidelberg New York Dordrecht London

Library of Congress Control Number: 2014955150

JEL Classification: C21, C22, C23, C26, C32, C53, C58, C18

Printed on acid-free paper

Springer is part of Springer Science+Business Media (www.springer.com)

Festschrift in Honour of
Professor Siegfried Heiler

Foreword

During the last four decades Siegfried Heiler has had a great influence on the development of Statistics in Germany and on the international community. On the one hand, he has been an active researcher. On the other hand, he held leading positions in statistical societies.

Siegfried has a wide research spectrum. His main research interests are in the fields of time series analysis and robust statistics. In many cases his research was motivated by empirical problems of relevance and he introduced new statistical methods to deal with. One of the most important examples is the Berlin Method that is inter alia used by the German Federal Statistical Office.

Over a long period Siegfried was very active in the German Statistical Society. From 1980 to 1988 he was Chairman of the Section "Neuere Statistische Methoden" renamed as "Statistical Theory and Methodology". Moreover, he was President of the Society from 1988 to 1992. This was the time of the German reunification and as well an important time for the Society. During the board meeting in Konstanz on January 19, 1990 there was an intensive discussion about the opportunity to communicate with statisticians from the GDR. The integration and promotion of this group was also topic of the board meeting in Trier on June 6, 1990. Due to the difficult implementation of regulations of the Article 38 of the Unification Treaty referring to science and research the German Statistical Society decided a Memorandum on the Development of Statistics at the Universities of the new federal states at the end of 1991. "Statistik im vereinten Deutschland" was also the main topic of the Annual Meeting of the Society in Berlin in 1991.

Very early Siegfried detected the importance of computers for statistics and particularly raised this point. In his time as President of the Society he intensified the contacts with international statistical societies. After his term as President he was Vice-President of the German Statistical Society from 1992 to 1996. Moreover, Siegfried was a board member of the European Course in Advanced Statistics over many years and its President from 1994 to 1997.

Siegfried has done much for the German Statistical Society and we are deeply indebted to him for his numerous activities.

Happy Birthday, Siegfried!

Frankfurt, Germany
October 2013

Wolfgang Schmid

Editorial

This edited book on recent advances in empirical economic and financial research was proposed as a Festschrift for celebrating the 75th Birthday of Prof. (em.) Siegfried Heiler, Department of Mathematics and Statistics, University of Konstanz, Germany. The contributions are written by his former students, friends, colleagues and experts whose research interests are closely related to his work. We are grateful to all authors for submitting their work, which ensured that this issue reflects the state of the art in the area. Our special acknowledgements go to Prof. Walter Krämer, Department of Statistics at TU Dortmund, Germany, and the corresponding colleagues of Springer-Verlag for kindly agreeing to publish this book in the Series "Advanced Studies in Theoretical and Applied Econometrics", which is a very suitable host for the current issue.

We would also like to thank Prof. Dr. Roland Jeske, Faculty of Business Administration, University of Applied Sciences Kempten, Germany, and a few other former students of Siegfried Heiler, who have provided us with details on his academic career and other useful information. Their kind help allowed us to carry out this project smoothly while keeping it a secret until its publication on his birthday.

Finally, we would like to thank Mr. Christian Peitz and Ms. Sarah Forstinger, both in the Faculty of Business Administration and Economics, University of Paderborn, Germany, for their invaluable help in editing this book. Mr. Peitz took over most of the technical tasks and parts of the organization. Ms. Forstinger integrated all single submissions into an entire LaTex file and, in particular, helped to retype two submissions in Word format into LaTex.

Konstanz, Germany — Jan Beran
Paderborn, Germany — Yuanhua Feng
Hamburg, Germany — Hartmut Hebbel
October 2013

Contents

Part III New Econometric Approaches

List of Contributors

Klaus Abberger Swiss Economic Institute, Zurich, Switzerland

Héctor Allende Depto. de Informática, Universidad Técnica Federico Santa María, Valparaíso, Chile and Facultad de Ingeniería, Universidad Adolfo Ibáñez, Viña del Mar, Chile

Héctor Allende-Cid Depto. de Informática, Universidad Técnica Federico Santa María, Valparaíso, Chile

Brian D.O. Anderson Research School of Information Sciences and Engineering, Australian National University, Canberra, ACT, Australia

Walter Assenmacher Department of Economics, Chair for Statistics and Econometrics, University of Duisburg-Essen, Essen, Germany

Ana Laura Badagián Statistics Department, Universidad Carlos III de Madrid, Madrid, Spain

Oskar Maria Baksalary Faculty of Physics, Adam Mickiewicz University, Poznań, Poland

Jan Beran Department of Mathematics and Statistics, University of Konstanz, Konstanz, Germany

Michael Bruckner University of Applied Sciences Kempten, Kempten, Germany

Domingo Pérez Cañete Indra. External Collaboration with the Bank of Spain

Robert Czudaj Department of Economics, Chair for Econometrics, University of Duisburg-Essen, Essen, Germany and FOM Hochschule für Oekonomie & Management, University of Applied Sciences, Essen, Germany

Beatrix Dart Rotman School of Management, University of Toronto, Toronto, Canada, M5S 3E1

Catherine Dehon ECARES, Université libre de Bruxelles, Brussels, Belgium

Manfred Deistler Institut für Wirtschaftsmathematik, Technische Universität Wien, Wien, Austria

Rodolphe Desbordes University of Strathclyde, Glasgow, UK

Bärbel Elpelt-Hartung Department of Statistics, TU Dortmund University, Dortmund, Germany

Yuanhua Feng Faculty of Business Administration and Economics, University of Paderborn, Paderborn, Germany

David Findley U.S. Census Bureau, Washington, DC, USA

Sucharita Ghosh Statistics Lab, Swiss Federal Research Institute WSL, Birmensdorf, Switzerland

Liudas Giraitis Queen Mary, University of London, London, UK

Claudia Grote Faculty of Economics and Management, Institute of Statistics, Leibniz University Hannover, Hannover, Germany

Alfred Hamerle Faculty of Business and Economics, University of Regensburg, Regensburg, Germany

Joachim Hartung Department of Statistics, TU Dortmund University, Dortmund, Germany

Uwe Hassler Goethe-Universität Frankfurt, Frankfurt, Germany

Hartmut Hebbel Helmut Schmidt University, University of the Federal Armed Forces Hamburg, Hamburg, Germany

Mehdi Hosseinkouchack Goethe-Universität Frankfurt, Frankfurt, Germany

Roland Jeske University of Applied Sciences Kempten, Kempten, Germany

Regina Kaiser Statistics Department, Universidad Carlos III de Madrid, Madrid, Spain

George Kapetanios Queen Mary, University of London, London, UK

Guido Knapp Institute of Applied Stochastics and Operations Research, TU Clausthal, Clausthal-Zellerfeld, Germany

Roger Koenker Department of Economics, University of Illinois, Champaign, IL, USA

Wolf Krumbholz Helmut-Schmidt-Universität/Universität der Bundeswehr Hamburg, Hamburg, Germany

Helmut Lütkepohl DIW Berlin and Freie Universität Berlin, Berlin, Germany

Mohaimen Mansur Queen Mary, University of London, London, UK

Agustín Maravall Research Department, Bank of Spain, Alcalá, Madrid, Spain

Tucker McElroy U.S. Census Bureau, Washington, DC, USA

Paul Michels University of Applied Sciences, Weidenbach, Germany

Pin T. Ng Frake College of Business, Northern Arizona University, Flagstaff, AZ, USA

Wolfgang Nierhaus Ifo Institute for Economic Research at the University of Munich, Munich, Germany

Osbert Pang U.S. Census Bureau, Washington, DC, USA

Roberto López Pavón Indra. External Collaboration with the Bank of Spain

Christian Peitz Faculty of Business Administration and Economics, University of Paderborn, Paderborn, Germany

Daniel Peña Statistics Department, Universidad Carlos III de Madrid, Madrid, Spain

Peter Pflaumer University of Applied Sciences Kempten, Kempten, Germany

Simon Price Bank of England, London, UK and City University, London, UK

Gerd Ronning Faculty of Economics and Social Sciences, University of Tübingen, Mohlstrasse, Tübingen, Germany

Alexander Samarov Massachusetts Institute of Technology, Cambridge, MA, USA

Gunther Schauberger Department of Statistics, LMU Munich, München, Germany

Christian Scherr Risk Research Prof. Hamerle GmbH & Co. KG, Regensburg, Germany

Wolfgang Scherrer Institut für Wirtschaftsmathematik, Technische Universität Wien, Wien, Austria

Rainer Schlittgen Institute of Statistics and Econometrics, University of Hamburg, Hamburg, Germany

Matthias Schmid Department of Statistics, University of Munich, Münich, Germany

Hans Schneeweiss Department of Statistics, University of Munich, Münich, Germany

Philipp Sibbertsen Faculty of Economics and Management, Institute of Statistics, Leibniz University Hannover, Hannover, Germany

James L. Smith Cox School of Business, Southern Methodist University, Dallas, TX, USA

Ingo Starke Helmut-Schmidt-Universität/Universität der Bundeswehr Hamburg, Hamburg, Germany

Detlef Steuer Helmut Schmidt University, University of the Federal Armed Forces Hamburg, Hamburg, Germany

Götz Trenkler Faculty of Statistics, Dortmund University of Technology, Dortmund, Germany

Gerhard Tutz Department of Statistics, LMU Munich, München, Germany

Gustavo Ulloa Depto. de Informática, Universidad Técnica Federico Santa María, Valparaíso, Chile

Vincenzo Verardi CRED, Université de Namur, Namur, Belgium

Peter-Th. Wilrich Institut für Statistik und Ökonometrie, Freie Universität Berlin, Berlin, Germany

Introduction

Jan Beran, Yuanhua Feng and Hartmut Hebbel

This edited volume consists of 30 original contributions in the two closely related research areas of empirical economic research and empirical financial research. Empirical economic research, also called empirical economics, is an important traditional sub-discipline of economics. The research activities in this area are particularly reflected by the journal "Empirical Economics" published by Springer-Verlag since 1976, and by the parallel series "Studies in Empirical Economics," which consists of 21 volumes published from 1989 to 2009 on different topics in this area. In recent years research in empirical economics has experienced another booming phase due to easy availability of very large data sets and the fast increase of computer power. This trend is reflected by the fact that the Econometric Society has published a new journal in quantitative/empirical economics, called "Quantitative Economics," since 2010. Stevenson and Wolfers (2012) note that the research in economics after the global financial crisis in 2008 is showing "a long-running shift toward a more empirical field, to the study of what hard data can tell us about the way the world really works." On the other hand, empirical financial research, also called empirical finance, has a relatively short tradition but the development in this area seems to be even faster than that of empirical economics, because, as indicated

J. Beran
Department of Mathematics and Statistics, University of Konstanz, Konstanz, Germany
e-mail: jan.beran@uni-konstanz.de

Y. Feng (✉)
Faculty of Business Administration and Economics, University of Paderborn, Paderborn, Germany
e-mail: yuanhua.feng@wiwi.upb.de

H. Hebbel
Helmut Schmidt University, University of the Federal Armed Forces Hamburg, 22043 Hamburg, Germany
e-mail: hartmut.hebbel@hsu-hh.de

J. Beran et al. (eds.), *Empirical Economic and Financial Research*,
Advanced Studies in Theoretical and Applied Econometrics 48,
DOI 10.1007/978-3-319-03122-4_1

by Campbell et al. (1996), "Financial economics is a highly empirical discipline, perhaps the most empirical among the branches of economics ... ... for financial markets are not mere figments of theoretical abstraction." The rapidly growing research in empirical finance is of course also pushed by the empirical success of ARCH (autoregressive conditional heteroskedasticity, Engle, 1982), GARCH (generalized ARCH, Bollerslev, 1986) and SV (stochastic volatility) models (Taylor, 1986), and a huge number of extensions with a wide range of applications in financial research. A detailed review in this context may be found, for instance, in Andersen and Bollerslev (1998). No doubt, empirical economic and financial research are closely related disciplines. Firstly, there is a clear overlap between statistical and econometric methods employed in both areas. Secondly, sometimes topics from the two disciplines are or must be studied together. This is in particular true when the impact of financial markets on economy is considered or when the economic sources of financial market volatility are studied. See, e.g., the recent study of Engle et al. (2008) on the latter topic. From a general point of view, finance can also be viewed as a sub-discipline of economics and hence empirical finance can be understood as a sub-area of empirical economics.

As an edited volume in honor of the 75th birthday of Siegfried Heiler, the selected subject areas reflect the broad range of his research. He worked on different topics of empirical economics since the late 1960s. One of his main areas was the analysis of macroeconomic time series. The Berlin Method (BV, Berliner Verfahren, Heiler, 1969, 1970) and further extended versions (Heiler, 1976, 1977) have become standard methods of the German Federal Statistical Office since the early 1970s for calculating major business-cycle indicators. Its fourth version (BV4) is used by the German Federal Statistical Office since 1983 (see Heiler and Michels, 1994; Speth, 2006 and references therein), and also by the DIW-Berlin (German Institute for Economic Research) and other institutes involved in empirical economic research. Since then, further improvements of the BV have been worked out by Heiler and his students. For instance, optimal decomposition of seasonal time series using spline-functions is discussed by Hebbel and Heiler (1978, 1987a), smoothing of time series in an error-in-variables model was studied by Hebbel and Heiler (1985), decomposition of seasonal time series based on polynomial and trigonometric functions is proposed in Hebbel and Heiler (1987b). Also a generalized BV has been developed (see the next chapter for a detailed description and applications). The application of local regression with polynomials and trigonometric functions as local regressors is discussed in Heiler and Michels (1994), algorithms for selecting the bandwidth based on this approach are developed in Heiler and Feng (1996, 2000) and Feng and Heiler (2000). Other significant contributions include robust estimation of ARMA models (Allende and Heiler, 1992; Heiler, 1990) and related topics in economic time series analysis.

Since the early 1990s, Prof. Heiler's research focused on further developments of nonparametric time series analysis, solving in particular the crucial problem of bandwidth selection (see Heiler, 2001 for an overview). New algorithms for bandwidth selection in nonparametric regression are published in Heiler and Feng (1998), Beran et al. (2009), and Feng and Heiler (2009). Nonparametric time series models for empirical financial research may be found in Abberger et al. (1998), Abberger and Heiler (2001, 2002), and Feng and Heiler (1998). Another area Prof. Heiler was involved in is environmental statistics. Results in this context are summarized, for instance, in Hebbel and Heiler (1988) and Heiler and Michels (1986, 1989) (also see his contribution in Ghosh et al., 2007). In the early years of his academic career, he also worked on some research topics in demography (Heiler, 1978, 1982). At that time, Heiler (1978) already indicated possible effects of the decline in the birthrate on the future of the German social security system.

The contributions to this volume are divided into three parts: (1) Empirical Economic Research; (2) Empirical Financial Research; (3) New Econometric Approaches. The first part, chapters "Decomposition of Time Series Using the Generalised Berlin Method (VBV)" through "The Precision of Binary Measurement Methods", consists of methods most suitable for empirical research in economics. Properties of the methods are discussed and applications are illustrated by real data examples. This part also includes two case studies to show how a project in empirical economics can be carried out using existing methods in the literature. In the second part, chapters "On EFARIMA and ESEMIFAR Models" through "Zillmer's Population Model: Theory and Application", different new models with a clear emphasis on applications in empirical financial research are introduced. Their theoretical properties and practical implementation are discussed in detail, together with applications to real financial data. A case study on the development of a currency crises monitoring system is also included. Finally, the third part, chapters "Adaptive Estimation of Regression Parameters for the Gaussian Scale Mixture Model" through "On a Craig–Sakamoto Theorem for Orthogonal Projectors", consists of general contributions to econometric and statistical methodology. Here the emphasis is on the discussion of theoretical properties. In some contributions theoretical results are confirmed by simulation studies.

The topics in the three parts are closely related to each other. Some contributions may be logically allocated to more than one part. Moreover, topics in environmental statistics and demography are also involved in some of the contributions, but these are not indicated separately. From the methodological perspective the contributions cover a wide range of econometric and statistical tools, including uni- and multivariate time series analysis, different forecasting methods, new models for volatility, correlations and high-frequency financial data, approaches in quantile regression, panel data analysis, instrument variables, and errors in variables models. The methodological characteristic was not a criterion for the allocation to Parts I, II, and III. Hence, contributions to specific statistical methods may occur in any of the three parts. Within each part, the contributions are, as far as possible, arranged following a methodological structure. In Part I the contributions are given in the following order (1) time series; (2) panel data; (3) other topics. Contributions in the second part are arranged in the sequence (1) univariate time series; (2) multivariate time series; (3) other financial data. The third part follows the sequence (1) cross-sectional data; (2) univariate time series; (3) multivariate time series; and (4) general econometric and statistical methods.

This book covers theory, methods, and applications of empirical economic and financial research. The purpose is to establish a connection between the well-developed area of empirical economic research and the emerging area of empirical financial research, and to build a bridge between theoretical developments in both areas and their application in practice. Most of the contributions in this book are originally published here. The book is a suitable reference for researchers, practitioners, and graduate and post-graduate students, and provides reading for advanced seminars in empirical economic and financial research.

References

[Part 1:] Common References

Andersen, T. G., & Bollerslev, T. (1998). Answering the skeptics: Yes, standard volatility models do provide accurate forecasts. *International Economic Review, 39*, 885–905.

Bollerslev, T. (1986). Generalized autoregressive conditional heteroskedasticity. *Journal of Econometrics, 31*, 307–327.

Campbell, J. Y., Lo, A. W., & MacKinlay, A. C. (1996). *The econometrics of financial markets*. Princeton: Princeton University Press.

Engle, R. F. (1982). Autoregressive conditional heteroskedasticity with estimates of the variance of United Kingdom. *Econometrica, 50*, 987–1007.

Engle, R. F., Ghysels, E., & Sohn, B. (2008). *On the economic sources of stock market volatility*. AFA 2008 New Orleans Meetings Paper.

Speth, H.-Th. (2006). *The BV4.1 procedure for decomposing and seasonally adjusting economic time series*. Wiesbaden: German Federal Statistical Office.

Stevenson, B., & Wolfers, J. (2012). Business is booming in empirical economics. *Opinion in Bloomberg*, August 6, 2012.

Taylor, S. J. (1986). *Modelling financial time series*. Chichester: Wiley.

[Part 2:] Selected Publications of Prof. Heiler Cited in this Chapter

Abberger, K., Feng, Y., & Heiler, S. (1998). Nonparametric smoothing and quantile estimation in time series. In G. Bol, G. Nakhaeizadeh, & K.-H. Vollmer (Eds.), *Risk measurement, econometrics and neural networks* (pp. 1–16). Heidelberg: Physica.

Abberger, K., & Heiler, S. (2001). Nonparametric quantile regression with application to stock returns. In J. Kunert & G. Trenkler (Eds.), *Mathematical statistics and biometrical applications*. Festschrift für Siegfried Schach. Lohmar: Josef Eul.

Abberger, K., & Heiler, S. (2002). Nonparametric quantile regression with applications to financial time series. In Y. Dodge (Ed.), *Statistical data analysis based on the L_1 norm and related methods* (pp. 149–160). Basel: Birkhäuser.

Allende, H., & Heiler, S. (1992). Recursive generalized M-estimates for ARMA-models. *Journal of Time Series Analysis, 13*, 1–18.

Beran, J., Feng, Y., & Heiler, S. (2009). Modifying the double smoothing bandwidth selector in nonparametric regression. *Statistical Methodology, 6*, 447–465.

Feng, Y., & Heiler, S. (1998). Locally weighted autoregression. In R. Galata & H. Küchenhoff (Eds.), *Econometrics in theory and practice*. Festschrift für Hans Schneeweiß (pp. 101–117). Heidelberg: Physica

Feng, Y., & Heiler, S. (2000, October). Eine datengesteuerte robuste Version des Berliner Verfahrens. *Wirtschaft und Statistik*, 10/2000, 786–795.

Feng, Y., & Heiler, S. (2009). A simple bootstrap bandwidth selector for local polynomial fitting. *Journal of Statistical Computation and Simulation*, *79*, 1425–1439.

Ghosh, S., Beran, J., Heiler, S., Percival, D., & Tinner, W. (2007). Memory, non-stationarity and trend: analysis of environmental time series. In F. Kienast, O. Wildi, & S. Ghosh (Eds.), *A changing world: Challenges for landscape research* (pp. 223–247). Netherlands: Springer.

Hebbel, H., & Heiler, S. (1978). Die Verwendung von Spline-Funktionen bei der Schätzung-von Spektraldichten. In K.-A. Schäffer (Ed.), *Splinefunktionen in der Statistik. Allgemeines Statistisches Archiv, Special Issue, 14*, 66–85.

Hebbel, H., & Heiler, S. (1985). Zeitreihenglättung in einem Fehler-in-den-Variablen-Modell. In G. Buttler, et al. (Eds), *Statistik zwischen Theorie und Praxis. Festschrift in Honour of K.-A. Schäffer* (pp. 105–117). Göttingen: Vandenhoeck & Ruprecht.

Hebbel, H., & Heiler, S. (1987a). Zeitreihenzerlegung über ein Optimalitätskriterium. *Allgemeines Statistisches Archiv*, *71*, 305–318.

Hebbel, H., & Heiler, S. (1987b). Trend and seasonal decomposition in discrete time. *Statistical Papers*, *28*, 133–158.

Hebbel, H., & Heiler, S. (1988). Statistische Analyse von Wassergütedaten. *Allgemeines Statistisches Archiv*, *72*, 24–39.

Heiler, S. (1969). Überlegungen zu einem statistischen Modell einer wirtschaftlichen Zeitreihe und einem daraus resultierenden Analyseverfahren. In B. Nullau, S. Heiler, P. Wäsch, B. Meisner, & D. Filip (Eds.), *"Das Berliner Verfahren" - Ein Beitrag zur Zeitreihenanalyse. DIW-Beiträge zur Strukturforschung* (Vol. 7, pp. 19–43). Berlin: Duncker & Humblot.

Heiler, S. (1970). Theoretische Grundlagen des "Berliner Verfahrens". In W. Wetzel (Ed.), *Neuere Entwicklungen auf dem Gebiet der Zeitreihenanalyse. Allgemeines Statistisches Archiv, Special Issue 1*, 67–93.

Heiler, S. (1976). Entwurf kausaler Filter zur Analyse ökonomischer Zeitreihen bei Vorschriften imFrequenzbereich. In K.-A. Schäffer (Ed.), *Beiträge zur Zeitreihenanalyse. Allgemeines Statistisches Archiv, Special Issue 9*, 7–33.

Heiler, S. (1977). Some recent developments in the analysis of component models for economic time series. *Statistische Hefte*, *18*, 154–180.

Heiler, S. (1978). Der Geburtenrückgang in der Bundesrepublik und seine Auswirkungen. Research Report. Department of Statistics, University of Dortmund.

Heiler, S. (1982). Die Verwendung von Zeitreihenverfahren und Verzweigungsprozessen zur Bevölkerungsvorhersage. In W. Piesch & W. Förster (Eds.), *Angewandte Statistik und Wirtschaftsforschung heute* (pp. 66–75). Göttingen: Vandenhoeck & Ruprecht.

Heiler, S. (1990). Robust estimation of ARMA-models. *Journal of Computing and Information*, *1*, 81–90.

Heiler, S. (2001). Nonparametric time series analysis: Nonparametric regression, locally weighted regression, autoregression, and quantile regression. In D. Peña, G. C. Tiao, & R. S. Tsay (Eds.), *A course in time series analysis* (pp. 308–347). New York: Wiley.

Heiler, S., & Feng, Y. (1996). Datengesteuerte Zerlegung saisonaler Zeitreihen. *IFO Studien: Zeitschrift für empirische Wirtschaftsforschung*, *42*, 337–369.

Heiler, S., & Feng, Y. (1998). A simple root n bandwidth selector for nonparametric regression. *Journal of Nonparametric Statistics*, *9*, 1–21.

Heiler, S., & Feng, Y. (2000). Data-driven decomposition of seasonal time series. *Journal of Statistical Planning and Inference*, *91*, 351–363.

Heiler, S., & Michels, P. (1986). FLUKON-Programm zur laufenden Kontrolle halbstündiger Meßwerte für Sauerstoffgehalt, pH-Wert, Leitfähigkeit und Wassertemperatur der Leine. Discussion Paper, University of Dortmund.
Heiler, S., & Michels, P. (1989). Die Wasserführung eines Flusses - Statistische Modellierungsversuche. Discussion Paper. University of Konstanz.
Heiler, S., & Michels, P. (1994). *Deskriptive und Explorative Datenanalyse*. München: Oldenbourg.

Part I
Empirical Economic Research

Decomposition of Time Series Using the Generalised Berlin Method (VBV)

Hartmut Hebbel and Detlef Steuer

Abstract The Generalised Berlin Method (Verallgemeinertes Berliner Verfahren, or VBV) is a flexible procedure to extract multiple unobservable components from a discrete or continuous time series. The finite number of observations doesn't have to be equidistant. For economic time series (mostly monthly or quarterly data) the interesting components are trend (economic cycle) and season. For financial data (daily, hourly, or even higher frequency data) two components are of interest: a long-time component (length of support, i.e. 201 observations) and a short-time component (length of support, i.e. 41–61 observations). The VBV has control parameters to result in components satisfying subjective preferences in the shape of these components. In a special case the solutions coincide with the known Berlin Method (Berliner Verfahren, or BV) in its base version.

1 Introduction

The decomposition of time series (particularly economic) in various components or their seasonal adjustment has a century long tradition. A large number of methods and procedures were developed to handle these problems. As examples for such methods and procedures a few shall be named: Census I, Census II, its variant Census X-11, X-11-ARIMA, X-12-ARIMA (starting 1997) and X-13-ARIMA-SEATS (starting 2006) in combination with RegARIMA and TRAMO (Time series Regression with ARIMA noise, Missing values and Outliers) or SEATS (Signal Extraction in ARIMA Time Series) program, see, for example, Shiskin et al. (1967), Dagum (1980), Findley et al. (1998), Deutsche Bundesbank (1999), Ladiray and Quenneville (2001), U.S. Census Bureau and Time Series Research Staff (2013), Bell (1998), Gómez and Maravall (1998).

Another method belonging to this group of procedures, which were defined initially by a series of algorithmic steps and later on translated into a model-based

H. Hebbel (✉) • D. Steuer
Helmut Schmidt University, University of the Federal Armed Forces Hamburg, 22043 Hamburg, Germany
e-mail: hartmut.hebbel@hsu-hh.de; detlef.steuer@hsu-hh.de

J. Beran et al. (eds.), *Empirical Economic and Financial Research*,
Advanced Studies in Theoretical and Applied Econometrics 48,
DOI 10.1007/978-3-319-03122-4_2

approach is SABL (Seasonal Adjustment at Bell Laboratories, see Cleveland et al. 1982).

Other exemplary methods are the Berliner Verfahren developed by Heiler in its recent version BV 4.1 (see Nullau et al. 1969; Speth 2006) and the robust, data-driven method of the Berliner Verfahren (Heiler and Feng 2004), further DAINTIES, developed by the European Commission 1997 as a tool to harmonise methods across the EU.

Furthermore worth to be noted are the model-based time discrete procedures by Schlicht (1976), Pauly and Schlicht (1983), BAYSEA of Akaike (cf. Akaike 1980 and Akaike and Ishiguro 1980), the generalisation of Hebbel and Heiler (1987), DECOMP (see Kitagawa 1985) and the software package STAMP (Structural Time Series Analyser, Modeller and Predictor) (see Koopman et al. 2010) in version 9 in 2013.

We can only start to list the vast amount of relevant literature about seasonal adjustment, see, e.g., Foldesi et al. (2007) or Edel et al. (1997) for a more complete overview. All methods and procedures were discussed extensively and controversial. Main points in these discussions were, if an approach in the time domain or in the frequency should be chosen, if the components are smooth enough or flexible enough for the respective application (see Statistisches Bundesamt 2013) or if seasonal adjustment or a decomposition of a time series is the goal.

This paper summarises the theory of the generalised Berliner Verfahren and its transfer to practical applications. VBV is a flexible method to decompose continuous or discrete time series of all kinds in various components. During talks and discussions in various working sessions and conferences with a multitude of different institutions (Statistisches Bundesamt, Deutsche Bundesbank, economical research institutes, environment agencies, partners in industry, universities) four important goals for a decomposition method arose.

First a method is sought which works fully automatic to handle even huge amounts of time series without manual intervention for tuning.

Second the method should work even with continuous variables observed at non-equidistant points in time *(missing data, irregular grid)*. Such behaviour is found in particular in environmental or technical time series.

Third the method should find its foundation in a plausible model *(demand for model)*. That way a discussion may be transferred to the domain of model selection. After selecting a proper model the method will result in reproducible outcomes concerning the parameters defining the model.

Fourth an implementation of the method as a usable computer program is required. Otherwise such a method wont be applied in practise *(demand for implementation)*.

While economic time series are defined by sampling some variable on a regular time grid (daily, weekly, monthly, quarterly) and consequently missing data are very rare, in technical settings measurements are often performed without relying on a regular time grid. Those time series are continuous by nature but often will only be observed on an irregular time grid. So most of the data in these series are missing, particularly all data in between two measurements.

The generalised Berlin Method (VBV), developed in the early 1980s, which is based on polynomial and trigonometric splines, see Hebbel (1982), approximately fulfils all those four requirements for a well-behaving method.

The idea to use spline functions for analysing time series was invented by Heiler. The name was motivated by Söll of the Statistisches Bundesamt Wiesbaden when it could be shown that the base version of the Berliner Verfahren IV, used by the Statistisches Bundesamt until the EU harmonised approaches throughout its member states, is a special case of VBV.

Finally this article aims for giving a complete and comprehensive presentation of VBV. Afterwards own experiments with VBV and modifications of VBV will be possible without too much effort. There are of course a lot of papers on decomposing time series using splines, e.g. Bieckmann (1987), Hebbel (1978, 1981, 1984, 1997), Hebbel and Heiler (1985, 1987), Hebbel and Kuhlmeyer (1983), but these mostly focused on a common smoothness parameter for trend and season. Furthermore some of these papers discuss the topic on an abstract level in some general Hilbert- or Banach-spaces only to derive the application as special case for some well-chosen function space. Only in 1997 the decomposition using two smoothness parameters for trend and season in some relevant function space was introduced. A general solution was given there, but no further research was conducted.

VBV also is very capable to do chart analysis on finance data. Usual chart analysis uses moving averages over (in most cases) 200 days, sometimes 30, 40, or 90 days, which are then identified with the current observation, not, as statistical theory would expect, with the mid-interval observation, seems plain wrong. In the same way all the different support lines and formations are missing a theoretical foundation. Most importantly classical chart technique is unable to give reliable results for the latest observations (direction of trend, change in trend). All these shortcomings are overcome by VBV if adequately used for time series of finance data.

In other domains VBV already found its applications, e.g. in water quality measurement, cf. Uhlig and Kuhbier (2001a,b), or in dendrology, cf. Heuer (1991).

2 Components and Base Model

For economic time series it is common to assume six different components: long-term development (trend), long-term cycles of trend (economic cycle), seasonal differences around the trend-cycles (season), calendar effects, an inexplicable rest and some extreme values and outliers, cf. Heiler and Michels (1994, pp. 331 ff). Those components are not observable directly.

2.1 Components of an Econometric Time Series

Trend Trend is explained by effects which change only slowly and continuously. Examples for such a long-term effect are slow changes in population or improvements in productivity.

Economic Cycle Economic cycle names the medium-term up and down movement of economic life. The phenomenons which are described by the whole multitude of the theory of the economic cycle show themselves as multi-year, not repeating fluctuations around the trend figure. The periods for these fluctuations are between 2 and 12 years, mostly 5–7 years.

Season All (nearly) regular periodic fluctuations with periods below 1 year (one base period) are called seasonal effects or season. The cause of these seasonal effects is mostly natural or institutional influences which unfold cyclically. Most important is the earth moving around the sun in 365.25 days. As is well known this period shows up in all kinds of natural variables like temperature, daily sunshine duration, rainfall, etc. Equally well known is the 24 h day–night sequence showing up in a lot of mostly ecological time series. More seldom the moon cycle shows up in data, i.e. the tides. Institutional causes contain regular dates, e.g. quarterly, tax or interest dates.

Calender Effects There are effects caused by the structure of the used calendar. Months have different lengths, the number of working days changes from month to month, holidays, etc. Sometimes a correction for these effects is possible. A simple factor may be enough to correct for different month lengths or number of working days. Nowadays these corrections are harder to perform, because working weekends or clerical holidays is much more common.

Rest The rest component subsumes all irregular movements, which are caused by inexplicable causes and do not work constantly in one direction. Most important are short-lived, unexpected influences and variances like special weather conditions, errors in the data collection processes, measurement errors and/or erroneous reactions.

Extreme Values, Outliers Relevant irregular discrepancies caused by extraordinary, often one-time events are called extreme values or outliers. Some examples are strikes, catastrophes or unexpected political changes. We differentiate between:

- Additive outliers: In one isolated point in time we see one value completely out of line with usual measurements.
- Innovative outliers: At some point in time a relevant change in the data generating systems happens. Possible results are level changes which slowly return to the old level, or which stay on the new level, or a change that defines a slowly increasing deviation from the old data structure to something different ("crash").

There is an additional problem if there are outliers in more or less regular distances. These may be caused by repeating events like fairs or holidays.

2.2 *Components of the Decomposition Model*

What is described in the following for economic time series is easily transferred into other domains by changing the natural base period length of a "season". The length of the base period helps to distinguish between trend (long-term) and (economic) cycle (medium-term).

We have to note that trend does not necessarily mean trend line. This often leads to discussions after analysis. Therefore it is strongly recommended to discuss these notions beforehand.

VBV assumes an additive composition of preferable three components in the variable under investigation. If the composition is multiplicative, the logarithm must be applied first.

2.2.1 Trend-Cycle (Short: Trend)

Often there are arguments against a strict distinction between trend and economic cycle. Such a distinction would only seem appropriate, if there were different sets of variables influencing trend and cycle. That is normally not the case. Therefore these two components, the long-term and the medium-term economic variations, are consolidated into one *smooth component*. In this paper the term smooth component is used in the context of smoothing a time series and is therefore reserved for a combined component of trend and season. Trend and cycle are one component in the following description. That component may contain singular innovative outliers. Splitting the component further would easily possible, cf. Michel (2008). Note that level changes remain in this component. So we call that combined variable in the following *trend* and it contains the mid-term and long-term course of a time series.

2.2.2 Season-Calendar (Short: Season)

For the above noted difficulties in identifying calendar components the Statistisches Bundesamt refrains from splitting the two components for some time already. We do alike in this paper. Additionally this combined component may contain cyclical innovative outliers. This way it is allowed that the pattern we simply call season is irregular and varying from one period to the next. This does not hinder splitting a calendar component afterwards if needed.

2.2.3 Rest- and Extreme Values (Short: Rest)

The third component is called rest for the sake of simplicity. It contains all irregular movements and all additive outliers. If a model looks sensitive against such outliers either the extreme values have to be removed before analysis or a robust approach of the model should be used, which doesn't require explicit removal of extreme values.

2.3 *Base Model*

Based on the above discussion a time series $x(t)$ with possibly continuous time index t in an interval $[a,b]$ will be analysed and additively decomposed in the unobservable important and interpretable components trend (and economic cycle) $x_1(t)$ and season (and calendar) $x_2(t)$. The rest $u(t)$ contains the unimportant, irregular unobservable parts, maybe containing additive outliers.

An "ideal" trend $\tilde{x}_1(t)$ is represented by a polynomial of given degree $p-1$ and an "ideal" season $\tilde{x}_2(t)$ is represented by a linear combination of trigonometric functions of chosen frequencies (found by exploration) $\omega_j = 2\pi/S_j$ with $S_j = S/n_j$ and $n_j \in \mathbb{N}$ for $j = 1,\ldots,q$. Here S is the known base period and S_j leads to selected harmonics, which can be defined by Fourier analysis.

Therefore holds

$$\tilde{x}_1(t) = \sum_{j=0}^{p-1} a_j t^j \quad \text{and} \quad \tilde{x}_2(t) = \sum_{j=1}^{q} (b_{1j} \cos \omega_j t + b_{2j} \sin \omega_j t), \quad t \in [a,b].$$

In applications the components $x_1(t)$ and $x_2(t)$ won't exist in ideal representation. They will be additively superimposed by random disturbances $u_1(t)$ and $u_2(t)$. Only at some points in time $t_1,\ldots,t_n$ in the time interval $[a,b]$ the sum $x(t)$ of components is observable, maybe flawed by further additive errors $\varepsilon_1,\ldots,\varepsilon_n$. The respective measurements are called $y_1,\ldots,y_n$.

Now we have following base model

$$\begin{aligned} x_1(t) &= \tilde{x}_1(t) + u_1(t) \\ x_2(t) &= \tilde{x}_2(t) + u_2(t) \end{aligned} \qquad t \in [a,b] \qquad \text{state equation}$$

$$y_k = x_1(t_k) + x_2(t_k) + \varepsilon_k\,, \quad k = 1,\ldots,n \qquad \text{observation equation}\,,$$

cf. Fig. 1.

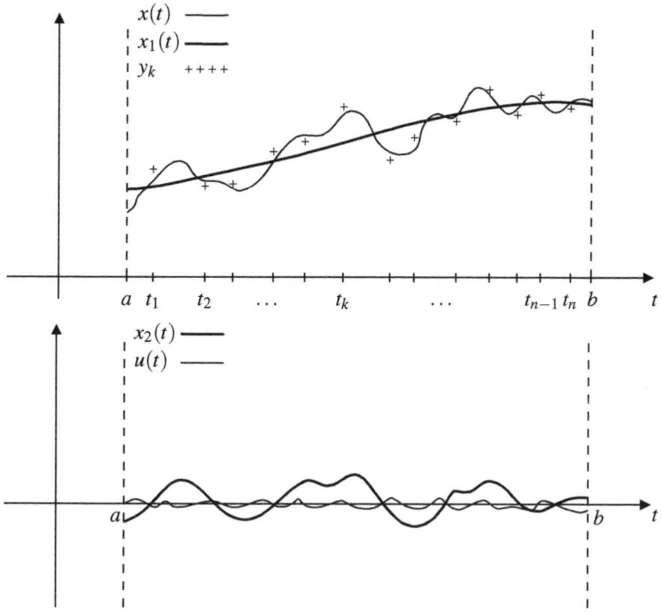

Fig. 1 Unknown original series $x(t)$, trend $x_1(t)$, seasonal component $x_2(t)$, rest $u(t)$ and observations y_k

3 Estimation Principle and Solutions

We are looking for appropriate estimations $\hat{x}_1(t)$, $\hat{x}_2(t)$ for unobservable components $x_1(t)$, $x_2(t)$ for all points in time in the interval $[a, b]$ not only at the observation points $t_1, \ldots, t_n$. The solution for the trend component $\hat{x}_1(t)$ shall replicate the medium and long-term course of the time series without being too smooth or too "rough". The seasonal estimator $\hat{x}_2(t)$ shall contain the important oscillations during a standard period S. It shall be flexible enough to catch pattern changes from period to period. In this component too much and too little smoothness must be avoided.

3.1 Construction of the Estimation Principle

For evaluation of smoothness (in contrast to flexibility) the following smoothness measures are constructed (actually these are roughness measures).

By differentiation $\mathrm{D} = \frac{\mathrm{d}}{\mathrm{d}t}$ the degree of a polynomial is reduced by 1. Therefore for a trend $x_1(t)$ as polynomial of degree $p-1$ always holds $\mathrm{D}^p x_1(t) = 0$. On the other hand, every function $x_1(t)$ with this feature is a polynomial of degree $p-1$. Therefore

$$Q_1(x_1) = \int_a^b |\mathrm{D}^p x_1(t)|^2 \,\mathrm{d}t \qquad \textit{measure of smoothness of trend}$$

is a measure of the smoothness of an appropriately chosen function x_1.

For any sufficiently often differentiable and quadratically integrable function x_1 in interval $[a,b]$ $Q_1(x_1)$ is zero iff x_1 is there a polynomial of degree $p-1$, i.e. $x_1(t) = \sum_{j=0}^{p-1} a_j t^j$, a smoothest (ideal) trend. The larger the value of Q_1 for a function x_1 in $[a,b]$ the larger is the deviation of x_1 from a (ideal) trend polynomial of degree $p-1$.

Two times differentiation of the functions $\cos\omega_j t$ and $\sin\omega_j t$ gives $-\omega_j^2 \cos\omega_j t$ and $-\omega_j^2 \sin\omega_j t$ such that $\prod_{j=1}^{q}(\mathrm{D}^2 + \omega_j^2 \mathrm{I})$ (I: identity) nullifies any linear combination $x_2(t)$ of all functions $\cos\omega_j t$ and $\sin\omega_j t$, $j = 1,\ldots,q$. That is because the following

$$(\mathrm{D}^2 + \omega_j^2\mathrm{I})(b_{1k}\cos\omega_k t + b_{2k}\sin\omega_k t) =$$
$$= b_{1k}(\omega_j^2 - \omega_k^2)\cos\omega_k t + b_{2k}(\omega_j^2 - \omega_k^2)\sin\omega_k t \quad \text{for} \quad j,k=1,\ldots,q,$$

nullifies for the case $j = k$ the respective oscillation. This also proves the exchangeability of the operators $\mathrm{D}^2 + \omega_j^2\mathrm{I}$, $j = 1,\ldots,q$.

If inversely $\prod_{j=1}^{q}(\mathrm{D}^2 + \omega_j^2\mathrm{I})x_2(t) = 0$ holds, the function $x_2(t)$ is a linear combination of the trigonometric functions under investigation. Consequently

$$Q_2(x_2) = \int_a^b \Big|\prod_{j=1}^{q}(\mathrm{D}^2 + \omega_j^2\mathrm{I})x_2(t)\Big|^2 \,\mathrm{d}t \qquad \textit{measure of seasonal smoothness}$$

is a measure for seasonal smoothness of the chosen function x_2. For any sufficiently often differentiable and quadratically integrable function x_2 in interval $[a,b]$ $Q_2(x_2)$ is zero iff x_2 is there a linear combination of the trigonometric functions $\cos\omega_j t$ and $\sin\omega_j t$, $j = 1,\ldots,q$, i.e. $x_2(t) = \sum_{j=1}^{q}(b_{1j}\cos\omega_j t + b_{2j}\sin\omega_j t)$, a smoothest (ideal) seasonal component. The larger the value of Q_2 for a function x_2 in $[a,b]$ the larger is the deviation of x_2 from an ideal seasonal component.

The goodness of fit of trend and season at observation times is measured by the usual least squares principle. With

$$Q(\mathbf{x}_1, \mathbf{x}_2; \mathbf{y}) = \sum_{k=1}^{n} |y_k - x_1(t_k) - x_2(t_k)|^2 \qquad \textit{Goodness of fit}$$

and vectors

$$\mathbf{y} = \begin{pmatrix} y_1 \\ \vdots \\ y_n \end{pmatrix}, \quad \mathbf{x}_1 = \begin{pmatrix} x_1(t_1) \\ \vdots \\ x_1(t_n) \end{pmatrix}, \quad \mathbf{x}_2 = \begin{pmatrix} x_2(t_1) \\ \vdots \\ x_2(t_n) \end{pmatrix},$$

is $Q(\mathbf{x}_1, \mathbf{x}_2; \mathbf{y}) = 0$ iff trend and season interpolate the data, i.e. $y_k = x_1(t_k) + x_2(t_k)$, $k = 1, \ldots, n$. Normally this results in too unruly "figures" for trend and season. Therefore a compromise between smoothness and fit must be sought. For that we introduce a weighted sum of smoothness measures and goodness of fit which must be minimised.

$$\min_{x_1, x_2} \left(\lambda_1\, Q_1(x_1) + \lambda_2\, Q_2(x_2) + Q(\mathbf{x}_1, \mathbf{x}_2; \mathbf{y})\right) .$$

Trend and season must be functions which p-th, respectively, $2q$-th differentiation exist and which are quadratic integrable in the Lebesgue-measure, i.e. stem from the Sobolev-spaces $H_{p2}[a, b]$, respectively, $H_{2q,2}[a, b]$.

The parameters λ_1 and λ_2, which must be given first, control smoothness of trend and season. The larger the parameter, the smoother (in the sense of the above given measurements) the respective component is chosen.

The minimum doesn't change if the functional to minimise is multiplied by a constant $c^2 \neq 0$ (factor of scale):

$$\min_{x_1,x_2} \left(\tilde{\lambda}_1\, Q_1(x_1) + \tilde{\lambda}_2\, Q_2(x_2) + c^2\, Q(\mathbf{x}_1, \mathbf{x}_2; \mathbf{y})\right) \quad \text{with} \quad \tilde{\lambda}_1 = c^2 \lambda_1\,, \quad \tilde{\lambda}_2 = c^2 \lambda_2\,.$$

With $\tilde{x}_1 = c\, x_1$, $\tilde{x}_2 = c\, x_2$ and $\tilde{\mathbf{y}} = c\, \mathbf{y}$ scaling and estimation may be interchanged (cf. Sect. 3.3.1). Without restriction a constraint is possible, e.g. $\tilde{\lambda}_1 = 1$ ($c^2 = 1/\lambda_1$), $\tilde{\lambda}_2 = 1$ ($c^2 = 1/\lambda_2$) or $\tilde{\lambda}_1 + \tilde{\lambda}_2 + c^2 = 1$ with $\tilde{\lambda}_1, \tilde{\lambda}_2, c^2 \in [0, 1]$.

The minimum remains constant, too, for all λ_1, λ_2 with $\lambda_1 \cdot \lambda_2 = 1$ (hyperbola, therefore for inverse λ_1, λ_2). Choosing $c^2 = 1/(\lambda_1 \cdot \lambda_2) = 1$, we get $\tilde{\lambda}_1 = 1/\lambda_2$ and $\tilde{\lambda}_2 = 1/\lambda_1$.

The extreme cases can easily be discussed looking at the minimisation problem to solve.

- For $\lambda_1 \to 0$ and $\lambda_2 > 0$ fixed, the optimisation is minimised with minimum 0 if season is smoothest (i.e. $Q_2(x_2) = 0$) and data are interpolated (i.e. $Q(\mathbf{x}_1, \mathbf{x}_2; \mathbf{y}) = 0$). Therefore the solutions consist of *most flexible trend* and *smoothest season*.
- In case of $\lambda_2 \to 0$ and $\lambda_1 > 0$ fixed we find in analogy solutions consisting of *smoothest trend* and *most flexible season*. (Following from interpolation of data with trend and season.)
- If at the same time $\lambda_1 \to \infty$ and $\lambda_2 \to \infty$ holds, then the goodness of fit loses its role in the minimisation. That way we get those smoothest trend and season figures which approximate the data best in the sense of the measure for goodness of fit. This is the same as a linear regression consisting of polynomial trend and trigonometric season (as given above), estimated with least squares methodology. (Base version of Berliner Verfahren IV, modified moving form.)

At least the first two extremal versions don't give acceptable solutions to our problem. In the first extremal case the trend is much to unruly, in the second the seasonal component has way too many oscillations. In the third case both trend and season are smooth, but the goodness of fit will normally be very low. Therefore the control parameters have to be chosen with care. For the special case if the base model consists only of a polynomial Whaba (1990) uses cross validation to find good parameter settings.

Now it becomes obvious that we look for an "optimum" in between least squares solution and interpolation. This "optimum" can be found selecting good control parameters. The problem therefore is a *calibration problem*, too.

If a so-called ρ-function is chosen instead of the quadratic "loss function", the problem is transformed in a rugged problem, which will only be solvable numerically.

To characterise the solution of the minimisation problem we need some notations. For arbitrary (maybe complex-valued) functions x, y which are quadratically integrable in interval $[a,b] \subset \mathbb{R}$ we write

$$\langle x, y\rangle = \int_a^b x(t)\,\overline{y(t)}\,\mathrm{d}t = \overline{\langle y, x\rangle} \quad \text{and} \quad \|x\|^2 = \langle x, x\rangle = \int_a^b |x(t)|^2\,\mathrm{d}t$$

(The bar means conjugated complex). If differential operators

$$T_1 = D^p \quad \text{and} \quad T_2 = \prod_{j=1}^{q}(D^2 + \omega_j^2 I)$$

are used, the target functional for a given data vector $\mathbf{y} \in \mathbb{R}_n$ can be written as

$$S(x_1, x_2; \mathbf{y}) = \lambda_1\,\|T_1 x_1\|^2 + \lambda_2\,\|T_2 x_2\|^2 + |\mathbf{y} - \mathbf{x}_1 - \mathbf{x}_2|^2\,.$$

For arbitrary given $\hat{x}_1 \in H_{p2}[a,b]$, $\hat{x}_2 \in H_{2q,2}[a,b]$ be $y_1 = x_1 - \hat{x}_1$, $y_2 = x_2 - \hat{x}_2$. Then follows

$$\begin{aligned} S(x_1, x_2; \mathbf{y}) = {} & \lambda_1\langle T_1\hat{x}_1 + T_1 y_1, T_1\hat{x}_1 + T_1 y_1\rangle + \lambda_2\langle T_2\hat{x}_2 + T_2 y_2, T_2\hat{x}_2 + T_2 y_2\rangle + \\ & +(\mathbf{y} - \hat{\mathbf{x}}_1 - \hat{\mathbf{x}}_2 - \mathbf{y}_1 - \mathbf{y}_2)'\overline{(\mathbf{y} - \hat{\mathbf{x}}_1 - \hat{\mathbf{x}}_2 - \mathbf{y}_1 - \mathbf{y}_2)}, \end{aligned}$$

where $\hat{\mathbf{x}}_1$, $\hat{\mathbf{x}}_2$ and $\mathbf{y}_1$, $\mathbf{y}_2$ (like $\mathbf{x}_1$, $\mathbf{x}_2$) are defined as vectors of function values at observation points $t_1, \ldots, t_n$.

Multiplication of the integrands gives

$$\begin{aligned} S(x_1, x_2; \mathbf{y}) = {} & S(\hat{x}_1, \hat{x}_2; \mathbf{y}) + \lambda_1\|T_1 y_1\|^2 + \lambda_2\|T_2 y_2\|^2 + |\mathbf{y}_1 + \mathbf{y}_2|^2 + \\ & +2\,\mathrm{Re}\big(\lambda_1\langle T_1\hat{x}_1, T_1 y_1\rangle + \lambda_2\langle T_2\hat{x}_2, T_2 y_2\rangle - (\mathbf{y} - \hat{\mathbf{x}}_1 - \hat{\mathbf{x}}_2)'\overline{(\mathbf{y}_1 + \mathbf{y}_2)}\big)\,, \end{aligned}$$

because for a complex number z always holds $z + \overline{z} = 2\,\mathrm{Re}(z)$ (Re: real part).

From that the following theorem follows easily

Theorem 1 (Characterisation Theorem) *Functions* $\hat{x}_1$, $\hat{x}_2$ *are a solution of the minimisation problem* $\min_{x_1,x_2} S(x_1, x_2; \mathbf{y})$, *i.e. it holds*

$$S(x_1, x_2; \mathbf{y}) \geq S(\hat{x}_1, \hat{x}_2; \mathbf{y}) \quad \textit{for all} \quad x_1 \in H_{p2}[a,b]\,, \; x_2 \in H_{2q,2}[a,b]$$

iff

$$\begin{matrix} Re\big(\lambda_1 \langle T_1\hat{x}_1, T_1 y_1\rangle - (\mathbf{y} - \hat{\mathbf{x}}_1 - \hat{\mathbf{x}}_2)' \overline{\mathbf{y}}_1\big) = 0 \\ Re\big(\lambda_2 \langle T_2\hat{x}_2, T_2 y_2\rangle - (\mathbf{y} - \hat{\mathbf{x}}_1 - \hat{\mathbf{x}}_2)' \overline{\mathbf{y}}_2\big) = 0 \end{matrix} \quad \textit{for all} \quad \begin{matrix} y_1 \in H_{p2}[a,b] \\ y_2 \in H_{2q,2}[a,b]\,. \end{matrix}$$

If $\hat{x}_1^{(1)}$, $\hat{x}_2^{(1)}$ *and* $\hat{x}_1^{(2)}$, $\hat{x}_2^{(2)}$ *are two solutions, then the relation holds*

$$\begin{matrix} \hat{x}_1^{(1)} = \hat{x}_1^{(2)} + y_1 \\ \hat{x}_2^{(1)} = \hat{x}_2^{(2)} + y_2 \end{matrix} \quad \textit{with} \quad \begin{matrix} T_1\, y_1 = 0 \\ T_2\, y_2 = 0 \end{matrix} \quad \textit{and} \quad \mathbf{y}_1 + \mathbf{y}_2 = 0\,,$$

i.e. y_1, y_2 *is solution of* $\min_{x_1,x_2} S(x_1, x_2; 0)$. *Therefore we get a unique solution iff for* $y_1 \in H_{p2}[a,b]$, $y_2 \in H_{2q,2}[a,b]$ *with*

$$T_1\, y_1 = 0\,, \quad T_2\, y_2 = 0 \quad \textit{and} \quad \mathbf{y}_1 + \mathbf{y}_2 = 0 \quad \textit{always} \quad y_1 = 0\,, \quad y_2 = 0$$

follows, i.e. if the null function is the only best approximating function for the null vector.

From this characterisation theorem a representation theorem follows directly.

Theorem 2 (Representation Theorem) *If* w_{1k}, w_{2k} *are a solution of the minimisation problem above with respect to the unity vector* $\mathbf{e}_k \in \mathbb{R}_n$, $k = 1, \ldots, n$, *then* $\hat{x}_1$, $\hat{x}_2$, *represented by*

$$\begin{matrix} \hat{x}_1(t) = \sum_{k=1}^{n} w_{1k}(t) y_k = \mathbf{w}_1(t)'\mathbf{y} \\ \hat{x}_2(t) = \sum_{k=1}^{n} w_{2k}(t) y_k = \mathbf{w}_2(t)'\mathbf{y} \end{matrix} \quad t \in [a,b]\,,$$

is a solution of the minimisation problem with respect to the data vector $\mathbf{y} = \sum_{k=1}^{n} y_k \mathbf{e}_k$ *and is characterised by*

$$\begin{matrix} \lambda_1 \int_a^b T_1 y_1(t) \cdot \overline{T_1 w_{1k}(t)}\, dt \overset{Re}{=} \mathbf{y}_1'(\mathbf{e}_k - \overline{\mathbf{w}}_k) \\ \lambda_2 \int_a^b T_2 y_2(t) \cdot \overline{T_2 w_{2k}(t)}\, dt \overset{Re}{=} \mathbf{y}_2'(\mathbf{e}_k - \overline{\mathbf{w}}_k) \end{matrix} \quad \textit{for all} \quad \begin{matrix} y_1 \in H_{p2}[a,b] \\ y_2 \in H_{2q,2}[a,b]\,, \end{matrix}$$

with $w_k = w_{1k} + w_{2k}$, *written as vectors and matrices*

$$\begin{aligned} \lambda_1 \int_a^b T_1 y_1(t) \cdot \overline{T_1 \mathbf{w}_1(t)}' \, dt &\overset{Re}{=} \mathbf{y}_1'(I - \overline{W}) \\ \lambda_2 \int_a^b T_2 y_2(t) \cdot \overline{T_2 \mathbf{w}_2(t)}' \, dt &\overset{Re}{=} \mathbf{y}_2'(I - \overline{W}) \end{aligned} \quad f0r\ all \quad \begin{aligned} y_1 &\in H_{p2}[a,b] \\ y_2 &\in H_{2q,2}[a,b] \end{aligned}$$

with unit matrix I, *where*

$$\mathbf{w}_1(t)' = \big(w_{11}(t) \cdots w_{1n}(t)\big), \qquad \mathbf{w}_2(t)' = \big(w_{21}(t) \cdots w_{2n}(t)\big)$$

$$W_1 = \begin{pmatrix} \mathbf{w}_1(t_1)' \\ \vdots \\ \mathbf{w}_1(t_n)' \end{pmatrix}, \quad W_2 = \begin{pmatrix} \mathbf{w}_2(t_1)' \\ \vdots \\ \mathbf{w}_2(t_n)' \end{pmatrix} \quad and \quad W = W_1 + W_2 .$$

The symbol $\overset{Re}{=}$ *means equality in the real part.*

3.2 Representation of Solutions

As we already noted in the introduction the solutions $\hat{x}_1$ and $\hat{x}_1$ for trend and season are natural polynomial and trigonometric spline functions. For each point in time with an observation t_k polynomial and trigonometric function are changed appropriately by the additional functions which are "cut" there

$$\begin{aligned} g_1(t - t_k) &= (t - t_k)^{2p-1} \\ g_2(t - t_k) &= \sum_{j=1}^{q} a_j \big(b_j \sin \omega_j (t - t_k) - (t - t_k) \cos \omega_j (t - t_k)\big) \end{aligned}$$

für $t > t_k$ und 0 für $t \leq t_k$, $k = 1, \ldots, n$, mit

$$a_j = \frac{1}{2\omega_j^2 \prod_{\substack{i=1 \\ i \neq j}}^{q} (\omega_i^2 - \omega_j^2)^2}, \quad b_j = \frac{1}{\omega_j} - 4\omega_j \sum_{\substack{i=1 \\ i \neq j}}^{q} \frac{1}{\omega_i^2 - \omega_j^2}, \quad j = 1, \ldots, q .$$

To find a solution also the weight function w_{1k} and w_{2k} of the representation theorem are chosen as natural polynomial and trigonometric spline functions. Written as vectors and matrices with

$$\mathbf{f}_1(t)' = \begin{pmatrix} 1\ t\ \ldots\ t^{p-1} \end{pmatrix} \qquad \mathbf{g}_1(t)' = \begin{pmatrix} g_1(t - t_1) \cdots g_1(t - t_n) \end{pmatrix}$$

$$F_1 = \begin{pmatrix} 1 & t_1 & \ldots & t_1^{p-1} \\ \vdots & \vdots & & \vdots \\ 1 & t_n & \ldots & t_n^{p-1} \end{pmatrix} \qquad G_1 = \begin{pmatrix} g_1(t_1 - t_1) & \cdots & g_1(t_1 - t_n) \\ \vdots & & \vdots \\ g_1(t_n - t_1) & \cdots & g_1(t_n - t_n) \end{pmatrix}$$

and

$$\mathbf{f}_2(t)' = \begin{pmatrix} \cos\omega_1 t & \sin\omega_1 t & \dots \cos\omega_q t & \sin\omega_q t \end{pmatrix}$$

$$F_2 = \begin{pmatrix} \cos\omega_1 t_1 & \sin\omega_1 t_1 & \dots \cos\omega_q t_1 & \sin\omega_q t_1 \\ \vdots & \vdots & \vdots & \vdots \\ \cos\omega_1 t_n & \sin\omega_1 t_n & \dots \cos\omega_q t_n & \sin\omega_q t_n \end{pmatrix},$$

$$\mathbf{g}_2(t)' = \begin{pmatrix} g_2(t - t_1) \dots g_2(t - t_n) \end{pmatrix}$$

$$G_2 = \begin{pmatrix} g_2(t_1 - t_1) & \dots & g_2(t_1 - t_n) \\ \vdots & & \vdots \\ g_2(t_n - t_1) & \dots & g_2(t_n - t_n) \end{pmatrix}.$$

The following representations hold (with real-valued coefficient matrices)

$$\mathbf{w}_1(t)' = \mathbf{f}_1(t)'B_1 + \mathbf{g}_1(t)'A_1\,, \text{ especially } W_1 = F_1B_1 + G_1A_1 \quad \text{with} \quad F_1'A_1 = 0\,,$$

$$\mathbf{w}_2(t)' = \mathbf{f}_2(t)'B_2 + \mathbf{g}_2(t)'A_2\,, \text{ especially } W_2 = F_2B_2 + G_2A_2 \quad \text{with} \quad F_2'A_2 = 0\,.$$

The constraints for A_1 and A_2 are typical for natural spline functions (special smoothness at borders) and it holds the
spline-orthogonality relation

$$\left.\begin{aligned} \int_a^b T_1 y_1(t) \cdot T_1\mathbf{w}_1(t)'\,\mathrm{d}t &= \mathbf{y}_1'A_1 \\ \int_a^b T_2 y_2(t) \cdot T_2\mathbf{w}_2(t)'\,\mathrm{d}t &= \mathbf{y}_2'A_2 \end{aligned}\right. \quad \text{for all} \quad \begin{aligned} y_1 &\in H_{p2}[a,b] \\ y_2 &\in H_{2q,2}[a,b]\,, \end{aligned}$$

cf. Hebbel (2000). Following the representation theorem now holds

$$\left.\begin{aligned} \lambda_1\,\mathbf{y}_1'A_1 &= \mathbf{y}_1'\,(I - W) \\ \lambda_2\,\mathbf{y}_2'A_2 &= \mathbf{y}_2'\,(I - W) \end{aligned}\right. \quad \text{bzw.} \quad A := I - W = \lambda_1\,A_1 = \lambda_2\,A_2\,,$$

because $\mathbf{y}_1, \mathbf{y}_2$ arbitrary. Consequently holds

$$\left.\begin{aligned} W_1 &= F_1B_1 + \tfrac{1}{\lambda_1}\,G_1A \\ W_2 &= F_2B_2 + \tfrac{1}{\lambda_2}\,G_2A \end{aligned}\right. \quad \text{with side condition} \quad \begin{pmatrix} F_1' \\ F_2' \end{pmatrix} A = 0$$

and therefore

$$I - A = W = W_1 + W_2 = \begin{pmatrix} F_1 & F_2 \end{pmatrix}\begin{pmatrix} B_1 \\ B_2 \end{pmatrix} + \left(\tfrac{1}{\lambda_1}\,G_1 + \tfrac{1}{\lambda_2}\,G_2\right)A\,.$$

After these considerations the following theorem holds:

Theorem 3 *The solutions of the minimisation problem which are linear homogeneous in the data are given by*

$$\hat{x}_1(t) = \mathbf{w}_1(t)'\mathbf{y}\,, \quad \hat{x}_2(t) = \mathbf{w}_2(t)'\mathbf{y}\,,$$

where

$$\begin{aligned} \mathbf{w}_1(t)' &= \mathbf{f}_1(t)'B_1 + \tfrac{1}{\lambda_1}\,\mathbf{g}_1(t)'A = \Big(\big(\mathbf{f}_1(t)'\ \ 0\big)\ \ \tfrac{1}{\lambda_1}\,\mathbf{g}_1(t)'\Big)\begin{pmatrix} B \\ A \end{pmatrix} \\ \mathbf{w}_2(t)' &= \mathbf{f}_2(t)'B_2 + \tfrac{1}{\lambda_2}\,\mathbf{g}_2(t)'A = \Big(\big(0\ \ \mathbf{f}_2(t)'\big)\ \ \tfrac{1}{\lambda_2}\,\mathbf{g}_2(t)'\Big)\begin{pmatrix} B \\ A \end{pmatrix} \end{aligned} \qquad B = \begin{pmatrix} B_1 \\ B_2 \end{pmatrix}$$

and matrices B and A are solutions of

$$\begin{pmatrix} 0 & F' \\ F & H \end{pmatrix}\begin{pmatrix} B \\ A \end{pmatrix} = \begin{pmatrix} 0 \\ I \end{pmatrix} \quad \textit{resp.} \quad \begin{aligned} F'A &= 0 \\ FB + HA &= I \end{aligned}$$

with identity matrix I and

$$F = \begin{pmatrix} F_1 & F_2 \end{pmatrix}, \quad H = I + \tfrac{1}{\lambda_1}\,G_1 + \tfrac{1}{\lambda_2}\,G_2\,.$$

Remark 1 Note that G_1 and G_2 contain only zeros above the diagonal and therefore H has the form of a lower triangular matrix with ones on the diagonal.

For the complete solution $\hat{x}(t) = \hat{x}_1(t) + \hat{x}_2(t)$ holds

$$\hat{x}(t) = \mathbf{w}(t)'\mathbf{y}\,,$$

where

$$\mathbf{w}(t)' = \mathbf{w}_1(t)' + \mathbf{w}_2(t)' = \Big(\mathbf{f}(t)'\ \ \tfrac{1}{\lambda_1}\,\mathbf{g}_1(t)' + \tfrac{1}{\lambda_2}\,\mathbf{g}_2(t)'\Big)\begin{pmatrix} B \\ A \end{pmatrix}, \quad \mathbf{f}(t)' = \big(\mathbf{f}_1(t)'\ \ \mathbf{f}_2(t)'\big)\,.$$

Especially for $t = t_1, \ldots, t_n$ the solutions are given in vector form as

$$\hat{\mathbf{x}}_1 = W_1\,\mathbf{y}\,, \quad \hat{\mathbf{x}}_2 = W_2\,\mathbf{y} \quad \text{and} \quad \hat{\mathbf{x}} = \hat{\mathbf{x}}_1 + \hat{\mathbf{x}}_2 = W\mathbf{y}$$

with

$$\begin{aligned} W_1 &= F_1\,B_1 + \tfrac{1}{\lambda_1}\,G_1A = \Big(\big(F_1\ \ 0\big)\ \ \tfrac{1}{\lambda_1}\,G_1\Big)\begin{pmatrix} B \\ A \end{pmatrix} \\ W_2 &= F_2\,B_2 + \tfrac{1}{\lambda_2}\,G_2A = \Big(\big(0\ \ F_2\big)\ \ \tfrac{1}{\lambda_2}\,G_2\Big)\begin{pmatrix} B \\ A \end{pmatrix} \end{aligned} \qquad W = W_1 + W_2 = I - A\,.$$

Remark 2 The theoretical-empirical rest component is given by

$$\hat{u}(t) = y(t) - \hat{x}_1(t) - \hat{x}_2(t) = y(t) - \hat{x}(t) = y(t) - \mathbf{w}(t)'\mathbf{y}\,, \quad t \in [a,b]\,.$$

But as only the observations $y_1, \ldots, y_n$ at points in time $t_1, \ldots, t_n$ of the theoretical measurement curve $y(t)$ exist, empirical rests can only be calculated at those points in time:

$$\hat{u}(t_k) = y_k - \hat{x}_1(t_k) - \hat{x}_2(t_k)\,, \quad k = 1, \ldots, n\,,$$

or as vectors

$$\hat{\mathbf{u}} = \mathbf{y} - \hat{\mathbf{x}}_1 - \hat{\mathbf{x}}_2 = \mathbf{y} - \hat{\mathbf{x}} = \mathbf{y} - W\mathbf{y} = (I - W)\mathbf{y} = A\mathbf{y}\,.$$

Because of $F'A = 0$ it holds especially

$$F'\hat{\mathbf{u}} = 0 \quad \text{and especially} \quad \mathbf{1}'\hat{\mathbf{u}} = 0 \quad \text{resp.} \quad \mathbf{1}'\mathbf{y} = \mathbf{1}'\hat{\mathbf{x}}\,,$$

because F has in its first column the vector of ones $\mathbf{1}$, i.e. the sum of the empirical rests is zero just like in a regression model with constant term.

Remark 3 With respect to the linear independence of the columns of F_2 special care is needed, especially for integer points in time (alias effect). At least in that case should

$$0 < \omega_j \leq \pi\,, \quad j = 1, \ldots, q$$

hold. If the harmonic π is used it is to note that for integer observation times the last column in F_2 contains only zeros. In such a case in the measure of smoothness of the seasonal component the operator $\mathrm{D}^2 - \pi^2\mathrm{I} = (\mathrm{D} - \mathrm{i}\pi\mathrm{I})(\mathrm{D} + \mathrm{i}\pi\mathrm{I})$ could be replaced with $\mathrm{D} - \mathrm{i}\pi\mathrm{I}$, which nullifies the function $\mathrm{e}^{\mathrm{i}\pi t} = \cos\pi t = (-1)^t$ in $\mathbb{Z}$. $\mathbf{f}_2(t)$ would only contain $\cos\pi t$ and not the null-function $\sin\pi t$. $g_2(t - t_k)$ should be modified analogously, cf. Hebbel (1997).

Remark 4 (Uniqueness and Matrix Properties) The system of equations above has a unique solution iff F has full rank $p + 2q \leq n$ in the columns. In that case exactly one solution of the spline optimisation problem exists. In this situation holds

$$\begin{pmatrix} 0 & F' \\ F & H \end{pmatrix}^{-1} = \begin{pmatrix} -(F'H^{-1}F)^{-1} & (F'H^{-1}F)^{-1}F'H^{-1} \\ H^{-1}F(F'H^{-1}F)^{-1} & H^{-1} - H^{-1}F(F'H^{-1}F)^{-1}F'H^{-1} \end{pmatrix}$$

$$= \begin{pmatrix} -D & B \\ C & A \end{pmatrix}$$

with

$$D = (F'H^{-1}F)^{-1}, \quad C = H^{-1}F(F'H^{-1}F)^{-1} = H^{-1}FD$$
$$B = (F'H^{-1}F)^{-1}F'H^{-1}, \quad A = H^{-1} - H^{-1}F(F'H^{-1}F)^{-1}F'H^{-1} = H^{-1}(I - FB)\,.$$

We get immediately

$$\begin{matrix} F'C = I & F'A = 0 \\ FD = HC & FB + HA = I \end{matrix} \quad \text{and} \quad \begin{matrix} BF = I & AF = 0 \\ DF' = BH & CF' + AH = I \end{matrix}$$

and especially

$$A'HA = A' \quad \text{resp.} \quad A'H'A = A \quad \text{and} \quad AHA = A\,, \; BHA = 0\,, \; AHC = 0\,.$$

In particular $AHAH = AH$ and $HAHA = HA$ holds and therefore AH and HA are idempotent with eigenvalues zero or one.

The inverse of

$$H = I + G \quad \text{with} \quad G = \tfrac{1}{\lambda_1}G_1 + \tfrac{1}{\lambda_2}G_2$$

may be calculated as $H^{-1} = I + \sum_{k=1}^{n-1}(-G)^k$, because $\big(I + \sum_{k=1}^{n-1}(-G)^k\big)(I + G) = I - (-G)^n$ and $G^n = 0$. With each power of G the null diagonal moves one diagonal further down. Nevertheless numerical problems may arise in the calculation of A using this formula, if λ_1, λ_2 are small.

Remark 5 Alternatively the solution of the system of equations

$$\begin{pmatrix} 0 & F' \\ F & H \end{pmatrix}\begin{pmatrix} B \\ A \end{pmatrix} = \begin{pmatrix} 0 \\ I \end{pmatrix} \quad \text{bzw.} \quad \left[\begin{pmatrix} 0 & F' \\ F & I \end{pmatrix} + \begin{pmatrix} 0 & 0 \\ 0 & G \end{pmatrix}\right]\begin{pmatrix} B \\ A \end{pmatrix} = \begin{pmatrix} 0 \\ I \end{pmatrix}$$

can be represented with respect to the smoothest solution according to BV (cf. item 0 below limiting cases in this subsection). This way of calculating turned out to be much more stable numerically. Multiplication with

$$\begin{pmatrix} 0 & F' \\ F & I \end{pmatrix}^{-1} = \begin{pmatrix} -(F'F)^{-1} & (F'F)^{-1}F' \\ F(F'F)^{-1} & I - F(F'F)^{-1}F' \end{pmatrix} = \begin{pmatrix} -(F'F)^{-1} & B^* \\ B^{*\prime} & A^* \end{pmatrix},$$

where $B^* = (F'F)^{-1}F'$ and $A^* = I - F(F'F)^{-1}F' = I - FB^*$ (with property $A^*A^* = A^*$, $B^*A^* = 0$), results in

$$\begin{pmatrix} I & B^*G \\ 0 & I + A^*G \end{pmatrix}\begin{pmatrix} B \\ A \end{pmatrix} = \begin{pmatrix} B^* \\ A^* \end{pmatrix} \quad \text{resp.} \quad \begin{matrix} B = B^*(I - GA) \\ (I + A^*G)A = A^*, \quad A = A^*(I - GA) \end{matrix}$$

therefore

$$A = (I + A^*G)^{-1}A^* \quad \text{with} \quad A^*A = AA^* = A\,.$$

Remark 6 If we choose a "symmetric" form for functions $g_1(t - t_k)$ and $g_2(t - t_k)$, such that the matrix H is symmetric and positive definite, then the estimation in the base model comes out as best linear forecast if the rest processes possess special covariance structures, see Hebbel (2000) and Michel (2008).

3.3 *Properties of Solutions*

The components found as solutions have interesting properties and many consequences can be formulated.

3.3.1 Properties of Linearity

Solutions are linear homogeneous in the date. If

$$\hat{x}_1^{(i)}(t) = \mathbf{w}_1(t)'\mathbf{y}^{(i)}\,, \quad \hat{x}_2^{(i)}(t) = \mathbf{w}_2(t)'\mathbf{y}^{(i)}$$

are solutions found for the observed single time series $\mathbf{y}^{(i)}$, $i = 1, \ldots, k$, then the "aggregated" components

$$\hat{x}_1(t) = \sum_{i=1}^{k} a_i\hat{x}_1^{(i)}(t) = \mathbf{w}_1(t)'\mathbf{y}\,, \qquad \hat{x}_2(t) = \sum_{i=1}^{k} a_i\hat{x}_2^{(i)}(t) = \mathbf{w}_2(t)'\mathbf{y}$$

are solutions for an "aggregated" observed time series $\mathbf{y} = \sum_{i=1}^{k} a_i\mathbf{y}^{(i)}$.

3.3.2 Spline Properties

The solutions

$$\begin{matrix} \hat{x}_1(t) = \mathbf{w}_1(t)'\mathbf{y} \\ \hat{x}_2(t) = \mathbf{w}_2(t)'\mathbf{y} \end{matrix} \quad \text{with} \quad \begin{matrix} \mathbf{w}_1(t)' = \mathbf{f}_1(t)'B_1 + \frac{1}{\lambda_1}\,\mathbf{g}_1(t)'A \\ \mathbf{w}_2(t)' = \mathbf{f}_2(t)'B_2 + \frac{1}{\lambda_2}\,\mathbf{g}_2(t)'A \end{matrix}$$

are, just like the weight functions, natural spline functions, because obviously the representation holds

$$\begin{matrix} \hat{x}_1(t) = \mathbf{f}_1(t)'\hat{\beta}_1 + \frac{1}{\lambda_1}\,\mathbf{g}_1(t)'\hat{\alpha} \\ \hat{x}_2(t) = \mathbf{f}_2(t)'\hat{\beta}_2 + \frac{1}{\lambda_2}\,\mathbf{g}_2(t)'\hat{\alpha} \end{matrix} \quad \text{with} \quad \begin{matrix} \hat{\beta}_1 = B_1\mathbf{y} \\ \hat{\beta}_2 = B_2\mathbf{y} \end{matrix} \quad \hat{\beta} = \begin{pmatrix} \hat{\beta}_1 \\ \hat{\beta}_2 \end{pmatrix} = B\mathbf{y}\,, \quad \hat{\alpha} = \hat{\mathbf{u}} = A\mathbf{y}\,.$$

and with $F'\hat{\alpha} = F'A\mathbf{y} = 0$, so $F_1'\hat{\alpha} = 0$ and $F_2'\hat{\alpha} = 0$, the necessary and sufficient side condition for natural splines is fulfilled, s. Hebbel (2000).

Because of

$$\begin{pmatrix}\hat{\beta}\\ \hat{\alpha}\end{pmatrix} = \begin{pmatrix}B\\ A\end{pmatrix}\mathbf{y} \quad \text{und} \quad \begin{pmatrix}0 & F'\\ F & H\end{pmatrix}\begin{pmatrix}B\\ A\end{pmatrix} = \begin{pmatrix}0\\ I\end{pmatrix}$$

the coefficients are a solution of

$$\begin{pmatrix}0 & F'\\ F & H\end{pmatrix}\begin{pmatrix}\hat{\beta}\\ \hat{\alpha}\end{pmatrix} = \begin{pmatrix}0\\ \mathbf{y}\end{pmatrix}.$$

3.3.3 Weight Properties

For the (spline-) weight functions

$$\begin{aligned}\mathbf{w}_1(t)' &= \Big(\big(\mathbf{f}_1(t)' \ 0\big) \ \ \tfrac{1}{\lambda_1}\mathbf{g}_1(t)'\Big)\begin{pmatrix}B\\ A\end{pmatrix}\\ \mathbf{w}_2(t)' &= \Big(\big(0 \ \mathbf{f}_2(t)'\big) \ \ \tfrac{1}{\lambda_2}\mathbf{g}_2(t)'\Big)\begin{pmatrix}B\\ A\end{pmatrix}\end{aligned} \qquad \text{with} \quad \begin{pmatrix}0 & F'\\ F & H\end{pmatrix}\begin{pmatrix}B\\ A\end{pmatrix} = \begin{pmatrix}0\\ I\end{pmatrix}$$

the following properties hold:

- Independence of origin

  Moving the origin along the time axis to $t_0 \in \mathbb{R}$ doesn't change weights.

  For the transformation $t \longmapsto \tilde{t} = t - t_0$ holds $(t - t_0)^j = \sum_{i=0}^{j}\binom{j}{i}t^i(-t_0)^{j-i}$ and therefore

$$\big(1 \ t - t_0 \ \cdots \ (t - t_0)^{p-1}\big) = \big(1 \ t \ \cdots \ t^{p-1}\big)\underbrace{\begin{pmatrix}1 & \binom{1}{0}(-t_0)^1 & \cdots\binom{p-1}{0}(-t_0)^{p-1}\\ & 1 & \cdots\binom{p-1}{1}(-t_0)^{p-1}\\ & \text{O} & \ddots \quad \vdots\\ & & 1\end{pmatrix}}_{M_1,\ \det M_1 = 1}$$

$$\mathbf{f}_1(\tilde{t})' = \mathbf{f}_1(t)'M_1\,, \quad \text{especially } \tilde{F}_1 = F_1 M_1\,,$$

and

$$\big(\cos\omega_j(t - t_0) \quad \sin\omega_j(t - t_0)\big) = \big(\cos\omega_j t \quad \sin\omega_j t\big)\underbrace{\begin{pmatrix}\cos\omega_j t_0 & -\sin\omega_j t_0\\ \sin\omega_j t_0 & \cos\omega_j t_0\end{pmatrix}}_{M_{2j},\ \det M_{2j} = 1}$$

and therefore

$$\begin{pmatrix}\cos\omega_1\tilde{t} & \sin\omega_1\tilde{t} & \cdots & \cos\omega_q\tilde{t} & \sin\omega_q\tilde{t}\end{pmatrix} =$$

$$= \begin{pmatrix}\cos\omega_1 t & \sin\omega_1 t & \cdots & \cos\omega_q t & \sin\omega_q t\end{pmatrix} \underbrace{\begin{pmatrix} M_{21} & & \mathrm{O} \\ & \ddots & \\ \mathrm{O} & & M_{2q}\end{pmatrix}}_{M_2,\ \det M_2 = 1}$$

$$\mathbf{f}_2(\tilde{t})' = \mathbf{f}_2(t)' M_2\,, \quad \text{especially } \tilde{F}_2 = F_2 M_2\,.$$

Consequently holds

$$\tilde{F} = \begin{pmatrix}\tilde{F}_1 & \tilde{F}_2\end{pmatrix} = \begin{pmatrix}F_1 & F_2\end{pmatrix} \underbrace{\begin{pmatrix} M_1 & 0 \\ 0 & M_2\end{pmatrix}}_{M,\ \det M = 1} = FM$$

and the transformation matrix M falls out of the weight vectors $\mathbf{w}_1(\tilde{t})'$ and $\mathbf{w}_2(\tilde{t})'$, so that it coincides with $\mathbf{w}_1(t)'$ and $\mathbf{w}_2(t)'$.

When calculating weights $\mathbf{w}_1(t)'$, $\mathbf{w}_2(t)'$ the independence of the origin can be used directly to move the origin, for example, in the middle of the interval $[a,b]$ or to design a local "moving" version of the method.

- Invariance and summation properties

Furthermore holds

$$\begin{aligned} \mathbf{w}_1(t)'F &= \begin{pmatrix}\mathbf{f}_1(t)' & 0\end{pmatrix} & W_1 F &= \begin{pmatrix}F_1 & 0\end{pmatrix} \\ \mathbf{w}_2(t)'F &= \begin{pmatrix}0 & \mathbf{f}_2(t)'\end{pmatrix} & W_2 F &= \begin{pmatrix}0 & F_2\end{pmatrix} \end{aligned} \qquad WF = F\,.$$

Because $\mathbf{f}_1(t)'$ has a one in the first position and therefore F has a vector of ones in the first column $\mathbf{1}$, in particular holds

$$\begin{aligned} \mathbf{w}_1(t)'\mathbf{1} &= 1 & W_1\mathbf{1} &= \mathbf{1} \\ \mathbf{w}_2(t)'\mathbf{1} &= 0 & W_2\mathbf{1} &= 0 \end{aligned} \qquad W\mathbf{1} = \mathbf{1}\,,$$

i.e. the sum of trend weights always is one and the sum of season weights always is zero.

- Values of smoothness

If the components from $\mathbf{w}_1$ or $\mathbf{w}_2$ are inserted into the spline orthogonality relation for y_1 or y_2, then in matrix notation follows (note the symmetry of the "smoothness matrices")

$$\begin{aligned}\int_a^b T_1\mathbf{w}_1(t)\cdot T_1\mathbf{w}_1(t)'\,\mathrm{d}t &= W_1'A_1 = \tfrac{1}{\lambda_1}W_1'A = \tfrac{1}{\lambda_1}A'W_1 \\ \int_a^b T_2\mathbf{w}_2(t)\cdot T_2\mathbf{w}_2(t)'\,\mathrm{d}t &= W_2'A_2 = \tfrac{1}{\lambda_2}W_2'A = \tfrac{1}{\lambda_2}A'W_2\end{aligned} \quad \text{and} \quad W'A = A'W\,,$$

because $W = W_1 + W_2$.

- Properties of symmetry and definiteness

  Therefore for above "smoothness-matrices" holds

$$W_1'A = \tfrac{1}{\lambda_1}A'G_1'A,\quad W_2'A = \tfrac{1}{\lambda_2}A'G_2'A,$$

$$W'A \quad \text{are symmetric and not negative definite.}$$

From $W = I - A$ follows after multiplication with A resp. A' in each case $W'A = A - A'A$, $A'W = A' - A'A$ and therefore $A = W'A + A'A = A'W + A'A = A'$, i.e.

$$A \quad \text{is symmetric not negative definite,}$$

because $W'A + A'A$ has this property. Herewith W is symmetric, too, because it is $W = I - A = I - A' = W'$ and from $0 \le \mathbf{z}'W'A\mathbf{z} = \mathbf{z}'W'(I - W)\mathbf{z} = \mathbf{z}'W'\mathbf{z} - \mathbf{z}'W'W\mathbf{z}$, i.e. $\mathbf{z}'W\mathbf{z} \ge \mathbf{z}'W'W\mathbf{z} \ge 0$ for any $\mathbf{z} \in \mathbb{R}_n$, follows

$$W \quad \text{is symmetric not negative definite.}$$

3.3.4 Property of Interpolation

If the data are interpolated by smoothest function consisting of a polynomial plus trigonometric sum, that is $\mathbf{y}$ is of the form

$$\mathbf{y} = F\beta\,, \quad \beta \text{ arbitrary,}$$

then holds, because of the invariance property of the weight function,

$$\hat{x}_1(t) = \mathbf{w}_1(t)'\mathbf{y} = \mathbf{w}_1(t)'F\beta = \begin{pmatrix}\mathbf{f}_1(t)' & 0\end{pmatrix}\beta = \mathbf{f}_1(t)'\beta_1$$

$$\hat{x}_2(t) = \mathbf{w}_2(t)'\mathbf{y} = \mathbf{w}_2(t)'F\beta = \begin{pmatrix}\mathbf{f}_2(t)' & 0\end{pmatrix}\beta = \mathbf{f}_2(t)'\beta_2$$

and with this trend and season will be completely reconstructed independent of the choice of λ_1, λ_2.

3.3.5 Values of Smoothness of Solutions

The solutions $\hat{x}_1(t) = \mathbf{w}_1(t)'\mathbf{y}$, $\hat{x}_2(t) = \mathbf{w}_2(t)'\mathbf{y}$ have smoothness values (cf. measurement of smoothness of weight functions)

$$Q_1(\hat{x}_1) = \int_a^b |T_1\hat{x}_1(t)|^2 \mathrm{d}t = \tfrac{1}{\lambda_1^2}\mathbf{y}'A'G_1'A\mathbf{y} = \tfrac{1}{\lambda_1}\mathbf{y}'W_1'A\mathbf{y} = \tfrac{1}{\lambda_1}\hat{\mathbf{x}}_1'\hat{\mathbf{u}} \geq 0\,,$$

$$Q_2(\hat{x}_2) = \int_a^b |T_2\hat{x}_2(t)|^2 \mathrm{d}t = \tfrac{1}{\lambda_2^2}\mathbf{y}'A'G_2'A\mathbf{y} = \tfrac{1}{\lambda_2}\mathbf{y}'W_2'A\mathbf{y} = \tfrac{1}{\lambda_2}\hat{\mathbf{x}}_2'\hat{\mathbf{u}} \geq 0\,.$$

If follows that estimations of components in observation points are always non-negative correlated with the empirical rests $\hat{\mathbf{u}} = \mathbf{y} - \hat{\mathbf{x}}$. Furthermore holds

$$\lambda_1 Q_1(\hat{x}_1) + \lambda_2 Q_2(\hat{x}_2) = \mathbf{y}'W'A\mathbf{y} = \hat{\mathbf{x}}'\hat{\mathbf{u}} \geq 0\,, \quad W = W_1 + W_2\,, \;\; \hat{\mathbf{x}} = \hat{\mathbf{x}}_1 + \hat{\mathbf{x}}_2$$
$$Q(\hat{\mathbf{x}}_1, \hat{\mathbf{x}}_2; \mathbf{y}) = |\mathbf{y} - \hat{\mathbf{x}}_1' - \hat{\mathbf{x}}_2|^2 = |\mathbf{y} - \hat{\mathbf{x}}|^2 = |\hat{\mathbf{u}}|^2 = \hat{\mathbf{u}}'\hat{\mathbf{u}} = \mathbf{y}'A'A\mathbf{y} \geq 0$$

and therefore for the minimum

$$S(\hat{x}_1, \hat{x}_2; \mathbf{y}) = \lambda_1 Q_1(\hat{x}_1) + \lambda_2 Q_2(\hat{x}_2) + Q(\hat{\mathbf{x}}_1, \hat{\mathbf{x}}_2; \mathbf{y}) = \hat{\mathbf{x}}'\hat{\mathbf{u}} + \hat{\mathbf{u}}'\hat{\mathbf{u}} = \mathbf{y}'\hat{\mathbf{u}} = \mathbf{y}'A\mathbf{y}$$
$$= \mathbf{y}'\mathbf{y} - \mathbf{y}'W\mathbf{y} \leq \mathbf{y}'\mathbf{y}\,.$$

3.3.6 Empirical Coefficient of Determination

From $\mathbf{y} = \hat{\mathbf{x}} + \hat{\mathbf{u}}$ and $\overline{\hat{\mathbf{u}}} = 0$ (i.e. $\overline{\mathbf{y}} = \overline{\hat{\mathbf{x}}}$) follows for empirical covariances or variances (for $\mathbf{x}, \mathbf{y} \in \mathbb{R}_n$ defined as $s_{\mathbf{xy}} = \frac{1}{n}\mathbf{x}'\mathbf{y} - \overline{\mathbf{x}}\,\overline{\mathbf{y}}$ and $s_{\mathbf{x}}^2 = s_{\mathbf{xx}}$. The bar stands for the arithmetical mean)

$$\begin{aligned}\mathbf{y}'\mathbf{y} &= \hat{\mathbf{x}}'\hat{\mathbf{x}} + \hat{\mathbf{u}}'\hat{\mathbf{u}} + 2\hat{\mathbf{x}}'\hat{\mathbf{u}} \\ 1 &= R_0^2 + \tfrac{\hat{\mathbf{u}}'\hat{\mathbf{u}}}{\mathbf{y}'\mathbf{y}} + 2\tfrac{\hat{\mathbf{x}}'\hat{\mathbf{u}}}{\mathbf{y}'\mathbf{y}}\end{aligned} \quad \text{resp.} \quad \begin{aligned}s_{\mathbf{y}}^2 &= s_{\hat{\mathbf{x}}}^2 + s_{\hat{\mathbf{u}}}^2 + 2s_{\hat{\mathbf{x}}\hat{\mathbf{u}}} \\ 1 &= R^2 + \tfrac{s_{\hat{\mathbf{x}}}^2}{s_{\mathbf{y}}^2} + 2\tfrac{s_{\hat{\mathbf{u}}}^2}{s_{\mathbf{y}}^2}\end{aligned}$$

with *"empirical coefficients of determination"*

$$R_0^2 = \frac{\hat{\mathbf{x}}'\hat{\mathbf{x}}}{\mathbf{y}'\mathbf{y}}\,, \quad R^2 = \frac{s_{\hat{\mathbf{x}}}^2}{s_{\mathbf{y}}^2} \quad \text{und} \quad 0 \leq R^2 \leq R_0^2 \leq 1\,, \quad 0 \leq \frac{\hat{\mathbf{x}}'\hat{\mathbf{u}}}{\mathbf{y}'\mathbf{y}} \leq \frac{s_{\hat{\mathbf{x}}\hat{\mathbf{u}}}}{s_{\mathbf{y}}^2} < \frac{1}{2}\,.$$

1. For $R_0^2 = 1$ or $R^2 = 1$ is $\hat{\mathbf{u}} = 0$ and $\hat{\mathbf{x}}'\hat{\mathbf{u}} = \lambda_1 Q_1(\hat{x}_1) + \lambda_2 Q_2(\hat{x}_2) = 0$. Therefore we have an interpolation of data with a smoothest solution (with $T_1\hat{x}_1 = 0$, $T_2\hat{x}_2 = 0$).

2. For $R^2 = 0$ resp. $\hat{\mathbf{x}} = \bar{\hat{\mathbf{x}}}\mathbf{1} = \bar{\mathbf{y}}\mathbf{1}$ is $s^2_{\hat{\mathbf{u}}} = s^2_{\mathbf{y}}$, $s_{\hat{\mathbf{x}}\hat{\mathbf{u}}} = 0$ resp. $\lambda_1 Q_1(\hat{x}_1) + \lambda_2 Q_2(\hat{x}_2) = 0$. Consequently $\hat{x}_1(t) = \bar{\mathbf{y}}$, $\hat{x}_2(t) = 0$ is a solution (with $T_1\hat{x}_1 = 0$, $T_2\hat{x}_2 = 0$, $\hat{\mathbf{x}} = \bar{\mathbf{y}}\mathbf{1}$), "consisting of no trend and no season".

3.3.7 Properties of Monotonicity

To investigate the monotonicity of the functions

$$Q_1(\hat{x}_1; \lambda_1, \lambda_2)\,, \quad Q_2(\hat{x}_2; \lambda_1, \lambda_2)\,, \quad Q(\hat{\mathbf{x}}_1, \hat{\mathbf{x}}_2; \mathbf{y}; \lambda_1, \lambda_2)\,, \quad \text{and} \quad S(\hat{x}_1, \hat{x}_2; \mathbf{y}; \lambda_1, \lambda_2)$$

we look at the partial derivatives in λ_1, λ_2. With the general rule of derivation

$$\frac{\mathrm{d}M^{-1}(x)}{\mathrm{d}x} = -M^{-1}(x)\frac{\mathrm{d}M(x)}{\mathrm{d}x}M^{-1}(x) \quad \text{and especially} \quad \frac{\partial G}{\partial \lambda_i} = -\tfrac{1}{\lambda_i^2}G_i$$

(because $G = \frac{1}{\lambda_1}G_1 + \frac{1}{\lambda_2}G_2$) after Remark 5 holds

$$\frac{\partial A}{\partial \lambda_i} = -(I + A^*G)^{-1}(-A^*\tfrac{1}{\lambda_i^2}G_i)(I + A^*G)^{-1}A^* = \tfrac{1}{\lambda_i^2}AG_iA = \tfrac{1}{\lambda_i}W_i{}'A\,, \quad i = 1, 2\,.$$

The result is the "matrix of smoothness" of the weight function $\mathbf{w}_i(t)$.

- For the minimum $S(\hat{x}_1, \hat{x}_2; \mathbf{y})$ holds

$$\frac{\partial S(\hat{x}_1, \hat{x}_2; \mathbf{y})}{\partial \lambda_i} = \tfrac{1}{\lambda_i}\mathbf{y}'W_i{}'A\mathbf{y} = Q_i(\hat{x}_i) \geq 0\,, \quad i = 1, 2\,.$$

Therefore $S(\hat{x}_1, \hat{x}_2; \mathbf{y}; \lambda_1, \lambda_2)$ is monotonically not falling in both directions λ_1, λ_2. Furthermore it is convex (cf. Hebbel 2000):
- For $Q(\hat{\mathbf{x}}_1, \hat{\mathbf{x}}_2; \mathbf{y})$ holds (because of symmetry)

$$\frac{\partial Q(\hat{\mathbf{x}}_1, \hat{\mathbf{x}}_2; \mathbf{y})}{\partial \lambda_i} = \mathbf{y}'\Big(A\frac{\partial A}{\partial \lambda_i} + \frac{\partial A}{\partial \lambda_i}A\Big)\mathbf{y} = \tfrac{2}{\lambda_i^2}\mathbf{y}'W_i{}'AA\mathbf{y} = \tfrac{2}{\lambda_i}\hat{\mathbf{x}}_i'A\hat{\mathbf{u}} \geq 0\,, \quad i = 1, 2\,.$$

- For $Q_i(\hat{x}_i)$ resp. $\lambda_i Q_i(\hat{x}_i) = \hat{\mathbf{x}}_i'\hat{\mathbf{u}} = \frac{1}{\lambda_i}AG_iA$ hold (because of symmetry) with application of

$$\frac{\partial(AG_1A)}{\partial \lambda_i} = \tfrac{1}{\lambda_i}W_i{}'AG_1A + \tfrac{1}{\lambda_i}AG_1AW_i = 2\tfrac{\lambda_1}{\lambda_i}W_i{}'AW_1\,, \qquad \frac{\partial(AG_2A)}{\partial \lambda_i} = 2\tfrac{\lambda_2}{\lambda_i}W_i{}'AW_2$$

the relationships

$$\frac{\partial(\hat{\mathbf{x}}_1'\hat{\mathbf{u}})}{\partial\lambda_1} = -\tfrac{1}{\lambda_1}\hat{\mathbf{x}}_1'\hat{\mathbf{u}} + \tfrac{2}{\lambda_1}\hat{\mathbf{x}}_1'A\hat{\mathbf{x}}_1\,, \qquad \frac{\partial(\hat{\mathbf{x}}_1'\hat{\mathbf{u}})}{\partial\lambda_2} = \tfrac{2}{\lambda_2}\hat{\mathbf{x}}_1'A\hat{\mathbf{x}}_2 \geq 0\,,$$

$$\frac{\partial(\hat{\mathbf{x}}_2'\hat{\mathbf{u}})}{\partial\lambda_1} = \tfrac{2}{\lambda_1}\hat{\mathbf{x}}_2'A\hat{\mathbf{x}}_1 \geq 0\,, \qquad \frac{\partial(\hat{\mathbf{x}}_2'\hat{\mathbf{u}})}{\partial\lambda_2} = -\tfrac{1}{\lambda_2}\hat{\mathbf{x}}_2'\hat{\mathbf{u}} + \tfrac{2}{\lambda_2}\hat{\mathbf{x}}_2'A\hat{\mathbf{x}}_2$$

and analogously

$$\frac{\partial Q_1(\hat{x}_1)}{\partial\lambda_1} = -\tfrac{2}{\lambda_1^2}\hat{\mathbf{x}}_1'\hat{\mathbf{u}} + \tfrac{2}{\lambda_1^2}\hat{\mathbf{x}}_1'A\hat{\mathbf{x}}_1 \leq 0\,, \qquad \frac{\partial Q_1(\hat{x}_1)}{\partial\lambda_2} = \tfrac{2}{\lambda_1\lambda_2}\hat{\mathbf{x}}_1'A\hat{\mathbf{x}}_2 \geq 0\,,$$

$$\frac{\partial Q_2(\hat{x}_2)}{\partial\lambda_1} = \tfrac{2}{\lambda_1\lambda_2}\hat{\mathbf{x}}_2'A\hat{\mathbf{x}}_1 \geq 0\,, \qquad \frac{\partial Q_2(\hat{x}_2)}{\partial\lambda_2} = -\tfrac{2}{\lambda_2^2}\hat{\mathbf{x}}_2'\hat{\mathbf{u}} + \tfrac{2}{\lambda_2^2}\hat{\mathbf{x}}_2'A\hat{\mathbf{x}}_2 \leq 0\,.$$

3.3.8 Limiting Cases

The limiting cases which already were considered shortly in Sect. 3.1. can now be investigated more thoroughly. As a base we use the (spline-)representation

$$\begin{aligned}\hat{x}_1(t) &= \mathbf{f}_1(t)'\hat{\beta}_1 + \tfrac{1}{\lambda_1}\mathbf{g}_1(t)'\hat{\mathbf{u}}\\ \hat{x}_2(t) &= \mathbf{f}_2(t)'\hat{\beta}_2 + \tfrac{1}{\lambda_2}\mathbf{g}_2(t)'\hat{\mathbf{u}}\end{aligned} \quad \text{with} \quad \begin{pmatrix}0 & F'\\ F & H\end{pmatrix}\begin{pmatrix}\hat{\beta}\\ \hat{\mathbf{u}}\end{pmatrix} = \begin{pmatrix}0\\ \mathbf{y}\end{pmatrix}, \quad \hat{\beta} = \begin{pmatrix}\hat{\beta}_1\\ \hat{\beta}_2\end{pmatrix}$$

and $\hat{\beta} = B\mathbf{y}$, $\hat{\mathbf{u}} = A\mathbf{y}$.

0. $\lambda_1 \to \infty$, $\lambda_2 \to \infty$ *(smoothest trend and smoothest season in the sense of best fit according to $Q(\hat{\mathbf{x}}_1, \hat{\mathbf{x}}_2; \mathbf{y})$):* Because of

$$H = I + \tfrac{1}{\lambda_1}G_1 + \tfrac{1}{\lambda_2}G_2 \to I$$

$$\begin{pmatrix}0 & F'\\ F & H\end{pmatrix}\begin{pmatrix}\hat{\beta}\\ \hat{\mathbf{u}}\end{pmatrix} = \begin{pmatrix}0\\ \mathbf{y}\end{pmatrix} \to \begin{pmatrix}0 & F'\\ F & I\end{pmatrix}\begin{pmatrix}\hat{\beta}^*\\ \hat{\mathbf{u}}^*\end{pmatrix} = \begin{pmatrix}0\\ \mathbf{y}\end{pmatrix}$$

holds

$$\hat{x}_1(t) \to \mathbf{f}_1(t)'\hat{\beta}_1^* =: \hat{x}_1^*(t)\,, \quad \hat{x}_2(t) \to \mathbf{f}_2(t)'\hat{\beta}_2^* =: \hat{x}_2^*(t)$$

with smoothness values

$$Q_1(\hat{x}_1^*) = 0\,, \quad Q_2(\hat{x}_2^*) = 0 \quad \text{and} \quad S(\hat{x}_1^*, \hat{x}_2^*; \mathbf{y}) = \mathbf{y}'\hat{\mathbf{u}}^* = \hat{\mathbf{u}}^{*\prime}\hat{\mathbf{u}}^*\,.$$

Hereby

$$\begin{matrix} F'\hat{\mathbf{u}}^* = 0 \\ F\hat{\beta}^* + \hat{\mathbf{u}}^* = \mathbf{y} \end{matrix} \quad \text{also} \quad F'F\hat{\beta}^* = F'\mathbf{y}\,, \;\; \hat{\beta}^* = (F'F)^{-1}F'\mathbf{y}\,, \;\; \hat{\mathbf{u}}^* = \mathbf{y} - F\hat{\beta}^*$$

is the classical least squares estimator. Because of this property BV 4.1 in its base version is a special case of the method introduced here.

1. $\lambda_1 \to 0$, $\lambda_2 > 0$ fixed *(most flexible trend and smoothest season in the interpolation case)*: The results are independent of λ_2. From

$$\lambda_1 H = \lambda_1 I + G_1 + \tfrac{\lambda_1}{\lambda_2} G_2 \to G_1\,, \quad \tfrac{1}{\lambda_1}\hat{\mathbf{u}} \to \hat{\alpha}^{(1)}, \quad \text{i. e.} \quad \hat{\mathbf{u}} \to 0$$

$$\begin{pmatrix} 0 & F' \\ F & \lambda_1 H \end{pmatrix}\begin{pmatrix} \hat{\beta} \\ \frac{1}{\lambda_1}\hat{\mathbf{u}} \end{pmatrix} = \begin{pmatrix} 0 \\ \mathbf{y} \end{pmatrix} \to \begin{pmatrix} 0 & F' \\ F & G_1 \end{pmatrix}\begin{pmatrix} \hat{\beta}^{(1)} \\ \hat{\alpha}^{(1)} \end{pmatrix} = \begin{pmatrix} 0 \\ \mathbf{y} \end{pmatrix}$$

(solution of the system of equations, e.g. following Remark 5 with $(G_1 - I)$ instead of G) follows

$$\hat{x}_1(t) \to \mathbf{f}_1(t)'\hat{\beta}_1^{(1)} + \mathbf{g}_1(t)'\hat{\alpha}^{(1)} =: \hat{x}_1^{(1)}(t)\,, \quad \hat{x}_2(t) \to \mathbf{f}_2(t)'\hat{\beta}_2^{(1)} =: \hat{x}_2^{(1)}(t)$$

with maximum and minimum smoothness values

$$Q_1(\hat{x}_1^{(1)}) = \hat{\mathbf{x}}_1^{(1)\prime}\hat{\alpha}^{(1)}\,, \quad Q_2(\hat{x}_2^{(2)}) = 0 \quad \text{and} \quad S(\hat{x}_1^{(1)}, \hat{x}_2^{(1)}; \mathbf{y}) = 0\,.$$

2. $\lambda_2 \to 0$, $\lambda_1 > 0$ fixed *(smoothest trend and most flexible season in case of interpolation)*: The results are independent of λ_1. From

$$\lambda_2 H = \lambda_2 I + + \tfrac{\lambda_2}{\lambda_1} G_1 + G_2 \to G_2\,, \quad \tfrac{1}{\lambda_2}\hat{\mathbf{u}} \to \hat{\alpha}^{(2)}, \quad \text{i. e.} \quad \hat{\mathbf{u}} \to 0$$

$$\begin{pmatrix} 0 & F' \\ F & \lambda_2 H \end{pmatrix}\begin{pmatrix} \hat{\beta} \\ \frac{1}{\lambda_2}\hat{\mathbf{u}} \end{pmatrix} = \begin{pmatrix} 0 \\ \mathbf{y} \end{pmatrix} \to \begin{pmatrix} 0 & F' \\ F & G_2 \end{pmatrix}\begin{pmatrix} \hat{\beta}^{(2)} \\ \hat{\alpha}^{(2)} \end{pmatrix} = \begin{pmatrix} 0 \\ \mathbf{y} \end{pmatrix}$$

(solution of the system of equations, e.g. following Remark 5 with $(G_2 - I)$ instead of G) follows

$$\hat{x}_1(t) \to \mathbf{f}_1(t)'\hat{\beta}_1^{(2)} =: \hat{x}_1^{(2)}(t)\,, \quad \hat{x}_2(t) \to \mathbf{f}_2(t)'\hat{\beta}_2^{(2)} + \mathbf{g}_2(t)'\hat{\alpha}^{(2)} =: \hat{x}_2^{(2)}(t)$$

with minimum and maximum smoothness values

$$Q_1(\hat{x}_1^{(2)}) = 0\,, \quad Q_2(\hat{x}_2^{(2)}) = \hat{\mathbf{x}}_2^{(2)\prime}\hat{\alpha}^{(2)} \quad \text{and} \quad S(\hat{x}_1^{(2)}, \hat{x}_2^{(2)}; \mathbf{y}) = 0\,.$$

3. $\lambda_1 \to \infty$, $\lambda_2 > 0$ fixed *(smoothest trend)*: The results are dependent on λ_2. Because of

$$H = I + \frac{1}{\lambda_1} G_1 + \frac{1}{\lambda_2} G_2 \to I + \frac{1}{\lambda_2} G_2$$

$$\begin{pmatrix} 0 & F' \\ F & H \end{pmatrix} \begin{pmatrix} \hat{\beta} \\ \hat{\mathbf{u}} \end{pmatrix} = \begin{pmatrix} 0 \\ \mathbf{y} \end{pmatrix} \to \begin{pmatrix} 0 & F' \\ F & I + \frac{1}{\lambda_2} G_2 \end{pmatrix} \begin{pmatrix} \hat{\beta}^{(3)} \\ \hat{\mathbf{u}}^{(3)} \end{pmatrix} = \begin{pmatrix} 0 \\ \mathbf{y} \end{pmatrix}$$

(solution of the system of equations e.g., following Remark 4 or 5 with $G = \frac{1}{\lambda_2} G_2$) holds

$$\hat{x}_1(t) \to \mathbf{f}_1(t)'\hat{\beta}_1^{(3)} =: \hat{x}_1^{(3)}(t)\,, \quad \hat{x}_2(t) \to \mathbf{f}_2(t)'\hat{\beta}_2^{(3)} + \frac{1}{\lambda_2}\mathbf{g}_2(t)'\hat{\mathbf{u}}^{(3)} =: \hat{x}_2^{(3)}(t)$$

with smoothness values

$$Q_1(\hat{x}_1^{(3)}) = 0\,, \quad Q_2(\hat{x}_2^{(3)}) = \frac{1}{\lambda_2}\hat{\mathbf{x}}_2^{(3)\prime}\hat{\mathbf{u}}^{(3)} \quad \text{and} \quad S(\hat{x}_1^{(3)}, \hat{x}_2^{(3)}; \mathbf{y}) = \mathbf{y}'\hat{\mathbf{u}}^{(3)}\,.$$

4. $\lambda_2 \to \infty$, $\lambda_1 > 0$ fixed *(smoothest season)*: The results depend on λ_1. Because of

$$H = I + \frac{1}{\lambda_1} G_1 + \frac{1}{\lambda_2} G_2 \to I + \frac{1}{\lambda_1} G_1$$

$$\begin{pmatrix} 0 & F' \\ F & H \end{pmatrix} \begin{pmatrix} \hat{\beta} \\ \hat{\mathbf{u}} \end{pmatrix} = \begin{pmatrix} 0 \\ \mathbf{y} \end{pmatrix} \to \begin{pmatrix} 0 & F' \\ F & I + \frac{1}{\lambda_1} G_1 \end{pmatrix} \begin{pmatrix} \hat{\beta}^{(4)} \\ \hat{\mathbf{u}}^{(4)} \end{pmatrix} = \begin{pmatrix} 0 \\ \mathbf{y} \end{pmatrix}$$

(solution of the system of equations, e.g. following Remark 4 or 5 with $G = \frac{1}{\lambda_1} G_1$) holds

$$\hat{x}_1(t) \to \mathbf{f}_1(t)'\hat{\beta}_1^{(4)} + \frac{1}{\lambda_1}\mathbf{g}_1(t)'\hat{\mathbf{u}}^{(4)} =: \hat{x}_1^{(4)}(t)\,, \quad \hat{x}_2(t) \to \mathbf{f}_2(t)'\hat{\beta}_2^{(4)} =: \hat{x}_2^{(4)}(t)$$

with smoothness values

$$Q_1(\hat{x}_1^{(4)}) = \frac{1}{\lambda_1}\hat{\mathbf{x}}_1^{(4)\prime}\hat{\mathbf{u}}^{(4)}\,, \quad Q_2(\hat{x}_2^{(4)}) = 0 \quad \text{and} \quad S(\hat{x}_1^{(4)}, \hat{x}_2^{(4)}; \mathbf{y}) = \mathbf{y}'\hat{\mathbf{u}}^{(4)}\,.$$

3.3.9 Property of Iteration

It is interesting to see what solution this method produces if it is applied on the "smoothed" solution $\hat{\mathbf{x}} = \hat{\mathbf{x}}_1 + \hat{\mathbf{x}}_2$ instead of $\mathbf{y}$ etc. After $m = 1, 2, \ldots$ iterations we get with "starting values" $\hat{x}_1^{(1)}(t) = \hat{x}_1(t)$, $\hat{x}_2^{(1)}(t) = \hat{x}_2(t)$ and $\hat{\mathbf{x}}^{(0)} = \mathbf{y}$

$$\begin{aligned} \hat{x}_1^{(m)}(t) &= \mathbf{w}_1(t)'\hat{\mathbf{x}}^{(m-1)} & & \lambda_1 Q_1(\hat{x}_1^{(m)}) = \hat{\mathbf{x}}_1^{(m)\prime}\hat{\mathbf{u}}^{(m)} \\ \hat{x}_2^{(m)}(t) &= \mathbf{w}_2(t)'\hat{\mathbf{x}}^{(m-1)} & \text{with} \quad & \lambda_2 Q_2(\hat{x}_2^{(m)}) = \hat{\mathbf{x}}_2^{(m)\prime}\hat{\mathbf{u}}^{(m)} \\ \hat{x}^{(m)}(t) &= \hat{x}_1^{(m)}(t) + \hat{x}_2^{(m)}(t) & & \lambda_1 Q_1(\hat{x}_1^{(m)}) + \lambda_2 Q_2(\hat{x}_2^{(m)}) = \hat{\mathbf{x}}^{(m)\prime}\hat{\mathbf{u}}^{(m)} \end{aligned}$$

and $\hat{\mathbf{u}}^{(m)} = \hat{\mathbf{x}}^{(m-1)} - \hat{\mathbf{x}}^{(m)}$. Now holds

$$\hat{x}_1^{(m)}(t) - \hat{x}_1^{(m+1)}(t) = \mathbf{w}_1(t)'\hat{\mathbf{u}}^{(m)}, \quad \hat{x}_2^{(m)}(t) - \hat{x}_2^{(m+1)}(t) = \mathbf{w}_2(t)'\hat{\mathbf{u}}^{(m)}, \quad t \in [a,b].$$

Because of the minimum property it is easy to see that $\lim_{n\to\infty} |\hat{\mathbf{u}}^{(m)}|^2 = 0$, that is $\hat{\mathbf{u}}^{(m)} \to 0$ converges. If $\hat{\mathbf{u}}^{(m)} = 0$ is already reached in step m the solutions remain in a fixed point and are smoothest solutions in the sense of this method. Otherwise the solution converge to the smoothest solutions in the sense of the method, see Hebbel (2000) or Bieckmann (1987, p. 57 ff).

3.4 Choice of Smoothing Parameters

The choice of smoothing parameters λ_1, λ_2 depends on the question how "smooth" trend function $\hat{x}_1$ and how "smooth" season function $\hat{x}_2$ should be to give at the same time a good fit to the data. Following the subsection on smoothness values of the solutions holds

$$S(\hat{x}_1, \hat{x}_2; \mathbf{y}) = \overbrace{\hat{x}_1'\hat{\mathbf{u}}}^{\lambda_1 Q_1(\hat{x}_1)} + \overbrace{\hat{x}_2'\hat{\mathbf{u}}}^{\lambda_2 Q_2(\hat{x}_2)} + \hat{\mathbf{u}}'\hat{\mathbf{u}} = \hat{\mathbf{x}}'\hat{\mathbf{u}} + \hat{\mathbf{u}}'\hat{\mathbf{u}} = \mathbf{y}'\hat{\mathbf{u}} = \mathbf{y}'\mathbf{y} + \hat{\mathbf{x}}'\mathbf{y} \leq \mathbf{y}'\mathbf{y}$$

resp.

$$\mathbf{y}'\mathbf{y} = \hat{\mathbf{x}}'\hat{\mathbf{x}} + \hat{\mathbf{u}}'\hat{\mathbf{u}} + 2\hat{\mathbf{x}}'\hat{\mathbf{u}} = \hat{\mathbf{x}}'\hat{\mathbf{x}} + \hat{\mathbf{x}}'\hat{\mathbf{u}} + S(\hat{x}_1, \hat{x}_2; \mathbf{y}) = \hat{\mathbf{x}}'\mathbf{y} + S(\hat{x}_1, \hat{x}_2; \mathbf{y})$$

The part of variation explained by the fit $\hat{\mathbf{x}}'\hat{\mathbf{x}}/\mathbf{y}'\mathbf{y}$ shall be large, therefore the parts explained by weighted smoothness values $\hat{x}_1'\hat{\mathbf{u}}/\mathbf{y}'\mathbf{y}$ and $\hat{x}_2'\hat{\mathbf{u}}/\mathbf{y}'\mathbf{y}$ must be relatively small. An obvious idea is to try to choose these two parts equal in size.

Generalised cross validation

$$\min_{\lambda_1,\lambda_2} V(\lambda_1, \lambda_2) = \quad \text{mit} \quad V = \frac{\hat{\mathbf{u}}'\hat{\mathbf{u}}}{\frac{1}{n}(\mathrm{tr}(A))^2}$$

doesn't produce satisfactory results in the following examples. Its solution tends to produce too rough seasonal components. Therefore it is recommended to choose values near the minimum such that weighted smoothness values are of same size or keep some predefined value.

4 Local, Moving Version

One can think of a lot of causes to modify the described method. May be it is irritating for a user that figures for the past change if new values enter the calculations. May be there occur numerical problems for long time series when very large matrices must be inverted. This problem may be avoidable if an iterative approach to estimation is chosen. In the following we will use the property of invariance against shifts in time, the same way BV 4.1 tries to avoid some of the problems.

It's natural, as in the Berliner Verfahren, to formulate the model not for the complete, possible observation time interval, but only for smaller parts of *support* of possible observation times, which "slides" over the time axis. This sliding technique is useful especially for equidistant (in time) data and *odd* number of observations. Estimations are performed for the first, second and finally last, moving window. As seen in Sect. 3.2 the weight vectors $\hat{\mathbf{w}}_1(t)$ and $\hat{\mathbf{w}}_2(t)$ resp. weight matrices W_1 and W_2 must be calculated and multiplied by the respective data vector for each moving support window. Trend and season in these observational point then are given by

$$\hat{\mathbf{x}}_1 = W_1 y \quad \text{and} \quad \hat{\mathbf{x}}_2 = W_2 y$$

in each support window.

The big advantage of this approach is that the weight matrices have to be calculated only once (invariance against shift). While estimating "in the middle" of the data there are m different supports areas around a point t which can be used for estimation in point t. Any of the rows of the weight matrix W_1 resp. W_2 could possibly be used to be multiplied with the data and generate an estimation. Naturally the question arises, if there is a good choice between the columns. Should some row be preferred?

The theory of filters suggests the use of a symmetric weight row. That way phase shifts in the oscillations can be avoided. Symmetric rows, on the other hand, are only found in the middle of the weight matrices W_1 resp. W_2, if m is odd. If m is even, the mean of the two middle rows of the weight matrices could be used.

Nearing the edges we simply use the next row of weights, therefore at the edges (of length $k = \frac{m-1}{2}$) we have a usual regression estimation (different weight rows, fixed data) and in the area away from the edges we have a sliding estimation (fixed weight rows (same filter), different data (shifted by one unit of time each)).

Thus the estimators of trend ($i = 1$) and season ($i = 2$) (m odd) in points in time $t = 1, \ldots, n$ can be written as follows:

$$\begin{pmatrix} \hat{x}_i(1) \\ \vdots \\ \hat{x}_i(k+1) \\ \vdots \\ \vdots \\ \hat{x}_i(n-k) \\ \vdots \\ \hat{x}_i(n) \end{pmatrix} = \begin{pmatrix} w^{(i)}_{-k,-k} & \cdots & w^{(i)}_{-k,k} & & & & \\ \vdots & & \vdots & & & & \\ w^{(i)}_{0,-k} & \cdots & w^{(i)}_{0,k} & & 0 & & \\ & \ddots & & & \ddots & & \\ & & \ddots & & & \ddots & \\ & & 0 & & w^{(i)}_{0,-k} & \cdots & w^{(i)}_{0,k} \\ & & & & \vdots & & \vdots \\ & & & & w^{(i)}_{k,-k} & \cdots & w^{(i)}_{k,k} \end{pmatrix} \begin{pmatrix} y_1 \\ \vdots \\ y_{k+1} \\ \vdots \\ \vdots \\ y_{n-k} \\ \vdots \\ y_n \end{pmatrix}$$

with weight matrix

$$W_i = \begin{pmatrix} w^{(i)}_{-k,-k} & \cdots & w^{(i)}_{-k,k} \\ \vdots & & \vdots \\ w^{(i)}_{k,-k} & \cdots & w^{(i)}_{k,k} \end{pmatrix}, \quad i = 1,2$$

for a support area of length $m = 2k + 1$.

For choosing a suitable length of support we can use the experiences from using the Berliner Verfahren. The choice of different lengths of support for different components (for example, 27 for trend and 47 for season in the case of monthly data see Speth 2006) seems inconsequential, just as the procedure at the edges.

At the edges we can't choose weights according to filter criteria, because filters are defined only for time intervals, not for points in time. Therefore it looks natural to change to "regression estimation" there according to the construction of the model. We recommend a support of length $m = 25 \ldots 31$. In that case only the last 12–15 values are "intermediate", because older values of components don't change any more if new data arrives.

5 Examples for Decompositions with VBV

We want to show two exemplary decompositions of time series performed with VBV as described in this paper. The source code implementing VBV in R (R Core Team 2013) is available from http://r-forge.r-project.org in package VBV.

5.1 Algorithm

The algorithm used follows the steps outlined below.

5.1.1 Parameter Settings

Time $t \in [a, b]$ is measured in units that are natural to the problem (e.g. sec, min, h, d, weeks, months, quarters).

- Observation times $t_1, \ldots, t_n$ with data $y_1, \ldots, y_n$
- Order of polynomial of trend function$p$, i. a. $p = 2$

- Order of trigonometric polynomial of the seasonal function $n_1, \dots, n_q \in \mathbb{N}$ for base period $S \le b-a$ (with $n_j < \frac{S}{2}$), results in "seasonal frequencies" $\omega_j = \frac{2\pi}{S} n_j$, set $\overline{n} = \frac{1}{q}\sum_{j=1}^{q} n_j$, $\overline{\omega} = \frac{2\pi}{S}\overline{n}$
- smoothness penalty parameter for trend λ_1
- smoothness penalty parameter for season λ_2 bzw. $\tilde{\lambda}_2 = 2\overline{\omega}^{4q-1}\lambda_2$

5.1.2 Truncated Functions

- Elements of trend, in dependence of p, t_k

$$g_1(t-t_k) = \left(t-t_k\right)^{2p-1}, \quad t > t_k$$

  and 0 for $t \le t_k$
- elements of season, in dependence of ω_j, t_k

$$\tilde{g}_2(t-t_k) = \sum_{j=1}^{q} \tilde{a}_j \left(\tilde{b}_j \sin\omega_j(t-t_k) - \overline{\omega}(t-t_k)\cos\omega_j(t-t_k)\right), \quad t > t_k$$

  and 0 for $t \le t_k$ with

$$\tilde{a}_j = \frac{1}{\left(\nu_j \prod_{\substack{i=1\\i\neq j}}^{q} (\nu_i^2 - \nu_j^2)\right)^2}, \quad \tilde{b}_j = \frac{1}{\nu_j} - 4\nu_j \sum_{\substack{i=1\\i\neq j}}^{q} \frac{1}{\nu_i^2 - \nu_j^2} \quad \text{and} \quad \nu_j = \frac{n_j}{\overline{n}}.$$

5.1.3 Vector Functions and Matrices

Preparation of

$$\mathbf{f}_{10}(t)' = (1 \quad t \quad \cdots \quad t^{p-1} \quad 0 \quad 0 \quad \cdots \quad 0 \quad 0), F_{10} = \begin{pmatrix} \mathbf{f}_{10}(t_1)' \\ \vdots \\ \mathbf{f}_{10}(t_n)' \end{pmatrix}$$

$$\mathbf{f}_{02}(t)' = (0 \; 0 \; \cdots \; 0 \; \cos\omega_1 t \;\; \sin\omega_1 t \; \cdots \; \cos\omega_q t \;\; \sin\omega_q t), \;\; F_{02} = \begin{pmatrix} \mathbf{f}_{02}(t_1)' \\ \vdots \\ \mathbf{f}_{02}(t_n)' \end{pmatrix}$$

and here, because of the independence of the origin the points in time t (and therefore the points in time $t_1, \dots, t_n$) can be replaced with $\tilde{t} = t - t_0$ with any t_0, i.e. $t_0 = \frac{1}{2}(a+b)$ or $t_0 = \frac{1}{2}(t_1 + t_n)$,

$$\mathbf{g}_1(t)' = \big(g_1(t-t_1) \cdots g_1(t-t_n)\big)\,, \quad G_1 = \begin{pmatrix} \mathbf{g}_1(t_1)' \\ \vdots \\ \mathbf{g}_1(t_n)' \end{pmatrix}$$

$$\tilde{\mathbf{g}}_2(t)' = \big(\tilde{g}_2(t-t_1) \cdots \tilde{g}_2(t-t_n)\big)\,, \quad \tilde{G}_2 = \begin{pmatrix} \tilde{\mathbf{g}}_2(t_1)' \\ \vdots \\ \tilde{\mathbf{g}}_2(t_n)' \end{pmatrix}$$

and

$$F = F_{10} + F_{02}\,, \quad \tilde{G} = \tfrac{1}{\lambda_1} G_1 + \tfrac{1}{\tilde{\lambda}_2} \tilde{G}_2\,.$$

5.1.4 Intermediate Calculations

$$B^* = (F'F)^{-1}F'\,, \quad A^* = I - FB^* \quad \text{gives} \quad A = \big(I + A^*\tilde{G}\big)^{-1} A^*\,.$$

5.1.5 Weight Functions and Weight Matrices

$$\begin{aligned} \mathbf{w}_1(t)' &= \mathbf{f}_{10}(t)'B + \tilde{\mathbf{g}}_1(t)'A \\ \mathbf{w}_2(t)' &= \mathbf{f}_{02}(t)'B + \tilde{\mathbf{g}}_2(t)'A \end{aligned} \quad \text{esp.} \quad W_1 = \begin{pmatrix} \mathbf{w}_1(t_1)' \\ \vdots \\ \mathbf{w}_1(t_n)' \end{pmatrix}, \quad W_2 = \begin{pmatrix} \mathbf{w}_2(t_1)' \\ \vdots \\ \mathbf{w}_2(t_n)' \end{pmatrix}$$

5.1.6 Solutions for Data-Vector

$$\begin{aligned} \hat{x}_1(t) &= \mathbf{w}_1(t)'\mathbf{y} \\ \hat{x}_2(t) &= \mathbf{w}_2(t)'\mathbf{y} \end{aligned} \quad \text{esp.} \quad \hat{\mathbf{x}}_1 = \begin{pmatrix} \hat{x}_1(t_1) \\ \vdots \\ \hat{x}_1(t_n) \end{pmatrix} = W_1\mathbf{y}\,, \quad \hat{\mathbf{x}}_2 = \begin{pmatrix} \hat{x}_2(t_1) \\ \vdots \\ \hat{x}_2(t_n) \end{pmatrix} = W_2\mathbf{y}\,.$$

5.2 Decomposition of Unemployment Numbers in Germany

We use the last 103 observations of German monthly unemployment numbers from the Federal Employment Agency (Statistik der Bundesagentur für Arbeit,

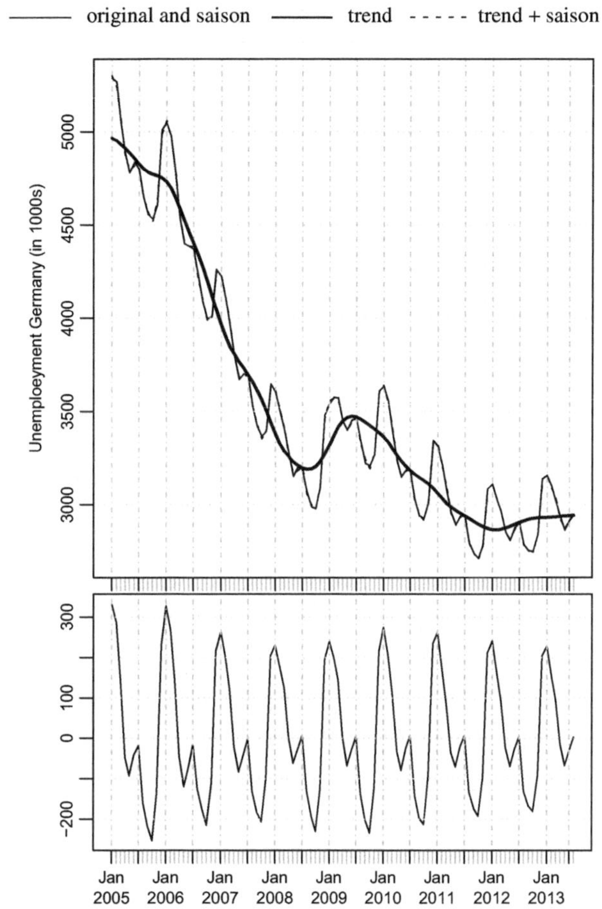

Fig. 2 Decomposition of unemployment numbers in Germany ($\lambda_1 = 6, \lambda_2 = 68$)

statistik.arbeitsagentur.de, Statistik nach Themen, Zeitreihen) starting in January 2005. The parameters used in Fig. 2 were $\lambda_1 = 6$, $\lambda_2 = 68$. These parameters were chosen near to a solution from generalised cross validation but improved using the constraint that the weighted smoothness values $\lambda_1 Q_1(\hat{x}_1) = \hat{\mathbf{x}}_1'\hat{\mathbf{u}}$ and $\lambda_2 Q_2(\hat{x}_2) = \hat{\mathbf{x}}_2'\hat{\mathbf{u}}$ are equal. The decomposition performed is the global version using all observations at the same time.

As a reference we use the same data to fit a local model (see Fig. 3) with $m = 31$ and the same λ_1, λ_2 as above.

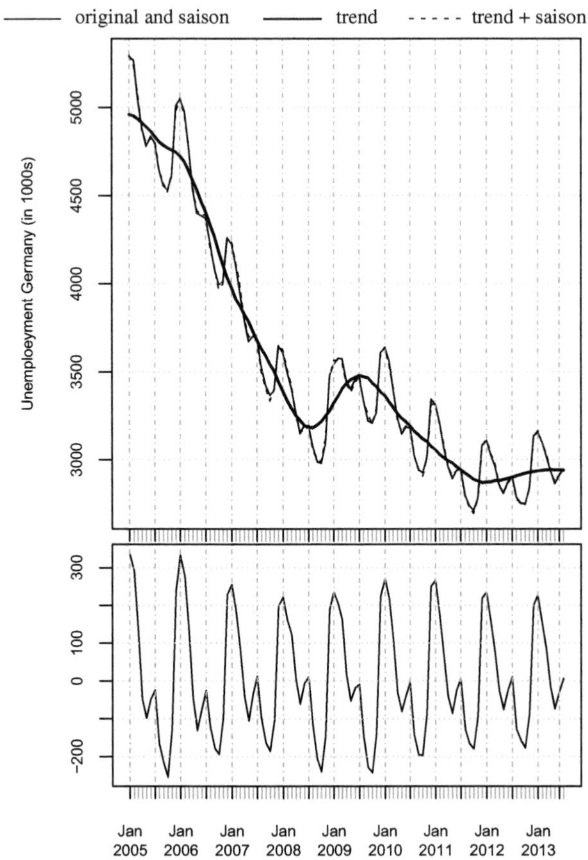

Fig. 3 Decomposition of unemployment numbers in Germany—a local model with $m = 31$ and $\lambda_1 = 6, \lambda_2 = 68$

5.3 *Decomposition of the DAX Closings*

We use the DAX closings since 2012-01-01 (from Yahoo Finance, created with quantmod) to show an example of VBV in its local variant using moving windows for local estimations (Fig. 4).

The parameters used were $m = 201, S = 56, \lambda_1 = 10{,}000, \lambda_2 = 1{,}000$.

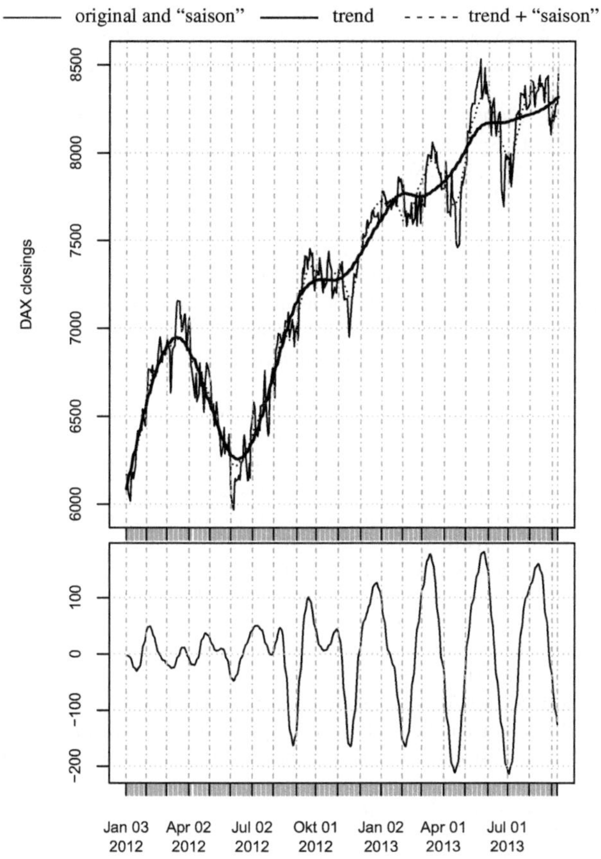

Fig. 4 Decomposition of the DAX closings ($m = 201$, $S = 56$, $\lambda_1 = 10{,}000$, $\lambda_2 = 1{,}000$)

References

Akaike, H. (1980). Seasonal adjustment by a bayesian modeling. *Journal of Time Series Analysis, 1*, 1–13.

Akaike, H., & Ishiguro, M. (1980). *BAYSEA, a bayesian seasonal adjustment program*. Computer Science Monographs (Vol. 13). Tokyo: The Institute for Statistical Methods.

Bell, W. R. (1998). An overview of regARIMA modeling. Research report. Statistical Research Division, U.S. Census Bureau.

Bieckmann, B. (1987). Ein allgemeines Modell zur Zeitreihenzerlegung. Diplomarbeit am Fachbereich Statistik, Universität Dortmund.

Cleveland, W. S., Devlin, S. J., & Terpenning, I. J. (1982). The SABL seasonal and calendar adjustment procedures. In O. D. Anderson (Ed.), *Time series analysis: Theory and practice* (Vol. 1, pp. 539–564). Amsterdam: North-Holland.

Dagum, E. B. (1980). The X-11-ARIMA seasonal adjustment method. Technical Report 12-564E. Statistics, Canada.

Deutsche Bundesbank. (1999). The changeover from the seasonal adjustment method Census X-11 to Census X-12-ARIMA. *Monthly Report, Deutsche Bundesbank, 51*(9), 39–50.
Edel, K., Schäffer, K.-A., & Stier, W. (Eds.). (1997). *Analyse saisonaler Zeitreihen*. Heidelberg: Physica.
European Commission. (2006). The joint harmonised EU programme of business and consumer surveys (pp. 113–114). Special report no 5, Annex A.2.
Findley, D. F., Monsell, B. C., Bell, W. R., Otto, M. C., & Chen, B.-C. (1998). New capabilities and methods of the X-12-ARIMA seasonal adjustment program. *Journal of Business and Economic Statistics, 16*(2), 127–176.
Foldesi, E., Bauer, P., Horvath, B., & Urr, B. (2007). Seasonal adjustment methods and practices. European Commission Grant 10300.2005.021-2005.709, Budapest.
Gómez, V., & Maravall, A. (1998). Guide for using the program TRAMO and SEATS. Working Paper 9805, Research Department, Banco de Espãna.
Hebbel, H. (1978). *Splines in linearen Räumen und Anwendungen in der Datenanalyse* (Dissertation). Universität Dortmund.
Hebbel, H. (1981). Exponentielle und trigonometrische Splinefunktionen. Forschungsbericht 1981/4 Fachbereich Statistik, Universität Dortmund.
Hebbel, H. (1982). Lineare Systeme, Analysen, Schätzungen und Prognosen (unter Verwendung von Splinefunktionen). Habilitationsschrift. Universität Dortmund.
Hebbel, H. (1984). Glättung von Zeitreihen über Zustandsraummodelle. Forschungsbericht 1984/17 Fachbereich Statistik, Universität Dortmund.
Hebbel, H. (1997). Verallgemeinertes Berliner Verfahren VBV. In K. Edel, K.-A. Schäffer, & W. Stier (Eds.), *Analyse saisonaler Zeitreihen* (pp. 83–93). Heidelberg: Physica.
Hebbel, H. (2000). *Weiterentwicklung der Zeitreihenzerlegung nach dem Verallgemeinerten Berliner Verfahren (VBV)*. Discussion Papers in Statistics and Quantitative Economics, Universität der Bundeswehr, Hamburg.
Hebbel, H., & Heiler, S. (1985). Zeitreihenglättung in einem Fehler-in-den-Variablen-Modell. In G. Buttler, H. Dickmann, E. Helten, & F. Vogel (Eds.), *Statistik zwischen Theorie und Praxis* (pp. 105–17). Festschrift für K-A Schäffer zur Vollendung seines 60. Lebensjahres. Göttingen:V&R.
Hebbel, H., & Heiler, S. (1987). Trend and seasonal decomposition in discrete time. *Statistische Hefte, 28*, 133–158.
Hebbel, H., & Heiler, S. (1987). Zeitreihenzerlegung über ein Optimalitätskriterium. *Allgemeines Statistisches Archiv, 71*, 305–318.
Hebbel, H., & Kuhlmeyer, N. (1983). Eine Weiterentwicklung von Heiler's Berliner Verfahren. Forschungsbericht 1983/9 Fachbereich Statistik, Universität Dortmund.
Heiler, S., & Feng, Y. (2004). A robust data-driven version of the Berlin method. In R. Metz, M. Lösch, & K. Edel (Eds.), *Zeitreihenanalyse in der empirischen Wirtschaftsforschung* (pp. 67–81). Festschrift für Winfried Stier zum 65. Geburtstag, Stuttgart: Lucius & Lucius.
Heiler, S., & Michels, P. (1994). *Deskriptive und Explorative Datenanalyse*. München/Wien: Oldenbourg.
Heuer, C. (1991). Ansätze zur simultanen Schätzung von Trend- und Klimaparametern in Jahrringreihen aus der Dendrologie. Diplomarbeit Fachbereich Statistik, Universität Dortmund.
Kitagawa, G. (1985). A smoothness priors-time varying AR coefficient modelling of nonstationary covariance time series. *The IEEE Transactions on Automatic Control, 30*, 48–56.
Koopman, S. J., Harvey, A. C., Doornik, J. A., & Shephard, N. (2010). *Structural time series analyser, modeller and predictor: STAMP 8.3*. London: Timberlake Consultants Ltd.
Ladiray, D., & Quenneville, B. (2001). *Seasonal adjustment with the X-11 method*. Lecture notes in statistics (Vol. 158). New York: Springer.
Michel, O. (2008). *Zeitreihenzerlegung mittels des mehrkomponentigen Verallgemeinerten Berliner Verfahrens* (Dissertation). Fachbereich Mathematik und Informatik, Universitt Bremen.

Nullau, B., Heiler, S., Wäsch, P., Meisner, B., & Filip, D. (1969). *Das "Berliner Verfahren". Ein Beitrag zur Zeitreihenanalyse*. Deutsches Institut für Wirtschaftsforschung (DIW), Beiträge zur Strukturforschung 7. Berlin: Duncker & Humblot.

Pauly, R., & Schlicht, E. (1983). Desciptive seasonal adjustment by minimizing pertubations. *Empirica, 1*, 15–28.

R Core Team. (2013). R: A language and environment for statistical computing. R Foundation for Statistical Computing. http://www.R-project.org/.

Schlicht, E. (1976). A seasonal adjustment principle and a seasonal adjustment method derived from this principle. *The Journal of the Acoustical Society of America, 76*, 374–378.

Shiskin, J., Young, A. H., & Musgrave, J. C. (1967). The X-11 variant of the census method II seasonal adjustment programm. Technical Paper 15, U.S. Department of Commerce, Bureau of the Census.

Speth, H.-Th. (2006). *The BV4.1 procedure for decomposing and seasonally adjusting economic time series*. Wiesbaden: Statistisches Bundesamt.

Statistisches Bundesamt. (2013). Volkswirtschaftliche Gesamtrechnungen. Fachserie 18 Reihe 1.3, 1. Vierteljahr 2013 Wiesbaden.

Uhlig, S., & Kuhbier, P. (2001a). Methoden der Trendabschätzung zur Überprüfung von Reduktionszielen im Gewässerschutz. Umweltbundesamt, Berlin (Texte 49/01, UBA-FB 00204).

Uhlig, S., & Kuhbier, P. (2001b). Trend methods for the assessment of effectiveness of reduction measures in the water system. Federal Environmental Agency (Umwelbundesamt), Berlin (Texte 80/01, UBA-FB 00204/e).

U.S. Census Bureau, Time Series Research Staff. (2013). *X-13ARIMA-SEATS Reference Manual*. Washington, DC: Statistical Research Division, U.S. Census Bureau.

Whaba, G. (1990). Spline models for observational data. In *CBMS-NSF Regional Conference Series in Applied Mathematics*. Philadelphia: SIAM.

Time Series Segmentation Procedures to Detect, Locate and Estimate Change-Points

Ana Laura Badagián, Regina Kaiser, and Daniel Peña

Abstract This article deals with the problem of detecting, locating, and estimating the change-points in a time series process. We are interested in finding changes in the mean and the autoregressive coefficients in piecewise autoregressive processes, as well as changes in the variance of the innovations. With this objective, we propose an approach based on the Bayesian information criterion (BIC) and binary segmentation. The proposed procedure is compared with several others available in the literature which are based on cusum methods (Inclán and Tiao, J Am Stat Assoc 89(427):913–923, 1994), minimum description length principle (Davis et al., J Am Stat Assoc 101(473):229–239, 2006), and the time varying spectrum (Ombao et al., Ann Inst Stat Math 54(1):171–200, 2002). We computed the empirical size and power properties of the available procedures in several Monte Carlo scenarios and also compared their performance in a speech recognition dataset.

1 Introduction

In this article we consider the problem of modelling a nonstationary time series by segmenting it into blocks which are fitted by stationary processes. The segmentation aims to: (1) find the periods of stability and homogeneity in the behavior of the process; (2) identify the moments of change, called change-points; (3) represent the regularities and features of each piece; and (4) use this information in order to determine the pattern in the nonstationary time series.

Time series segmentation and change-point detection and location has many applications in several disciplines, such as neurology, cardiology, speech recognition, finance, and others. Consider questions like: What are the main features of the brain activity when an epileptic patient suffers a seizure? Is the heart rate variability reduced after ischemic stroke? What are the most useful phonetic features to recognizing speech data? Is the conditional volatility of the financial assets constant? These questions can often be answered by performing segmentation analysis. The

A.L. Badagián (✉) • R. Kaiser • D. Peña
Statistics Department, Universidad Carlos III de Madrid, Madrid, Spain
e-mail: abadagia@est-econ.uc3m.es; kaiser@est-econ.uc3m.es; dpena@est-econ.uc3m.es

J. Beran et al. (eds.), *Empirical Economic and Financial Research*,
Advanced Studies in Theoretical and Applied Econometrics 48,
DOI 10.1007/978-3-319-03122-4_3

reason is that many series in these fields do not behave as stationary, but can be represented by approximately stationary intervals or pieces.

Segmentation analysis aims to answer the following questions: Did a change occur? When did the changes occur? If more than one change occurs, how can we locate them? Whereas the first two questions refer to the problem of defining a statistical criteria for detecting, estimating, and locating a change-point, the last one is related with the difficult task of creating a strategy, implemented in an algorithm, in order to search for multiple change-points.

When multiple change-points are expected, as its number and location are usually unknown, the multiple searching issue is very intricate. It is a challenge to jointly estimate the number of structural breaks and their location, and also provide a estimation of the model representing each interval. This problem has received considerably less attention than the detection and estimation of a single change-point, due to the difficulty in handling the computations. Many algorithms exist to calculate the optimal number and location of the change-points, some of them were presented by Scott and Knott (1974), Inclán and Tiao (1994), Auger and Lawrence (1989), Jackson et al. (2005), and Davis et al. (2006)

The main contributions of this paper are: (a) proposing a procedure based on the BIC joint with the binary segmentation algorithm to look for changes in the mean, the autoregressive coefficients, and the variance of perturbation in piecewise autoregressive processes, by using a procedure; (b) comparing this procedure with several others available in the literature, which are based on cusum methods (Inclán and Tiao 1994; Lee et al. 2003), minimum description length (MDL) principle (Davis et al. 2006), and the time varying spectrum (Ombao et al. 2002). For that, we compute the empirical size and the power properties in several scenarios and we apply them to a speech recognition dataset.

The article is organized as follows. In Sect. 2 we present the change-point problem. Following, in Sect. 3, we briefly present cusum methods, Auto-PARM and Auto-SLEX procedures. The final part of this section is dedicated to the informational approach procedures and the proposed procedure based on BIC is presented. Section 4 presents different algorithms that are useful to search for multiple change-points. In Sect. 5 we compute and compare the size and the power of the presented approaches. In Sect. 6 they are applied to real data of speech recognition, and finally, the final section presents the conclusions.

2 The Change-Point Problem

The problem we deal is the following. Suppose that $x_1, x_2, \ldots, x_T$ is a time series process with m change-points at the moments $k_1^*, \ldots, k_m^*$, with $1 \leq k_1^* \leq \ldots \leq k_m^* \leq T$. The density function $f\ (x_t/\theta)$, with θ the vector of parameters, is assumed to be

$$f(x_t/\theta) = \begin{cases} f(x_t/\theta_1), & t = 1,\ldots,k_1^*, \\ f(x_t/\theta_2), & t = k_1^*+1,\ldots,k_2^*, \\ \vdots & \\ f(x_t/\theta_{m+1}), & t = k_m^*+1,\ldots,T. \end{cases} \quad \text{for } \theta_1 \neq \theta_2 \neq \ldots \neq \theta_{m+1}.$$

The values of $\theta_i,\ i = 1, 2, \ldots, m+1$ can be a priori known or unknown and the goal is to detect and locate $k_1^*, k_2^*, \ldots, k_m^*$, and also estimate θ_i's when they are unknown.

Then, in general, the change-point problem consists of testing

$$\begin{aligned} &H_0: x_t \sim f(x_t/\theta), t = 1,\ldots,T \\ &H_1: x_t \sim f(x_t/\theta_1), t = 1,\ldots,k_1^*,\ x_t \sim f(x_t/\theta_2), t = k_1^*+1,\ldots,k_2^*,\ldots \quad (1) \\ &\qquad \ldots, x_t \sim f(x_t/\theta_{m+1}), t = k_m^*+1,\ldots,T, \text{for } \theta_1 \neq \theta_2 \neq \ldots \neq \theta_{m+1}. \end{aligned}$$

If the distributions $f(x_t/\theta_1),\ f(x_t/\theta_2), \ldots, f(x_t/\theta_m + 1)$ belong to a common parametric family, then the change-point problem in (1) is equivalent to test the null hypothesis:

$$\begin{aligned} H_0: &\quad \theta_1 = \theta_2 = \ldots = \theta_{m+1} = \theta \\ H_1: &\quad \theta_1 = \ldots = \theta_{k_1^*} \neq \theta_{k_1^*+1} = \ldots = \theta_{k_2^*} \neq \ldots \\ &\quad \ldots \neq \theta_{k_{m-1}+1} = \ldots = \theta_{k_m} \neq \theta_{k_m+1} = \ldots = \theta_T. \end{aligned} \quad (2)$$

Most of the parametric methods proposed in the literature for change-point problems consider a normal model. If the density function is constant over time, the change-point problem consists on testing whether the mean or the variance registered a change over the period analyzed.

3 Segmentation Procedures to Detect, Locate, and Estimate Change-Points

There are many approaches for solving the problem of detecting, estimating, and locating a change-point for independent or linear autocorrelated random variables that can be based on parametric (Chen and Gupta 2001, 2011) and non-parametric methods (Brodsky and Darkhovsky 1993; Heiler 1999, 2001). The main idea consists of minimizing a loss function which involves some criteria or statistic selected to measure the goodness of the segmentation performed. The computation of those statistics is useful to detect a potential change-point, by comparing the corresponding statistic computed under the hypothesis of no changes with the one assuming a change-point at the most likely period (Kitagawa and Gersch 1996; Chen and Gupta 1997; Al Ibrahim et al. 2003; Davis et al. 2006).

3.1 Cusum Methods

One of the statistics most often used to segment a time series is the cumulative sum or cusum (Page 1954). In fact, many procedures for change-point detection are based on cusum statistics (Inclán and Tiao 1994; Lee et al. 2003; Kokoszka and Leipus 1999; Lee et al. 2004 among others). The procedure in Inclán and Tiao (1994) is useful to test the null hypothesis of constant unconditional variance of a Gaussian uncorrelated process x_t, against the alternative of multiple change-points. The test statistic is defined as:

$$IT = \sqrt{T/2} \max_k D_k \tag{3}$$

where

$$D_k = \frac{\sum_{t=1}^{k} x_t^2}{\sum_{t=1}^{T} x_t^2} - \frac{k}{T}, \tag{4}$$

with $0 < k < T$. The asymptotic distribution of the statistic IT is the maximum of a Brownian bridge ($B(k)$):

$$IT \rightarrow_{D[0,1]} \max\{B(k) : k \in [0, 1]\}$$

This establishes a Kolmogorov–Smirnov type asymptotic distribution. The null hypothesis is rejected when the maximum value of the function IT is greater than the critical value and the change-point is located at period $k = \hat{k}$ where the maximum is achieved:

$$\hat{k} = \{k : IT > \text{c.v.}\}.$$

where c.v. is the corresponding critical value.

3.2 Automatic Procedure Based on Parametric Autoregressive Model (Auto-PARM)

In Davis et al. (2006) an automatic procedure called Auto-PARM is proposed for modelling a nonstationary time series by segmenting the series into blocks of different autoregressive processes.

Let k_j the breakpoint between the j-th and the $(j+1)$-st AR processes, with $j = 1, \ldots, m$, $k_0 = 1$ and $k_m < T$. Thus, the j-th piece of the series is modelled as:

$$X_t = x_{t,j}, \qquad k_{j-1} \leq t < k_j, \tag{5}$$

where $\{x_{t,j}\}$ is an AR(p_j) process.

$$x_{t,j} = \gamma_j + \phi_{j1} x_{t-1,j} + \ldots + \phi_{j,p_j} x_{t-p_j,j} + \sigma_j \epsilon_t,$$

where $\boldsymbol{\theta}_j := \left(\gamma_j, \phi_{j1}, \ldots, \phi_{j,p_j}, \sigma_j^2\right)$ is the parameter vector corresponding to this AR(p_j) process and the sequence $\{\epsilon_t\}$ is iid with mean 0 and variance 1. This model assumes that the behavior of the time series is changing at various times. Such a change might be a shift in the mean, a change in the variance, and/or a change in the dependence structure of the process.

The best segmentation is the one that makes the maximum compression of the data possible measured by the MDL principle of Rissanen (1989). *MDL* is defined as[1]:

$$MDL\,(m, k_1, \ldots, k_m, p_1, \ldots, p_{m+1}) = \tag{6}$$

$$\log m + (m+1)\log T + \sum_{j=1}^{m+1} \log p_j + \sum_{j=1}^{m+1} \frac{p_j + 2}{2} \log T_j + \sum_{j=1}^{m+1} \frac{T_j}{2} \log\left(2\pi\hat{\sigma}_j^2\right).$$

where m is the number of change-points located at $k_1, k_2, \ldots, k_m$, T_j is the number of observation in each segment j, p_j is the order of the autoregressive model fitted to the segment j, and $\hat{\sigma}_j^2$ is the Yule Walker estimator of σ_j^2 (Brockwell and Davis 1991).

3.3 *Automatic Procedure Based on Smooth Localized Complex EXponentials (Auto-SLEX) Functions*

In Adak (1998), Donoho et al. (1998), Ombao et al. (2002), and Maharaj and Alonso (2007) the segmentation is performed by using a cost function based on the spectrum, called evolutionary spectrum, because the calculation is made by the spectrum of each stationary interval. Ombao et al. (2002) created SLEX vectors which are calculated by applying a projection operator on the Fourier vectors, to get a basis which is simultaneously orthogonal and localized in time and frequency and is useful to compute the spectrum of nonstationary time series.

[1]For more details see Davis et al. (2006).

The cost function of the block $S_j = [k_j, k_{j+1}]$ is given by

$$\text{Cost}\,(S) = \sum_{S_j} \log \hat{\alpha}_{S_j} + \beta \sqrt{m_j}, \tag{7}$$

where $\hat{\alpha}_{S_j}$ is the SLEX periodogram, β is a penalty parameter generally equal to 1 (Donoho et al. 1998), and m_j is the number of breaks in the block. The cost for a particular segmentation of the time series is the sum of the costs at all the blocks defining that segmentation. The best segmentation is the one having the smallest cost.

3.4 *Informational Approach*

Information criteria, which commonly are useful as a measure of goodness of fit of a model, can be used to detect and estimate change-points. The first and most popular of the information criteria is the Akaike information criterion (AIC), which was introduced in 1973 for model selection in statistics. This criterion has found many applications in time series, outliers detection, robustness and regression analysis. AIC is defined as:

$$\text{AIC} = T \log \hat{\sigma}^2_{MV} + 2p.$$

where $\hat{\sigma}^2_{MV}$ is the maximum likelihood estimator of σ^2, and p is the number of free parameters. A model that minimizes the AIC is considered the appropriate model. The limitation of the minimum estimated AIC is that it is not an asymptotically consistent estimator of the model order (Schwarz 1978).

Another information criterion was introduced by Schwarz in 1978, and commonly is referred to as BIC or SIC. The fundamental difference with the AIC is the penalization function, which penalizes more the number of model parameters and leads to an asymptotically consistent estimate of the order of the true model. BIC is defined as

$$\text{BIC} = T \log \hat{\sigma}^2_{MV} + p \log T,$$

where $\hat{\sigma}^2_{MV}$ is the maximum likelihood estimator of σ^2, p is the number of free parameters, and T is the length of the time series. In this setting, we have two models corresponding to the null and the alternative hypotheses.

Let $\text{BIC}_0(T)$ the BIC under H_0 in (2) where no changes occur in the process along whole the sample and $\text{BIC}_1(k)$ the criterion assuming that there is a change-point at $t = k$, where k could be, in principle, $1, 2, \ldots, T$.

The rejection of H_0 is based on the principle of minimum information criterion. That is, we do not reject H_0 if $\text{BIC}_0(T) < \min_k \text{BIC}_1(k)$, because the BIC computed assuming no changes is smaller than the BIC calculated supposing the existence of a change-point at the most likely k, that is, in the value of k where the minimum BIC is achieved. On the other hand, H_0 is rejected if $\text{BIC}_0(T) > \text{BIC}_1(k)$ for some k and estimate the position of the change-point k^* by $\hat{k}$ such that

$$\text{BIC}(\hat{k}) = \min_{2<k<T} \text{BIC}_1(k).$$

In Chen and Gupta (1997) a procedure which combine BIC and the binary segmentation is proposed[2] to test for multiple change-points in the marginal variance, assuming independent observations. In this article BIC is used for locating the number of breaks in the variance of stock returns. Liu et al. (1997) modified the BIC by adding a larger penalty function and Bai and Perron (1998) considered criteria based on squared residuals. In the following section we present the approach of Chen and Gupta (1997) for testing a single change-point in the variance of independent normal data. In Al Ibrahim et al. (2003) the BIC is used to detect change-points in the mean and autoregressive coefficients of an AR(1).

3.5 A Proposed Procedure to Detect Changes in Mean, Variance, and Autoregressive Coefficients in AR Models

In this section, we propose an informational approach procedure for detecting changes in mean, variance, and autoregressive coefficients for AR(p) processes. Let $x_1, x_2, \ldots, x_T$ be the T consecutive observations from a Gaussian autoregressive process of order p given by:

$$x_t = \begin{cases} c_1 + \phi_{11}x_{t-1} + \ldots + \phi_{1p}x_{t-p} + \sigma_1\epsilon_t, & -\infty < t \leq k_1 \\ c_2 + \phi_{21}x_{t-1} + +\phi_{2p}x_{t-p} + \sigma_2\epsilon_t, & k_1 < t \leq k_2 \\ \cdot & \\ \cdot & \\ \cdot & \\ c_m + \phi_{m1}x_{t-1} + \ldots + \phi_{mp}x_{t-p} + \sigma_m\epsilon_t, & k_{m-1} < t \leq k_m \\ c_{m+1} + \phi_{m+1,1}x_{t-1} + \ldots + \phi_{m+1,p}x_{t-p} + \sigma_{m+1}\epsilon_t, & k_m < t \leq \infty \end{cases} \tag{8}$$

The null hypothesis is that

$$H_0 : c_1 = \ldots = c_{m+1}, \ \ \phi_{11} = \ldots = \phi_{m+1,1}, \ \ \phi_{1p} = \ldots = \phi_{m+1,p} \ \text{and}$$
$$\sigma_1^2 = \ldots = \sigma_{m+1}^2.$$

Under the null hypothesis, the formula for the BIC, denoted as $\text{BIC}_0(T)$, is given by:

---

[2]Binary segmentation is a searching procedure in order to detect multiple change-points in one time series. We will explain it in Sect. 4.

$$BIC_0(T) = (T-p)\,\hat{\sigma}_0^2 + (p+2)\log(T-p)\,, \tag{9}$$

where $\hat{\sigma}_0^2 = \frac{1}{T-p}\sum_{t=p+1}^{T}\left(x_t - \hat{c}_1 - \hat{\phi}_1 x_{t-1} - \ldots - \hat{\phi}_p x_{t-p}\right)^2$, $\hat{c}$, $\hat{\phi}_1, \ldots, \hat{\phi}_p$ are the conditional maximum likelihood estimators of σ^2, c_1, and the autoregressive parameters, respectively.

The $\mathrm{BIC}_1(k)$ for the piecewise AR(p) model under the alternative hypothesis is given by:

$$\mathrm{BIC}_1(k) = (k_1-1)\log\hat{\sigma}_1^2 + \ldots + (T-k_m)\log\hat{\sigma}_{m+1}^2 + (m+1)(p+2)\log T. \tag{10}$$

where $\hat{\sigma}_1^2 = \frac{1}{k_1-1}\sum_{t=2}^{k_1}(x_t - \tilde{c}_1 - \tilde{\phi}_{11}x_{t-1} - \ldots - \tilde{\phi}_{1p}x_{t-p})^2, \ldots, \hat{\sigma}_{m+1}^2 = \frac{1}{T-k_m}\sum_{t=k_m+1}^{T}(x_t - \tilde{c}_{m+1} - \tilde{\phi}_{m+1,1}x_{t-1} - \ldots - \tilde{\phi}_{m+1,p}x_{t-p})^2$, $\tilde{c}_1, \ldots, \tilde{c}_{m+1}$, $\tilde{\phi}_{11}, \ldots, \tilde{\phi}_{m+1,p}$ are the conditional maximum likelihood estimators of the variances, $\sigma_1^2, \ldots, \sigma_{m+1}^2$, the constants, $c_1, \ldots, c_{m+1}$ and the autoregressive parameters, $\phi_{11}, \ldots, \phi_{m+1,p}$, respectively.

H_0 is not rejected if $\mathrm{BIC}_0(T) < \min_k \mathrm{BIC}_1(k) + c_\alpha$, where c_α, and α have the relationship $1-\alpha = P[\mathrm{BIC}_0(T) < \min_k \mathrm{BIC}_1(k) + c_\alpha / H_0]$.

4 Multiple Change-Point Problem

When multiple change-points are expected, as its number and location are usually unknown, it is a challenge to jointly estimate the number of structural breaks, their location, and also provide a estimation of the model representing each interval. Many algorithms exist to calculate the optimal number and location of the change-points, some of them were presented by Scott and Knott (1974), Inclán and Tiao (1994), Davis et al. (2006), and Stoffer et al. (2002).

Binary segmentation (Scott and Knott 1974; Sen and Srivastava 1975; Vostrikova 1981) addresses the issue of multiple change-points detection as an extension of the single change-point problem. The segmentation procedure sequentially or iteratively applies the single change-point detection procedure, i.e. it applies the test to the total sample of observations, and if a break is detected, the sample is then segmented into two sub-samples and the test is reapplied. This procedure continues until no further change-points are found. This simple method can consistently estimate the number of breaks (e.g., Bai 1997; Inclán and Tiao 1994) and is computationally efficient, resulting in an $O(T\log T)$ calculation (Killick et al. 2012). In practice, binary segmentation becomes less accurate with either small changes or changes that are very close on time. Inclán and Tiao (1994) applied a such of modified binary segmentation in its Iterative Cusums of Square (ICSS) algorithm, by sequentially applying the statistic IT presented in Sect. 3.1.

In Davis et al. (2006) a genetic algorithm is used for detecting the optimal number and location of multiple change-points by minimizing the MDL. These algorithms make a population of individuals or chromosomes "to evolve" subject to random actions similar to those that characterize the biologic evolution (i.e., crossover and genetic mutation), as well as a selection process following a certain criteria which determines the most adapted (or best) individuals who survive the process, and the less adapted (or the "worst" ones), who are ruled out. In general, usual methods for applying genetic algorithm encode each parameter using binary coding or gray coding. Parameters are concatenated together in a vector to create a chromosome which evolve to a solution of the optimization problem.

Finally, other algorithms set a priori the segmentation structure. For instance, some procedures perform a dyadic segmentation to detect multiple change-points. Under this structure, time series can be divided into a number of blocks which are a power of 2. The algorithm begins setting the smallest possible size of the segmented blocks or the maximum number of blocks. Ideally, the block size should be small enough so that one can ensure the stationary behavior, but not too small to guarantee good properties of the estimates. Stoffer et al. (2002) recommended a block size greater or equal than 2^8. Then, the following step is to segment the time series in $2^8, 2^7, \ldots, 2^1, 2^0$ blocks, which is equivalent to consider different resolution levels $j = 8, 7, \ldots, 1, 0$, respectively. At each level j, we compare a well-defined cost function computed in that level j (father block) with respect to that computed in the level $j - 1$ (two children blocks). The best segmentation is that which minimizes the cost function.

Some papers focusing on multiple change-point problem for autocorrelated data are Andreou and Ghysels (2002) and Al Ibrahim et al. (2003). In Andreou and Ghysels (2002) an algorithm similar to ICSS (Inclán and Tiao 1994) is applied to detect multiple change-points in financial time series using cusum methods. In the first step the statistic is applied to the total sample and if a change-point is detected, the sampled is segmented and the test is applied again to each subsample up to five segments. Other algorithms are applied in this paper, using a grid search approach or methods based on dynamic programming. In Al Ibrahim et al. (2003) the binary segmentation algorithm combined with the BIC is used for piecewise autoregressive models.

Given the merits of binary segmentation saving a lot of computational time and the better performance with respect to ICSS algorithm, in order to design the simulation experiments, and, for empirical applications below, we propose to combine the BIC statistic assuming the model in Eq. (8) with binary segmentation (referred as BICBS).

5 Monte Carlo Simulation Experiments

In this section we evaluate the performance of the methods presented above, by computing the empirical size and power under different hypotheses. We have used four methods: ICSS (Inclán and Tiao 1994), BICBS (BIC for model in (8) with binary segmentation), Auto-PARM (Davis et al. 2006), and Auto-SLEX (Ombao et al. 2002). In the tables below, where these procedures are compared, the results for BICBS, which is the proposed procedure, are highlighted with bold font.

5.1 Empirical Size

First, we compute the empirical size, that is, how many times the corresponding methodology incorrectly segments a stationary process. The length of the simulated series is set equal to 4,096. Table 1 presents the results for 1,000 replications for a Gaussian white noise with unitary variance, and for AR(1) and MA(1) stationary processes.

All the procedures analyzed seems to appear undersized in finite samples. Applying them to stationary processes we obtain only one block or segment in most of the cases, and only a very small percentage of processes are segmented in two blocks. For example, for ICSS, BICBS, and Auto-PARM the rate of wrong segmented stationary processes is almost zero. The hypothesis that the type of autocorrelation (i.e., autoregressive and moving average) could influence the segmentation is rejected, given that the results for MA(1) and AR(1) processes are similar leading to the conclusion that the type of serial correlation seems to be not important for the size of these procedures.

5.2 Power for Piecewise Stationary Processes

We compute the power of the methods by counting how many times the corresponding methodology correctly segments piecewise stationary processes in 1,000 replications. Two stationary segments or blocks are assumed. We observe if the procedure finds the correct number of segments or blocks and if the changes occur in a narrow interval centered on the correct breakpoint ($k^* \pm 100$). For a time series of length $T = 4096$, we evaluate the performance of the procedures when the data present serial correlation and the perturbation's variance changes. The simulated process is an AR(1) with autoregressive parameter $\phi \in (-1, 1)$ changing the perturbation variance from 1 to 2 in $k^* = 2048$.

Table 1 Size of ICSS, BICBS, Auto-PARM, and Auto-SLEX

Processes	ICSS	**BICBS**	Auto-PARM	Auto-SLEX
White noise	0.000	**0.04**	0.000	0.000
AR(1) $\phi \in (-1, 1)$	0.000	**0.000**	0.005	0.025
MA(1) $\theta \in (-1, 1)$	0.000	**0.000**	0.001	0.011

Table 2 Power of the procedures segmenting piecewise autoregressive processes with $\phi \in (-1, 1)$, where the perturbation's variance changes from 1 to 2 in $t = 2048$

Processes	ICSS	**BICBS**	Auto-PARM	Auto-SLEX
Precise detection	0.951	**0.960**	0.961	0.923
Oversegmentation	0.001	**0.040**	0.039	0.077
No segmentation	0.048	**0.000**	0.000	0.000

In Table 2 we present the results, where the autoregressive coefficient is generated as $\phi \in (-1, 1)$, and the perturbation term is a white noise with unitary variance in the first piece ($t = 1, \ldots, 2048$), shifting to 2 in the second piece ($t = 2049, \ldots, 4096$).

All the procedures obtained excellent results when the perturbation's term variance changes, where the best results were for Auto-PARM and BICBS.

Finally, we analyze the performance of the tests detecting multiple change-points in three processes. The first one is given by:

$$x_t = \begin{cases} \epsilon_t, & 1 < t \leq 1365 \\ 2\epsilon_t, & 1366 < t \leq 2730 \\ 0.5\epsilon_t, & 2731 < t \leq 4096, \end{cases} \tag{11}$$

where we are interested in changes in the scale of the perturbation term, when the process does not have autocorrelation. The second is:

$$x_t = \begin{cases} 0.5x_{t-1} + \epsilon_t, & 1 < t \leq 1365 \\ 0.8x_{t-1} + \epsilon_t, & 1366 < t \leq 2730 \\ -0.5x_{t-1} + \epsilon_t, & 2731 < t \leq 4096, \end{cases} \tag{12}$$

where it is introduced first order autocorrelation in the process and the change-points are due to the autoregressive coefficient. The third process is given by:

$$x_t = \begin{cases} 0.5x_{t-1} + \epsilon_t, & 1 < t \leq 1365 \\ 0.8x_{t-1} + \epsilon_t, & 1366 < t \leq 2730 \\ 0.8x_{t-1} + 2\epsilon_t, & 2731 < t \leq 4096, \end{cases} \tag{13}$$

where also is introduced autocorrelation in the data and there is both a change-point in the autoregressive coefficient and another one in the variance of the perturbation. It is assumed that $\epsilon_t \sim$ N(0,1) and $x_0 = 0$. The results are presented in Table 3.

When multiple change-points are present in the time series, some procedures performed well only if the data have no serial correlation [process (11)]. That is the case of ICSS, BICBS, and Auto-PARM. Auto-SLEX detected the change-point, but with a big rate of oversegmentation. For autocorrelated data, the procedures with the best performance were BICBS and Auto-PARM, with powers greater than 0.91. ICSS has smaller power and often it does not segment or only finds one of the two

Table 3 Proportion of detected change-points in piecewise stationary processes with two changes presented in Eqs. (11)–(13)

	ICSS	**BICBS**	Auto-PARM	Auto-SLEX
Process with no autocorrelation as in (11)				
Precise detection	0.999	**0.910**	1.000	0.626
One change-point	0.000	**0.000**	0.000	0.000
Oversegmentation	0.000	**0.005**	0.000	0.372
No segmentation	0.001	**0.085**	0.000	0.000
Process AR(1) as in (12)				
Precise detection	0.673	**0.992**	0.995	0.029
One change-point	0.000	**0.000**	0.000	0.000
Oversegmentation	0.001	**0.001**	0.000	0.914
No segmentation	0.326	**0.007**	0.005	0.057
Process AR(1) in (13)				
Precise detection	0.753	**0.910**	0.954	0.023
One change-point	0.206	**0.028**	0.045	0.000
Oversegmentation	0.013	**0.062**	0.001	0.945
No segmentation	0.000	**0.000**	0.000	0.032

change-points that the process exhibits. Finally, Auto-SLEX performed badly, again detecting more than the right number of change-points.

In summary, Monte Carlo simulation experiments showed that Auto-PARM and the proposed BICBS have the better performance, with high power in the different simulation experiments. Thus, the proposed method provides an intuitive and excellent tool to detect and locate the change-points and has the advantage with respect to Auto-PARM of the simplicity, without the need of a complex searching method as the genetic algorithm.

6 Application to a Speech Recognition Dataset

The performance of the procedures is illustrated by applying them to a speech dataset consisting in the recordings of the word GREASY with 5,762 observations. GREASY has been analyzed by Ombao et al. (2002) and Davis et al. (2006). The resulting segmentations of the four procedures are presented in Fig. 1. Breakpoints are showed with vertical dashed lines.

GREASY appears in the figure as nonstationary, but it could be segmented into approximately stationary blocks. Note that in the behavior of the time series we can identify blocks corresponding to the sounds G, R, EA, S, and Y (Ombao et al. 2002). Auto-SLEX was the procedure which found more breakpoints also for this time series. The performance of ICSS, BICBS, and Auto-PARM seems to be better, finding 6–13 change-points, most of them limiting intervals corresponding to the sounds compounding the word GREASY.

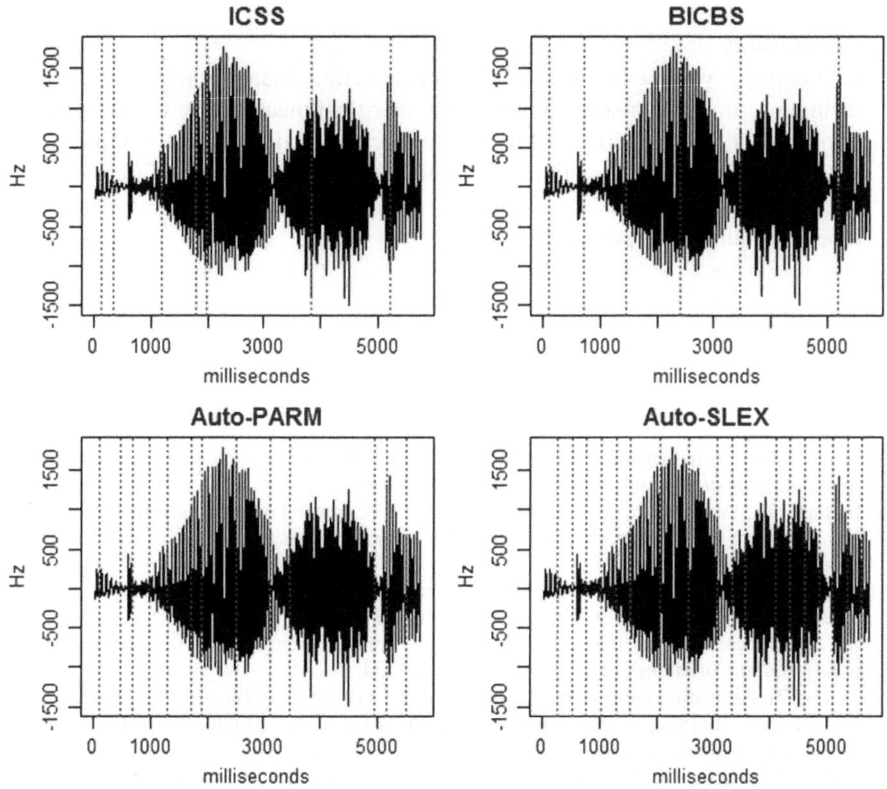

Fig. 1 Changepoints of GREASY estimated by ICSS, BICBS, Auto-PARM, and Auto-SLEX

Table 4 Standard deviation, AIC, BIC, and number of change-point in the segmentation by each methodology

	ICSS	BICBS	Auto-PARM	Auto-SLEX
Std. dev.	*51.97*	52.44	118.32	137.84
AIC	*4.0409*	*4.0409*	4.0486	4.0898
BIC	4.0763	*4.0759*	4.1178	4.1712
# change-points	7	6	13	18

In order to compare the goodness of the segmentation, we compute the standard deviation, Akaike and Bayesian Information criteria for the resulting segmentation by each method. We present the results in Table 4, where the best values of the statistics proposed are highlighted with italic font.

Although the segmentation with less standard deviation is reached by ICSS, the information criteria selected as the best the segmentation performed by BICBS.

Conclusions
In this paper we handled the problem of detecting, locating, and estimating a single or multiple change-points in the marginal mean and/or the marginal variance for both uncorrelated and serial correlated data. By combining the BIC with binary segmentation we propose a very simple procedure, which does not need a complex searching algorithms, with excellent performance in several simulation experiments.

References

Adak, S. (1998). Time-dependent spectral analysis of nonstationary time series. *Journal of the American Statistical Association, 93*(444), 1488–1489.
Al Ibrahim, A., Ahmed, M., & BuHamra, S. (2003). Testing for multiple change-points in an autoregressive model using SIC criterion. In *Focus on applied statistics* (pp. 37–51). New York: Nova Publishers.
Andreou, E., & Ghysels, E. (2002). Detecting multiple breaks in financial market volatility dynamics. *Journal of Applied Econometrics, 17*(5), 579–600.
Auger, I., & Lawrence, C. (1989). Algorithms for the optimal identification of segment neighborhoods. *Bulletin of Mathematical Biology, 51*(1), 39–54.
Bai, J. (1997). Estimating multiple breaks one at a time. *Econometric Theory, 13*, 315–352.
Bai, J., & Perron, P. (1998). Estimating and testing linear models with multiple structural changes. *Econometrica, 66*(1), 47–78.
Brockwell, P., & Davis, R. (1991). *Time series: Theory and methods*. New York: Springer.
Brodsky, B., & Darkhovsky, B. (1993). *Nonparametric methods in change-point problems* (Vol. 243). Dordrecht: Springer.
Chen, J., & Gupta, A. (1997). Testing and locating variance changepoints with application to stock prices. *Journal of the American Statistical Association, 92*(438), 739–747.
Chen, J., & Gupta, A. (2011). *Parametric statistical change point analysis: With applications to genetics, medicine, and finance*. Boston: Birkhauser.
Chen, J., & Gupta, A. K. (2001). On change point detection and estimation. *Communications in Statistics-Simulation and Computation, 30*(3), 665–697.
Davis, R., Lee, T., & Rodriguez-Yam, G. (2006). Structural break estimation for nonstationary time series models. *Journal of the American Statistical Association, 101*(473), 229–239.
Donoho, D., Mallat, S., & von Sachs, R. (1998). *Estimating covariances of locally stationary processes: Rates of convergence of best basis methods* (Vol. 517, pp. 1–64). Technical Report. Stanford, CA: Department of Statistics, Stanford University.
Heiler, S. (1999). *A survey on nonparametric time series analysis*. Fakultät für Wirtschaftswissenschaften und Statistik, Universität Konstanz.
Heiler, S. (2001). Nonparametric time series analysis: Nonparametric regression, locally weighted regression, autoregression, and quantile regression. In *A course in time series analysis*. Wiley and sons, (pp. 308–347).
Inclán, C., & Tiao, G. (1994). Use of cumulative sums of squares for retrospective detection of changes of variance. *Journal of the American Statistical Association, 89*(427), 913–923.
Jackson, B., Scargle, J., Barnes, D., Arabhi, S., Alt, A., Gioumousis, P., et al. (2005). An algorithm for optimal partitioning of data on an interval. *Signal Processing Letters, IEEE, 12*(2), 105–108.
Killick, R., Fearnhead, P., & Eckley, I. (2012). Optimal detection of changepoints with a linear computational cost. *Journal of the American Statistical Association, 107*(500), 1590–1598.

Kitagawa, G., & Gersch, W. (1996). *Smoothness priors analysis of time series*. New York: Springer.

Kokoszka, P., & Leipus, R. (1999). Testing for parameter changes in ARCH models. *Lithuanian Mathematical Journal, 39*(2), 182–195.

Lee, S., Ha, J., Na, O., & Na, S. (2003). The cusum test for parameter change in time series models. *Scandinavian Journal of Statistics, 30*(4), 781–796.

Lee, S., Tokutsu, Y., & Maekawa, K. (2004). The CUSUM test for parameter change in regression models with ARCH errors. *Journal of the Japanese Statistical Society, 34*, 173–188.

Liu, J., Wu, S., & Zidek, J. (1997). On segmented multivariate regression. *Statistica Sinica, 7*, 497–526.

Maharaj, E., & Alonso, A. (2007). Discrimination of locally stationary time series using wavelets. *Computational Statistics & Data Analysis, 52*(2), 879–895.

Ombao, H., Raz, J., von Sachs, R., & Guo, W. (2002). The SLEX model of a non-stationary random process. *Annals of the Institute of Statistical Mathematics, 54*(1), 171–200.

Page, E. (1954). Continuous inspection schemes. *Biometrika, 41*(1/2), 100–115.

Rissanen, J. (1989). *Stochastic complexity in statistical inquiry theory*. Singapore: World Scientific Publishing.

Schwarz, G. (1978). Estimating the dimension of a model. *The Annals of Statistics, 6*(2), 461–464.

Scott, A., & Knott, M. (1974). A cluster analysis method for grouping means in the analysis of variance. *Biometrics, 30*(3), 507–512.

Sen, A., & Srivastava, M. (1975). On tests for detecting change in mean. *The Annals of Statistics, 3*(1), 98–108.

Stoffer, D., Ombao, H., & Tyler, D. (2002). Local spectral envelope: An approach using dyadic treebased adaptive segmentation. *Annals of the Institute of Statistical Mathematics, 54*(1), 201–223.

Vostrikova, L. (1981). "Disorder" in multidimensional random processes. *Soviet Mathematics Doklady 24*, 55–59.

Regularization Methods in Economic Forecasting

Gunther Schauberger and Gerhard Tutz

Abstract Modern regularization techniques are able to select the relevant variables and features in prediction problems where much more predictors than observations are available. We investigate how regularization methods can be used to select the influential predictors of an autoregressive model with a very large number of potentially informative predictors. The methods are used to forecast the quarterly gross added value in the manufacturing sector by use of the business survey data collected by the ifo Institute. Also ensemble methods, which combine several forecasting methods are exemplarily evaluated.

1 Introduction

Regularization methods are a major topic in current statistical research. Many models and algorithms have been proposed that are designed to deal with complex regression problems where conventional methods are severely restricted, as in the case of correlated covariates or large data sets. Shrinkage methods like the Lasso estimator allow for a biased but less variable estimation. Frequently, regularization is combined with a dimension reduction of the covariates space. For a broad introduction to regularization methods see, for example, Hastie et al. (2001). Regularization methods can be very helpful in forecasting problems since a large amount of available predictors that potentially can contribute to predictions, can be handled easily. As a useful side effect, some regularization methods also automatically perform variable selection, which enforces interpretability.

There is a wide body of literature on the analysis of time series and forecasting methods with a small number of predictors, including Feng and Heiler (1998) and Heiler and Feng (2000). Forecasting problems in which the number of covariates exceeds the number of observations were mostly solved by factor forecasting. This strategy was addressed, for example, by Bai and Ng (2002), Stock and Watson (2006) and Stock and Watson (2011). Methods that perform variable selection

G. Schauberger • G. Tutz (✉)
Department of Statistics, LMU Munich, München, Germany
e-mail: gunther.schauberger@stat.uni-muenchen.de; gerhard.tutz@stat.uni-muenchen.de

J. Beran et al. (eds.), *Empirical Economic and Financial Research*,
Advanced Studies in Theoretical and Applied Econometrics 48,
DOI 10.1007/978-3-319-03122-4_4

have been discussed in the forecasting literature more rarely. Recently, Bai and Ng (2009) and Buchen and Wohlrabe (2011) used the newly developed method of boosting, whereas De Mol et al. (2008) studied shrinkage forecasting from a Bayesian view. Bai and Ng (2008) used shrinkage methods to perform variable selection for forecasting with targeted predictors. Shafik and Tutz (2009) and Robinzonov et al. (2012) examined boosting for additive time series models from a rather technical point of view. The objective of the present paper is to evaluate exemplarily how modern shrinkage and selection methods can be used to improve prediction accuracy.

2 Data and Model

The data we are considering were provided by the Munich ifo Institute. The objective is to forecast the quarterly gross added value in the manufacturing sector in Germany. Since 1949, the ifo Institute for Economic Research conducts the ifo Business Survey. Based on these data, since 1972 it monthly releases the ifo Business Climate Index, one of the most followed early indicators for economic development in Germany. It is based on roughly 7,000 monthly responses from all economic areas. As the two central questions of the survey, the companies are asked for their assessments of the current business situation and their expectations for the next 6 months. From these two questions the Business Climate Index is calculated. These two and all other questions that are asked are measured on a 3-level scale (e.g. "good", "satisfactory" or "poor"). The companies that are part of the manufacturing sector are classified into $r = 68$ branches. For every single branch and for each question, a (metric) balance value is calculated as the difference of fractions of positive and negative answers. In the case of a branch with 40 % positive, 50 % undecided and 10 % negative answers, a balance value of $40 - 10 = 30$ results. For further information on the data pool of the ifo Business Survey, see Becker and Wohlrabe (2007).

Since the time series of the gross added value is released once per quarter, the arithmetic means of the monthly values corresponding to one quarter are used as predictors. We only use the data from the manufacturing sector in the period from 1991 to 2010. As forecasting series, the rate of change per quarter $y_t \leftarrow \frac{y_t - y_{t-1}}{y_{t-1}} \cdot 100$ and a forecasting horizon of $h = 1$ are used. The learning set for the first forecast encompasses 40 observations from 1991 to 2000, the first forecast is calculated for the first quarter of 2001. For every forecast, the information set is enlarged by one observation and a new forecasting model is calculated.

The basic model that is used is the autoregressive model with exogenous covariates, denoted as AR-X model,

$$\mathbb{E}(y_t) = \alpha_0 + \sum_{i=1}^{q} \alpha_i y_{t-i} + \sum_{j=1}^{r \cdot m} \sum_{i=1}^{q} \gamma_i^{(j)} z_{t+1-i}^{(j)} = \boldsymbol{x}_t \boldsymbol{\beta}. \tag{1}$$

Here, $\boldsymbol{\beta}$ denotes the parameter vector $\boldsymbol{\beta}^T = (\alpha_0, \alpha_1, \ldots, \alpha_q, \gamma_1^{(1)}, \ldots, \gamma_q^{(r\cdot m)})$ and $\boldsymbol{x}_t = (1, y_{t-1}, \ldots, y_{t-q}, z_t^{(1)}, \ldots, z_{t+1-q}^{(r\cdot m)})$ is the number of used covariates. The predictors that are included are the q lags of the forecasting series $y_{t-1}, \ldots, y_{t-q}$ and the exogenous covariates $x_s^{(j)}$, $s = t, \ldots, t-q+1$, where j refers to one specific combination of the r branches and m questions. We choose $q = 4$ to cover the period of one year. The exogenous covariates can be used from the current date t since they are available long enough before the forecasting is released.

Assuming one question ($m = 1$) to be the only exogenous covariate, the total number of coefficients, that is, the dimension of $\boldsymbol{\beta}$, is 277 ($r = 68$, $q = 4$; $1 + 4 + 4 \cdot 68 = 277$). For the largest setting from this study including five questions from the ifo data pool, 1,365 coefficients have to be estimated. Therefore, one has a rather low number of observations and a comparatively high number of predictors.

3 Regularization Methods

In the following, the regularization methods used in forecasting are shortly sketched. To simplify notation, we assume the data to have the form $(\boldsymbol{y}, \boldsymbol{X})$, where $\boldsymbol{y} = (y_1, \ldots, y_n)^T$ denotes the response vector and $\boldsymbol{X} = (\boldsymbol{1}, \boldsymbol{x}_1, \ldots, \boldsymbol{x}_p)$, $\boldsymbol{x}_j = (x_{1j}, \ldots, x_{nj})^T$, denote the data matrix and the observations of the jth variable, which are assumed to be standardized. Therefore, we represent the AR-X model as a simple linear model and estimate the parameter vector $\boldsymbol{\beta}^T = (\beta_0, \beta_1, \ldots, \beta_p)$ from the model $E(y) = \beta_0 + \sum_{j=1}^{p} \beta_j x_j$ or, equivalently, $E(\boldsymbol{y}) = \boldsymbol{X}\boldsymbol{\beta}$.

3.1 *L2-Boosting*

L2-Boosting, as outlined by Bühlmann and Hothorn (2007), uses the method of stepwise gradient descent for parameter estimation. It is based on AdaBoost, which was proposed by Freund and Schapire (1996), and extended by Bühlmann and Yu (2003). Generally, Boosting is an algorithm for a stepwise solution of the problem

$$f^*(\boldsymbol{x}) = \underset{f(\boldsymbol{x})}{argmin}\, \mathbb{E}(\rho(y, f(\boldsymbol{x}))),$$

where $\rho(.,.)$ is a differentiable loss function. In our case of L2-Boosting, the quadratic loss

$$\rho_{L_2}(y, f) = \frac{1}{2}|y - f|^2$$

is used. L2-Boosting uses the following algorithm:

Step 1 Initialize offset $\hat{f}^{[0]} = \overline{y}, \hat{\boldsymbol{\beta}}^{[0]} = 0, m = 0$

Step 2 $m \rightarrow m + 1$: Compute residuals $u_i = y_i - \hat{f}^{[m-1]}(\boldsymbol{x}_i),\ i = 1, \ldots, n$, which is the negative gradient of the loss function (3.1).

Step 3 Choose $\hat{\delta}$ by

$$\hat{\delta} = \underset{0 \leq j \leq p}{argmin} \sum_{i=1}^{n} \left(u_i - \hat{\beta}_j x_{ij}\right)^2$$

as the variable that causes the greatest reduction of prediction by simple regression of the variable on the residuals.

Step 4 The parameter of variable $\hat{\delta}$ is updated by

$$\hat{f}^{[m]}(\boldsymbol{X}) = \hat{f}^{[m-1]}(\boldsymbol{X}) + \nu \cdot \sum_{i=1}^{n} \hat{\beta}_{\hat{\delta}} x_{i\hat{\delta}},$$

where ν, $0 < \nu \leq 1$, is a shrinkage factor which prevents overfitting.

Step 5 Iterate steps 2–4 until $m = M$.

The maximal number of steps M has to be chosen sufficiently high. Afterwards, the optimal number of Boosting steps m_{opt} has to be chosen, it is the main tuning parameter in the Boosting procedure. Like all the tuning parameters for the regularization methods we used, m_{opt} will be chosen by ten-fold cross validation. Boosting automatically performs variable selection as only those variables remain in the model that have been chosen at least once by the iteration m_{opt}. Therefore, the smaller m_{opt} is chosen the more variables are excluded and the more parameters are shrinked. Computation will be done by use of the R package `mboost`.

3.2 *Lasso*

The Lasso estimator has been proposed by Tibshirani (1996) and is described in Hastie et al. (2009). It simultaneously shrinks the parameter estimates and performs variable selection. It is defined by

$$\hat{\boldsymbol{\beta}}^{lasso} = \underset{\boldsymbol{\beta}}{argmin} \sum_{i=1}^{n} \left(y_i - \beta_0 - \sum_{j=1}^{p} \beta_j x_{ij}\right)^2, \quad \text{where} \sum_{j=1}^{p} |\beta_j| \leq t$$

or, equivalently, in Lagrange form by

$$\hat{\boldsymbol{\beta}}^{lasso} = \underset{\boldsymbol{\beta}}{argmin} \left(\frac{1}{2} \sum_{i=1}^{n} \left(y_i - \beta_0 - \sum_{j=1}^{p} \beta_j x_{ij} \right)^2 + \lambda \sum_{j=1}^{p} |\beta_j| \right).$$

In contrast to the least squares estimator, the Lasso estimator is biased but more robust. It tends to generate parameter estimates with lower variance and therefore to reduce the prediction error. The tuning parameter λ determines the amount of regularization. With growing λ the number of variables that are included in the model reduces. For $\lambda = 0$ (and $p \leq n$), the least squares estimator is obtained. For $\lambda > 0$, a unique solution for the parameter estimates can be computed also in the $p > n$ case.

3.3 Elastic Net

The Ridge estimator, proposed by Hoerl and Kennard (1970), is very similar to the Lasso approach. Instead of penalizing the L1-norm of the parameter vector, the L2-norm is penalized. It is defined by

$$\hat{\boldsymbol{\beta}}^{ridge} = \underset{\boldsymbol{\beta}}{argmin} \sum_{i=1}^{n} \left(y_i - \beta_0 - \sum_{j=1}^{p} \beta_j x_{ij} \right)^2, \quad \text{where} \sum_{j=1}^{p} \beta_j^2 \leq t$$

or, in Lagrangian form, by

$$\hat{\boldsymbol{\beta}}^{ridge} = \underset{\boldsymbol{\beta}}{argmin} \left(\sum_{i=1}^{n} \left(y_i - \beta_0 - \sum_{j=1}^{p} \beta_j x_{ij} \right)^2 + \lambda \sum_{j=1}^{p} \beta_j^2 \right)$$

In contrast to the Lasso, Ridge does not perform variable selection, it is a shrinkage method only. The higher the tuning parameter λ, the more the parameter estimates are shrinked towards zero.

Zou and Hastie (2005) proposed the Elastic Net estimator

$$\hat{\boldsymbol{\beta}}^{elasticnet} = \underset{\boldsymbol{\beta}}{argmin} \left(\sum_{i=1}^{n} \left(y_i - \beta_0 - \sum_{j=1}^{p} \beta_j x_{ij} \right)^2 + \lambda \sum_{j=1}^{p} ((1-\alpha)\frac{1}{2}\beta_j^2 + \alpha|\beta_j|) \right).$$

as a combination of the approaches of Lasso and Ridge, simultaneously penalizing the L1-norm and the L2-norm of the parameter vector. The total amount

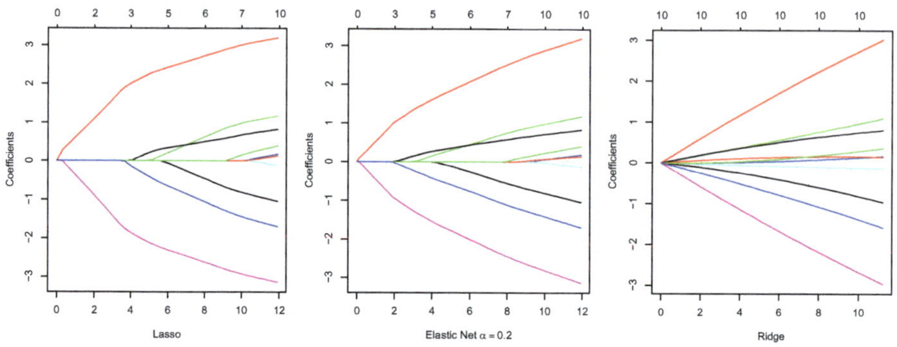

Fig. 1 Parameter paths for simulated data for estimating procedures Lasso, Ridge and Elastic Net ($\alpha = 0.2$). The x-axes represent the L1-norm of the parameter estimates. The axes above the plots represent the current numbers of covariates in the model

of regularization is again controlled by the tuning parameter λ. To control the weighting of L1- and L2-penalty, the additional tuning parameter α, $0 \leq \alpha \leq 1$, is used. $\alpha = 0$ generates the Ridge estimator, $\alpha = 1$ generates the Lasso estimator. For $\alpha \neq 0$, Elastic Net can perform variable selection.

Figure 1 shows exemplarily the parameter paths for a simulated data set for Lasso, Ridge and Elastic Net ($\alpha = 0.2$). The paths represent the parameter estimates of the corresponding method depending on the current value of the tuning parameter λ. The x-axis represents the L1-norm of the parameter vector. Therefore, λ is reduced along the x-axis with the ML estimates being seen at the right-hand side. It can be seen that Ridge does not enforce variable selection and therefore all parameter paths start at the same point. In contrast, Elastic Net with $\alpha = 0.2$ performs variable selection, but not as strictly as Lasso. The parameter paths for Elastic Net start for higher values of λ.

For the estimation of Lasso or Elastic Net estimators, various algorithms have been developed, e.g. by Efron et al. (2004) or Goeman (2010). We will use the R package `glmnet`, an implementation of an algorithm using coordinate descent proposed by Friedman et al. (2010).

3.4 *Generalized Path Seeking*

Friedman (2012) proposed to extend the Elastic Net to the so-called Generalized Elastic Net. It is defined as

$$\hat{\beta} = \underset{\beta}{argmin} \left(\sum_{i=1}^{n} \left(y_i - \beta_0 - \sum_{j=1}^{p} \beta_j x_{ij} \right)^2 + \lambda \sum_{j=1}^{p} ((\gamma - 1)\frac{\beta_j^2}{2} + (2 - \gamma)|\beta_j|) \right)$$

for $1 \le \gamma \le 2$ and

$$\hat{\boldsymbol{\beta}} = \underset{\boldsymbol{\beta}}{argmin} \left(\sum_{i=1}^{n} \left(y_i - \beta_0 - \sum_{j=1}^{p} \beta_j x_{ij} \right)^2 + \lambda \sum_{j=1}^{p} \log((1-\gamma)|\beta_j| + \gamma) \right)$$

for $0 < \gamma < 1$. For $1 \le \gamma \le 2$, this matches the definition of Elastic Net as defined above and bridges the penalties from Lasso ($\gamma = 1$) to Ridge ($\gamma = 2$). For $0 < \gamma < 1$, this bridges the penalties from the so-called all-subset regression ($\gamma \to 0$) to Lasso ($\gamma \to 1$). All-Subset regression is a penalty performing quite strict variable selection by penalizing the number of nonzero parameters. Since the penalties for $0 < \gamma < 1$ are non-convex, they usually are rather hard to optimize. Friedman (2012) proposed an algorithm called Generalized Path Seeking to easily approximate all penalties within the Generalized Elastic Net family without repeatedly solving (possibly non-convex) optimization problems. Generally, this algorithm is applicable for all penalties where

$$\frac{\partial P(\boldsymbol{\beta})}{\partial |\beta_j|} > 0 \quad \forall\, j = 1, \ldots, p$$

holds. This requirement is met for the Generalized Elastic Net where $P(\boldsymbol{\beta})$ is denoted as

$$P(\boldsymbol{\beta}) = \begin{cases} \sum_{j=1}^{p} ((\gamma - 1)\frac{\beta_j^2}{2} + (2-\gamma)|\beta_j|) & 1 \le \gamma \le 2 \\ \sum_{j=1}^{p} \log((1-\gamma)|\beta_j| + \gamma) & 0 < \gamma < 1. \end{cases}$$

All parameters are initialized to be zero and are updated stepwise during the algorithm. In every loop, for every variable it is checked how much the quadratic loss can be reduced and how much the penalty term would increase simultaneously. The variable with the best compromise (i.e. the largest ratio) between these two aspects is updated. For more details on this algorithm, see Friedman (2012). The GPS algorithm (implementation for R available on http://www-stat.stanford.edu/~jhf/R-GPS.html) can be used to approximate solutions for the family of Generalized Elastic Net penalties using the penalties from the set $\gamma \in \{0.0, 0.1, 0.2, \ldots, 1.9, 2.0\}$.

3.5 *Group Lasso*

An important extension of the Lasso is the so-called Group Lasso, proposed by Yuan and Lin (2006) and Meier et al. (2008). If the covariates are grouped within the data set (for example, all the dummy variables for one categorical predictors form a group), it can be useful to focus selection on groups of variables. In our case, the different lags for one covariate are seen as one group. Group Lasso deals with groups in the data set as a whole. Either, the group is left out completely or every covariate within the group is taken into the model. Group Lasso is defined as

$$\hat{\boldsymbol{\beta}} = \underset{\boldsymbol{\beta}}{argmin} \left(||y - \beta_0 \mathbf{1} - \sum_{l=1}^{L} \boldsymbol{X}_l \boldsymbol{\beta}_l||_2^2 + \lambda \sum_{l=1}^{L} \sqrt{K_l} ||\boldsymbol{\beta}_l||_2 \right),$$

where $\boldsymbol{X}_l$ represents the predictor matrix for group l out of L groups. $\boldsymbol{\beta}_l$ and K_l represent the parameter vector and the group size for group l, $||\boldsymbol{a}||_2$ denotes the Euclidian norm

$$||\boldsymbol{a}||_2 = \sqrt{\langle \boldsymbol{a}, \boldsymbol{a} \rangle} = \sqrt{a_1^2 + \ldots + a_n^2}$$

of an n-dimensional vector $\boldsymbol{a}$. The Euclidian norm can only be zero if all the components of the corresponding vector are zero. Therefore, a group only can be excluded from the model as a whole. We apply Group Lasso by treating all lags $x_t^{(j)}, \ldots, x_{t+1-q}^{(j)}$ corresponding to one covariate j as a group, also the autoregressive terms are treated as a group. Group Lasso estimates will be computed with help of the R package `grplasso`, see also Meier (2009).

3.6 Principal Components Regression

Principal Components Regression (PCR) is a well-established alternative to least squares regression, described, e.g., in Kendall (1957). PCR uses the principal components of the data matrix instead of the original covariates. The principal components are linear combinations of the covariates that are orthogonal and are chosen to capture as much variance within the data set as possible.

Principal components can be used for dimension reduction in regression. As every principal component captures the maximal amount of variance within the data, typically most of the information can be captured by a few principal components. These principal components are used as regressors, the number of regressors is used as tuning parameter in this case. This dimension reduction does not include variable selection, as every principal component is a linear combination of all underlying covariates. Principal components can be calculated by eigendecomposition where the eigenvalues represent the amount of variance that is represented by the corresponding eigenvector. It should be mentioned that the extraction of the principal components does not use the regression model which is called unsupervised learning in the learning community.

3.7 Partial Least Squares Regression

Partial Least Squares Regression (PLSR), first proposed by Wold (1975), is strongly related to PCR. While principal components only maximize the fraction of explained variance within the data matrix of the explanatory variables, partial least squares creates linear combinations of the explanatory variables maximizing the covariance of the data matrix and the response variable. Thus, it can be assured that the information captured by the linear combinations is correlated to the response variable.

Apart from that, PLSR has the same characteristics as PCR. It performs dimension reduction without variable selection because linear combinations out of the original variables are used as explanatory covariates. The number of linear combinations is used as tuning parameter. PCR and PLSR will be calculated with help of the functions `pcr` and `plsr` from the `pls` package, see also Mevik et al. (2011).

4 Comparison of Forecasts

All the methods presented above will be used to fit model (1) as a forecasting model. For benchmarking, we will use the AR-4 model

$$\hat{y}_t = \sum_{i=1}^{4} \beta_i y_{t-i} + \epsilon_t.$$

with four autoregressive terms and the more general AR-p model

$$\hat{y}_t = \sum_{i=1}^{p} \beta_i y_{t-i} + \epsilon_t, \quad j = 1, \ldots, p_{max}$$

where $p \leq p_{max}$ is determined by AIC and p_{max} equals q from (1). In R, these models are calculated by the function `ar` from the `stats` package.

To measure the forecasting accuracy, the most popular choice is the relative mean squared forecasting error (RMSFE)

$$RMSFE(\hat{y}_t) = \frac{\sum_{t=1}^{T} (\hat{y}_t - y_t)^2}{\sum_{t=1}^{T} (\hat{y}_{Bt} - y_t)^2},$$

where $\hat{y}_t$, $t = 1, \ldots, T$, is the predicted value for y_t. The RMSFE is calculated as the ratio of the mean squared forecasting errors of the corresponding method and the benchmark model $\hat{y}_{Bt}$ (AR-p). Additionally, we will use the geometric mean relative absolute error (GMRAE)

$$GMRAE(\hat{y}_t) = \left(\prod_{t=1}^{T} \frac{|\hat{y}_t - y_t|}{|\hat{y}_{Bt} - y_t|} \right)^{\frac{1}{T}}$$

as recommended by Armstrong and Collopy (1992). Here, corresponding forecasts are directly compared to each other and therefore the mean growth rate of the absolute forecasting error is compared to the benchmark forecast $\hat{\boldsymbol{y}}_B = (\hat{y}_{B1}, \ldots, \hat{y}_{BT})$.

Harvey et al. (1998) proposed the so-called HLN-Test as a test on equal forecasting accuracy of two competing forecasts. It is based on the popular Diebold-Mariano-Test (DM-Test), proposed by Diebold and Mariano (1995). The vector $\boldsymbol{d} = (d_1, \ldots, d_T), d_t = (\hat{y}_t - y_t)^2 - (\hat{y}_{Bt} - y_t)^2$, contains the differences of quadratic loss between the forecasts and the true values. The HLN-Test is used to test the null hypothesis

$$H_0: \ \mathbb{E}(\boldsymbol{d}) = 0$$

assuming equal forecasting accuracy for the competing forecasts. Following Harvey et al. (1998), the test statistic (assuming a forecasting horizon $h = 1$) is

$$DM = (T - 1) \frac{\overline{d}}{\sqrt{\hat{V}(\overline{d})}} \tag{2}$$

and will be compared to the $T - 1$ t-distribution.

Clements and Harvey (2007) stated that a similarly constructed test statistic (2) can also be used to perform encompassing tests. Assuming two forecasting series $\hat{y}_{1t}$ and $\hat{y}_{2t}$ one wants to test the null hypothesis

$$H_0: \quad \lambda = 0$$

referring to a combination of the two series,

$$\hat{y}_{ct} = (1 - \lambda)\hat{y}_t + \lambda \hat{y}_{Bt}, \quad 0 \leq \lambda \leq 1.$$

If the null hypothesis holds, it is assumed that $\hat{y}_{Bt}$ does not contain any additional information to that from $\hat{y}_t$. Then, $\hat{y}_t$ encompasses $\hat{y}_{Bt}$. The test statistic DM is used with d_t defined by $d_t = (\hat{y}_t - y_t)^2 - (\hat{y}_t - y_t)(\hat{y}_{Bt} - y_t)$.

5 Results

In the following, forecasting results for all the methods are given. The methods AR-p and AR-4 are used as benchmarks: PLSR and PCR represent the more traditional techniques of forecasting with dimension reduction by aggregating information into

Table 1 Relative mean squared forecasting errors (RMSFE) of forecasting the gross added value relative to the AR-p Model; lowest values per setting in boldface

	Business situations	Business expectations	Business climate	All covariates[a]
AR-p	1.000	1.000	1.000	1.000
AR-4	1.062	1.062	1.062	1.062
Lasso	1.175	0.604	0.742	0.758
Elastic Net	0.969	0.713	0.844	0.690
Group Lasso	**0.702**	0.737	**0.632**	0.680
GPS	1.038	0.775	0.748	0.805
Boosting	1.130	0.618	0.648	**0.612**
PLSR	1.005	**0.567**	0.649	0.816
PCR	0.857	0.746	0.703	0.707

[a] *All covariates* encompass the variables business expectations, business situations, past and current volume of orders and the current business climate

Table 2 Geometric mean relative absolute errors (GMRAE) of forecasting the gross added value relative to the AR-p Model; lowest values per setting in boldface

	Business situations	Business expectations	Business climate	All covariates[a]
AR-p	1.000	1.000	1.000	1.000
AR-4	1.006	1.006	1.006	1.006
Lasso	1.169	0.904	1.125	**0.658**
Elastic Net	0.943	0.846	0.912	0.902
Group Lasso	**0.790**	0.868	0.934	1.105
GPS	0.937	0.864	1.107	0.905
Boosting	0.997	0.960	**0.784**	1.048
PLSR	1.097	**0.803**	0.901	0.981
PCR	1.215	1.086	1.045	0.939

[a] *All covariates* encompass the variables business expectations, business situations, past and current volume of orders and the current business climate

factor variables. Finally, the methods Lasso, Elastic Net, Group Lasso, GPS and Boosting represent regularization methods with the feature of variable selection. Tables 1, 2 and 3 show the results, namely the forecasting errors RMSFE and GMRAE and the p-values for the HLN-Tests on equal forecasting accuracy. In total, four different covariate settings were considered. The first three settings only used one exogenous covariate from every branch, namely the covariates business situations, business expectations and business climate. The last setting, denoted as **all covariates**, uses all three covariates as well as the past and current volume of orders simultaneously for all branches as exogenous covariates. In Tables 1 and 2

Table 3 p-Values for HLN-Tests on equal forecasting accuracy of forecasting the gross added value relative to the AR-p Model; lowest values per setting in boldface

	Business situations	Business expectations	Business climate	All covariates[a]
AR-p	0.500	0.500	0.500	0.500
AR-4	0.953	0.953	0.953	0.953
Lasso	0.734	0.074	0.143	0.161
Elastic Net	0.461	0.091	0.256	0.115
Group Lasso	**0.012**	**0.023**	**0.007**	**0.014**
GPS	0.548	0.028	0.119	0.052
Boosting	0.687	0.039	0.072	0.075
PLSR	0.507	0.028	0.053	0.260
PCR	0.235	0.061	0.066	0.090

[a]*All covariates* encompass the variables business expectations, business situations, past and current volume of orders and the current business climate

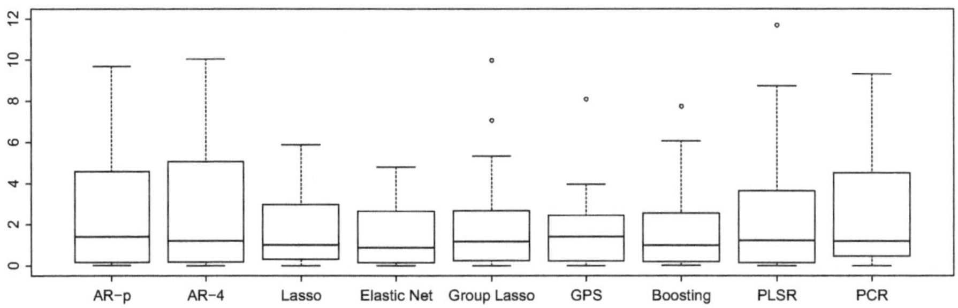

Fig. 2 Boxplots for squared forecasting errors for different methods of forecasting of the gross added value by use of the exogeneous covariate business expectations

values smaller than 1 denote better forecasting performance than AR-p. The best method is given in boldface.

In general, the methods including exogenous covariates distinctly dominate the benchmark methods AR-p and AR-4 in terms of RMSFE. Most of them also perform better in terms of GMRAE. The regularization methods easily compete with PLSR and PCR. The p-values for the HLN-Tests are most distinct for the Group Lasso. It turns out to have a significant higher forecasting accuracy for all settings, even for the setting business situations which turned out to be the one with the lowest gain of additional information.

Figure 2 shows boxplots of the squared forecasting errors for the setting with the business expectations as the only exogenous covariates. This setting turned out to be the one with the most additional information when compared to the simple autoregressive model. All methods including exogenous covariates decrease the forecasting errors when compared to the benchmark models AR-p and AR-4. The regularization methods achieve remarkably more stable forecasts than PCR and PLSR.

6 Ensemble Methods

As an extension, we consider the combination of the presented methods into one joint forecast. Combining forecasts has become a well-accepted principle in the forecasting community. In Clemen (1989), a comprehensive overview on combination methods and related literature is presented. Armstrong (2001) provides some practical instructions for the correct combination of forecasts. More recently, Stock and Watson (2006) presented and evaluated an extensive collection of combination methods. The main issue addressed by forecasting combinations is to gain more stable results than by restricting the forecast to one single method.

6.1 Methods

The combination methods we use differ with regard to their complexity. Simple methods to combine a list of n time series, $\hat{y}_{1t}, \ldots, \hat{y}_{nt}$, for observation t are the

Arithmetic Mean

$$\hat{y}_{ct} = \frac{1}{n} \sum_{i=1}^{n} \hat{y}_{it}, \tag{3}$$

the *Median*

$$\hat{y}_{ct} = \begin{cases} \hat{y}_{(\frac{n+1}{2})t} & n \text{ uneven} \\ \frac{1}{2}\left(\hat{y}_{(\frac{n}{2})t} + \hat{y}_{(\frac{n}{2}+1)t}\right) & n \text{ even} \end{cases} \tag{4}$$

and the *Trimmed Mean*

$$\hat{y}_{ct} = \frac{1}{n - 2 \cdot \lfloor \alpha n \rfloor} \sum_{i=\lfloor \alpha n \rfloor + 1}^{n - \lfloor \alpha n \rfloor} \hat{y}_{(i)t}, \tag{5}$$

where $\hat{y}_{(1)t}, \hat{y}_{(2)t}, \ldots, \hat{y}_{(n)t}$ represents the order statistic for observation t and α represents the proportion of the highest and lowest forecasts eliminated in the trimmed mean. In our application, $\alpha = 0.1$ is used.

The three methods do not use any information from former forecasts and can therefore also be used for rather small data sets. All the following methods try to use some information on the forecasting accuracy of the single methods in former forecasts.

6.1.1 Weighted Means

One possibility to use information from the forecasting accuracy of the respective methods is to use weighted means of the forecasted values. Using weights w_{it}, $i = 1,\ldots,n$, where $\sum_{i=1}^{n} w_{it} = 1$, the combined forecast for observation t can be calculated by

$$\hat{y}_{ct} = \sum_{i=1}^{n} w_{it}\hat{y}_{it}.$$

The weights can be calculated in numerous ways:.

6.1.2 Ridge-Weights

For the combination method *Ridge-Weights*, a linear model

$$\mathbb{E}(y_s) = \beta_0 + \sum_{i=1}^{n} \hat{y}_{is}\beta_{it}, \quad s = 1,\ldots,t-1$$

is calculated by Ridge estimation. The estimated parameters $\hat{\beta}_{1t},\ldots,\hat{\beta}_{nt}$ are used to calculate the weights by

$$w_{it} = \frac{\hat{\beta}_{it}}{\sum_{j=1}^{n} \hat{\beta}_{jt}}.$$

6.1.3 Shrinkage-Forecast

The method of *Shrinkage-Forcast*, adapted from Stock and Watson (2004), uses the *Ridge-Weights* from above and seeks to get a compromise between the method of *Ridge-Weights* and the simple *Arithmetic Mean*. The weights are calculated by

$$w_{it} = \alpha\frac{\hat{\beta}_{it}}{\sum_{j=1}^{n} \hat{\beta}_{jt}} + (1-\alpha)\frac{1}{n}.$$

Therefore, depending on the tuning parameter α, the weights will be a weighted mean between the equal weights from the *Arithmetic Mean* and the *Ridge-Weights*. We will use $\alpha = 0.5$ and $\alpha = 0.75$ in our application.

6.1.4 MSFE and MAFE

The forecasting accuracy of the single methods can be measured by the mean squared forecasting error or the mean absolute forecasting error (MSFE and MAFE). For method i, the MSFE for observations $1, \ldots, t-1$ is calculated by

$$m_{i,t-1} = \frac{1}{t-1} \sum_{s=1}^{t-1} (y_s - \hat{y}_{is})^2,$$

whereas the MAFE is calculated by

$$m_{i,t-1} = \frac{1}{t-1} \sum_{s=1}^{t-1} |y_s - \hat{y}_{is}|.$$

The forecasting accuracy is measured by the inverse of the respective error. Therefore, the weights are calculated by

$$w_{it} = \frac{m_{it-1}^{-1}}{\sum_{j=1}^{n} m_{jt-1}^{-1}},$$

respectively. See also Stock and Watson (2004) for these combination methods.

6.1.5 HLN-Test

The last method of combining forecasts is the so-called *HLN-Test* method, proposed by Kisinbay (2010). An algorithm is used that tests the single forecasting methods against each other by the encompassing test (see Sect. 4) from Clements and Harvey (2007). The algorithm has the following structure:

Step 1: Calculate the MSFE m_{it-1}, $i = 1, \ldots, n$, (see above) for every forecast and choose $\hat{y}_{bt}$ such, that $b = \underset{i}{argmin}(m_{it-1})$

Step 2: Test $\hat{y}_{bt}$ against all other forecasts using the encompassing test and delete all forecasts with no significant additional information (for a given level of significance α)

Step 3: Repeat **Step 2** with the forecast with the lowest MSFE within the remaining forecasts

Step 4: Repeat with the third-best forecast and so on until there is no needless forecast left

Last step: Calculate the arithmetic mean from the remaining forecasts

For our application, α will be taken from the set $\alpha \in (0.01, 0.05, 0.1, 0.2, 0.3, 0.4)$.

6.2 Results

In Sect. 5, the business expectations turned out to be the most informative covariate. Therefore, we used these forecasts and combined them by the afore-mentioned methods. Figure 3 shows the boxplots of the squared forecasting errors for all combination methods and the AR-p model as benchmark model.

Table 4 shows the RMSFE, the GMRAE and the p-values for the HLN-tests on equal forecasting accuracy against the benchmark model AR-p. Both Fig. 3 and Table 4 show that the mean squared forecasting errors are reduced significantly by most of the combination methods compared to the AR-p model. The smallest p-values are found for the simple methods *Arithmetic Mean*, *Median* and *Trimmed Mean* and by the methods *MSFE* and *MAFE*. Therefore, also very simple methods seem to be able to improve the forecasting performance of a combination of forecast over the performance of the single forecasts. However, the rather complicated method *HLN-Test* does not seem to be the best choice.

The combination methods have also been applied to the forecasts where all available covariates (setting *All covariates*) have been used. Table 5 shows the accuracy measures for these combinations. Again, several methods have significant improvement over the benchmark model with the simple methods among the best ones.

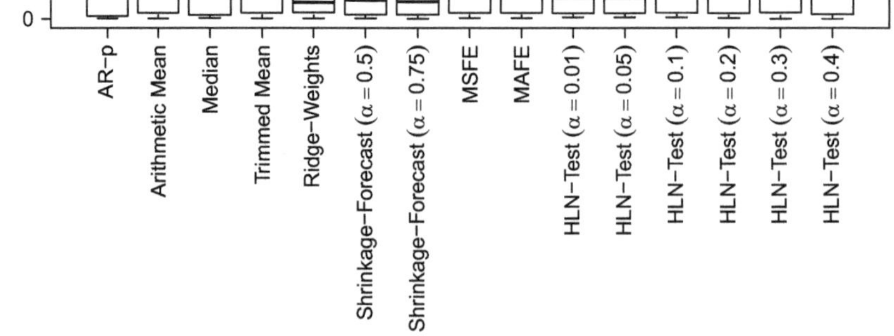

Fig. 3 Boxplots of squared forecasting errors for combinations of the forecasts of the gross added value by use of the exogenous covariate business expectations

Table 4 Accuracy measures for combinations of the forecasts of the gross added value by use of the exogenous covariate business expectations; lowest values per setting in boldface

	RMSFE	GMRAE	p-Value
Arithmetic mean	0.682	1.026	**0.020**
Median	**0.647**	1.032	0.021
Trimmed mean	0.686	1.072	0.022
Ridge-Weights	0.786	1.005	0.247
Shrinkage-Forecast ($\alpha = 0.5$)	0.700	0.955	0.076
Shrinkage-Forecast ($\alpha = 0.75$)	0.734	0.912	0.148
MSFE	0.665	1.024	0.025
MAFE	0.676	1.029	0.022
HLN-Test ($\alpha = 0.01$)	0.681	1.080	0.099
HLN-Test ($\alpha = 0.05$)	0.683	1.082	0.101
HLN-Test ($\alpha = 0.1$)	0.662	1.112	0.068
HLN-Test ($\alpha = 0.2$)	0.656	1.046	0.053
HLN-Test ($\alpha = 0.3$)	0.695	0.973	0.066
HLN-Test ($\alpha = 0.4$)	0.725	**0.889**	0.073

Table 5 Accuracy measures for combinations of the forecasts of the gross added value by use of the exogenous covariates business expectations, business situations, past and current volume of orders and the current business climate; lowest values per setting in boldface

	RMSFE	GMRAE	p-Value
Arithmetic mean	0.698	0.839	**0.039**
Median	**0.652**	1.022	0.056
Trimmed mean	0.692	0.788	0.043
Ridge-Weights	0.679	0.933	0.078
Shrinkage-Forecast ($\alpha = 0.5$)	0.684	0.873	0.056
Shrinkage-Forecast ($\alpha = 0.75$)	0.680	0.882	0.067
MSFE	0.694	0.810	0.048
MAFE	0.699	0.827	0.042
HLN-Test ($\alpha = 0.01$)	0.779	0.941	0.194
HLN-Test ($\alpha = 0.05$)	0.779	0.941	0.194
HLN-Test ($\alpha = 0.1$)	0.779	0.941	0.194
HLN-Test ($\alpha = 0.2$)	0.656	0.975	0.069
HLN-Test ($\alpha = 0.3$)	0.765	0.963	0.073
HLN-Test ($\alpha = 0.4$)	0.784	**0.770**	0.102

Concluding Remarks
We used several regularization methods to forecast the quarterly added value in the manufacturing sector by using data provided by the Munich ifo Institute. The used methods are well established in the statistical literature but are still rarely used in the forecasting community. The methods turned out to be very strong competitors for the established forecasting methods. Especially, Group Lasso turned out to have a strong performance in terms of forecasting. Group Lasso has also an advantage when it comes to interpretation of the forecasting models. Because of its feature of group-wise variable selection, it can uncover the sectors which do or do not have influence upon the gross added value. We also found that ensemble methods can improve the accuracy of forecasting. Especially in cases where none of the methods is obviously dominating, combinations can provide more robust forecasts than a single method. In our application, the weighted means with respect to previous forecasting errors (MSFE or MAFE) and the simple methods of arithmetic mean, median and trimmed mean turned out to perform best.

Acknowledgements We thank the Munich ifo Institute for providing the data from the surveys of the ifo Business Climate Index. Especially, we thank Kai Carstensen, Johannes Mayr, Klaus Wohlrabe, Teresa Buchen and Steffen Henzel from the ifo Institute for helpful discussions.

References

Armstrong, J. (2001). Combining forecasts. *International Series in Operations Research and Management Science, 30*, 417–440.

Armstrong, J. S., & Collopy, F. (1992). Error measures for generalizing about forecasting methods: Empirical comparisons. *International Journal of Forecasting, 8*, 69–80.

Bai, J., & Ng, S. (2002). Determining the number of factors in approximate factor models. *Econometrica, 70*(1), 191–221.

Bai, J., & Ng, S. (2008). Forecasting economic time series using targeted predictors. *Journal of Econometrics, 146*(2), 304–317.

Bai, J., & Ng, S. (2009). Boosting diffusion indices. *Journal of Applied Econometrics, 24*(4), 607–629.

Becker, S. O., & Wohlrabe, K. (2007). Micro Data at the Ifo Institute for Economic Research - The "Ifo Business Survey", Usage and Access. Ifo Working Paper Series Ifo Working Paper No. 47, Ifo Institute for Economic Research at the University of Munich.

Buchen, T., & Wohlrabe, K. (2011). Forecasting with many predictors: Is boosting a viable alternative? *Economics Letters, 113*(1), 16–18.

Bühlmann, P., & Hothorn, T. (2007). Boosting algorithms: Regularization, prediction and model fitting (with discussion). *Statistical Science, 22*, 477–505.

Bühlmann, P., & Yu, B. (2003). Boosting with the L2 loss: Regression and classification. *Journal of the American Statistical Association, 98*, 324–339.

Clemen, R. T. (1989). Combining forecasts: A review and annotated bibliography. *International Journal of Forecasting, 5*(4), 559–583.

Clements, M. P., & Harvey, D. I. (2009). Forecast combination and encompassing. In *Palgrave handbook of econometrics. Volume 2: Applied econometrics* (pp. 169–198). London: Palgrave Macmillan.

De Mol, C., Giannone, D., & Reichlin, L. (2008). Forecasting using a large number of predictors: Is bayesian shrinkage a valid alternative to principal components? *Journal of Econometrics, 146*(2), 318–328.

Diebold, F. X., & Mariano, R. S. (1995). Comparing predictive accuracy. *Journal of Business & Economic Statistics, 13*, 253–263.

Efron, B., Hastie, T., Johnstone, I., & Tibshirani, R. (2004). Least angle regression. *Annals of Statistics, 32*, 407–499.

Feng, Y., & Heiler, S. (1998). Locally weighted autoregression. In *Econometrics in theory and practice* (pp. 101–117). Heidelberg: Springer.

Freund, Y., & Schapire, R. E. (1996). Experiments with a new boosting algorithm. In *Proceedings of the Thirteenth International Conference on Medicine Learning* (pp. 148–156). San Francisco: Morgan Kaufmann.

Friedman, J. H. (2012). Fast sparse regression and classification. *International Journal of Forecasting, 28*(3), 722–738.

Friedman, J. H., Hastie, T., & Tibshirani, R. (2010). Regularization paths for generalized linear models via coordinate descent. *Journal of Statistical Software, 33*(1), 1–22.

Goeman, J. J. (2010). L1 penalized estimation in the Cox proportional hazards model. *Biometrical Journal, 52*, 70–84.

Harvey, D. I., Leybourne, S. J., & Newbold, P. (1998). Tests for forecast encompassing. *Journal of Business & Economic Statistics, 16*, 254–259.

Hastie, T., Tibshirani, R., & Friedman, J. H. (2001). *The elements of statistical learning*. New York: Springer.

Hastie, T., Tibshirani, R., & Friedman, J. H. (2009). *The elements of statistical learning* (2nd ed.). New York: Springer.

Heiler, S., & Feng, Y. (2000). Data-driven decomposition of seasonal time series. *Journal of Statistical Planning and Inference, 91*(2), 351–363.

Hoerl, A. E., & Kennard, R. W. (1970). Ridge regression: Bias estimation for nonorthogonal problems. *Technometrics, 12*, 55–67.

Kendall, M. G. (1957). *A course in multivariate analysis*. New York: Hafner Pub. Co.

Kisinbay, T. (2010). The use of encompassing tests for forecast combinations. *Journal of Forecasting, 29*, 715–727.

Meier, L. (2009). *grplasso: Fitting user specified models with Group Lasso penalty*. R package version 0.4-2.

Meier, L., van de Geer, S., & Bühlmann, P. (2008). The group lasso for logistic regression. *Journal of the Royal Statistical Society, Series B, 70*, 53–71.

Mevik, B.-H., Wehrens, R., & Liland, K. H. (2011). *pls: Partial Least Squares and Principal Component regression.* R package version 2.3-0.

Robinzonov, N., Tutz, G., & Hothorn, T. (2012). Boosting techniques for nonlinear time series models. *AStA Advances in Statistical Analysis, 96*, 99–122.

Shafik, N., & Tutz, G. (2009). Boosting nonlinear additive autoregressive time series. *Computational Statistics and Data Analysis, 53*, 2453–2464.

Stock, J. H., & Watson, M. W. (2004). Combination forecasts of output growth in a seven-country data set. *Journal of Forecasting, 23*, 405–430.

Stock, J. H., & Watson, M. W. (2006). Forecasting with many predictors. In C. G. G. Elliott & A. Timmermann (Eds.), *Handbook of economic forecasting* (Vol. 1, pp. 515–554). Amsterdam: Elsevier.

Stock, J. H., & Watson, M. W. (2011, February). Generalized shrinkage methods for forecasting using many predictors generalized shrinkage methods for forecasting using many predictors. Manuscript, Harvard University, 0-62.

Tibshirani, R. (1996). Regression shrinkage and selection via the lasso. *Journal of the Royal Statistical Society B, 58*, 267–288.

Wold, H. (1975). Soft Modeling by latent variables; The nonlinear iterative partial least squares approach. *Perspectives in probability and statistics*. Papers in Honour of M. S. Bartlett. London: Academic Press.

Yuan, M., & Lin, Y. (2006). Model selection and estimation in regression with grouped variables. *Journal of the Royal Statistical Society B, 68*, 49–67.

Zou, H., & Hastie, T. (2005). Regularization and variable selection via the elastic net. *Journal of the Royal Statistical Society B, 67*, 301–320.

Investigating Bavarian Beer Consumption

Michael Bruckner and Roland Jeske

Abstract This article investigates various influencing factors such as weather conditions and economic factors which are considered to determine the monthly beer consumption in Bavaria. Therefore, two regression models are used to identify influencing factors. The results indicate that besides seasonal effects, sunshine duration and beer price are the main influencing factors of the Bavarian beer consumption.

1 Introduction

While many parts of Germany appear to be interchangeable concerning their attitudes, behaviors, and mentalities, the image of Bavaria and Bavarian lifestyle seems to be dominated by some outstanding properties and products such as King Louis' castles, FC Bayern Munich, some special rural dishes, and of course Bavarian beer. This perception of Bavaria and the Bavarians by themselves but also from abroad makes this country somehow special.

Hardly any item of food production is that important for Bavaria rather than beer (Bayerischer Brauerbund 2012b). Bavarian beer consists of some 4,000 trademarks (Bayerischer Brauerbund 2012c), standing for about three quarters of the German total, while more than 600 production facilities of Bavarian beer amounting nearly half of all German breweries (Bayerischer Brauerbund 2012a,d). Therefore, the question arises what makes Bavarian beer special and what are possible influence factors on Bavarian beer consumption.

M. Bruckner • R. Jeske (✉)
University of Applied Sciences Kempten, Bahnhofstraße 61, 87435 Kempten, Germany
e-mail: roland.jeske@hs-kempten.de

J. Beran et al. (eds.), *Empirical Economic and Financial Research*,
Advanced Studies in Theoretical and Applied Econometrics 48,
DOI 10.1007/978-3-319-03122-4_5

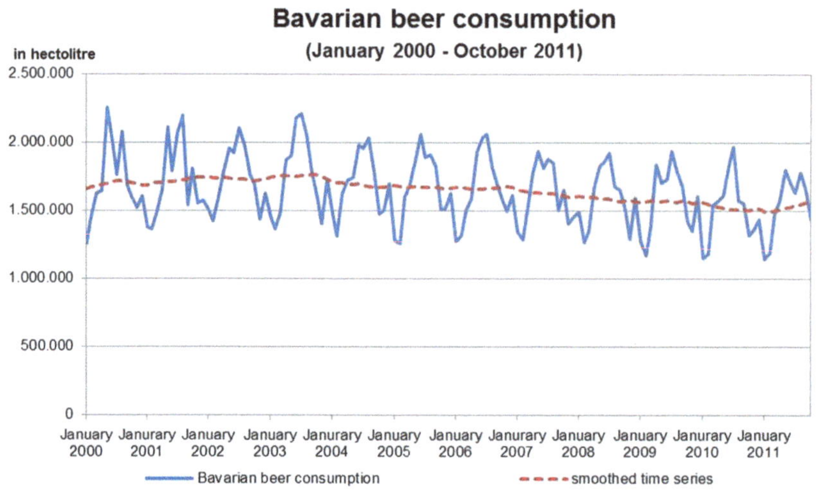

Fig. 1 Monthly beer consumption in Bavaria Jan 2000 to Oct 2011

2 Data

The concrete Bavarian beer consumption is not collected by German official statistics. As compensation the monthly taxable sales volume of alcohol-containing beer in Bavaria between January 2000 and October 2011 was considered.[1] Figure 1 shows this monthly beer consumption for the given time period. This time series obviously seems to have a remarkable seasonal pattern. Therefore, a smoothing by Berlin method (see, e.g., Heiler 1970) was added.

Even graphically the greater beer consumption during the summer is visible while beer consumption during the winter months seems to decrease. Therefore, one might expect some climatic influences on the Bavarian beer consumption. As possible covariables, monthly sunshine duration, air temperature, wind velocity, precipitation amount, and cloud coverage[2] were taken into consideration. Since these climatic indicators were provided for 16 single Bavarian weather stations (see Fig. 2), simple averages of these indicators were calculated except for three stations due to their exposed positions.

Another important aspect might be the influence of tourism since Bavaria is one of the most popular regions in Germany for making holidays. In order to measure this influence of tourism industry, the amount of overnight guests (only in

[1]Source: Bavarian State Office for Statistics and Data Processing.

[2]Source: German Meteorological Service (DWD), Offenbach.

Fig. 2 Weather stations in Bavaria (annotation: those marked with *filled star* were excluded)

hostels with capacity exceeding eight beds) and the monthly turnover development in Bavarian gastronomy index were taken into consideration.[3]

Finally, the beer price index[4] was considered concerning its influences on beer consumption.

In addition, a trend variable was considered in the first model in order to accommodate the declining sales volumes. Last but not least due to the seasonal fluctuations in beer consumption the season was modelled with 11 monthly dummy variables.

[3]Both Sources: Bavarian State Office for Statistics and Data Processing.

[4]Source: Bavarian State Office for Statistics and Data Processing.

3 Considered Models

Focus was put on the following two models:

Model 1: At a first step a regression model with all mentioned covariables and additional monthly dummies was performed by using OLS. This model was reduced by variable selection in a top down modelling approach.

Model 2: A two-stage model was performed. At first a factor analysis of the described covariables was performed in order to use these factors as independent variables once again in an OLS approach.

Bruckner (2012) additionally performed a distributed lag model, which however yielded worse results and therefore is not mentioned here.

4 Results

Concerning the unreduced model 1 several indicators turned out to be insignificant such as trend, wind velocity, cloud coverage, precipitation amount as well as overnight guests and gastronomy index. Surprisingly the latter two indicators did not have a significant influence on beer consumption at all. This might be due to several aspects. On the one hand, for both indicators it could be argued that non-negligible carry-over effects and substitution effects exist. On the other hand, it might be due to data's quality. The gastronomy index is sampled more or less unchanged since 1995 neglecting any economic dynamics in the tourism sector. Concerning the time series of the overnight guests it has to be seen critical that only accommodations with nine beds and more are considered while a lot of Bavarian regions—as well as areas in Rhineland-Palatine and along the German sea side—are highly dependent on accommodations with less than nine beds.

The variable-reduced model was well fitted with an adjusted $R^2 = 0.88$ and consisted of three components: the sunshine duration, measuring the weather impact, the beer price index as the structural component, and the season which reflected the yearly fluctuations in the sales volumes. An increase in the sunshine duration had a highly positive impact whereas increasing beer prices influenced the beer consumption negatively (see Table 1).

Further investigations of the reduced model did not provide any indication of multicollinearity: neither the variance inflation factors nor the condition index or the proportions of variance showed abnormalities. Moreover the QQ-Plot of standardized residuals did not stand for a violation of the Gaussian distributional assumption (Fig. 3). Based on the Breusch–Pagan LM-test the null hypothesis that homoscedasticity exists could not be denied ($p = 0.709$). Last but not least the Durbin–Watson-Statistic with 2.5 turned out to be unobtrusive.

Secondly, a two-step model was performed. Here, in a first step, a principal component analysis (PCA) was made. Therefore the weather indicators, the

Table 1 Regression results for reduced model 1

Variable	Coefficient	Standard error	t-Statistic	*p*-Value
(Constant)	2,478,441.79	95,928.560	−25.836	0.000
Sunshine duration	1,514.80	227.104	6.670	0.000
Price index of beer	−9,836.85	941.213	−10.451	0.000
Dummies				
January	−278,381.49	36,086.80	−7.714	0.000
February	−344,959.63	36,659.58	−9.410	0.000
March	−187,062.61	39,299.06	−4.760	0.000
April	−80,717.52	45,145.76	−1.788	0.076
May	78,888.10	47,933.45	1.646	0.102
June	86,285.07	50,075.33	1.723	0.087
July	132,762.14	49,223.26	2.697	0.008
August	97,830.88	47,421.77	2.063	0.041
September	−59,581.67	42,145.73	−1.414	0.160
October	−118,747.37	38,206.00	−3.108	0.002
November	−163,985.57	36,814.49	−4.454	0.000

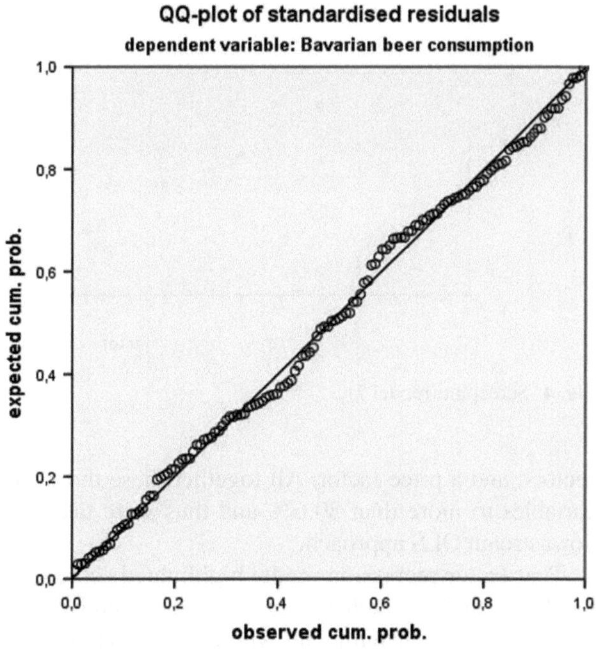

Fig. 3 QQ-plot of standardized residuals (model 1)

gastronomy index, the overnight guests, and the beer price index were used as input data. Within the PCA the Varimax-method was used as rotation-method in order to derive orthogonal factors (see Table 2). Based on the screeplot (Fig. 4) three underlying factors could be identified: A weather factor, a factor of weather-depending

Table 2 Rotated component matrix of factor analysis

Variable	Component 1	Component 2	Component 3
Cloud coverage	−0.899	−0.054	−0.009
Sunshine duration	0.790	0.446	−0.094
Wind velocity	−0.663	−0.055	−0.154
Precipitation amount	−0.364	0.867	0.018
Overnight guests	0.485	0.793	0.163
Air temperature	0.583	0.759	−0.023
Gastronomy index	0.392	0.681	−0.284
Beer price index	0.093	−0.019	0.974

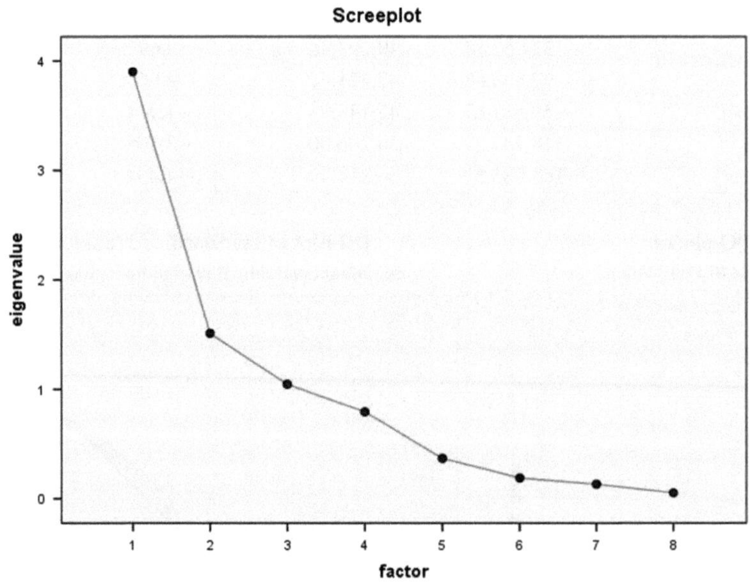

Fig. 4 Screeplot (model 2)

sectors, and a price factor. All together these three factors reproduced the original variables to more than 80.6 % and thus were taken as dependent variables in the downstream OLS approach.

That factor-regression model highlighted some interesting findings. On the one hand, the factor which included the gastronomy index and the overnight guests time series was insignificant whereas the weather and the beer price factor were significant. Moreover the goodness of fit was not attached (adjusted $R^2 = 0.88$). Thus model 2 supports the findings of model 1 (see Table 3).

Table 3 Regression results for reduced model 2

Variable	Coefficient	Standard error	t-Statistic	p-Value
(Constant)	1,610,228.24	27,652.12	−58.232	0.000
Weather factor	42,136.72	9,251.18	4.555	0.000
Price factor	−83,438.654	7,541.60	−11.064	0.000
Dummies				
January	−233,410.77	37,051.86	−6.3	0.000
February	−276,163.53	37,085.74	−7.447	0.000
March	−82,615.27	37,053.75	−2.23	0.028
April	41,327.88	38,946.50	1.061	0.291
May	247,524.36	38,187.62	6.482	0.000
June	278,741.32	38,872.58	7.171	0.000
July	323,514.30	38,525.30	8.397	0.000
August	272,128.94	39,233.64	6.936	0.000
September	42,616.72	39,313.60	1.084	0.280
October	−59,115.55	38,321.19	−1.543	0.125
November	−130,944.39	37,860.95	−3.459	0.001

5 Summary

Bavarian beer consumption can be fairly well described by linear regression modelling. Both considered models show good performances and result in qualitatively similar results: they indicate sunshine duration, beer price index, and seasonal dummies as explaining variables. There is high evidence that sunshine duration has a deep positive impact on Bavarian beer consumption, whereas beer price index influences beer consumption negatively. The seasonal effects in both models point out that the beer garden seasons led to over averaged beer consumption in Bavaria.

References

Bayerischer Brauerbund e.V. (2012a). Absatz und Ausstoß.

Bayerischer Brauerbund e.V. (2012b). Der Bierkonsum.

Bayerischer Brauerbund e.V. (2012c). Bierwissen: Bier in Zahlen: Die Biersorten.

Bayerischer Brauerbund e.V. (2012d). Die Brauereien.

Bavarian State Office for Statistics and Data Processing. (2012). Tourismus in Bayern im September 2011

Bruckner, M. (2012). Einflussfaktoren auf den bayerischen Bierabsatz - Eine empirische Analyse mit SPSS, Bachelorarbeit, Hochschule Kempten.

Heiler, S. (1970). Theoretische Grundlagen des Berliner Verfahrens. In: Wetzel, W. (Ed.) (pp. 67–93).

Sources of Data

- Bayerisches Landesamt für Statistik und Datenverarbeitung, www.statistik.bayern.de
- Deutscher Wetterdienst, www.dwd.de
- Statistisches Bundesamt, www.destatis.de

The Algebraic Structure of Transformed Time Series

Tucker McElroy and Osbert Pang

Abstract Invertible transformations are often applied to time series data to generate a distribution closer to the Gaussian, which naturally has an additive group structure. Estimates of forecasts and signals are then typically transformed back to the original scale. It is demonstrated that this transformation must be a group homomorphism (i.e., a transformation that preserves certain arithmetical properties) in order to obtain coherence between estimates of quantities of interest in the original scale, and that this homomorphic structure is ensured by defining an induced group structure on the original space. This has consequences for the understanding of forecast errors, growth rates, and the relation of signal and noise to the data. The effect of the distortion to the additive algebra is illustrated numerically for several key examples.

1 Introduction

The analysis of time series data is often focused on producing estimates of signals, forecasts, and/or growth rates, all of which are typically estimated by methodologies that assume an additive group structure of the data. For example, many signal extraction estimates assume that the sum of signal and noise equals the original data process; forecasts have their performance evaluated by taking their difference with the future value (this defines the forecast error). However, it is not uncommon for data to be initially transformed by an invertible function so as to make a Gaussian distribution more plausible. Any signal estimates, forecasts, or growth rates would then be transformed back into the original scale by inverting the transformation. This mapping necessarily distorts the additive group structure.

For example, many monthly retail series exhibit dramatic seasonal behavior and hence are candidates for seasonal adjustment (Bell and Hillmer, 1984; McElroy, 2012). Due to the underlying linkage of retail to inflation, exponential growth is not uncommon, and typically a logarithmic transformation is suitable for producing a more symmetric, light-tailed marginal distribution. Seasonal adjustments, which

T. McElroy (✉) • O. Pang
U.S. Census Bureau, Washington, DC, USA
e-mail: tucker.s.mcelroy@census.gov; osbert.c.pang@census.gov

J. Beran et al. (eds.), *Empirical Economic and Financial Research*,
Advanced Studies in Theoretical and Applied Econometrics 48,
DOI 10.1007/978-3-319-03122-4_6

are an application of signal extraction techniques, can then be produced using an additive group structure. Inverting the initial transformation by exponentiation maps the addition operator to the multiplication operator. That is, in the original data scale the seasonal and nonseasonal estimates no longer sum to the data process, but instead their product equals the data process.

This is the only transformation with an intuitive induced algebra on the original space. All transformations induce a group structure on the original space, which can be used to understand how the data process is decomposed into signal and noise, or how growth rates are to be properly understood; however, multiplication is the only familiar induced group structure.[1] The main result of this paper is to explicitly derive the induced group structure, and study its impact on several examples, such as the hyperbolic sine and logistic transformations.

Section 2 gives background concepts, with a brief discussion of the statistical motivation for our results, which arise from time series data that have been affected by the use of transformations. Section 3 contains our main results, and develops the algebra of the parent space, which is induced by the additive group structure of the transformed space. Section 4 continues the main examples and provides plots of level curves for the new group operations. Section 5 gives two empirical examples that compare the new group operator to addition in the parent space for the square root and logistic transformations. Section 6 provides our conclusions and discusses the implications for interpreting signal extractions, forecasts, and growth rates.

2 Statistical Background

Let us label the original domain of the data as the "parent space," and all variables will be written in bold. The "transformation space" arises from application of a one-to-one mapping φ, which is chosen so as to reduce heteroscedasticity, skewness, and kurtosis in an effort to produce data that is closer to having a Gaussian structure. For Gaussian time series variables, the additive group structure is extremely natural: optimal mean square error estimates of quantities of interest (such as future values, missing values, unknown signals, etc.) are linear in the data, and hence are intimately linked to the addition operator. Errors in estimation are assessed by comparing estimator and target via subtraction—this applies to signal extraction, forecasting, and any other Gaussian prediction problem. Therefore the additive operator is quite natural for relating quantities in the transformation space.

It is for the above reasons (the linearity of estimators when the data is Gaussian) that the sum of signal and noise estimates equals the data process; no other algebraic operation is natural for relating Gaussian signal and noise. Given an observed time series $\{\mathbf{X}_t\}$ in the parent space, say for $1 \leq t \leq n$, the analyst would select φ

[1]The original use of the logarithm, as invented by John Napier, was to assist in the computation of multiplications of numbers (McElroy, 2005).

via exploratory analysis such that $X_t = \varphi(\mathbf{X}_t)$ is representable as a sample from a Gaussian process. Most of the classical results on signal extraction (Bell, 1984; McElroy, 2008) and projection (Brockwell and Davis, 1991) are interpretable in terms of a Gaussian distribution. More precisely, the estimates commonly used in time series applications minimize the mean squared prediction error among all linear estimators, and are also conditional expectations when the process is Gaussian. If φ does not produce a Gaussian distribution, at a minimum it should reduce skewness and kurtosis in the marginal distributions.

Also, it is necessary that φ be invertible, and it will be convenient for it to be a continuously differentiable function. Denoting the joint probability distribution function (pdf) of the transformed data by $p_{X_1,\cdots,X_n}(x_1,\cdots,x_n)$, the joint pdf of the original data is then

$$p_{\mathbf{X}_1,\cdots,\mathbf{X}_n}(\mathbf{x}_1,\cdots,\mathbf{x}_n) = p_{X_1,\cdots,X_n}(x_1,\cdots,x_n) \cdot \Pi_{t=1}^{n} \frac{\partial\varphi(\mathbf{x}_t)}{\partial x}. \tag{1}$$

Of course, here $x_t = \varphi(\mathbf{x}_t)$. If we select a parametric family to model $p_{X_1,\cdots,X_n}$, e.g., a multivariate Gaussian pdf, then (1) can be viewed as a function of model parameters rather than of observed data, and we obtain the likelihood. It is apparent that the Jacobian factor does not depend on the parameters, and hence is irrelevant for model fitting purposes. That is, the model parameter estimates are unchanged by working with the likelihood in the parent space.

There may be estimates of interest in the transformation space, which are some functions of the transformed data. Typically we have some quantity of interest Z that we estimate via $\hat{Z}$ in the transformed space, perhaps computed as a linear function of the transformed data (though the linearity of the statistic is not required for this discussion). If we have a measure of the uncertainty in $\hat{Z}$, we can compute probabilities such as $\mathbb{P}[a \leq \hat{Z} \leq b]$ and $\mathbb{P}[a \leq \hat{Z} - Z \leq b]$. Since φ is invertible, the former probability can be immediately converted into a confidence interval for the parent space, via

$$\mathbb{P}\left[\varphi^{-1}(a) \leq \varphi^{-1}(\hat{Z}) \leq \varphi^{-1}(b)\right].$$

This assumes that φ is increasing (else the inequalities will be flipped around). Then our estimate of $\mathbf{Z} = \varphi^{-1}(Z)$ would be $\varphi^{-1}(\hat{Z})$, with uncertainty interval given by the above equation; a knowledge of the probability in the transformed space immediately provides the probability in the parent space. However, when uncertainty about an estimate is assessed in terms of its relation to a target quantity Z, which may be stochastic, it is less obvious how to proceed. This is typically the situation in time series analysis, where Z is often a signal or a future value of the data process, and so is a stochastic quantity. If we apply the inverse transformation to $\mathbb{P}[a \leq \hat{Z} - Z \leq b]$, we obtain

$$\mathbb{P}\left[\varphi^{-1}(a) \leq \varphi^{-1}(\hat{Z} - Z) \leq \varphi^{-1}(b)\right], \tag{2}$$

which tells us nothing of the relationship of $\mathbf{Z}$ to its estimate $\varphi^{-1}(\hat{Z})$. That is, there should be some algebraic relation between $\mathbf{Z}$ and $\varphi^{-1}(\hat{Z})$ such that a suitable notion of their discrepancy can be assessed probabilistically, and (2) can become interpretable in terms of natural quantities in the parent domain. Supposing that some operator $\oplus$ were defined such that $\varphi^{-1}(\hat{Z} - Z) = \varphi^{-1}(\hat{Z}) \oplus \mathbf{Z}^{-1}$, for an appropriate notion of the inverse of $\mathbf{Z}$, then we could substitute into (2) and obtain a confidence interval for the statistical error. The next section develops the unique operator $\oplus$ possessing the requisite properties.

3 Algebraic Structure of the Parent Space

Given an additive operation in the transformed space, e.g., $x_t + x_{t-1}$, it is crucial to define a corresponding composition rule $\oplus$ in the parent domain such that φ is a group homomorphism. A group is a set together with an associative composition law, such that an identity element exists and every element has an inverse (Artin, 1991). A homomorphism is a transformation of groups such that the laws of composition are respected. The groups under consideration are $\mathscr{R} = (\mathbb{R}, +)$ for the transformed space, and $\mathscr{G} = (\varphi^{-1}(\mathbb{R}), \oplus)$ for the parent space. Consider the situation of latent components in the transformed space, where $X_t = S_t + N_t$ is a generic signal-noise decomposition. Then the components in the parent space are $\varphi^{-1}(S_t) = \mathbf{S}_t$ and $\varphi^{-1}(N_t) = \mathbf{N}_t$, which can be quantities of interest in their own right. How do we define an algebraic structure that allows us to combine $\mathbf{S}_t$ and $\mathbf{N}_t$, such that the result is always $\mathbf{X}_t$? What is needed is a group operator $\oplus$ such that

$$\mathbf{S}_t \oplus \mathbf{N}_t = \mathbf{X}_t = \varphi^{-1}(S_t + N_t) = \varphi^{-1}(\varphi(\mathbf{S}_t) + \varphi(\mathbf{N}_t)).$$

This equation actually suggests the definition of $\oplus$: any two elements $\mathbf{a}, \mathbf{b}$ in the parent group $\mathscr{G}$ are summed via the rule

$$\mathbf{a} \oplus \mathbf{b} = \varphi^{-1}(\varphi(\mathbf{a}) + \varphi(\mathbf{b})). \tag{3}$$

This definition "lifts" the additive group structure of $\mathscr{R}$ to $\mathscr{G}$ such that: (1) $\varphi^{-1}(0) = 1_G$ is the unique identity element of $\mathscr{G}$; (2) $\mathscr{G}$ has the associative property; (3) the unique inverse of any $\mathbf{a} \in \mathscr{G}$ is given by $\mathbf{a}^{-1} = \varphi^{-1}(-\varphi(\mathbf{a}))$. These properties are verified below, and establish that $\mathscr{G}$ is indeed a group. Moreover, the group is Abelian and φ is a group isomorphism.

First, $\mathbf{a} \oplus \varphi^{-1}(0) = \varphi^{-1}(\varphi(\mathbf{a}) + 0) = \mathbf{a}$, which together with the reverse calculation shows that $\varphi^{-1}(0)$ is an identity; uniqueness similarly follows. Associativity is a book-keeping exercise. For the inverse, note that $\mathbf{a} \oplus \varphi^{-1}(-\varphi(\mathbf{a})) = \varphi^{-1}(\varphi(\mathbf{a}) - \varphi(\mathbf{a})) = \varphi^{-1}(0) = 1_{\mathscr{G}}$. This shows that $\mathscr{G}$ is a group, and commutativity follows from (3) and the commutativity of addition; hence, $\mathscr{G}$ is an Abelian group. Finally, φ is a bijection as well as a homomorphism, i.e., it is an isomorphism.

What goes wrong if we use another composition rule to define $\mathscr{G}$? We would lose the group structure, and more importantly we no longer have the important property that $\varphi(\mathbf{X}_t) = \varphi(\mathbf{S}_t) + \varphi(\mathbf{N}_t)$. For example, suppose that $\varphi(x) = \text{sign}(x)\sqrt{|x|}$, and for illustration suppose that $\mathbf{X}_t, \mathbf{S}_t, \mathbf{N}_t$ are all positive. But if an additive structure is assigned to the parent space, then we would have $\mathbf{X}_t = \mathbf{S}_t + \mathbf{N}_t$, and as a consequence $\sqrt{\mathbf{X}_t} = \sqrt{\mathbf{S}_t + \mathbf{N}_t} \neq \sqrt{\mathbf{S}_t} + \sqrt{\mathbf{N}_t}$. Instead, $\oplus$ should be defined via (for positive inputs $\mathbf{a}$ and $\mathbf{b}$) the following: $\mathbf{a} \oplus \mathbf{b} = \mathbf{a} + \mathbf{b} + 2\sqrt{\mathbf{ab}}$. Now this example results in an unfamiliar operator for $\oplus$, but when φ is the logarithm, we obtain multiplication. Although some conceptual realignment is required, the requisite algebraic structure is uniquely determined by φ and cannot be wished away.

Example 1: Logarithm

Suppose that $\varphi(x) = \log x$ and the domain is all positive real numbers. Then $\mathbf{a} \oplus \mathbf{b} = \exp\{\log \mathbf{a} + \log \mathbf{b}\} = \mathbf{a} \cdot \mathbf{b}$, i.e., the group operator is multiplication. The identity element of $\mathscr{G}$ is unity, and inverses of elements are their reciprocals. This is a familiar case, and it works out nicely; the homomorphic property of the logarithm is well known. In application, seasonal noise is viewed in the parent domain as a "seasonal factor" that divides the data, with the residual being the seasonally adjusted data.

Example 2: Box–Cox

Suppose that $\varphi(x) = \text{sign}(x)|x|^{\lambda}$, which is essentially a Box–Cox transform (see Box and Jenkins 1976) when $\lambda \in (0, 1]$. The case $\lambda = 1$ is trivial, and $\lambda \to 0$ essentially encompasses the case of logarithmic transformation. Typically the transform is utilized on positive data, but we include the sign operator to ensure the homomorphic property, as well as invertibility of φ. The composition law in $\mathscr{G}$ is then

$$\mathbf{a} \oplus \mathbf{b} = \text{sign}\left(\text{sign}(\mathbf{a})|\mathbf{a}|^{\lambda} + \text{sign}(\mathbf{b})|\mathbf{b}|^{\lambda}\right) \cdot \left|\text{sign}(\mathbf{a})|\mathbf{a}|^{\lambda} + \text{sign}(\mathbf{b})|\mathbf{b}|^{\lambda}\right|^{1/\lambda}.$$

The identity is also zero, and $\mathbf{a}^{-1} = \text{sign}(-\mathbf{a})|\mathbf{a}|$. When we restrict the spaces to $\mathbb{R}^{+}$, the rule simplifies to $\mathbf{a} \oplus \mathbf{b} = (\mathbf{a}^{\lambda} + \mathbf{b}^{\lambda})^{1/\lambda}$ (but then additive inverses are not well defined, and $\mathscr{R}$ becomes a semi-group).

Example 3: Logistic

Suppose that $\varphi(x) = \log(x) - \log(1-x)$ defined on $(0, 1)$, with inverse $e^{x}/(1+e^{x})$. This transform is sometimes used for bounded data that represents a percentage or rate. The composition law is

$$\mathbf{a} \oplus \mathbf{b} = \frac{\mathbf{ab}}{1 - \mathbf{a} - \mathbf{b} + 2\mathbf{ab}}$$

with identity element $1/2$ and inverses $\mathbf{a}^{-1} = 1 - \mathbf{a}$. This rule tells one way that percentages may be composed so as to ensure the result is again a percentage.

Example 4: Hyperbolic Sine

The function $\varphi(x) = (e^x - e^{-x})/2$ is the hyperbolic sine transformation, which maps $\mathbb{R}$ to $\mathbb{R}$, with inverse $\varphi^{-1}(y) = \log(y + \sqrt{y^2 + 1})$. Then the composition law is

$$\mathbf{a} \oplus \mathbf{b} = \varphi^{-1}\left((e^{\mathbf{b}} - e^{-\mathbf{a}})(1 + e^{\mathbf{a}-\mathbf{b}})/2\right).$$

The identity element is zero, and inverses are the same as in $\mathscr{R}$, i.e., $\mathbf{a}^{-1} = -\mathbf{a}$.

Example 5: Distributional Transforms

Any random variable with continuous invertible cumulative distribution function (cdf) F can be transformed to a standard Gaussian variable via $\varphi = \Xi \circ F$, where Ξ is the quantile function of the standard normal. Letting Φ denote the Gaussian cdf and $Q = F^{-1}$ the given variable's quantile function, clearly $\varphi^{-1} = Q \circ \Phi$. This transform takes a random variable with cdf F in the parent domain to a Gaussian variable, and the corresponding composition rule is

$$\mathbf{a} \oplus \mathbf{b} = Q\left\{\Phi\left(\Xi[F(\mathbf{a})] + \Xi[F(\mathbf{b})]\right)\right\}.$$

For example, F might correspond to a χ^2, student t, uniform, or Weibull distribution. A χ^2 variable on 2 degrees of freedom (i.e., an exponential variable) has $F(x) = 1 - e^{-x}$, with $Q(u) = -\log(1 - u)$. Then

$$\mathbf{a} \oplus \mathbf{b} = -\log\left\{1 - \Phi\left(\Xi[1 - e^{-\mathbf{a}}] + \Xi[1 - e^{-\mathbf{b}}]\right)\right\}$$

defines the composition law.

4 Numerical Illustrations

In order to assess the degree of distortion that $\oplus$ generates in quantities, in comparison with the $+$ operator, one can examine the level curves $\mathbf{c} = \mathbf{a} \oplus \mathbf{b}$ for various values of $\mathbf{c}$, i.e.,

$$L_{\mathbf{c}} = \{(\mathbf{a}, \mathbf{b}) : \mathbf{a} \oplus \mathbf{b} = \mathbf{c}\} = \{(\mathbf{a}, \mathbf{c} \oplus \mathbf{a}^{-1}) : \mathbf{a}, \mathbf{c} \in \varphi^{-1}(\mathbb{R})\}.$$

When φ is the identity mapping, the level curves are just the lines of slope -1, with y intercepts given by various values of $\mathbf{c}$. By plotting the various level curves $L_{\mathbf{c}}$ in comparison with the straight lines for the operator $+$, we can form a notion of the extent of distortion involved to the group structure of $\mathscr{R}$.

To compute the level curves, we must calculate $\mathbf{c} \oplus \mathbf{a}^{-1}$ in each case, which we write as $f_{\mathbf{c}}(\mathbf{a})$ for short; then the level curve is the graph of $f_{\mathbf{c}}$. For the logarithmic transform, $f_{\mathbf{c}}(\mathbf{a}) = \mathbf{c}/\mathbf{a}$. For the Box–Cox, the general formula is cumbersome. For example, when $\mathbf{a}, \mathbf{c} > 0$ and $\lambda = 1/2$ we obtain $f_{\mathbf{c}}(\mathbf{a}) = \text{sign}(\sqrt{\mathbf{c}} - \sqrt{\mathbf{a}}) \cdot |\sqrt{\mathbf{c}} - \sqrt{\mathbf{a}}|^2$. For the logistic, we have

$$f_{\mathbf{c}}(\mathbf{a}) = \frac{\mathbf{c}(1-\mathbf{a})}{\mathbf{a} - \mathbf{c} + 2\mathbf{c}(1-\mathbf{a})}.$$

For hyperbolic sine, we have $f_{\mathbf{c}}(\mathbf{a}) = \varphi^{-1}((e^{-\mathbf{a}} - e^{-\mathbf{c}})(1 + e^{\mathbf{c}+\mathbf{a}})/2)$, which does not simplify neatly. For distributional transforms,

$$f_{\mathbf{c}}(\mathbf{a}) = Q\left\{\Phi\left(\Xi[F(\mathbf{c})] - \Xi[F(\mathbf{a})]\right)\right\}.$$

Various level curves are plotted in Figs. 1, 2, 3, and 4. We focus on values of $\mathbf{c} = i/10$ for $1 \leq i \leq 10$, and all values of $\mathbf{a} \in [0, 1]$. We consider Examples 1 and 2 in Fig. 1, Examples 3 and 4 in Fig. 2, and Example 5 in Figs. 3 and 4, where the distributional transforms include student t with 2 degrees of freedom, χ^2 with 1 degree of freedom, the uniform (on [0, 1]) distribution, and the Weibull with shape parameter 1.5 and unit scale.

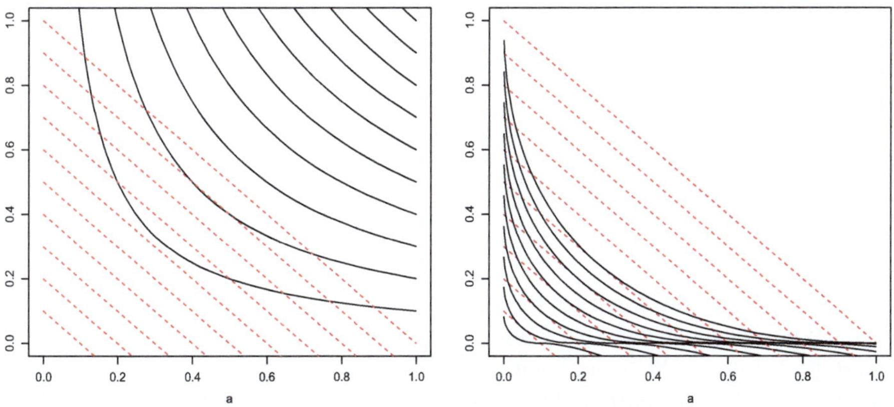

Fig. 1 Level curves L_c for the logarithmic (*left panel*) and square root Box–Cox (*right panel*) transformations. The *red* (*dotted*) *lines* are level curves for $a + b$, while the *black* (*solid*) *lines* are level curves for $a \oplus b$, where $c = 0.1, 0.2, 0.3, 0.4, 0.5, 0.6, 0.7, 0.8, 0.9, 1.0$

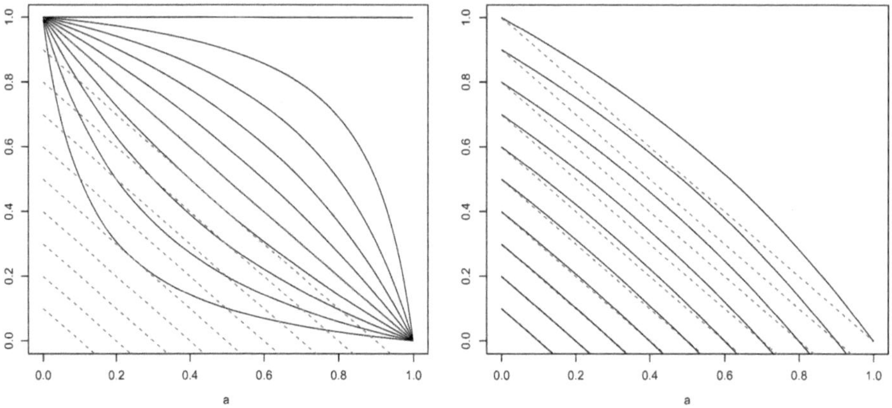

Fig. 2 Level curves L_c for the logistic (*left panel*) and hyperbolic sine (*right panel*) transformations. The *red* (*dotted*) *lines* are level curves for $a + b$, while the *black* (*solid*) lines are level curves for $a \oplus b$, where $c = 0.1, 0.2, 0.3, 0.4, 0.5, 0.6, 0.7, 0.8, 0.9, 1.0$

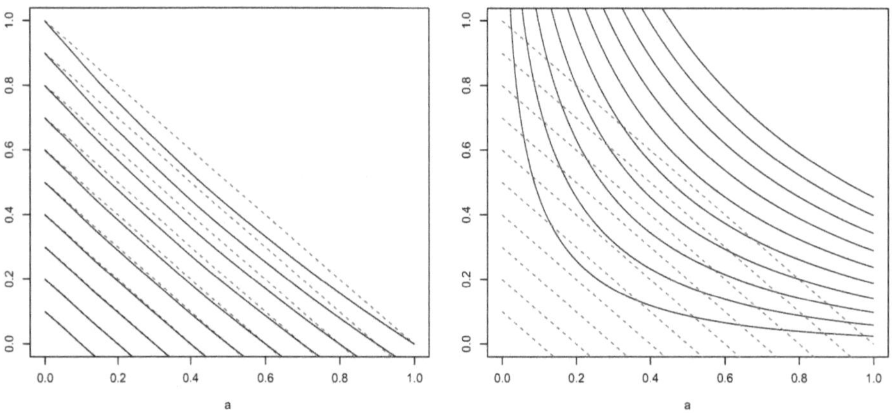

Fig. 3 Level curves L_c for the student t (*left panel*) and χ^2 (*right panel*) transformations. The *red* (*dotted*) *lines* are level curves for $a + b$, while the *black* (*solid*) *lines* are level curves for $a \oplus b$, where $c = 0.1, 0.2, 0.3, 0.4, 0.5, 0.6, 0.7, 0.8, 0.9, 1.0$

We see that the level curves for the logistic and uniform transforms are similar (though not identical, see Figs. 2 and 4), which is intuitive since they both map the space $[0, 1]$ into $\mathbb{R}$. Also, the logarithmic (Fig. 1), χ^2 (Fig. 3), and Weibull (Fig. 4) are quite similar. The hyperbolic sine (Fig. 2) and student t (Fig. 3) both offer little distortion, but have opposite curvature.

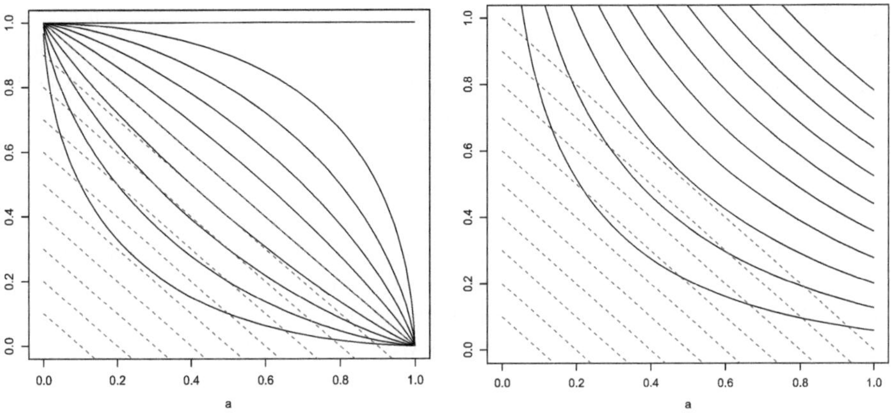

Fig. 4 Level curves L_c for the uniform (*left panel*) and Weibull (*right panel*) transformations. The *red* (*dotted*) *lines* are level curves for $a + b$, while the *black* (*solid*) *lines* are level curves for $a \oplus b$, where $c = 0.1, 0.2, 0.3, 0.4, 0.5, 0.6, 0.7, 0.8, 0.9, 1.0$

5 Empirical Illustrations

How much does the $\oplus$ operator differ from addition in practice? To answer this query we provide two data illustrations. In these examples, a data set $\{X_t\}$ that has undergone some transformation φ will be seasonally adjusted using X-12-ARIMA (Findley et al., 1998), being applied to $X_t = \varphi(\mathbf{X}_t)$ in the transformed space. We then demonstrate that the additive decomposition into seasonal and nonseasonal components in the transformed space does not reproduce an additive decomposition of these inverted components in the parent space. For this application, if X_t decomposes into a trend-cycle C_t, seasonal S_t, and irregular component I_t, then we have $X_t = C_t + S_t + I_t$. The nonseasonal component will be composed of the trend-cycle and the irregular effect, so let us label the adjusted component N_t as $N_t = C_t + I_t$. Note that while the signal-noise decomposition uses S_t to denote signal and N_t to denote noise, for the additive seasonal decomposition described here, the nonseasonal portion N_t is the signal, and the seasonal component S_t is the noise. What we show is that although $X_t = N_t + S_t$ and $\mathbf{X}_t = \varphi^{-1}(X_t)$ are both true, $\varphi^{-1}(X_t)$ can be quite a bit different from $\varphi^{-1}(N_t) + \varphi^{-1}(S_t) = \mathbf{N}_t + \mathbf{S}_t$ when φ is not a linear transformation.

5.1 Example 1: Square Root Transform

The first example is the U.S. Census Bureau monthly series of total inventory of nonmetallic mineral products in the USA, between the years 1992 and 2011. The default square root transform in X-12-ARIMA is $0.25 + 2(\sqrt{\mathbf{X}_t} - 1)$, which is

Table 1 Comparison of log likelihoods and AICCs for three transforms of total inventory data

Transform	(Adj.) log likelihood	AICC
None	−1,353.0860	2,712.2800
Logarithm	−1,352.1446	2,710.3974
Square root	−1,350.8787	2,707.8655

a shifted and scaled version of the basic $\sqrt{\mathbf{X}_t}$ square root transform, and the two adjusted log likelihoods are identical. Using X-12-ARIMA's automdl and transform specs, we compare the square root transform to both a logarithmic transform and to no transform at all. Typically, the model with the smallest AICC would be preferred over other contenders, but since the same SARIMA (0 2 1)(0 1 1) model was found to fit all three transforms of the data, the best transform would equivalently be indicated by the highest log likelihood. Table 1 displays the log likelihoods (adjusted for the transformations) along with the corresponding AICC. We see that the square root transform yields the highest log likelihood in the parent space and also the lowest value for AICC; this leads us to prefer the use of a square root transform for this total inventory series.

We proceed by using X-12-ARIMA to obtain an additive decomposition of the series $\{X_t\}$, where X_t is just the square root of $\mathbf{X}_t$. In checking the difference series $X_t - (N_t + S_t)$, we note that the differences appear to be centered around 0, with a maximum magnitude no greater than 5×10^{-13}; numerical error from rounding and computer precision explains why this difference is not identically 0. Similar results hold for the difference between $\mathbf{X}_t$ and $\mathbf{N}_t \oplus \mathbf{S}_t$, which is just the application of φ^{-1} to $N_t + S_t$. However, there are substantial discrepancies between $\mathbf{X}_t$ and $\mathbf{N}_t + \mathbf{S}_t$, as expected. For $\mathbf{N}_t = \varphi^{-1}(N_t)$ and $\mathbf{S}_t = \varphi^{-1}(S_t)$, Fig. 5 shows a plot of the untransformed series $\mathbf{X}_t$ along with $\mathbf{N}_t + \mathbf{S}_t$ on the top panel, and on the bottom panel, we have the difference series obtained by subtracting $\mathbf{N}_t + \mathbf{S}_t$ from $\mathbf{X}_t$. The top panel of Fig. 5 confirms that the additive decomposition in transformed space does not translate to an additive decomposition in parent space, and the bottom panel shows that the deviations from 0 in this case are quite pronounced. Furthermore, while the lower panel of Fig. 5 indicates that the differences are roughly unbiased (the series is centered around zero), it also displays a highly seasonal pattern evincing some heteroskedasticity. We explain this behavior below.

Noting that the seasonal S_t can be negative, it follows that $\mathbf{S}_t$ can be negative as well; however, if the original data $\mathbf{X}_t$ is always positive, it follows that

$$\mathbf{S}_t \oplus \mathbf{N}_t = \mathbf{S}_t + \mathbf{N}_t + \text{sign}(\mathbf{S}_t \mathbf{N}_t)\, \sqrt{|\mathbf{S}_t|\,|\mathbf{N}_t|}.$$

Typically $\mathbf{N}_t$ is positive as well, so that

$$\mathbf{S}_t \oplus \mathbf{N}_t - (\mathbf{S}_t + \mathbf{N}_t) = \text{sign}(\mathbf{S}_t)\, \sqrt{|\mathbf{S}_t|}\, \sqrt{\mathbf{N}_t}.$$

Thus, the discrepancy between $\oplus$ and the addition operator is equal to the square root of the product of the seasonal and nonseasonal, multiplied by the sign of the

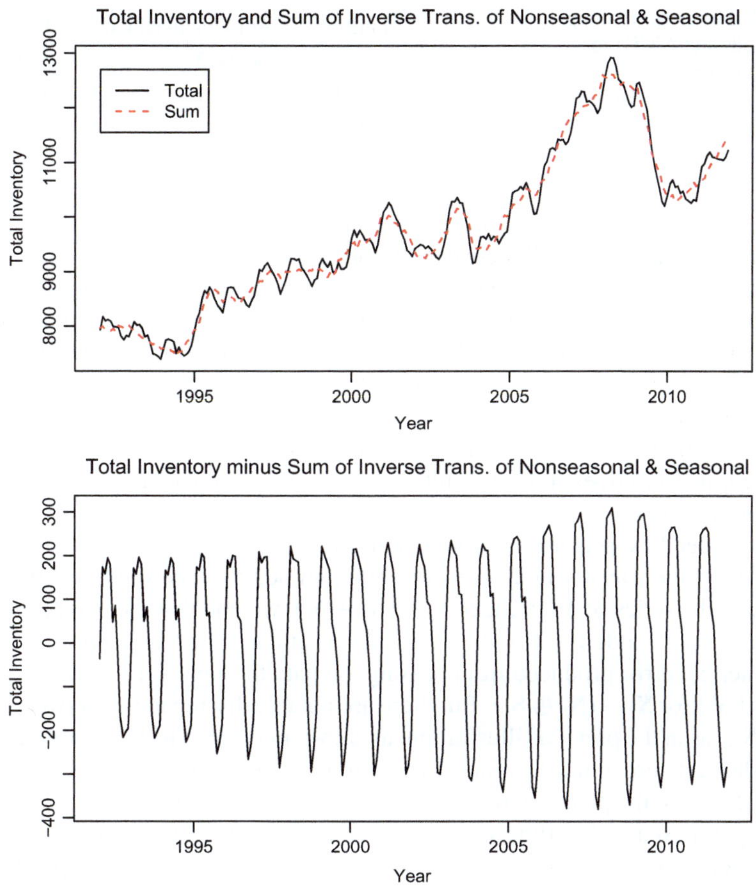

Fig. 5 The *top* plot shows $\mathbf{X}_t$ and $\mathbf{N}_t + \mathbf{S}_t$ together, while the *bottom* plot displays $\mathbf{X}_t - (\mathbf{N}_t + \mathbf{S}_t)$, where $\mathbf{X}_t$ is the series for U.S. total inventory of nonmetallic mineral products between 1992 and 2011. $\mathbf{N}_t$ and $\mathbf{S}_t$ are the signed squares of N_t and S_t, the nonseasonal and seasonal components from an additive decomposition of $X_t = \sqrt{\mathbf{X}_t}$

seasonal; we can expect this time series to be centered around zero, because S_t is centered around zero. This explains the seasonal behavior of the lower panel in Fig. 5.

5.2 *Example 2: Logistic Transform*

The second example is the monthly unemployment rate for 16–19-year-old individuals of Hispanic origin between the years 1991 and 2011; the data was obtained from the Bureau of Labor Statistics. For rate data, the logistic transform $\varphi(\mathbf{a}) =$

Table 2 Comparison of log likelihoods and AICCs for three transforms of unemployment rate data

Transform	(Adj.) log likelihood	AICC
None	506.2443	−1,006.3864
Logarithm	508.9064	−1,011.7107
Logistic	511.0460	−1,015.9900

$\log(\mathbf{a}) - \log(1 - \mathbf{a})$ is sometimes warranted, as it ensures fits and predictions that are guaranteed to fall between 0 and 1. As in the previous example, we use X-12-ARIMA's automdl and transform specs to help us compare the logistic transform to both a logarithmic transform and to no transform at all. Again, the procedure selects the same SARIMA (0 1 1)(0 1 1) model for all three transforms, so whichever transform has the highest log likelihood in the parent space will also have the lowest AICC. Table 2 displays the log likelihoods (adjusted for the transformations) along with the corresponding AICC, and we see that the logistic transform does indeed result in a better model compared to the other two transformations.

We proceed by performing a logistic transform on $\mathbf{X}_t$ and then running X-12-ARIMA on the transformed series to obtain an additive seasonal decomposition. Checking the series of differences $X_t - (N_t + S_t)$, we find that the magnitude of the differences is bounded by 6×10^{-15}. These deviations from 0 are entirely explained by numerical error produced from passing the data through X-12-ARIMA. Similar results hold for $\mathbf{X}_t - (\mathbf{N}_t \oplus \mathbf{S}_t)$. But there are notable discrepancies between $\mathbf{X}_t$ and $(\mathbf{N}_t + \mathbf{S}_t)$, as in the previous illustration, as shown in Fig. 6. The top panel shows that the additive nature of the decomposition in transformed space is not preserved when mapped back to the parent space, while the bottom panel shows that this discrepancy (in the parent space) is a time series centered around −0.5. Also, the lower panel of discrepancies $\mathbf{X}_t - (\mathbf{N}_t + \mathbf{S}_t)$ exhibits seasonal structure; we explain this phenomenon next.

For the logistic transform, the composition operator $\oplus$ is defined as

$$\mathbf{S}_t \oplus \mathbf{N}_t = \frac{\mathbf{S}_t \cdot \mathbf{N}_t}{1 - \mathbf{S}_t - \mathbf{N}_t + 2\mathbf{S}_t \cdot \mathbf{N}_t},$$

where $\mathbf{S}_t$ and $\mathbf{N}_t$ in the parent space are mapped using $1/(1+e^{-S_t})$ and $1/(1+e^{-N_t})$ from the transformed space. To explain the behavior of the lower panel in Fig. 6, we calculate the difference:

$$\begin{aligned}\mathbf{S}_t \oplus \mathbf{N}_t - (\mathbf{S}_t + \mathbf{N}_t) &= \frac{\mathbf{S}_t \cdot \mathbf{N}_t}{1 - (\mathbf{S}_t + \mathbf{N}_t) + 2\mathbf{S}_t \cdot \mathbf{N}_t} - (\mathbf{S}_t + \mathbf{N}_t) \\ &= -\frac{1}{2} + \frac{1}{2}(\mathbf{S}_t + \mathbf{N}_t - 1)\left\{\frac{1}{1 - (\mathbf{S}_t + \mathbf{N}_t) + 2\mathbf{S}_t \cdot \mathbf{N}_t} - 2\right\}.\end{aligned}$$

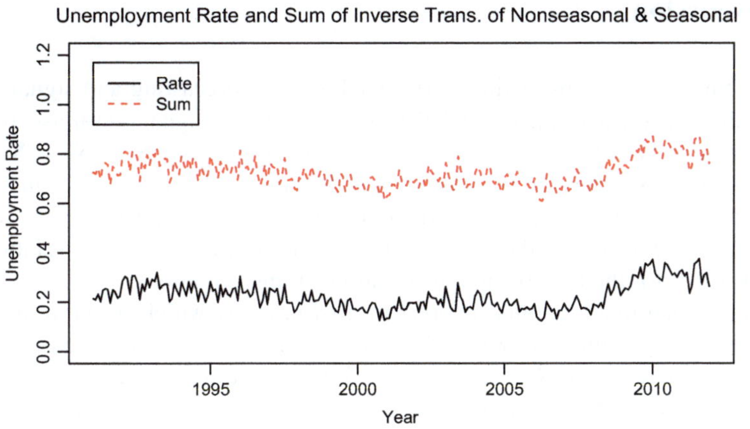

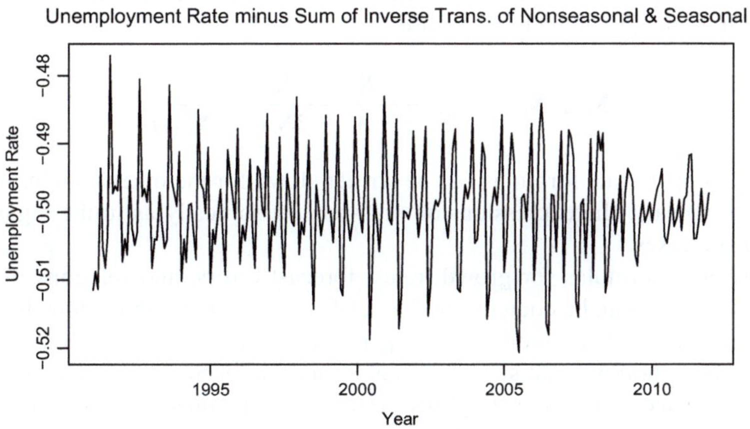

Fig. 6 The *top panel* shows $\mathbf{X}_t$ and $\mathbf{N}_t + \mathbf{S}_t$ together, while the *bottom panel* displays $\mathbf{X}_t - (\mathbf{N}_t + \mathbf{S}_t)$, where $\mathbf{X}_t$ is the unemployment rate among 16–19 year old Hispanic individuals between 1991 and 2011. $\mathbf{N}_t$ and $\mathbf{S}_t$ are the inverse transforms of the N_t and S_t from the additive decomposition of $X_t = \log(\mathbf{X}_t) - \log(1 - \mathbf{X}_t)$

Given that $\mathbf{S}_t$ and $\mathbf{N}_t$ are both restricted between 0 and 1, the second term in the final expression above is a time series that fluctuates about zero (we cannot claim that its expectation is zero). This explains why the discrepancies in parent space were centered around -0.5. The second part of the sum helps account for the variation around the -0.5 center in the discrepancies $\mathbf{S}_t \oplus \mathbf{N}_t - (\mathbf{S}_t + \mathbf{N}_t)$.

6 Discussion

The primary applications of time series analysis are forecasting and signal extraction. In the transformed space, the data process is equal to signal plus noise, but their proper relation is different in the parent space, being given by $\mathbf{S}_t \oplus \mathbf{N}_t = \mathbf{X}_t$. Also, for Gaussian time series the forecast error is defined via $\hat{X}_{t+1} - X_{t+1}$, which in the parent space becomes $\hat{\mathbf{X}}_{t+1} \oplus \mathbf{X}_{t+1}^{-1}$. If the transformation is logarithmic, the forecast error in the parent space is the ratio of estimate and future value. Other relations can be worked out for the logistic and distributional transformations.

There is also much applied interest in growth rates, which in the transformed space is given by definition as $X_t - X_{t-1}$ (these might also be computed in terms of a signal of interest, say $S_t - S_{t-1}$). For a logarithmic transform, the growth rate becomes $\mathbf{X}_t / \mathbf{X}_{t-1}$ in the parent space, which might be interpreted as a percent increase over the previous value. But a growth rate for another transformation looks much different, e.g., in the logistic case

$$\mathbf{X}_t \oplus \mathbf{X}_{t-1}^{-1} = \frac{\mathbf{X}_t(1 - \mathbf{X}_{t-1})}{\mathbf{X}_{t-1} - \mathbf{X}_t + 2\mathbf{X}_t(1 - \mathbf{X}_{t-1})}.$$

Likewise, growth rate formulas can be written down for the other transformations, although typically the expressions do not simplify so neatly as in the logarithmic and logistic cases.

These new formulas for growth rates, forecast errors, and relations of signal and noise to data can be counterintuitive. Only with the logarithmic transformation we do attain a recognizable group operation, namely multiplication. In order for φ to be a homomorphism of groups—which is needed so that quantities in the parent space can be meaningfully combined—one must impose a new group operator on the parent space, and oftentimes this operator $\oplus$ results in unfamiliar operations. However, there seems to be no rigorous escape from the demands of the homomorphism, and familiarity can develop from intimacy.

To illustrate a particular conundrum resolved by our formulation, consider the case alluded to in Sect. 2, where $\mathbf{Z}$ represents a forecast or signal of interest in the parent domain, and $\varphi^{-1}(\hat{Z})$ is its estimate. Note that $\varphi^{-1}(Z) = \mathbf{Z}^{-1}$, and the corresponding error process is then $\varphi^{-1}(\hat{Z}) \oplus \mathbf{Z}^{-1}$. The probability (2) becomes

$$\mathbb{P}\left[\varphi^{-1}(a) \leq \varphi^{-1}(\hat{Z}) \oplus \mathbf{Z}^{-1} \leq \varphi^{-1}(b)\right].$$

Hence the confidence interval for the statistical error (in the parent domain) is expressed as $[\varphi^{-1}(a), \varphi^{-1}(b)]$, which exactly equals the probability that in the transformed domain $\hat{Z} - Z$ lies in $[a, b]$. This type of interpretation is not possible unless φ is a homomorphism, which the particular definition of $\oplus$ guarantees.

We can also manipulate $\mathbb{P}[a \leq \hat{Z} - Z \leq b]$ to obtain an interval for $\mathbf{Z}$:

$$\mathbb{P}\left[a \leq \hat{Z} - Z \leq b\right] = \mathbb{P}\left[\hat{Z} - b \leq Z \leq \hat{Z} - a\right]$$
$$= \mathbb{P}\left[\varphi^{-1}(\hat{Z} - b) \leq \mathbf{Z} \leq \varphi^{-1}(\hat{Z} - a)\right].$$

Although the last expression allows us to easily compute the interval for $\mathbf{Z}$, it is not directly expressed in terms of the parent estimate $\varphi^{-1}(\hat{Z})$. Using the homomorphism property, the interval can be written as

$$\left[\varphi^{-1}(\hat{Z}) \oplus \mathbf{b}^{-1}, \varphi^{-1}(\hat{Z}) \oplus \mathbf{a}^{-1}\right].$$

In summary, the chief applications of time series analysis dictate that quantities in the parent space of a transformation must satisfy certain algebraic relations, and the proper way to ensure this structure is to define a group operator $\oplus$ via (3). As a consequence, the notions of statistical error (for forecasts, imputations, signal extraction estimates, etc.) are altered accordingly, as are the definitions of growth rates and the relations of signal and noise to data. Such relations are already intuitive and well accepted when the transformation is logarithmic, but for other transforms there remains quite a bit of novelty.

Disclaimer

This article is released to inform interested parties of research and to encourage discussion. The views expressed on statistical issues are those of the authors and not necessarily those of the U.S. Census Bureau.

References

Artin, M. (1991). *Algebra*. Upper Saddle River, NJ: Prentice Hall.

Bell, W. (1984). Signal extraction for nonstationary time series. *The Annals of Statistics, 12*, 646–664.

Bell, W., & Hillmer, S. (1984). Issues involved with the seasonal adjustment of economic time series. *Journal of Business and Economic Statistics, 2*, 291–320.

Box, G., & Jenkins, G. (1976). *Time series analysis, forecasting and control*. San Francisco: Holden-Day.

Brockwell, P., & Davis, R. (1991). *Time series: Theory and methods* (2nd ed.). New York: Springer

Findley, D., Monsell, B., Bell, W., Otto, M., & Chen, B. (1998). New capabilities and methods of the X-12-ARIMA seasonal adjustment program. *Journal of Business and Economic Statistics, 16*, 127–177.

McElroy, T. (2005). *A to Z of mathematicians*. New York: Facts on File.

McElroy, T. (2008). Matrix formulas for nonstationary ARIMA signal extraction. *Econometric Theory, 24*, 1–22.

McElroy, T. (2012). An alternative model-based seasonal adjustment that reduces over-adjustment. *Taiwan Economic Forecast & Policy, 43*, 35–73.

Reliability of the Automatic Identification of ARIMA Models in Program TRAMO

Agustín Maravall, Roberto López-Pavón, and Domingo Pérez-Cañete

Abstract In so far that—as Hawking and Mlodinow state—"there can be no model-independent test of reality," time series analysis applied to large sets of series needs an automatic model identification procedure, and seasonal adjustment should not be an exception. In fact, the so-called ARIMA model-based seasonal adjustment method (as enforced in programs TRAMO and SEATS) is at present widely used throughout the world by data producers and analysts. The paper analyzes the results of the automatic identification of ARIMA models of program TRAMO. Specifically, the question addressed is the following. Given that many ARIMA models are possible, how likely is it that (default) use of TRAMO yields a satisfactory result? Important requirements are proper detection of seasonality, of non-stationarity (i.e., of the proper combination of unit autoregressive roots), and of the stationary ARMA structure, and eventual identification of either the correct model, or a relatively close one that provides zero-mean normally identically independently distributed residuals and good out-of-sample forecasts. A comparison with the default AMI procedure in the present X12-ARIMA and DEMETRA+ programs (based on older versions of TRAMO) is made.

The simulation exercise shows a satisfactory performance of the default automatic TRAMO procedure applied to very large sets of series; certainly, it can also provide good benchmark or starting point when a careful manual identification is intended.

1 Introduction

Seasonality, i.e., the seasonal component of a time series, is never directly observed, nor does it have a generally accepted and precise definition, and these limitations obscure proper treatment and analysis. In the early 1980s, a seasonal adjustment

A. Maravall
Research Department, Bank of Spain, Alcalá 48, 28014 Madrid, Spain
e-mail: maravall@bde.es

R. López-Pavón (✉) • D. Pérez-Cañete (✉)
Indra. External collaboration with the Bank of Spain

J. Beran et al. (eds.), *Empirical Economic and Financial Research*,
Advanced Studies in Theoretical and Applied Econometrics 48,
DOI 10.1007/978-3-319-03122-4_7

based on minimum mean squared error (MMSE) estimation of unobserved components in linear stochastic time series models—namely, ARIMA models—was proposed by Hillmer and Tiao (1982) and Burman (1980). The approach came to be known as the ARIMA-model-based (AMB) seasonal adjustment. The proposal seemed interesting because it would provide the analyst with a precise definition of seasonality (as well as of the other unobserved components) by means of a model consistent with the model identified for the observed series. The approach would further permit model-derived diagnostics and parametric inference. Some extensions of the approach are found in, for example, Pierce (1979), Bell and Hillmer (1984), Maravall (1987), Gómez and Maravall (2001b), Bell and Martin (2004), and McElroy (2008). However, application of the approach when many series are to be treated was discarded because it seemed to imply exceedingly heavy computational and time series analyst resources. Besides, many series need some preadjustment before they can be assumed the output of an ARIMA process: perhaps the series requires some transformation (such as the log), non-periodic calendar effects—such as TD—may need removal, and the series may be contaminated by outliers and/or by other special effects. Because not all users need to be time series modeling experts, and because—even if they are—the number of series that need treatment may be too big, an automatic model identification (AMI) procedure is needed. The procedure should address both preadjustment of the series and identification of the ARIMA model.

In the 1990s, Gómez and Maravall presented a first version of two linked programs that enforced the AMB approach and contained an AMI option. The first program, TRAMO ("Time series Regression with ARIMA Noise, Missing Observations and Outliers") performed preadjustment and ARIMA model identification. The second program, SEATS ("Signal Extraction in ARIMA Time Series") decomposed the series into unobserved components and, in particular, performed seasonal adjustment (Gómez and Maravall, 1996).

The two programs are widely used throughout the world, most notably at statistical offices, central banks, and agencies involved with analysis and production of economic data; see, for example, European Statistical System (2009) and United Nations (2011). Together with X12, they are part of the new X13-ARIMA-SEATS program (U.S. Census Bureau 2012), and of the Eurostat-supported program DEMETRA+ (Grudkowska 2012).

Over the years, the empirical performance of TRAMO and SEATS has been discussed, and a large-scale analysis of their (early) AMI performance is contained in Fischer and Planas (2000). (This work had led to a recommendation for its use in official production; Eurostat 1998.) New versions of the programs have just been released, and the new version of TRAMO (to be referred to as TRAMO+) incorporates modifications and improvements in the AMI procedure. In what follows, the performance of this procedure is analyzed in terms of the following questions: if a series has been generated by an ARIMA model, will AMI properly detect presence/absence of seasonality, stationarity or the lack thereof (i.e., unit roots), the ARMA structure (i.e., model orders)? Will the identified model provide normally, identically, independently distributed (n.i.i.d.) residuals? Will the out-of-sample forecast performance be acceptable?

Program TSW+ (the Windows version of TRAMO-SEATS+) has been used, in all cases in an entirely automatic mode.

2 Summary of the Automatic Identification Procedure

2.1 *The Regression-ARIMA Model*

Let the observed time series be $z = (z_{t_1}, z_{t_2}, \ldots, z_{t_m})$ where $1 = t_1 < t_2 < \cdots < t_m = T$. (There may be missing observations and the original observations may have been log transformed.) The Reg-ARIMA model is

$$z_t = y_t'\beta + x_t \tag{1}$$

where y_t is a matrix with n regression variables, and β is the vector with the regression coefficients. The variable x_t follows a (possibly nonstationary) ARIMA model. Hence, in (1), $y_t'\beta$ represents the deterministic component, and x_t the stochastic one.

If B denotes the backward shift operator, such that $B^j z_t = z_{t-j}$, the ARIMA model for x_t is of the type

$$\nu_t = \delta(B)x_t, \tag{2}$$

$$\phi(B)[\nu_t - \mu_\nu] = \theta(B)a_t, \qquad a_t \sim niid(0, V_a), \tag{3}$$

where ν_t is the stationary transformation of x_t, μ_ν its mean, $\delta(B)$ contains regular and seasonal differences; $\phi(B)$ is a stationary autoregressive (AR) polynomial in B; $\theta(B)$ is an invertible moving average (MA) polynomial in B. For seasonal series, the polynomials typically have a "multiplicative" structure. Letting s denote the number of observations per year, in TRAMO+, the polynomials in B factorize as

$$\delta(B) = (1 - B)^d (1 - B^s)^{d_s} = \nabla^d \nabla_s^{d_s}$$

where ∇ and ∇_s are the regular and seasonal differences, and

$$\phi(B) = \phi_p(B)\Phi_{p_s}(B^s) = (1 + \phi_1 B + \ldots + \phi_p B^p)(1 + \phi_s B^s) \tag{4}$$

$$\theta(B) = \theta_q(B)\Theta_{q_s}(B^s) = (1 + \theta_1 B + \ldots + \theta_q B^q)(1 + \theta_s B^s) \tag{5}$$

Stationarity and invertibility imply that all the roots of the polynomials in B in the right-hand-side of (4) and (5) lie outside the unit circle. In what follows, the variable x_t will be assumed centered around its mean and the general expression for the model will be the ARIMA $(p, d, q)(p_s, d_s, q_s)_s$ model:

$$\phi_p(B)\Phi_{p_s}(B^s)\nabla^d \nabla_s^{d_s} x_t = \theta_q(B)\Theta_{q_s}(B^s)a_t, \tag{6}$$

where p, q $= 0, 1, 2, 3$; d $= 0, 1, 2$; $d_s, p_s, q_s = 0, 1$.

In what follows, the only regression variables will be the outliers that may have been automatically identified by the program run in a default mode. Three types of possible outliers are considered: additive outlier (AO), i.e., a single spike; transitory change (TC), i.e., a spike that takes some time to return to the previous level; and level shift (LS), i.e., a step function. TRAMO+ will pre-test for the log/level transformation and perform automatic ARIMA model identification joint with automatic outlier detection, estimate by exact maximum likelihood the model, interpolate missing values, and forecast the series.

2.2 AMI in the Presence of Outliers

The algorithm iterates between the following two stages.

1. Automatic outlier detection and correction: The procedure is based on Tsay (1986) and Chen and Liu (1993) with some modifications (see Gómez and Maravall 2001a,b). At each stage, given the ARIMA model, outliers are detected one by one, and eventually jointly estimated.
2. AMI: TRAMO+ proceeds in two steps: First, it identifies the differencing polynomial $\delta(B)$ that contains the unit roots. Second, it identifies the ARMA model, i.e, $\phi_p(B)$, $\Phi_{p_s}(B^s)$, $\theta_q(B)$, and $\Theta_{q_s}(B^s)$. A pre-test for possible presence of seasonality determines the default model, used at the beginning of AMI and at some intermediate stages (as a benchmark comparison). For seasonal series the default model is the so-called Airline model, given by the equation

$$\nabla\nabla_s x_t = (1 + \theta_1 B)(1 + \theta_s B^s)a_t \tag{7}$$

i.e., the *IMA*$(0, 1, 1)(0, 1, 1)_s$ model. For nonseasonal series the default model is

$$\nabla x_t = (1 + \theta B) + \mu, \tag{8}$$

i.e., the IMA (1,1) plus mean model.

Identification of the ARIMA model is performed with the series corrected for the outliers detected at that stage. If the model changes, the automatic detection and correction of outliers is performed again from the beginning.

2.2.1 Identification of the Nonstationary Polynomial $\delta(B)$

To determine the appropriate differencing of the series, we discard standard unit root tests. First, when MA roots are not negligible, the standard tests have low power. Second, a run of AMI for a single series may try thousands of models, where the next try depends on previous results. There is, thus, a serious data mining problem: the size of the test is a function of prior rejections and acceptances, and its correct value is not known.

We follow an alternative approach that relies on the superconsistency results of Tiao and Tsay (1983), and Tsay (1984). Sequences of multiplicative AR(1) and ARMA(1,1) are estimated, and instead of a fictitious size, the following value is fixed "a priori": How large the modulus of an AR root should be in order to accept it as 1? By default, in the sequence of AR(1) and ARMA(1,1) estimations, when the modulus of the AR parameter is above 0.91 and 0.97, respectively, it is made 1. Unit AR roots are identified one by one; for MA roots invertibility is strictly imposed.

2.2.2 Identification of the Stationary ARMA Polynomials

Identification of the stationary part of the model attempts to minimize the Bayesian information criterion given by

$$BIC_{P,Q} = ln(\hat{\sigma}^2_{P,Q}) + (P + Q)\frac{ln(N - D)}{N - D}.$$

where $P = p + p_s$, $Q = q + q_s$, and $D = d + d_s$. The search is done sequentially: for fixed regular polynomials, the seasonal ones are obtained, and vice versa. A more complete description of the AMI procedure and of the estimation algorithms can be found in Gómez and Maravall (1993, 1994, 2001a); Gómez et al. (1999); and Maravall and Pérez (2012).

3 Performance of AMI on Simulated Series

3.1 Simulation of the Series

Monthly series of n.i.i.d.(0,1) innovations $[a_t]$ were simulated in MATLAB, and $(d + d_s)$ arbitrary starting conditions were set (see Bell, 1984). For 50 ARIMA models, 500 series with 120 observations ("short" series) and 500 "long" series with 240 observations were generated. Thus two sets of 25,000 series each were obtained. Each set was divided into three subsets as follows:

- The first subset is formed by 8,500 series simulated with *Airline-type models*, as in (7). The combinations of MA parameters (θ_1, θ_s) were (–0.9,–0.7), (–0.8,–0.4), (–0.7,–0.3), (–0.6,–0.4), (–0.6,0), (–0.5,–0.95), (–0.5,–0.5), (–0.4,–0.6), (–0.4,0), (–0.3,–0.7), (0,–0.7), (0,–0.5), (0.3,–0.6), (0.3,0), (0.4,–0.8), and (0.5,–0.6).
- The second set contains 8,000 series simulated from the following *non-seasonal models*.
  Stationary models: $x_t = a_t$; $(1-0.7B)x_t = a_t$; $x_t = (1+0.6B^2)a_t$; $(1-0.8B)x_t = (1-0.5B)a_t$; $(1-B+0.6B^2)x_t = a_t$; $(1-0.41B-0.37B^2)x_t = (1-0.30B)a_t$; $(1+0.3B^2-0.5B^3)x_t = a_t$. *Non-stationary models*: $\nabla x_t = (1-0.7B)a_t$; $\nabla x_t = (1-0.3B)a_t$; $\nabla x_t = a_t$; $(1-0.7B)\nabla x_t = a_t$; $(1-0.6B)\nabla x_t = (1+0.5B+0.7B^2)a_t$; $(1-0.40B+0.42B^2)\nabla x_t = a_t$; $(1+0.7B^{12})\nabla x_t = a_t$; $\nabla^2 x_t = (1-0.8B)a_t$; $\nabla^2 x_t = (1-0.31B+0.36B^2)a_t$.
- The third set is formed by 8,500 seasonal series not of the Airline-type; it will be referred to as the *"Other-seasonal models"* set.

  Stationary models: $(1-0.6B)(1-0.6B^{12})x_t = a_t$; $(1-0.8B^{12})x_t = (1-0.4B^{12})a_t$; $(1-0.7B)(1-0.85B^{12})x_t = (1-0.3B)a_t$; $(1-0.7B^{12})\nabla x_t = (1-0.4B+0.7B^2)a_t$.
  Non-stationary models: $\nabla_{12}x_t = (1-0.5B^{12})a_t$; $(1-1.4B+0.7B^2)\nabla_{12}x_t = (1-0.5B^{12})a_t$; $(1+0.4B^{12})\nabla_{12}x_t = (1-0.5B^{12})a_t$; $\nabla\nabla_{12}x_t = (1-0.23B-0.19B^2)(1-0.56B^{12})a_t$; $(1-0.5B^{12})\nabla\nabla_{12}x_t = (1-0.4B)a_t$; $(1-0.4B)\nabla\nabla_{12}x_t = (1+0.4B+0.4B^2)(1-0.4B^{12})a_t$;$(1-0.3B)\nabla\nabla_{12}x_t = (1-0.6B^{12})a_t$; $(1+0.3B)\nabla\nabla_{12}x_t = (1-0.6B)(1-0.3B^{12})a_t$; $(1+0.4B^{12})\nabla\nabla_{12}x_t = (1-0.5B)(1-0.5B^{12})a_t$; $(1-0.6B+0.5B^2)\nabla\nabla_{12}x_t = (1-0.8B^{12})a_t$; $(1+0.5B-0.3B^3)\nabla\nabla_{12}x_t = (1-0.4B^{12})a_t$; $(1+0.1B-0.17B^2-0.34B^3)\nabla\nabla_{12}x_t = (1-0.48B^{12})a_t$; $(1+0.4B^{12})\nabla^2\nabla_{12}x_t = (1-0.4B)a_t$.

Therefore, 16 % of the models are stationary (40 % of them seasonal), and 84 % are non-stationary (75 % of them seasonal). The models' orders cover the following ranges:
$p = 0, 1, 2, 3$; $d = 0, 1, 2$; $q = 0, 1, 2$; $p_s = 0, 1$; $d_s = 0, 1$; $q_s = 0, 1$;
so that the maximum order of differencing is $\nabla^2\ \nabla_{12}$ and 384 models are possible. Factorizing the AR polynomials, real and complex roots are present, with varying moduli and frequencies. In particular, identification of unit roots implies identification of one of the pairs $(d, d_{12}) = (0,0), (1,0), (2,0), (0,1), (1,1)$, and (2,1).

The complete set contains many models often found in practice. Non-seasonal series are possibly over represented, yet it was thought important to detect reliably which series have seasonality and which ones do not. Some models with awkward structures are also included. As a simple example, the model with seasonal orders $(1,0,0)_{12}$ and seasonal AR polynomial $(1+\phi_{12}B^{12})$ with $\phi_{12} > 0$ displays spectral holes at seasonal frequencies. Not being associated with seasonality, nor with trend-cycle, the spectral peaks will generate a transitory component. Such an

AR structure may appear, for example, when modeling SA series: the spectral holes induced by seasonal adjustment are associated with negative autocorrelation for seasonal lags in the seasonally adjusted series and are implied by "optimal" MMSE estimation (see, for example, Gómez and Maravall, 2001b).

3.2 *AMI Results*

TSW+ was applied to the simulated series in automatic mode with no trading-day pre-testing.

3.2.1 Preadjustment

Log-Level Test

The 50,000 simulated series were exponentiated, then the log/level (likelihood ratio) test was applied to the total 100,000 series. Table 1 presents the results.

The test is accurate (averaging all groups, the error percentage is 0.4 %), and shows a slight bias that favors levels. It can be seen that most errors occur for models with $d = 2$ (often, appropriate for models with smooth trend-cycle component).

Seasonality Detection

Next, the series were pre-tested for possible presence of seasonality. The pre-test is based on four separate checks. One is a χ^2_{11} non-parametric rank test similar to the one in Kendall and Ord (1990), one checks the autocorrelations for seasonal lags (12 and 24) in the line of Pierce (1978), and uses a χ^2_2; one is an F-test for the significance of seasonal dummy variables similar to the one in Lytras et al. (2007), and one is a test for the presence of peaks at seasonal frequencies in the spectrum of the differenced series. The first three tests are applied at the 99 % critical value. The fourth test combines the results of two spectrum estimates: one, obtained with an AR(30) fit in the spirit of X12-ARIMA (Findley et al., 1998); the second is a non-parametric Tuckey-type estimator, as in Jenkins and Watts (1968), approximated by an F distribution.

Table 1 Errors in log/level test (in % of series)

	Series is in levels		Series is in logs	
Series length	120	240	120	240
Airline model	0.1	0.0	0.2	0.0
Other-seasonal	0.4	0.1	1.1	0.1
Non-seasonal	0.0	0.0	1.6	1.0
Total average	**0.2**	**0.0**	**1.0**	**0.4**

The results of the four tests have to be combined into a single answer to the question: Is there seasonality in the series? The tests are first applied to the original series, and determine the starting model in AMI. Once the series has been corrected for outliers, the tests are applied again to the "linearized" series; these are the results reported in Table 2. The first four columns show the percentage of series (in each of the six groups) for which the tests have made an error (not detecting seasonality when there is some, or detecting seasonality when there is none). Leaving aside the Airline model case, for which all tests are close to perfect, in all other cases the spectral test performs worse. The "overall test" in column 5 combines the results of the previous four tests, assigning weights broadly in accordance with their relative performance: more weight is given to the autocorrelation and F tests, and little weight is given to the spectral one. The overall test assumes seasonality even when the evidence is weak; its role is to orient AMI, but the final decision as to whether seasonality is present in the series is made by the AMI itself, i.e., by the final model obtained by TRAMO+, and the way it is decomposed by SEATS+. The errors in this final decision are displayed in the last column of Table 2. It is seen that the test implied by AMI outperforms all other tests, including the overall one. On average, for the short series, this final test fails one out of 200 cases; when the series is long, the proportion becomes 1 out of 500, well below the 1 % critical value used in the individual tests.

It can be seen that most errors in Table 2 are failures of the test to detect highly stationary seasonality, and that a slight over detection of seasonality in non-seasonal series is also present.

Outlier Detection

No outliers were added to the simulated series and hence detected outliers can be seen as spurious; the average number detected per series is shown in Table 3.

Table 2 Errors in the detection-of-seasonality-in-series tests (in % of series in group)

	Series length	Non-parametric test	Auto-correlation test	Spectral test	F-test	Overall test	Model produced by AMI
Airline	120	0.0	0.0	0.0	0.1	0.0	0.0
Model	240	0.0	0.0	0.0	0.1	0.0	0.0
Other-seasonal	120	2.9	0.2	6.2	2.0	0.1	0.3
Models	240	1.9	0.0	4.9	1.4	0.0	0.1
Non-seasonal	120	1.5	1.6	2.5	0.8	2.1	1.3
Models	240	1.9	1.8	3.1	0.7	2.4	0.7
Total	**120**	**1.5**	**0.6**	**2.9**	**1.0**	**0.7**	**0.5**
	240	**1.2**	**0.6**	**2.6**	**0.7**	**0.8**	**0.2**

Table 3 Average number of outliers per series

Series length	120	240
Airline model	0.18	0.11
Other-seasonal	0.16	0.10
Non-seasonal	0.17	0.09
Total	**0.17**	**0.10**

However, because our interest is automatic use of TRAMO+ with input parameters set at default values and this use includes automatic outlier detection and correction, outliers may show up in the identified model. These spurious outliers may cause some distortion in AMI, yet this distortion is likely to be minor. (In 9,000,000 generated observations some are bound to exceed the critical value for outlier detection. For example, approximating the probability of detecting an AO (the most frequently detected type of outlier) in random samples of 120 and 240 observations, or an LS in random walks of equal lengths, the results of Table 3 are below the proportion of outliers that could be expected from the critical values used in the outlier detection tests (close to 3.5) and the fact that three types of outliers are tested for each observation. The numbers in Table 3 can be seen as type I errors of the test; they are seen to decrease significantly for the long series, in accordance with the increase in accuracy of AMI.

Identification of the Differencing Polynomial (Unit Root Detection)

An important part of AMI is identification of the non-stationary roots (i.e., the orders d and d_s of the regular and seasonal differencing). Given that $d = 0, 1, 2$, and d_s=0,1, six combinations (d,d_s) are possible. Table 4 displays the % of errors made when detecting unit roots in the six groups of series, short and long, separating the errors made in the detection of d from the errors in the detection of d_s, and distinguishing between errors due to over—or to under—detection. First, it is seen that the results improve considerably for the long series: doubling the number of observations cuts—on average—in more than half the proportion of errors. In terms of identification of the complete differencing polynomial, the % of errors decrease from 5.6 % (series with 120 observations) to 2.6 % (series with 240 observations). For all groups, when present, seasonal unit AR roots are captured with less than 1 % of errors; spurious seasonal unit roots occur with the same frequency (<1 %), except for the case of "non-seasonal model" short series (2.3 %).

As for regular unit AR roots, over-estimation of d in "Other seasonal models" and under estimation of d in the "Airline model" group for short series present the highest proportion of errors (about 4 and 3.5 %, respectively). In all other cases the percentage of errors is below 2.5 % (short series) and 1.5 % (long series).

Table 5 is as Table 4, but the errors are classified according to the orders of the differencing polynomial of the model generating the series. The largest proportion of errors is due to regular over-differencing of stationary series (i.e., the group with

Table 4 Errors in unit root detection (in % of series grouped by type of model)

Group	# observ.	# of series in group	Regular unit roots (d): Under estimation	Regular unit roots (d): Over estimation	Seasonal unit roots (d_s): Under estimation	Seasonal unit roots (d_s): Over estimation	Complete differencing polynomial (d and/or d_s)
Airline model	120	8,500	3.5	0.2	0.4	0	4.0
Other-seasonal models	120	8,500	1.6	4.2	0	0.6	6.3
Non-seasonal model	120	8,000	2.4	2.1	0.8	2.3	6.8
Total	**120**	**25,000**	**2.5**	**2.1**	**0.4**	**1.0**	**5.6**
Airline model	240	8,500	0.6	0.1	0	0	0.7
Other seasonal models	240	8,500	0.2	3.8	0	0.6	4.6
Non-seasonal model	240	8,000	0.6	1.4	0	0.8	2.6
Total	**240**	**25,000**	**0.4**	**1.7**	**0**	**0.4**	**2.6**

Table 5 Errors in differencing polynomials (in % in grouped by orders of differencing)

Simulated model: Regular differences d	Simulated model: Seasonal differences d_s	# of obs. in series	# of series in group	Errors in d: Under diff.	Errors in d: Over diff.	Errors in d_s: Under diff.	Errors in d_s: Over diff.	Total errors in diff. polynomial
0	0	120	4,500	–	7.4	–	4.4	10.4
		240	4,500	–	6.6	–	1.7	7.8
1	0	120	4,000	0.0	1.5	–	1.0	2.5
		240	4,000	0.0	0.8	–	0.5	1.2
2	0	120	1,000	12.8	–	–	0.6	13.1
		240	1,000	1.8	–	–	1.2	3.0
0	1	120	1,500	–	4.2	0.7	–	4.9
		240	1,500	–	3.2	0.0	–	3.2
1	1	120	13,500	3.7	0.5	0.6	–	4.6
		240	13,500	0.8	0.4	0.0	–	1.2
2	1	120	500	3.2	–	1.2	–	4.4
		240	500	0.4	–	0.0	–	0.4
Total		**120**	**25,000**	**2.5**	**2.1**	**0.4**	**1.0**	**5.6**
		240	**25,000**	**0.5**	**1.7**	**0.0**	**0.4**	**2.6**

d=d_s=0), and of short series with (d = 0,d_s=1), to regular under-differencing of short series with (d = 2,d_s = 0), and to seasonal over-differencing of short stationary series. In all other cases the percentage of errors is in the range (0–3.7 %).

Altogether, the proportion of successes in identifying correctly the complete differencing polynomial is 94.4 % for the series with 120 observations, and 97.4 % for those with 240 observations. Most of the errors concern regular differencing in short series, in particular stationary ones, and are concentrated in the series generated with models that have a large and positive AR real root (for example, 0.8, or 0.85). By default, when the estimated root in the model finally obtained is above 0.92 (seasonal roots) or 0.95 (regular roots), the program sets it equal to 1 and re-estimates the model. Thus, when a stationary and non-stationary specification seem both possible, AMI tends to favor non-stationarity. This (slight) bias towards non-stationarity is justified by the fact that ARIMA models are basically short-term tools, that IMA(1,1) structures are more stable than ARMA(1,1) ones, and that non-stationary models tend to yield more regular seasonal component and smoother trend-cycle.

ARMA Model Parameters

Concerning the stationary ARMA model given by (3), Table 6 presents the average number of parameters per model. This number is remarkably close to the average number of parameters in the models used to generate the series.

Identification of the ARIMA Model Orders

Next, exact identification of the ARIMA model orders (p,d,q) $(p_s,d_s,q_s)_{12}$ is considered. The first and fourth columns of Table 7 show (in bold values) the percentage of series in each group for which identification has produced the correct values for the six-order parameters. It should be kept in mind that by default, the AMI of TRAMO+ considers 384 possible combinations of model orders. Some of

Table 6 Average number of stationary parameters per series

	120	240	In simulation model
Airline model	1.9	1.8	1.7
Other-seasonal	2.4	2.6	2.6
Non-seasonal	1.5	1.5	1.5
Total	**1.93**	**1.97**	**1.94**

Table 7 Correct identification of the ARIMA model

	# obs.	Complete model orders			Differencing polynomial (d and d_s)		
	in series	TSW+	X13A-S	Demetra+	TSW+	X13A-S	Demetra+
Airline-type	120	**78.0**	68.6	71.6	**96.0**	94.8	96.4
Models	240	**85.6**	79.9	79.9	**99.3**	98.9	99.3
Other-seasonal	120	**47.4**	37.3	43.3	**93.2**	86.5	85.9
Models	240	**71.7**	50.8	66.3	**97.4**	86.8	88.5
Non-seasonal	120	**69.1**	37.8	54.0	**93.7**	70.4	76.6
models	240	**79.4**	36.3	64.5	**95.4**	68.1	80.4
Total	**120**	**64.8**	**48.1**	**56.4**	**94.5**	**84.2**	**86.8**
	240	**78.9**	**56.1**	**70.3**	**97.4**	**84.9**	**89.6**

these models are close and hence difficult to distinguish when the series is relatively short. Simple examples are the ARMA(1,1) and IMA(1,1) when the AR parameter is close to -1; the ARMA(1,1,1) and ARMA(2,1,0) when the roots of the AR(2) are real and not large; or the ARI(1,1) and IMA(1,1) models when the AR parameter is small in modulus.

The average group performance varies between a minimum of 1 out of 2 and a maximum of 6 out of 7 correct identifications of the complete model (short series with non-seasonal models and long series with Airline-type models, respectively). Averaging all groups, automatic default run of TRAMO+ yields the following results: the model is correctly identified 2/3 of the time for the series with 120 observations and 4/5 of the time for series with 240 observations.

Identification of unit roots is considerably accurate (the range of success varies between 93.2 and 99.3 %). Therefore, most of the failures in the identification of the full model affect the smaller roots of the ARMA polynomials and, as Table 6 suggests, the effect of the misspecification is likely to be moderate.

A Remark on the Default Model

It is a well-known fact that, in practice, the default model (namely, the Airline model of Eq. (7)) provides a good fit to many economic time series. Table 8 presents the errors in model identification having to do with cases in which an Airline model is identified for a series generated with a different model, and in which the generating model was an Airline model, yet the identified model is not. Table 8 evidences that, contrary to an often expressed belief, there is no over-detection of Airline models; rather the opposite is true.

A Comparison of Results

Up to the year 2011, programs TRAMO and SEATS (and TSW) maintained the basic structure of the Gómez and Maravall (1996) programs, and revisions were kept moderate. In the year 2001 work was started on new versions that corrected, completed, and extended the standard ones. This paper presents the AMI results of the new versions, TRAMO+, SEATS+, and TSW+.

The TRAMO and SEATS programs made available for the routine RegARIMA in X12-ARIMA and X13-ARIMA-SEATS, and for DEMETRA+, were older versions

Table 8 Errors in airline model detection (in % of series in group)

	120	240
Airline model	21.9	14.4
Other-seasonal	15.0	6.1
Non-seasonal	0.3	0.2
Total	**12.6**	**7.0**

of the new programs that will eventually be updated (at least, partially). Over the last 2 years, considerable amount of work has been done on the AMI procedure. (Most notably, the old versions had a tendency to over-difference the series, over-detect outliers, and over-adjust for seasonality.)

To get a feeling for the differences in AMI between the older and present versions, X13-ARIMA-SEATS (release version 1.0, build 150) and DEMETRA+ (version 1.0.4.323) were applied to the set of 50,000 series and compared to the results of TSW+ (version 750). Table 7 presents the comparison. It should be mentioned that the difference between the three AMIs is not simply due to revisions in the TRAMO+ versions. In both, DEMETRA+ and X12-ARIMA, when adopting TRAMO's AMI, some modifications were made. Still, Table 7 provides a fair idea of the effects of the TRAMO+ revisions on the AMI procedure, and of the relevance of updating older versions.

TSW+ yields the best results. For the Airline-type group, the percentage of correctly identified models increases by an amount between 6 and 10 percent points (p.p.). For the groups Other-Seasonal and Non-seasonal the improvement is considerably larger, most notably when the comparison is made with X12-ARIMA. (This reflects the fact that the TRAMO+ version in the present DEMETRA+ program is more recent.) Notice that the improvement is largest for the group of Non-seasonal models where the % of successful identification is between 15 and 40 p.p. higher for the case of TSW+. Further, contrary to the case of the Airline-model group, for the Other-seasonal and Non-seasonal groups, improvement in unit root detection accounts for an important fraction of the total improvement. In any event, identification of unit roots is always more successful than identification of the stationary orders.

3.2.2 Model Diagnostics

Residual Diagnostics and Out-of-Sample Performance

TSW+ offers two types of diagnostics. One is aimed at testing the n.i.i.d. assumption on the residuals; the other performs out-of-sample forecast tests. The Normality assumption is checked with the Behra-Jarque Normality test, plus the skewness and kurtosis t-tests; the autocorrelation test is the standard Ljung–Box test (with 24 autocorrelations); independence is further checked with a non-parametric t-test on randomness of the residual sign runs; and the identical distribution assumption is checked with the constant mean and variance test, that tests, first, for equality of means between the first and second half of the series residuals; if accepted, equality of variances is then tested. The out-of-sample checks are, first, a test whereby one-period-ahead forecast errors are sequentially computed for the model estimated for the series with the last 18 observations removed (with the model fixed), and an F-test compares the variance of these errors with the variance of the in-sample residuals. The second test computes the standardized out-of-sample one-period-ahead forecast error for each of the series in the group, and computes the proportion that lie beyond the 1 % critical value of a t distribution. (The option TERROR, i.e., "TRAMO for errors," applied to the full group, directly provides the answer.)

The diagnostic checks for n.i.i.d. residuals are presented in Table 9. Each entry shows the % of series in the group that fail the test at the 1 % size. All residual tests perform satisfactorily. The empirical size falls, in all cases, within the range (0.2–1.3 %), with the N test at the top of the range, and randomness in signs and lack of autocorrelation lying at the bottom. For 32 of the 36 groups, the empirical sizes are smaller than the theoretical 1 % one. Sample variation may cause that a slightly misspecified ARMA model produces slightly better diagnostics, and hence is selected by AMI. Because of this fact, a bias towards smaller empirical sizes in the in-sample tests for the simulated series could be expected. Given that the effect of sample variation should decrease with the length of the series, it seems reasonable that the long series—as seen in Table 9—are closer to the 1 % (approximate) theoretical size.

However, the better performance of the misspecified model is unlikely to extend out of sample, so that the bias towards a smaller size induced by the sampling variation should be smaller in out-of-sample tests. In fact, as Table 10 shows the proportion of errors in the out-of-sample forecast tests lies in the interval (1.1–2.3 %) for the short series. For the long series the interval becomes (0.9–1.5 %), in agreement with the increased accuracy in model identification.

Seasonality in Residuals

When the models are to be used in seasonal adjustment, it is important to check for whether seasonality may still remain in the model residuals. Table 11 exhibits the % of series in each group that show evidence of seasonality according to the same

Table 9 Simulated series: model diagnostics; % of series in group that fail the test

	n.i.i.d. assumption on residuals						
	Series length	Constant mean and variance	Auto-correlation	Random signs	Normality	Skewness	Kurtosis
Airline model	120	0.8	0.2	0.2	0.9	0.8	0.6
(8,500)	240	0.8	0.3	0.2	1.3	0.8	0.8
Other-seasonal	120	0.6	0.3	0.3	1.2	0.8	0.8
(8,500)	240	0.8	0.4	0.2	1.3	0.9	1.0
Non-seasonal	120	0.7	0.6	0.3	0.7	0.6	0.5
(8,000)	240	0.8	0.6	0.2	0.7	0.7	0.5
Total	**120**	**0.7**	**0.4**	**0.3**	**1.0**	**0.7**	**0.6**
(25,000)	**240**	**0.8**	**0.4**	**0.2**	**1.1**	**0.8**	**0.7**

Table 10 Out-of-sample forecast tests (% of series that fail the test)

Out-of-sample forecast			
	Series length	F-test (18 final periods)	t-test (1-period-ahead)
Airline model	120	1.7	1.5
(8,500)	240	1.1	1.2
Other-seasonal	120	2.3	1.2
(8,500)	240	1.5	0.9
Non-seasonal	120	1.9	1.1
(8,000)	240	1.1	0.9
Total	**120**	**2.0**	**1.3**
(25,000)	**240**	**1.2**	**1.0**

Table 11 Seasonality and calendar residual effects (% of residual series in group that show evidence)

	Evidence of seasonality in residuals					
	Series length	Seasonal autocorrel.	Non-parametric test	Spectral evidence	Overall test	Spectral evidence of TD effects in residuals
Airline model	120	0.0	0.1	0.1	0.0	0.1
(8,500)	240	0.0	0.0	0.1	0.0	0.1
Other-seasonal	120	0.1	0.1	0.1	0.1	0.1
(8,500)	240	0.1	0.2	0.1	0.1	0.1
Non-seasonal	120	0.1	0.2	0.2	0.0	0.1
(8,000)	240	0.1	0.2	0.2	0.1	0.1
Total	**120**	**0.1**	**0.1**	**0.2**	**0.0**	**0.1**
(25,000)	**240**	**0.1**	**0.1**	**0.1**	**0.1**	**0.1**

set of tests as those in Table 2 with the exception of the F-test. For all cases, the frequency of detecting seasonality in the model residuals is—at most—1 every 500 series; for the overall test, it is—at most—1 every 1,000.

Summary and Conclusions

In so far as time series have different dynamic structures, an appropriate model for each series needs to be identified. Because all analysts need not be time series modeling experts, or because, even if they are, the number of series to be treated is too big—as is often the case in seasonal adjustment—an AMI procedure is required.

In this paper some evidence on the performance of the AMI procedure in TRAMO+ is discussed. The question addressed is: does the AMI procedure captures well series that follow ARIMA models? To answer the question,

(continued)

50,000 series that follow 50 different ARIMA models (stationary and non-stationary, seasonal and non-seasonal) were simulated. For each model, 500 series with 120 observations and 500 series with 240 observations were generated.

The series were exponentiated and the resulting 50,000 series were added to the original ones; then, the log/level test was applied to the 100,000 series. On average, an error is made every 250 series. As for the detection-of-seasonality sequence of tests, the final result yields, on average, one error for every 200 series (short series) and one error for every 500 series (long series). Further, the full model is correctly identified 2 out of 3 cases (short series) and 4 out of 5 cases (long series). The complete differencing polynomial (that allows for regular differencing of order 0, 1, or 2, and seasonal differencing of order 0 or 1) is correctly identified 94.4 % of the time (short series) and 97.4 % of the time (long series). Model diagnostics that test the n.i.i.d. assumption for the residuals are excellent (the size of the test is always 1 %, and the empirical size is below 1.3 % in all 36 groups), and the two out-of-sample forecast tests perform satisfactorily (between 1 and 2 % of errors). Concerning seasonality, no seasonality and no evidence of trading-day effect is left in the residuals (one error every 1,000 series in about all groups). In conclusion, the AMI in TRAMO+ is a reliable tool for modeling series that follow ARIMA models.

TRAMO+ has been applied in automatic mode with all input parameters set at default values. The automatic procedure can be maintained while some parameters are changed to non-default values. For example, for series that fail the Normality test and have no outliers, lowering the critical value for outlier detection is likely to improve Normality at the price of some additional outlier. As another example, if favoring non-stationarity is desired, one may change the default critical value of the unit root parameters. Or, to get better results for the longer series, one may remove some of the early periods. But the purpose of this paper was to show the performance of TRAMO+ when run automatically by default, i.e. blindly, on a large number of series.

References

Bell, W. R. (1984). Signal extraction for nonstationary time series. *Annals of Statistics, 12*, 646–664.

Bell, W. R., & Hillmer, S. C. (1984). Issues involved with the seasonal adjustment of economic time series. *Journal of Business and Economic Statistics, 2*, 291–320.

Bell, W. R., & Martin, D. E. K. (2004). Computation of asymmetric signal extraction filters and mean squared error for ARIMA component models. *Journal of Time Series Analysis, 25*, 603–625.

Burman, J. P. (1980). Seasonal adjustment by signal extraction. *Journal of the Royal Statistical Society A, 143*, 321–337.

Chen C., & Liu, L. M. (1993). Joint estimation of model parameters and outlier effects in time series. *Journal of the American Statistical Association, 88*, 284–297.
EUROSTAT. (1998). *Seasonal adjustment methods: A comparison*. Luxembourg: Office for Official Publications of the European Communities.
EUROSTAT. (2009). *European statistical system guidelines on seasonal adjustment*. Luxembourg: Office for Official Publications of the European Communities.
Findley, D. F., Monsell, B. C., Bell, W. R., Otto, M. C., & Chen, B. C. (1998). New capabilities and methods of the X12 ARIMA seasonal adjustment program (with discussion). *Journal of Business and Economic Statistics, 12*, 127–177. http://www.census.gov/srd/www/sapaper/jbes98_abs.html.
Fischer, B., & Planas, C. (2000). Large scale fitting of regression models with ARIMA errors. *Journal of Official Statistics, 16*, 173–184 (see also Eurostat Working Paper no. 9/1998/A/8).
Gómez, V., & Maravall, A. (1993). Initializing the Kalman filter with incompletely specified initial conditions. In G. R. Chen (Ed.), Approximate Kalman filtering (series on approximation and decomposition) (pp. 39–62). London: World Scientific Publication.
Gómez, V., & Maravall, A. (1994). Estimation, prediction and interpolation for non-stationary series with the Kalman filter. *Journal of the American Statistical Association, 89*, 611–624.
Gómez, V., & Maravall, A. (1996). Programs TRAMO and SEATS. Instructions for the User (with some updates). Working Paper 9628, Servicio de Estudios, Banco de España. http://www.bde.es/webbde/SES/servicio/software/tramo/manualdos.pdf.
Gómez, V., & Maravall, A. (2001a). Automatic modeling methods for univariate series. In D. Peña, G. C. Tiao, & R. S. Tsay (Eds.), *A course in time series analysis*. New York: Springer.
Gómez, V., & Maravall, A. (2001b). Seasonal adjustment and signal extraction in economic time series. In D. Peña, G. C. Tiao, & R. S. Tsay (Eds.), *A course in time series analysis*. New York: Springer.
Gómez, V., Maravall, A., & Peña, D. (1999). Missing observations in ARIMA models: Skipping approach versus additive outlier approach. *Journal of Econometrics, 88*, 341–364.
Grudkowska, S. (2012). *Demetra+ user manual*. National Bank of Poland. http://www.crosportal.eu/sites/default/files/Demetra$%2B%20User%20Manual%20March%$202012.pdf.
Hillmer, S. C., & Tiao, G. C. (1982). An ARIMA model based approach to seasonal adjustment. *Journal of the American Statistical Association, 77*, 63–70.
Jenkins, G. M., & Watts, D. G. (1968). *Spectral analysis and its applications*. San Francisco: Holden Day
Kendall, M., & Ord, J. K. (1990). *Time series*. London: Edward Arnold
Lytras, D. P., Feldpausch, R. M., & Bell, W. R. (2007). Determining seasonality: A comparison of diagnostics from X-12-ARIMA. U.S. Census Bureau. http://www.census.gov/ts/papers/ices2007dpl.pdf.
Maravall, A. (1987). On minimum mean squared error estimation of the noise in unobserved component models. *Journal of Business and Economic Statistics, 5*, 115–120.
Maravall, A., & Pérez, D. (2012). Applying and interpreting model-based seasonal adjustment. The euro-area industrial production series. In W. R. Bell, S. H. Holan, & T. S. McElroy (Eds.), *Economic time series: Modeling and seasonality*. New York: CRC Press.
McElroy, T. S. (2008). Matrix formulas for nonstationary signal extraction. *Econometric Theory, 24*, 988–1009.
Pierce, D. A. (1978). Seasonal adjustment when both deterministic and stochastic seasonality are present. In A. Zellner (Ed.), *Seasonal analysis of economic time series*. Washington, DC: U.S. Department of Commerce-Bureau of the Census.
Pierce, D. A. (1979). Signal extraction error in nonstationary time series. *Annals of Statistics, 7*, 1303–1320.
Tiao, G.C., & Tsay, R. S. (1983). Consistency properties of least squares estimates of autoregressive parameters in ARIMA models. *Annuals of Statistics, 11*, 856–871.
Tsay, R. S. (1984). Regression models with time series errors. *Journal of the American Statistical Association, 79*, 118–124.

Tsay, R. S. (1986). Time series model specification in the presence of outliers. *Journal of the American Statistical Association, 81*, 132–141.

United Nations Economic Comission for Europe. (2011). *Practical guide to seasonal adjustment with Demetra+*. New York/Geneva: United Nations. http://www.unece.org/fileadmin/DAM/stats/publications/Practical_Guide_to_Seasonal_Adjustment_final_web.pdf.

U.S. Census Bureau. (2012). *X-13ARIMA-SEATS reference manual, version 1.0, time series research staff, center for statistical research*. Washington, DC: U.S. Census Bureau. http://www.census.gov/ts/x13as/docX13ASHTML.pdf.

Panel Model with Multiplicative Measurement Errors

Hans Schneeweiss, Gerd Ronning, and Matthias Schmid

Abstract The analysis of panel data is a common problem in economic research. Because panel data are often subject to measurement error, it is important to develop consistent statistical estimation techniques that take the measurement error into account. A related problem is given when statistical offices anonymize confidential panel data before publication. In this case, artificial "measurement" errors are often imposed on the data to prevent the disclosure of the identity of observations. Consequently, the anonymized data can be analyzed by using the same statistical techniques as those for measurement error models. While most articles in the literature deal with the analysis of additive measurement errors, this paper is concerned with the estimation of a panel data model when multiplicative error is present. Using the generalized method of moments (GMM), we construct consistent estimators of the parameters of the panel data model and compare them to traditional estimators that are based on the least squares principle.

1 Introduction

In this paper we analyze the effect of the superposition of multiplicative measurement errors on the estimation of a panel data model. Panel data consists of doubly indexed random variables like x_{nt} and y_{nt}, $n = 1, \dots, N$, $t = 1, \dots, T$, where N is the number of items (e.g., individuals, households, companies) and T is the number of time periods (waves). A linear relation between x_{nt} and y_{nt} is assumed to hold, which is the subject of the analysis. Typically N is large and T is small. So asymptotic results will always be concerned with N going to infinity. A main assumption is the independence assumption between items n.

H. Schneeweiss • M. Schmid (✉)
Department of Statistics, University of Munich, Ludwigstrasse 33, 80539 Münich, Germany
e-mail: hans.schneeweiss@stat.uni-muenchen.de; schmid@imbie.meb.uni-bonn.de

G. Ronning
Faculty of Economics and Social Sciences, University of Tübingen, Mohlstrasse 36, 72074 Tübingen, Germany
e-mail: gerd.ronning@uni-tuebingen.de

J. Beran et al. (eds.), *Empirical Economic and Financial Research*,
Advanced Studies in Theoretical and Applied Econometrics 48,
DOI 10.1007/978-3-319-03122-4_8

The variables x_{nt} and y_{nt} are assumed to be contaminated with measurement errors, which are independent of the underlying true values ξ_{nt} and η_{nt}, respectively. The problem is to estimate the true linear relation between ξ_{nt} and η_{nt} when the variables can only be observed as error contaminated variables x_{nt} and y_{nt}, respectively. The errors may be of an additive or a multiplicative nature. Here we are mainly concerned with multiplicative measurement errors.

The variances (and covariance) of the errors may be known or unknown. Both cases occur in practice. In particular, known error variances occur when errors are deliberately added to the original true data by data collecting agencies in order to protect them from identification. Because the majority of officially collected data are confidential and can therefore not be distributed to data users in their original form, statistical offices often anonymize data before publication by using a number of anonymization techniques (Hundepool 2012; Ronning et al. 2005; Schmid 2007; Willenborg and de Waal 2001. One such technique, applicable to continuous variables, is to superimpose random errors on the original data either in an additive or a multiplicative way (Abowd et al. 2005). The error contaminated data are then released to the (scientific) public together with the error variances. An advantage of this anonymization technique is that econometricians can analyze the data in the same way as they would analyze data with measurement errors (Biewen and Ronning 2008; Ronning et al. 2005). Multiplicative errors are preferred to additive errors because they protect large values of the true variables, which are often the more sensitive values, better than additive errors. Multiplicative errors have, for example, been recommended as anonymization technique for statistical offices in Germany (Ronning et al. 2005). This is the case we are investigating in the present paper.

There are a number of papers on panel data models with *additive* measurement errors (Biorn 1996; Biorn and Krishnakumar 2008; Griliches and Hausman 1986; Hsiao and Taylor 1991; Wansbeek 2001; Wansbeek and Koning 1991). However, there are much fewer papers on *multiplicative* errors in panel data (Ronning and Schneeweiss 2009; Schneeweiss and Ronning 2010; Ronning and Schneeweiss 2011). Multiplicative measurement errors in other models are treated in, e.g., Carroll et al. (2006), Hwang (1986), and Lin (1989).

In the papers by Ronning and Schneeweiss on multiplicative errors, the parameter estimation is based on a correction of within least squares. The present paper goes beyond this approach in so far as it adds more estimating equations resulting from the use of lagged variables as instrumental variables. The estimating equations are then aggregated in order to yield a GMM estimator. This approach is very similar to Wansbeek (2001) approach except that here multiplicative errors instead of additive errors are the subject of the study. This, however, implies that some additional nuisance parameters, which do not occur in the additive case, have to be dealt with.

For the sake of simplicity, we deal only with one error ridden exogenous (and one endogenous) variable just as in Wansbeek (2001). A further simplification as compared to Wansbeek is that we do not include error free variables in the model equation in addition to the error contaminated variables and we assume serial independence in the errors. On the other hand, we incorporate in our model the possibility of a correlation between the measurement errors of the exogenous and the endogenous variables. We also construct a different weighted GMM estimator.

The paper is organized as follows: in Sect. 2 we formally introduce the panel data model and provide details on anonymization by multiplicative errors. In Sects. 3 and 4 we derive new GMM estimators for the error contaminated panel data model. Section 5 contains some remarks on related estimators, especially on the least squares estimator derived in Ronning and Schneeweiss (2011). Section 6 contains a simulation study on the theoretical results derived in Sect. 3. Section 7 considers a real-world example on the econometric analysis of an officially collected data set. A summary and discussion of the results is given in section "Conclusion and Discussion".

2 The Model

A panel consists of a sample of N items, $n = 1, \dots, N$, observed in T waves, $t = 1, \dots, T$. For each pair (n, t) we have a pair of real variables (ξ_{nt}, η_{nt}), which, however, are not directly observable. We assume a linear relation between ξ_{nt} and η_{nt} as follows:

$$\eta_{it} = \alpha_n + \xi_{nt}\beta + \varepsilon_{nt}, \tag{1}$$

where α_n is the individual effect, giving rise to unobserved heterogeneity. β is the slope parameter to be estimated. All variables including the α_n are assumed to be random.

The "errors in the equation" ε_{nt} follow the usual assumptions: they are iid with mean 0 and variance σ_ε^2, and they are independent of the α_n and ξ_{nt} and also independent of the measurement errors to be introduced below.

We assume that the vectors $(\alpha_n, \xi_{n1}, \cdots, \xi_{nT})$, $n = 1, \dots, N$, are iid. We therefore often simply omit the index n in the sequel (i.e., we study a randomly drawn arbitrary item n from the sample).

We make no assumptions about the joint distribution of $(\alpha_n, \xi_{n1}, \dots, \xi_{nT})$ except that the moments as far as necessary exist. In particular, the ξ_{nt} may be autocorrelated and the α_n may be correlated with the ξ_{nt}.

Instead of the latent variables ξ_{nt} and η_{nt}, we observe error ridden manifest variables x_{nt} and y_{nt}, which are the original variables contaminated with error. In the case of *additive errors* they are given by

$$\begin{aligned} x_{nt} &= \xi_{nt} + v_{nt}, \\ y_{nt} &= \eta_{nt} + w_{nt}, \end{aligned} \tag{2}$$

and for *multiplicative errors* by

$$\begin{aligned} x_{nt} &= \xi_{nt} V_{nt}, \\ y_{nt} &= \eta_{nt} W_{nt}, \end{aligned} \tag{3}$$

with $V_{nt} = 1 + v_{nt}$ and $W_{nt} = 1 + w_{nt}$. In both cases, the pairs (v_{nt}, w_{nt}) are iid with mean vector (0, 0) and variances σ_v^2, σ_w^2, and with covariance σ_{vw}. In the case of masking the data by error perturbation, which is the case we are considering here, these parameters are supposed to be known. The errors are assumed to be independent of all the (ξ_{nt}, η_{nt}).

Note that in the case of multiplicative errors v_{nt} and w_{nt} are dimensionless. They should be greater than -1, but this property will not be used in the sequel.

3 Estimating Equations for β

Here we mainly study multiplicative errors; additive errors will be mentioned only as an aside.

We first have to eliminate the individual effects α_n. We do this by switching to deviations from the time mean. Let $m_{xn} = \frac{1}{T}\sum_{t=1}^{T} x_{nt}$ and $\tilde{x}_{nt} = x_{nt} - m_{xn}$. The same notation is used for all the other variables. The model equations (1) and (3) then become

$$\begin{aligned} \tilde{\eta}_{nt} &= \tilde{\xi}_{nt}\beta + \tilde{\varepsilon}_{nt}, \\ \tilde{x}_{nt} &= \tilde{\xi}_{nt} + \widetilde{\xi_{nt} v_{nt}}, \\ \tilde{y}_{nt} &= \tilde{\eta}_{nt} + \widetilde{\eta_{nt} w_{nt}}. \end{aligned} \tag{4}$$

In the following we omit the index n, i.e., we write x_t instead of x_{nt} *etc.*

In order to derive a GMM estimator, we first collect all the mixed moments of x_t and $\tilde{y}_s$, $t = 1, \ldots, T$, $s = 1, \ldots, T$. Using (4) and the independence assumptions between measurement errors, equation error, and latent variables, we find

$$\begin{aligned} \mathbb{E}x_t\tilde{y}_s &= \mathbb{E}x_t(\tilde{\eta}_s + \widetilde{\eta_s w_s}) \\ &= \mathbb{E}x_t\tilde{\xi}_s\beta + \mathbb{E}x_t\widetilde{\eta_s w_s} \\ &= \mathbb{E}x_t(\tilde{x}_s - \widetilde{\xi_s v_s})\beta + \mathbb{E}\xi_t v_t\widetilde{\eta_s w_s} \\ &= [\mathbb{E}x_t\tilde{x}_s - \mathbb{E}\xi_t v_t\widetilde{\xi_s v_s}]\beta + \mathbb{E}\xi_t v_t\widetilde{\eta_s w_s} \\ &= [\mathbb{E}x_t\tilde{x}_s - \sigma_v^2\mathbb{E}\xi_t^2(\delta_{ts} - \tfrac{1}{T})]\beta + \sigma_{vw}\mathbb{E}\xi_t\eta_t(\delta_{ts} - \tfrac{1}{T}). \end{aligned}$$

Under the assumption that σ_v^2 and σ_{vw} are known, we thus have the following provisional set of T^2 equations for the unknown scalar parameter β:

$$\mathbb{E}x_t\tilde{y}_s - \sigma_{vw}\mathbb{E}\xi_t\eta_t(\delta_{ts} - \tfrac{1}{T}) = [\mathbb{E}x_t\tilde{x}_s - \sigma_v^2\mathbb{E}\xi_t^2(\delta_{ts} - \tfrac{1}{T})]\beta. \tag{5}$$

However, they contain the nuisance parameters $\mathbb{E}\xi_t^2$ and $\mathbb{E}\xi_t\eta_t$, which have to be eliminated.

The equation $x_t = \xi_t + \xi_t v_t$ implies

$$\mathbb{E}x_t^2 = \mathbb{E}\xi_t^2(1+\sigma_v^2)$$

and thus

$$\mathbb{E}\xi_t^2 = \frac{1}{1+\sigma_v^2}\mathbb{E}x_t^2.$$

Similarly,

$$\mathbb{E}\xi_t\eta_t = \frac{1}{1+\sigma_{vw}}\mathbb{E}x_t y_t.$$

Substituting these identities into (5) we finally get the following set of T^2 equations:

$$\mathbb{E}x_t\tilde{y}_s - \frac{\sigma_{vw}}{1+\sigma_{vw}}\mathbb{E}x_t y_t(\delta_{ts} - \tfrac{1}{T}) = \left[\mathbb{E}x_t\tilde{x}_s - \frac{\sigma_v^2}{1+\sigma_v^2}\mathbb{E}x_t^2(\delta_{ts} - \tfrac{1}{T})\right]\beta. \tag{6}$$

There are redundancies in these equations. To see this more clearly and also for the further development, it is helpful to write (6) in matrix form. To this end, given any particular item n, let us introduce a time series vector x for the x_t, i.e., $x := (x_1, \dots, x_T)^\top$, again omitting the index n. The vectors $y, \tilde{y}, \tilde{x}$, etc. are similarly defined. Let $A = I - \frac{1}{T}\iota\iota^\top$ be the centralization matrix such that, e.g., $\tilde{y} = Ay$. Here $I = I_T$ is the unit matrix and $\iota = \iota_T$ is the T-dimensional vector consisting of ones. For any square matrix S let diag$S$ be a diagonal matrix of the same size and having the same diagonal elements as S. Then (6) can be written as

$$A\left[\mathbb{E}yx^\top - \frac{\sigma_{vw}}{1+\sigma_{vw}}\text{diag}(\mathbb{E}yx^\top)\right] = A\left[\mathbb{E}xx^\top - \frac{\sigma_v^2}{1+\sigma_v^2}\text{diag}(\mathbb{E}xx^\top)\right]\beta. \tag{7}$$

The redundancies in this equation system are now clearly seen: Multiplying both sides of (7) from the left by $\iota^\top$ results in T-dimensional zero-vectors on both sides.

The next step will be to arrange the T^2 equations for β in a column. We do this by applying the vec operator to (7). For any matrix B, vec$B$ is the vector consisting of the columns of B stacked one underneath the other. Let D and C denote the matrices on the left and right sides of (7), respectively, without the expectation sign, so that (7) reads

$$\mathbb{E}D = \mathbb{E}C\beta.$$

Let $d = \text{vec}D$ and $c = \text{vec}C$, then (7) turns into

$$\mathbb{E}d = \mathbb{E}c\beta. \tag{8}$$

There are several ways to write c and d. For example, using the identities $\text{vec}(A_1A_2) = (I \otimes A_1)\text{vec}A_2$ for matrices and $\text{vec}(a_1a_2^\top) = a_2 \otimes a_1$ for vectors,

$$c := (I_T \otimes A)\left[x \otimes x - \frac{\sigma_v^2}{1+\sigma_v^2}\text{vec diag}(xx^\top)\right],$$

$$d := (I_T \otimes A)\left[x \otimes y - \frac{\sigma_{vw}}{1+\sigma_{vw}}\text{vec diag}(xy^\top)\right]. \tag{9}$$

Note that

$$(I \otimes \iota^\top)c = (I \otimes \iota^\top)d = 0, \tag{10}$$

in accordance with the remark after (7).

Now we derive the GMM estimator for β from (8), written in the form

$$\mathbb{E}(d - c\beta) = 0.$$

We replace the expectation sign $\mathbb{E}$ by the averaging operator $\frac{1}{N}\sum_n$, i.e., we replace $\mathbb{E}d$ by $\bar{d} = \frac{1}{N}\sum_{n=1}^N d_n$ and $\mathbb{E}c$ by $\bar{c} = \frac{1}{N}\sum_{n=1}^N c_n$, and minimize the quadratic form

$$(\bar{d} - \bar{c}\beta)^\top V(\bar{d} - \bar{c}\beta) \tag{11}$$

with some positive definite weight matrix V that has to be chosen. The simplest choice is $V = I$, yielding the unweighted GMM estimator as a least squares solution:

$$\hat{\beta} = (\bar{c}^\top\bar{c})^{-1}\bar{c}^\top\bar{d}. \tag{12}$$

Under general conditions, the unweighted GMM estimator is consistent and asymptotically normal. Its asymptotic variance can be derived from the estimating error

$$\hat{\beta} - \beta = (\bar{c}^\top\bar{c})^{-1}\bar{c}^\top(\bar{d} - \bar{c}\beta).$$

and is given by

$$\text{asvar}(\hat{\beta}) = \tfrac{1}{N}(\bar{c}^\top\bar{c})^{-1}\bar{c}^\top W\bar{c}(\bar{c}^\top\bar{c})^{-1}$$

with

$$W = \mathbb{E}(d - c\beta)(d - c\beta)^\top,$$

which can be consistently estimated by

$$\hat{W} = \overline{(d - c\hat{\beta})(d - c\hat{\beta})^\top}.$$

According to general GMM theory, W^{-1} (or rather its estimate $\hat{W}^{-1}$) would be an optimal weight matrix. However, in this particular case, W (and also $\hat{W}$) turns out to be singular and therefore cannot be used as a weight matrix. Indeed, because of (10), $(I \otimes \iota')W = 0$ (and also $(I \otimes \iota')\hat{W} = 0$). A way out might be to use certain reduced vectors c^* and d^* instead of c and d. Let the $(T-1) \times T$ matrix J be defined by $J = (I_{T-1}, 0)$, where 0 is a (T-1)-dimensional zero-vector, and let $c^* = Kc$ and $d^* = Kd$, where $K = I_T \otimes J$. The vector c^* is derived from c by deleting every T'th element from c and similarly for d^*. Obviously,

$$\mathbb{E}(d^* - c^*\beta) = 0,$$

and thus

$$\beta^* := (\bar{c}^{*\top}\bar{c}^*)^{-1}\bar{c}^{*\top}\bar{d}^* \tag{13}$$

is a consistent asymptotically normal estimator of β with

$$\text{asvar}(\beta^*) = \tfrac{1}{N}(\bar{c}^{*\top}\bar{c}^*)^{-1}\bar{c}^{*\top}W^*\bar{c}^*(\bar{c}^{*\top}\bar{c}^*)^{-1}, \tag{14}$$

where $W^* = \mathbb{E}(d^* - c^*\beta)(d^* - c^*\beta)^\top$, which can be estimated by

$$\hat{W}^* = \overline{(d^* - c^*\beta^*)(d^* - c^*\beta^*)^\top}. \tag{15}$$

Note that $\beta^* = \hat{\beta}$ for $T = 2$.

A weighted GMM estimator can now be constructed by

$$\hat{\beta}_{GMM} := (\bar{c}^{*\top}\hat{W}^{*-1}\bar{c}^*)^{-1}\bar{c}^{*\top}\hat{W}^{*-1}\bar{d}^* \tag{16}$$

with asymptotic variance

$$\text{asvar}(\hat{\beta}_{GMM}) = \tfrac{1}{N}(\bar{c}^{*\top}W^{*-1}\bar{c}^*)^{-1}, \tag{17}$$

where again W^* is estimated by (15). (Another estimator of W^* may be used by replacing β^* with $\hat{\beta}$ in (15), but we will not do so here.)

4 Estimating σ_ε^2

For any of the time series of the model, say for $x = (x_1, \ldots, x_T)$, define the variance $s_x^2 = \frac{1}{T-1}\sum_t \tilde{x}_t^2$, adjusted for degrees of freedom, and the quadratic moment $m_{xx} = \frac{1}{T}\sum_t x_t^2$. Then the model equations (4) together with (3) imply

$$\begin{aligned}
\mathbb{E}s_\eta^2 &= \mathbb{E}s_\xi^2\beta^2 + \sigma_\varepsilon^2,\\
\mathbb{E}s_y^2 &= \mathbb{E}s_\eta^2 + \sigma_w^2\mathbb{E}m_{\eta\eta},\\
\mathbb{E}s_x^2 &= \mathbb{E}s_\xi^2 + \sigma_v^2\mathbb{E}m_{\xi\xi},\\
\mathbb{E}m_{yy} &= (1+\sigma_w^2)\mathbb{E}m_{\eta\eta},\\
\mathbb{E}m_{xx} &= (1+\sigma_v^2)\mathbb{E}m_{\xi\xi}.
\end{aligned}$$

Putting these equations together, we get

$$\sigma_\varepsilon^2 = \mathbb{E}s_y^2 - \frac{\sigma_w^2}{1+\sigma_w^2}\mathbb{E}m_{yy} - \left(\mathbb{E}s_x^2 - \frac{\sigma_v^2}{1+\sigma_v^2}\mathbb{E}m_{xx}\right)\beta^2, \tag{18}$$

which implies the following estimator of σ_ε^2:

$$\hat{\sigma}_\varepsilon^2 = \overline{s_y^2} - \frac{\sigma_w^2}{1+\sigma_w^2}\overline{m_{yy}} - \left(\overline{s_x^2} - \frac{\sigma_v^2}{1+\sigma_v^2}\overline{m_{xx}}\right)\hat{\beta}^2, \tag{19}$$

where again the bar indicates averaging over the items n. Here $\hat{\beta}$ may be any of the above estimates of β, preferably $\hat{\beta}_{GMM}$.

5 Remarks

5.1 Additive Measurement Errors

If we have additive measurement errors (2) instead of multiplicative errors (3), Eq. (8) is replaced with

$$\mathbb{E}d_a = \mathbb{E}c_a\beta,$$

where

$$\begin{aligned}
c_a &:= (I_T \otimes A)\left[x \otimes x - \sigma_v^2 \mathrm{vec} I\right],\\
d_a &:= (I_T \otimes A)\left[x \otimes y - \sigma_{vw} \mathrm{vec} I\right],
\end{aligned}$$

from which the various estimators of β follow in the same way as in Sect. 3. For instance, the unweighted GMM of β is

$$\hat{\beta}_a = (\bar{c}_a^\top \bar{c}_a)^{-1}\bar{c}_a^\top \bar{d}_a, \tag{20}$$

and σ_ε^2 is estimated by

$$\hat{\sigma}_\varepsilon^2 = \overline{s_y^2} - \sigma_w^2 - \left(\overline{s_x^2} - \sigma_v^2\right)\hat{\beta}^2. \tag{21}$$

Note that $\hat{\sigma}_\varepsilon^2$ may become negative. To avoid this, one can modify the estimator along the line of Cheng et al. (2000), but we will not follow up this line.

5.2 The Within Least Squares Estimator

It is always possible to omit some of the equations (6). In particular, if we retain only the equations with $t = s$, these are

$$\mathbb{E}x_t\tilde{y}_t - \frac{\sigma_{vw}}{1+\sigma_{vw}}\mathbb{E}x_t y_t(1-\tfrac{1}{T}) = \left[\mathbb{E}x_t\tilde{x}_t - \frac{\sigma_v^2}{1+\sigma_v^2}\mathbb{E}x_t^2(1-\tfrac{1}{T})\right]\beta. \tag{22}$$

Summing over t and dividing by $T-1$ we get

$$\mathbb{E}s_{xy} - \frac{\sigma_{vw}}{1+\sigma_{vw}}\mathbb{E}m_{xy} = \left[\mathbb{E}s_x^2 - \frac{\sigma_v^2}{1+\sigma_v^2}\mathbb{E}m_{xx}\right]\beta, \tag{23}$$

from which we derive the following estimating equation for the error-corrected Within Least Squares (LS) estimator of β:

$$\overline{s_{xy}} - \frac{\sigma_{vw}}{1+\sigma_{vw}}\overline{m}_{xy} = \left[\overline{s_x^2} - \frac{\sigma_v^2}{1+\sigma_v^2}\overline{m}_{xx}\right]\hat{\beta}_{LS}, \tag{24}$$

the solution of which is

$$\hat{\beta}_{LS} = \frac{\overline{s_{xy}} - \frac{\sigma_{vw}}{1+\sigma_{vw}}\overline{m}_{xy}}{\overline{s_x^2} - \frac{\sigma_v^2}{1+\sigma_v^2}\overline{m}_{xx}}. \tag{25}$$

This is the same estimator as in Ronning and Schneeweiss (2011). Its efficiency as compared to the (weighted) GMM estimator $\hat{\beta}_{GMM}$ of (16) is one of the issues of the ensuing simulation study. Its asymptotic variance can be estimated by

$$\widehat{\text{asvar}}(\hat{\beta}_{LS}) = \frac{1}{N}(\overline{s_x^2} - \frac{\sigma_v^2}{1+\sigma_v^2}\overline{m_{xx}})^{-2}\overline{[s_{xy} - \frac{\sigma_{vw}}{1+\sigma_{vw}}m_{xy} - (s_x^2 - \frac{\sigma_v^2}{1+\sigma_v^2}m_{xx})\hat{\beta}_{LS}]^2}. \tag{26}$$

In an error free panel model $\hat{\beta}_{LS}$ is optimal, as it is simply the LS estimator of a linear model with N dummy variables, one for each α_n, e.g., Baltagi (2005).

This might imply that $\hat{\beta}_{GMM}$ would be inferior to $\hat{\beta}_{LS}$. However, one can show that in the error free panel model $\hat{\beta}_{LS}$ and $\hat{\beta}_{GMM}$ have the same asymptotic properties, in particular they have the same asymptotic variance (see Appendix). This does not mean that the same holds true for error contaminated panel models in general, though for some models, depending on the ξ_t-process, it may well be so, while for others the two estimators differ in their asymptotic properties. They may also differ in their finite sample properties, as is shown in the subsequent simulation study.

6 Simulation Study

In order to investigate the finite sample behavior of the proposed estimators and also to study the dependence of the asymptotic variances of the estimators on the model parameters, we carried out a simulation study using different sample sizes and parameter settings. All simulations are based on a first order autoregressive panel model with normally distributed variables ξ_{nt} with variance $\mathbb{V}(\xi_{nt}) = 2^2$ and with correlation coefficients $\text{cor}(\xi_{nt}, \xi_{n(t-s)}) = \rho^{t-s}$, $|\rho| < 1$, for all $s \leq t$ (i.e., we assume the ξ_{nt} to follow a stationary AR(1)-process). The slope parameter β in model (1) was set to 1 throughout, and the residual variance was kept fixed at $\sigma_\epsilon^2 = 1$. The individual effects α_n were generated from a normal distribution with mean 1 and standard deviation 2.

Concerning the correlation parameter ρ, we considered two values ($\rho = 0.5, 0.7$), which corresponded to the realistic case of positively autocorrelated data. Also, we note that similar values of ρ were observed in a real-world study on panel data conducted by Biewen and Ronning (2008). We further considered three values of the standard deviation σ_v ($\sigma_v = 0.2, 0.3, 0.4$, corresponding to measurement errors of 20, 30, and 40 %, respectively, on average). Note that we assume σ_v to be known in advance; this setting is typical in situations where a statistical office (or some other data holder) releases a set of anonymized data and communicates the value of σ_v to data analysts. As we were solely interested in the effect of measurement errors in the regressor variable, we did not contaminate the response variable with measurement errors, implying that we set $\sigma_w^2 = \sigma_{vw} = 0$. For each parameter combination 1,000 simulation runs were carried out.

Qualitatively, due to the multiplicative nature of the measurement errors, we expect the effect of the multiplicative error on the performance of the estimators to depend on the expression

$$\kappa = \sigma_v^2 \frac{\mathbb{E}(m_{\xi\xi})}{\mathbb{E}(s_\xi^2)}, \tag{27}$$

so that both the variance of the ξ_t, $t = 1, \ldots, T$, and the arithmetic mean of their squares affect the estimation results. This expression may be contrasted with the similar construct of the noise-to-signal ratio σ_v^2/σ_ξ^2 in the context of a linear cross section model with additive measurement errors, e.g., Cheng and Van Ness (1999). The new panel variant κ of the noise-to-signal ratio can be justified by the following reasoning: When we consider a linear cross section model $\eta_n = \alpha + \beta\xi_n + \varepsilon_n$ with multiplicative measurement error and write the measurement equation in the form $x_n = \xi_n + \xi_n v_n$, it is seen that the term $\xi_n v_n$ corresponds to an additive (though heteroscedastic) measurement error. The noise-to-signal ratio would then turn into $\mathbb{E}\xi^2\sigma_v^2/\sigma_\xi^2$. In the panel model with multiplicative measurement errors we then simply replace σ_ξ^2 with $\mathbb{E}s_\xi^2$ and $\mathbb{E}\xi^2$ with $\mathbb{E}m_{\xi\xi}$. We thus obtain the panel variant (27) of the noise-to-signal ratio. It can be estimated by replacing the expectation sign in (27) with the averaging operator $\frac{1}{N}\sum_n$. In the special case of a stationary AR(1) ξ_t-process with $\mathbb{E}\xi_{nt} = \mu_\xi$ and $\mathbb{V}\xi_{nt} = \sigma_\xi^2$, κ becomes

$$\kappa = \sigma_v^2(1 + \tfrac{\mu_\xi^2}{\sigma_\xi^2}) \Big/ \left[1 - \tfrac{2}{T-1}\{(1 - \tfrac{1}{T})\rho + (1 - \tfrac{2}{T})\rho^2 + \cdots + \tfrac{1}{T}\rho^{T-1}\}\right]. \quad (28)$$

Clearly κ increases with increasing σ_v, increasing μ_ξ/σ_ξ and increasing ρ, and one can show that it decreases with increasing T.

To start with, we set $\mathbb{E}(\xi_{nt}) = 0$ and considered the small sample behavior of the proposed estimators for $N = 100$. In this case, for $T = 2$, the expression (28) becomes equal to $\kappa = 2 \cdot \sigma_v^2$ if $\rho = 0.5$ and equal to $\kappa = 3.33 \cdot \sigma_v^2$ if $\rho = 0.7$. Similarly, for $T = 8$, (28) becomes equal to $\kappa = 1.27 \cdot \sigma_v^2$ if $\rho = 0.5$ and equal to $\kappa = 1.68 \cdot \sigma_v^2$ if $\rho = 0.7$. Consequently, we expect the magnitude of the estimation error to be positively correlated with ρ and to be negatively correlated with the value of T. Tables 1 (corresponding to $T = 2$) and 2 (corresponding to $T = 8$) show the mean estimates of β, as obtained from the weighted GMM estimator $\hat{\beta}_{GMM}$ in (16) and the LS estimator $\hat{\beta}_{LS}$ in (25). In addition, Tables 1 and 2 contain the standard deviation estimates of the estimators (that were obtained by computing the finite sample variances of the 1,000 values of $\hat{\beta}_{GMM}$ and $\hat{\beta}_{LS}$) and the respective mean squared error (MSE) values. Also, they contain the average estimated asymptotic standard deviations of the two estimators (as obtained from estimating the asymptotic variances given in (17) and (26)).

Table 1 Results of the simulation study, as obtained from 1,000 simulation runs with $\mathbb{E}(\xi_{nt}) = 0$, $T = 2$ and $N = 100$

		$\hat{\beta}_{GMM}$				$\hat{\beta}_{LS}$			
ρ	σ_v	Mean	sd	MSE	as. sd	Mean	sd	MSE	as. sd
0.5	0.2	1.00	0.085	0.0072	0.079	1.00	0.084	0.0071	0.080
	0.3	1.00	0.098	0.0096	0.091	1.00	0.098	0.0096	0.094
	0.4	1.02	0.120	0.0148	0.110	1.01	0.120	0.0145	0.110
0.7	0.2	1.01	0.110	0.0122	0.110	1.01	0.110	0.0122	0.110
	0.3	1.02	0.130	0.0173	0.130	1.01	0.130	0.0170	0.130
	0.4	1.02	0.180	0.0328	0.160	1.02	0.180	0.0328	0.170

Table 2 Results of the simulation study, as obtained from 1,000 simulation runs with $\mathbb{E}(\xi_{nt}) = 0$, $T = 8$ and $N = 100$

		$\hat{\beta}_{GMM}$				$\hat{\beta}_{LS}$			
ρ	σ_v	Mean	sd	MSE	as. sd	Mean	sd	MSE	as. sd
0.5	0.2	1.00	0.030	0.0009	0.015	1.00	0.026	0.0007	0.025
	0.3	1.00	0.034	0.0012	0.016	1.00	0.030	0.0009	0.029
	0.4	1.00	0.039	0.0015	0.018	1.00	0.034	0.0012	0.033
0.7	0.2	1.00	0.036	0.0013	0.016	1.00	0.029	0.0008	0.029
	0.3	1.00	0.041	0.0017	0.018	1.00	0.034	0.0012	0.033
	0.4	0.99	0.046	0.0022	0.020	1.00	0.040	0.0016	0.039

From Table 1 it is seen that the two estimators $\hat{\beta}_{GMM}$ and $\hat{\beta}_{LS}$ are almost unbiased, even if the sample size is as small as $N = 100$. However, there is a clearly visible pattern in the standard error estimates: As expected, the variances of the estimators (and also their MSE values) become larger as the correlation ρ between the panel waves increases from $\rho = 0.5$ to $\rho = 0.7$. The same result is observed if the variance σ_v^2 is increased for fixed ρ. Interestingly, the least squares estimator $\hat{\beta}_{LS}$ performs better than the weighted GMM estimator $\hat{\beta}_{GMM}$ w.r.t. to the MSE criterion, although the former estimator is based on less information (i.e., fewer moments) than $\hat{\beta}_{GMM}$. Apparently, $\hat{\beta}_{LS}$ is more robust than $\hat{\beta}_{GMM}$ w.r.t. to random variations in the data. The same results hold true if T is increased from $T = 2$ to $T = 8$ (see Table 2), where the standard errors and the MSE values of the estimators decreased because of the larger number of waves (and the resulting increase of information contained in the data). Concerning the estimation of the asymptotic standard deviations of the estimators, it is seen that the estimators of asvar($\hat{\beta}_{GMM}$) and asvar($\hat{\beta}_{LS}$) tend to underestimate the true variances of $\hat{\beta}_{GMM}$ and $\hat{\beta}_{LS}$, respectively, the former more so than the latter. This is apparently a small-sample phenomenon as it almost completely vanishes for $N = 1{,}000$, see Table 3. Note that the estimates of the asymptotic variances depend on forth moments of the data [see (17) and (26)], and these are notoriously rather unstable.

Tables 3 and 4 show the behavior of the estimators $\hat{\beta}_{LS}$ and $\hat{\beta}_{GMM}$ if the sample size is increased from $N = 100$ to $N = 1{,}000$. Our hypothesis was that, given the increased amount of information contained in the data, the weighted GMM estimator $\hat{\beta}_{GMM}$ exploits this information to a larger degree than the least squares estimator $\hat{\beta}_{LS}$ and hence results in smaller standard errors and MSE values. However, as seen from Tables 3 and 4, the least squares estimator still shows a very good behavior. In fact, the results obtained from $\hat{\beta}_{GMM}$ and $\hat{\beta}_{LS}$ are almost identical.

In addition to the results presented in Tables 1, 2, 3, and 4, we also compared the weighted GMM estimator to the unweighted GMM estimator $\hat{\beta}$ in (12). We do not present the respective simulation results here, as the unweighted GMM estimator performed worse than the weighted GMM estimator in all analyzed settings (w.r.t. both bias and variance) and is hence not recommended for practical use.

Table 3 Results of the simulation study, as obtained from 1,000 simulation runs with $\mathbb{E}(\xi_{nt}) = 0$, $T = 2$ and $N = 1{,}000$

		$\hat{\beta}_{GMM}$				$\hat{\beta}_{LS}$			
ρ	σ_v	Mean	sd	MSE	as. sd	Mean	sd	MSE	as. sd
0.5	0.2	1.00	0.025	0.0006	0.026	1.00	0.025	0.0006	0.026
	0.3	1.00	0.032	0.0010	0.030	1.00	0.032	0.0010	0.030
	0.4	1.00	0.036	0.0013	0.036	1.00	0.036	0.0013	0.036
0.7	0.2	1.00	0.035	0.0012	0.034	1.00	0.035	0.0012	0.034
	0.3	1.00	0.043	0.0018	0.042	1.00	0.042	0.0018	0.042
	0.4	1.00	0.054	0.0029	0.053	1.00	0.054	0.0029	0.054

Table 4 Results of the simulation study, as obtained from 1,000 simulation runs with $\mathbb{E}(\xi_{nt}) = 0$, $T = 8$ and $N = 1{,}000$

		$\hat{\beta}_{GMM}$				$\hat{\beta}_{LS}$			
ρ	σ_v	Mean	sd	MSE	as. sd	Mean	sd	MSE	as. sd
0.5	0.2	1.00	0.0081	0.0000656	0.0076	1.00	0.0079	0.0000624	0.0080
	0.3	1.00	0.0095	0.0000903	0.0087	1.00	0.0093	0.0000865	0.0092
	0.4	1.01	0.0110	0.0002210	0.0098	1.00	0.0100	0.0001000	0.0106
0.7	0.2	1.00	0.0094	0.0000884	0.0087	1.00	0.0090	0.0000810	0.0091
	0.3	1.00	0.0110	0.0002210	0.0099	1.00	0.0110	0.0002210	0.0106
	0.4	1.01	0.0130	0.0002690	0.0110	1.00	0.0130	0.0001690	0.0120

Table 5 Results of the simulation study, as obtained from 1,000 simulation runs with $\mathbb{E}(\xi_{nt}) = 8$, $T = 2$ and $N = 100$

		$\hat{\beta}_{GMM}$				$\hat{\beta}_{LS}$			
ρ	σ_v	Mean	sd	MSE	as. sd	Mean	sd	MSE	as. sd
0.5	0.2	1.04	0.33	0.1105	0.26	1.11	0.62	0.3965	0.42
	0.3	0.95	2.25	5.0650	2.15	1.44	6.58	43.4900	26.09
	0.4	0.66	3.65	13.4381	5.66	1.27	17.12	293.1673	191.03
0.7	0.2	0.96	1.29	1.6657	0.82	1.94	23.70	562.5736	210.30
	0.3	0.62	1.57	2.6093	1.63	−4.11	100.03	10,032.11	10,173.44
	0.4	0.27	0.95	1.4354	1.15	−0.20	18.88	357.8944	393.88

Next, we increased $\mathbb{E}(\xi_{nt})$ from 0 to 8, implying that the expression (28) increased by the factor 17. The results for $N = 100$ and $T = 2$ are presented in Table 5. Obviously, according to the MSE values, the weighted GMM estimator is clearly preferable to the LS estimator (which is now extremely volatile). If T is increased to 8, however, the LS estimator performs better than the weighted GMM estimator w.r.t. the MSE criterion (Table 6). This is mostly due to the relatively large bias of the weighted GMM estimator, whereas the LS estimator shows only little bias in this case.

Table 6 Results of the simulation study, as obtained from 1,000 simulation runs with $\mathbb{E}(\xi_{nt}) = 8$, $T = 8$ and $N = 100$

		$\hat{\beta}_{GMM}$				$\hat{\beta}_{LS}$			
ρ	σ_v	Mean	sd	MSE	as. sd	Mean	sd	MSE	as. sd
0.5	0.2	0.76	0.150	0.0801	0.034	1.00	0.066	0.0044	0.065
	0.3	0.68	0.170	0.1313	0.039	1.00	0.130	0.0169	0.127
	0.4	0.54	0.140	0.2312	0.038	1.02	0.250	0.0629	0.232
0.7	0.2	0.45	0.173	0.3324	0.037	1.03	0.089	0.0088	0.084
	0.3	0.36	0.170	0.4385	0.039	1.05	0.190	0.0386	0.171
	0.4	0.28	0.140	0.5380	0.035	1.08	0.370	0.1433	0.343

Table 7 Results of the simulation study, as obtained from 1,000 simulation runs with $\mathbb{E}(\xi_{nt}) = 8$, $T = 2$ and $N = 1{,}000$

		$\hat{\beta}_{GMM}$				$\hat{\beta}_{LS}$			
ρ	σ_v	Mean	sd	MSE	as. sd	Mean	sd	MSE	as. sd
0.5	0.2	1.01	0.08	0.0065	0.08	1.01	0.08	0.0065	0.08
	0.3	1.01	0.17	0.0290	0.15	1.03	0.18	0.0333	0.17
	0.4	1.04	0.38	0.1460	0.28	1.15	1.62	2.6469	1.05
0.7	0.2	1.01	0.13	0.0170	0.12	1.02	0.14	0.0200	0.14
	0.3	1.06	0.55	0.3061	0.27	1.12	0.66	0.4500	0.43
	0.4	0.95	0.77	0.5954	0.50	1.30	14.92	222.6233	90.04

Table 8 Results of the simulation study, as obtained from 1,000 simulation runs with $\mathbb{E}(\xi_{nt}) = 8$, $T = 8$ and $N = 1{,}000$

		$\hat{\beta}_{GMM}$				$\hat{\beta}_{LS}$			
ρ	σ_v	Mean	sd	MSE	as. sd	Mean	sd	MSE	as. sd
0.5	0.2	1.00	0.022	0.000484	0.017	1.00	0.021	0.000441	0.021
	0.3	0.98	0.036	0.001696	0.027	1.00	0.038	0.001444	0.039
	0.4	0.92	0.058	0.009764	0.038	1.01	0.067	0.004589	0.065
0.7	0.2	0.99	0.026	0.000776	0.020	1.00	0.026	0.000676	0.026
	0.3	0.96	0.045	0.003625	0.030	1.00	0.051	0.002601	0.051
	0.4	0.87	0.069	0.021661	0.040	1.01	0.086	0.007496	0.087

Finally, we increased the sample size from $N = 100$ to $N = 1{,}000$. The results (presented in Tables 7 and 8) show a very similar pattern as the results for $N = 100$: For small T, the weighted GMM estimator is clearly preferable to the LS estimator due to its smaller MSE values. Conversely, if T is increased from 2 to 8, the LS estimator performs better w.r.t. the MSE criterion (which is mostly due to the smaller bias of the LS estimator if compared to the weighted GMM estimator).

Based on the results of the simulation study, we conclude that the LS estimator performs surprisingly well, but also that the weighted GMM estimator is to be preferred if the amount of measurement error is large and if the number of waves (and hence the amount of available information in the data) is small.

7 An Empirical Example

We illustrate our results obtained from simulations by an empirical example. The data have first been used by Dahlberg and Johansson (2000) and can be obtained from the data archive of Journal of Applied Econometrics.[1] They consider the—dynamic—impact of both tax income and grants (from the central government) on the expenditure behavior of 265 municipalities in Sweden during $T = 9$ subsequent years (1979–1987). The authors were primarily interested in the lag structure of the two kinds of revenues. Their main finding based on bootstrapped test statistics was that tax income has an 1-year lagged impact whereas no dynamic effect was found in case of grants. Since our own analysis is constrained to the case of a single regressor, we will aggregate both revenue categories, which, by the way, has also been suggested by Dahlberg and Johansson (2000, p. 407). We call the resulting regressor variable x "total revenues," which is related to the dependent variable "total expenditures" denoted by y. Furthermore, we will consider only the contemporaneous relation disregarding any dynamic structure.

In order to illustrate our theoretical results, we anonymize the Swedish data set by multiplicative errors with various values of σ_v (in the same way as in Sect. 6) and compare the results from this panel regression with results obtained from the original data. The mean of the eight first order autocorrelation coefficients of the ξ_{nt}, $t = 1, \ldots, 9$, was estimated to be 0.89. The expressions $\mathbb{E}(m_{\xi\xi})$ and $\mathbb{E}(s_\xi^2)$ were estimated to be 0.0003583428 and 0.0000028918, respectively. Consequently, the coefficient κ was estimated with the help of (27) to be $123.92 \cdot \sigma_v^2$. Because the value 123.92 is very large, we subtracted the overall empirical mean of the total revenues (which was estimated to be 0.01865859) from both the regressor and the dependent variable. This will not change the value of β in the model. If all ξ_{nt} are replaced with $\xi_{nt}^* = \xi_{nt} + c$, where c is a constant, then κ changes to

$$\kappa^* = \kappa \left(1 + \frac{2c\mathbb{E}m_\xi + c^2}{\mathbb{E}m_{\xi\xi}} \right), \tag{29}$$

with $m_\xi = \frac{1}{T} \sum_t \xi_{nt}$, as can be seen from (27). As a result, with $c = -0.01865859$, κ became approximately equal to $3.53 \cdot \sigma_v^2$. This value is comparable to $\kappa = 3.28 \cdot \sigma_v^2$, which is the value that we would have obtained from (28) for $\rho = 0.89$, $T = 9$, and $\mu_\xi = 0$. Note that $T = 9$ is in close agreement with the value $T = 8$ used in the simulations. Last but not least it should be noticed that the estimated regression coefficient β will be close to 1.0 since total expenditures consist mainly of tax and grants.[2]

---

[1] See http://econ.queensu.ca/jae/.

[2] The estimated coefficient obtained from a pooled regression is 0.955.

The results obtained from the weighted GMM estimator $\hat{\beta}_{GMM}$ and from the least squares estimator $\hat{\beta}_{LS}$ are presented in Table 9. As expected, the values of the estimators are close to 1.0 in case the data are not anonymized ($\sigma_v = 0$). Also, there is almost no difference between the estimates based on the non-anonymized data ($\sigma_v = 0$) and the estimates based on the anonymized data ($\sigma_v > 0$). This result indicates that on average the original estimates can be preserved very well by the two estimators, despite the anonymization of the data. On the other hand, anonymization causes an efficiency loss that is expressed in the asymptotic variance estimates shown in Table 9: As expected, the estimated asymptotic variances of both estimators increase as σ_v increases. It is also seen from Table 9 that the weighted GMM estimator is superior to the LS estimator in this case, as the estimated asymptotic variance of the latter estimator is larger for all values of σ_v.

Interestingly, there is quite a large difference between the two estimators even in the non-anonymized case. This result is somewhat surprising, as the weighted GMM and the LS estimators should be equal in the limit. A possible explanation for this result might be that the sample size ($N = 265$) is too small for the asymptotic theory (on which the two estimators are based) to become effective. Another explanation might be that some of the assumptions on which the estimators are based are not satisfied in case of the data by Dahlberg and Johansson. For example, errors might be heteroscedastic, or the effect of the total revenues on total expenditures might vary across the municipalities (implying that β depends on n). To investigate this issue, it would be possible, for example, to base statistical analysis on a mixed-model approach with flexible error structure (Verbeke and Molenberghs 2000). To our knowledge, however, no estimators for mixed models that take into account multiplicative measurement errors have been developed yet.

In the final step, we standardized the data such that the expression (27) increased by the factor 17 (as in the second part of our simulation study, so that $\kappa = 17 \cdot 3.53 \cdot \sigma_v^2$). This was done by subtracting the constant 0.0058835 from the values of both the original regressor and the dependent variable and referring to (29). The results are presented in Table 10. Obviously, with the amount of noise being much larger than in Table 9, there is a clear effect of the error variance σ_v^2 on the finite-sample bias of both estimators. While anonymization seems to induce a downward bias in the weighted GMM estimator, the LS estimator seems to be upward-biased. On the other hand, the asymptotic variance estimates shown in Table 10 again suggest that the weighted GMM estimator is probably superior to the LS estimator in case of the data by Dahlberg and Johansson.

Table 9 Results obtained from the analysis of the data set by Dahlberg and Johansson (2000)

	$\hat{\beta}_{GMM}$		$\hat{\beta}_{LS}$	
σ_v	Mean	sd (asymptotic)	Mean	sd (asymptotic)
0.0	**0.88**	**0.0093**	**0.81**	**0.0171**
0.0	0.87	0.0090	0.81	0.0170
0.1	0.87	0.0096	0.81	0.0181
0.2	0.87	0.0110	0.81	0.0210
0.3	0.87	0.0130	0.82	0.0270
0.4	0.87	0.0150	0.82	0.0350

The estimated standard deviations were obtained by applying formulas (17) and (26). As explained in Sect. 7, data values were standardized such that the expression (27) became equal to $3.53 \cdot \sigma_v^2$. All estimates represent the mean results obtained from 1,000 randomly generated sets of the error variable v_{nt}. The first data line (in bold face) contains the estimates that were obtained from the original data with $\sigma_v^2 = 0$ and without standardization

Table 10 Results obtained from the analysis of the data set by Dahlberg and Johansson (2000)

	$\hat{\beta}_{GMM}$		$\hat{\beta}_{LS}$	
σ_v	Mean	sd (asymptotic)	Mean	sd (asymptotic)
0.0	**0.88**	**0.0093**	**0.81**	**0.0171**
0.0	0.88	0.0093	0.81	0.0171
0.1	0.89	0.0180	0.82	0.0300
0.2	0.86	0.0320	0.82	0.0780
0.3	0.81	0.0420	0.85	0.1780
0.4	0.76	0.0490	1.07	6.0030

The estimated standard deviations were obtained by applying formulas (17) and (26). As explained in Sect. 7, data values were standardized such that the expression (27) became equal to $17 \cdot 3.53 \cdot \sigma_v^2$. All estimates represent the mean results obtained from 1,000 randomly generated sets of the error variable v_{nt}. The first data line (in bold face) contains the estimates that were obtained from the original data with $\sigma_v^2 = 0$ and without standardization

Conclusion and Discussion

We have proposed a new estimation method for a linear panel model with multiplicative measurement errors. Despite some similarity to corresponding methods for panel models with *additive* measurement errors, the new method is more involved as it has to deal with certain nuisance parameters.

Multiplicative measurement errors turn up, in particular, when confidential data have been masked by error superposition before being released to the scientific public. In such a case the error variances are typically communicated to the researcher, so that these can be used in the estimation process. We have therefore developed methods for known error variances. It should be noted, however, that unknown error variances may also occur. Developing estimators for this case might be a project for future research.

(continued)

We have constructed a weighted GMM estimator for the slope parameter of the panel model along similar lines as in Wansbeek (2001) for additive measurement errors. In contrast to the method by Wansbeek, however, we used a different weight matrix for the GMM estimator. In a next step, we compared the GMM estimator to the Within LS estimator, which has been proposed in a previous paper by Ronning and Schneeweiss (2011).

Our simulation study suggests that both estimators work equally well in large samples, but in small to medium sized samples they seem to differ in their stochastic properties. Depending on the model parameters, sometimes GMM outperforms LS while in other cases GMM is inferior.

In Sect. 7, we have also analyzed a real data problem with these estimation methods. To evaluate the error proneness of the data, we have introduced a new error-to-signal ratio adapted to panel models with multiplicative measurement errors. It turns out that this ratio is extremely high in the empirical data. We therefore subtracted a constant from the data values and obtained a better manageable data set without changing the slope parameter. The results confirmed those obtained from simulations experiments.

Acknowledgements The work of Matthias Schmid was supported by Deutsche Forschungsgemeinschaft (DFG) (www.dfg.de), grant SCHM 2966/1-1.

Appendix: Equivalence of GMM and LS in the Error Free Panel Model

We want to prove the following proposition:

Proposition *In the error free panel model the estimators $\hat{\beta}_{LS}$ and $\hat{\beta}_{GMM}$ have equal asymptotic variances.*

Proof The error free panel model is characterized by the model equation

$$y_{nt} = \alpha_n + x_{nt}\beta + \varepsilon_{nt}.$$

The LS estimator is given by $\hat{\beta}_{LS} = \overline{s_{xy}} \;/\; \overline{s_x^2}$. Its asymptotic variance can be computed as follows:

$$\text{asvar}(\hat{\beta}_{LS}) = \frac{\mathbb{E}(s_{xy} - \beta s_x^2)^2}{N(\mathbb{E}s_x^2)^2} = \frac{\mathbb{E}(s_{x\varepsilon})^2}{N(\mathbb{E}s_x^2)^2}.$$

Now

$$\mathbb{E}(s_{x\varepsilon})^2 = \frac{1}{(T-1)^2}\mathbb{E}(\tilde{x}^\top \varepsilon)^2 = \frac{\sigma_\varepsilon^2}{T-1}\mathbb{E}s_x^2$$

and thus

$$\text{asvar}(\hat{\beta}_{LS}) = \frac{\sigma_\varepsilon^2}{N(T-1)\mathbb{E}s_x^2}.$$

As to the GMM estimator, we first note that in the error free model the vectors c and d of (9) reduce to

$$\begin{aligned} c &= (I \otimes A)(x \otimes x), \\ d &= (I \otimes A)(x \otimes y) = (I \otimes A)[(x \otimes x)\beta + (x \otimes \varepsilon)] \end{aligned}$$

and thus

$$\begin{aligned} W &= \mathbb{E}(d - c\beta)(d - c\beta)^\top \\ &= (I \otimes A)\mathbb{E}[(xx^\top) \otimes (\varepsilon\varepsilon^\top)](I \otimes A) \\ &= \sigma_\varepsilon^2 (I \otimes A)[\mathbb{E}(xx^\top) \otimes I](I \otimes A) \\ &= \sigma_\varepsilon^2 \mathbb{E}(xx^\top) \otimes A. \end{aligned}$$

With $K = I \otimes J$ it follows that

$$W^* = KWK^\top = \sigma_\varepsilon^2 \mathbb{E}(xx^\top) \otimes (JAJ^\top)$$

and consequently

$$W^{*-1} = \frac{1}{\sigma_\varepsilon^2}(\mathbb{E}xx^\top)^{-1} \otimes (JAJ^\top)^{-1}.$$

With $c^* = Kc = (I \otimes JA)(x \otimes x) = (I \otimes JA)\text{vec}(xx^\top)$ we get

$$\mathbb{E}c^{*\top} W^{*-1}\mathbb{E}c^* = \frac{1}{\sigma_\varepsilon^2}\text{vec}^\top(\mathbb{E}xx^\top)[(\mathbb{E}xx^\top)^{-1} \otimes M]\text{vec}(\mathbb{E}xx^\top)$$

with the projection matrix $M := AJ^\top(JAJ^\top)^{-1}JA$. Using the identity $(A \otimes B)\text{vec}C = \text{vec}(BCA^\top)$ for matching matrices A, B, C, we get

$$\mathbb{E}c^{*\top} W^{*-1}\mathbb{E}c^* = \frac{1}{\sigma_\varepsilon^2}\text{vec}^\top(\mathbb{E}xx^\top)\text{vec}[M\mathbb{E}xx^\top(\mathbb{E}xx^\top)^{-1}]$$

$$= \frac{1}{\sigma_\varepsilon^2}\mathrm{tr}(\mathbb{E}xx^\top M)$$
$$= \frac{1}{\sigma_\varepsilon^2}\mathbb{E}\mathrm{tr}[Mx(Mx)^\top].$$

It turns out that $M = A$, so that $Mx = Ax = \tilde{x}$ and thus by (17)

$$\mathrm{asvar}(\hat{\beta}_{GMM}) = \frac{\sigma_\varepsilon^2}{N\mathbb{E}\mathrm{tr}(\tilde{x}\tilde{x}^\top)} = \frac{\sigma_\varepsilon^2}{N\mathbb{E}\tilde{x}^\top\tilde{x}} = \frac{\sigma_\varepsilon^2}{N(T-1)\mathbb{E}s_x^2},$$

which is just $\mathrm{asvar}(\hat{\beta}_{LS})$.

In order to prove that $M = A$ first note that

$$JAJ^\top = I_{T-1} - \frac{1}{T}\iota_{T-1}\iota_{T-1}^\top$$

and consequently,

$$(JAJ^\top)^{-1} = I_{T-1} + \iota_{T-1}\iota_{T-1}^\top.$$

Now define the $(T \times T)$-matrix I_0 and the T-vector ι_0 by

$$I_0 = \begin{pmatrix} I_{T-1} & 0 \\ 0 & 0 \end{pmatrix} \quad \text{and} \quad \iota_0 = \begin{pmatrix} \iota_{T-1} \\ 0 \end{pmatrix},$$

Then clearly

$$J^\top(JAJ^\top)^{-1}J = I_0 + \iota_0\iota_0^\top.$$

With some algebra one can now verify that

$$M = A(I_0 + \iota_0\iota_0^\top)A = (I - \tfrac{1}{T}\iota\iota^\top)(I_0 + \iota_0\iota_0^\top)(I - \tfrac{1}{T}\iota\iota^\top) = I - \tfrac{1}{T}\iota\iota^\top = A.$$

References

Abowd, J. M., Stephens, B. E., & Vilhuber, L. (2005). *Confidentiality Protection in the Census Bureau's Quarterly Workforce Indicators*. Unpublished manuscript. Available at http://www.vrdc.cornell.edu/news/description-of-qwi-confidentiality-protection-methods/.

Baltagi, B. H. (2005). *Econometric analysis of panel data* (3rd ed.). Chichester: Wiley.

Biewen, E., & Ronning, G. (2008). Estimation of linear models with anonymised panel data. *Advances in Statistical Analysis (AStA), 92*, 423–438.

Biorn, E. (1996). Panel data with measurement errors. In L. Matyas & P. Sevestre (Eds.), *The econometrics of panel data: A handbook of the theory with applications* (2nd ed.) (pp. 236–279). Dodrecht: Kluwer.

Biorn, E., & Krishnakumar, J. (2003). Measurement errors and simultaneity. In L. Matyas & P. Sevestre (Eds.), *The econometrics of panel data* (3rd ed.) (pp. 323–367). Heidelberg: Springer.

Carroll, R. J., Ruppert, D., Stefanski, L. A., & Crainiceanu, C. M. (2006). *Measurement error in nonlinear models* (2nd ed.). London: Chapman and Hall.

Cheng, C.-L., Schneeweiss, H., & Thamerus, M. (2000). A small sample estimator for a polynomial regression with errors in the variables. *Journal of the Royal Statistical Society, Series B, 62*, 699–709.

Cheng, C.-L., & Van Ness, J. W. (1999). *Statistical regression with measurement error*. New York: Oxford University Press.

Dahlberg, M., & Johansson, E. (2000). An examination of the dynamic behavior of local governments using GMM bootstrapping methods. *Journal of Applied Econometrics, 15*, 401–416.

Griliches, Z., & Hausman, J. A. (1986). Errors in variables in panel data. *Journal of Econometrics, 31*, 93–118.

Hsiao, C., & Taylor, G. (1991). Some remarks on measurement errors and the identification of panel data models. *Statistica Neerlandica, 45*, 187–194.

Hundepool, A., Domingo-Ferrer, J., Franconi, L., Giessing, S., Schulte Nordholt, E., Spicer, K., et al. (2012). *Statistical disclosure control*. New York: Wiley.

Hwang, J. T. (1986). Multiplicative errors-in-variables models with applications to recent data released by the U.S. Department of Energy. *Journal of the American Statistical Association, 81*, 680–688.

Lin, A. (1989). Estimation of multiplicative measurement error models and some simulation results. *Economics Letters, 31*, 13–20.

Ronning, G., & Schneeweiss, H. (2009). Panel regression with random noise. CESifo Working Paper 2608.

Ronning, G., & Schneeweiss, H. (2011). Panel regression with multiplicative measurement errors. *Economics Letters, 110*, 136–139.

Ronning, G., Sturm, R., Höhne, J., Lenz, R., Rosemann, M., Scheffler, M., et al. (2005). *Handbuch zur Anonymisierung wirtschaftsstatistischer Mikrodaten. Statistik und Wissenschaft* (Vol. 4). Wiesbaden: Statistisches Bundesamt.

Schmid, M. (2007). *Estimation of a linear regression with microaggregated data*. Munich: Verlag Dr. Hut.

Schneeweiss, H., & Ronning, G. (2010). Multiple linear panel regression with multiplicative random noise. In T. Kneib & G. Tutz (Eds.), *Statistical modelling and regression structures. Festschrift in honour of Ludwig Fahrmeir* (pp. 399–417). Heidelberg: Physica-Verlag.

Verbeke, G., & Molenberghs, G. (2000). *Linear mixed models for longitudinal data*. New York: Springer.

Wansbeek, T. (2001). GMM estimation in panel data models with measurement error. *Journal of Econometrics, 104*, 259–268.

Wansbeek, T. J., & Koning, R. H. (1991). Measurement error and panel data. *Statistica Neerlandica, 45*, 85–92.

Willenborg, L., & de Waal, T. (2001). *Elements of statistical disclosure control*. New York: Springer.

A Modified Gauss Test for Correlated Samples with Application to Combining Dependent Tests or *P*-Values

Joachim Hartung, Bärbel Elpelt-Hartung, and Guido Knapp

Abstract In combining several test statistics, arising, for instance, from econometrical analyses of panel data, often a direct multivariate combination is not possible, but the corresponding p-values have to be combined. Using the inverse normal and inverse chi-square transformations of the p-values, combining methods are considered that allow the statistics to be dependent. The procedures are based on a modified Gauss test for correlated observations which is developed in the present paper. This is done without needing further information about the correlation structure. The performance of the procedures is demonstrated by simulation studies and illustrated by a real-life example from pharmaceutical industry.

1 Introduction

To judge whether, for example, a whole panel of economical or financial time series can be considered as stationary, the individual Dickey–Fuller unit root tests on stationarity may be combined in a suitable way. A difficulty arises from the fact that the several single test statistics from the same panel data are, in general, not independent. So a solution of this problem is provided by the results presented in the following.

Given normally distributed random variables with variances known or estimated with high precision, a question of interest is whether at least one of them has a mean value greater than zero. An answer can be given by the common Gauss test if the random variables are assumed to be uncorrelated. A Gauss test statistic is one which

J. Hartung
Department of Statistics, TU Dortmund University, 44221 Dortmund, Germany

B. Elpelt-Hartung
Department of Statistics, TU Dortmund University, Dortmund, Germany
e-mail: jghartung@aol.com

G. Knapp (✉)
Institute of Applied Stochastics and Operations Research, TU Clausthal,
Erzstraße 1, 38678 Clausthal-Zellerfeld, Germany
e-mail: guido.knapp@tu-clausthal.de

J. Beran et al. (eds.), *Empirical Economic and Financial Research*,
Advanced Studies in Theoretical and Applied Econometrics 48,
DOI 10.1007/978-3-319-03122-4_9

is $\mathcal{N}(0, 1)$-distributed. Now suppose the variables are correlated, e.g. the variables can arise from observations in identical or overlapping populations, as, for instance, so-called multiple endpoints in empirical studies. A method is introduced that is able to draw enough information, just only from the given variables, about a possible correlation structure in order to extend the Gauss test to the case of dependent observations. If at first individual tests, e.g. t-tests, are performed and the resulting p-values under the null-hypotheses are transformed to (at least approximately) standard normally distributed variables, then the method is applicable also in situations where the variance estimates are not of high precision.

Most methods for combining tests, or p-values, assume independence of tests, which might not be fulfilled. In this case a direct multivariate combination might not be possible. The proposed methods allow the use of the inverse normal and inverse χ^2-transformations of the resulting p-values where the independence assumption is dropped. Furthermore, in the χ^2-case, the properties of the procedures for combining independent p-values to be sensitive and sturdy, or not fragile, in the sense of Marden (1991), are preserved.

Simulation studies in Sect. 4 show a convincing behaviour of the proposed method with respect to significance level and power. A real-life example from pharmaceutical industry in Sect. 5 illustrates the application.

A first (inverse normal) combining proposal, derived under more restrictive assumptions, is given by Hartung (1999). Demetrescu et al. (2006) extensively used this proposal in the econometrical applications mentioned above, and for further considerations, see Hartung et al. (2009).

In the meta-analysis for combining the results of several studies or forecasts, the studies or forecasts are usually assumed to be independent, cf. e.g. Hartung (2008), Hartung et al. (2009). By the main result in the present paper, namely the modified Gauss test for correlated observations, possibilities are offered to consider also non-independent studies or forecasts. Essentially just two possibilities are discussed in detail in the following.

Let us denote for a vector $\mathbf{a} \in \mathbf{R}^n$ by $\mathbf{a}' = (a_1, \ldots, a_n)$ its transpose and $\mathbf{a}^2 := (a_1^2, \ldots, a_n^2)'$. For $i = 1, \ldots, n$ denote $\boldsymbol{\iota}_i := (0, \ldots, 0, 1, 0, \ldots, 0)' \in \mathbf{R}^n$, with the 1 at the i-th place, the i-th unit vector in $\mathbf{R}^n$, $\boldsymbol{\iota} := \sum_{i=1}^n \boldsymbol{\iota}_i$ the vector of ones, $\mathbf{I}_i := \boldsymbol{\iota}_i \boldsymbol{\iota}_i'$, and $\mathbf{I} = \sum_{i=1}^n \mathbf{I}_i$ the identity matrix in $\mathbf{R}^{n \times n}$. On $\mathbf{R}^n$ we take the natural semi-order induced by componentwise ordering, $\mathbf{R}^n_{\geq 0}$ be the nonnegative and $\mathbf{R}^n_{>0}$ the positive orthant of $\mathbf{R}^n$. With $\mathbf{A} \in \mathbf{R}^{n \times n}$ stands tr $\mathbf{A}$ for the trace of $\mathbf{A}$.

2 A Modified Gauss Test

Here the Gauss test is extended to deal with correlated variables, too. Let $\mathbf{x} = (x_1, \ldots, x_n)'$, $n \geq 2$, be an n-dimensional normally distributed random variable with unknown mean $\boldsymbol{\mu} = (\mu_1, \ldots, \mu_n)' \in \mathbf{R}^n$ and variance–covariance matrix $\operatorname{cov}(\mathbf{x}) = \mathbf{C} = \left(\{c_{ij}\}_{\substack{i=1,\ldots,n \\ j=1,\ldots,n}}\right)$ being an unknown correlation matrix, i.e.

$$\mathbf{x} \sim \mathcal{N}(\boldsymbol{\mu}, \mathbf{C}), \qquad \text{with } \operatorname{var}(x_i) = c_{ii} = 1, \text{ for } i = 1, \ldots, n. \tag{1}$$

Of interest are the hypotheses

$$H_{0,\mathbf{x}} : \boldsymbol{\mu} = \mathbf{0} \text{ vs. } H_{1,\mathbf{x}} : \boldsymbol{\mu} \geq \mathbf{0}, \ \boldsymbol{\mu} \neq \mathbf{0}, \tag{2}$$

where the alternative may be written more suggestively as: $\boldsymbol{\mu} \geq 0$ and $\sum_{i=1}^n \mu_i > 0$. Let $\boldsymbol{\lambda}$ be a vector of positive normed weights,

$$\boldsymbol{\lambda} \in \mathbf{R}^n_{>0}, \quad \boldsymbol{\lambda}'\boldsymbol{\lambda} = 1, \quad \boldsymbol{\lambda} = (\lambda_1, \ldots, \lambda_n)', \tag{3}$$

defining the transformation

$$\mathbf{x}_{\boldsymbol{\lambda}} := \left(\sum_{i=1}^n \lambda_i \, \mathbf{I}_i \right) \mathbf{x} \ \sim \ \mathcal{N}(\boldsymbol{\mu}_{\boldsymbol{\lambda}}, \mathbf{C}_{\boldsymbol{\lambda}}) \tag{4}$$

with $\boldsymbol{\mu}_{\boldsymbol{\lambda}} := \sum_{i=1}^n \mu_i \, \lambda_i \, \boldsymbol{\iota}_i$, $\qquad \mathbf{C}_{\boldsymbol{\lambda}} := \left(\sum_{i=1}^n \lambda_i \, \mathbf{I}_i\right) \mathbf{C} \left(\sum_{i=1}^n \lambda_i \, \mathbf{I}_i\right)$, and

$$\boldsymbol{\lambda}'\mathbf{x}_{\boldsymbol{\lambda}} = \boldsymbol{\lambda}^{2\prime}\mathbf{x} \sim \mathcal{N}\left(\boldsymbol{\lambda}^{2\prime}\boldsymbol{\mu}, \boldsymbol{\lambda}^{2\prime}\mathbf{C}\boldsymbol{\lambda}^2\right). \tag{5}$$

We need now a further statistic for getting information about the variance of $\boldsymbol{\lambda}'\mathbf{x}_{\boldsymbol{\lambda}}$. Desirable would be to have a statistic that is stochastically independent of $\boldsymbol{\lambda}'\mathbf{x}_{\boldsymbol{\lambda}}$, but this is not possible since $\mathbf{C}$ is unknown. So we consider for the present a sub-model of (4), assuming $\boldsymbol{\mu}$ to be one-parametric: $\boldsymbol{\mu} = \mu_0 \cdot \boldsymbol{\iota}$, $\mu_0 \in \mathbf{R}$. This leads to $\mathrm{E}\mathbf{x}_{\boldsymbol{\lambda}} = \mu_0 \cdot \boldsymbol{\lambda}$, and a maximal invariant linear statistic with respect to the group of one-parametric mean value translations is given now by Seely (1971) and Hartung (1981)

$$\mathbf{x}_{[\mathbf{M}_{\boldsymbol{\lambda}}]} := (\mathbf{I} - \boldsymbol{\lambda}\boldsymbol{\lambda}')\mathbf{x}_{\boldsymbol{\lambda}} =: \mathbf{M}_{\boldsymbol{\lambda}}\mathbf{x}_{\boldsymbol{\lambda}}. \tag{6}$$

Now this was just for motivating the projector $\mathbf{M}_{\boldsymbol{\lambda}}$ to be used in the following, and we return to the general model (1), or (4). Let us refer to, e.g., Mathai and Provost (1992) for moments of quadratic forms, and note that the i-th diagonal element of $\mathbf{C}_{\boldsymbol{\lambda}}$, cf. (4), is given by $c_{\boldsymbol{\lambda},ii} = \lambda_i^2$, $i = 1, \ldots, n$, then the desired variance estimator is characterized by the following theorem.

Theorem 1 *In model (1) there holds with respect to* $var(\boldsymbol{\lambda}^{2\prime}\mathbf{x})$, *cf. (4)–(6),*

1. *under the null-hypothesis* $H_{0,\mathbf{x}}$*:*

$$E_{H_{0,x}}\left(1 - \mathbf{x}_{\boldsymbol{\lambda}}'\mathbf{M}_{\boldsymbol{\lambda}}\mathbf{x}_{\boldsymbol{\lambda}}\right) = var\left(\boldsymbol{\lambda}^{2\prime}\mathbf{x}\right), \tag{7}$$

2. *under the alternative hypothesis* $H_{1,\mathbf{x}}$*:*

$$E_{H_{1,x}}\left(1 - \mathbf{x}_{\boldsymbol{\lambda}}'\mathbf{M}_{\boldsymbol{\lambda}}\mathbf{x}_{\boldsymbol{\lambda}}\right) \leq var\left(\boldsymbol{\lambda}^{2\prime}\mathbf{x}\right). \tag{8}$$

Proof We have, with $\boldsymbol{\lambda}'\boldsymbol{\lambda} = 1$ and (5),

$$\begin{aligned} \mathrm{E}\left(1 - \mathbf{x}_{\lambda}'\mathbf{M}_{\lambda}\mathbf{x}_{\lambda}\right) &= 1 - \mathrm{tr}(\mathbf{M}_{\lambda}\mathbf{C}_{\lambda}) - \boldsymbol{\mu}_{\lambda}'\mathbf{M}_{\lambda}\boldsymbol{\mu}_{\lambda} \\ &= 1 - \mathrm{tr}(\mathbf{I}\mathbf{C}_{\lambda}) + \mathrm{tr}(\boldsymbol{\lambda}\boldsymbol{\lambda}'\mathbf{C}_{\lambda}) - \boldsymbol{\mu}_{\lambda}'\mathbf{M}_{\lambda}\boldsymbol{\mu}_{\lambda} \\ &= 1 - \mathrm{tr}\mathbf{C}_{\lambda} + \boldsymbol{\lambda}'\mathbf{C}_{\lambda}\boldsymbol{\lambda} - \boldsymbol{\mu}_{\lambda}'\mathbf{M}_{\lambda}\boldsymbol{\mu}_{\lambda} \qquad (9) \\ &= 1 - \sum_{i=1}^{n}\lambda_i^2 + \boldsymbol{\lambda}^{2\prime}\mathbf{C}\boldsymbol{\lambda}^2 - \boldsymbol{\mu}_{\lambda}\mathbf{M}_{\lambda}\boldsymbol{\mu}_{\lambda} \\ &= \mathrm{var}(\boldsymbol{\lambda}^{2\prime}\mathbf{x}) - \boldsymbol{\mu}_{\lambda}'\mathbf{M}_{\lambda}\boldsymbol{\mu}_{\lambda}\,, \end{aligned}$$

where $\boldsymbol{\mu}_{\lambda}'\mathbf{M}_{\lambda}\boldsymbol{\mu}_{\lambda}$ is zero under $H_{0,\mathbf{x}}$ and nonnegative under $H_{1,\mathbf{x}}$ since $\mathbf{M}_{\lambda}$ as a projector is positive semidefinite. Note that $\mathbf{M}_{\lambda}\boldsymbol{\mu}_{\lambda}$ stays zero if $\boldsymbol{\mu}_{\lambda}$ has only one parameter under $H_{1,\mathbf{x}}$, cf. (6), as in the usual Gauss test. □

So a suitable test statistic would be

$$(\boldsymbol{\lambda}^{2\prime}\mathbf{x})/(1 - \mathbf{x}_{\lambda}'\mathbf{M}_{\lambda}\mathbf{x}_{\lambda})^{1/2}\,, \qquad (10)$$

provided the denominator is positive, which leads in expectation by use of (8) to higher values under $H_{1,\mathbf{x}}$ than under $H_{0,\mathbf{x}}$. We notice that the normality assumption is not necessary for this statement, respectively, for Theorem 1.

Now in (10), we have to recognize that the square root function is concave, leading by Jensen's inequality $\mathrm{E}\{(1 - \mathbf{x}_{\lambda}'\mathbf{M}_{\lambda}\mathbf{x}_{\lambda})^{1/2}\} \le \{\mathrm{E}(1 - \mathbf{x}_{\lambda}'\mathbf{M}_{\lambda}\mathbf{x}_{\lambda})\}^{1/2}$ and by (7), even under $H_{0,\mathbf{x}}$, to an underestimation of the denominator, which additionally has to be assured to stay positive. For both reasons, a small amount of an estimate for the standard deviation of the variance estimator will be added in the denominator of (10). We get this desired estimate via an approximation of $\mathbf{C}$ by the easier to handle matrix of an equicorrelation.

Theorem 2 *Let be*

$$\mathbf{D} := (1-\rho)\mathbf{I} + \rho\,\boldsymbol{\iota}\boldsymbol{\iota}', \quad \rho \in \mathbf{R}: \quad -1/(n-1) \le \rho \le 1\,, \qquad (11)$$

and assume cov$(\mathbf{x}) = \mathbf{D}$, *then with* $\boldsymbol{\mu} = \mathbf{0}$ *there holds*

$$E\left\{\gamma_{\lambda}(\gamma_{\lambda}+1)^{-1}\left(\mathbf{x}_{\lambda}'\mathbf{M}\mathbf{x}_{\lambda}\right)^2\right\} = var\left\{1 - \mathbf{x}_{\lambda}'\mathbf{M}_{\lambda}\mathbf{x}_{\lambda}\right\}, \qquad (12)$$

where $\gamma_{\lambda} := 2\{\sum_{i=1}^{n}(\lambda_i^4 - \lambda_i^6)\}/(1 - \boldsymbol{\lambda}^{2\prime}\boldsymbol{\lambda}^2)^2$.

Proof Note that corresponding to (4) there is, interchanging $\mathbf{C}$ by $\mathbf{D}$,

$$\mathbf{D}_{\lambda} = (1-\rho)\sum_{i=1}^{n}\lambda_i^2\mathbf{I}_i + \rho\boldsymbol{\lambda}\boldsymbol{\lambda}'\,. \qquad (13)$$

For $\text{cov}(\mathbf{x}) = \mathbf{D}$ we get

$$\text{var}(\boldsymbol{\lambda}^{2\prime}\mathbf{x}) \;=\; (1-\rho)\boldsymbol{\lambda}^{2\prime}\boldsymbol{\lambda}^2 + \rho(\boldsymbol{\lambda}'\boldsymbol{\lambda})^2 \;=\; \boldsymbol{\lambda}^{2\prime}\boldsymbol{\lambda}^2 - \rho(\boldsymbol{\lambda}^{2\prime}\boldsymbol{\lambda}^2 - 1), \tag{14}$$

and with (7): $\text{var}(\boldsymbol{\lambda}^{2\prime}\mathbf{x}) = \text{E}(1 - \mathbf{x}_\lambda'\mathbf{M}_\lambda\mathbf{x}_\lambda)$, so that by equating to (14) we get

$$1 - \rho = (1 - \boldsymbol{\lambda}^{2\prime}\boldsymbol{\lambda}^2)^{-1}\text{E}\left(\mathbf{x}_\lambda'\mathbf{M}_\lambda\mathbf{x}_\lambda\right). \tag{15}$$

Then we have with this and (13), by noting that $\mathbf{M}_\lambda^2 = \mathbf{M}_\lambda$, $\mathbf{M}_\lambda\boldsymbol{\lambda} = \mathbf{0}$, cf. (6),

$$\begin{aligned}
\text{var}(1 - \mathbf{x}_\lambda'\mathbf{M}_\lambda\mathbf{x}_\lambda) &= \text{var}(\mathbf{x}_\lambda'\mathbf{M}_\lambda\mathbf{x}_\lambda)\\
&= 2\text{tr}(\mathbf{M}_\lambda\mathbf{D}_\lambda)^2\\
&= 2(1-\rho)^2\text{tr}(\sum_{i=1}^{n}\lambda_i^2\mathbf{I}_i\mathbf{M}_\lambda)^2\\
&= 2(1-\rho)^2\text{tr}((\sum_{i=1}^{n}\lambda_i^2\mathbf{I}_i)^2\mathbf{M}_\lambda)\\
&= 2(1-\rho)^2\text{tr}(\sum_{i=1}^{n}\lambda_i^4(\mathbf{I}_i - \mathbf{I}_i\boldsymbol{\lambda}\boldsymbol{\lambda}')) \qquad (16)\\
&= 2(1-\rho)^2\sum_{i=1}^{n}(\lambda_i^4 - \lambda_i^6)\\
&= 2(1 - \boldsymbol{\lambda}^{2\prime}\boldsymbol{\lambda}^2)^{-2}\{\sum_{i=1}^{n}(\lambda_i^4 - \lambda_i^6)\}\left\{\text{E}(\mathbf{x}_\lambda'\mathbf{M}_\lambda\mathbf{x}_\lambda)\right\}^2\\
&= \gamma_\lambda\left\{\text{E}(\mathbf{x}_\lambda'\mathbf{M}_\lambda\mathbf{x}_\lambda)\right\}^2\\
&= \gamma_\lambda(\gamma_\lambda + 1)^{-1}\text{E}\left\{(\mathbf{x}_\lambda'\mathbf{M}_\lambda\mathbf{x}_\lambda)^2\right\},
\end{aligned}$$

where the last equality follows analogously to the "general lemma" in Hartung and Voet (1986), which completes the proof. □

Regarding $\mathbf{D}$ as an approximation to the arbitrary $\mathbf{C}$ in the sense that ρ may represent the mean correlation, we use now the estimate implied by (12) also for the general case. Further we have to see that the estimator $\mathbf{x}_\lambda'\mathbf{M}_\lambda\mathbf{x}_\lambda$ is useless if it takes on values greater than one, since then the variance would be estimated negatively. Therefore we replace now everywhere $\mathbf{x}_\lambda'\mathbf{M}_\lambda\mathbf{x}_\lambda$ by

$$m_{\mathbf{x},\lambda} := \min\left\{1\,,\, \mathbf{x}_\lambda'\mathbf{M}_\lambda\mathbf{x}_\lambda\right\}. \tag{17}$$

That means under $H_{0,\mathbf{x}}$, $v^2 := 1 - m_{\mathbf{x},\lambda}$ is the truncated nonnegative estimator of $\sigma^2 := \text{var}(\boldsymbol{\lambda}^{2\prime}\mathbf{x})$ and $s^2(v^2) := \gamma_\lambda(\gamma_\lambda + 1)^{-1}m_{\mathbf{x},\lambda}^2$ is an estimate of $\text{var}(v^2)$. Both σ^2 and v^2 are bounded by 1, and if $v^2 \to 1$, then $s^2(v^2) \to 0$. The idea is now to introduce a regularization parameter or function κ, $0 < \kappa < 1$, and to take $v_\kappa := \{v^2 + \kappa s(v^2)\}^{1/2}$ as an admissible, positive estimator of σ that corrects for the concavity of the square root function, where $\kappa\{\gamma_\lambda/(\gamma_\lambda + 1)\}^{1/2} \leq v_\kappa \leq 1$. So an optimal choice of κ under $H_{0,\mathbf{x}}$ would always satisfy $\mathrm{E}(v_\kappa) = \sigma$, yielding, by (8), to an underestimation of σ under the alternative $H_{1,\mathbf{x}}$. But since we have to assure v_κ to stay positive under $H_{0,\mathbf{x}}$, we cannot avoid an overestimation if σ becomes small, which particularly occurs for a negative correlation of $\mathbf{x}$. On the other hand, choosing κ too low leads even under $H_{0,\mathbf{x}}$ to an underestimation of σ in the other situations. Now $\boldsymbol{\lambda}^{2\prime}\mathbf{x}/\sigma \sim \mathcal{N}(\boldsymbol{\mu}, 1)$, and replacing σ by its admissible estimator v_κ, we get the following test statistic:

$$S_{\mathbf{x},\kappa} := (\boldsymbol{\lambda}^{2\prime}\mathbf{x}) \big/ \left[1 - m_{\mathbf{x},\lambda} + \kappa\{\gamma_\lambda/(\gamma_\lambda + 1)\}^{1/2} m_{\mathbf{x},\lambda}\right]^{1/2}, \tag{18}$$

which under $H_{0,\mathbf{x}}$ is approximately $\mathcal{N}(0, 1)$-distributed.

Our general proposals are $\kappa = \kappa_1 := 0.2$, being somewhat conservative for nonpositive equicorrelations, and $\kappa = \kappa_2 := 0.1\,\{1 + (n-1)\,m_{\mathbf{x},\lambda}\}/(n-1)$ for a less regularization than with κ_1, working mainly in case of smaller correlations. So κ_2 is more liberal holding the level better for larger n in the independent case and for negative equicorrelations. But both κ_1 and κ_2 are well performing with respect to level and power, particularly if the correlations are varying within one sample, cf. the simulation results in Sect. 4. $H_{0,\mathbf{x}}$ is rejected at level α in favour of $H_{1,\mathbf{x}}$ if $S_{\mathbf{x},\kappa}$ exceeds the $(1-\alpha)$-quantile $u_{1-\alpha}$ of the $\mathcal{N}(0, 1)$-distribution.

3 Combining Tests or p-Values

The modified Gauss test is now applied to combine dependent test statistics. Let for $i = 1, \ldots, n$, $n \geq 2$, be T_i one-sided test statistics for testing the null-hypothesis $H_{i,0} : \vartheta_i = \vartheta_{i,0}$ for some real valued parameters ϑ_i, against the one-sided alternatives $H_{i,1} : \vartheta_i > \vartheta_{i,0}$, where large values of T_i may lead to a rejection of $H_{i,0}$. It is desired to test the global, combined null-hypothesis, denoting $\boldsymbol{\vartheta} = (\vartheta_1, \ldots, \vartheta_n)'$, $\boldsymbol{\vartheta}_0 = (\vartheta_{1,0}, \ldots, \vartheta_{n,0})'$,

$$H_{0,G} : \boldsymbol{\vartheta} = \boldsymbol{\vartheta}_0, \text{ vs. } H_{1,G} : \boldsymbol{\vartheta} \geq \boldsymbol{\vartheta}_0, \quad \boldsymbol{\vartheta} \neq \boldsymbol{\vartheta}_0. \tag{19}$$

Under $H_{i,0}$, T_i may have a continuous distribution function $F_{i,0}$, such that the p-values

$$p_i := 1 - F_{i,0}(T_i), \quad i = 1, \ldots, n, \tag{20}$$

under $H_{i,0}$ are uniformly distributed on the open interval $(0, 1)$, cf. e.g. Hedges and Olkin (1985), Marden (1991), and Hartung et al. (2008), also for the following. The

T_i's arising, for instance, from multivariate problems may be arbitrarily stochastically dependent, and consequently the p_i's are also stochastically dependent, $i = 1, \ldots, n$. Based on the fact that stochastical dependence and correlation coincide in the normal case we can handle the dependent case if the p-values are transformed to normal, or approximately normal, variables. Applying then the test of Sect. 2, $H_{0,G}$ is rejected in favour of $H_{1,G}$ if, with the transformed variables, $H_{0,\mathbf{x}}$ is rejected in favour of $H_{1,\mathbf{x}}$ in Sect. 2.

The inverse normal transformation

$$z_i := -\Phi^{-1}(p_i), \quad i = 1, \ldots, n, \tag{21}$$

suggests itself, where Φ denotes the $\mathscr{N}(0,1)$-distribution function, leading under $H_{0,G}$ to $z_i \sim \mathscr{N}(0,1)$ so that with $\mathbf{z} = (z_1, \ldots, z_n)'$ instead of $\mathbf{x}$ in Sect. 2 we get the test statistic $S_{\mathbf{z},\kappa}$, cf. (18). Here $\boldsymbol{\lambda}^{2\prime}\mathbf{z}$ is considered as approximately normally distributed if the z_i's are not claimed to be jointly normal under $H_{0,G}$.

Prominent transformations are delivered by the family of χ^2-distributions. Let denote $F_{\chi^2(\nu)}$ the distribution function of the (central) χ^2-distribution with ν degrees of freedom, then

$$q_i(\nu) := F^{-1}_{\chi^2(\nu)}(1 - p_i), \quad i = 1, \ldots, n, \tag{22}$$

belongs under $H_{0,G}$ to a $\chi^2(\nu)$-distribution. To these variables, we apply now the very well approximating transformation of Wilson and Hilferty (1931), respectively, its inverse, cf. e.g. also Mathai and Provost (1992), in order to get under $H_{0,G}$ nearly $\mathscr{N}(0,1)$-distributed variables

$$y_i(\nu) := \left[\{q_i(\nu)/\nu\}^{1/3} + 2/(9\nu) - 1\right](9\nu/2)^{1/2}, \quad i = 1, \ldots, n, \tag{23}$$

such that with $\mathbf{y}(\nu) = \{y_1(\nu), \ldots, y_n(\nu)\}'$ instead of $\mathbf{x}$ in Sect. 2 we get the test statistic $S_{\mathbf{y}(\nu),\kappa}$, cf. (18). We may also choose $\nu = \nu_i$ differently for $i = 1, \ldots, n$.

A combining method may be called to possess the Marden (1991) property if in his sense the method is "sensitive" and "sturdy", or not "fragile". This property is met if the convergence of a sequence of one of the p-values to 0 leads after a finite number of steps to a rejection of $H_{0,G}$, irrespectively of the behaviour of the other p-values. The corresponding, equivalent statement is given in the last passage on p. 927 of Marden (1991); [note that by an mistake there the term "rejection region" has to be interchanged by "acceptance region"].

Looking now at our test statistic (18), we see that the denominator is bounded by some positive constants. Further we perceive $q_i(\nu)$ in (22) and consequently $y_i(\nu)$ in (23), contrarily to z_i in (21), to be bounded below, $i = 1, \ldots, n$. If now for a sequence $\{p_{i_0,j}\}_{j \in \mathbb{N}}$, with $p_{i_0,j} \in (0,1)$, $j \in \mathbb{N}$, of one of the p-values, $i_0 \in \{1, \ldots, n\}$, we have $p_{i_0,j} \to 0$, for $j \to \infty$, $j \in \mathbb{N}$, then the corresponding sequence of values of the test statistic $\{S_{\mathbf{y}(\nu)_j,\kappa}\}_{j \in \mathbb{N}}$ converges uniformly to infinity, i.e. for some $j^* \in \mathbb{N}$: $S_{\mathbf{y}(\nu)_{j*},\kappa} > u_{1-\alpha}$. So we can say: For inverse $\chi^2(\nu)$-transformed p-values our method preserves the Marden property as known for combining independent p-values.

Essentially based on Tippett's combining statistic $p_{[n]} = \min\{p_1, \ldots, p_n\}$, rejecting $H_{0,G}$ if $p_{[n]}$ lies below some critical value, Berk and Jones (1978) give a general approach to combine dependent test statistics observed in the same sample for testing a common hypothesis. To realize the proposed procedures, the main work consists of getting the asymptotic null distribution. So like in our approach, which is based on the inverse normal and inverse chi-square combining statistics, if one does not assume to observe a running sequence of the family of test statistics, one has to find some suitable statistics characterizing the dependency in the only once observed multiple test statistics. With this information, the null distribution then may be got, for instance, by Monte Carlo methods. However, in our approach by use of (7) and (12) for simulating the null distribution, we could not obtain better results than those to be presented in the next section. Further we remark that the combining statistics considered here are constructed to be more sensitive for alternatives with large $\sum_{i=1}^{n} \vartheta_i$ caused not only by a single parameter. In the latter case Tippett's combining statistic, if applicable, is more powerful. In these considerations note that by going over to the p-values we have a standardization in the sense that the ϑ_i implicitly are transformed to parameters of the same possible size.

4 Simulation Results

Now let us come to some simulation results, confirming the good performance of the proposed method. We consider the inverse normal transformed $\mathbf{z}$, since this under $H_{0,G}$ meets here in the simulations the assumptions of Sect. 2 exactly, and so we get generally valid results of our method for dependent observations. From the inverse $\chi^2(\nu)$—transformations we choose the case $\nu = 2$, because this leads in the case of independent p-values to the Fisher method. For a better representation in the tables we introduce the following notation, cf. (18) with the subsequent remark, and (21), (22), (23),

$$Y_1 = S_{\mathbf{y}(2),\kappa_1}\,, \quad Y_2 = S_{\mathbf{y}(2),\kappa_2}\,; \quad Y_0 = \sum_{i=1}^{n} q_i(2)\,, \tag{24}$$

$$Z_1 = S_{\mathbf{z},\kappa_1}\,, \quad Z_2 = S_{\mathbf{z},\kappa_2}\,; \quad Z_0 = n^{-1/2} \sum_{i=1}^{n} z_i\,. \tag{25}$$

We notice that Y_0 and Z_0 are the correct combining statistics in the case of independent p-values, where at size $\alpha H_{0,G}$ is rejected by Y_0, if Y_0 exceeds the $(1-\alpha)$-quantile $\chi^2(2n)_{1-\alpha}$ of the $\chi^2(2n)$-distribution. The other statistics have all $u_{1-\alpha}$ as critical value. Further we take everywhere the unweighted version, i.e. we put $\boldsymbol{\lambda}^2 = (1/n)\boldsymbol{\iota}$, leading to $\gamma_{\boldsymbol{\lambda}}/(1+\gamma_{\boldsymbol{\lambda}}) = 2/(n+1)$ and $m_{\mathbf{x},\boldsymbol{\lambda}} = \min\{1, (1/n)\sum_{i=1}^{n}[x_i - (1/n)\sum_{j=1}^{n} x_j]^2\}$ in (18).

In the simulations now we receive dependent p-values p_i by the transformation $p_i = \Phi(t_i)$, $i = 1,\ldots,n$, where $\mathbf{t} = (t_1,\ldots,t_n)'$ are generated according to $\mathbf{t} \sim \mathcal{N}(\mathbf{0},\mathbf{C})$, $\mathbf{C}$ being a correlation matrix. Our methods are then applied to $p_1,\ldots,p_n$ to test $H_{0,G}$ vs. $H_{1,G}$ at level $\alpha = 0.05$. For $n = 2,3,5,10,25$ at first, by 10,000 runs each, the levels are estimated for the independent case and several equicorrelations ρ of $\mathbf{t}$, i.e. $\mathbf{C}$ is chosen as $(1-\rho)\mathbf{I} + \rho\boldsymbol{\iota}\boldsymbol{\iota}'$, cf. Table 1. We observe a satisfying behaviour of our statistics Y_k, Z_k for $k = 1, 2$, with main differences for

Table 1 Estimated sizes $\hat{\alpha}\%$, respectively, ranges of $\hat{\alpha}\%$, of the statistics Y_k, Z_k, cf. (24), (25), for testing the global hypothesis $\mathrm{H}_{0,G}$ at nominal size $\alpha = 5\,\%$, for several cases of equicorrelation ρ, as well as for randomly chosen correlation matrices; correlations and correlation matrices are taken for $\Phi^{-1}(p_1),\ldots,\Phi^{-1}(p_n)$

Estimated sizes $\hat{\alpha}\%$											
		Number n of hypotheses $\mathrm{H}_{1,0},\ldots,\mathrm{H}_{n,0}$									
$\alpha = 5\,\%$		2		3		5		10		25	
ρ	k	Y_k	Z_k	Y_k	Z_k	Y_k	Z_k	Y_k	Z_k	Y_k	Z_k
	0	2.6	1.1	2.3	1.0	2.1	1.1	2.0	1.0	1.6	1.0
$-\frac{1}{2(n-1)}$	1	3.2	2.6	2.5	2.0	1.7	1.4	0.7	0.6	0.2	0.2
	2	3.2	2.6	3.5	3.2	3.6	3.0	2.6	2.2	1.7	1.0
	0	4.8	5.0	4.8	4.8	5.2	4.9	5.1	5.1	5.2	4.9
0.0	1	5.1	5.0	4.7	4.6	4.2	3.8	2.8	2.6	1.6	1.1
	2	5.1	5.1	5.7	5.6	6.1	5.8	5.4	5.0	4.4	3.5
	0	5.0	5.4	5.5	5.6	6.0	6.5	7.5	8.8	11.2	13.4
0.05	1	5.1	5.0	5.1	4.9	4.9	4.5	4.2	4.0	4.1	4.0
	2	5.2	5.1	6.0	5.8	6.6	6.5	6.8	6.6	7.0	7.0
	0	5.2	5.8	6.2	6.4	7.0	8.0	9.7	11.5	15.1	18.4
0.1	1	5.2	5.2	5.3	5.1	5.2	5.0	5.1	5.0	5.6	5.6
	2	5.3	5.2	6.3	6.1	7.1	6.9	7.6	7.5	8.3	8.3
	0	5.8	6.7	7.0	8.2	8.7	10.9	12.9	16.6	19.6	24.7
0.2	1	5.3	5.2	5.5	5.5	5.9	5.8	6.0	5.8	6.5	6.7
	2	5.4	5.3	6.4	6.3	7.6	7.4	8.3	8.1	8.5	8.4
	0	7.3	8.9	9.4	12.5	12.4	17.3	18.0	24.6	24.5	35.6
0.5	1	5.2	5.1	5.5	5.5	5.8	5.7	5.7	5.6	5.1	5.0
	2	5.4	5.2	6.2	6.1	6.5	6.4	6.3	6.1	5.6	5.4
	0	9.3	12.2	12.5	17.2	16.2	23.3	21.1	31.2	26.1	37.5
1	1	5.1	5.0	4.9	4.8	4.9	4.9	5.2	5.1	5.1	4.9
	2	5.1	5.0	4.9	4.8	4.9	4.9	5.2	5.1	5.1	4.9
Randomly											
chosen	1	4.5–5.5		4.5–5.5		4.5–5.5		4.5–6		4–6	
correlation	2	4.5–6		4.5–6		4.5–6		4.5–6.5		4–7	
matrices											

low ρ and large n between Y_1, Z_1 and Y_2, Z_2, respectively. In those constellations the latter ones hold the level better, with the consequence of being somewhat liberal in the other situations.

Furthermore, correlation matrices $\mathbf{C}$ are randomly chosen, between 50 for $n = 2$ and 500 for $n = 25$, and for each matrix the level is estimated by 10,000 independent replications of the methods. Now, the results are so similar that we restrict ourselves and report only the ranges of the observed $\hat{\alpha}$, cf. the last row in Table 1. As expected, the extreme cases we have for some constellations with an equicorrelation do not occur if the correlations are varying within one sample. The results are quite convincing. Some different simulations for the inverse normal combining method are reported by Hartung (1999) showing also quite satisfying results.

Now to get an impression of the power of the tests we consider for $n = 5$ hypotheses in the independent and in the various equicorrelated situations the case that the expectation of just one of the p-values is getting smaller, say of p_1. For this we take the equicorrelated $t_1, t_2, \ldots, t_n$ as above and get the p-values $p_1 = \Phi(t_1 - \mu_1), p_2 = \Phi(t_2), \ldots, p_n = \Phi(t_n)$, on which our methods Y_k and Z_k, $k = 1, 2$, are now applied. For $\mu_1 = 0, 1, 2, 3, 5$ the results, by 10,000 runs each, are given in Table 2, where in the independent case for comparison besides Fisher's Y_0 also the common inverse normal combining statistic Z_0 is considered, cf. (24), (25). We see that Z_0 is dominated by Y_0 clearly, by Y_1 mostly, by Y_2, and in particular, being a consequence of (8), also by Z_1 mostly and by Z_2, where with regard to Y_2, Z_2 the higher levels as starting points of the power functions

Table 2 Estimated values of the power functions [in %] at $\mu_1 = -\mathrm{E}\{\Phi^{-1}(p_1)\}$ and $0 = \mathrm{E}\{\Phi^{-1}(p_h)\}$, $h = 2, \ldots, n$; with: $\mathrm{cov}\left\{\Phi^{-1}(p_i), \Phi^{-1}(p_j)\right\} = \rho, i \neq j$

$n = 5$		μ_1									
$\alpha = 5\,\%$		0		1		2		3		5	
ρ	k	Y_k	Z_k	Y_k	Z_k	Y_k	Z_k	Y_k	Z_k	Y_k	Z_k
	0	5.2	4.9	12	11	34	22	65	38	98	72
0.0	1	4.2	3.8	10	10	26	26	49	49	82	84
	2	6.1	5.8	14	14	34	34	58	58	89	89
	1	1.7	1.4	6.9	6.5	22	22	50	50	91	92
-0.125	2	3.6	3.0	11	11	33	32	62	62	96	96
	1	4.9	4.5	11	11	27	27	49	49	80	81
0.05	2	6.6	6.5	15	15	34	34	57	57	86	87
	1	5.2	5.0	12	12	28	28	49	49	78	79
0.1	2	7.1	6.9	15	15	35	35	57	57	84	85
	1	5.9	5.8	13	12	30	29	49	49	75	77
0.2	2	7.6	7.4	16	16	35	35	56	56	81	82
	1	5.8	5.7	13	12	30	30	49	50	70	71
0.5	2	6.5	6.4	14	14	35	34	55	55	75	76
	1	4.9	4.9	9.3	9.2	24	25	51	52	65	67
1.0	2	4.9	4.9	9.5	9.4	26	26	56	57	69	71

have to be taken into consideration. For $k = 1, 2$ the statistics show also a good behaviour in the correlated situations. Only for $\mu_1 = 5$ the increasing correlation markedly diminishes the power, but on a high level. The behaviour of our statistics is surprising for negative equicorrelation. Although they have here only a small size, the power grows most quickly, above the values obtained for nonnegative correlations.

Summarizing the simulation results, we can state that the proposed test procedures prove to possess a quite satisfying performance. It should be noticed that, besides for $\boldsymbol{\mu} = \mathbf{0}$ and $\rho \leq 0$, the statistics Y_1, Z_1 and Y_2, Z_2, respectively, show a nearly identical behaviour. This speaks for the good approximation by the Wilson and Hilferty transformation, yielded already in the case of only $\nu = 2$ degrees of freedom for the χ^2-variables involved here in the transformation.

5 An Example

In an Alzheimer's disease multi-centre study ($N = 450$ patients) of a drug named idebenone, we have three treatment groups j consisting of: patients who receive placebo ($j = 1$), patients who receive idebenone 90 mg tid ($j = 2$), and patients who receive idebenone 120 mg tid ($j = 3$). According to the Alzheimer-Disease-Guideline, the cognitive part of the Alzheimer's Disease Assessment Scale, ADAS cog, is the dominating primary variable, and thus the ADAS cog: baseline ($i = 1$) value of the patients becomes a main risk factor. The two other risk factors are age ($i = 2$) and sex ($i = 3$) of the patients, cf. Weyer et al. (1996) for a detailed description of the study and of these subjects. The characteristic values of the risk factors in the three treatment groups are put together in Table 3. The resulting p-values of the homogeneity tests are:

$$p_1 = 0.044\,, \qquad p_2 = 0.463\,, \qquad p_3 = 0.172\,.$$

Let θ_{ij} denote the expected value of the risk variable i in the j-th group, then we put formally $\vartheta_i = \sum_{j=1}^{3} \left(\theta_{ij} - \frac{1}{3} \sum_{k=1}^{3} \theta_{ik} \right)^2 \geq 0$, and the test on homogeneity of the i-th risk factor with respect to the three treatment groups can be written as $H_{i,0}$: $\vartheta_i = 0$ vs. $H_{i,1}$: $\vartheta_i > 0$, $i = 1, 2, 3$, which fits our general formulation given in Sect. 3. To be tested now at size $\alpha = 0.05$ is the global hypothesis $H_{0,G}$: $\vartheta_1 = \vartheta_2 = \vartheta_3 = 0$ vs. $H_{1,G}$: at least one of $\vartheta_1, \vartheta_2, \vartheta_3$ is positive, or: $\sum_{i=1}^{3} \vartheta_i > 0$.

For a better comparison the test values of the statistics in our example are put together in Table 4. Whereas the "independence statistics" Y_0 and Z_0 are close to a rejection, the other statistics considering the dependence in the data stay far away from rejecting the global homogeneity hypothesis $H_{0,G}$ with respect to the three risk factors ADAS cog: baseline, age, and sex.

Table 3 Characteristic values of the risk factors in the treatment groups and the p-values of the homogeneity tests

N total 450	Risk factor					
Treatment group (N)	ADAS cog: baseline		Age		Sex	
	Mean	Standard deviation	Mean	Standard deviation	Male	Female
Placebo group (153)	34.27	9.32	68.93	11.38	55	98
Idebenone 90 mg tid (148)	35.26	9.33	70.33	11.55	42	106
Idebenone 120 mg tid (149)	32.68	8.10	70.39	11.85	57	92
p-Value	$p_1 = 0.044$		$p_2 = 0.463$		$p_3 = 0.172$	
Test	F-test		F-test		χ^2-test	

Table 4 Test values of the statistics Y_k and Z_k, $k = 0, 1, 2$, cf. (24), (25), for testing the global homogeneity hypothesis $H_{0,G}$ at size $\alpha = 0.05$ in the data of Table 3

Test statistic	Y_0	Z_0	Y_1	Z_1	Y_2	Z_2
Test value	11.31	1.58	1.17	1.16	1.20	1.19
Critical value	12.59 $(\chi^2(6)_{0.95})$	1.65 $(u_{0.95})$				

Acknowledgements Thanks are due to Takeda Euro Research and Development Centre for the permission to publish the homogeneity results presented in Sect. 5.

References

Berk, R. H., & Jones, D. H. (1978). Relatively optimal combinations of test statistics. *Scandinavian Journal of Statistics, 5*, 158–162.

Demetrescu, M., Hassler, U., & Tarcolea, A.-I. (2006). Combining significance of correlated statistics with application to panel data. *Oxford Bulletin of Economics and Statistics, 68*, 647–663.

Hartung, J. (1981). Nonnegative minimum biased invariant estimation in variance component models. *The Annals of Statistics, 9*, 278–292.

Hartung, J. (1999). A note on combining dependent tests of significance. *Biometrical Journal, 41*, 849–855.

Hartung, J., Elpelt, B.,& Klösener, K.-H. (2009). Chapter XV: Meta-Analyse zur Kombination von Studien. Experimenten und Prognosen. In *Statistik Lehr- und Handbuch der angwandten Statistik* (15th ed.). München: Oldenbourg.

Hartung, J., Knapp, G., & Sinha, B. K. (2008). *Statistical meta-analysis with applications*. New York: Wiley.

Hartung, J., & Voet, B. (1986). Best invariant unbiased estimators for the mean squared error of variance component estimators. *Journal of the American Statistical Association, 81*, 689–691.

Hedges, L.V., & Olkin, I. (1985). *Statistical methods for meta-analysis*. Orlando: Academic Press.

Marden, J. I. (1991). Sensitive and sturdy p-values. *The Annals of Statistics, 19*, 918–934.

Mathai, A. M., & Provost, S. B. (1992). *Quadratic forms in random variables*. New York: Marcel Dekker.

Seely, J. (1971). Quadratic subspaces and completeness. *The Annals of Mathematical Statistics, 42*, 710–721.

Weyer, G., Erzigkeit, H., Hadler, D., & Kubicki, S. (1996). Efficacy and safety of idebenone in the longterm treatment of Alzheimer's disease: A double-blind, placebo controlled multi-centre study. *Human Psychopharmacology, 11*, 53–65.

Wilson, E. B., & Hilferty, M. M. (1931). The distribution of chi-square. *Proceedings of the National Academy of Sciences, 17*, 684–688.

Panel Research on the Demand of Organic Food in Germany: Challenges and Practical Solutions

Paul Michels

Abstract Since the demand structure of organic food and beverages markets was rather non-transparent, the German Government funded the development of a reporting system covering all important retail channels. We suggested a puzzle approach merging three commercial panels in Germany. In close collaboration with the panel institutes, we met a lot of challenges like confusion of consumers when classifying organic fresh food, or missing intensive buyers of organic products in consumer panels. Up to now, parts of the system are used by manufacturers and retailers, national and federal administration bodies as well as by researchers. Selected examples of applications, based on our fundamental work, are quoted in this paper. Finally, the necessity for an adaptation of the methods is outlined to meet today's market situation and information requirements.

1 Introduction

Retail and consumer panels play an important role in commercial market research on fast moving consumer goods (fmcg). The operation of these panels requires high investments as well as a very specific know-how in collecting, processing, analyzing, and interpretation of data. Hence, worldwide there are only few companies operating fmcg panels. In order to defend their competitive advantages, the research institutes usually do not share their know-how and their data with public research institutions. For this reason, there is a lack of methodological literature concerning commercial panel research.

From the beginning of the twenty-first century, organic food and beverages are strongly emerging segments within the fmcg markets of Northern and Western Europe. The largest among them is the German organic market, which achieved a sales volume of 7 billion Euros in the year 2012.

However, up to 2007, neither in official statistics nor in major fmcg panels, organic and conventional products were distinguishable. Fmcg-producers are not

P. Michels
University of Applied Sciences, Steingruber Str. 2, 91746 Weidenbach, Germany
e-mail: paul.michels@hswt.de

J. Beran et al. (eds.), *Empirical Economic and Financial Research*,
Advanced Studies in Theoretical and Applied Econometrics 48,
DOI 10.1007/978-3-319-03122-4_10

legally obligated to distinguish between organic and conventional products, when reporting production and sales data to the bureaus of official statistics. Also, customs numbers for foreign trade do not differentiate between the two forms of producing food. Before 2007, the commercial panel operators showed little engagement in building up appropriate tools to record the demand for organic food, because a lot of detailed work is necessary and the prospective clients are few and rather poor. For the years 2000 to 2008 the total sales volume of organic food and beverages was yearly estimated by Hamm and Rippin (2007) based on expert interviews. These figures were well accepted among the stakeholders of the organic sector, but did not deliver detailed data concerning products and channels of distribution.

Thus, any specific information on the demand side of the organic markets was missing. To overcome this shortage, the German Government funded the development of a reporting system covering all important retail channels. ZMP[1] suggested a puzzle approach merging three suitable panels in Germany. In this paper we provide some insights into the handling of commercial panel data by describing challenges and solutions of this project. After quoting selected examples of applications, the necessity for an adaptation of the methods is outlined.

2 Commercial FMCG Panels in Germany

In Germany three important panel institutes provide insights into fmcg markets for manufacturers and retailers:

- GfK[2] drives a panel with 30,000 households called *ConsumerScan*. They collect their purchases of fmcg via in-home scanning of the bar codes on the product packages. Obviously, the method is not suitable for products without bar code. This occurs especially in categories like meat, sausage, cheese, fruit, vegetables, potatoes, eggs, and bread. Therefore, 13,000 households record fresh food items by scanning bar codes out of a code book provided by GfK. This subsample is named *ConsumerScan-Fresh Food*. The GfK panels are considered to be representative for the universe of all 40 million German households.
- Nielsen[3] runs two fmcg panels. Within the retail panel *MarketTrack* Nielsen receives scanner data from a sample of about 1,000 fmcg retail stores. Nielsen *Homescan* is based on 20,000 households recording their purchases using a

[1]**Z**entrale **M**arkt- und **P**reisberichtstelle für Erzeugnisse der Land-, Forst- und Ernährungswirtschaft GmbH, a provider of market and price information for agriculture, food industry, and forestry. The author was responsible for the project as head of the division "market research, consumer-prices-panel, food service" at ZMP. Most of the analyses were carried out by Barbara Bien, research assistant at ZMP.

[2]GfK SE is a full service market research institute, market leader in Germany, no. 4 worldwide.

[3]Nielsen is the global market leader in market research and the market leader in panel research for fmcg in Germany.

methodology comparable to GfK ConsumerScan. However, Nielsen does not collect fresh food items as detailed as GfK. The hard discounters Aldi, Lidl, and Norma do not cooperate with Nielsen. The missing data are estimated via Nielsen Homescan and integrated into Nielsen MarketTrack in order to achieve a full coverage of the grocery and drug stores in Germany.
- SymphonyIRI also conducts a retail panel using a technique comparable to Nielsen MarketTrack.

The above panels are designed to measure the sales of conventional retailers only. However, within organic food market a significant part of the sales is generated by special organic food stores. These outlets are not represented in Nielsen's retail sample. Furthermore, they are covered poorly by household panels for reasons described later.

Since 2004 the startup enterprise *bioVista* discovered the blank area in panel research and built up its own retail panel of organic food stores delivering aggregated sales statistics free-accessible for the participating retailers and selling analyses to manufacturers. By now, bioVista has access to scanner data of 400 organic and health stores. In 2004 they started with less than 100 participants.

3 Building Up an Information System for Organic Food and Beverages

Decision makers are not willing to invest money in non-transparent markets. At least, they need information on the development of purchase volumes, sales, and prices. A reliable evaluation of the demand side provides farmers, administration, retailers, and manufacturers with information to better match the future needs of the organic markets. In the following a selection of applications for the different stakeholders is denoted:

- *Benchmarking and new business development for manufacturers*: manufacturers can benchmark their own business comparing it with the development of the total market, i.e. they can determine their current market share. Furthermore, they can identify consumer trends, which are worth to invest in by creating new products or building up new production facilities.
- *Decision making support for farmers considering a conversion from conventional to organic farming*: usually, the quantitative yield of organic farming is lower than that of conventional farming. In a conversion period of 2 or 3 years the product prices remain on the level of conventional products, because in the meantime it is not permitted to use organic labels. Significantly higher prices for organic food in the long run have to exceed the effect of the initial poor returns. Steadily growing demand is essential for high prospective farm prices.
- *Controlling of political targets*: politicians like to formulate ambitious targets, e.g. achieving a certain growth for the organic market within a given period. In

case of deviations from the desired course, suitable measures can be undertaken, e.g. rise of funding during the conversion period.

In order to improve the level of transparency of the demand side of organic food and beverages in Germany, the Federal Program of Organic Farming[4] announced a call for research projects. The proposal of ZMP,[5] based on the integration of the existing panels described above, was accepted and funded. Hence, from November 2004 to June 2007, ZMP in cooperation with the panel providers developed a reporting system. We decided to use a mixture of existing panels using their strengths of capturing certain retail segments of the market.

Nielsen was charged to deliver data for important categories of *packaged food and beverages for the food retailers and drug discounters.* The main reason for this decision was the higher number of purchases represented by a retail panel as compared to a household panel: Nielsen MarketTrack recorded purchase transactions from about 1,000 retail stores sampled proportional to the their sales. According to Nielsen, these stores represented about 2–3 % of the fmcg retail sales. Thirty thousand GfK sample households in a universe of 40 million German households correspond to a sampling fraction of $\frac{3}{4}$ per mill. This comparatively low sampling fraction leads to high standard errors in volume, value, and price estimations for products with low penetration rates.[6] This was especially true for most of the organic packaged goods. The second provider of retail panel technology, SymphonyIRI, was not interested in building up an organic reporting.

Nielsen's retail panel MarketTrack had no access to organic food stores. Therefore, we had to apply the scanner panel bioVista for packaged goods from organic food stores.

GfK is the only panel provider operating a fresh food panel. In the subpanel ConsumerScan-Fresh Food, 13,000 panelists collect detailed information on the categories fruits, vegetables, potatoes, eggs, meat, sausage, bread, and cheese. Due to the lack of alternatives, the decision for GfK ConsumerScan-Fresh Food was mandatory. Fortunately, fresh organic food was better penetrated compared to packaged products such that the standard errors of the estimations remained on an acceptable level, especially when total categories were observed. GfK data were used for all retail channels.

Table 1 summarizes the choices of the panel providers within the puzzle approach. For fresh food data collection, there was no alternative to GfK ConsumerScan in all types of stores. For packaged food and beverages Nielsen was adequate for food retailers and drug discounters, bioVista for organic food stores. At bakeries, butcheries, markets, and farms the packaged goods could be neglected.

[4]In German: Bundesprogramm Ökologischer Landbau, BÖL. In the meantime extended to Federal Program of Organic Farming and other forms of Sustainable Farming, in German: Bundesprogramm Ökologischer Landbau und andere Formen nachhaltiger Landwirtschaft, BÖLN.

[5]See Footnote 1.

[6]The penetration rate is defined as percentage of buying household of all sample households.

Table 1 Choice of suitable panel providers for different segments of stores and products.

Type of product	Type of stores				
	Food retailers, drug discounters	Organic food stores	Bakeries, butcheries	Markets	Farmers
Fresh food[a]	GfK	GfK	GfK	GfK	GfK
Packaged food and beverages[b]	Nielsen	bioVista	Negligible	Negligible	Negligible

[a] In the project the fresh food categories meat, sausage, cheese, fruits, vegetables, potatoes, eggs, and bread were considered

[b] The categories of interest in this project were the packaged goods milk, yogurt, curd, butter, baby food, baby formula, cereals, pasta, frozen vegetables, flour, vegetable spreads, cookies, fruit and vegetable juices

In each of the three panels miscellaneous problems had to be solved during the setup of the information system. A selection of problems and solutions is presented in the next section.

4 Challenges and Solutions

The following challenges had to be overcome during the project:

1. How can organic products with bar codes be identified?
2. How can organic products without bar codes be identified by panel households?
3. How can sales data be projected in case of missing information on the universe?
4. How can projections based on the different sources be combined to total market estimates?

4.1 How Can Organic Products with Bar Codes be Identified?

Bar codes like the common Global Trade Item Number (GTIN, former EAN) do not contain the information whether a product is organic or not. The first seven digits of a 13-digit GTIN refer to the country of origin and the manufacturer who had packaged the product, digits 8–12 are defined individually by the manufacturers and the last digit is a control digit. Thus, only for exclusive organic manufacturers the GTIN leads back to the way of production (i.e., organic or conventional). Nielsen cooperates with food retailers who provide scanner-based data from a sample of their stores. The delivered product information corresponds more or less to that on the shoppers' checkout slips, i.e. bar code, product description, number of packages, price per package, and total amount for the product.

At the beginning of the project Nielsen's product description database had not contained the characteristic "organic or not." Hence, a lot of detailed work was necessary to establish a classification process. Initially, all products of a category had to be classified using checkout slip descriptions, price lists of manufacturers, internet tools, and personal store checks. After building up the initial classification for the product categories specified in the project,[7] the identification process could be concentrated on new products. The projected sales volumes were presented to experts, who judged their sizes and trends. In many cases reworks were necessary—mainly when organic products were missing, but also when conventional products were misclassified as organic.

Many packaged goods are included in the fresh food categories, too (e.g., packaged sausage, bread, and cheese). Hence, GfK had to use the similar techniques of classification as mentioned above.

4.2 How Can Organic Products Without Bar Codes be Identified by Panel Households?

Fruits and vegetables, cheese, eggs, and bread belong to the pioneer categories of organic production. Bar codes are often not available, because many of these products are not pre-packed. Therefore, the GfK panelists are provided with manual containing bar codes for fresh food items defined by GfK. After scanning one of these codes, the household is prompted on the scanner display to enter the price and the volume of the product as well as to classify whether the item is organic or not. In this manual the common seals (e.g., labels of EU-organic or of an association for organic agriculture like Bioland, Demeter, or Naturland) are displayed in order to facilitate the identification of organic fresh food by the panelist. New panelists are instructed how to classify organic food and beverage. For existing panelists the instruction is repeated once a year.

All these measures did not prove sufficiently successful, because in the case of unpacked food items the home-scanning panelist has to remember the product information from the point of sale. If products are positioned naturally or offered in a natural surrounding people tend to believe that they are organic. From a psychological point of view, purchasing organic products is socially desirable and causes a feeling of being a good soul protecting animals, nature, and environment. The highest degree of confusion is observed when products are purchased at farms, weekly markets, regional butcheries or bakeries. However, in usual grocery shops organic and conventional products are also mixed up. Consequently, in case of relying on the classification capabilities of the panelists the volume share of organic food in fresh food categories would be overestimated to an unrealistically high extent.

Therefore, we had to establish a validation step before processing the raw data from the panelists. In order to check the correctness of the panelists' classification

[7] See footnote "b" in Table 1.

we used their price entries. As organic food is pretty expensive we were able to fix lower price limits and accepted as organic only purchases beyond these limits, otherwise the entry was switched to "nonorganic." The records were checked monthly for all important fresh food products separately for different store types. Eggs and carrots are the major organic fresh food items and suit well to explain the classification procedure.

Eggs are offered in packages with six or ten units. However, the identification of the bar codes is complex and time-consuming, because there are a lot of small regional packagers using their individual codes. Basically, the prices of eggs depend on the way of hen keeping, the size of eggs, the package size, and the shop type. Panelists tend to mix up organic eggs and eggs from free-range hens. Figure 1 shows the entries of purchases in discounters assigned to these two ways of hen farming. There are four clusters of prices belonging to eggs from caged hens, barn eggs, eggs from free range hens and organic eggs. Evidently, the 258 entries of €2.20 and more are plausible for organic eggs. According to experts, the price range from €1.20 to €1.59 belongs to eggs from free-range hens. For these prices organic eggs cannot even be produced. However, there are 101 entries of organic eggs in this price range. Objectively, the panelists performed rather well, because they misclassified as organic only 101 of 2,232 purchases, which corresponds to a share of 4.5 %. In 2005, 43 % of eggs at German retailers came from caged hens, 26 % from barn,

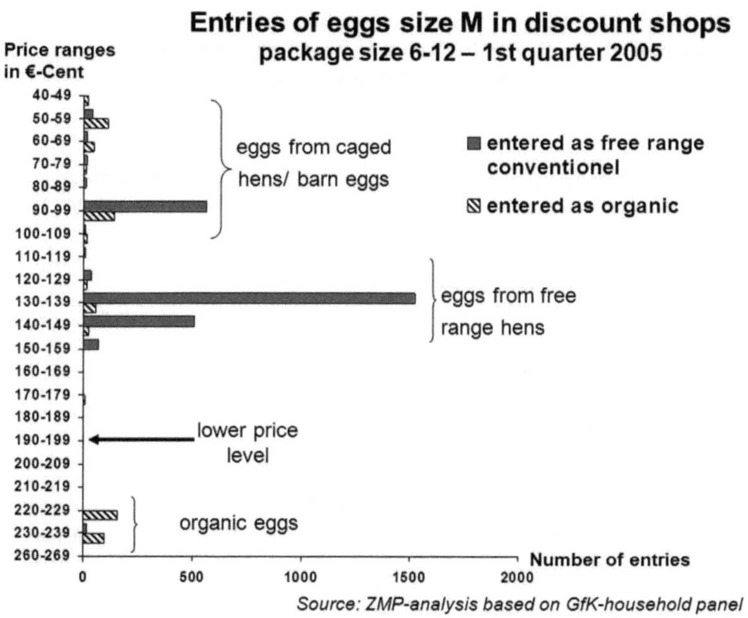

Fig. 1 Distribution of consumer prices of eggs from purchases classified as organic or as free range, 1st. Quarter 2005. Previously published by ZMP Zentrale Markt- und Preisberichtstelle für Erzeugnisse der Land-, Forst- und Ernährungswirtschaft GmbH

22 % from free-range hens, and only 4 % from organic farming. Even if the panelists have low misclassification rates, when purchasing conventional eggs, the absolute number of misclassified organic eggs is high as compared to the absolute number of plausible entries of organic eggs. In this case we defined a lower price level of €1.90 and classified only purchases beyond this level as organic. The lower price limit for eggs is checked quarterly and adopted if necessary.

In the meantime the panelists use the first digit of the stamp on the egg to classify the way of hen keeping (0 for organic, 1 for free-range, 2 for barn, 3 for cage).

Figure 2 shows a typical distribution of prices of carrots classified as organic or conventional. When the share of organic food entries in a price class was low, we assumed misclassification and processed the corresponding purchase as conventional. The lower price level is fixed at the lower class limit of the first class, where the percentage grows considerably (in this case €0.60 per kilo). Vegetable prices seasonally vary in large scale. Consequently, the lower price limit has to be checked and adopted monthly. For the majority of products the discounter distributions of organic and conventional entries permit clear decisions for the lower price limits. In supermarkets the distributions are overlapping to a greater extent, because they offer a wide range of products, e.g. conventional regional products in the price range of organic food. The situation for weekly markets and farm stores is even more difficult. Here we defined a lower price level by adding a certain amount to the level of supermarket prices. The classification work was done

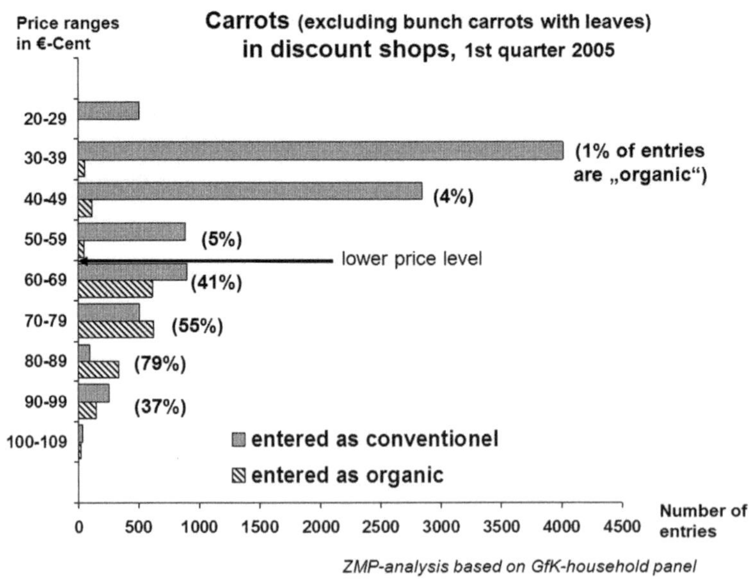

Fig. 2 Distribution of consumer prices of carrots from purchases in discounters, 1st quarter 2005. In *brackets*: percentage of organic entries in the price class. In brackets: percentage of organic entries in the price class. Previously published by ZMP Zentrale Markt- und Preisberichtstelle für Erzeugnisse der Land-, Forst- und Ernährungswirtschaft GmbH

manually by looking at suitable tables for all important fresh food items. In the case of uncertainty experts were consulted.

For items with lower penetrations and purchase frequencies an algorithm was developed. It selected those panelists that had no or few problems in classifying organic fresh food. The products with manually defined lower price limits were used to judge the classification performance of the panelists. Households were selected reporting organic food only in case of prices beyond the lower price level. Among the 13,000 panel household we found approximately 1,000 with good classification skills. For low penetrated organic products we defined the lower price limit as the minimum price[8] that these 1,000 panelists entered.

The procedure described above proved to be suitable for regular prices. Problems occurred when retailers used bargain offers to stimulate their sales of organic food. In this case, the bargain prices often fell below the lower price limits and the corresponding purchases were wrongfully classified as conventional ones. The effect was not negligible, because the purchase volumes are very high when significant price offs are offered by big retailers. To avoid these effects, we bought promotion data from a supplier that collected information from offer brochures and newspaper ads. The lower price limit was reduced exclusively for the retailer in the identified promotion weeks.

After we had installed the above described routines the main hurdle of the project was jumped over. Finally we succeeded in extracting the truly organic purchases from the panelists. The methods were developed in close cooperation with GfK who offered ZMP deep insights into the processing of raw data which went far beyond the usual business practice of market research institutes. GfK and ZMP developed a well-working division of labor: the data validation process was taken over by ZMP and the projection of the validated data was done by GfK.

4.3 How Can Sales Data be Projected in Case of Missing Information on the Universe?

Usually panel operating companies project their sample data to a well-known universe. Nielsen uses data from official statistics and own surveys to define a universe as the base of its projection system. In 2007, the universe for the special organic food stores was unknown. Estimates for the number of organic stores ranged from 2,500 to 3,500. Sales estimates showed a comparable range. Because of missing universe information, bioVista's panel for organic food stores did not offer projected data. However, for our project, projection to the universe of organic stores was crucial.

Therefore the following method was tested: bioVista asked a selection of manufacturers for the volumes of their brands realized with organic retailers and

[8]To achieve more robustness against outliers we replaced the minimum by an appropriate rank statistic.

wholesalers in Germany. The attempt was successful for most of the categories of our interest.[9] Based on the delivered data, a projection factor for each category was calculated as

$$\frac{\textit{volume} \text{ of coop.manufacturers in the universe}}{\textit{volume} \text{ of coop.manufacturers} \textit{in the bioVista sample}} \tag{1}$$

These projection factors were applied to cooperating and non-cooperating manufacturers of the corresponding categories. Thus, the projected category volumes could be calculated. The method works, because organic retailers emphasize on brands exclusively sold in organic shops. Therefore, the sales to organic and conventional retailers can be easily separated.

4.4 How Can Projections Based on the Different Sources be Combined to Total Market Estimates?

Up to now we had solved special issues of the three involved panel methods. Below, we come to the challenge of combining the different approaches to an estimate of total sales, volumes, and market shares.

Concerning the two retail panels from Nielsen and bioVista, we did not expect a considerable bias in measuring sales volumes and values. Therefore, we considered the projected values of these panels as unbiased estimates and used them without bias corrections. Consequently, for packaged food and beverages we could simply consolidate sales volumes and values by summing up the respective figures from the two instruments. In contrast, the situation of household panel data in the fresh food sector was more difficult.

Household panels tend to underestimate the market volume. There is a variety of reasons for the missing coverage of household panels, e.g.

- panelists consciously or unconsciously skip purchases,
- purchases for out-of-home consumption are not likely to be scanned,
- purchases of re-sellers, gastronomists, and caterers are represented by retail panels but not regarded by household panels.

Among the clients of household panel data these shortcomings are well known and will not be treated in this paper. Instead of it we examine the question to what extent the coverages of conventional and organic products differ. These differences are crucial, especially when calculating market shares of organic products. Unfortunately, in the current project a direct comparison of household and retail panels was not feasible, because Nielsen's and bioVista's retail panels do not provide information on fresh food. Hence, the coverage analysis had to be carried out

[9]See Footnote 7.

for selected dairy categories instead of fresh food. Both, dairy and fresh food are characterized by high purchase frequencies and considerable relevance of organic products. Furthermore, the products of both categories are usually brought home directly after shopping. For these reasons and the lack of alternatives, we assumed similar coverage pattern of the considered dairy and fresh food categories.

For the universe of conventional food retailers, the coverage is defined by

$$\frac{\textit{projected sales of GfK household panel}}{\textit{projected sales of Nielsen retail panel}} \times 100 \tag{2}$$

For the examined dairy categories milk, yogurt, curd, and butter the coverage values for conventional products at conventional food retailers were close to each other, the average is about 90 %. For organic products the coverage proved to be much smaller, on average 66 %. This relatively poor coverage could be explained by the following two arguments:

- Organic products are expensive and panelists use to be more price-sensitive as compared to the universe of all households in Germany.
- The intensive buyers of organic food show a distinctive anonymity requirement. Hence, many of them are not willing to report their purchase behavior to commercial panel institutes.

Taking account of the above coverage figures, sales of conventional products (cp) measured by the GfK household panel should be expanded by the factor $1/0.9 = 1.11$ and sales of organic products by the factor $1/0.66 = 1.52$. With these coverage correction factors, the market share of organic products (op) at conventional stores (cs) like supermarkets, consumer markets, and discounters can by calculated by

$$\frac{\textit{sales of op in cs} \times \textit{1.52}}{\textit{sales of op in cs} \times \textit{1.52} + \textit{sales of cp in cs} \times \textit{1.11}}, \tag{3}$$

using sales estimates from the GfK household panel.

The coverage analyses of GfK household panel with respect to organic stores (small bio shops and bio supermarkets) are based on further data sources. Hamm and Rippin (2007) published sales figures of different market segments based on interviews with experts from retailers and direct marketers. For the year 2005 they estimated the sales volume for organic stores of about 1 billion Euros. The share of the most important fresh food categories is quantified by Klaus Braun Kommunikationsberatung,[10] a consulting agency using operating data from a sample of organic retailers including category-specific sales figures. Combining the two results yields a sales volume of 425 million Euros for fresh food of which the GfK household panel covers about 50 %. The reasons for the coverage gap are

[10]Klaus Braun Kommunikationsberatung collects data from its clients (e.g., organic store owners). The sample is stratified by the sales values of the organic stores. For more information see www.klausbraun.de.

quoted above. They can be applied for the clients of organic shops (os) to an even higher extent. Thus, we have the formula

$$\frac{\textit{sales of op in cs} \times 1.52 + \textit{sales of op in os} \times 2.00}{\textit{sales of op in cs} \times 1.52 + \textit{sales of cp in cs} \times 1.11 + \textit{sales of op in os} \times 2.00} \quad (4)$$

for a coverage corrected market share of organic fresh food products. Again, the sales figures are based on the GfK household panel. Similar correction factors can be derived using purchase volume instead of sales estimates. Actually, the volume-based coverage proves to be slightly higher, because of the price sensitivity of the panelists mentioned above.

5 Applications of Panel Data for Organic Food and Beverages

In the project report, Bien and Michels (2007) presented many examples of the use of the developed reporting facilities for specific analysis on the organic market. Up to now parts of our fundamental research have been used to describe the purchase behavior on the organic markets.

The sales of organic food and beverages have steadily increased from 3.9 billion Euros in 2005 to 7.0 billion Euros in the year 2012. The corresponding average growth rate of 8.7 % is definitely remarkable in the German food and beverage sector. Once a year the change rates and the corresponding sales values of the total organic market are estimated by a working team[11] using the sources of our proposed puzzle approach and taking into account the strengths and weaknesses derived in this paper. Every year in February, the results are published at the world's largest trade fair for organic products Biofach in Nuremberg. The new market figures are widely distributed by mass media and special media reporting on the occasion of the Biofach.

After implementation of the classification and validation processes as described above, especially the data of GfK household panel offer a large potential for the further research. A follow-up project proposal from the University of Kassel and ZMP was funded again by the Federal Program of Organic Farming and other forms of Sustainable Agriculture. This project treated the dynamics in purchase behavior for organic food with descriptive and inductive statistical methods (Buder et al. 2010).

[11]Members of the working team: Hamm, U., University of Kassel, Michels, P., University of Applied Sciences Weihenstephan-Triesdorf, representatives from the research institutes GfK, Nielsen, bioVista, Klaus Braun Kommunikationsberatung, Agrarmarktinformations-Gesellschaft (coordinating) and from the umbrella organization Bund Ökologischer Lebensmittelwirtschaft BÖLW.

Within this project, about 40 million purchase acts were investigated. For the years 2004–2008 they reflect the food and beverage demand of 20,000 GfK panel households in 41 product categories. Selected results are given below:

- Household segmentation by loyalty showed that only 17 % of the shoppers stood for 76 % of the sales of organic food and beverages. Hence the organic market was strongly dependent on few loyal customers. Growth potential was identified especially in the group of occasional buyer. This result had to be handled with caution, because of the findings of the above coverage analyses. Missing heavy intensive buyers in the GfK sample may lead to an underestimation of the share of loyal shoppers.
- Once a year, the GfK panelists answer to questionnaires on socio-demographics, attitudes, media, and leisure behavior. The results can be used to analyze the motivation of buying organic food. By using structural equation models, significant factors of influence were discovered: the purchase behavior was primarily determined by selfish buying motives. Consumers bought organic products, because they find that they taste better, contain fewer residues, and are considered to be healthier.
- Classical consumer segmentation criteria like "income" and "education" were not significant.
- Up to now, a blank area of the organic market is the target group with positive attitudes towards fast food and snacks. Useful offers in this field may attract young people to organic food.

In a project for the Bavarian Ministry for Food, Agriculture and Forestry, Michels et al. (2013) quantified the development and the structure of the demand for organic food and beverages in Bavaria by using GfK household panel data and considering the learnings of the above coverage analyses. This is a part of a current evaluation of the Bavarian organic sector and the basis of future funding strategies of the Bavarian state government. The analyses showed that Bavarians are above-average affine to organic food as compared to other German regions. Their demand is rather resistant to economic crisis. Furthermore, food categories and shop types that Bavarians prefer are identified. This information can be used to support the development and the marketing of regional organic food.

6 Further Research Requirements

The basic research project dates back to the year 2007 (Bien and Michels 2007). Until today the solutions proposed in this paper are adopted still to GfK data. In the meantime the sales volume of the organic market has doubled. Further methodological work is needed with respect to the following issues:

- In 2012 GfK has generally improved the coverage by applying a different projection technology. In the meantime, the universe of organic shops has been surveyed. The corresponding sales values have been applied to the yearly estimations of the total market mentioned above. Furthermore, today organic food and special organic stores are closer to mainstream. Therefore, the question is obvious whether the coverage values derived in this paper are still valid.

- The methods of this paper only work for bias reduction of volume, sales (including related shares), and price estimations. However, the facts like penetrations, purchase frequencies, or shares of requirement are very important for deeper consumer insights. Here further research is needed, too.
- The coverage of GfK household panel for fresh food in the small trade sector (bakeries, butcheries, weekly markets, or farmers) is completely unknown, because there are no further sources that can serve as benchmarks.

References

Bien, B., & Michels, P. (2007). Aufbau einer kontinuierlichen Berichterstattung zum Einkaufsverhalten bei ökologisch erzeugten Produkten in Deutschland. Final Report of the Research Project 02OE367/F of the German Federal Program of Organic Farming and Other Forms of Sustainable Farming. Available via organic eprints. http://orgprints.org/11096/ Accessed 19.01.13.

Buder, F., Hamm, U., Bickel, M., Bien, B., & Michels, P. (2010). Dynamik des Kaufverhaltens im Bio-Sortiment. Final Report of the Research Project 09OE014 of the German Federal Program of Organic Farming and Other Forms of Sustainable Farming. Available via organic eprints. http://orgprints.org/16983/ Accessed 19.01.13

Hamm, U., & Rippin, M. (2007). Marktdaten aktuell: Öko-Lebensmittelumsatz in Deutschland 2006. Available via http://www.agromilagro.de Accessed 09.06.13

Michels, P. (2013). Entwicklung des Öko-Marktes. Evaluation des Ökologischen Landbaus in Bayern. In Internal Preliminary Report. Forschungsgruppe Agrar- und Regionalentwicklung, Triesdorf, Ecozept GbR, Freising (eds.).

The Elasticity of Demand for Gasoline: A Semi-parametric Analysis

Pin T. Ng and James L. Smith

Abstract We use a semi-parametric conditional median as a robust alternative to the parametric conditional mean to estimate the gasoline demand function. Our approach protects against data and specification errors, and may yield a more reliable basis for public-policy decisions that depend on accurate estimates of gasoline demand. As a comparison, we also estimated the parametric translog conditional mean model. Our semi-parametric estimates imply that gasoline demand becomes more price elastic, but also less income elastic, as incomes rise. In addition, we find that demand appears to become more price elastic as prices increase in real terms.

1 Introduction

Projections of future gasoline consumption are conditioned by the elasticity of demand. Thus, the design and success of various energy and environmental policy initiatives that pertain to gasoline necessarily involve judgments regarding this important aspect of consumer behavior. The magnitude of price elasticity, for example, largely determines the potency of excise taxes as a tool for raising government revenues, discouraging consumption and emissions, encouraging conservation and fuel switching, and attaining certain national security goals regarding energy independence. Moreover, the magnitude of income elasticity may influence the way in which economic growth and development affect progress towards achieving specific policy goals over time.

Numerous empirical studies have contributed to our understanding of the elasticity of demand for gasoline; see, e.g., Baltagi and Griffin (1997), Brons et al. (2008), Espey (1998), Kayser (2000), Nicol (2003), Puller and Greening

P.T. Ng (✉)
Frake College of Business, Northern Arizona University, Flagstaff, AZ 86011-5066, USA
e-mail: pin.ng@nau.edu

J.L. Smith
Cox School of Business, Southern Methodist University, Dallas, TX 75275, USA
e-mail: jsmith@mail.cox.smu.edu

J. Beran et al. (eds.), *Empirical Economic and Financial Research*,
Advanced Studies in Theoretical and Applied Econometrics 48,
DOI 10.1007/978-3-319-03122-4_11

(1999), Schmalensee and Stoker (1999), and Wadud et al. (2010). Dahl and Thomas (1991)'s very useful survey of previous research encompasses an almost bewildering variety of models, but finds a certain general consistency of results. They show, for example, that when appropriate allowances are made for differences in the treatment of dynamic adjustment processes and the effect of intervening variables, the preponderance of evidence suggests that gasoline demand is slightly inelastic with respect to price (the long-run elasticity being in the neighborhood of –0.9), but elastic with respect to income (approximately 1.2 in the long-run).

Although this body of previous research may suggest plausible consensus values that reflect the tendencies of representative consumers, the evidence is less conclusive on the question of whether it is appropriate to regard demand elasticities as being constant across groups of consumers who face different price and income levels. A study by McRae (1994), for example, shows that the demand for gasoline in the developing countries of Southeast Asia is somewhat less price elastic, but more income elastic, than that in the industrialized countries of the OECD. If this difference is due to variation in income levels between the two groups, we would then expect the rapid rate of increase in gasoline consumption that has been observed in the Asian countries to moderate as their incomes continue to rise. Wadud et al. (2010) also find substantial heterogeneity in price and income elasticities based on demographic characteristics and income groupings. A more precise forecast, however, would require further knowledge of how elasticities vary with respect to price and income levels.

Most studies of gasoline consumption rely on models of the form:

$$Q = g(P, Y, Z) + \epsilon \tag{1}$$

which specifies the quantity of gasoline demanded Q as some unknown parametric function $g(\cdot)$ of the price of gasoline P, disposable income Y, and a vector of other explanatory variables Z, e.g., demographic characteristics, plus the disturbance term ϵ which captures the unexplained portion of demand. Economic theory provides information on the signs of partial derivatives of g, but not its functional form nor the specific nature of ϵ. Almost all analyses of gasoline demand to date, however, utilize some form of parametric specification on g (most notably linear, log-linear, or translog) and assume the distribution of ϵ to be normal with zero mean and fixed variance. The demand function g is then estimated by the conditional mean of Q using least-squares regression.

Although easy to apply, this method is not well suited for studying the potential variation in the elasticity of demand. The problem, of course, is that each functional specification "sees" a different pattern of variation in elasticities and imposes rigid constraints on what can be deduced from a given set of data. Reliance on the linear form forces estimated elasticities to vary hyperbolically, regardless of what the data might look like. Reliance on the log-linear form, on the other hand, is tantamount to assuming that elasticities are constant.

In this paper, we utilize a semi-parametric extension of the quantile regression technique of He and Ng (1999), He et al. (1998), and Koenker et al. (1994) to study gasoline demand in the USA. This approach, which is based on tensor product polynomial splines, protects against misspecification in the demand functional form and achieves robustness against departures of the disturbance term from normality. Because we do not impose any predetermined structure on the demand function, the resulting estimates of demand elasticities, and their variation across price and income levels, reflect patterns of consumer choice that are inherent in the underlying data. We also develop and report confidence intervals that reflect the degree of uncertainty that is associated with the estimates that result from this semi-parametric procedure.

One of the earlier studies that attempt a non-parametric specification of the gasoline demand function is Goel and Morey (1993). They estimate the conditional *mean* using a kernel estimator and report considerable variation in the price elasticity of U.S. demand across the range of gasoline prices observed before and after the 1973 Arab oil embargo. However, they attribute all fluctuations in demand to variations in gasoline prices and ignore the influence of income and other variables. Therefore, the price elasticities which they report, which are sometimes *positive*, are probably contaminated by the confounding effects of omitted variables. Hausman and Newey (1995) also discuss a kernel estimator of the gasoline demand function, but since they do not report on elasticities, we cannot compare our results to theirs. Schmalensee and Stoker (1999) also specify the functional form of the income component non-parametrically in their semi-parametric model and find no evidence that income elasticity falls at high income levels. Similar to Goel and Morey (1993), Schmalensee and Stoker (1999)'s conclusions are also drawn from estimation of the conditional *mean* functions instead of the robust conditional *median* that we use in this paper.

2 Theory and Data

Economic theory suggests a negative relationship between prices and quantity consumed. In addition, there is a positive income effect on consumption, at least if gasoline is a normal good. For the cross-sectional time-series data we use in this study, variations in population density across states also play an important role in determining consumption. For sparsely populated states like Montana, Nevada, New Mexico, and Wyoming, where alternative forms of public transportation are not readily available, people rely heavily on the automobile as a means of transportation. The lack of close substitutes for automobile transportation suggests a relatively inelastic demand function.

The raw data spans from 1952 to 1978 for 48 states. Alaska and Hawaii are dropped from the sample due to lack of data on gasoline prices. After 1978, gasoline was reclassified into regular, leaded, and unleaded grades, as well as full-service and self-service. Our sample, therefore, ends in 1978 to avoid inconsistent calibration in the data set. The gasoline prices and consumption used in this study are essentially those of Goel and Morey (1993). Quantity demanded is measured by gasoline consumption subject to taxation, as compiled by the *Federal Highway Administration*. Prices are the average service station gasoline prices within each state, as reported by *Platt's Oil Price Handbook and Oilmanac*. Annual per-capita personal income is taken from the *Survey of Current Business*. Population density is computed from state population divided by geographic areas, using figures from the *Statistical Abstract of the United States*. The price deflator is the consumer price index (1967 dollars) also from the *Statistical Abstract of the United States*.

Figure 1 presents scatter plots of annual gasoline consumption per capita in gallons (Q), prices per gallon in 1967 dollars (P), annual incomes per capita in 1967 dollars (Y), and population densities in 1,000 persons per square mile (D). To ameliorate the nonlinearity of the data, we show a second set of scatter plots in Fig. 2 with all variables measured in logarithmic form. In both figures, there appears to be a negative relationship between quantity and prices, a positive income effect, and a negative relationship between quantity and population density. There also seems to be a strong interaction between prices and income. The states with extremely sparse population (less than 50 persons per square mile) and high gasoline consumption (more than 750 gallons per person) are Montana, Nevada, New Mexico, and Wyoming. In these states few means of alternative transportation are readily available. The scatter plot between Q and its one period lag Q_{-1} also suggests a significant inertia in gasoline consumption adjustment.

To illustrate the effect of per-capita income and population density on the demand curve, we present a series of conditional scatter plots of consumption per capita on prices over various intervals of income and density in Fig. 3. The conditional plots allow us to see how quantity depends on prices given relatively constant values of the other variables (income and density). The different income ranges are given in the top panel while the given density levels are in the right panel in the figure. As we move from left to right, across a single row, income increases. Population densities rise as we move from the bottom to the top of each column. Also superimposed in the conditional scatter plots are cubic *basis spline* (B-spline) fits to the data in each panel; see de Boor (1978) or Schumaker (1981) for definition and construction of B-spline. Figure 3 gives us a rough idea of how the demand curve looks over different income and population density regions. The conditional plots seem to suggest that both very low and very high income states have relatively price inelastic demand functions while the middle income and the moderately populated states have more elastic demand functions. Moving left to right horizontally across each row shows the positive income effect on consumption. Moving from bottom to top also reveals the negative population density effect on consumption. The highly populated states seem to have lower gasoline consumption per capita holding all else constant. We should, of course, emphasize that the conditional plots in Fig. 3 only provide a very crude and tentative picture of the demand surface behavior.

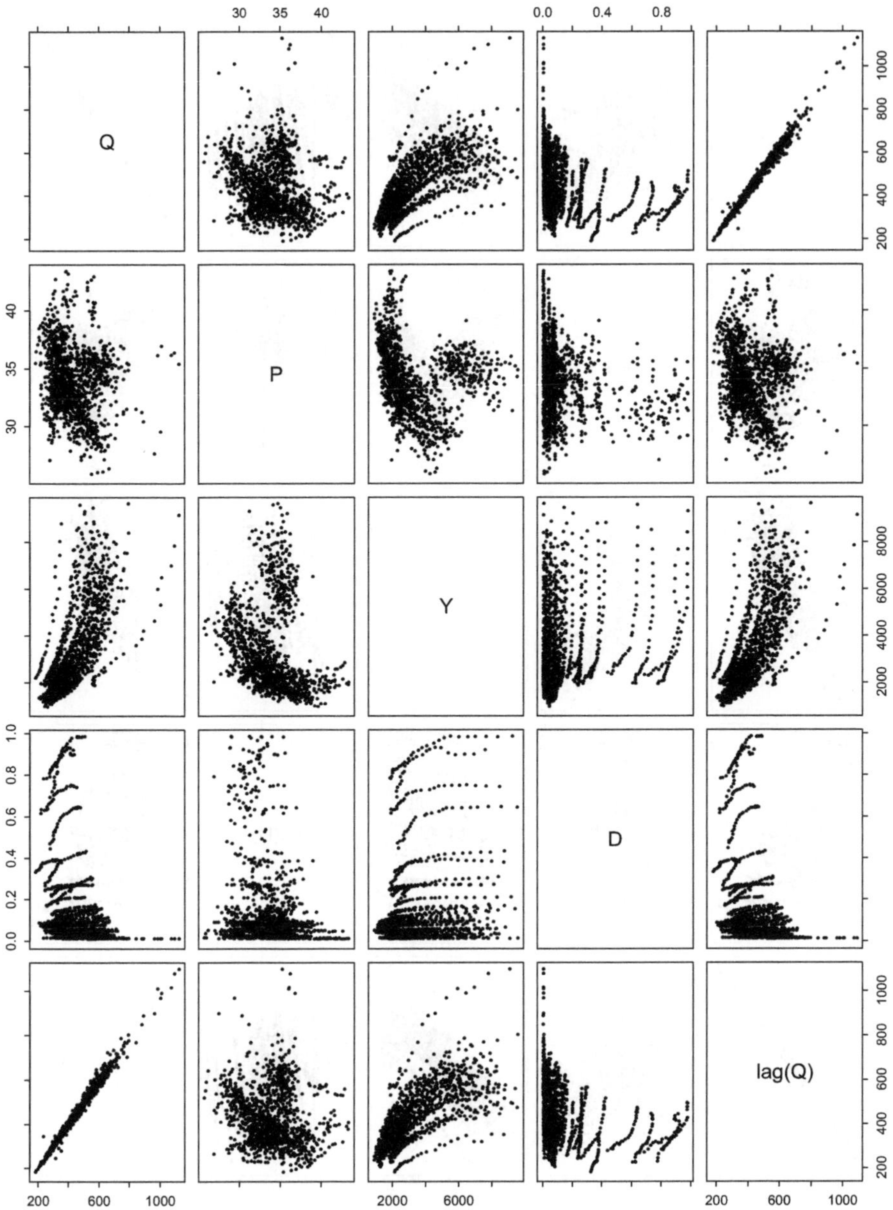

Fig. 1 Scatter plots of raw data

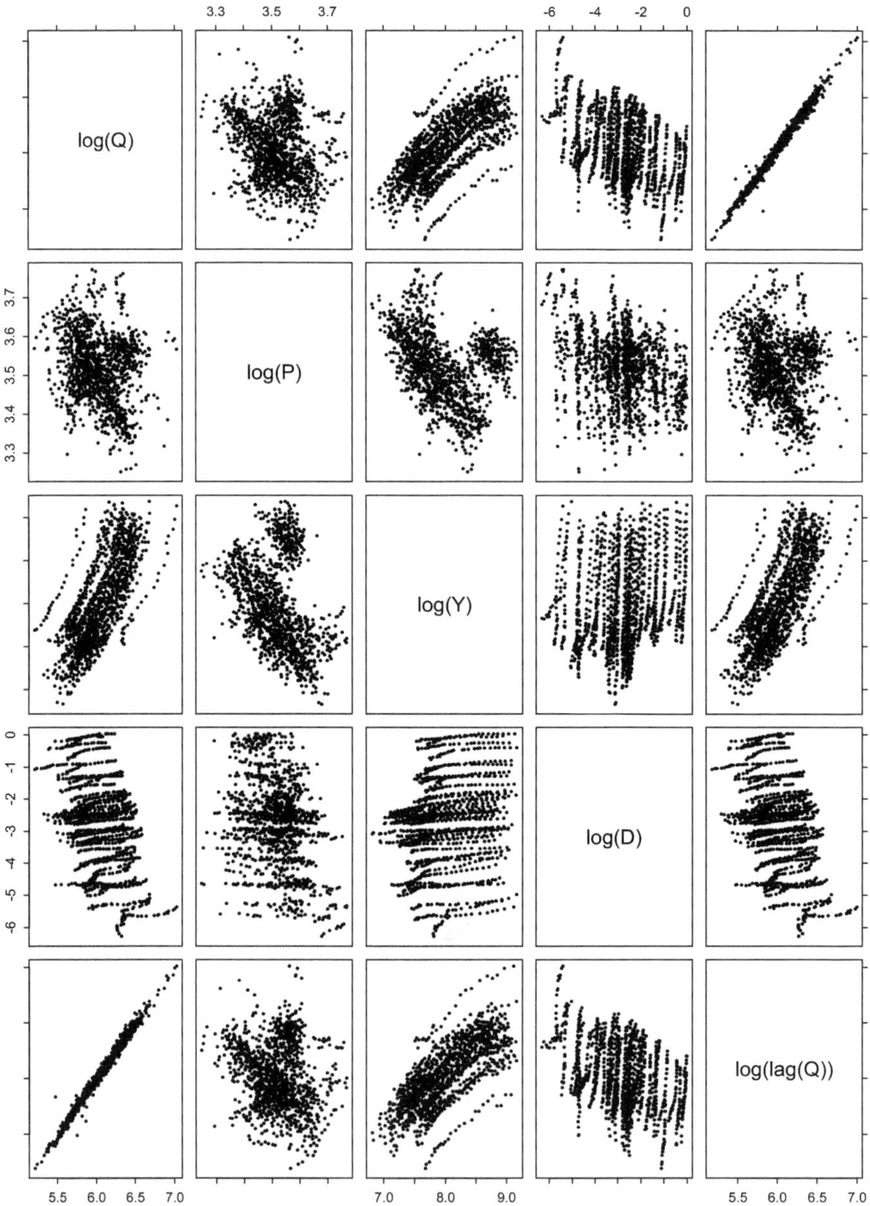

Fig. 2 Scatter plots of logarithmic transformed raw data

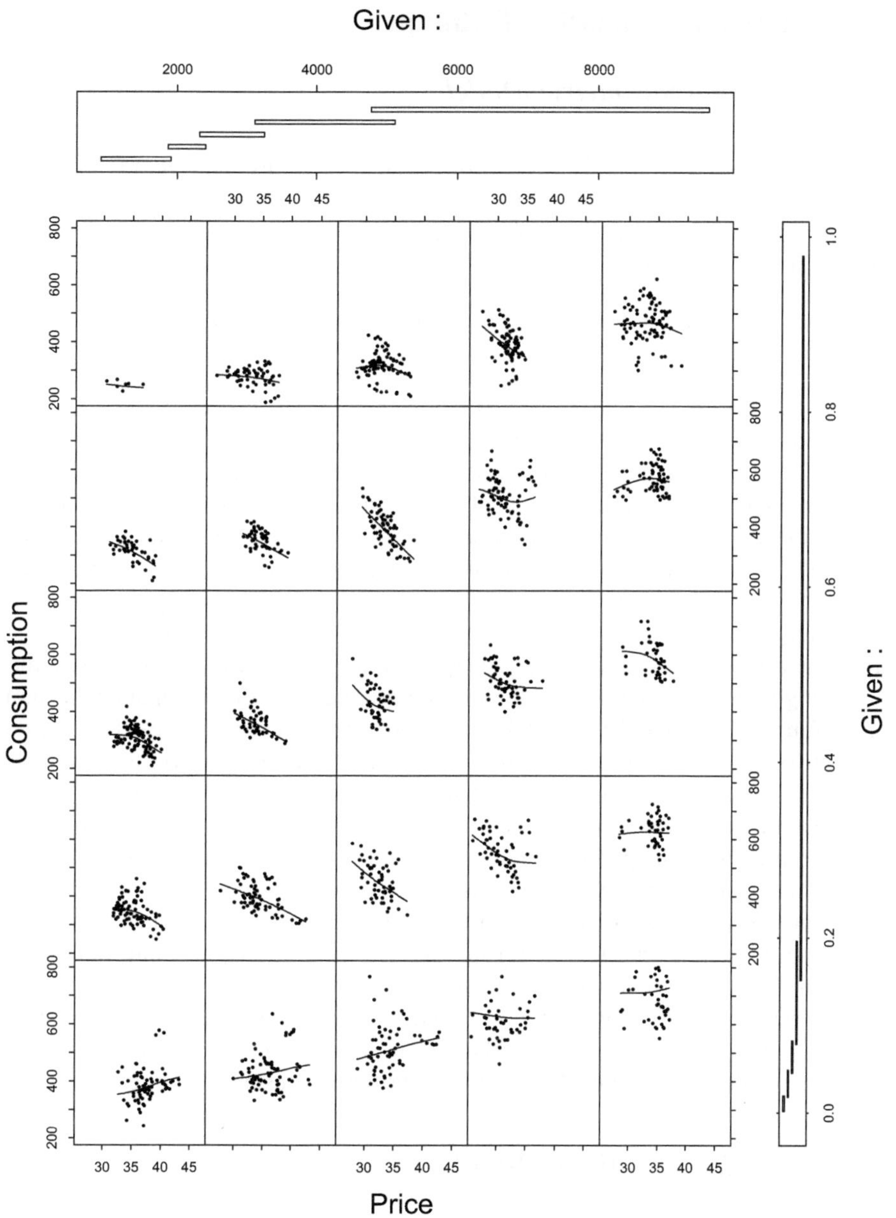

Fig. 3 Conditional plots

3 Models and Estimation Techniques

3.1 *The Semi-parametric Model*

As we have seen in Fig. 2, logarithmic transformations manage to remove a considerable amount of nonlinearity from the data. Using lowercase to denote logarithmically transformed variables, we adopt the following semi-parametric form of the demand equation:

$$q_i = \delta + g_{12}(p_i, y_i) + g_3(d_i) + \alpha q_{-1,i} + \epsilon_i \tag{2}$$

for $i = 1, \cdots, N$, where g_3 is a univariate continuous function, g_{12} is a bi-variate smooth function, α is a scalar, and δ is the intercept term. The fact that g_3 and g_{12} are not confined to any specific parametric family provides flexibility to the model while the linear lag consumption component facilitates the traditional adaptive expectation dynamic analysis. The analysis of variance (ANOVA) decomposition in (2) has the virtue of separating the contributions of the covariates into main effects captured by the univariate functions and joint effect represented by the bi-variate function; see He and Ng (1999). It also provides a parsimonious representation of a potentially much more complex functional. Stone (1994) provides a theoretical justification for the use of ANOVA-type decomposition in multivariate function estimation using polynomial splines and their tensor products. We do not separate the main effect functions g_1 and g_2 for p and y from the joint-effect function g_{12} because the estimate of g_{12}, a tensor product bi-linear B-spline, spans the spaces of the univariate B-spline estimates $\hat{g}_1$ and $\hat{g}_2$; see He et al. (1998). Including these main effect functions would introduce perfect multicollinearity and pose an identification problem during estimation. The population density d does not enter in interaction form because both economic theory and the data in Fig. 1 seem to suggest that no interaction with other explanatory variables is warranted. Our parametric model chosen by the Akaike information criterion (AIC) in Sect. 3.5 does not suggest any interaction between d and other explanatory variables either. We also estimated a fully nonparametric version of (2) with $\alpha\, q_{-1,i}$ replaced by a univariate continuous function $g_4(q_{-1,i})$. The result is identical to that of the semi-parametric specification. This supports our decision to model the lag of logarithmic consumption linearly.

3.2 *Quantile Smoothing B-Splines*

The demand equation (2) is estimated by solving the following optimization problem:

$$\min_{(\delta,\alpha)\in R^2; g_3, g_{12}\in\mathcal{G}} \sum_{i=1}^{N} \rho_\tau\left(q_i - \delta - g_{12}(p_i, y_i) - g_3(d_i) - \alpha q_{-1,i}\right)$$
$$+\lambda\left\{V_{12}\left(\tfrac{\partial g_{12}}{\partial p}\right) + V_{21}\left(\tfrac{\partial g_{12}}{\partial y}\right) + V_3\left(g_3'\right)\right\} \tag{3}$$

where $\mathcal{G}$ is some properly chosen functional space, $\tau \in [0, 1]$ specifies the desired conditional quantile, $\rho_\tau(u) = u(\tau - I(u < 0))$ is the check function which assigns a weight of τ to positive u and $\tau - 1$ otherwise, $\lambda \in (0, \infty)$ is the smoothing parameter, and V_3, V_{12}, and V_{21} are measures of roughness defined in He et al. (1998) and Koenker et al. (1994). For a given τ and λ, the estimated τth conditional quantile consumption function is

$$\hat{q}_{\tau,i} = \hat{\delta}_\tau + \hat{g}_{12_{\tau,\lambda}}(p_i, y_i) + \hat{g}_{3_{\tau,\lambda}}(d_i) + \hat{\alpha} q_{-1,i}$$

The special case of $\tau = 0.5$ yields the estimated conditional median consumption function. The portion in (3) associated with the check function controls the fidelity of the solution to the data.

For an appropriately chosen $\mathcal{G}$, Koenker et al. (1994) show that, in the special case where there is only one covariate, the solution, which they call the τth quantile smoothing spline, is a linear smoothing spline, i.e. continuous piecewise linear function with potential breaks in the derivatives occurring at the knots of the mesh. With the linear smoothing spline characterization, the objective function (3) can be written in the form similar to that of the linear regression quantile in Koenker and Bassett (1978). This facilitates computation of the τth conditional quantile via modified versions of some familiar linear programs; see Koenker and Ng (1992) for a simplex algorithm, and Koenker and Ng (2005) for a Frisch-Newton algorithm. Convergence rates of the quantile smoothing splines are given in He and Shi (1994), Portnoy (1997), and Shen and Wong (1994).

Even though computation of the quantile smoothing splines is feasible with an efficient linear program, it is still quite formidable for even a moderately large data set. In this paper, we suggest a B-spline approximation to the solution which utilizes a much smaller number of uniform knots in each mesh, hence saving tremendous memory and computing cycles as suggested in He and Ng (1999).

The fact that the solution is computed via a linear program leads to a very useful by-product—the entire family of unique conditional quantile estimates corresponding to the whole spectrum of τ can be computed efficiently by parametric programming; see Koenker et al. (1994) for details. The same is true for the whole path of λ. This property will be exploited later in determining the optimal smoothing parameter and constructing the confidence interval of the conditional median estimate.

3.3 *Choice of the Smoothing Parameter*

The smoothing parameter λ in (3) balances the trade-off between fidelity and roughness of the objective function. Its choice dictates the smoothness of the estimated conditional quantile. As $\lambda \to \infty$, the paramount objective is to minimize the roughness of the fit and the solution becomes the linear regression quantile of Koenker and Bassett (1978). On the other hand, when $\lambda \to 0$, we have a linear spline which interpolates every single q_i. We could, of course, assign different smoothing parameters to V_3, V_{12}, and V_{21} to produce different degrees of roughness along the direction of the separate covariates. Doing so, however, would complicate the choice of the correct smoothing parameters. In the single covariate problem, Koenker et al. (1994) suggest using a modified version of Schwarz (1978)'s information criterion (*SIC*) for choosing λ. The procedure is computationally feasible due to the univariate parametric programming nature of the problem in (3). Introducing more than one λ would require higher dimensional parametric programming.

The single smoothing parameter in the conditional median is chosen to minimize

$$SIC(\lambda) = \log\left(\frac{1}{N}\sum_{i=1}^{N}\left|q_i - \hat{\delta}_\tau - \hat{g}_{12_{\tau,\lambda}}(p_i, y_i) - \hat{g}_{3_{\tau,\lambda}}(d_i) - \hat{\alpha}_\tau q_{-1,i}\right|\right) + \frac{k(\lambda)}{2N}\log(N) \quad (4)$$

where k, which is inversely proportional to λ, is the effective dimensionality of the solution defined in Koenker et al. (1994).[1] The fidelity part of (4) can be interpreted as the log-likelihood function of the Laplace density. The second portion is the conventional dimension penalty for over-fitting a model.

The piecewise linear nature of the spline solution is particularly convenient for elasticity analysis. If the demand function is in fact log-linear, the optimal choice of λ will be very large and the demand function will be that characterized by the conventional log-linear model. If the demand function is only piecewise linear, the chosen λ will be relatively small and our quantile smoothing spline will produce a piecewise linear structure.

3.4 Confidence Set

Zhou and Portnoy (1996) suggests a *direct method* to construct confidence sets in the linear regression model

$$y_i = x_i'\beta + \epsilon_i \quad (5)$$

The $100(1-2\alpha)\%$ point-wise confidence interval for the τth conditional quantile at x' is given by

$$I_n = \left[x'\hat{\beta}_{\tau-b_n}, x'\hat{\beta}_{\tau+b_n}\right]$$

[1]The effective dimension of the estimated conditional median function is the number of interpolated q_i. Its value varies between N and the number of explanatory variables in (3) plus one (for the intercept). We can treat k as the equivalent number of independent variables needed in a fully parametric model to reproduce the semi-parametric estimated conditional median. When $k = N$, there is no degree of freedom and the estimated conditional median function passes through every response observation.

where $b_n = z_\alpha \sqrt{x' Q^{-1} x \tau (1-\tau)}$, $Q = \sum_{i=1}^{n} x_i x_i'$, z_a is the $(1-\alpha)$ quantile of the standard normal distribution, and $\hat{\beta}_{\tau - b_n}$ and $\hat{\beta}_{\tau + b_n}$ are the $(\tau - b_n)$th and $(\tau + b_n)$th regression quantiles of the linear regression model, respectively. Utilizing the compact formulation of the pseudodesign matrix $\tilde{X}$ in Eq. (13) of Appendix A in He et al. (1998), we can adapt the direct method to compute the confidence sets of our estimated quantiles by treating the upper partitioned matrix B of $\tilde{X}$ as the design matrix of (5). The lower partitions V^y and V^x of $\tilde{X}$ determine only the smoothness of the fitted quantile function and is irrelevant once an optimal λ has been chosen.

3.5 A Parametric Conditional Mean Model

To see how much our semi-parametric conditional median estimate differs from the conventional parametric conditional mean estimation, we fit the following translog model to the same data set:

$$q_{it} = \delta + \beta_1 p_{it} + \beta_2 y_{it} + \beta_{12} p_{it} y_{it} + \beta_3 d_{it} + \beta_4 d_{it}^2 + \alpha q_{it-1} + \epsilon_{it} \tag{6}$$

The model is chosen by minimizing the AIC in a stepwise model selection procedure.

4 Estimation Results

The minimizing λ is 0.418 which occurs at an *SIC* of 0.021. The corresponding effective dimension k of the semi-parametric quantile smoothing B-splines fit is 17.

The quantile smoothing B-splines estimated α is 0.959 and hence the long-run elasticity multiplier is 24.4. As we have observed from the scatter plots in both Figs. 1 and 2, the inertia of short-run adjustment is quite high.

The dimension of the translog model (6) is 7, which is about $2/5$ of the dimension ($k = 17$) of the semi-parametric model. This suggests that the semi-parametric model prefers a more complex structure than the translog model can offer. The least squares estimate of α is 0.95 and the long-run elasticity multiplier is 20 which is only slightly smaller than the semi-parametric estimate of 24.4.

We compute the perspective plot of the estimated semi-parametric and translog demand surfaces conditioned at the median population density and lag consumption. There are altogether 25 grid points along both the price and income axes. The slightly positively sloped demand curves over the very low income region are the result of a boundary effect. There is just not enough data to make an accurate estimation near the boundary. As a result, in Figs. 4 and 5, we discard the first and last five grid points (the boundaries) and slice through the demand surface at

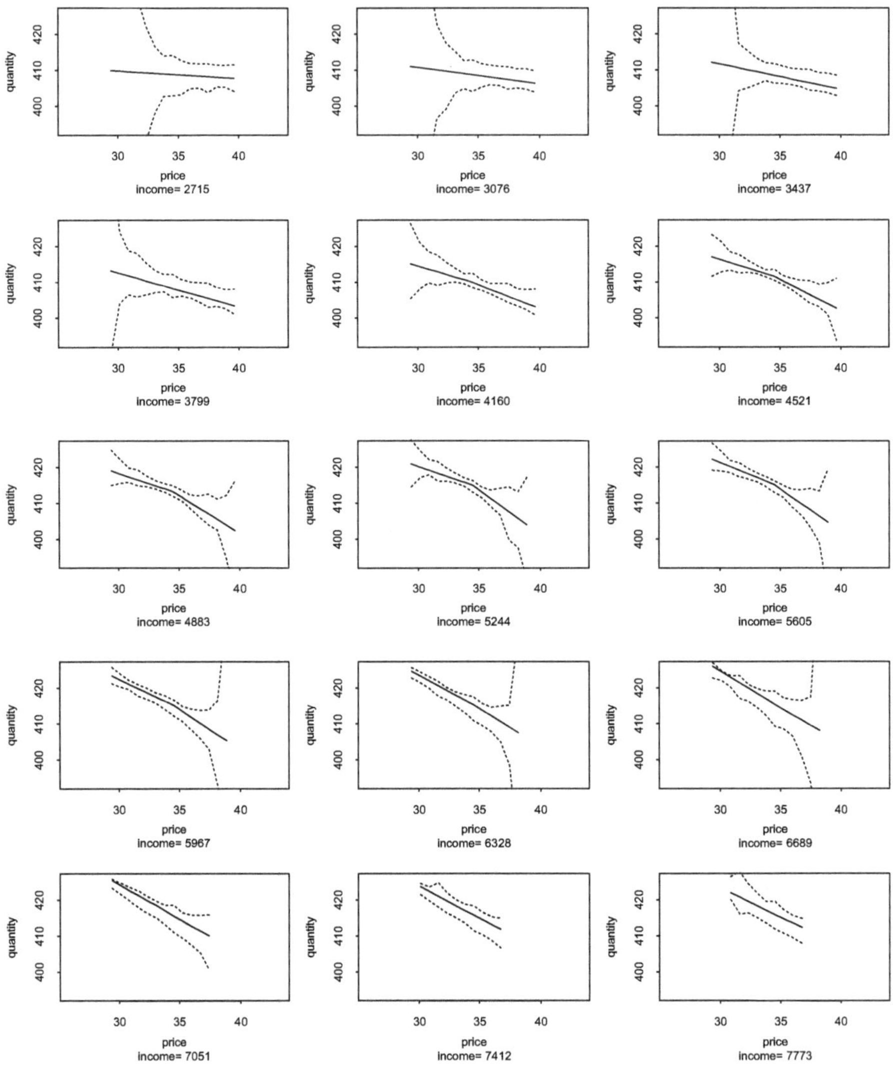

Fig. 4 Smoothing B-splines confidence intervals for the demand curves: magnitude of price effect observed at increasing income levels

the different income grid points starting at the sixth and ending at the twentieth when plotting quantity on the vertical axis and price on the horizontal axis. Also superimposed in the figures are the 95 % point-wise confidence intervals. The boundary effect along the price direction is also reflected as wider intervals near the edges in each panel. The effect is more drastic for the semi-parametric model reflecting the slower convergence rate of the nonparametric approach.

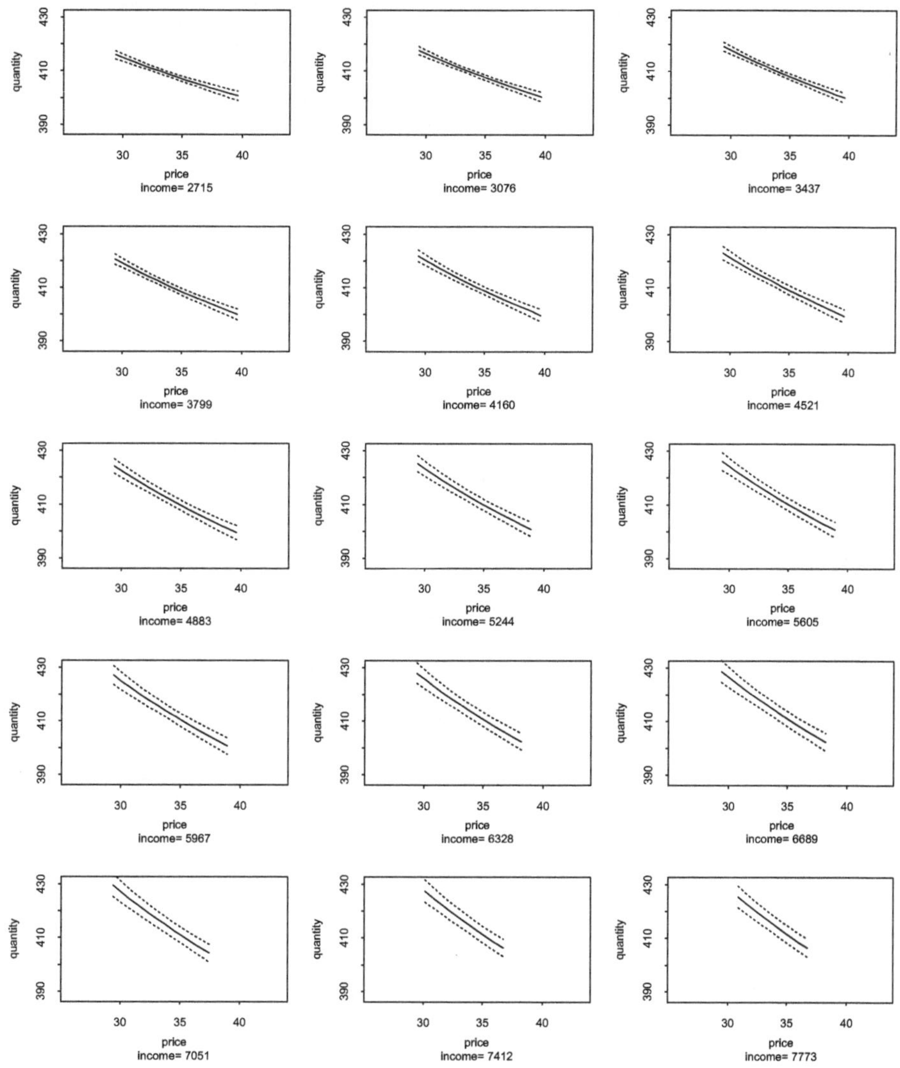

Fig. 5 Confidence intervals for the translog demand curves: magnitude of price effect observed at increasing income levels

Figure 4 depicts the phenomenon we observed in the conditional plots in Fig. 3. The price elasticity seems to be lower (in magnitude) when income is lower. As income increases, demand generally becomes more price sensitive. This confirms for U.S. consumers the type of income effect that McRae (1994) discovered in comparing price elasticities in industrialized and developing nations. Short-run price elasticity plots of the demand slices are shown in Fig. 6. The price elasticity functions are step functions reflecting the piecewise linear nature of our quantile

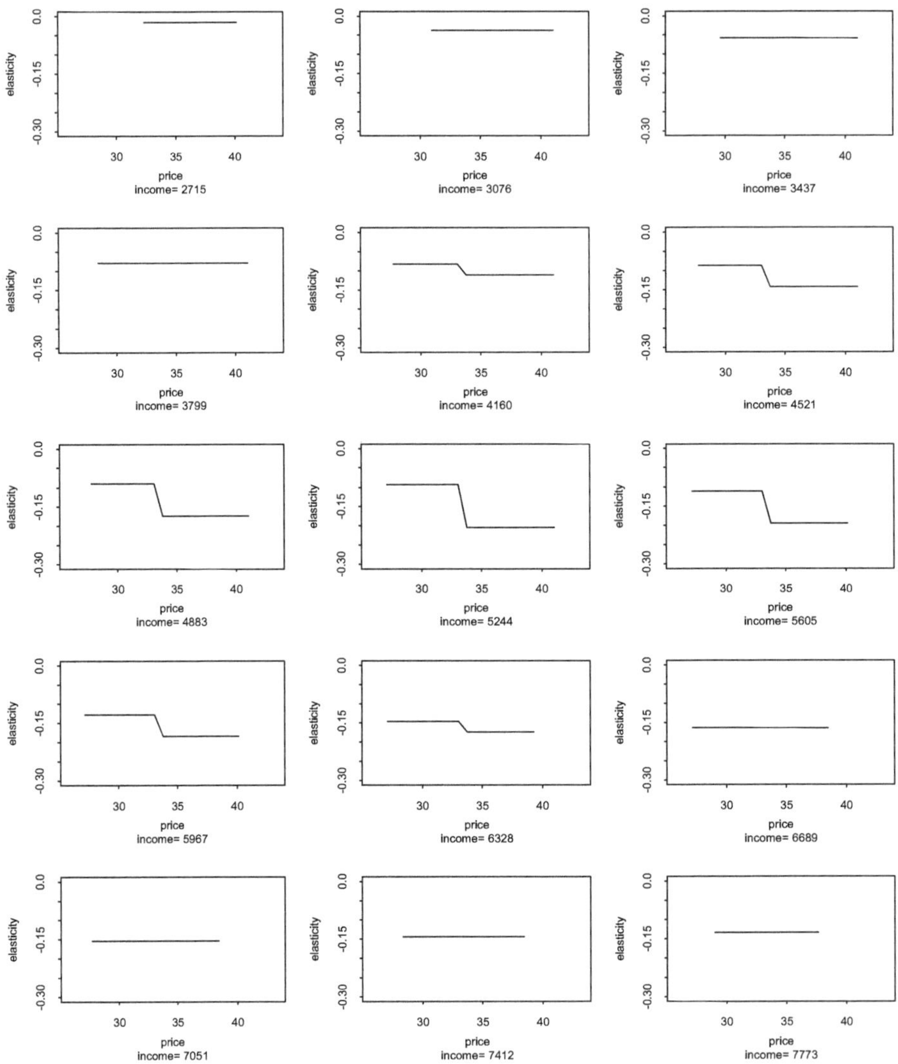

Fig. 6 Smoothing B-splines short-run price elasticity

smoothing B-splines.[2] Short-run demand also seems to be less price elastic at lower prices and to become more elastic as prices increase. The translog model produces somewhat different result, as shown in Fig. 7. As before, the price elasticity of demand appears to increase with income. However, the estimated price elasticity generally increases with price, which contradicts the semi-parametric estimates.

[2]Since we have measured all variables in logarithmic form, the slope of each log-linear segment of the demand curve corresponds to the elasticity.

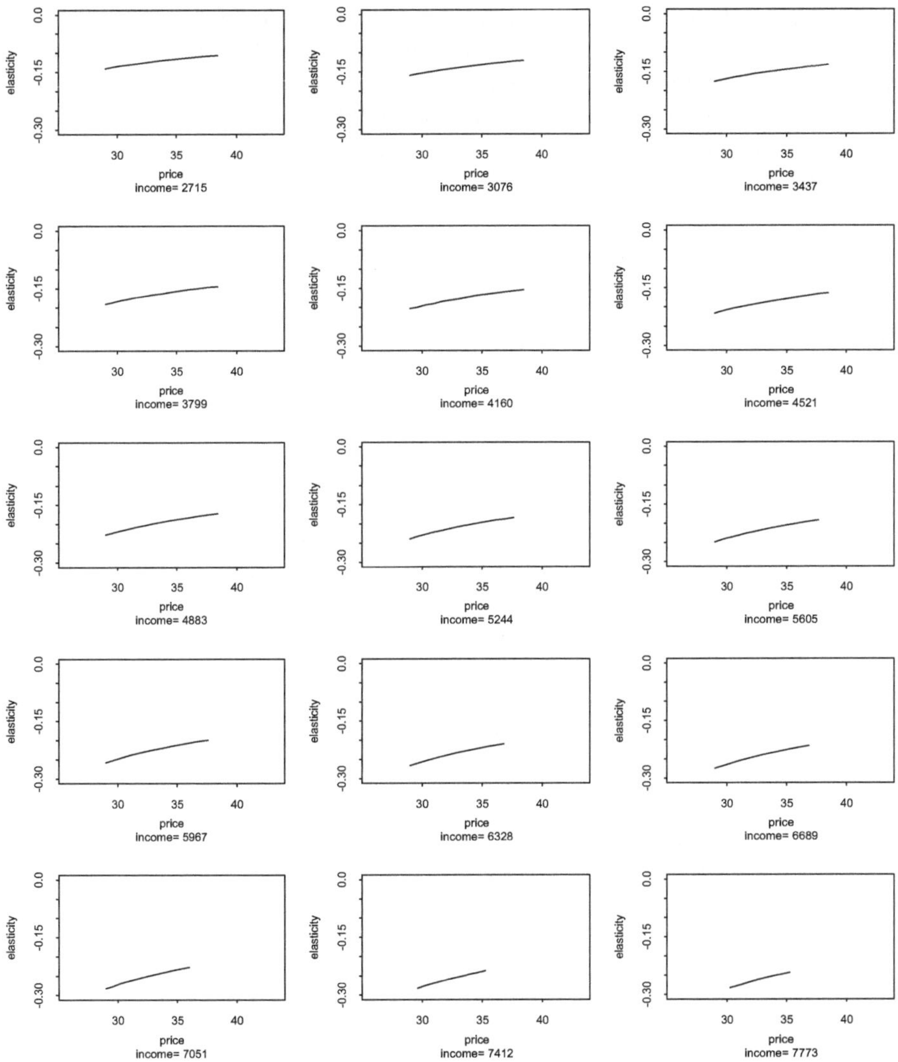

Fig. 7 Short-run price elasticity for the translog model

Our semi-parametric estimates of short-run price elasticity range (across price and income levels) from −0.205 to −0.017 with a median of −0.134. This compares to the average value of −0.24 reported by Dahl and Thomas (1991) for models that use a comparable partial adjustment mechanism. Our short-run price elasticity evaluated at the median of the data is −0.205, which is even closer to the number reported by Dahl and Thomas (1991). Our estimates of long-run price elasticity range from −5.02 to −0.415, which extends well beyond the highest long-run price elasticities reported by Dahl and Thomas (1991). Our median estimate of −3.27 is about four times the magnitude of their average long-run elasticity.

Estimates of short-run price elasticity we obtain from the parametric translog model range from −0.295 to −0.045 with a median of −0.189. The elasticity at the median of the data is −0.206. In general, gasoline demand appears slightly more elastic when fitted to the translog model instead of the semi-parametric model.

A generally positive effect of income on consumption is also apparent in Figs. 8 and 9, in which we slice through the demand surface at fixed price levels to illustrate the Engel curves, and again superimpose the 95 % confidence intervals in the plots.

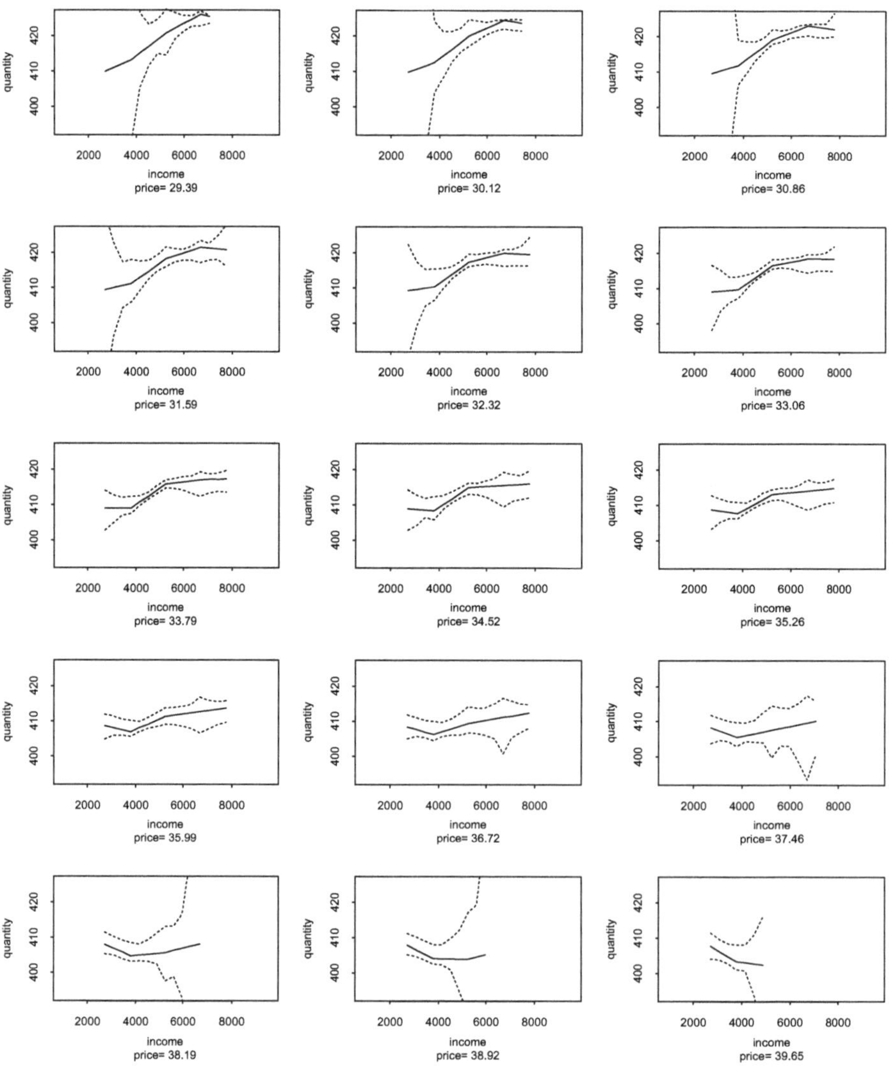

Fig. 8 Smoothing B-splines confidence interval for the demand curves: magnitude of income effect observed at increasing price levels

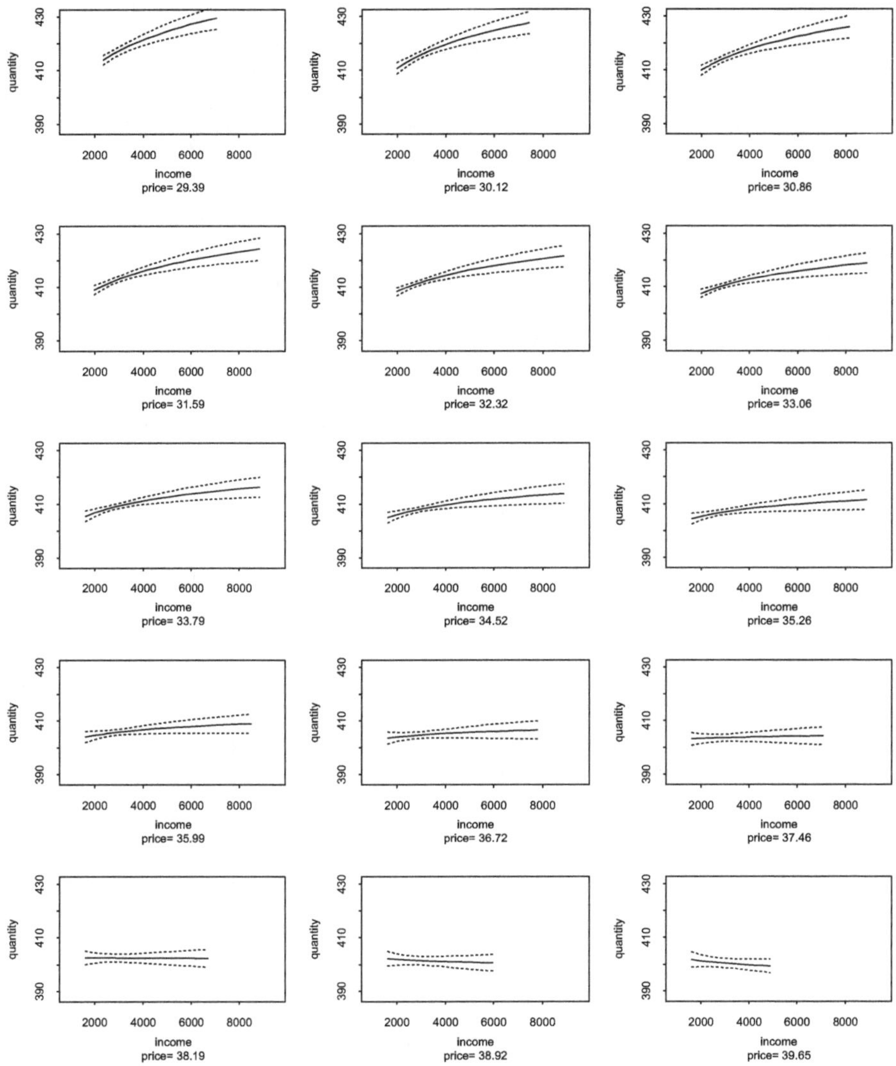

Fig. 9 Confidence interval for the translog demand curves: magnitude of income effect observed at increasing price levels

The slight negative income effects evident at extremely high price levels are artifacts of the data that cannot be taken too seriously in view of the very wide confidence intervals that are found at the boundaries of the data set. The quantile smoothing B-splines estimates of short-run income elasticity corresponding to each panel in Fig. 8 are presented in Fig. 10 while estimates derived from the translog model are shown in Fig. 11. Apart from the boundary effects noted above, short-run income elasticities seem to fall as income rises. This finding is also consistent with McRae

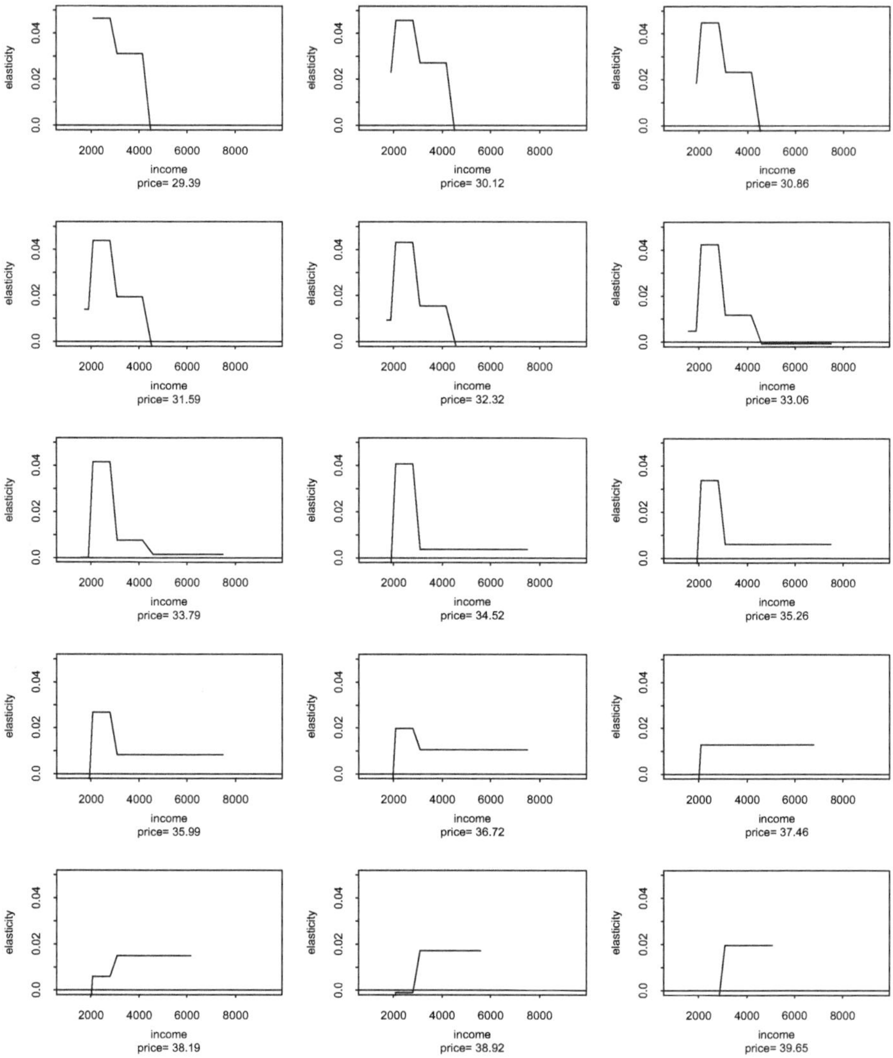

Fig. 10 Smoothing B-splines short-run income elasticity

(1994)'s conclusion that income elasticities are generally lower in the relatively prosperous industrialized countries than in the developing countries of South East Asia.

Discarding the negative values near the boundary, our semi-parametric estimates of short-run income elasticity fall between 0 and 0.048, with a median value of 0.008. The short-run income elasticity evaluated at the median of the data is 0.042 which is substantially lower than the average short-run income elasticity of 0.45 reported by Dahl and Thomas (1991). Our estimates of long-run income elasticity

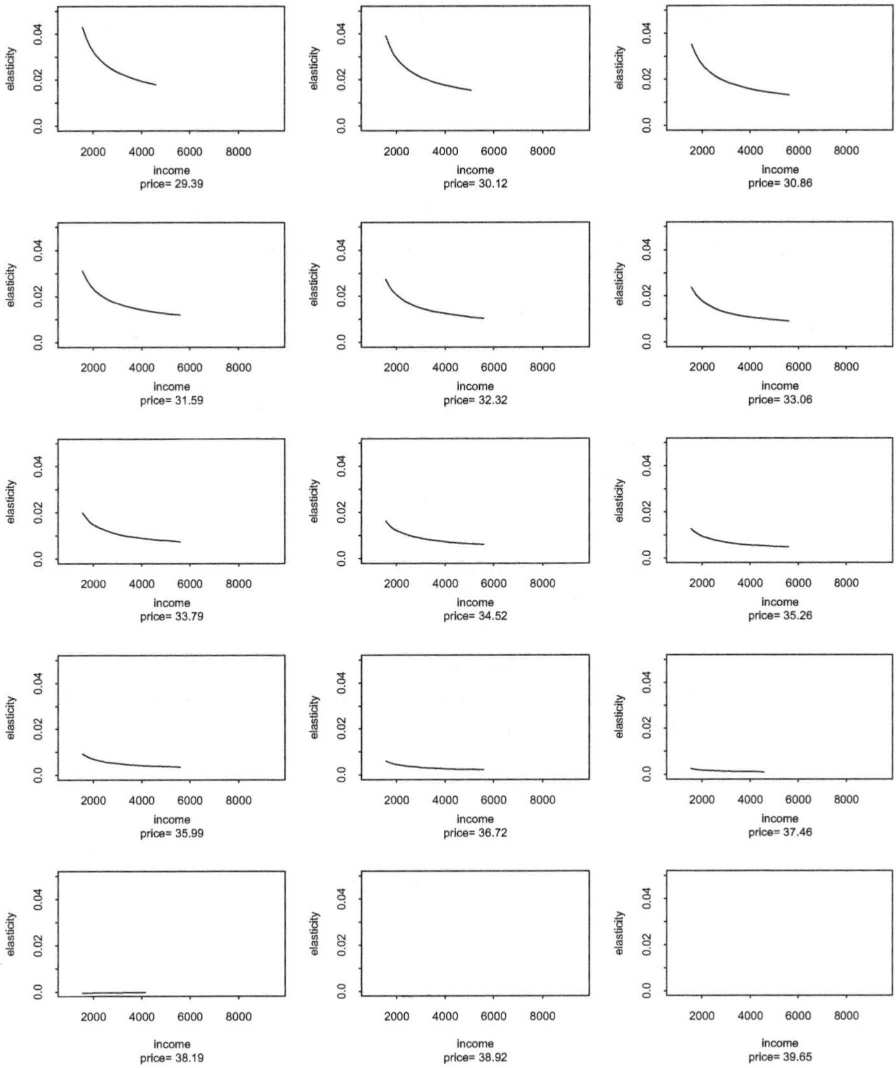

Fig. 11 Short-run income elasticity for the translog model

range from 0 to 1.17, with a median value of 0.195. Our long-run income elasticity of 1.03 evaluated at the median of the data is fairly close to the average long-run elasticity of 1.31 which Dahl and Thomas (1991) reports.

The estimates of short-run income elasticity we derive from the translog model range between 0 and 0.06 with a median of 0.01. These values are quite close to our semi-parametric estimates. They also confirm again the general tendency of income elasticities to decline as incomes rise. At the median of the data, the short-run income elasticity is 0.012, which is only 1/4 of that of the semi-parametric model.

Conclusion

We have applied a new, semi-parametric estimator to test the hypothesis that the elasticity of gasoline demand varies systematically across price and income levels. The approach we take uses the conditional median to produce a robust alternative to conventional parametric models that rely on the conditional mean. Our results tend to confirm, with different data and methods, both of McRae (1994)'s suggestions: gasoline demand appears to become more price elastic, but also less income elastic, as incomes rise. In addition, we find that demand appears to become more price elastic as prices increase in real terms.

In comparison with previous parametric estimates of gasoline demand, our results tend to indicate that long-run adjustments are quite large relative to short-run effects. Regarding the effect of prices on demand, our short-run estimates are generally consistent with the consensus of previous short-run elasticities. Regarding the income effect, however, our long-run estimates tend to be much more consistent with the results of previous studies than are our short-run estimates. Further empirical research would be useful in helping to clarify what appears to be an important difference in the nature of dynamic adjustments to income versus price changes.

Acknowledgements We thank Steve Craig for sharing his data on population and income, which was incorporated into the data set used in this study. We are also very grateful to Rajeev Goel for sending us his gasoline and consumption data. Any remaining errors in the data are, of course, our own responsibility.

References

Baltagi, B. H., & James, M. G. (1997). Pooled estimators vs. their heterogeneous counterparts in the context of dynamic demand for gasoline. *Journal of Econometrics, 77*, 303–327.

Brons, M., Nijkampa, P., Pelsa, E., & Rietveld, P. (2008). A meta-analysis of the price elasticity of gasoline demand. A SUR approach. *Energy Economics, 30*(5), 2105–2122.

Dahl, C., & Sterner, T. (1991). Analysing gasoline demand elasticities: A survey. *Energy Economics, 13*(3), 203–210.

de Boor, C. (1978). *A practical guide to splines*. New York: Springer.

Espey, M. (1998). Gasoline demand revisited: An international meta-analysis of elasticities. *Energy Economics, 20*(3), 273–295.

Goel, R. K., & Morey, M. J. (1993). Effect of the 1973 oil price embargo: A non-parametric analysis. *Energy Economics, 15*(1), 39–48.

Hausman, J. A., & Newey, W. K. (1995). Nonparametric estimation of exact consumers surplus and deadweight loss. *Econometrica, 63*(6), 1445–1476.

He, X., & Ng, P. T. (1999). Quantile splines with several covariates. *Journal of Statistical Planning and Inference, 75*, 343–352.

He, X., Ng, P. T., & Portnoy, S. (1998). Bivariate quantile smoothing splines. *Journal of the Royal Statistical Society(B), 60*, 537–550.

He, X., & Shi, P. (1994). Convergence rate of B-spline estimators of nonparametric conditional quantile function. *Journal of Nonparametric Statistics, 3*, 299–308.

Kayser, H. A. (2000). Gasoline demand and car choice: Estimating gasoline demand using household information. *Energy Economics, 22*, 331–348.

Koenker, R., & Bassett, G. W. (1978). Regression quantiles. *Econometrica, 46*, 33–50.

Koenker, R., & Ng, P. T. (1992). Computing quantile smoothing splines. *Computing Science and Statistics, 24*, 385–388.

Koenker, R., & Ng, P. T. (2005). Frisch-Newton algorithm for sparse quantile regression. *Acta Mathematicae Applicatae Sinica (English Series), 21*, 225–236.

Koenker, R., Ng, P., & Portnoy, S. (1994). Quantile smoothing splines. *Biometrika, 81*, 673–680.

McRae, R. (1994). Gasoline demand in developing Asian countries. *The Energy Journal, 15*, 143–155.

Nicol, C. J. (2003). Elasticities of demand for gasoline in Canada and the United States. *Energy Economics, 25*(2), 201–214.

Portnoy, S. (1997). Local asymptotics for quantile smoothing splines. *Annals of Statistics, 25*(1), 414–434.

Puller, S., & Greening, L. A. (1999). Household adjustment to gasoline price change: An analysis using 9 years of US survey data. *Energy Economics, 21*(1), 37–52.

Schmalensee, R., & Stoker, T. M. (1999). Household gasoline demand in the United States. *Econometrica, 69*(3), 645–662.

Schumaker, L. L. (1981). *Spline functions: Basic theory*. New York: Wiley.

Schwarz, G. (1978). Estimating the dimension of a model. *Annals of Statistics, 6*(2), 461–464.

Shen, X., & Wong, W. H. (1994). Convergence rate of sieve estimates. *Annals of Statistics, 22*(2), 580–615.

Stone, C. J. (1994). The use of polynomial splines and their tensor products in multivariate function estimation. *Annals of Statistics, 22*, 118–171.

Wadud, Z., Graham, D. J., & Noland, R. B. (2010). Gasoline demand with heterogeneity in household responses. *Energy Journal, 31*(1), 47–74.

Zhou, Q., & Portnoy, S. L. (1996). Direct use of regression quantiles to construct confidence sets in linear models. *Annals of Statistics, 24*(1), 287–306.

The Pitfalls of Ignoring Outliers in Instrumental Variables Estimations: An Application to the Deep Determinants of Development

Catherine Dehon, Rodolphe Desbordes, and Vincenzo Verardi

Abstract The extreme sensitivity of instrumental variables (IV) estimators to outliers is a crucial problem too often neglected or poorly dealt with. We address this issue by making the practitioner aware of the existence, usefulness, and inferential implications of robust-to-outliers instrumental variables estimators. We describe how the standard IV estimator can be made robust to outliers, provide a brief description of alternative robust IV estimators, simulate the behaviour of both the standard IV estimator and each robust IV estimator in presence of different types of outliers, and conclude by replicating a celebrated study on the deep determinants of development in order to establish the danger of ignoring outliers in an IV model.

1 Introduction

In 1977, Nobel Prize laureate George Stigler compiled a list of the most common comments heard at Economics conferences. Among them figures prominently worry about the lack of identification of the parameters. Indeed, while the applied researcher is usually interested in uncovering a causal relationship between two variables, there is no guarantee that the parameter of interest will be consistently estimated due to reverse causality, measurement error in the explanatory variable or an omitted confounding variable. For this reason, instrumental variables (IV) estimations have become a cornerstone of empirical economic research. However, despite their widespread use in empirical applications, little attention has been paid to a key condition underlying IV estimators: the absence of outliers, i.e. observations which are substantially different from the others and whose presence in the sample

C. Dehon (✉)
ECARES, Université libre de Bruxelles, Brussels, Belgium
e-mail: cdehon@ulb.ac.be

R. Desbordes
University of Strathclyde, Glasgow, UK
e-mail: rodolphe.desbordes@strath.ac.uk

V. Verardi
CRED, Université de Namur, Namur, Belgium
e-mail: vverardi@fundp.ac.be

J. Beran et al. (eds.), *Empirical Economic and Financial Research*,
Advanced Studies in Theoretical and Applied Econometrics 48,
DOI 10.1007/978-3-319-03122-4_12

can strongly influence the estimates. Unfortunately, even one outlier may cause an IV estimator to be heavily biased. In the jargon of the statistics literature, the IV estimator is said to be not a robust estimator. Although it must be acknowledged that some studies report having paid attention to outliers, it is unlikely that they have successfully dealt with this issue. They used outlier diagnostics based on least squares residuals. Given that the least squares estimator is extremely non-robust to outliers, these diagnostics share the same fragility and very often fail to detect atypical observations (this effect is called the masking effect). Furthermore, their approach did not take into account the combined influence of outliers in the first and second stages of their IV estimations. Hence, to the already long list compiled by George Stigler should be added a question about the robustness of the results to the potential presence of outliers in the sample.

The purpose of this paper is to make the practitioner aware of the distorting effects that outliers can have on the standard IV estimator since the latter is shown to be very sensitive to contamination of the dependent variable, the endogenous variable(s), the exogenous variable(s) and/or the instrument(s). Consequently, we motivate the usefulness and inferential implications of robust-to-outliers instrumental variables (ROIV) estimators. We first explain how the standard IV estimator can be adapted to be robust to outliers by describing a two-stage methodology. We focus on this estimator because it is relatively simple and efficient, is strongly resistant to all types of outliers and allows access to robustified versions of the tests for the quality of the instruments. Afterwards, we offer a brief description of the other robust IV estimators suggested in the literature and we present Monte Carlo simulations, which assess the relative performance of six alternative robust IV estimators in presence of different types of outliers. The method that we propose appears to behave the best, with a low mean squared error in whatever scenario is devised. Finally, we revisit the findings of Rodrik et al. (2004) on the deep determinants of development, in order to illustrate the distorting effects of outliers in the data. We show that the specification used become under-identified once outliers are removed from the sample, as their instrument for institutional quality, "settler mortality", loses its relevance.

The remainder of the paper is organized as follows: Sect. 2 reviews the standard IV estimator. Section 3 presents the new ROIV. Section 4 describes alternative robust IV estimators and provides Monte Carlo simulations to assess the relative performance of each IV estimator in presence of various types of outliers. Section 5 replicates an early study to demonstrate that outliers are a common feature in most data and that their presence can frequently result in misleading econometric inferences. The final section concludes.

2 Classical IV Estimator

The multiple linear regression model is used to study the relationship between a dependent variable and a set of regressors using the simplest relation, the linear function. The linear regression model is given by:

$$y_i = \mathbf{x}_i^t \boldsymbol{\theta} + \varepsilon_i \qquad i = 1, \ldots, n, \tag{1}$$

where y_i is the scalar dependent variable and $\mathbf{x}_i$ is the $(p \times 1)$ vector of covariates observed.[1] Vector $\boldsymbol{\theta}$ of size $(p \times 1)$ contains the unknown regression parameters and needs to be estimated. On the basis of an estimated parameter $\hat{\boldsymbol{\theta}}$, it is then possible to fit the dependent variable by $\hat{y}_i = \mathbf{x}_i^t \hat{\boldsymbol{\theta}}$, and to estimate the residuals $r_i(\hat{\boldsymbol{\theta}}) = y_i - \hat{y}_i$ $\forall i = 1, \ldots, n$. Although $\boldsymbol{\theta}$ can be estimated in several ways, the underlying idea is always to try to get as close as possible to the true regression hyperplane by reducing the total magnitude of the residuals, as measured by an aggregate prediction error. In the case of the well-known ordinary least squares (LS) estimator, this aggregate prediction error is defined as the sum of squared residuals. The vector of parameter estimated by LS is then

$$\hat{\boldsymbol{\theta}}_{LS} = \arg\min_{\theta} \sum_{i=1}^{n} r_i^2(\boldsymbol{\theta}) \tag{2}$$

with $r_i(\boldsymbol{\theta}) = y_i - \mathbf{x}_i^t \boldsymbol{\theta}$ for $i = 1, \ldots, n$.

Using matrix notations with $\mathbf{X}$ the $(n \times p)$ matrix containing the values for the p regressors (constant included) and $\mathbf{y}$ as the $(n \times 1)$ vector containing the value of the dependent variable for all the observations, the solution of Eq. (2) leads to the well-known formula

$$\hat{\boldsymbol{\theta}}_{LS} = \left(\mathbf{X}^t\mathbf{X}\right)^{-1} \mathbf{X}^t \mathbf{y}. \tag{3}$$

However, if at least one regressor is correlated with the error term, the parameter estimated by *LS* is inconsistent. To tackle this problem the method of instrumental variables (IV) is generally used. More precisely, define $\mathbf{Z}$ as the $(n \times m)$ matrix (where $m \geq p$) containing instruments. This matrix is composed of two blocks: the included instruments (i.e. the variables in $\mathbf{X}$ that are not correlated with the error term) and the excluded instruments (i.e. variables not in $\mathbf{X}$ that are correlated with the endogenous regressors but independent of the error term). Continuous variables are in submatrix $(n \times m_1)$ $\mathbf{Z_C}$ and dummies in submatrix $(n \times m_2)$ $\mathbf{Z_D}$, with $m = m_1 + m_2$. The standard IV estimator is given by

$$\hat{\boldsymbol{\theta}}_{IV} = (\mathbf{X}^t\mathbf{Z}(\mathbf{Z}^t\mathbf{Z})^{-1}\mathbf{Z}^t\mathbf{X})^{-1}\mathbf{X}^t\mathbf{Z}(\mathbf{Z}^t\mathbf{Z})^{-1}\mathbf{Z}^t\mathbf{y}, \tag{4}$$

which can be interpreted as a two-step estimation procedure where the first step is needed to purge the endogenous regressors of their correlation with the error term before a standard linear regression is run in the second stage.

A serious drawback of this IV method is that if outliers are present in the data, all the estimated parameters are distorted, possibly causing the IV estimators to take

[1]For the sake of clarity, vectors and matrices are in bold font and scalars are in normal font.

on values arbitrarily far from the true values of the regression parameters. These outliers can be present in the dependent variable, the endogenous variable, and/or in the included and excluded instruments.

3 Robust IV Estimator

In order to deal with this issue, several robust-to-outliers estimators have been proposed. Some authors, e.g. Amemiya (1982) or Wagenvoort and Waldmann (2002) suggest using robust estimators in each step of the two-stage instrumental variables procedure. Others, such as Lee (2007) and Chernozhukov et al. (2010), adopt the same logic but employ the control function approach.[2] A third group of authors, among others Lucas et al. (1997), Ronchetti and Trojani (2001), Wagenvoort and Waldmann (2002) and Honore and Hu (2004), propose to achieve robustness by modifying the moment conditions of general method of moments (GMM) estimators. While the theory behind all these estimators is appealing, not all of them behave well in presence of all types of outliers. For example, Amemiya (1982), Lee (2007) and Chernozhukov et al. (2010) rely on quantile regressions that, though being resistant to the presence of vertical outliers (i.e. points lying far away from the regression hyperplane in the vertical dimension but having standard values in the space of the explanatory variables) behave poorly in the case of existence of bad leverage points (i.e. points associated with outlying values in the space of the explanatory variables and lying far away from the regression hyperplane). Similarly, Honore and Hu (2004) propose several GMM estimators considering moment conditions based on the median or the rank of the error term. Here again, we expect these estimators to be fairly robust against vertical outliers but not necessarily with respect to bad leverage points.

Another idea proposed by Cohen-Freue et al. (2013) is based on the robustification of the IV's closed-form formula (see Eq. (4)). Instead of using the classical covariance matrices in Eq. (4), the authors replace it by robust multivariate location and scatter S-estimator (see Maronna et al. 2006 for further details on this method)[3] that withstand the contamination of the sample by outliers. The advantage of this estimator is that it takes simultaneously into account all the possible types of outliers: outliers in the response variable, in the regressors, or in the instruments.

However, we adopt a slightly different approach here. Our approach is a two-step procedure. We first identify outlying observations simultaneously in the response, the regressors, or the instruments variables, using the Stahel (1981) and Donoho (1982) univariate projections estimator and then apply Eq. (4) on this contamination-

[2]Note that these authors were more interested in the advantages offered by quantile regressions to study the distribution of a given variable than in the resistance of a median regression-type estimator to certain types of outliers.

[3]We have implemented Cohen-Freue et al. (2013)-type RIV estimators in *Stata*, see Desbordes and Verardi (2013) for a description of the ready-to-use—-robivreg—package.

free subsample. Three main reasons motivate our strategy. First, standard tests for the strength and validity of the excluded instruments are readily available, since we end up by running a standard IV estimation on a sample free of outliers. Second, a substantial gain in efficiency with respect to the robust IV estimator proposed by Cohen-Freue et al. (2013) can be attained. Third, the Stahel and Donoho estimator can easily be adapted to cope with the presence of dummies in the data, in contrast to the sub-sampling algorithms used to compute S-estimates that can easily fail if various dummies are among the regressors, due to perfect collinearity within subsamples. Welsh and Ronchetti (2002) point out that the "cleaning process" which takes place in the first step could lead to an underestimation of the standard errors of the final stage. However, in the simulation section, we show that this effect is negligible.

The logic of the Stahel and Donoho estimator is that a multivariate outlier must also be a univariate outlier in some one-dimensional projection of the data. Hence, the data cloud is projected in all possible directions and the degree of outlyingness of each point is measured as its maximal univariate robust standardised distance from the centre of a given projection. For example, the data for each projection can be centred around the median and standardised by the median absolute deviation. As hinted above, special attention needs to be paid to dummies. Maronna and Yohai (2000) highlight that if the size of one (or several) of the groups identified by a dummy is much smaller than the others, all of the points belonging to this group might be considered as outliers when dummies are neglected from the outlier identification step on the grounds that they do not generate themselves outlyingness. Following the logic of these authors, for each projection, we partial out the effect of dummies on the basis of a regression M-estimator. The M-estimator of regression is a generalisation of the least squares estimator. When another function $\rho(\cdot)$ of the residuals is minimised instead of the square function, this results in M-estimators of regression, which have been introduced by Huber (1964). Function $\rho(\cdot)$ must be even, non-decreasing for positive values and less increasing than the square function. The vector of parameters estimated by an M-estimator is then

$$\hat{\boldsymbol{\theta}}_M = \arg\min_{\theta} \sum_{i=1}^{n} \rho(\frac{r_i(\boldsymbol{\theta})}{\hat{\sigma^M}}) \tag{5}$$

where $\hat{\sigma^M}$ is robustly estimated beforehand and is needed to guarantee scale equivariance. M-estimators are called monotonic if $\rho(\cdot)$ is convex over the entire domain and redescending if $\rho(\cdot)$ is bounded.

Defining $\mathbf{X}_C$ the $(n \times p_1)$ submatrix of $\mathbf{X}$ containing only continuous variables, $\mathbf{X}_D$ the $(n \times p_2)$ submatrix of $\mathbf{X}$ containing only dummy variables (with $p = p_1 + p_2$), $\mathbf{Z}_C^E$ the $(n \times m_3)$ submatrix of $\mathbf{Z}_C$ containing only excluded continuous instruments and $\mathbf{Z}_D^E$ the $(n \times m_4)$ submatrix of $\mathbf{Z}_D$ containing only excluded dummy instruments, the matrix $\mathbf{M} = (\mathbf{y}, \mathbf{X}_C, \mathbf{Z}_\mathbf{C}^\mathbf{E})$ of dimension $n \times q$ (where $q = 1 + p_1 + m_3$) is projected in "all" possible directions. Given a direction $a \in R^{q\times 1}$, with $\|a\| = 1$, the projection of the dataset $\mathbf{M}$ along a is $k(a) = a'\mathbf{M}$, and we define the outlyingness with respect to $\mathbf{M}$ of a point $m_i \in R^{q\times 1}$ along a, partialling out $\mathbf{X}_D$ and $\mathbf{Z}_D^E$, as

$$\delta_i(\mathbf{M})\vdots_{(\mathbf{X}_D,\mathbf{Z}_D^E)} = \max_{\|a\|=1} \frac{\left|\tilde{k}_i(a) - m(\tilde{k}(a))\right|}{s(\tilde{k}(a))} \tag{6}$$

where, as suggested by Maronna and Yohai (2000), $\tilde{k}(a)$ is the result of partialling out the effect of the dummies from k, i.e. $\tilde{k}(a) = k(a) - \hat{k}(a)$ with $\hat{k}(a)$ being the predicted value of $k(a)$ obtained by regressing it on the set of dummies using a monotonic M-estimator. The notation $\vdots_{(\mathbf{X}_D,\mathbf{Z}_D^E)}$ indicates the partialling out of $\mathbf{X}_D$ and $\mathbf{Z}_D^E$. $\tilde{k}(a)$ is thus the part of $k(a)$ not explained by the dummies figuring in the econometric model, m is a measure of location and s is a measure of dispersion of $\tilde{k}(a)$. The partialling out of the dummies is done for each projection and not only done once before using the Stahel–Donoho estimator, as it would otherwise lead to a regression but not affine equivariant estimate, i.e. an estimate that does not change in accord with a linear transformation of the explanatory variables. When $\mathbf{X}_D$ contains only the intercept, $\hat{k}(a)$ is the predicted value of $k(a)$ obtained by regressing it on a constant. It is therefore a robust location parameter. Finally if $\rho(.)$ used in Eq. (5) is the absolute value function, it is easy to show that the location parameter will be the median and the measure of dispersion will be the median absolute deviation. As stated by Maronna et al. (2006), the square of the outlyingness distance is approximatively distributed as χ_q^2. We can therefore define an observation as being an outlier if $\delta_i^2(\mathbf{M})\vdots_{(\mathbf{X}_D,\mathbf{Z}_D^E)}$ is larger than a chosen quantile of a χ_q^2 distribution. Having identified outliers, it is now easy to estimate a robust counterpart of Eq. (4). The robust instrumental variable estimator is:

$$\hat{\boldsymbol{\theta}}_{IV}^{R} = (\tilde{\mathbf{X}}'\tilde{\mathbf{Z}}(\tilde{\mathbf{Z}}'\tilde{\mathbf{Z}})^{-1}\tilde{\mathbf{Z}}'\tilde{\mathbf{X}})^{-1}\tilde{\mathbf{X}}'\tilde{\mathbf{Z}}(\tilde{\mathbf{Z}}'\tilde{\mathbf{Z}})^{-1}\tilde{\mathbf{Z}}'\tilde{\mathbf{y}} \tag{7}$$

where the tilde symbol indicates that only non-outlying observations are considered.[4]

4 Alternative Robust IV Estimators and Monte Carlo Simulations

4.1 *Alternative Robust IV Estimators*

The proposed two-step estimator is by no means the only robust IV estimators available in the literature. We nevertheless believe that our robust-to-outlier IV

[4]Ready-to-use *Stata* code for the Stahel and Donoho estimator is available upon request to the authors.

estimator is particularly well suited for the applied researcher because of (1) its simplicity and efficiency (2) its strong resistance to all types of outliers and (3) the immediate availability of robustified versions of the tests for the quality of the instruments.

In order to better grasp the behaviour of existing estimators with our ROIV in presence of outliers, we run some Monte Carlo simulations. We compare our proposed estimator with:

(1) A standard IV estimator. We do not expect this estimator to resist to any type of outlier.
(2) The Cohen-Freue et al. (2013) estimator based on the robustification of the IV's closed-form formula. We expect this estimator to resist to any type of outlier but with low efficiency.
(3) The Lee (2007) estimator based on a control function approach estimator. This estimator follows a two-stage procedure. In the first stage, the endogenous regressor(s) is (are) regressed on the instruments calling on a median regression estimator. The first stage residuals are fitted and, using again a median regression estimator, the dependent variable is regressed in a second stage on the set of explanatory variables and a flexible function of the first stage residuals. We do not expect this two-stage median regression estimator to be very resistant to bad leverage points, neither in the first nor in the second stage of the procedure, given that median regression estimators are known to be not robust to this type of outliers.[5]
(4) Honore and Hu (2004) GMM estimator. This is a GMM estimator where the moment conditions have been modified to increase robustness against outliers. Indeed the standard IV estimator can be naturally interpreted as a GMM estimator with moment conditions $E[\varepsilon Z] = 0$. Since this estimator is fragile to outliers, Honore and Hu (2004) propose to modify the moment conditions using rank of variables instead of the values. This generalized method-of-moment estimator based on ranks should make the IV estimator less sensitive to extreme values. We expect this estimator to behave reasonably well in the case of vertical outliers. However, given that resistance to leverage points is not guaranteed by the moment conditions as they are written, it is possible that this estimator will not always be resistant to outliers in the included instruments when the regressors are uncorrelated (such as in our simulations), and to outliers in the endogenous regressor(s) or the excluded instruments when the regressors are correlated.
(5) Lucas et al. (1997) GMM-type estimator. This estimator is also based on a modification of the moment conditions of the standard GMM-IV estimator to make it resistant to outliers. In contrast to Honore and Hu (2004), robustness

[5] We have implemented this estimator using the -cqiv- *Stata* code written by Chernozhukov et al. (2010), given that other interested practitioners are likely to turn to the same source. However, note that we obtain similar results when we adopt a more flexible function of the first-stage residuals in the second stage. Results are available upon request.

to outliers is achieved by using weights in the moment conditions. More specifically, their idea is to use two types of weights: (a) weight ω to reduce the importance of leverage outliers among the explanatory variables and excluded instruments and (b) weight ϕ to reduce the importance of vertical outliers.[6] Being based on weighted moment conditions where the weights minimise the influence of outlying values in (a) the regressors and the excluded instruments and (b) the residuals, we expect this estimator to behave reasonably well under all contamination scenarios.

(6) Wagenvoort and Waldmann (2002) estimator. This estimator is a two-stage procedure. In the first stage, the endogenous regressor(s) is (are) regressed on both the included and excluded instruments calling on a generalised M-estimator. The generalised M-estimator considered in this first stage is a weighted M-estimator with a Huber loss function.[7] The weighting of leverage points is needed since a monotonic M-estimator (such as the median regression estimator or the one used here) cannot withstand contamination of the sample by bad leverage outliers. The endogenous regressor(s) is (are) predicted for all the individuals. In the second stage, the parameters are estimated minimising again a Huber function of the residuals while considering only non-outlying observations. Being based on a two-stage procedure where both stages are estimated using highly robust estimators, we expect this estimator to resist to all types of outliers.

4.2 Monte Carlo Simulations

The simulation set-up considered here is similar to that of Cohen-Freue et al. (2013). We first generate 1,000 observations for five random variables $(\mathbf{x}_0, \mathbf{u}, \mathbf{v}, \mathbf{z}, \mathbf{w})$ drawn from a multivariate normal distribution with mean $\mu = (0, 0, 0, 0, 0)$ and covariance

$$\Sigma = \begin{pmatrix} 1 & 0 & 0 & 0.5 & 0 \\ 0 & 0.3 & 0.2 & 0 & 0 \\ 0 & 0.2 & 0.3 & 0 & 0 \\ 0.5 & 0 & 0 & 1 & 0 \\ 0 & 0 & 0 & 0 & 1 \end{pmatrix}.$$

The considered data generating process (DGP) is $\mathbf{y} = 1 + 2\mathbf{x}_0 + \mathbf{w} + u$. We then assume that only variable $\mathbf{x}$, measured with error ($\mathbf{x} = \mathbf{x}_0 + \mathbf{v}$), can be observed. If we

[6] For the simulation, we define $\omega_i = I\left(\delta_i\,(\mathbf{X}_C.\mathbf{Z}_\mathbf{C}^\mathbf{E})^{\vdots}_{(\mathbf{X}_D,\mathbf{Z}_D^E)} < \sqrt{\chi^2_{p_1+m_3,0.95}}\right)$, $\phi_i = \sigma\frac{\psi_i(\frac{r_i}{\sigma})}{r_i}$, $\psi_i(u) = u\left[1 - \left(\frac{u}{1.546}\right)^2\right]^2 I\,(|u| \leq 1.546)$ where I is the indicator function.

[7] The loss function is defined as $\rho(u) = \frac{u^2}{2} I\,(|u| \leq 4.685) + \left(4.685\,|u| - \frac{u^2}{2}\right) I\,(|u| > 4.685)$.

simply regressed **y** on **x** and **w**, we would obtain biased and inconsistent estimators since **x** and **u** are not independent (the correlation coefficient r between **u** and **v** is about 0.70). We therefore have to call on an instrumental variable estimator using instrument **z**. The latter is a good instrument because it is independent of **u** and strongly correlated with **x** ($r = 0.50$).

We start the simulations with a dataset without contamination. We then contaminate the data by generating 10 % of outliers consecutively in the **x**, the **y**, the **w** and the **z** variables. In each case the outliers are generated by taking the simulated value observed for the variable of interest in the clean sample and by increasing it by 2 units in a first scenario, by 5 units in a second scenario and by 20 units in a third scenario. For example, in the first scenario, when we consider contamination of the **x** variable, we replace **x** by $\mathbf{x} + 2$ for 100 observations without modifying neither **w**, **y** or **z**. In this way we create different types of outliers, be they in the first or in the second stage. We then estimate the model using alternatively the classical IV estimator or one of the six RIV estimators. We re-do this exercise 1,000 times and calculate the Bias and Mean Squared Error (MSE) for all the estimated regression parameters of the final equation.

Table 1 presents the simulation results. For the sake of brevity, we do not report the results associated with the clean sample as all estimators perform comparably well.[8] The upper part of Table 1 clearly shows that neither the standard IV estimator nor the Lee (2007) or the Honore and Hu (2004) estimators behave well in the presence of outliers. While the last two estimators appear robust to vertical outliers (except for the estimation of the constant), they tend to suffer from a large bias when the outliers are in other variables than **y**. For the three estimators, it is likely that all coefficients would have been biased in most simulations if X, w and Z had been correlated and leverage points had been present in any of these variables. The lower part of Table 1 shows that the Lucas et al. (1997) estimator, the Wagenvoort and Waldmann (2002) estimator, the modified Cohen-Freue et al. (2013) estimator and the robust two-stage estimator we propose behave much better than the Lee (2007) or the Honore and Hu (2004) estimators. The bias remains low in all contamination scenarios for these three estimators. But on the basis of the MSE criterion, our proposed ROIV estimator performs the best.

Overall, we have shown in this section that outliers in IV estimations can be a serious source of bias and that among robust IV estimators, the robust two-step IV estimator we propose offers a very good protection against the distorting influence of outlying observations in the dependent variable, the endogenous variable, and/or in the included and excluded instruments. We now turn to an empirical example, which illustrates how outliers can result in misleading econometric inference.

[8]Obviously, in the absence of contamination, the standard IV estimator should be adopted.

Table 1 Robust IV estimators: Monte Carlo simulations

	Standard IV						Lee (2007)						Honore and Hu (2004)					
Strength	2		5		20		2		5		20		2		5		20	
	Bias	MSE	Bias	MSE	Bias	MSE	Bias	MSE	Bias	MSE	Bias	MSE	Bias	MSE	Bias	MSE	Bias	MSE
10 % contamination in X																		
X	0.005	0.010	0.021	0.047	**−2.318**	**4,000**	0.012	0.000	**−0.851**	**0.725**	**−2.181**	**4.755**	0.001	0.004	0.009	0.004	0.000	0.005
w	−0.001	0.002	−0.002	0.010	0.067	60.472	−0.013	0.000	0.018	0.000	−0.007	0.000	0.005	0.005	0.006	0.009	0.000	0.009
constant	**−0.400**	**0.161**	**−1.010**	**1.033**	**0.627**	**16,000**	**−0.243**	**0.059**	−0.050	0.002	**0.374**	**0.140**	**−0.248**	**0.067**	**−0.259**	**0.073**	**−0.283**	**0.086**
10 % contamination in Y																		
X	0.001	0.004	0.001	0.011	0.000	0.148	0.066	0.004	0.067	0.004	0.067	0.004	0.011	0.006	0.005	0.004	0.010	0.005
w	−0.001	0.001	−0.001	0.003	0.000	0.038	0.033	0.001	0.032	0.001	0.032	0.001	0.007	0.005	0.021	0.009	0.010	0.010
constant	**0.201**	**0.041**	**0.501**	**0.252**	**2.002**	**4.007**	0.086	0.007	0.087	0.008	0.087	0.008	**0.219**	**0.056**	**0.309**	**0.103**	**0.291**	**0.092**
10 % contamination in w																		
X	0.001	0.004	0.001	0.006	0.001	0.007	0.085	0.007	0.052	0.003	0.031	0.001	−0.001	0.003	0.003	0.007	0.001	0.007
w	**−0.266**	**0.071**	**−0.693**	**0.481**	**−0.973**	**0.947**	**−0.193**	**0.037**	**−0.591**	**0.349**	**−0.971**	**0.944**	**−0.261**	**0.072**	**−0.693**	**0.481**	**−0.974**	**0.948**
constant	**−0.146**	0.022	**−0.152**	0.024	−0.052	0.005	**−0.130**	**0.017**	**−0.158**	**0.025**	−0.076	0.006	**−0.120**	**0.018**	**−0.141**	**0.027**	−0.027	0.009
10 % contamination in Z																		
X	0.002	0.004	0.005	0.011	0.242	19.105	0.040	0.002	0.001	0.000	**−0.179**	**0.032**	0.009	0.004	0.000	0.006	0.005	0.005
w	−0.001	0.001	−0.001	0.001	0.002	0.045	0.004	0.000	0.030	0.001	0.028	0.001	0.011	0.004	−0.001	0.007	0.001	0.027
constant	0.001	0.001	0.001	0.001	0.011	0.028	−0.035	0.001	−0.046	0.002	−0.038	0.001	0.032	0.006	0.025	0.008	0.049	0.019

	Lucas et al. (1997)						Wagenvoort and Waldmann (2002)						Cohen-Freue et al. (2013)					
Strength	2		5		20		2		5		20		2		5		20	
	Bias	MSE	Bias	MSE	Bias	MSE	Bias	MSE	Bias	MSE	Bias	MSE	Bias	MSE	Bias	MSE	Bias	MSE
10 % contamination in X																		
X	0.000	0.003	0.001	0.002	0.001	0.002	0.005	0.010	0.006	0.016	0.006	0.015	0.001	0.010	−0.010	0.011	0.005	0.009
w	−0.052	0.020	−0.048	0.019	−0.048	0.019	0.000	0.003	0.000	0.004	0.000	0.004	0.003	0.002	−0.001	0.002	−0.003	0.003
constant	−0.001	0.002	0.000	0.002	0.000	0.002	**−0.325**	**0.107**	**−0.405**	**0.167**	**−0.405**	**0.167**	−0.003	0.002	0.000	0.002	0.002	0.002
10 % contamination in Y																		
X	0.001	0.003	0.000	0.002	0.001	0.002	0.006	0.006	0.008	0.012	0.009	0.013	0.012	0.012	0.007	0.011	0.004	0.012
w	−0.050	0.020	−0.050	0.019	−0.048	0.019	−0.001	0.001	−0.001	0.003	−0.001	0.003	−0.004	0.002	−0.006	0.002	−0.006	0.002
constant	0.027	0.004	0.000	0.002	0.000	0.002	**0.186**	**0.036**	**0.337**	**0.115**	**0.357**	**0.129**	0.046	0.004	0.001	0.002	−0.003	0.002
10 % contamination in w																		
X	−0.033	0.004	0.001	0.002	0.001	0.002	0.004	0.005	0.005	0.004	0.005	0.004	0.005	0.008	0.006	0.009	0.006	0.009
w	−0.061	0.021	−0.048	0.019	−0.048	0.019	**−0.194**	**0.039**	−0.007	0.001	−0.001	0.001	−0.027	0.003	−0.002	0.003	−0.002	0.003
constant	−0.020	0.003	0.000	0.002	0.000	0.002	**−0.116**	**0.015**	−0.003	0.001	−0.001	0.001	−0.018	0.002	−0.004	0.001	−0.004	0.001
10 % contamination in Z																		
X	0.001	0.003	0.002	0.003	0.002	0.003	0.013	0.006	0.006	0.004	0.005	0.004	0.008	0.009	0.008	0.009	0.008	0.009
w	−0.093	0.029	−0.057	0.020	−0.059	0.021	−0.001	0.001	−0.001	0.001	−0.001	0.001	−0.003	0.003	−0.003	0.003	−0.003	0.003
constant	0.003	0.003	0.000	0.003	0.000	0.003	0.002	0.001	0.000	0.001	−0.001	0.001	−0.004	0.001	−0.004	0.001	−0.004	0.001

(continued)

Table 1 (continued)

	ROIV					
Strength	2		5		20	
	Bias	MSE	Bias	MSE	Bias	MSE
10 % contamination in X						
X	0.002	0.004	0.002	0.004	0.002	0.004
w	−0.001	0.001	−0.001	0.001	−0.001	0.001
constant	−0.017	0.001	0.001	0.001	0.001	0.001
10 % contamination in Y						
X	0.003	0.004	0.002	0.004	0.002	0.004
w	−0.002	0.001	−0.001	0.001	−0.001	0.001
constant	**0.140**	**0.021**	0.001	0.001	0.001	0.001
10 % contamination in w						
X	0.001	0.004	0.002	0.004	0.002	0.004
w	**−0.118**	**0.015**	−0.001	0.001	−0.001	0.001
constant	−0.077	0.007	0.001	0.001	0.001	0.001
10 % contamination in Z						
X	0.002	0.005	0.002	0.004	0.002	0.004
w	−0.002	0.001	−0.001	0.001	−0.001	0.001
constant	0.001	0.001	0.001	0.001	0.001	0.001

5 Empirical Example: The Deep Determinants of Development

In a seminal paper, Rodrik et al. (2004) investigate the separated contributions of geography, international trade and institutions in explaining cross-sectional variation in income levels measured by the logarithm of GDP per capita. Conscious that their measures of international integration and institutional quality may be endogenous, they use as instruments the variables proposed by Frankel and Romer (1999) (constructed "natural" openness) and Acemoglu et al. (2001) (settler mortality). They find that "the quality of institutions 'trumps' everything else" (p. 131).

Using the data made available by Dani Rodrik on his website,[9] we replicate their preferred specification, based on Acemoglu et al. (2001)'s extended sample.[10] Column (1) of Table 2 shows that institutions appear indeed to exert a statistically and economically strong positive effect on income, while the coefficients on geography and openness are negative and statistically insignificant. According to these estimates, a one standard deviation increase in institutional quality would increase income by a factor of about $e^{1.98} - 1 \simeq 6$. The multivariate first-stage F-statistics suggest that the regression parameters are identified as the instruments appear to be relevant, even though the F-statistic for "settler mortality" is slightly below the Staiger and Stock (1997)'s rule of thumb value of 10.[11]

To demonstrate that their results are robust to outliers, Rodrik et al. (2004) use the DFBETA statistics proposed by Belsley et al. (1980), to identify influential observations.[12] They find that their main results hold once the outliers (Ethiopia and Singapore) are discarded from the sample. Although these observations have not been formally flagged as outliers, a similar conclusion is reached when neo-European countries (Australia, Canada, New-Zealand, the USA) are omitted from the sample. Unfortunately, common outlier diagnostics, including DFBETAs, are themselves not robust to the presence of several outliers in the data as they fundamentally rely on the non-robust LS estimator. Furthermore, these diagnostics are ill-suited in an IV model, which combines multiple stages.

For these two reasons, we re-estimate their IV regression using our robust IV estimator. In the first stage, observations with an outlyingness distance exceeding the squared root of the 90th quantile of a χ^2_6 distribution are considered to be

[9]http://www.hks.harvard.edu/fs/drodrik/research.html.

[10]As in Rodrik et al. (2004), regressors have been scaled by expressing them as deviations from their mean divided by their standard deviation.

[11]The first-stage F-statistics measure the correlation of the excluded instruments with the endogenous regressors, adjusted for the presence of two endogenous regressors. With weak identification, the classical IV estimator can be severely biased.

[12]The DFBETA statistics measure how each regression coefficient changes when each observation is deleted in turn.

Table 2 Determinants of development

Second stage (I)	IV	ROIV	ROIV	ROIV	IV	ROIV
Log GDP per capita	(1)	(2)	(3)	(4)	(5)	(6)
Geography (DISTEQ)	−0.72	−13.64	−2.92	0.74***	−1.49	−0.03
	(0.51)	(50.78)	(2.72)	(0.17)	(2.79)	(0.23)
Institutions (RULE)	1.98***	18.77	5.17		3.90	1.01***
	(0.55)	(66.35)	(3.84)		(5.80)	(0.19)
Integration (LCOPEN)	−0.31	−10.98		0.24	−0.98	−0.36
	(0.25)	(40.31)		(0.28)	(1.94)	(0.25)
Neo-Europes dummy					−4.83	
					(9.31)	
Africa dummy					0.18	
					(1.94)	
Asian Tigers dummy					−3.53	
					(7.04)	
Second stage (IIa)	IV	ROIV	ROIV	ROIV	IV	ROIV
Institutions (RULE)	(1)	(2)	(3)	(4)	(5)	(6)
Geography (DISTEQ)	0.55***	0.67***	0.63***		0.40***	
	(0.16)	(0.15)	(0.16)		(0.13)	
Settler mortality (LOGEM4)	−0.35***	−0.14	−0.11		−0.09	
	(0.10)	(0.09)	(0.09)		(0.09)	
Constructed Openness (LOGFRANKROM)	0.19**	0.34***			0.24***	
	(0.09)	(0.12)			(0.08)	
Neo-Europes dummy					1.67***	
					(0.28)	

Second stage (IIa)	IV	ROIV	ROIV	ROIV	IV	ROIV
Institutions (RULE)	(1)	(2)	(3)	(4)	(5)	(6)
Africa dummy					−0.31	
					(0.20)	
Asian Tigers dummy					1.64***	
					(0.39)	

Second stage (IIb)	IV	ROIV	ROIV	ROIV	IV	ROIV
Integration (LCOPEN)	(1)	(2)	(3)	(4)	(5)	(6)
Geography (DISTEQ)	−0.18	−0.13		−0.01	−0.20	−0.30*
	(0.13)	(0.14)		(0.13)	(0.13)	(0.15)
Settler mortality (LOGEM4)	−0.27***	−0.18*			−0.10	
	(0.09)	(0.11)			(0.10)	
Constructed Openness (LOGFRANKROM)	0.80***	0.56***		0.55***	0.78***	0.43***
	(0.08)	(0.09)		(0.09)	(0.08)	(0.09)
Neo-Europes dummy					0.54	
					(0.40)	
Africa dummy					-0.23	
					(0.19)	
Asian Tigers dummy					1.52***	
					(0.22)	
AP F-test LOGEM4	7.39	0.12	1.43	–	0.43	–
AP F-test LOGFRANKROM	56.96	0.18	–	36.71	3.21	24.10
Observations	79	60	60	60	79	60

Heteroskedasticity-robust standard errors in parentheses. Significant at *10 %, **5 %, ***1 %. All regressions include an unreported constant

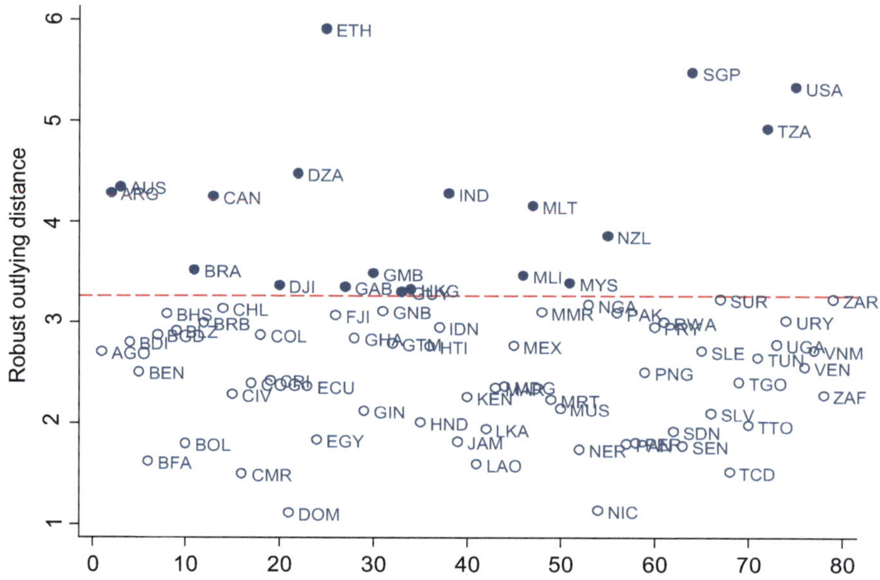

Fig. 1 Identification of outliers

outliers.[13] Column (2) of Table 2 indicates that the results of Rodrik et al. (2004) are extremely sensitive to outliers. Once we account for them, the multivariate first-stage F-statistics become extremely small and we cannot reject the joint insignificance of all the explanatory variables in the second-stage regression (panel (I)). Columns (3) and (4) show that the culprit is the instrument "settler mortality", which loses its relevance once outliers are omitted from the sample. In other words, the model estimated in column (2) is underidentified because there is only one valid instrument for two endogenous variables, as underlined by the absence of a statistically significant impact of "settler mortality" on institutions in the first-stage regression (panel (IIa)) in columns (2) and (3). Interestingly, in column (4), even when omitting the institutional variable and despite "constructed openness" being a strong instrument (panel (IIb)), we do not find any statistical evidence that greater international integration raises income.

Figures 1 and 2 provide a graphical identification of the outlying observations. In Fig. 1, the robust outlyingness distance of each observation is plotted against the index of the observation. The full points above the horizontal line, which intersects the vertical axis at the critical cut-off value above which an observation is considered

[13]The value for the degrees of freedom of the Chi-Square distribution corresponds to the presence in the IV model of one dependent variable, three explanatory variables and two excluded instruments with $1 + 3 + 2 = 6$.

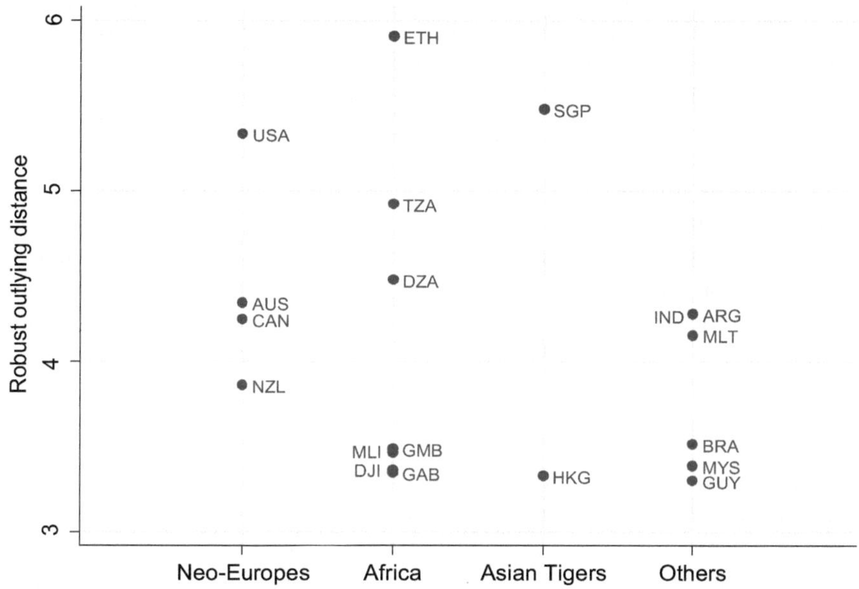

Fig. 2 Common features of outliers

to be a potential outlier, are the outliers in the sample. In Fig. 2, we group the 19 outlying observations according to geographical or historical common features. In agreement with Rodrik et al. (2004), we also find that Ethiopia and Singapore are strong outliers, with large outlyingness distances. On the other hand, contrary to what their DFBETA statistics indicated, the four Neo-European countries also appear to be outliers, in addition to a number of African countries, the other Asian Tiger figuring in the sample (Hong Kong) and six other countries. Hence, once we use robust diagnostic tools and take into account that outliers may be present both in the first and second stages of the IV estimations, we find many more outliers than Rodrik et al. (2004). It is worthwhile to note that, in a disparate way, these outlying observations have frequently been recognised as problematic by studies exploiting these data and an IV strategy, e.g. Frankel and Romer (1999) for Singapore, Dollar and Kraay (2003) for the four neo-European countries or Albouy (2012) for several African countries.

An imperfect way of controlling for these outliers is to identify the first three groups (Neo-Europes, Africa, Asian Tigers) with a separate regional dummy indicator in an econometric model estimated with a standard IV estimator.[14] Column

[14]Note that these dummies take the value of one for all countries in a specific group. They are not restricted to the identified outliers. These dummies capture therefore common group (regional) effects.

(5) of Table 2 shows that the introduction of these dummies generates qualitative findings very similar to those obtained using the RIV estimator. Once these dummies are included, settler mortality becomes an irrelevant instrument for institutional quality (panel (IIa)), while panels (IIa) and (IIb) suggest that Neo-Europes and Asian Tigers are indeed strong first-stage outliers. Furthermore, as in column (2), panel (I) shows that none of the "deep determinants" of differences in income levels is statistically significant.

Finally, in column (6), we follow Dollar and Kraay (2003) and treat institutions as exogenous, using the outlier-free sample. Under this heroic assumption, we find, once again, that the quality of institutions trumps everything else, including geography and trade openness. However, the impact of institutions on income is lower than that obtained in column (1) and there is no guarantee that simultaneity, an omitted variable or measurement error do not invalidate these results.

Conclusion

We have shown in this paper that outliers can be a real danger for the validity of Instrumental Variables (IV) estimations. Hence, we believe that testing for their presence in the sample should be as common as testing for the relevance and exogeneity of the excluded instruments. Fortunately, this can easily be done by the practitioner through the use of a robust two-stage IV estimator resistant to all types of outliers that we have described and implemented in various forms in *Stata*.

Acknowledgements Catherine Dehon gratefully acknowledges research support from the IAP research network grant nr. P7/06 of the Belgian government (Belgian Science Policy) and from the ARC contract of the Communauté Française de Belgique. Catherine Dehon is also member of ECORE, the association between CORE and ECARES.

References

Acemoglu, D., Johnson,S., & Robinson, J. A. (2001). The colonial origins of comparative development: An empirical investigation. *American Economic Review, 91*(5), 1369–1401.

Albouy, D. Y. (2012). The Colonial origins of comparative development: An investigation of the settler mortality data. *American Economic Review, 102*(6), 3059–3076.

Amemiya, T. (1982). Two stage least absolute deviations estimators. *Econometrica, 50*(3), 689–711.

Belsley, D. A., Kuh, E., & Welsch, R. E. (1980). *Regression diagnostics: Identifying influential data and sources of collinearity*. Hoboken, NJ: Wiley-Interscience.

Chernozhukov, V., Fernandez-Val, I., & Kowalski, A. E. (2010). *Quantile regression with censoring and endogeneity*. Working Paper 2009–012, Department of Economics, Boston University.

Cohen-Freue, G. V., Ortiz-Molina, H., & Zamar, R. H. (2013). A natural robustification of the ordinary instrumental variables estimator. *Biometrics*. doi:10.1111/biom.12043.

Desbordes, R., & Verardi, V. (2013). A robust instrumental variables estimator. *Stata Journal, 12*(2), 169–181.

Dollar, D., & Kraay, A. (2003). Institutions, trade, and growth. *Journal of Monetary Economics, 50*(1), 133–162.

Donoho, D. (1982). *Breakdown properties of multivariate location estimators*. Qualifying Paper, Harvard University, Boston.

Frankel, J. A., & Romer, D. (1999). Does trade cause growth? *American Economic Review, 89*(3), 379–399.

Honore, B. E., & Hu, L. (2004). On the performance of some robust instrumental variables estimators. *Journal of Business & Economic Statistics, 22*(1), 30–39.

Huber, P. J. (1964). Robust estimation of a location parameter. *Annals of Mathematical Statistics, 35*, 73–101.

Lee, S. (2007). Endogeneity in quantile regression models: A control function approach. *Journal of Econometrics, 141*(2), 1131–1158.

Lucas, A., Van Dijk, R., & Kloek, T. (1997). *Outlier robust GMM estimation of leverage determinants in linear dynamic panel data models*. Working Paper, Department of Financial Sector Management and Tinbergen Institute, ECO/BFS, Vrije Universiteit.

Maronna, R., Martin, D., & Yohai, V. (2006). *Robust statistics*. New York, NY: Wiley.

Maronna, R. A., & Yohai, V. J. (2000). Robust regression with both continuous and categorical predictors. *Journal of Statistical Planning and Inference, 89*(1–2), 197–214.

Rodrik, D., Subramanian, A., & Trebbi, A. (2004). Institutions rule: The primacy of institutions over geography and integration in economic development. *Journal of Economic Growth, 9*(2), 441–443.

Ronchetti, E., & Trojani, F. (2001). Robust inference with GMM estimators. *Journal of Econometrics, 101*(1), 37–69.

Stahel, W. (1981). *Robuste Schätzungen: Infinitesimale Optimalität und Schätzungen von Kovarianzmatrizen* (Ph.D. thesis). ETH Zürich, Zürich.

Staiger, D., & Stock, J. H. (1997). Instrumental variables regression with weak instruments. *Econometrica, 65*(3), 557–586.

Wagenvoort, R., & Waldmann, R. (2002). On B-robust instrumental variable estimation of the linear model with panel data. *Journal of Econometrics, 106*(2), 297–324.

Welsh, A. H., & Ronchetti, E. (2002). A journey in single steps: robust one-step M-estimation in linear regression. *Journal of Statistical Planning and Inference, 103*(1–2), 287-310. http://archive-ouverte.unige.ch/unige:23228.

Evaluation of Job Centre Schemes: Ideal Types Versus Statistical Twins

Rainer Schlittgen

Abstract Control groups for evaluation studies are mostly constructed by matching. Propensity score matching is the preferred method. With it a control group is constructed which has mean values of covariates close to that of the treated group. A summary statistic based on Cox regression was used when job centre schemes were evaluated. In that situation it is possible to use the centre of the covariates of the treatment group itself. This is elaborated here. Both methods are applied to a simulated data set mimicking the one which was used in the real evaluation.

1 Problem

The reorganisation of the social system in Germany, the so called Hartz reform, took place in 2003–2005. An evaluation of it was performed in 2004–2006. One part of research dealt with job centre schemes, ABM (Arbeitsbeschaffungsmaßnahmen). Here, the question was if there could be shown a positive effect with respect to the statutory goals, especially if and how much the chances of the participants were enhanced to become reintegrated into the labour market again.

There are several studies dealing with the reintegration into the labour market, see, for example, Lechner (2002), Caliendo et al. (2003, 2004) and Reinowski et al. (2003). But only in 2004 the integrated employment biographies of the Labor Institute became available. This large database makes it possible to do an evaluation on a broad basis for whole Germany.

For the evaluation it is important that the outcome variable is chosen properly. First and foremost it has to reflect the goal of the job centre schemes. This is as formulated in the SGB III §260 and is the occupational stabilisation and the qualification of employees to enhance their opportunities for regular work. Therefore, a suitable outcome variable is the time of regular employment after the participation in ABM. With the help of this variable the question can be answered

R. Schlittgen (✉)
Institute of Statistics and Econometrics, University of Hamburg, Von-Melle-Park 5, 20146 Hamburg, Germany
e-mail: rainer.schlittgen@uni-hamburg.de

J. Beran et al. (eds.), *Empirical Economic and Financial Research*,
Advanced Studies in Theoretical and Applied Econometrics 48,
DOI 10.1007/978-3-319-03122-4_13

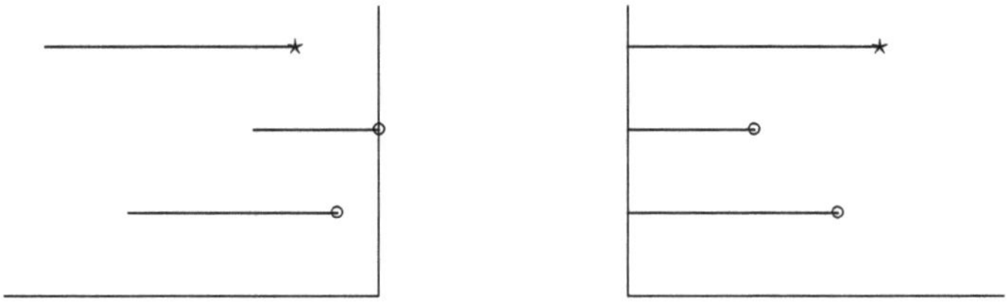

Fig. 1 Duration time and censoring (*filled star* = transition into first labour market, *open circle* = censoring due to moving, death, etc. or end of observation time, respectively)

if a participant who has been in ABM gets easier a regular employment than an employee who did not participate in ABM. Unfortunately, because of the data that are available it is not possible to use this as outcome variable. Instead the duration is used that a person is registered as seeking employment, ASU (arbeitssuchend). One has to take into account that a person who participated in ABM usually had an ASU phase before. Therefore, the time periods ASU phase, time in ABM and following ASU time (if any) are considered as one ASU phase.

Let's suppose that at the end of all ASU times the persons get a job in the "first labour market" (the "second labour market" consists of subsidised jobs) and that these times were completely observed. Then it is easy to calculate the proportion of the probands remaining longer than time t in ASU. It is

$$S(t) = \frac{\text{Number of ASU times} \geq t}{\text{number of all probands}}. \tag{1}$$

But not all ASU phases end during the time period under consideration that way. Additionally, not few probands became dropouts from the cohort for reasons not connected with the topic of the study. The related times are called censored times (Fig. 1).

The proportions are to be determined with the help of the methods of survival analysis, cf. Klein and Moeschberger (1997). Using these methods also implies that $S(t)$ cannot be interpreted any more as a simple proportion. Instead it must be considered as probability that a single proband who is randomly selected from the group of all probands under consideration has a survival time larger than t. These probabilities would approximately result however, when one would many times randomly select a proband from this group and calculate eventualy the proportions.

2 Determination of Twins by Propensity Score Matching

Any evaluation of a labour policy is to be based on a comparison of a group of people attaining the consequences of the policy and another group not obtaining them. The groups are called treatment group and control group, respectively. The statistical comparison is done by using summary statistics of the outcome variable. Even then it is not obvious that it is possible to interpret a difference of the summaries as causal effects. Only groups of people that are identical with respect to all other features allow to interpret them that way. In the context of evaluation of job centre schemes the summary statistic is $S(t)$.

To come to that requirement as close as possible for every proband in the treatment group a statistical twin is chosen from the control group. A statistical twin is one who has the same values of all relevant covariates. Differences of the values in the outcome variable for a pair of twins are interpreted as being causal. The resulting causal effect is interpreted as individual net effect from the job centre schemes. It cannot be attributed to the whole population, see Rosenbaum and Rubin (1985, S. 103).

The determination of the statistical twins is done by matching, cf. Rässler (2002). Matching means that to every proband a statistical twin is chosen randomly from his twins in the control group. It can be successful only if all relevant covariates are considered and if for all probands there are twins in the control group. This is a possible weak point of the matching approach. Only those covariates can be taken into account that were observed. There is some danger that the selection problem cannot be resolved completely due to unobserved heterogeneity resulting from the characteristics not observed.

A second issue at stake is high dimensionality when all relevant covariates are taken into account. With m binary covariates there are 2^m combinations of their values that are to be dealt with to find statistical twins. Fortunately the propensity score offers a way to overcome this curse of dimensionality. The propensity score p is a one dimensional constructed variable, $p = p(\boldsymbol{x})$, for a row vector $\boldsymbol{x}$ of realised values of the covariates. In the context of simple random sampling from the set of probands and controls it is the conditional probability that a proband is selected. The condition is that the values of the covariates are held fixed. The propensity score is usually computed by logistic or probit regression. The dependent variable in the regression is the indicator which takes the value 1 for probands and 0 for controls. For the logistic regression the underlying model is

$$q(\boldsymbol{x}) = \ln\left(\frac{p(\boldsymbol{x})}{1 - p(\boldsymbol{x})}\right) = \alpha + \boldsymbol{x}\boldsymbol{\beta}\,, \tag{2}$$

where $\boldsymbol{\beta}$ is a column vector of parameters. Since $q(\boldsymbol{x})$ is in a one-to-one relation to $p(\boldsymbol{x})$ it can be used instead.

The basis of the propensity score are results by Rosenbaum and Rubin (1983). They showed that it is possible to choose twins in such a way that the mean values of the covariates tend to be equal. This balance is only a tendency. In an application it is necessary to check if it is true. Otherwise it is necessary to improve it with the help of additional criteria, see Rosenbaum and Rubin (1985).

Matching with the propensity score is based on adjusting the centres of the groups. It does not choose statistical twins. Propensity score twins can be quite different with respect to the values of the covariates because different linear combinations can result in the same value $q(\boldsymbol{x})$. Therefore, using propensity score matching means that the initial idea of choosing statistical twins to approximate individual effects has been given up.

An other justification of the matching via propensity score is the insinuation that a twin determined that way has at least the same chance to participate in the treatment as his twin in the treatment group. This would avoid a selection bias that would result from consideration of all people in the control group. To enter the treatment a person had to fulfill some prerequisites. This seems not to hit the point. The prerequisites may be accepted realised when the vector of covariate values fulfill some side conditions. In the same way as argued above the propensity score results from a linear combination of these values and the same score can be the result from quite different values. Also the idea of the propensity score as a probability is not convincing. The size of $\hat{p}$ depends essentially on the size of the control group. And that can be chosen quite large. In fact, $\hat{p}(\boldsymbol{x})$ is an estimate of a proportion determined from already chosen groups.

On the other hand, consideration of the propensity score may be very helpful. The common support condition states that the values of the propensity score in both groups must be in the same range. A serious infringement of this condition shows that there are a large number of people in the control group showing quite different values of the covariates. Comparison of such groups can be problematic.

3 Cox Regression and Ideal Types

The statistical behaviour of duration times T are described with the help of a survivor function $S(t) = P(T > t)$. Influence of covariates to duration is incorporated by suitably modifying a baseline survivor function $S_0(t)$. Proportional hazard rate models result from the assumption that the covariates act through a linear combination $\boldsymbol{x\beta}$ in the following way:

$$S(t|\boldsymbol{x}) = S_0(t)^{\exp(x\boldsymbol{\beta})}. \tag{3}$$

This is also called Cox regression model.

The exponent is greater than zero. This ensures that $S(t|\boldsymbol{x})$ always fulfil the formal conditions imposed to survivor functions. It is not necessary to specify the functional form of the baseline survivor function. No ex ante distributional assumptions must be stated. Only covariates are considered that are fixed over the time.

The usual goal of a Cox regression model is the determination of the influence of the covariates. It would be possible to model the treatment as covariate itself. But that is not suitable. This model would impose to strong restrictions. For example, this approach implies that the baseline survivor functions are the same in the treatment and control group. Therefore one has to estimate the models for the two groups separately.

A comparison may be based on the survivor functions computed at the respective centres of the covariate values $\bar{\boldsymbol{x}}$ and $\bar{\boldsymbol{x}}'$ for the treatment and control group. These means represent ideal types of the two groups. "Ideal type" means that all characteristics are the average characteristic of the corresponding group. With S_T and S_C being the respective survivor functions one has to compare $S_T(t|\bar{\boldsymbol{x}}) = S_{0T}(t)^{\exp(\bar{\boldsymbol{x}}\boldsymbol{\beta})}$ and $S_C(t|\bar{\boldsymbol{x}}') = S_{0C}(t)^{\exp(\bar{\boldsymbol{x}}'\boldsymbol{\beta}')}$. The survivor functions differ in form (S_{0T} and S_{0C}), in the parameters ($\boldsymbol{\beta}$ and $\boldsymbol{\beta}'$), and in the centres ($\bar{\boldsymbol{x}}$ and $\bar{\boldsymbol{x}}'$).

This approach compares the ideal types of the treatment and the control groups. As is explained above such a comparison may be biased since the ideal type of the control group may be influenced too much from that part of the group that is not eligible. Instead for an unbiased comparison it is essential that also the group centre of the control group is the same as of the treatment group. The ideal types are then indistinguishable with respect to the covariates and a remaining difference in the survivor functions can be attributed solely to the outcome variable. A way to do that is to compute the survivor function of the control group at the point $\bar{\boldsymbol{x}}$, the centre of the covariates of the treatment group. So the comparison is to be based on the two baseline survival functions to the powers $\exp(\bar{\boldsymbol{x}}\hat{\boldsymbol{\beta}})$ and $\exp(\bar{\boldsymbol{x}}\hat{\boldsymbol{\beta}}')$, respectively.

Figure 2 illustrates the two approaches of matching and using ideal types. The upper part shows the matching approach. Corresponding to the (small) group of treatments a comparable group of controls is determined. For both groups the survivor functions are estimated. They are adjusted for the centres of these two groups. The lower part shows the ideal type approach. For both groups, the treatments and controls, the survivor functions are estimated. They are both adjusted for the centre of covariates given by the treatment group.

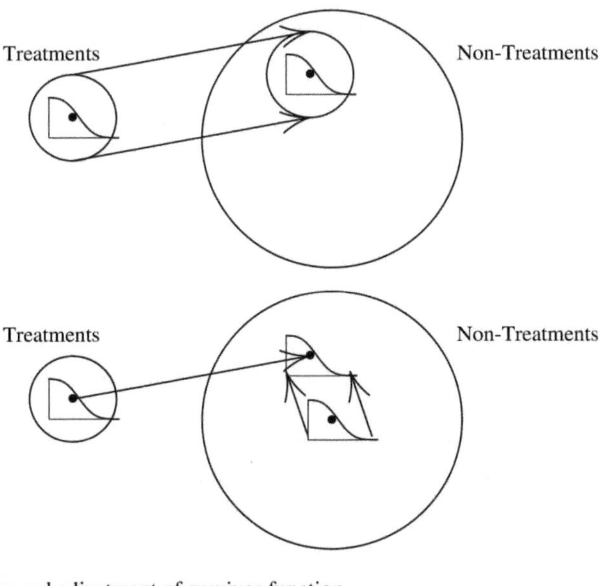

Fig. 2 Matching and adjustment of survivor function

The ideal type approach is advantageous compared to matching. The matching approach starts with the goal to establish a net effect by allowing comparison of people who can be considered as statistical twins. But since the matching is almost always performed via propensity score matching, one can only hope that the centres are almost equal. On the other hand, the ideal type approach ensures this completely. Also, it does not lead to erroneous interpretations which are often seen by writers who are not quite clear about the limitations of matching. Additionally, a rule of thumb says that there should be 25 times the treatments in the control group to get a satisfactory matching. They can all be used to estimate the survivor function for the control group. So that can be based on a larger number of observations. This allows also to consider subgroups. For those it is often more difficult to get matches belonging to the group of matchings since there need not to be real statistical twins.

4 Application of the Two Methods

The original data from the large database cannot be used here because of data-protection. Instead data were simulated taking the situation of the year 2002 for the so-called region III as a basis.

For the simulation the original data were transformed to become normally distributed. With the resulting covariance matrix normally distributed random variates were generated. These were inversely transformed. Censored and non-censored data were generated separately since they differ considerably, 1200 data for male participants in job centre schemes and 20 times of that for controls. The ratio of censored to non-censored observation is 1.75:1. Matching was done in a way that controls could not be selected more than once.

The variables of the data set are:
education with categories NA (= without any school-leaving qualifications), MH (= completed secondary modern school), MR (= intermediate school-leaving certificate), FH (= technical college degree), and HR (= university degree), *age* (years), *employment*, duration of employment before unemployment in days, *begin*, the beginning quartal of unemployment, *benefits*, daily benefits.

The means of the covariates in the two groups of treated and non-treated persons differ naturally. Because of the theoretical properties the subgroup determined by propensity score matching should have a centre much closer to that of the treated persons. But as the figures in Table 1 show propensity score matching does not always lead to a remarkable reduction of these differences.

In the original evaluation the means of the covariate values of the treated group and the matched group were much closer. The reduction of mean differences seems to be greater for larger groups. This corresponds with the theoretical properties of propensity score matching.

Figure 3 illustrates that persons who attended job centre schemes have a tendency to finish their unemployment phase earlier than the other. This results from the

Table 1 Standardised differences of the mean values of the covariates

Covariate	All non-treated	Propensity score match
Education MH	−0.01229	−0.00863
Education MR	−0.22300	0.06167
Education FR	−0.05594	0.13526
Education HR	−0.00216	0.07095
Benefits	−0.46082	0.06635
Age	−0.01388	−0.01336
Employment	−0.31817	0.17152
Begin	−1.18835	−0.10309
$\hat{q}(\boldsymbol{x})$	1.17799	0.00041
$\hat{p}(\boldsymbol{x})$	1.01966	0.00046

Fig. 3 Survivor functions versus time (days); people in ABM (*lowermost curve*), matched group (*uppermost curve*) and non-ABM with the centre of the ABM group (*middle curve*)

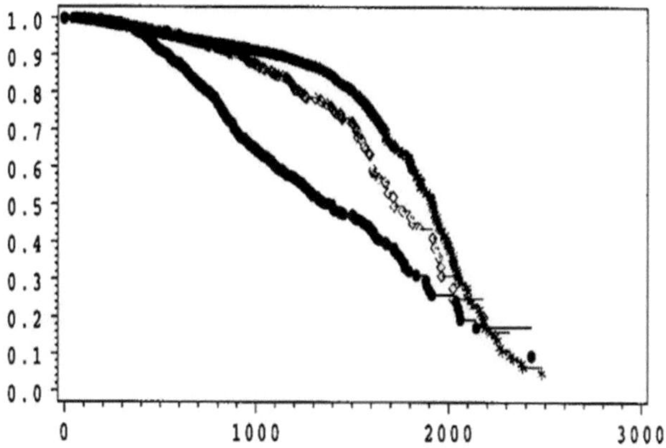

comparison of the lowermost curve with each of the other two. They show the results for the two approaches, propensity score matching and using the survivor function of all people not in ABM but for the centre values of the treated group. The last one is nearer to that of the treated group.

References

Caliendo, M., Hujer, R., & Thomsen, S. L. (2003). Evaluation individueller Netto-Effekte von ABM in Deutschland, Ein Matching-Ansatz mit Berücksichtigung von regionalen und individuellen Unterschieden. IAB Werkstattbericht, Diskussionsbeiträge des Instituts für Arbeitsmarkt- und Berufsforschung der Bundesanstalt für Arbeit.

Caliendo, M., Hujer, R., & Thomsen, S. L. (2004). Evaluation der Eingliederungseffekte von Arbeitsbeschaffungsmaßnahmen in reguläre Beschäftigung für Teilnehmer in Deutschland. *Zeitschrift für ArbeitsmarktForschung, 3*, 211–237.

Klein, J. P., & Moeschberger, M. L. (1997). *Survival analysis*. Berlin: Springer.

Lechner, M. (2002). Some practical issues in the evaluation of heterogenous labour market programmes by matching methods. *Journal of the Royal Statistical Society - Series A, 165*, 59–82.

Rässler, S. (2002). *Statistical matching*. Berlin: Springer.
Reinowski, E., Schultz, B., & Wiemers, A. (2003). Evaluation von Maßnahmen der aktiven Arbeitsmarktpolitik mit Hilfe eines iterativen Matching-Algorithmus; Eine Fallstudie über Langzeitarbeitslose Maßnahmeteilnehmer in Sachsen. Diskussionspapier Nr. 173, Institut für Wirtschaftsforschung, Halle.
Rosenbaum, P. R., & Rubin, D. P. (1983). The central role of the propensity-score in observational studies for causal effects. *Biometrika, 70*, 41–55
Rosenbaum, P. R., & Rubin, D. P. (1985). The bias due to incomplete matching. *Biometrics, 41*, 103–116.

The Precision of Binary Measurement Methods

Peter-Th. Wilrich

Abstract In analogy to quantitative measurement methods the precision of binary measurement methods used in a population of laboratories can be characterised by the repeatability standard deviation and the reproducibility standard deviation of the probability of detection, POD. In order to estimate these standard deviations an interlaboratory experiment with k laboratories, each performing n repeated binary measurements at identical samples, is carried out according to ISO 5725-2 and analysed with a one-way analysis of variance. The variance estimates are, e.g., used for a test of equal POD of all laboratories and for the determination of a 90 %-expectation tolerance interval for the PODs of the laboratories.

1 Introduction

"Qualitative analysis is often used to determine whether or not a particular feature appears or is absent in tests, in quality control procedures, identification scans, go/no go measurements and many other fields. Generally, such analysis uses simple measuring methods that classify the analyzed property value into two comprehensive and exclusive classes/categories. The performance reliability of such binary measurement systems (BMSs) is usually assessed by false positive and false negative rates" Bashkansky and Gadrich (2013, p. 1922). In this paper we are not interested in the misclassification rates of binary measurement methods but in a problem that particularly arises in the application of these methods in microbiology.

Microbiological tests form an important part of quality control for a wide range of industries, covering products as diverse as food, cosmetics, detergents and packaging. They help to assess the safety or efficacy of raw materials, components, ingredients and final products and to avoid the contamination of goods under normal use conditions. A large number of microbiological tests are carried out in order to determine the absence or the occurrence of specified pathogenic microorganisms in

P.-Th. Wilrich (✉)
Institut für Statistik und Ökonometrie, Freie Universität Berlin, Garystrasse 21, 14195 Berlin, Germany
e-mail: wilrich@wiwiss.fu-berlin.de

J. Beran et al. (eds.), *Empirical Economic and Financial Research*,
Advanced Studies in Theoretical and Applied Econometrics 48,
DOI 10.1007/978-3-319-03122-4_14

a substance, e.g. a particular food product or a source of drinking water or process water. A single application of such a test gives the binary measurement result "specified microorganism detected" or "specified microorganism not detected".

We deal with the problem of determination of the precision of such binary measurement methods, expressed as the components of standard deviation within and between laboratories.

2 The Model

We deal with the case of binary measurements where the measurement value x of a single measurement is either 1 (positive result, detected) or 0 (negative result, not detected).

The probability p of obtaining a measurement result 1 in a laboratory that is randomly chosen from a population of laboratories, its probability of detection POD, is modelled as the realisation of the continuous[1] random variable P that has the probability density $f_P(p)$ with $E(P) = \pi_0$ and

$$\begin{aligned}\sigma_L^2 = V(P) &= \int_0^1 (p - \pi_0)^2 f_P(p)dp \\ &= \int_0^1 p^2 f_P(p)dp - \pi_0^2 \\ &\leq \int_0^1 p f_P(p)dp - \pi_0^2 = \pi_0 - \pi_0^2 = \pi_0(1 - \pi_0); \end{aligned} \tag{1}$$

σ_L^2 is called the between-laboratory variance. The equality sign in $\sigma_L^2 \leq \pi_0(1 - \pi_0)$ holds if $f_P(p)$ is a two-point distribution at $p = 0, 1$.

Given that the POD of a randomly chosen laboratory is p, a measurement value x obtained in this laboratory is the realisation of the random variable X that is, under the condition $P = p$, Bernoulli distributed, i.e. it has the probability function

$$f_{X|P}(x|p) = P(X = x|P = p) = p^x(1 - p)^{1-x}; x = 0, 1. \tag{2}$$

Expectation and variance of $X|P$ are

$$E(X|P) = p;\ V(X|P) = p(1 - p). \tag{3}$$

The measurement value x obtained in a randomly chosen laboratory is the realisation of a random variable X that has the unconditional probability function

[1]The following results also hold for discrete random variables P. However, for the sake of simplicity only the case of a continuous random variable P is considered.

$$f_X(x) = P(X = x) = \int_0^1 f_{X|P}(x|p) f_P(p)dp$$
$$= \int_0^1 p^x(1-p)^{1-x} f_P(p)dp; x = 0, 1. \tag{4}$$

X has expectation

$$E(X) = E(E(X|P)) = E(P) = \pi_0 \tag{5}$$

and variance

$$\begin{aligned}\sigma_R^2 = V(X) &= E(V(X|P)) + V(E(X|P))\\ &= E(P(1-P)) + V(P) = E(P) - E(P^2) + V(P)\\ &= E(P) - V(P) - E^2(P) + V(P) = E(P) - E^2(P)\\ &= \pi_0(1-\pi_0).\end{aligned} \tag{6}$$

In a particular laboratory with probability of detection p the within-laboratory variance is $p(1-p)$, i.e. the within-laboratory variances of laboratories with different p are also different. We define the repeatability variance of the measurement method as the expectation of the within-laboratory variances,

$$\begin{aligned}\sigma_r^2 = E(P(1-P)) &= \int_0^1 p(1-p) f_P(p)dp\\ &= \int_0^1 p f_P(p)dp - \int_0^1 p^2 f_P(p)dp\\ &= \pi_0 - (\sigma_L^2 + \pi_0^2) = \pi_0(1-\pi_0) - \sigma_L^2.\end{aligned} \tag{7}$$

We find

$$\sigma_r^2 + \sigma_L^2 = \pi_0(1-\pi_0) - \sigma_L^2 + \sigma_L^2 = \pi_0(1-\pi_0) = \sigma_R^2. \tag{8}$$

σ_R^2, the reproducibility variance, is a function of the expectation π_0 of the probability of detection of the laboratories, i.e. for a given expectation π_0 of the probability of detection it is a constant. However, depending on the variation between the probabilities of detection of the laboratories it splits differently into its components, the between-laboratory variance σ_L^2 and the repeatability variance σ_r^2.

In cases where the measurand X is continuous the variation between laboratories in relation to the variation within laboratories is often described by the ratio of the reproducibility variance to the repeatability variance, σ_R^2/σ_r^2. Since this does not make sense for binary measurands we propose to use instead the ratio of the between-laboratory variance to the reproducibility variance,

$$\frac{\sigma_L^2}{\sigma_R^2} = \frac{\sigma_L^2}{\pi_0(1-\pi_0)}; \tag{9}$$

it is 0 if all laboratories have the same POD π_0, and it is 1 if the fraction π_0 of the laboratories has the POD 1 and the fraction $1-\pi_0$ of the laboratories has the POD 0.

Given that the POD of a randomly chosen laboratory is p and that it performs n independent measurements $X_1, X_2, \ldots, X_n$, the conditional distribution of the number $Y = \sum_{i=1}^n X_i$ of positive measurement results is the binomial distribution with the probability function

$$f_{Y|P}(y|p) = \binom{n}{y} p^y (1-p)^{n-y}; 0 \le p \le 1, n \in \mathbb{N}, y = 0, 1, \ldots, n \tag{10}$$

with expectation $E(Y|P) = np$ and variance $V(Y|P) = np(1-p)$.

The number of positive measurement results, $Y = \sum_{i=1}^n X_i$, in a series of n independent measurements $X_1, X_2, \ldots, X_n$ obtained in a randomly chosen laboratory has the unconditional probability function

$$f_Y(y) = \int_0^1 f_{Y|P}(y|p) f_P(p)dp = \int_0^1 \binom{n}{y} p^y (1-p)^{n-y} f_P(p)dp. \tag{11}$$

Y has expectation

$$E(Y) = E(E(Y|P)) = E(nP) = nE(P) = n\pi_0 \tag{12}$$

and variance

$$\begin{aligned} V(Y) &= E(V(Y|P)) + V(E(Y|P)) \\ &= E(nP(1-P)) + V(nP) = nE(P) - nE(P^2) + n^2V(P) \\ &= nE(P) - nV(P) - nE^2(P) + n^2V(P) \\ &= n\pi_0(1-\pi_0) + n(n-1)\sigma_L^2. \end{aligned} \tag{13}$$

The fraction of positive measurement results among the n measurement results of a laboratory, $\hat{P} = Y/n$, has expectation and variance

$$E(\hat{P}) = E(Y/n) = E(Y)/n = \pi_0 \tag{14}$$

and

$$V(\hat{P}) = V(Y/n) = V(Y)/n^2 = \frac{\pi_0(1-\pi_0)}{n} + \left(1 - \frac{1}{n}\right)\sigma_L^2, \tag{15}$$

respectively. From (1) and (15) we see that $V(\hat{P})$ is bounded:

$$\frac{\pi_0(1-\pi_0)}{n} \leq V(\hat{P}) \leq \pi_0(1-\pi_0). \tag{16}$$

Of course, the variance $V(\hat{P})$ is equal to $\pi_0(1-\pi_0) = \sigma_R^2$ for $n = 1$ and tends to σ_L^2 for $n \to \infty$.

3 The Determination of the Precision of a Binary Measurement Method

In order to determine the precision of a binary measurement method we perform an interlaboratory experiment. k laboratories are randomly selected from a large population of laboratories, and each of the laboratories obtains n independent measurement results under repeatability conditions. The measurement series y_{ij} ; $j = 1, \ldots, n$ in laboratory i is a series of ones and zeros. We apply the one-way analysis of variance as described in ISO 5725-2 (1994) to these binary measurements and find (see Wilrich 2010) the ANOVA Table 1.

$$\hat{p}_i = \bar{y}_i = \frac{1}{n}\sum_{j=1}^{n} y_{ij} \tag{17}$$

is the fraction of positive measurement results in laboratory i and

$$\bar{p} = \frac{1}{k}\sum_{i=1}^{k}\hat{p}_i = \bar{\bar{y}} = \frac{1}{kn}\sum_{i=1}^{k}\sum_{j=1}^{n} y_{ij} = \frac{1}{k}\sum_{i=1}^{k}\bar{y}_i \tag{18}$$

Table 1 ANOVA table of the statistical analysis of the interlaboratory experiment for the determination of the precision of a binary measurement method

(1)	(2)	(3)	(4)	(5)
Source	Sum of squares	Degrees of freedom	Mean square	Expected mean square
	SQ	f	$MS = SQ/f$	$E(MS)$
Between laboratories	$n\sum_{i=1}^{k}(\hat{p}_i - \bar{p})^2$	$k-1$	s_{II}^2	$n\sigma_L^2 + \sigma_r^2$
Within laboratories	$n\sum_{i=1}^{k}\hat{p}_i(1-\hat{p}_i)$	$k(n-1)$	s_{I}^2	σ_r^2
Total	$kn\bar{p}(1-\bar{p})$	$kn-1$	–	–

is the average fraction of positive measurement results in all k laboratories participating in the interlaboratory experiment.

An unbiased estimate of the repeatability variance σ_r^2 is

$$s_r^2 = s_{\mathrm{I}}^2 = \left(\frac{n}{n-1}\right) \cdot \frac{1}{k} \sum_{i=1}^{k} \hat{p}_i (1 - \hat{p}_i) = \left(\frac{n}{n-1}\right) \overline{s_r^2} \tag{19}$$

where

$$\overline{s_r^2} = \frac{1}{k} \sum_{i=1}^{k} \hat{p}_i (1 - \hat{p}_i) \tag{20}$$

is the average of the estimated within-laboratory variances $s_{ri}^2 = \hat{p}_i (1 - \hat{p}_i)$ of the laboratories.

The expectation of $s_{ri}^2 = \hat{p}_i (1 - \hat{p}_i)$ is

$$E(s_{ri}^2) = \frac{n-1}{n} p_i (1 - p_i) = \frac{n-1}{n} \sigma_{ri}^2; \tag{21}$$

s_{ri}^2 is a biased estimate of σ_{ri}^2; its bias is corrected by multiplying $\hat{p}_i (1 - \hat{p}_i)$ with $n/(n\text{-}1)$.

An unbiased estimate of the between-laboratory variance σ_L^2 is

$$\begin{aligned} s_{L,0}^2 &= (s_{\mathrm{II}}^2 - s_{\mathrm{I}}^2)/n \\ &= \frac{\sum_{i=1}^{k} (\hat{p}_i - \bar{p})^2}{k-1} - \frac{\sum_{i=1}^{k} \hat{p}_i (1 - \hat{p}_i)}{k(n-1)} \\ &= s_{\hat{p}}^2 - \frac{\overline{s_r^2}}{n-1} = s_{\hat{p}}^2 \left(1 - \frac{\overline{s_r^2}/s_{\hat{p}}^2}{n-1}\right) = s_{\hat{p}}^2 \left(1 - \frac{1}{c(n-1)}\right) \end{aligned} \tag{22}$$

where

$$s_{\hat{p}}^2 = \frac{1}{k-1} \sum_{i=1}^{k} (\hat{p}_i - \bar{p})^2 \tag{23}$$

is the variance of the fractions of positive measurement results $\hat{p}_i$ of the laboratories and

$$c = s_{\hat{p}}^2 / \overline{s_r^2} \,. \tag{24}$$

This estimator $s_{L,0}^2$ is unadmissable because it is negative if $c < 1/(n-1)$. We consider two modifications of this estimator. In the first modification we replace negative values of $s_{L,0}^2$ by 0, i.e.

$$s_{L,1}^2 = \max\left(0, s_{\hat{p}}^2\left(1 - \frac{1}{c(n-1)}\right)\right). \tag{25}$$

However, if the PODs of the laboratories are not extremely different, there is a high probability of obtaining the value $s_{L,1}^2 = 0$ with the erroneous conclusion that the PODs of all laboratories are equal. Hence, we do not use this modification. Instead we follow a proposal of Federer (1968) and Wang and Ying (1967),

$$s_L^2 = s_{\hat{p}}^2\left(1 - \frac{\exp(1 - c(n-1))}{c(n-1)}\right). \tag{26}$$

We observe that $s_{L,0}^2 \le s_{L,1}^2 \le s_L^2$ and, since $E(s_{L,0}^2) = \sigma_L^2$ the estimator $s_{L,1}^2$ is positively biased and s_L^2 is slightly more positively biased than $s_{L,1}^2$.

The estimate of the reproducibility variance $\sigma_R^2 = \pi_0(1-\pi_0)$ [see (6)] is

$$s_R^2 = s_r^2 + s_L^2; \tag{27}$$

it does not carry information on the variation of measurement results within or between laboratories. We use it for the definition of the ratio

$$LR = \frac{s_L^2}{s_R^2}; \tag{28}$$

LR is 0 if the interlaboratory experiment does not show any variation of the PODs of the laboratories and it approaches 1 if the variation of the PODs of the laboratories becomes extremely large.

4 The Interlaboratory Variation of the PODs

Wilrich (2010) presents a Chisquared test of the null hypothesis that the PODs of all laboratories are equal, $H_0 : p_i = p$ for all laboratories $i = 1, 2, \ldots$. Its test statistic is

$$\chi_{k-1}^2 = \frac{n(k-1)}{\bar{p}(1-\bar{p})} s_{\hat{p}}^2; \tag{29}$$

at the significance level α the null hypothesis H_0 is rejected if $\chi_{k-1}^2 > \chi_{k-1;1-\alpha}^2$.

However, as indicated in Macarthur and von Holst (2012) practitioners are more interested in an interval that covers a particular fraction of the PODs of the population of laboratories. As such an interval we choose the $(1 - \gamma)$-expectation tolerance interval, i.e. the interval calculated with the results of the interlaboratory experiment that is expected to cover the fraction $(1 - \gamma)$ of the PODs of the population of laboratories.

Generally, a $(1 - \gamma)$-expectation tolerance interval can be constructed (1) if the type of distribution of the PODs of the laboratories is unknown as a nonparametric tolerance interval or (2) if the type of distribution of the PODs of the laboratories is known as a parametric tolerance interval.

(1) If the PODs $p_i; i = 1, \ldots, k$ of the k randomly chosen laboratories included in the interlaboratory experiment could be directly observed, we could use the interval $[p_{min} = \min(p_i), p_{max} = \max(p_i)]$ as a nonparametric $(1 - \gamma)$-expectation tolerance interval with the expectation $(1 - \gamma) = (k - 1)/(k + 1)$, see Graf et al. (1987). For example, if $k = 10$ laboratories would participate in the interlaboratory experiment, this interval were expected to cover $9/11 = 0.8 = 80\,\%$ of the PODs of the population of laboratories. However, the PODs p_i of the laboratories cannot be observed. Instead, we observe the fractions $\hat{p}_i = y_i/n$ of positive results among the n repeated measurements in each of the laboratories; y_i is binomial distributed with the parameter p_i. The $(1 - \gamma)$-expectation tolerance interval $[\hat{p}_{min} = \min(\hat{p}_i), \hat{p}_{max} = \max(\hat{p}_i)]$ is expected to cover $(1-\gamma) = (k-1)/(k+1)$ of the fractions $\hat{p}_i = y_i/n$, but not of the p_i. Hence, we cannot construct a nonparametric tolerance interval for the PODs p_i of the laboratories.

(2) In order to construct a parametric tolerance interval for the PODs of the laboratories we have to assume a particular type of distribution of these PODs. Macarthur and von Holst (2012) assume a Beta distribution with probability density

$$f_P(p; \alpha, \beta) = \frac{p^{\alpha-1}(1-p)^{\beta-1}}{B(\alpha, \beta)}; 0 \leq p \leq 1 \tag{30}$$

with parameters $\alpha > 0, \beta > 0$, where $B(\alpha, \beta)$ denotes the (complete) Beta function. The Beta distribution is a flexible distribution model: it includes unimodal distributions for $(\alpha > 1, \beta > 1)$, J-shaped distributions for $(\alpha = 1, \beta > 1)$ or $(\alpha > 1, \beta = 1)$, U-shaped distributions for $(\alpha < 1, \beta < 1)$ and the rectangular distribution for $(\alpha = 1, \beta = 1)$, however, it does not include multimodal distributions.

Expectation and variance of P are $\pi_0 = E(P) = \alpha/(\alpha + \beta)$ and $\sigma_L^2 = V(P) = \pi_0(1-\pi_0)/(\alpha+\beta+1)$, respectively. The parameters α and β, expressed as functions of π_0 and σ_L^2, are

$$\alpha = \pi_0 \left(\frac{\pi_0(1-\pi_0)}{\sigma_L^2} - 1 \right); \; \beta = (1-\pi_0) \left(\frac{\pi_0(1-\pi_0)}{\sigma_L^2} - 1 \right). \tag{31}$$

The number of positive measurement results, $Y = \sum_{i=1}^{n} X_i$, in a series of n independent measurements $X_1, X_2, \ldots, X_n$ obtained in a randomly chosen laboratory follows the Beta-Binomial distribution with the probability function

$$\begin{aligned} f_Y(y; n, \alpha, \beta) &= \int_0^1 f_{Y|P}(y|p) f_P(p) dp \\ &= \int_0^1 \binom{n}{y} p^y (1-p)^{n-y} \frac{p^{\alpha-1}(1-p)^{\beta-1}}{B(\alpha, \beta)} dp \\ &= \binom{n}{y} \frac{B(y+\alpha, n-y+\beta)}{B(\alpha, \beta)}. \end{aligned} \tag{32}$$

Y has expectation and variance

$$E(Y) = n\pi_0 = n\frac{\alpha}{\alpha+\beta}, \quad V(Y) = \frac{n\alpha\beta(\alpha+\beta+n)}{(\alpha+\beta)^2(\alpha+\beta+1)}, \tag{33}$$

respectively.

The fraction of positive measurements among the n measurement results, $\hat{P} = Y/n$, has expectation and variance

$$E(\hat{P}) = \frac{\alpha}{\alpha+\beta} = \pi_0; \; V(\hat{P}) = \frac{\alpha\beta(\alpha+\beta+n)}{n(\alpha+\beta)^2(\alpha+\beta+1)}, \tag{34}$$

respectively.

Macarthur and von Holst (2012) calculate estimates $\hat{\alpha}$ and $\hat{\beta}$ of α and β of the Beta distribution of the PODs p_i by substituting π_0 by the estimate $\bar{p}$ and σ_L^2 by the estimate $s_{\hat{p}}^2$ in Eq. (31), take these estimates as being the true values α and β and calculate the 90 %-expectation tolerance interval A as

$$[b_{\alpha,\beta;0.05}, \; b_{\alpha,\beta;0.95}] \tag{35}$$

where $b_{\alpha,\beta;0.05}$ and $b_{\alpha,\beta;0.95}$ are quantiles of the Beta distribution. This interval would cover 90 % of the PODs of the laboratories if they were distributed according to this Beta distribution with $\alpha = \hat{\alpha}$ and $\beta = \hat{\beta}$. However, the coverage of this tolerance interval is unknown because (a) the estimation method uses Eq. (31) for the Beta distribution of the PODs p_i instead of equation (34) for the Beta-Binomial distribution of the observed $\hat{p}_i$, (b) the variance σ_L^2 in (31) is substituted by $s_{\hat{p}}^2$ and not by its estimate s_L^2, (c) the estimates $\hat{\alpha}$ and $\hat{\beta}$ that are seriously biased are taken as the true values of the Beta-distribution of the PODs p_i of the laboratories and (d) it is uncertain whether the distribution of the PODs p_i is at all a Beta distribution.

(3) We propose directly to use $\bar{p}$ and s_L for the calculation of a 90 %-expectation tolerance interval for the PODs of the laboratories with lower limit $\bar{p}-2s_L$ and upper limit $\bar{p}+2s_L$. If the lower limit is negative we substitute it by 0, and if the upper

limit is larger than 1 we substitute it by 1. Hence, the proposed 90 %-expectation tolerance interval B for the PODs of the laboratories is

$$[\max(0, \bar{p} - 2s_L),\ \min(1, \bar{p} + 2s_L)]. \tag{36}$$

If the estimates of the PODs, $\hat{p}_i = y_i/n_i$, of all laboratories are equal we have $s^2_{\hat{p}} = 0$ and $s^2_L = 0$ and hence, the tolerance intervals A and B degenerate to the single point $\bar{p}$. Macarthur and von Holst (2012) recommend to use in such cases the total number of positive measurements, $y_{total} = \sum_{i=1}^{k} \sum_{j=1}^{n} y_{ij}$ and the total number of measurements, kn, for the calculation of a confidence interval for the mean π_0 of the PODs of the laboratories, under the assumption of a binomial distribution of y_{total}.

In order to investigate the coverage of the tolerance intervals A and B according to (35) and (36), respectively, we run a simulation experiment with $k = 5, 10$ laboratories each performing $n = 5, 10, 20$ repeated measurements where the PODs of the laboratories are Beta distributed with means $\pi_0 = 0.5, 0.75, 0.95$ and standard deviations $\sigma_L = (0.25, 0.5, 0.75) \cdot \sqrt{\pi_0(1 - \pi_0)}$. For each of these 54 scenarios 5,000 simulation runs have been carried out and the coverage of the tolerance intervals calculated. Each point in Fig. 1 represents the average of the 5,000 coverages of A as abscissa and of B as ordinate. Red symbols represent $k = 5$, green symbols $k = 10$, open circle $n = 5$, open triangle $n = 10$, plus symbol $n = 20$. The average of the coverages over all scenarios is 0.88 for A and 0.89 for B (solid straight lines). A has a little larger spread than B. The coverage for $k = 10$ is slightly larger than for $k = 5$. Dependencies on the other parameters are not visible.

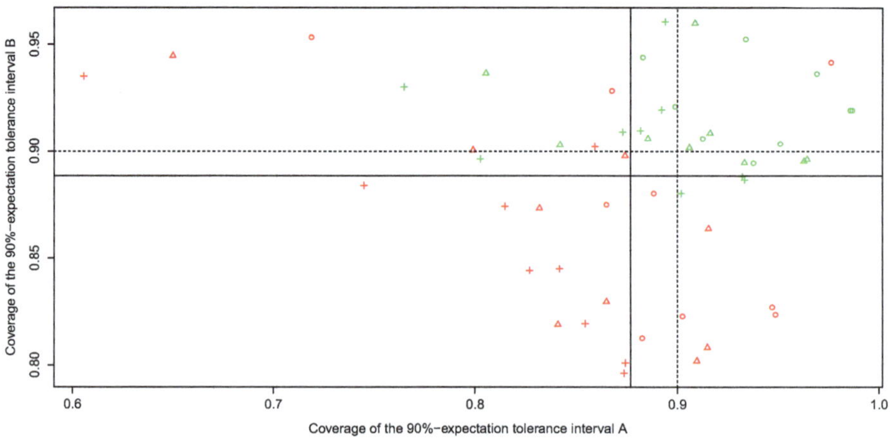

Fig. 1 Plot of coverage of the 90 %-expectation tolerance interval B against that of the 90 %-expectation tolerance interval A for various Beta-distributed PODs of the laboratories. *Red symbols* represent $k = 5$, *green symbols* $k = 10$, *open circle* $n = 5$, *open triangle* $n = 10$, *plus symbol* $n = 20$. The average of the coverages over all scenarios is 0.88 for A and 0.89 for B (*solid straight lines*)

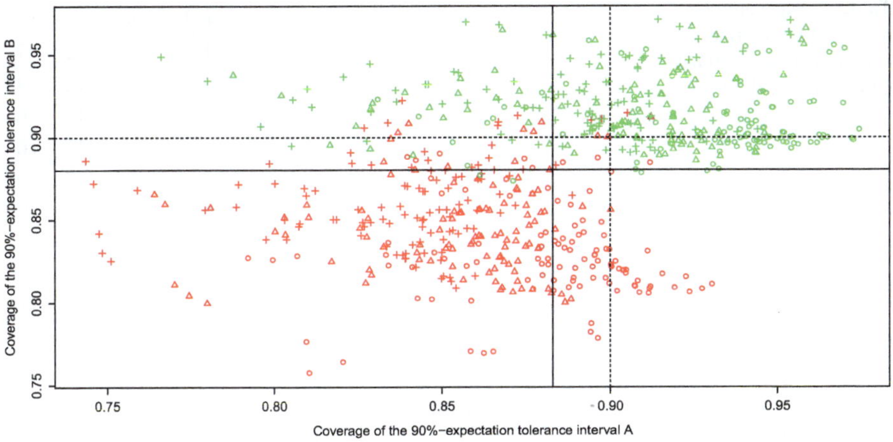

Fig. 2 Plot of coverage of the 90 %-expectation tolerance interval B against that of the 90 %-expectation tolerance interval A for various mixed distributions of the PODs of the laboratories consisting of two Beta-distributed components. *Red symbols* represent $k = 5$, *green symbols* $k = 10$, *open circle* $n = 5$, *open triangle* $n = 10$, *plus symbol* $n = 20$. The average of the coverages over all scenarios is 0.88 for both A and B (*solid straight lines*)

In order to find out what happens if the distribution of the PODs is not a Beta distribution as assumed for the tolerance interval A we run a simulation experiment with $k = 5, 10$ laboratories and $n = 5, 10, 20$ repeated measurements in each laboratory and with two mixed Beta distributions, the first one being chosen with probability $\omega_1 = 0.25, 0.5, 0.75$ and having mean $\mu_1 = 0.25, 0.5$ and standard deviation $\sigma_{L,1} = (0.25, 0.5, 0.75) \cdot \sqrt{\mu_1(1-\mu_1)}$, the second one having mean $\mu_2 = 0.75, 0.99$ and standard deviation $\sigma_{L,2} = (0.25, 0.5, 0.75) \cdot \sqrt{\mu_2(1-\mu_2)}$. For each of these 648 scenarios 5,000 simulation runs have been carried out and the coverage of the tolerance intervals calculated. Each point in Fig. 2 represents the average of 5,000 coverages of A as abscissa and of B as ordinate. The average of the coverages over all scenarios is 0.88 for A and B, and again, A has a little larger spread than B, the coverage for $k = 10$ is slightly larger than for $k = 5$ and dependencies on the other parameters are not visible.

We conclude that the tolerance intervals A and B are roughly equivalent and have an average coverage almost identical to the desired value of 90 %. However, since the tolerance interval B uses directly the estimate s_L of the standard deviation of the PODs of the laboratories and is much easier to calculate than the tolerance interval A we recommend to use the tolerance interval B.

5 An Example

We analyse an example that is presented in AOAC Guidelines (2012, pp. 40–42). Each of $k = 12$ laboratories has performed $n = 12$ measurements of a bacterial contamination. Table 2 shows the measurement results and Table 3 the results of the statistical analysis.

Table 2 Measurement results of an interlaboratory experiment (from AOAC Guidelines (2012))

Laboratory	n	y
1	12	7
2	12	9
3	12	6
4	12	10
5	12	5
6	12	7
7	12	5
8	12	7
9	12	11
10	12	9

Table 3 Results of the statistical analysis of the data of Table 2

Equation	Estimate
18	$\bar{p} = 0.6333$
19	$s_r = 0.4735$
23	$s_{\hat{p}} = 0.1721$
25	$s_{L,1} = 0.1046$
26	$s_L = 0.1215$
27	$s_R = 0.4850$
28	$LR = 0.063$
29	$\chi^2_{k-1} = 13.78$
	$\chi^2_{k-1;1-\alpha} = \chi^2_{9;0.95} = 16.92$
31	$\hat{\alpha} = 4.330$
31	$\hat{\beta} = 2.507$
35	$[b_{\hat{\alpha},\hat{\beta};0.05} = 0.328,\ b_{\hat{\alpha},\hat{\beta};0.95} = 0.892]$
36	$[\max(0, \bar{p} - 2s_L) = 0.390,\ \min(1, \bar{p} + 2s_L)$ $= 0.876]$

The estimate s_L^2 of the laboratory variance is only 6.3 % of the estimate of the reproducibility variance and the Chisquared test does not reject the null hypothesis of no variation of the PODs of the laboratories at the significance level $\alpha = 0.05$ ($\chi^2_{k-1} = 13.78 < \chi^2_{k-1;1-\alpha} = \chi^2_{9;0.95} = 16.92$). The 90 %-expectation tolerance intervals for the PODs of the laboratories according to method A and B are almost equal. We prefer B because it is not based on the assumption of a Beta distribution of the PODs and its calculation is very simple.

6 Summary

In analogy to quantitative measurement methods the precision of binary measurement methods used in a population of laboratories can be characterised by the repeatability standard deviation and the reproducibility standard deviation of the probability of detection, POD. In order to estimate these standard deviations an interlaboratory experiment with k laboratories, each performing n repeated binary measurements at identical samples, is carried out according to ISO 5725-2 and analysed with a one-way analysis of variance. The variance estimates are, e.g., used for a test of equal POD of all laboratories and for the determination of a 90 %-expectation tolerance interval for the PODs of the laboratories. A simulation experiment shows that the tolerance interval $[\max(0, \bar{p} - 2s_L),\ \min(1, \bar{p} + 2s_L)]$ (where $\bar{p}$ is the estimate of the mean of the PODs of the laboratories and s_L^2 is an estimate of the between-laboratory variance proposed by Federer (1968) and Wang and Ying (1967)) has an average coverage near to 90 %.

References

AOAC Guidelines. (2012). AOAC guidelines for validation of microbiological methods for food and environmental surfaces. AOAC INTERNATIONAL Methods Committee.

Bashkansky, E., & Gadrich, T. (2013). Some statistical aspects of binary measuring systems. *Measurement, 46*, 1922–1927.

Federer, W. T. (1968). Non-negative estimators for components of variance. *Applied Statistics, 17*, 171–174.

Graf, U., Henning, H.-J., Stange, K., & Wilrich, P.-Th. (1987). *Formeln und Tabellen der angewandten mathematischen Statistik*. Berlin/Heidelberg/New York: Springer.

ISO 5725-2. (1994). *Accuracy (trueness and precision) of measurement methods and results – Part 2: Basic method for the determination of repeatability and reproducibility of a standard measurement method*. Geneva: International Organization for Standardization.

Macarthur, R., & von Holst, C. (2012). A protocol for the validation of qualitative methods for detection. *Analytical Methods, 4*, 2744–2754.

Wang, Y. Y. (1967). A comparison of several variance component estimators. *Biometrika, 54*, 301–305.

Wilrich, P.-Th. (2010). The determination of precision of qualitative measurement methods by interlaboratory experiments. *Accreditation and Quality Assurance, 15*, 439–444.

Part II
Empirical Financial Research

On EFARIMA and ESEMIFAR Models

Jan Beran, Yuanhua Feng, and Sucharita Ghosh

Abstract An exponential FARIMA (EFARIMA) and an exponential SEMIFAR (ESEMIFAR) model for modelling long memory in duration series are introduced. The EFARIMA model avoids using unobservable latent processes and can be thought of as an exponential long-memory ACD model. The semiparametric extension, ESEMIFAR, includes a nonparametric scale function for modelling slow changes of the unconditional mean duration. Estimation and model selection can be carried out with standard software. The approach is illustrated by applications to average daily transaction durations and a series of weekly means of daily sunshine durations.

1 Introduction

Duration analysis refers to event history when a sequence of event occurrences are observed over time. We are concerned with positive random variables termed durations that correspond to the length of time between two consecutive occurrences of an event. In this paper, we refer mostly to the financial literature although this topic is dealt with in reliability engineering, survival analysis, political science, economics, and other fields, as, for instance, in the study of natural event occurrences. In financial econometrics, the autoregressive conditional duration (ACD) model was introduced in Engle and Russell (1998). For extensions and further details see, e.g., Bauwens and Giot (2000), Dufour and Engle (2000), Fernandes and Grammig

J. Beran (✉)
Department of Mathematics and Statistics, University of Konstanz, Konstanz, Germany
e-mail: jan.beran@uni-konstanz.de

Y. Feng
Faculty of Business Administration and Economics, University of Paderborn, Paderborn, Germany
e-mail: yuanhua.feng@wiwi.upb.de

S. Ghosh
Statistics Lab, Swiss Federal Research Institute WSL, Birmensdorf, Switzerland
e-mail: rita.ghosh@wsl.ch

J. Beran et al. (eds.), *Empirical Economic and Financial Research*,
Advanced Studies in Theoretical and Applied Econometrics 48,
DOI 10.1007/978-3-319-03122-4_15

(2006), Bauwens and Hautsch (2007), Hautsch (2012), Pacurar (2008), and Russell and Engle (2010).

Most extensions of the ACD model can only capture short-range dependence in conditional durations. In practice however durations are often found to exhibit long-range dependence (see, e.g., Jasiak 1998, Sun et al. 2008, Deo et al. 2009, 2010, Hautsch 2012). Early work on long-memory duration models can be found in Jasiak (1998), Koulikov (2003), and Karanasos (2004). Modelling durations is also important in other scientific fields beyond financial applications (see Fig. 2).

In this paper we will introduce an EFARIMA (exponential FARIMA) model and extended it to the semiparametric ESEMIFAR (exponential SEMIFAR) model that allows for simultaneous modelling of systematic changes, and short- and long-range dependence in duration data. Statistical properties of the models are derived. Estimation and model selection can be carried out with standard software. The approach is illustrated by applications to average daily transaction durations and a series of weekly averages of daily sunshine durations.

The paper is organized as follows. The EFARIMA model is introduced in Sect. 2. The relationship between the EFARIMA and EACD_1 models as well as statistical properties and estimation is discussed in Sect. 3. The ESEMIFAR model is introduced in Sect. 4, and its properties and estimation are discussed. Applications to data sets illustrated the methods in Sect. 5. Final remarks in Sect. 6 conclude the paper.

2 The Exponential FARIMA Model

Let X_t $(t = 1, \ldots, T)$ denote the duration process of interest. We define a multiplicative error model (MEM, see Engle 2002) as follows. Let

$$X_t = \nu\lambda_t\eta_t, \tag{1}$$

where $\nu > 0$ is a scale parameter, $\lambda_t > 0$ denotes the conditional mean of X_t/ν determined by the σ-algebra of past observations, and η_t are positive i.i.d. random variables such that all moments of $\epsilon_t = \log(\eta_t)$ exist and $E(\epsilon_t) = 0$. It will be assumed that

$$Z_t = \log X_t - \log\nu = \log\lambda_t + \epsilon_t$$

follows a zero mean FARIMA(p, d, q) model with innovations ϵ_t, i.e.

$$(1 - B)^d\phi(B)Z_t = \psi(B)\epsilon_t, \tag{2}$$

where $0 < d < 0.5$ is the memory parameter, and $\phi(z) = 1 - \phi_1 z - \ldots - \phi_p z^p$ and $\psi(z) = 1 + \psi_1 z + \ldots + \psi_q z^q$ are MA- and AR-polynomials with all roots outside the unit circle. It should be noted that, in contrast, for instance, to stochastic volatility models (SV models), the ϵ_t in Z_t coincides with the innovations on the right hand side defining the FARIMA process. Therefore, no unobservable latent process (which would make estimation more difficult) is involved here. Let $\zeta_t = \log \lambda_t$ denote the conditional mean of Z_t. Then the equation can be rewritten as

$$\zeta_t = \left[\phi^{-1}(B)\psi(B)(1-B)^{-d} - 1\right]\epsilon_t. \tag{3}$$

In particular, due to the FARIMA assumption (2) on Z_t we have $E(\zeta_t) = 0$. Models defined by (1) and (2) will be called exponential FARIMA (EFARIMA) model, and in the special case where the ϵ_t are normal the model will be called a Gaussian EFARIMA model. (Note that Taqqu and Teverovsky 1998 used the same term "*exponential FARIMA*" for a different model, namely a FARIMA process with exponentially distributed innovations.)

It is well known that the stationary solution of (2) is given by

$$Z_t = \sum_{j=0}^{\infty} a_j \epsilon_{t-j} \tag{4}$$

where $a_j \sim c_a j^{d-1}$ for large j with $c_a > 0$, with $\sim$ indicating that the ratio of both sides tends to one. The autocorrelations of Z_t are not summable, since they are of the form $\rho_Z(k) \sim c_\rho^Z |k|^{2d-1}$, where $c_\rho^Z > 0$ is a constant. Under sufficient moment conditions on η_t we obtain the stationary solution by taking the exponential transformation

$$X_t = \nu \prod_{i=0}^{\infty} \eta_{t-i}^{a_i}. \tag{5}$$

To simplify further discussion we define $X_t^* = X_t/\nu = \exp(Z_t)$. In summary we have the following result:

Lemma 1 *Assume that $Z_t = \ln(X_t^*)$ is a FARIMA(p,d,q) process as defined in (2) with zero mean, $0 < d < 0.5$ and all roots of $\phi(B)$ and $\psi(B)$ outside the unit circle. Then*

$$X_t^* = \prod_{i=0}^{\infty} \eta_{t-i}^{a_i}$$

is a weakly and strictly stationary process and $X_t = \nu X_t^*$ is a stationary solution of (1) and (2).

Remark 1 In particular, if $Z_t = \ln(X_t^*)$ is a Gaussian FARIMA(p,d,q) process, then $X_t^* = \prod_{i=0}^{\infty} \eta_{t-i}^{a_i}$ is a weakly and strictly stationary process with an $LN(0,\sigma^2)$ marginal distribution, where $\sigma^2 = \sigma_\epsilon^2 \sum_{i=0}^{\infty} a_i^2$.

3 Properties and Estimation of the EFARIMA Model

3.1 Relationship Between EFARIMA and EACD$_1$

The so-called EACD$_1$ model (Bauwens and Giot, 2000; Karanasos, 2008) is a short-memory version of the EFARIMA model defined above. More specifically, (1) and (2) with $d = 0$ correspond to an EACD$_1$ defined by Eqs. (4) and (7) in Bauwens et al. (2003) or Eqs. (5) and (6) in Karanasos (2008).

To show the connection to the definitions in Bauwens et al. (2003) and Karanasos (2008), note that

$$\zeta_t = \ln(\lambda_t) = \ln(X_t^*) - \ln(\eta_t) = Z_t - \epsilon_t$$

and $E(\zeta_t) = 0$. Define

$$\Theta(B) = (1-B)^d \phi(B) = 1 - \sum_{i=1}^{\infty} \theta_i B^i$$

and

$$\Omega(B) = \psi(B) - \Theta(B) = \sum_{j=1}^{\infty} \omega_j B^j$$

where $\omega_j = \theta_j + \psi_j$, for $1 \le j \le q$, and $\omega_j = \theta_j$, for $j > q$. By rewriting (2) we obtain the representation

$$\Theta(B)\ln(\lambda_t) = \Omega(B)\ln(\eta_t) \tag{6}$$

which is a fractional extension of Eq. (5) in Karanasos (2008). Equation (6) can also be represented as an extension of Eq. (7) in Bauwens et al. (2003),

$$\ln(\lambda_t) = \sum_{i=1}^{\infty} \theta_i \ln(\lambda_{t-i}) + \sum_{j=1}^{\infty} \omega_j \ln(\eta_{t-j}). \tag{7}$$

For $0 < d < 0.5$, the hyperbolic decay of θ_i and ω_j implies long memory in $\ln(\lambda_t)$. This can be seen more clearly from the MA(∞) representation of ζ_t. Taking the first term on the right-hand side of (7) to the left, and applying the inverse operator $\Theta^{-1}(B)$ we obtain

$$\zeta_t = \sum_{j=1}^{\infty} a_j \epsilon_{t-j} \tag{8}$$

with nonsummable coefficients a_j. It is clear that ζ_t is a stationary process with mean zero and variance $var(\zeta_t) = \sigma_\zeta^2 = \sigma_\epsilon^2 \sum_{i=1}^{\infty} a_i^2$. Under sufficient moment conditions on η_t, (8) implies that a strictly stationary solution of λ_t is given by

$$\lambda_t = \prod_{i=1}^{\infty} \eta_{t-i}^{a_i}. \tag{9}$$

Note that in general some coefficients a_j may be negative, although this is not the case as $j \to \infty$. Nevertheless, the conditional mean in Eq. (9) is always positive, as required for a reasonable ACD-type model. A further attractive feature is that the distribution of the conditional mean duration is completely known. In particular, if $\epsilon_t = \log \eta_t$ are normal, then λ_t has an $LN(0, \sigma_\lambda^2)$ marginal distribution.

3.2 *Moments, acf and Persistence of the EFARIMA Model*

Now we will discuss some detailed statistical properties of the proposed model. Following the definition, the memory parameter d is fixed for the Gaussian FARIMA process Z_t. An important question concerns the relationship between long memory in Z_t and X_t. In other words, if we have obtained an estimate of d from Z_t, can we use this as an estimator of the memory parameter in X_t? Fortunately, the answer is yes. Due to the transformation $X_t = \nu \exp(Z_t)$ that is of Hermite rank one, and well-known results on Hermite polynomials (see, e.g., Taqqu 1975, Beran 1994, Dittmann and Granger 2002) the process X_t with ϵ_t Gaussian has the same long-memory parameter d as Z_t. For non-Gaussian innovations, the same is true under suitable additional assumptions on the distribution of ϵ_t (see, e.g., Giraitis and Surgailis 1989, Surgailis and Vaiciulis 1999). In the Gaussian case, more specific formulas for moments, autocovariances

$$\gamma_{X^*}(k) = cov(X_t^*, X_{t+k}^*)$$

and autocorrelations $\rho_X(k) = \rho_{X^*}(k)$ can be obtained.

Theorem 1 *Under the same assumptions in Lemma 1 and ϵ_t Gaussian, we have*

i)
$$E[(X_t^*)^s] = \exp\left\{s^2\sigma^2/2\right\}.$$

ii)
$$var(X_t^*) = e^{\sigma^2}\left(e^{\sigma^2} - 1\right),$$

$$\gamma_{X^*}(k) = e^{\sigma^2}\left[\exp\left(\sigma_\epsilon^2 \sum_{i=0}^{\infty} a_i a_{i+k}\right) - 1\right].$$

iii)

$$\rho_X(k) = \left[\exp\left(\sigma_\epsilon^2 \sum_{i=0}^{\infty} a_i a_{i+k}\right) - 1\right]\left(e^{\sigma^2} - 1\right)^{-1}.$$

iv) For $k \to \infty$ we have

$$\rho_X(k) \sim c_\rho^X |k|^{2d-1},$$

where $c_\rho^X = c_\rho^{\mathrm{e}} \cdot c_\rho^Z$ is a positive constant and $0 < c_\rho^{\mathrm{e}} < 1$.

Items *i*)–*iii*) mean that the moments of any order and the correlations of X_t^* (or X_t) are completely known, and that these processes are weakly stationary. This is in contrast to most duration and volatility models where conditions for the existence of high order moments, the correlation structure, and the unconditional distribution are usually very complex or even unknown. Furthermore, a simple estimation procedure is implied since the long-memory parameters of X_t^* (or X_t) and Z_t are the same and no unobservable latent process is present. As we will see, a Gaussian MLE coincides with the ML estimators for the original non-negative process. The last result *iv*) means that, although the persistence levels in X_t and Z_t are the same, the autocorrelations of X_t are asymptotically smaller than those of Z_t. Finally note that the results of Theorem 1 hold for $d < 0$. In particular, using Theorem 1 *iv*) it can be shown that $\sum \rho_X(k) > 0$ for $d < 0$, i.e. X_t does not exhibit antipersistence; for related findings see, e.g., Dittmann and Granger (2002).

Of particular interest is the autocorrelation function of the conditional mean duration λ_t. First the following asymptotic formula can be obtained:

Lemma 2 *Under the assumptions of Theorem 1 and ϵ_t Gaussian, the asymptotic formula of the autocorrelations of ζ_t is given by*

$$\rho_\zeta(k) \sim c_\rho^\zeta |k|^{2d-1} \ (k \to \infty)$$

where $c_\rho^\zeta = c_\rho^Z c_\rho^\lambda$ and where $c_\rho^\lambda = \sigma^2/\sigma_\zeta^2 > 1$.

In particular we conclude that for $d > 0$, ζ_t has the same long-memory parameter as Z_t. However the constant in $\rho_\zeta(k)$ is slightly larger than that for $\rho_Z(k)$. For $\rho_\lambda(k)$ a result similar to Theorem 1 can be obtained:

Corollary 1 *Under the assumptions of Theorem 1 and if ϵ_t are Gaussian we have*

i)

$$\rho_\lambda(k) = \left[\exp\left(\sigma_\epsilon^2 \sum_{i=1}^{\infty} a_i a_{i+k}\right) - 1\right]\left(e^{\sigma_\lambda^2} - 1\right)^{-1}$$

ii) For $k \to \infty$ we have

$$\rho_\lambda \sim c_\rho^\lambda |k|^{2d-1}$$

where $c_\rho^\lambda = \tilde{c}_\rho^{\mathrm{e}} * c_\rho^\zeta$ is a positive constant and $0 < \tilde{c}_\rho^{\mathrm{e}} < 1$.

We conclude again that λ_t has the same long-memory parameter d, however with a slightly higher constant than in $\rho_\xi(k)$. Other properties of λ_t can be obtained by combining Theorem 1 and Corollary 1. In particular moments of λ_t of any order exist and the sth moment of λ_t is given by $E(\lambda_t^s) = \exp\{s^2\sigma_\lambda^2/2\}$.

3.3 Estimation of the Model

Suppose that we observe X_t $(t = 1, 2, \ldots, n)$ generated by an EFARIMA process with an unknown parameter vector

$$\vartheta = \left(\nu, \sigma_\varepsilon^2, d, \phi_1, \ldots, \phi_p, \psi_1, \ldots, \psi_q\right)^T.$$

Recall that, due to (3), X_t is *not* an SV model with unobservable latent random components so that maximum likelihood estimation does not cause any major difficulty. Suppose, for instance, that the innovations ϵ_t are normal. By assumption, $Y_t = \log X_t$ has expected value $\mu = \log \nu$ and $Z_t = Y_t - \mu$ is a centered Gaussian FARIMA process. Given a consistent estimator $\hat{\mu}$ of μ, the FARIMA parameter vector

$$\beta = \left(\sigma_\epsilon^2, d, \phi_1, \ldots, \phi_p, \psi_1, \ldots, \psi_q\right)^T$$

can be estimated by applying a Gaussian MLE for FARIMA models to $\hat{Z}_t = \log Y_t - \hat{\mu}$ $(t = 1, 2, \ldots, n)$. The asymptotic distribution of $\hat{\beta}_{MLE}$ is known (see, e.g., Fox and Taqqu 1986, Giraitis and Surgailis 1990, Beran 1995) and various approximate ML-methods and algorithms exist (Haslett and Raftery 1989; Fox and Taqqu 1986; Beran 1995). Furthermore, the generally unknown orders p and q can be chosen using one of the known model selection criteria such as the BIC. For results on the BIC in the context of stationary and integrated FARIMA models see Beran et al. (1998). For practical purposes it is often sufficient to set $q = 0$, so that model choice reduces to estimating p only. This will be the approach taken here.

4 The Exponential SEMIFAR Model

Duration series may exhibit a nonstationarity in the mean which can be modelled by a nonparametric multiplicative scale function. Let $\tau_t = t/n$ denote rescaled time and $\mu(\tau)$ a smooth function of τ. We then replace the constant $\mu = \log \nu$ in the EFARIMA model by a nonparametric regression function, i.e.

$$Y_t = \mu(\tau_t) + Z_t, \tag{10}$$

where Z_t is the zero mean FARIMA(p, d, q) process defined in (2). Model (10) can be thought of as a SEMIFAR process (Beran and Feng, 2002a) with integer differencing parameter $m = 0$ (and the possible addition of an MA part). Note however that, as before, we have the additional structural assumption $Z_t = \log \lambda_t + \epsilon_t$ implying (3).

Using the notation

$$\nu(\tau_t) = \exp[\mu(\tau_t)]$$

the observed series $X_t = \exp(Y_t)$ is of the form

$$X_t = \nu(\tau_t) X_t^* = \nu(\tau_t)\lambda_t \eta_t = g(\tau_t)\eta_t, \tag{11}$$

where $\lambda_t > 0$ is the conditional mean as defined before, $\nu(\tau) > 0$ is a positive nonparametric scale function (or local mean function), $X_t^* = \exp(Z_t)$ is the log-normally distributed stationary long-memory process as defined before and

$$g(\tau_t) = \nu(\tau_t)\lambda_t$$

will be called the *total mean* in the original process. Under suitable regularity conditions X_t defined in (11) is a locally stationary process as defined in Dahlhaus (1997). In what follows (11) will be called an ESEMIFAR (exponential SEMIFAR) model.

By analogous arguments as before, it can be seen that the ESEMIFAR model is a semiparametric long-memory EACD_1 model. It allows for simultaneous modelling of slowly changing scaling factors, long-range dependence, and short-range dependence. As for the EFARIMA model, different conditional distributions can be used for the ESEMIFAR model. Such modifications are of particular interest when analyzing intraday trade durations.

In analogy to the earlier discussion, fitting ESEMIFAR models can be done by applying algorithms for SEMIFAR processes. This involves, for instance, kernel or local polynomial regression for estimating the trend function g and maximum likelihood estimation of the other parameters from the residuals. Theoretical results on estimators of g may be found, for example, in Hall and Hart (1990) and Beran and Feng (2002a,c). For properties of estimated parameters based on residuals see, e.g., Beran and Feng (2002a). Data-driven algorithms for selecting the bandwidth are proposed in Ray and Tsay (1997) and Beran and Feng (2002a,b). The algorithm of Beran and Feng (2002b) is implemented in the S-Plus module FinMetrics (see Zivot and Wang 2003).

After fitting an ESEMIFAR model, one obtains $\hat{\mu}(\tau_t)$, the estimate of the local mean in Y_t. The estimated local mean of X_t is given by $\hat{\nu}(\tau_t) = \exp[\hat{\mu}(\tau_t)]$. Another important task is the computation of conditional and local total means. Note that under the conditions of Lemma 1 the process Z_t is invertible with AR(∞) representation

$$Z_t = \sum_{j=1}^{\infty} b_j Z_{t-j} + \epsilon_t, \tag{12}$$

where $b_j \sim c_b j^{-d-1}$ (as $j \to \infty$), $0 < d < 0.5$ and $\sum_{j=1}^{\infty} b_j \equiv 1$. This leads to

$$\zeta_t = \sum_{j=1}^{\infty} b_j Z_{t-j} = \sum_{j=1}^{\infty} b_j (Z_{t-j} + \mu) - \mu \tag{13}$$

$$= \sum_{j=1}^{\infty} b_j \log X_{t-j} - \log \nu = \sum_{j=1}^{\infty} b_j \log X_{t-j}^* \tag{14}$$

and

$$\lambda_t = \exp(\zeta_t) = \prod_{j=1}^{\infty} (X_{t-j}^*)^{b_i}. \tag{15}$$

The conditional means ζ_t and λ_t can be approximated based on these results. Let $\hat{b}_j$ be the estimated values of b_j. Set $\hat{\xi}_1 = 0$,

$$\hat{\xi}_t = \sum_{j=1}^{t-1} \hat{b}_j [y_{t-j} - \hat{\mu}(\tau_{t-j})] \; (t = 2, \ldots, n) \tag{16}$$

and

$$\hat{\lambda}_t = \exp(\hat{\zeta}_t) = \prod_{j=1}^{t-1} [y_{t-j} - \hat{\mu}(\tau_{t-j})]^{\hat{b}_i}.$$

Finally

$$\hat{X}_t = \hat{g}(\tau_t) = \hat{\nu}(\tau_t)\hat{\lambda}_t = \exp[\hat{\mu}(\tau_t) + \hat{\zeta}_t] \tag{17}$$

are the estimated total means. Similarly, forecasts of total means can be obtained by combining the forecasts of both conditional and unconditional parts.

5 Data Examples

In this section we analyze two data sets: (1) a daily average trade duration data set from Germany and (2) a sunshine duration data set from Switzerland.

5.1 Daily Average Trade Durations

We consider daily average trade durations of Deutsche Post AG (DPA) observed on XETRA (source: Thomson Reuters Corporation). Using the notation x_{ti} ($i = 1, \ldots, N_t$) for intraday durations observed on day t, where N_t is the random number of observations on that day, the daily average duration on day t is defined by $x_t = \sum x_{ti}/N_t$. This definition leads to an equidistant duration series whose features differ from nonequidistant intraday duration series. In particular, we will see that long-range dependence tends to occur in these series. The duration data are displayed in Fig. 1a.

Figure 1a indicates that the marginal distribution is asymmetric, however, due to averaging of a large number of intraday durations, only a few observations are close to zero. In particular, distributions with a peak at zero, such as the exponential distribution, are not suitable. Furthermore, there appears to be a systematic trend in the mean, and the variability tends to be higher where the trend function assumes higher values. A log-transformation therefore seems to be appropriate. The transformed data together with an estimated nonparametric trend function $\hat{\mu}(\tau)$ (with a data-driven bandwidth of 0.1943) are shown in Fig. 1b. A local linear estimator with the Epanechnikov kernel as weight function was used. For the Gaussian parametric part, an EFARIMA$(0, d, 0)$ model with $\hat{d} = 0.398$ is selected by the BIC for $\hat{\xi}_t$. The long-memory parameter is clearly significant with a 95 %-confidence interval of $[0.357, 0.440]$. The estimated conditional means $\hat{\zeta}_t$ and the total means $\hat{X}_t$ calculated according to formulae (16) and (17) are shown in Fig. 1c, d. Note that $\hat{\zeta}_t$ looks stationary whereas this is not the case for $\hat{X}_t$.

5.2 Average Sunshine Durations

Figure 2a shows logarithms of weekly averaged daily sunshine durations (after seasonal adjustment) in the city of Basel (Switzerland) between January 1900 to December 2010. Fitting an ESEMIFAR model (with the BIC for model choice) leads to no significant trend function and an EFARIMA$(0, d, 0)$ process with $d = 0.1196$ (95 %-confidence interval $[0.0994, 0.1398]$). Thus, there is no evidence of any systematic change regarding sunshine duration, however dependence between sunshine durations appears to be far reaching. For a confirmation of the fit, Fig. 2 shows the log–log-periodogram of the data together with the fitted spectral density (in log–log-coordinates), Fig. 2c displays the histogram of $\hat{\varepsilon}_t$. Here, the residuals are not exactly normally distributed, but do not appear to be particularly long-tailed. As mentioned above, the asymptotic behavior of autocorrelations is still the same in such cases, the Gaussian MLE (and the semiparametric SEMIFAR algorithm) can be used (as a QMLE) and parameter estimates have the same asymptotic properties.

As a general comment we may add that the lack of a significant trend could be due to having considered one time series only. In some recent empirical studies based on large numbers of sunshine duration series at various geographic locations, it has

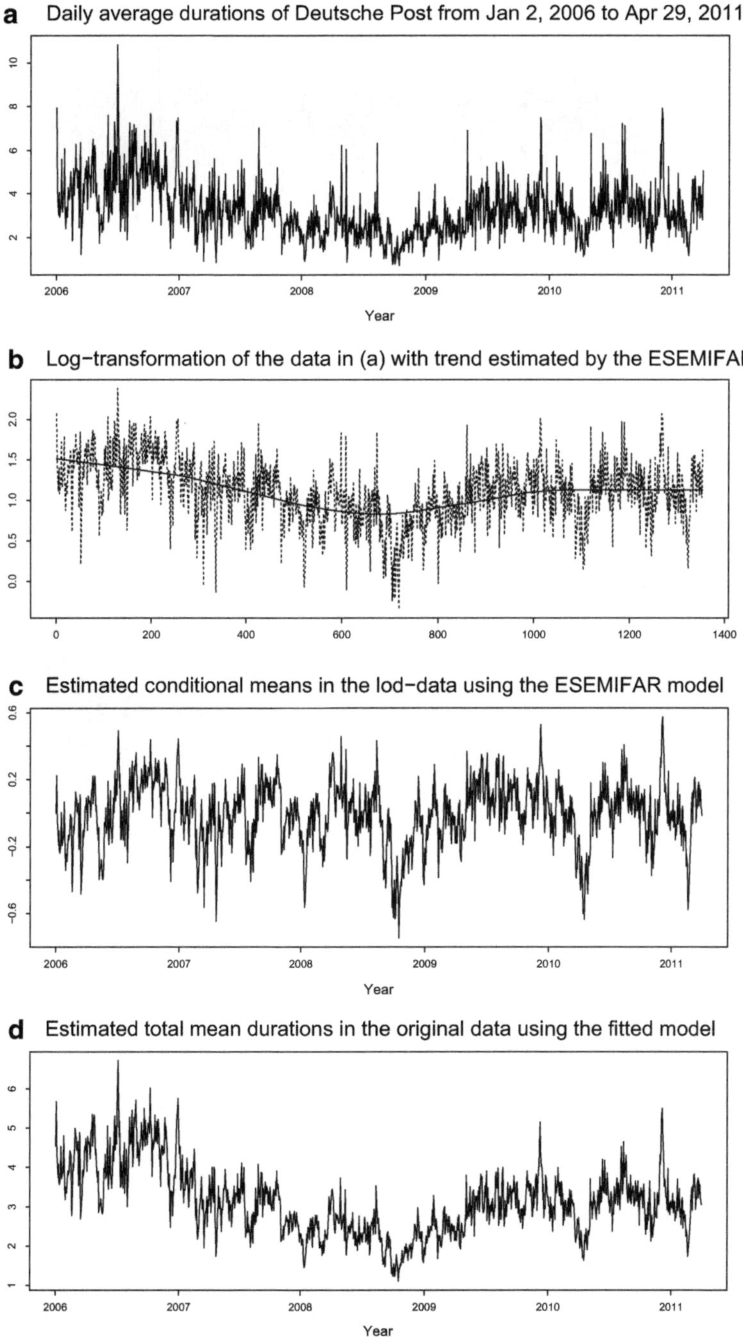

Fig. 1 Daily average durations of Deutsche Post (**a**); log-transformation together with the estimated trend (**b**); estimated conditional means in the log-data (**c**); estimated total means in the original data (**d**)

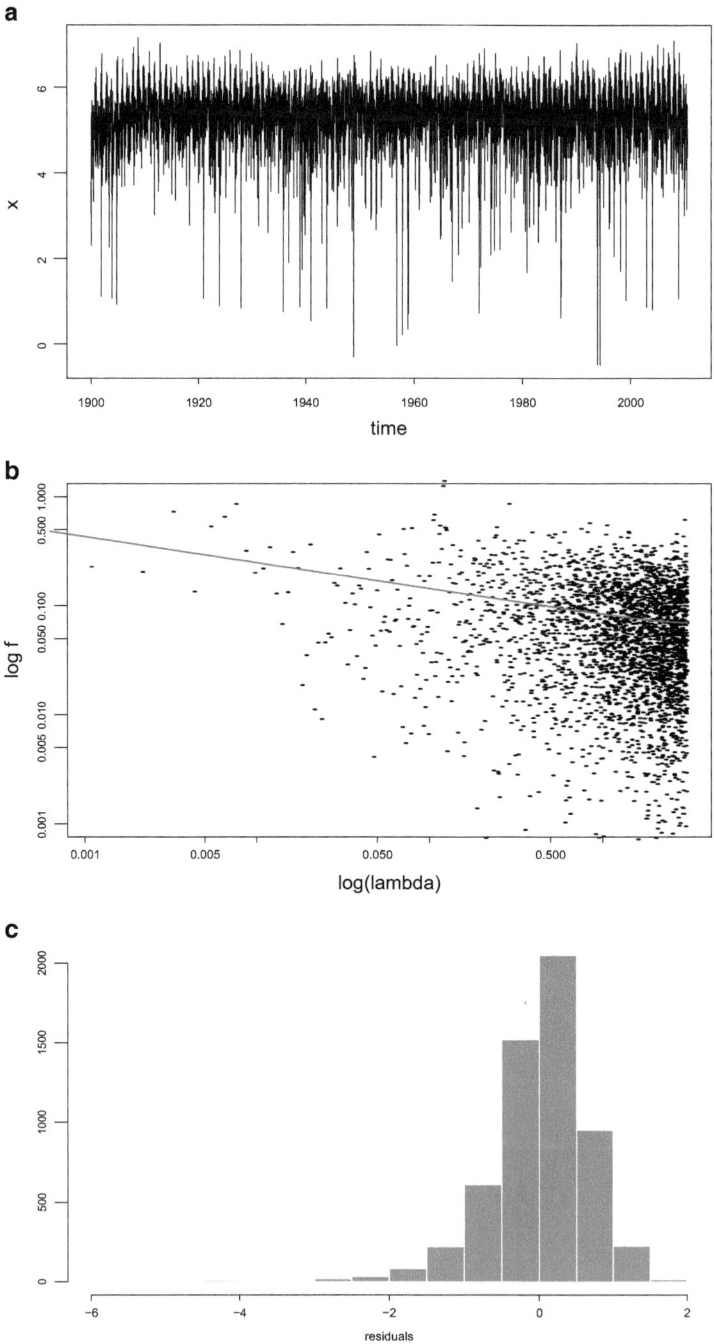

Fig. 2 (**a**) Logarithms of weekly averaged daily sunshine durations (seasonally adjusted) in Basel between January 1900 and December 2010; (**b**) log–log periodogram and fitted spectral density for the sunshine durations in figure (**a**); (**c**) histogram of $\hat{\varepsilon}_t$

been argued that there may be evidence for an increase in average sunshine durations in the last few decades (see, e.g., Raichijk 2012). These studies did however not take into account the possibility of long-range dependence. A systematic empirical spatial-temporal study using ESEMIFAR models would be useful to examine the conjecture of global dimming and brightening.

6 Final Remarks

In this paper we introduced an EFARIMA model and extended it to the semiparametric ESEMIFAR model that allows for simultaneous modelling of systematic changes, and short- and long-range dependence in duration data. Fitting these models can be done using existing software. The usefulness of the approach was illustrated by applications to duration data from finance and environmental sciences.

It might be possible to apply the same ideas to modelling volatility in financial returns. Note that the Log-ACD_1 (or $EACD_1$) is defined following the idea of the Log-GARCH (see, e.g., Geweke 1986). It may be expected that a long-memory Log-GARCH model can be defined by applying the idea of an EFARIMA to the Log-GARCH model. Another well-known long-memory exponential GARCH, which is closely related to the EFARIMA model, is the FIEGARCH (fractionally integrated exponential GARCH) introduced by Bollerslev and Mikkelsen (1996). This is a long-memory extension of the EGARCH model proposed by Nelson (1991). The relationship between the EFARIMA and the FIEGARCH models should be clarified in future research. Recently, Lopes and Prass (2012) proved that under mild conditions a FIEGARCH(p, d, q) process can be rewritten as a FARIMA(p, d, 0) process. This indicates in particular that a semiparametric extension of the FIEGARCH model after introducing a scale function should be an ESEMIFAR model (without the MA part). It will therefore be worthwhile to discuss a possible combination of FIEGARCH and SEMIFAR models. If an ESEMIFAR model can be successfully defined as a semiparametric extension of the FIEGARCH model, then it should also be possible to apply the existing data-driven SEMIFAR algorithms to these models.

Acknowledgements The financial data were prepared by Mr. Christian Peitz and Mr. Kan Wang, University of Paderborn. We are very grateful for their support. The sunshine duration data are courtesy of the Federal Office of Meteorology and Climatology MeteoSwiss, Switzerland.

References

Bauwens, L., Galli, F., & Giot, P. (2003). The moments of log-ACD models. Discussion Paper 2003/11, Université Catholique de Louvain.

Bauwens, L., & Giot, P. (2000). The logarithmic ACD model: An application to the bid-ask quote process of three NYSE stocks. *Annales d'Économie et de Statistique, 60*, 117–149.

Bauwens, L., & Hautsch, N. (2007). Modelling financial high frequency data using point processes. CRC Discussion paper no. 2007–066.

Beran, J. (1994). *Statistics for long-memory processes*. New York: Chapman & Hall.

Beran, J. (1995). Maximum likelihood estimation of the differencing parameter for invertible short- and long-memory ARIMA models. *Journal of the Royal Statistical Society, Series B, 57*, 659–672.

Beran, J., Bhansali, R. J, & Ocker, D. (1998). On unified model selection for stationary and nonstationary short- and long-memory autoregressive processes. *Biometrika, 85*(4), 921–934.

Beran, J., & Feng, Y. (2002a). SEMIFAR models—A semiparametric framework for modelling trends, long-range dependence and nonstationarity. *Computational Statistics & Data Analysis, 40*, 393–419.

Beran, J., & Feng, Y. (2002b). Iterative plug-in algorithms for SEMIFAR models - definition, convergence and asymptotic properties. *Journal of Computational and Graphical Statistics, 11*, 690–713.

Beran, J., & Feng, Y. (2002c). Local polynomial fitting with long-memory, short-menory and antipersistent errors. *Annals of the Institute of Statistical Mathematics, 54*, 291–311.

Bollerslev, T., & Mikkelsen, H. (1996). Modeling and pricing long memory in stock market volatility. *Journal of Econometrics, 73*, 151–184.

Dahlhaus, R. (1997). Fitting time series models to nonstationary processes. *The Annals of Statistics, 25*, 1–37.

Deo, R., Hsieh, M., & Hurvich, C. (2010). Long memory in intertrade durations, counts and realized volatility of nyse stocks. *Journal of Statistical Planning and Inference, 140*, 3715–3733.

Deo, R., Hurvich, C. Soulier, P., & Wang, Y. (2009). Conditions for the propagation of memory parameter from durations to counts and realized volatility. *Econometric Theory, 25*, 764–792.

Dittmann, I., & Granger, C. (2002). Properties of nonlinear transformations of fractionally integrated processes. *Journal of Econometrics, 110*, 113–133.

Dufour, A., & Engle, R. F. (2000). The ACD model: Predictability of the time between consecutive trades. Discussion papers in finance. ISMA Centre, 59.

Engle, R. F. (2002), New frontiers for ARCH models. *The Journal of Applied Econometrics, 17*, 425–446.

Engle, R. F., & Russell, J. R. (1998). Autoregressive conditional duration: A new model for irregularly spaced transaction data. *Econometrica, 66*, 1127–1162.

Fernandes, M., & Grammig, J. (2006). A family of autoregressive conditional duration models. *Journal of Econometrics, 130*, 1–23.

Fox, R., & Taqqu, M. S. (1986). Large-sample properties of parameter estimates for strongly dependent stationary Gaussian time series. *The Annals of Statistics, 14*, 517–532.

Geweke, J. (1986). Modelling the persistence of conditional variance: A comment. *Econometric Reviews, 5*, 57–61.

Giraitis, L., & Surgailis, D. (1989). Limit theorem for polynomials of a linear process with long-range dependence. *Lithuanian Mathematical Journal, 29*(2), 128–145.

Giraitis, L., & Surgailis, D. (1990). A central limit theorem for quadratic forms in strongly dependent linear variables and its application to asymptotical normality of Whittle's estimate. *Probability Theory and Related Fields, 86*(1), 87–104.

Hall, P., & Hart, J. D. (1990). Nonparametric regression with long-range dependence. *Stochastic Processes and Applications, 36*, 339–351.

Haslett, J., & Raftery, A. E. (1989). Space-time modelling with long-memory dependence: Assessing Ireland's wind power resource. *Applied Statistics, 38*, 1–50.

Hautsch, N. (2012). *Econometrics of financial high-frequency data*. Berlin: Springer.

Jasiak, J. (1998). Persistence in intertrade durations. *Finance, 19*, 166–195.

Karanasos, M. (2004). Statistical properties of long-memory ACD models. *WESEAS Transactions on Business and Economics, 1*, 169–175.

Karanasos, M. (2008). The statistical properties of exponential ACD models. *Quantitative and Qualitative Analysis in Social Sciences, 2*, 29–49.

Koulikov, D. (2003). Modeling sequences of long memory non-negative stationary random variables. Working Paper 331100. Social Science Research Network.

Lopes, S., & Prass, T. (2012). Theoretical results on FIEGARCH processes. Preprint, Mathematics Institute - UFRGS.

Nelson, D. B. (1991). Conditional heteroskedasticity in asset returns: A new approach. *Econometrica, 59*, 347–370.

Pacurar, M. (2008). Autoregressive conditional duration (ACD) models in finance: A survey of the theoretical and empirical literature. *Journal of Economic Surveys, 22*, 711–751.

Raichijk, C. (2012). Observed trends in sunshine duration over South America. *International Journal of Climatology, 32*(5), 669–680.

Ray, B. K., & Tsay, R. S. (1997). Bandwidth selection for kernel regression with long-range dependence. *Biometrika, 84*, 791–802.

Russell, J. R., Engle, R. F. (2010). Analysis of high frequency data. In Y. Ait-Sahalia & L. P. Hansen (Eds.), *Handbook of financial econometrics* (Vol. 1, pp. 383–426). Amsterdam: Elsevier.

Sun, W., Rachev, S., Fabozzi, F., & Kalev, P. (2008). Fractals in trade duration: Capturing long-range dependence and heavy tailedness in modeling trade duration. *Annals of Finance, 4*, 217–241.

Surgailis, D., & Vaičiulis, M. (1999). Convergence of appell polynomials of long range dependent moving averages in martingale differences. *Acta Applicandae Mathematicae, 58*(1–3), 343–357.

Taqqu, M. S. (1975).Weak convergence to fractional Brownian motion and to the Rosenblatt process. *Z. Wahrsch. und Verw. Gebiete, 31*, 287–302.

Taqqu, M. S., & Teverovsky, V. (1998). On estimating the intensity of long-range dependence in finite and infinite variance series. In R. Adler, R. Feldman, & M. S. Taqqu (Eds.), *A practical guide to heavy tails: Statistical techniques and applications* (pp. 177–217). Boston: Birkhäuser.

Zivot, E., & Wang, J. (2003). *Modeling financial time series with S-PLUS*. New York: Springer.

Prediction Intervals in Linear and Nonlinear Time Series with Sieve Bootstrap Methodology

Héctor Allende, Gustavo Ulloa, and Héctor Allende-Cid

Abstract Forecasting is one of the main goals in time series analysis and it has had a great development in the last decades. In forecasting, the prediction intervals provide additional assessment of the uncertainty compared with a point forecast, which can better guide risk management decisions. The construction of prediction intervals requires fitting a model and the knowledge of the distribution of the observed data, which is typically unknown. Hence, data are usually assumed to follow some hypothetical distribution, and the resulting prediction interval can be adversely affected by departures from that assumption (Thombs and Schucany, J Am Stat Assoc 85:486–492, 1990). For this reason, in the last two decades several works based on free distributions have been proposed as an alternative for the construction of prediction intervals. Some alternatives consist in the sieve bootstrap approach, which assumes that the linear process admits typically an autoregressive AR representation, and it generates "new" realizations from the same model but with the resampled innovations (Alonso et al., J Stat Plan Inference 100:1–11, 2002; Chen et al., J Forecast 30:51–71, 2011). The linear nature of the models has not limited the implementation of the sieve bootstrap methodology in nonlinear models such as GARCH, since the squared returns can also be represented as linear ARMA process (Shumway and Stoffer, Time series analysis and its applications with R examples (2nd ed.). New York: Springer, 2006; Francq and Zakoian, GARCH Models: Structure, statistical inference and financial applications. Chichester: Wiley, 2010; Chen et al., J Forecast 30:51–71, 2011).

H. Allende (✉)
Depto. de Informática, Universidad Técnica Federico Santa María, Valparaíso, Chile

Facultad de Ingeniería, Universidad Adolfo Ibáñez, Viña del Mar, Chile
e-mail: hallende@inf.utfsm.cl

G. Ulloa • H. Allende-Cid
Depto. de Informática, Universidad Técnica Federico Santa María, Valparaíso, Chile
e-mail: gulloa@inf.utfsm.cl; vector@inf.utfsm.cl

J. Beran et al. (eds.), *Empirical Economic and Financial Research*,
Advanced Studies in Theoretical and Applied Econometrics 48,
DOI 10.1007/978-3-319-03122-4_16

The focus of this chapter will be on the construction of prediction intervals with sieve bootstrap. Linear and nonlinear models in time series like AR, ARIMA, ARCH, and GARCH will be analyzed as well as their sieve bootstrap versions. We evaluate their performance with current techniques using Monte Carlo simulations and real data used as benchmark. Finally future research directions will be included, as the application to hybrid models, missing data in time series, and applications in others areas in which the time series have shown great promise.

1 Stochastic Processes

A stochastic process is a family of random variables $\{X_t\}_{t\in T}$ defined over a probability space (Ω, Σ, P), which is indexed by an index set T. The index set T usually corresponds to the integer set $\mathbb{Z} = \{0, \pm 1, \pm 2, \dots\}$ or the real set $\mathbb{R}(\mathbb{C})$, which indicates if the process is discrete or continuous. In the rest of this chapter we assume $T = \mathbb{Z}$.

Stochastic processes are represented by a space of states (range of possible values of the random variables X_t), by its index set T and by the relation of dependency between the random variables X_t. According to the Kolmogorov theorem a stochastic process $\{X_t\}_{t\in T}$ can be specified if we know the finite-dimensional distributions

$$F(x_1, \dots x_n; t_1, \dots, t_n) = P(X_{t_1} \le x_1, \dots, X_{t_n} \le x_n), \tag{1}$$

for all $n \ge 1$.

A stochastic process can also be represented by $X = \{X_{t,\omega}\}_{t\in T, \omega\in\Omega}$, whose domain is the cartesian product between index set T and the sample set Ω. A stochastic process $\{X_t\}_{t\in T}$ is strictly stationary if all its finite-dimensional distributions are invariant to translations over time t (Eq. (1)). This definition of stationarity is too strict for the majority of the applications and is difficult to evaluate in a single data set. A less strict version corresponds to the weak stationarity. A stochastic process $\{X_t\}_{t\in T}$ is weakly stationary if the mean and covariance between X_t and X_{t+h} its invariant in $t \in T$, where h is an arbitrary integer. This process is also known as a second degree stationary process, since it requires the existence of the first two population moments.

More specifically $\{X_t\}_{t\in T}$ is weakly stationary if:

(i) $E(X_t^2) < \infty, \ \forall t \in \mathbb{Z}$,
(ii) $E(X_t) = \mu, \ \forall t \in \mathbb{Z}$,
(iii) $Cov(X_t, X_{t+h}) = \gamma_X(h) \ \forall t, h \in \mathbb{Z}$.

The function $\gamma_X(\cdot)$ is called also autocovariance function of $\{X_t\}_{t\in T}$. Note that condition (iii) also implies that $Var(X_t) = \sigma^2, \ \forall t \in \mathbb{Z}$.

2 Time Series

A time series corresponds to a realization or a trajectory of a stochastic process where the index set T corresponds to time. In practical terms, time series are a sequence of numerical data points in successive order, usually occurring in uniform intervals.

2.1 Linear Models in Time Series

Linear time series models are stochastic processes with a high degree of temporal dependence which admits a general linear representation or MA(∞)

$$x_t = \mu + \varepsilon_t + \sum_{j=1}^{\infty} \psi_j \varepsilon_{t-j}, \tag{2}$$

where μ is the mean of x_t and $\{\varepsilon_t\}_{t\in T}$ is a white noise process with $E[\varepsilon_t] = 0$ and variance σ^2. In order that the latter process is stationary, it is necessary that the coefficients ψ_t are absolutely addable $\sum_{j=0}^{\infty} |\psi_j| < \infty$. Since we can always center the process around the mean μ, we can assume without loss of generality that X is zero mean.

$$x_t = \varepsilon_t + \sum_{j=1}^{\infty} \psi_j \varepsilon_{t-j}, \tag{3}$$

Linear models can also be described as a function of past and present observations of random shocks $\{\varepsilon_t\}_{t\in T}$

$$x_t = f(\varepsilon_t, \varepsilon_{t-1}, \ldots), \tag{4}$$

where $f(\cdot)$ is a linear function.

Other representation for time series models that can be found in the literature (Tsay, 2005) is the one that takes into account the first two conditional moments until the time step $t-1$,

$$x_t = g(F_{t-1}) + \sqrt{h(F_{t-1})}\epsilon_t, \tag{5}$$

where F_{t-1} is the σ-algebra generated in terms of the information available until time $t-1$ and $g(\cdot)$ and $h(\cdot)$ are well-defined functions with $h(\cdot) > 0$ and $\epsilon_t = \frac{\varepsilon_t}{\sigma_t}$. For linear series (2), $g(\cdot)$ is a linear function of elements of F_{t-1} and $h(\cdot) = \sigma_\varepsilon^2$.

3 Parametric Time Series Models

General linear time series models are often insufficient for explaining all of the interesting dynamics of a time series. So, the introduction of correlation as a phenomenon that may be generated through lagged linear relations leads to proposing the well-known autoregressive moving average (ARMA) models. Adding nonstationarity to the model leads to the autoregressive integrated moving average model (ARIMA). In this subsection we will present the ARIMA model and its extensions, the long memory ARMA and Fractional Differencing ARIMA (ARFIMA). In addition we discuss the nonlinear generalized autoregressive conditionally heteroscedastic models GARCH. This models are motivated by finance time series and assume a nonconstant variance.

3.1 ARMA Model

The ARMA stationary processes can be represented by

$$\Phi(B)X_t = \Theta(B)\varepsilon_t, \tag{6}$$

where $\Phi(B)$ and $\Theta(B)$ are backward shift polynomials of operator B, which are defined by

$$\Phi(B) = \phi_0 - \phi_1 B - \phi_2 B^2 - \cdots - \phi_p B^p, \quad \phi_0 = 1, \phi_p \neq 0, \phi_j \in \mathbb{R}, \tag{7}$$

and

$$\Theta(B) = \theta_0 + \theta_1 B + \theta_2 B^2 + \cdots + \theta_q B^q, \quad \theta_0 = 1, \theta_q \neq 0, \theta_j \in \mathbb{R}, \tag{8}$$

where

$$B^k : \mathbb{R}^{\mathbb{Z}} \to \mathbb{R}^{\mathbb{Z}} \tag{9}$$

$$X_t \to X_{t-k}. \tag{10}$$

and $k \in \mathbb{Z}$.

An ARMA(p, q) model is causal and stationary if it can be expressed by a linear combination of its past innovations as

$$X_t = \sum_{j=0}^{\infty} \psi_j \varepsilon_{t-j}, \tag{11}$$

where its backward shift polynomial operator is $\Psi(B) = \sum_{j=0}^{\infty} \psi_j B^j$, which must comply the restriction of being absolutely addable $\sum_{j=0}^{\infty} |\psi_j| < \infty$. Complying the former restrictions of stability, it is possible, with the Z transform, to express the polynomial $\Psi(B)$ as a rational function

$$\psi(z) = \sum_{j=0}^{\infty} \psi_j z^j = \frac{\Theta(z)}{\Phi(z)}, \ |z| \leq 1, \quad z \in \mathbb{C} \tag{12}$$

with which the infinite coefficients of the linear process can be calculated by means of two finite polynomials of order q and p.

To ensure the restriction of causality it is necessary that $\Phi(z) \neq 0$ for $|z| \leq 1$, or that its roots are outside the unity circle.

An ARMA(p,q) model is invertible if it can be expressed as an infinite autoregressive process AR(∞)

$$\pi(B)X_t = \sum_{j=0}^{\infty} \pi_j x_{t-j} = \varepsilon_t, \tag{13}$$

this is equivalent to asking that the moving average polynomial has its roots outside the unity circle $\Theta(z) \neq 0$, for $|z| \leq 1$ with $\theta_q \neq 0$. The coefficients of $\pi(B)$ can be calculated by solving equation

$$\pi(z) = \sum_{j=0}^{\infty} \pi_j z^j = \frac{\Phi(z)}{\Theta(z)}, \quad z \in \mathbb{C}. \tag{14}$$

Note that the invertibility property or AR(∞) representation guarantees the unity in the determination of the model.

3.2 ARIMA and ARFIMA Models

The ARIMA(p,d,q) models are represented as

$$\Psi(B)Z_t = \Theta(B)\varepsilon_t, \tag{15}$$

where $\Psi(B)$ is an autoregressive linear shift operator of the form

$$\Psi(B) : \mathbb{R}^{\mathbb{Z}} \to \mathbb{R}^{\mathbb{Z}} \tag{16}$$

$$Z_t \to \Psi(B)Z_t. \tag{17}$$

The $\Psi(B)$ autoregressive operator has to satisfy the following condition: d of its roots $\Psi(B) = 0$ have value of 1, found in the limit of the unity circle, and the rest are outside of the circle.

We can express the model (15) in the following way

$$\Psi(B)Z_t = \Phi(B)(1-B)^d X_t = \Theta(B)\varepsilon_t, \tag{18}$$

where $\Phi(B)$ is an autoregressive stationary operator and $d \in \mathbb{Z}_0^+$. Once the series X_t has been derived d times, we can assume that it can be represented by a stationary *ARMA* process

$$\Phi(B)W_t = \Theta(B)\varepsilon_t, \tag{19}$$

where $W_t = (1-B)^d X_t$.

The ARFIMA(p,d,q) models, in comparison with the ARIMA(p,d,q) models, have a fractionary differentiation, where $-\frac{1}{2} < d < \frac{1}{2}$.

3.3 GARCH Model

The *GARCH* models are a generalization of autoregressive conditional heteroscedastic (ARCH) models, a family of models proposed in 1986 by Bollerslev. This models are nonlinear, because the observations X_t are nonlinear functions of past and present random shocks

$$x_t = f(\varepsilon_t, \varepsilon_{t-1}, \ldots),$$

where $f(\cdot)$ is a nonlinear function with respect to the variance σ_t^2, which is expressed as a function of time t.

We can define the *GARCH*(p,q) model as

$$y_t = \sigma_t \varepsilon_t, \tag{20}$$

$$\sigma_t^2 = \alpha_0 + \sum_{i=1}^{p} \alpha_i y_{t-i}^2 + \sum_{j=1}^{p} \beta_j \sigma_{t-j}^2, \tag{21}$$

where $\{\varepsilon_t\}_{t\in T}$ is an i.i.d. process with mean zero and variance $\sigma^2 = 1$. This generalization adds to the model the past q conditional volatilities, introducing q new parameters β (a change in the restrictions)

$$\alpha_0 \geq 0,\ \alpha_i \geq 0 \text{ and } \beta_j \geq 0,\ \text{ for } i = 1, \ldots, p \text{ y } j = 1, \ldots q \tag{22}$$

and

$$\sum_{i=1}^{\max(p,q)} (\alpha_i + \beta_i) < 1. \tag{23}$$

Despite the nonlinear nature of the *GARCH* models, these can be represented as a linear *ARMA* model, which presents linearity in the mean and variance Shumway and Stoffer (2006); Francq and Zakoian (2010).

$$y_t^2 = \alpha_0 + \sum_{i=1}^{m}(\alpha_i + \beta_i)y_{t-i}^2 + \eta_t - \sum_{j=1}^{q}\beta_j \eta_{t-j} \tag{24}$$

where $\{y\}_{i=1}^{T}$ is a $ARMA(m,q)$ model with $m = \max(p,q)$ and $\{\eta\}_{i=1}^{T}$ is a white noise. The latter expression is not generally i.i.d. unless one assumes the strict stationarity of $\{y\}_{i=1}^{T}$ (Chen et al., 2011) .

4 Bootstrap in Time Series

In many statistical procedures it is necessary to know the sample distribution of the statistics or the used estimators. For example, for the construction of confidence intervals and hypothesis tests it is necessary to know the quantiles of the distribution of the estimator, and for estimation problems it is necessary to know a precision measure like the variance, skew, or mean squared error (Alonso et al., 2002b).

The classic approach to determine the quantiles of the estimator distributions is by means of the use of pivotal statistics, which converges asymptotically to a known distribution when the law of probability of the observed process satisfies some assumptions, e.g. gaussian distribution.

For the case of precision measures of an estimator, the estimation is performed by means of the empirical analogous of the analytic formulas obtained from a determined model. These approximations require some assumptions and simplifications of the model. If these assumptions do not hold, the approximations produce wrong results. On the other hand, it is difficult or impossible to obtain analytic formulas of the precision measure for most of the statistics.

Resampling methods evaluate the statistics of the obtained resamples from the original sample, where these values are used to estimate the distribution function of the estimators, in order to avoid analytic derivations based on assumptions that may not be true. The most popular resampling method is bootstrap, a method based on resamples of an i.i.d. sample. Due to the fact that the structure of correlations of the time series violates the independence assumption of the observed data, several extensions to the classic bootstrap method for time series models, like block bootstrap and sieve bootstrap, need to take into account the structure of temporal dependence (Efron and Tibshirani, 1995; Bühlmann, 2002).

The classic approach to time series analysis and the generation of prediction intervals corresponds to the Box–Jenkins methodology. This methodology relies on assumptions of normality for the distribution of the innovative process. The obtained prediction intervals are affected in a malicious way when there are deviations from the normality assumption. To treat this problem, several methods based on bootstrap techniques have been proposed, which give more robust results than the classic approach (Bühlmann, 2002; Politis, 2003; Härdle, 2003; Pascual et al., 2004).

There are several works about bootstrap in time series estimation in the literature over the years. The authors in Stine (1987) proposed a bootstrap method to estimate the mean squared error of the prediction, of a linear $AR(p)$ model, where p is known. In 1990, Thombs and Schucany proposed a backward and forward bootstrap method for prediction intervals of an $AR(p)$ also with a known p value. In 1997, Cao et al. proposed a faster alternative, which consists in generating resamples only from future realizations (forwards), without obtaining bootstrap estimations of the autoregressive parameters. After that, Pascual et al. (2004) generalized the Cao approximation for $ARMA(p, q)$ models with known parameters. Alonso et al. (2002a) proposed an $AR(\infty)$ sieve bootstrap procedure, which consists in inverting a mean average stationary process of order infinity.

5 Bootstrap

The bootstrap method is a method based on resampling with substitution from a random sample $X_1, X_2, \ldots, X_n$, which allows us to estimate the distribution of some statistic $G(x)$ of interest. This method also allows to estimate the precision of the estimations and the statistical tests performed based on a methodology, that uses less or no structural and parametric assumptions of the process under analysis. The bootstrap method was proposed in 1979 by Bradley Efron. The algorithm can be summarized in the following steps:

1. Generate B samples with replacement $X_1^*, \ldots, X_n^*$ from $X_1, \ldots, X_n$.
2. Compute B times the statistic of interest $\hat{\theta}$.
3. Estimate the distribution $G(x^*)$ from (2).

Step 1 consists in generating B resamples with replacement from a random sample $X_1, \ldots, X_n$. The usual number of B is ≥ 1000 to estimate the expected value and the variance of one statistic. This resampling is performed from the estimated distribution function $\hat{F}(x)$, which can be obtained in two ways, one parametric and one nonparametric. The parametric bootstrap assumes that the distribution function that was generated from the random sample $X_1, \ldots, X_n$, comes from a known parametric or theoretical family $F(x, \theta)$, and estimates $\hat{F}$ as $\hat{F}(x) = F(x, \hat{\theta})$, where $\hat{\theta}$ is a Fisher estimator. The obtained resamples $X_1^*, \ldots, X_n^*$ can take values within the range of $F(x, \hat{\theta})$, which can be continuous or discrete. The nonparametric bootstrap instead uses the empirical function distribution, estimated from the sample $X_1, X_2, \ldots, X_n$, which assigns the same probability $\frac{1}{n}$ to each element of the sample. That is why in the resample $X_1^*, \ldots, X_n^*$ only elements of the original sample appear. In the nonparametric resampling case, each element of the random sample $X_1, \ldots, X_n$ can appear more than once in the resample $X_1^*, \ldots, X_n^*$.

In step 2, with every resample we estimate the statistic of interest by means of its empirical version $\hat{\theta}(x^*)$. Finally, with the bootstrap estimation of the statistics of interest we can obtain an estimation of distribution $G(x^*)$ by means of $\hat{G}(x^*, \hat{F})$ and some characteristics of its population moments. For example, if we need to estimate the expected value and precision of a specific statistic $\hat{\theta}$, we can obtain its estimations in the following way:

$$\hat{\mu}^*_{\hat{\theta}} = \frac{1}{B}\sum_{b=1}^{B}\hat{\theta}^*_b$$

for the expected value of $\hat{\theta}$ and the estimation of the standard error is

$$\hat{\sigma}^*_{\hat{\theta}} = \sqrt{\frac{1}{B-1}\sum_{b=1}^{B}\left(\hat{\theta}^*_b - \hat{\mu}^*_{\hat{\theta}}\right)}$$

5.1 Bootstrap Confidence Intervals

Confidence intervals correspond to random sets with limits which do not depend on unknown quantities (θ, F), including the real unknown parameter θ with a specific probability (e.g., 95 %).

$$P\left(\hat{\theta}_\alpha \leq \theta \leq \hat{\theta}_{1-\alpha}\right) = 1 - 2\alpha$$

The approximation of the intervals by means of bootstrap is based mainly on the empirical quantiles obtained from the B estimations $\hat{\theta}^*$ obtained from the resamplings.

The percentile intervals can be obtained in the following way:

$$\left[\hat{\theta}^*_{\frac{\alpha}{2}};\hat{\theta}^*_{1-\frac{\alpha}{2}}\right] \tag{25}$$

where $\hat{\theta}^*_\alpha$ corresponds to the $100 \cdot \alpha$ empirical percentile of the $\hat{\theta}^*$.

The percentile intervals, being based on the empirical quantiles, estimate in a more reliable way the probability distribution of the estimator $\hat{\theta}$ than the classic symmetric intervals, which are valid only when the distributional assumptions are met (Davison and Hinkley, 1997).

The BCa (Bias Corrected accelerated) confidence intervals are also based on the bootstrap percentiles, but with the difference that the selected percentiles take into account the skew and asymmetry of the empirical distribution of the estimator (Efron and Tibshirani, 1995; Davison and Hinkley, 1997)

$$\left[\hat{\theta}^*_{\alpha_1};\hat{\theta}^*_{\alpha_2}\right]$$

where in general the percentiles $\hat{\theta}^*_{\alpha_1}$ and $\hat{\theta}^*_{\alpha_2}$ have not the same probability in the tails. These differences make that the obtained intervals are more precise than the percentile intervals.

6 Bootstrap Methods in Time Series

In this subsection we will present two of the main bootstrap methods for time series: block bootstrap and sieve bootstrap.

6.1 *Block Bootstrap*

The block bootstrap method uses an i.i.d. resampling method with replacement from blocks of l observations of the time series. It uses blocks $X_{t+1}, \ldots, X_{t+l}$ in order to preserve the dependence structure of the time series in each block, where its length must be adequate to capture the structure and to keep independence between them (Bühlmann, 2002). This idea was first proposed in Hall (1992), but the formal proposition can be found in the work of Künsch (1989).

The obtained blocks can have overlapping observations, which increments the quantity of generated blocks in comparison with a version with nonoverlapping blocks. The B bootstrap resamples generate B trajectories or series that are designed to preserve the structure of the original series. Before applying an estimator $\hat{\theta}$ of a parameter of the time series, it is important to consider the dimension of the distribution function of parameter θ, which is a functional of the m-dimensional distribution of the time series, so we can estimate it as $\hat{\theta} = T(\hat{F}^m)$. The dimension will depend on which parameter we are interested, for example, if we want to determine the autocorrelation of the time series in one step ahead, $\rho(X_t, X_{t+1})$, the dimension is $m = 2$, so before generating the necessary blocks we need to vectorize the consecutive observations $Y_t = (X_{t-m}, \ldots, X_t)$ $t = m, \ldots, n$ with which we will build the overlapped blocks $(Y_m, \ldots, Y_{m+l-1}), (Y_{m+1}, \ldots, Y_{m+l}), \ldots, (Y_{n-l+1}, \ldots, Y_n)$, where $l \in \mathbb{N}$ is the length of the blocks. This vectorization avoids the separation, and posterior union of the blocks that will affect the estimation of the statistics, because consecutive observations, for example, $\rho(X_t, X_{t+1})$ may be altered.

This method does not assume that the observed time series belongs to any parametric family, so we could say that this method is not parametric and, in this sense, more general than the sieve bootstrap method that will be explained in the following subsection.

6.2 *Sieve Bootstrap*

Sieve bootstrap, as Block bootstrap, is a bootstrap method to generate trajectories from the original time series maintaining its probabilistic structure. The sieve bootstrap method is based on resampling with replacement from the residuals obtained from estimating the stochastic process that generated the observed time series. The sieve bootstrap method is based on the approximation of an infinite dimensional or nonparametric model by means of a sequence of finite dimensional parametric models, due that the order of the model converges to infinity as $n \to \infty$ (Bühlmann, 1997). The sieve bootstrap method is based on the Wold theorem, which establishes that if we decompose a stationary stochastic process $\{X_t\}_{t\in\mathbb{Z}}$, and we take the stochastic part, it can be represented as a stochastic mean average stationary process $\{X_t\}_{t\in\mathbb{Z}}$ of order infinity or general linear model

$$X_t - \mu_X = \sum_{j=0}^{\infty} \psi_j \varepsilon_{t-j}, \qquad \psi_0 = 1,\, t \in \mathbb{Z} \tag{26}$$

where $\{\varepsilon_t\}_{t\in\mathbb{Z}}$ is an i.i.d. process with $E[\varepsilon_t] = 0$ y $\sum_{j=0}^{\infty} \psi_j^2 < \infty$. This general linear representation plus some assumptions allow us to use the sieve method in linear autoregressive and mean average autoregressive models.

7 Sieve Bootstrap Confidence Intervals

The sieve bootstrap confidence intervals are built from the empirical quantiles obtained from the B bootstrap observations X^*_{T+h}. These observations, h steps ahead, are part of the B bootstrap trajectories generated by means of the sieve bootstrap algorithm for prediction intervals, with which we estimate the conditional distribution of X_{T+h}, given the known or past observations until a time T.

In Fig. 1 we observe an ARMA(1,1) time series together with the trajectories obtained with sieve bootstrap. The new trajectories approximate the probabilistic structure of the original time series.

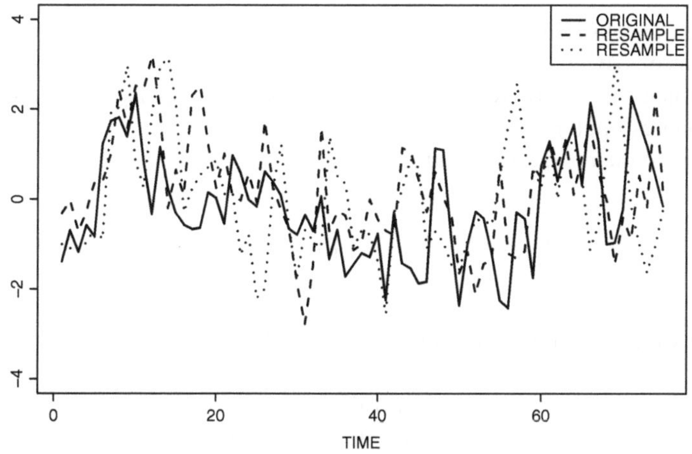

Fig. 1 Original series and bootstrap trajectories

Despite the fact that the sieve bootstrap procedure has been proven more efficient than the classic methodology of Box and Jenkins, the prediction intervals obtained are affected by the presence of innovative outliers, generating an inflation in the length of the prediction intervals. This effect is unwanted, because what we expect from a prediction interval is that it concentrates a high probability of containing a future observation and at the same time that its length is as short as possible.

7.1 Winsorized Sieve Bootstrap

The innovative outliers present in the time series affect the estimated residuals and then the bootstrap time series and its respectives obtained prediction intervals, where they suffer from an increase of its lengths, thus losing precision.

One way to deal with this problem is to add a stage to the existing sieve bootstrap algorithms for interval prediction, like AR-sieve bootstrap (Alonso et al., 2002a) and GARCH-sieve bootstrap (Chen et al., 2011). This stage consists in using a winsorized filter of order k, over the residuals that have been obtained after adjusting a high order linear process over the observed time series, *AR* or *ARMA* respectively. The difference between the winsorized filter and the truncated filters is that the winsorized filter replaces the k statistics of extreme orders with statistics of order $X_{(k+1)}$ and $X_{(n-k-1)}$, which correspond to the extreme values of the remaining ordered residual samples. In both algorithms the winsorized filter is added at stage 4.

The winsorized sieve bootstrap algorithms for prediction intervals for linear and nonlinear GARCH models are the following:

7.2 Winsorized AR-Sieve Bootstrap

(1) Given an observed time series $\{X_1, \ldots, X_T\}$, and an estimated order p by means of AICc.
(2) Estimate the autoregressive coefficients $(\hat{\phi}_1, \cdots, \hat{\phi}_{\hat{p}})$ by mean of the Yule–Walker estimators.
(3) Estimate the residuals $\hat{\varepsilon}_t$ with:

$$\hat{\varepsilon}_t = X_t - \sum_{j=1}^{\hat{p}} \hat{\phi}_j (X_{t-j} - \hat{\mu}_X) \text{ for } t = \hat{p}+1, \hat{p}+2, \cdots, T \tag{27}$$

(4) Apply the winsorized filter of order k over the residuals

$$\hat{\varepsilon}_{(t)} = \begin{cases} \hat{\varepsilon}_{(\hat{p}+k+1)} \text{ if } t < \hat{p}+k+1 \\ \hat{\varepsilon}_{(t)} \text{ if } \hat{p}+k+1 \le t \le T-k \\ \hat{\varepsilon}_{(T-k)} \text{ if } t > T-k \end{cases} \tag{28}$$

where $\hat{\varepsilon}_{(t)}$ represents the order statistic t.

(5) Obtain the empirical distribution of the centered residuals

$$\hat{F}_{\tilde{\varepsilon}}(x) = \frac{1}{T - \hat{p}} \sum_{p+1}^{T} 1_{\{\tilde{\varepsilon}_t \leq x\}} \tag{29}$$

where: $\tilde{\varepsilon}_t = \hat{\varepsilon}_t - \hat{\varepsilon}^{(\cdot)}$ y $\hat{\varepsilon}^{(\cdot)} = \frac{1}{T-\hat{p}} \sum_{p+1}^{T} \hat{\varepsilon}_t$

(6) Generate a resample of the residuals ε_t^* with i.i.d. observations from $\hat{F}_{\tilde{\varepsilon}}$.

(7) Generate a new series $\{X_1^*, \ldots, X_n^*\}$ with the following recursion:

$$X_t^* - \hat{\mu}_X = \sum_{j=1}^{\hat{p}} \hat{\phi}_j (X_{t-}^* - \hat{\mu}_X) + \varepsilon_t^* \tag{30}$$

where the first $\hat{p}$ values are: $(X_1, \cdots, X_{\hat{p}}) = (\hat{\mu}_X, \cdots, \hat{\mu}_X)$.

In practice series of length $n + 100$ are generated, discarding the first 100 observations.

(8) Estimate the autoregressive bootstrap coefficients $(\hat{\phi}_1^*, \cdots, \hat{\phi}_{\hat{p}}^*)$ as in step 2.

(9) Calculate the future bootstrap observation with the following recursion:

$$X_{T+h}^* - \hat{\mu}_X = \sum_{j=1}^{\hat{p}} \hat{\phi}_j^* (X_{T+h-j}^* - \hat{\mu}_X) + \varepsilon_t^* \tag{31}$$

where $h > 0$ and $X_t^* = X_t$, for $t \leq T$

(10) Repeat steps 6–9, B times.

(11) Finally, using $F^*_{X^*_{T+h}}$ obtain the prediction interval of $100(1-\alpha)\%$ for X_{T+h} given by $[Q^*_{(\alpha/2)}, Q^*_{(1-\alpha/2)}]$ where $Q^*_{(\cdot)}$ is a quantile of the estimated bootstrap distribution.

7.3 *Winsorized GARCH-Sieve Bootstrap*

(1) Estimate the ARMA coefficients $\hat{\alpha}_0$, $(\widehat{\alpha_1 + \beta_1}), \ldots, (\widehat{\alpha_m + \beta_m})$, $\hat{\beta}_1, \ldots, \hat{\beta}_q$, by means of the mean square algorithm. Then estimate $\hat{\alpha}_i = (\widehat{\alpha_1 + \beta_1}) - \hat{\beta}_i$ for $i = 1, \ldots, p$.

(2) Estimate the residuals $\{\hat{\nu}_t\}_{t=m+1}^{T}$ with

$$\hat{\nu}_t = y_t^2 - \hat{\alpha}_0 - \sum_{i=1}^{m} (\widehat{\alpha_i + \beta_i}) y_{t-i}^2 + \sum_{j=1}^{q} \hat{\beta}_j \nu_{t-j} \text{ for } t = m+1, \cdots, T \tag{32}$$

(3) Center the estimated residuals with

$$\tilde{\nu}_t = \left(\hat{\nu}_t - \frac{1}{T-m} \sum_{t=m+1}^{T} \hat{\nu}_t \right) \tag{33}$$

where the empirical distribution is

$$\hat{F}_{\nu,T}(y) = \sum_{m+1}^{T} 1_{\{\tilde{\nu}_t \leq y\}} \tag{34}$$

(4) Apply the winsorized filter of order k over the residuals

$$\tilde{\nu}_{(t)} = \begin{cases} \tilde{\nu}_{(p+k+1)} \text{ if } t < p+k+1 \\ \tilde{\nu}_{(t)} \text{ if } p+k+1 \leq t \leq T-k \\ \tilde{\nu}_{(T-k)} \text{ if } t > T-k \end{cases} \tag{35}$$

where $\tilde{\nu}_{(t)}$ represents the statistic of order t.

(5) Generate a resample $\{\nu_t^*\}_{t=1}^T$ from $\hat{F}_{\nu,T}(y)$.

(6) Generate a bootstrap resample of the squared $\{y_t^{2*}\}_{t=1}^T$ with

$$y_t^{2*} = \hat{\alpha}_0 + \sum_{i=1}^{m} \widehat{(\alpha_i + \beta_i)} y_{t-i}^{2*} + \nu_t^* - \sum_{j=1}^{q} \hat{\beta}_j \nu_{t-j}^* \tag{36}$$

where $y_k^{2*} = \frac{\hat{\alpha}_0}{1-\sum_{i=1}^{m}\widehat{(\alpha_i+\beta_i)}}$ y $\nu_k^* = 0$ for $k \leq 0$

(7) Given $\{y_t^{2*}\}_{t=1}^T$ from step 6, estimate the coefficients $\hat{\alpha}_0^*$, $\widehat{(\alpha_1 + \beta_1)}^*, \ldots,$ $\widehat{(\alpha_m + \beta_m)}^*$, $\hat{\beta}_1^*, \ldots, \hat{\beta}_q^*$, $\hat{\alpha}_i^* = \widehat{(\alpha_1 + \beta_1)}^* - \hat{\beta}_i^*$ para $i = 1, \ldots, p$. The bootstrap sample for the volatility is$\{\sigma_t^{2*}\}_{t=1}^T$ and is obtained by means of

$$\sigma_t^{2*} = \hat{\alpha}_0^* + \sum_{i=1}^{p} \hat{\alpha}_i^* y_{t-i}^{2*} + \sum_{j=1}^{q} \hat{\beta}_j^* \sigma_{t-j}^{2*} \text{ for } t = m+1, \cdots, T \tag{37}$$

with $\sigma_t^{2*} = \frac{\hat{\alpha}_0}{1-\sum_{i=1}^{m}(\hat{\alpha}_i+\hat{\beta}_i)}$, for $t = 1, \cdots, m$.

(8) Resample with replacement from $\hat{F}_{\nu,T}(y)$ to obtain the error process of the bootstrap prediction $\{\nu_{t+h}^*\}_{h=1}^s$ where $s \geq 1$.

(9) Be $y_{T+h}^* = y_{T+h}$, $\nu_{T+h}^* = \tilde{\nu}_{T+h}$ y $\sigma_{T+h}^{2*} = \sigma_{T+h}^{2*}$ for $h \leq 0$

$$y_{T+h}^{2*} = \hat{\alpha}_0^* + \sum_{i=1}^{m} \widehat{(\alpha_i + \beta_i)}^* y_{T+h-i}^{2*} + \nu_{T+h}^* - \sum_{j=1}^{q} \hat{\beta}_j^* \nu_{T+h-j}^* \tag{38}$$

$$\sigma^{2*}_{T+h} = \hat{\alpha}^*_0 + \sum_{i=1}^{p} \hat{\alpha}^*_i y^{2*}_{T+h-i} + \sum_{j=1}^{q} \hat{\beta}^*_j \sigma^{2*}_{T+h-j} \text{ f } h = 1, \ldots, s \tag{39}$$

(10) Repeat steps 4–8, B times.
(11) Finally, we obtain prediction intervals $100(1-\alpha)\%$ for y_{T+h} and σ^2_{T+h} using $\hat{F}^*_{y^{2*}_{T+h}}$ and $\hat{F}^*_{\sigma^{2*}_{T+h}}$.

- For y_{T+h}:

$$\left[-\sqrt{H^*_{(1-\alpha)}}, \sqrt{H^*_{(1-\alpha)}}\right], h = 1, \cdots, s \tag{40}$$

where $H^*_{(1-\alpha)}$ is the quantile $1-\alpha$ of $\hat{F}^*_{y^{2*}_{T+h}}$

- For σ^2_{T+h}:

$$\left[0, K^*_{(1-\alpha)}\right], h = 1, \cdots, s \tag{41}$$

where $K^*_{(1-\alpha)}$ is the quantile $1-\alpha$ of $\hat{F}^*_{\sigma^{2*}_{T+h}}$

7.4 Simulations

The outliers in the innovative process (IO) tend to generate a bigger impact on the time series than the additive outliers (AO), because its effect is related strongly with the order of the process (deterministic part of the process). The innovative outlier model was proposed in 1972 by Fox

$$F_{\varepsilon_t} = (1-\zeta)N(0, \sigma_0^2) + \zeta N(0, \sigma_1^2) \tag{42}$$

where $\sigma_1^2 \gg \sigma_0^2$ and ζ corresponds to the contamination level.

Next, some results showing the performance of algorithms based on sieve bootstrap for interval prediction are presented.

The simulated processes are the following:

- ARMA(1,1):

$$X_t = 0.4X_{t-1} + 0.3\varepsilon_{t-1} + \varepsilon_t \tag{43}$$

- ARCH(2):

$$y_t = \sigma_t \cdot \varepsilon_t \tag{44}$$

$$\sigma_t^2 = 0.1 + 0.2y_{t-1}^2 + 0.15y_{t-2}^2 \tag{45}$$

Table 1 Simulate results with innovative process $F_{\varepsilon_t} = (1-\zeta)N(0,1) + \zeta N(0,10)$

h	k	Method	Coverage (s.d.)	Length (s.d.)	CQM
h = 1	–	BJ	96.36 (0.24)	4.54 (0.04)	0.173
	–	SB	95.32 (0.19)	4.51 (0.05)	0.150
	1	WSB	95.31 (0.19)	4.54 (0.05)	0.153
	2	WSB	94.39 (0.21)	4.22 (0.04)	0.080
	3	**WSB**	93.21 (0.24)	4.01 (0.04)	**0.039**
	4	WSB	91.72 (0.22)	3.72 (0.03)	0.086
	5	WSB	90.22 (0.24)	3.53 (0.03)	0.150
h = 3	–	BJ	96.34 (0.15)	5.62 (0.05)	0.447
	–	SB	95.40 (0.19)	5.58 (0.07)	0.136
	1	WSB	94.91 (0.19)	5.37 (0.05)	0.087
	2	**WSB**	94.03 (0.20)	5.06 (0.05)	**0.033**
	3	WSB	93.14 (0.22)	4.85 (0.04)	0.039
	4	WSB	92.19 (0.21)	4.63 (0.03)	0.093
	5	WSB	91.67 (0.22)	4.55 (0.03)	0.115

The parameters of the simulation were:

- $S = 1,000$ time series simulated for ARMA and ARCH processes.
- $B = 1,000$ sieve bootstrap trajectories.
- $R = 1,000$ simulations of future observations X_{T+h} for both processes and for the ARCH process we add σ^2_{T+h} for h steps ahead.

The following tables show the results of the comparison of the models regarding coverage and length of the intervals, in addition to the combined metric CQM proposed in Alonso et al. (2002a), which depends on the theoretical coverage and length, and the empirical values obtained with the bootstrap prediction intervals. This metric is a discrepancy metric between the theoretical aim and the empirical performance, for that, a smaller value obtained in this metric indicates a better performance of the prediction interval.

In Table 1 we can see for $h = 1$ and $h = 3$ steps-ahead, that the methods (SB) and (WSB) perform better than the classical method (BJ), with respect to the metric CQM. We observe an inflection point in $k = 3$ for $h = 1$ step-ahead and in $k = 2$ for $h = 3$ steps-ahead, which is observed in the combined metric CQM. The method (WSB) has better results for $h = 1$ and $h = 3$ steps-ahead than the method (SB) and (WSB) when $k > 1$, because the winsorized filter diminishes the impact of the outliers. We can see the best results in bold.

In Table 2 we observe that under the presence of contamination in the innovative process the prediction intervals of the algorithm (SB) are clearly affected by the coverture of the returns and volatility, and also the increment in the length of them. Also it is observed that the method (WSB) has a positive impact on the performance of the prediction intervals of the returns and volatility. It seems that if the filter order of algorithm WSB increases, the covertures and lengths of the prediction intervals converge to the theoretical covertures and lengths.

Table 2 Simulate results with ARCH(2) model Simulate with innovative process $F_{\varepsilon_t} = (1-\zeta)N(0,1) + \zeta N(0,100)$

h	k	Method	Coverage return (d.e.)	Length return (d.e.)	CQM return	Coverage volatility (d.e.)	Length volatility (d.e.)	CQM volatility
h = 1	–	EMP	95 %	2.44	–	95 %	–	–
	–	SB	98.34 (6.11)	7.86 (15.71)	2.248	98.40 (12.55)	112.43 (1236.36)	–
	1	WSB	97.33 (8.24)	4.57 (3.59)	0.898	97.90 (14.34)	14.85 (81.14)	–
	2	WSB	96.52 (9.76)	2.94 (2.59)	0.647	97.80 (14.67)	7.74 (34.23)	–
	3	**WSB**	96.26 (9.78)	3.71 (2.04)	**0.544**	97.70 (14.99)	4.99 (15.92)	–
h = 5	–	EMP	95 %	1.78	–	95 %	0.94	–
	–	SB	99.73 (0.84)	10.55 (18.51)	4.969	99.74 (1.31)	144.36 (1537.29)	152.633
	1	WSB	99.51 (2.51)	6.99 (4.95)	2.970	99.62 (1.97)	20.85 (107.61)	21.186
	2	WSB	99.52 (1.83)	6.35 (3.71)	2.616	99.57 (2.16)	11.44 (56.02)	11.292
	3	**WSB**	99.48 (2.10)	5.97 (2.65)	**2.397**	99.52 (2.34)	7.28 (16.23)	**6.792**
h = 10	–	EMP	95 %	1.61	–	95 %	0.29	–
	–	SB	99.83 (0.18)	10.89 (18.87)	5.803	99.89 (0.17)	149.95 (1579.38)	507.893
	1	WSB	99.77 (0.34)	7.38 (5.49)	3.627	99.84 (0.21)	23.06 (113.41)	77.270
	2	WSB	99.55 (3.24)	6.67 (4.36)	3.187	99.82 (0.23)	13.56 (67.12)	45.054
	3	**WSB**	99.51 (3.03)	6.25 (3.35)	**2.92**	99.79 (0.25)	8.79 (19.69)	**28.800**

8 Closing Remark

The inference bootstrap proposed by Efron for independent data can be extended for dependent data, in particular it can be used on time series, where two of the main approximations correspond to: block bootstrap and sieve bootstrap.

The block bootstrap is the most general method but has several disadvantages. It is necessary to perform a prevectorization of the data, and the resampling could exhibit artifacts where resampled blocks are linked together, implying that the plug-in rule for bootstrapping an estimator is not appropriate. Double bootstrapping, which could give us more precision, does not seem promising (Bühlmann, 2002). Instead, sieve bootstrap, where the resampling is performed from a reasonable time series model, implies that the plug-in rule makes sense for defining and computing the bootstrapped estimator. Double bootstrap potentially leads to higher order accuracy, which has led this model to become much more popular.

Inference techniques based on bootstrap have demonstrated to have better results, in comparison with classic inference techniques, which assume a known distribution of the underlying process. The prediction intervals obtained with sieve bootstrap have shown, by means of simulations, to obtain better results in coverage and shorter lengths, which has been studied in Alonso et al. (2002a) together with the performance of the combined metric CQM.

Despite the fact that sieve bootstrap is widely used in linear time series modeling, specially the AR sieve bootstrap, this method can be used in nonlinear models ARCH/GARCH, because the squared returns can be represented as AR/ARMA processes (Chen et al., 2011). Hence, we can adopt a sieve bootstrap procedure to estimate the prediction intervals for the returns and volatility of GARCH models, which can be less expensive, from a computational cost, than other bootstrap proposals, as those presented in Pascual et al. (2006).

In this chapter we presented the impact produced in interval prediction by the presence of innovative outliers in time series, which produces a loss in precision and efficiency, because the length of the intervals is affected. We also showed that the use of a winsorized filter over the estimated residuals can diminish the impact of isolated outliers, which is perceived in a lower value of the combined metric CQM.

In order to reduce the impact of outliers over the prediction, it may be interesting to study the effect that the incorporation of robust statistic approaches could produce, not only over the estimated residuals, but also in stages of parameter estimation of the models or even for the estimation of their structural parameters. Also it is necessary to investigate the effect that patch outliers could produce.

Acknowledgements This work was supported by the following Research Grants: Fondecyt 1110854 and FB0821 Centro Científico Tecnológico de Valparaíso. Partial support was also received from Mecesup FSM 0707. We also want to thank Dr. Ricardo Ñanculef for his important contribution in the realization of this chapter.

References

Alonso, A., Peña, D., & Romo, J. (2002). Forecasting time series with sieve bootstrap. *Journal of Statistical Planning and Inference*, *100*, 1–11.
Alonso, A., Peña, D., & Romo, J. (2002). Una revisi6n de los métodos de remuestreo en series temporales. *Estadística Española*, *44*(150), 133–159.
Bollerslev, T. (1986). Generalized autoregressive conditional heteroskedasticity. *Journal of Econometrics*, *31*, 307–327.
Bühlmann, P. (1997). Sieve bootstrap for time series. *Bernoulli*, *2*(3), 123–148.
Bühlmann, P. (2002). Bootstrap for time series. *Statistical Science*, *17*(1), 52–72.
Cao, R., Febrero-Bande, M., Gonzalez-Manteiga, W., & Garcia-Jurado, I. (1997). Saving computer time in constructing consistent bootstrap prediction intervals for autoregressive processes. *Communications in Statistics—Simulation and Computation*, *26*, 961–978.
Chen, B., Gel, Y., Balakrishna, N., & Abraham, B. (2011). Computationally efficient bootstrap prediction intervals for returns and volatilities in arch and garch processes. *Journal of Forecasting*, *30*, 51–71.
Davison, A., & Hinkley, D. (1997). *Bootstrap methods and their application*. Cambridge University Press.
Efron, B., & Tibshirani, R. (1995). *An introduction to the bootstrap*. Chapman and Hall.
Fox, A. J. (1972). Outliers in time series. *Journal of the Royal Statistical Society*, *34*(B), 350–363.
Francq, C., & Zakoian, J. (2010). *GARCH Models: Structure, statistical inference and financial applications*. Wiley.
Hall, P. (1992). *The bootstrap and Edgeworth expansion*. Springer.
Härdle, W. (2003). Bootstrap methods for time series. *International Statistical Review*, *71*, 435–459.
Künsch, H. (1989). The jackknife and the bootstrap for general stationary observations. *Statistic*, *17*, 1217–1241.
Pascual, L., Romo, J., & Ruiz, E. (2004). Bootstrap predictive inference for arima processes. *Journal of Time Series Analysis*, *25*, 449–465.
Pascual, L., Romo, J., & Ruiz, E. (2006). Bootstrap prediction for returns and volatilities in garch models. *Computational Statistics and Data Analysis*, *50*, 2293–2312.
Politis, D. N. (2003). The impact of bootstrap methods on time series analysis. *Statistical Science*, *28*, 219–230.
Shumway, R., & Stoffer, D. (2006). *Time series analysis and its applications with R examples* (2nd ed.). Springer.
Stine, R. A. (1987). Estimating properties of autoregressive forecasts. *Journal of the American Statistical Association*, *82*(400), 1072–1078.
Thombs, L. A., & Schucany, W. R. (1990). Bootstrap prediction intervals for autoregression. *Journal of the American Statistical Association*, *85*, 486–492.
Tsay, R. (2005). *Analysis of financial time series* (2nd ed.). Wiley.

Do Industrial Metals Prices Exhibit Bubble Behavior?

Walter Assenmacher and Robert Czudaj

Abstract Between 2004 and 2008, prices for industrial metals increased significantly but they experienced a subsequent decline after the turmoil of the financial crisis. A crucial question is if the prices of internationally traded metals have been driven by an explosive speculative bubble or if such a huge price increase was fundamentally justified. Based on data from the Dow Jones UBS Commodity Index, which uses metals traded on the London Metal Exchange and US exchanges, this study attempts to answer this question by applying the sup ADF test proposed by Phillips et al. (Int Econ Rev 52(1):201–226, 2011) which allows to test for explosive bubbles and to date the origin and collapse of the bubbles. Overall, our findings indicate that prices of industrial metals have shown explosive bubble behavior. More precisely, prices for copper and nickel have been subject to a speculative bubble around 2006 and 2008 whereas the evidence for the accumulation of a bubble in zinc prices is weak and aluminum prices do not exhibit any indication of a speculative bubble.

1 Introduction

The large swings in the prices of several commodities including industrial metals especially between 2004 and 2008 have recently become the subject of an extensive debate in the media and in academia. For instance, nickel prices increased by nearly 500 % from May 2004 until May 2007 and then dropped sharply by around 83 %

W. Assenmacher (✉)
Department of Economics, Chair for Statistics and Econometrics, University of Duisburg-Essen, Universitätsstr. 12, 45117 Essen, Germany
e-mail: walter.assenmacher@uni-due.de

R. Czudaj
Department of Economics, Chair for Econometrics, University of Duisburg-Essen, Universitätsstr. 12, 45117 Essen, Germany

FOM Hochschule für Oekonomie & Management, University of Applied Sciences, Herkulesstr. 32, 45127 Essen, Germany
e-mail: robert.czudaj@uni-due.de

J. Beran et al. (eds.), *Empirical Economic and Financial Research*,
Advanced Studies in Theoretical and Applied Econometrics 48,
DOI 10.1007/978-3-319-03122-4_17

until December 2008. Besides other factors such as the increasing importance of emerging economies like China and India as market players, the engagement of speculative capital has been identified as a main source of those swings (Chen 2010). Among others, Masters (2008), Masters and White (2008), and Gensler (2009) argue that extensive buy-side pressure from index funds recently created a speculative bubble in commodity prices, with the consequence that prices heavily exceeded their fundamental values at the highest level. Such a volatility increase evokes risk for both producers and consumers and should therefore be observed carefully by researchers and policymakers (Beckmann and Czudaj 2013).

The idea that asset or commodity prices have the potential to deviate from their intrinsic values based on market fundamentals due to speculative bubbles is already well established in the literature (Tirole 1982, 1985) and could be outlined by Stiglitz's famous definition:

> [I]f the reason that the price is high today is *only* because investors believe that the selling price is high tomorrow – when "fundamental" factors do not seem to justify such a price – then a bubble exists (see Stiglitz, 1990, p.13).

In this vein, the number of speculative traders which are active in a market and their potential impact on the evolution of prices could be time-varying. Thus, in periods where a large number of such traders are active the data generating process of prices possibly changes from a mean-reverting process consistent with the real demand and supply for this commodity to an explosive bubble process.

Based upon this idea Phillips et al. (2011) suggest an approach that allows testing for the presence of speculative bubbles. Basically, this methodology relies on the estimation of recursive unit root test regressions. However, unlike the application of standard unit root tests where the applicant concerns to test the unit root null against the alternative of stationarity, which is located on the left-side of the probability distribution of the test statistic, testing the alternative of an explosive root yields a test statistics that is located on the right-side of the probability distribution. The main advantages of this procedure are that (1) it does not require the estimation of a fundamental value of the certain asset or commodity, which is a notoriously difficult task in the latter case, and (2) it not only provides a tool for identifying bubble behavior, but also the dating of its origin and collapse.

Therefore, the aim of this study is to apply this methodology to test if the prices of industrial metals exhibit a speculative bubble. To do so, we use data from January 2, 1991 to October 19, 2011 for prices of aluminum, copper, nickel, and zinc, as well as a composite index. Seen as a whole, our results indicate that prices of industrial metals have shown explosive bubble behavior. However, this finding is not clear-cut for each metal price. While prices for copper and nickel have been subject to a speculative bubble around 2006 and 2008, the evidence for a bubble in zinc prices is weak and aluminum prices do not exhibit any indication of a speculative bubble.

The reminder of this paper is organized as follows. The following section provides a brief presentation of the testing approach while Sect. 3 intends to state a behavioral foundation for the testing procedure. Section 4 describes our dataset and presents our findings. The last section concludes.

2 Testing Approach

In this study we follow the approach recently proposed by Phillips et al. (2011), which is based on the classical present value theory of finance. In terms of the latter the fundamental prices for industrial metals could be represented by the sum of the present discounted values of the expected future dividend sequence. Therefore the standard no arbitrage condition should hold:

$$P_t = \frac{E_t(P_{t+1} + \Psi_{t+1})}{1+R}, \tag{1}$$

where P_t refers to the price for any industrial metal at time t, Ψ_t denominates the convenience yield from storing this commodity from $t-1$ to t,[1] R gives the constant and nonnegative discount rate, and E_t is the expectations operator conditional on information available at time t. In order to achieve an empirically more tractable representation and to decompose the price for an industrial metal in a fundamental component (p_t^f) and a bubble component (b_t), a log-linear approximation of Eq. (1) is used as follows[2]:

$$p_t = p_t^f + b_t, \tag{2}$$

with

$$\begin{aligned} p_t^f &= \frac{\kappa - \gamma}{1-\rho} + (1-\rho)\sum_{i=0}^{\infty} \rho^i E_t \psi_{t+1+i}, \\ b_t &= \lim_{i\to\infty} \rho^i E_t p_{t+i}, \\ E_t(b_{t+1}) &= \frac{1}{\rho} b_t = (1 + \exp(\overline{\psi - p}))b_t, \\ p_t &= \ln(P_t), \quad \psi_t = \ln(\Psi_t), \\ \gamma = \ln(1+R), &\quad \rho = 1/(1+\exp(\overline{\psi - p})), \\ \kappa &= -\ln(\rho) - (1-\rho)\ln\left(\frac{1}{\rho} - 1\right), \end{aligned} \tag{3}$$

[1] See, among others, Kaldor (1939) or Working (1949) for details regarding the convenience yield.

[2] See Campbell and Shiller (1988, 1989) for details. In addition, it should be noted that the concept presented in Eq. (2) is notationally very similar to various types of fad models, which are also often used in the literature to explain bubble behavior in asset prices. The basic idea is that markets could sometimes be driven by animal spirits unrelated to fundamentals. See, for instance, Summers (1986).

where $\overline{\psi - p}$ indicates the average convenience yield-price ratio and $0 < \rho < 1$. If the growth rate of the natural logarithm of the bubble $\exp(\overline{\psi - p}) > 0$, then the so-called rational bubble b_t is a submartingale process, which is explosive in expectation[3]:

$$b_t = \frac{1}{\rho} b_{t-1} + \varepsilon_{b,t} = (1 + g) b_{t-1} + \varepsilon_{b,t} \ , \tag{4}$$

where $E_{t-1}(\varepsilon_{b,t}) = 0$, $g = \frac{1}{\rho} - 1 = \exp(\overline{\psi - p}) > 0$, and $\varepsilon_{b,t}$ is a martingale difference sequence, since its autoregressive coefficient is larger than unity. In case of $b_t = 0 \ \forall t$, i.e. a bubble does not exist, the price for an industrial metal is determined solely by fundamental factors and thus by the discounted expected future convenience yield ψ_t, as can be seen from Eq. (3). Phillips et al. (2011) show that if p_t and ψ_t are both integrated of order one, $b_t = 0$ ensures that both are cointegrated. This becomes evident if the first equation in (3) is inserted into Eq. (2) and rearranged. On the contrary, if $b_t \neq 0$, i.e. in the presence of a bubble, p_t will show explosive behavior, as shown in Eq. (4). Therefore, Δp_t can never be stationary, no matter if ψ_t is integrated of order one or of order zero.

Hence, Diba and Grossman (1988) have firstly motivated the application of unit root tests on Δp_t, i.e. the return of an asset, which in our case is a specific industrial metal, to check for the existence of a bubble in the price series p_t. If the unit root null on Δp_t can be rejected, then the prices for industrial metals do not exhibit any indication of explosive behavior. In case of the latter p_t should be cointegrated with the convenience yield, if ψ_t is integrated of order one, i.e. $I(1)$. However, Evans (1991) claimed that a periodically collapsing bubble process cannot be detected using standard unit root tests, since it could behave like an $I(1)$ process or even like a stationary process. While looking at the historical patterns of many financial assets, it seems plausible that explosiveness of p_t is a temporary phenomenon.

Therefore, Phillips et al. (2011) suggest looking at sub-sample periods and propose a recursive application of the augmented Dickey–Fuller (ADF; Dickey and Fuller, 1979) test for a unit root against the alternative of an explosive root (the right-tailed). The latter is based upon the following test regression:

$$y_t = \mu + \delta y_{t-1} + \sum_{j=1}^{J} \phi_j \Delta y_{t-j} + \varepsilon_{y,t}, \quad t = 1, \ldots, T \ , \tag{5}$$

where y_t indicates a time series for which the bubble hypothesis should be checked and $\varepsilon_{y,t}$ is an independently and normally distributed random error term with zero mean and constant variance. As stated above, the null hypothesis being tested is $H_0 : \delta = 1$ and the right-tailed alternative is $H_1 : \delta > 1$. In the empirical part of

[3]The expression "rational" used by many authors referring to bubble behavior indicates that this concept is consistent with rational expectations.

this study the test regression given in Eq. (5) is estimated recursively by starting with $\tau_0 = [Tr_0]$ observations and incrementing the sample period by one observation at each step. r_0 indicates a sufficient fraction of the whole sample period T and $[\cdot]$ denotes an integer-valued function. Thus, Eq. (5) is estimated for each fraction $\tau = [Tr]$ with $r_0 \leq r \leq 1$ and the corresponding test statistic is denoted by ADF_r. Under the unit root null it follows:

$$\sup_{r\in[r_0,1]} ADF_r \Rightarrow \sup_{r\in[r_0,1]} \frac{\int_0^r \tilde{W} dW}{\left(\int_0^r \tilde{W}^2\right)^{1/2}} , \tag{6}$$

where W denotes the Brownian motion and $\tilde{W}(r) = W(r) - \frac{1}{r}\int_0^1 W$ denominates the demeaned Brownian motion (see Phillips et al. 2011 for details). The unit root null is rejected, if the test statistic $\sup_r ADF_r$ exceeds the corresponding right-tailed critical value. In order to locate the date of the origin (r_e) and the burst (r_f) of the bubble in case of a rejection, one can simply match the series of the recursive test statistic ADF_r against the right-tailed critical values of the standard ADF test. Estimates can be achieved as follows:

$$\hat{r}_e = \inf_{s\geq r_0} \left\{s : ADF_s > cv_\alpha^{ADF}(s)\right\}, \quad \hat{r}_f = \inf_{s\geq \hat{r}_e} \left\{s : ADF_s < cv_\alpha^{ADF}(s)\right\} , \tag{7}$$

where $cv_\alpha^{ADF}(s)$ indicates the right-tailed critical values of the standard ADF test with significance level α.[4] For the critical value $cv_\alpha^{ADF}(s)$, Phillips et al. (2011) propose the following choice: $cv_\alpha^{ADF}(s) = \ln[\ln(Ts)]/100$ with $s \in [0.1, 1]$.

3 Behavioral Motivation

Recently, Baur and Glover (2012) have provided a behavioral foundation for the testing approach introduced in Sect. 2, which should be explained in the following. The baseline assumption for the latter is given by the type of the structural model for the price formation stated below:

$$p_{t+1} = p_t + \theta\left(\sum_{h=1}^{H} d_t^h - s_t\right) + \varepsilon_{p,t} , \tag{8}$$

where d_t^h denotes the demand for an industrial metal by an agent of type h and s_t denominates the supply of this commodity. As it is the case for several other

[4]Homm and Breitung (2012) show that this testing procedure is much more robust against multiple breaks than alternative tests. For a summary of alternative bubble detection tests see Homm and Breitung (2012). For a rolling window version and a bootstrap approach for this test see also Gutierrez (2013).

commodities as well, the demand for industrial metals can be subdivided into industrial demand (d_t^I) and speculative demand. The latter is modeled by two different types of chartists behavior, viz. "trend followers" (d_t^{TF}) and "threshold traders" (d_t^{TT}).

Supply and industrial demand is simply modeled by the following equations:

$$d_t^I = \alpha_d - \beta_d p_t, \quad s_t = \alpha_s + \beta_s p_t, \quad \beta_i > 0, \quad i = d, s\,. \tag{9}$$

However, both types of chartists' demands depend on the heterogeneous beliefs of each agent as given below:

$$d_t^h = \sum_{j=1}^{N_t^h} \alpha_j^h \left[E_t^{h,j}(p_{t+1}) - p_t \right], \quad h = TF, TT\,. \tag{10}$$

where N_t^h indicates that the number of agents of type h, which are active in the market at time t, could be time-varying. Each agent's subjective beliefs are reflected in their expectations $E_t^{h,j}(p_{t+1})$ as follows:

$$E_t^{TF,j}(p_{t+1}) = p_t + \beta_j^{TF}(p_t - p_{t-k_j}), \quad E_t^{TT,j}(p_{t+1}) = p_t + \beta_j^{TT}(p_t - c_t^j)\,, \tag{11}$$

where the time window over which trend followers extrapolate past trends is given by k_j and c_t^j denotes the threshold value, which indicates that the beliefs of a threshold trader depend on the fact whether today's price is above or below a certain value that could also be time-varying. Both values, k_j and c_t^j, could differ for several agents.[5]

It can easily be shown that inserting Eqs. (9), (10), and (11) into Eq. (8) yields the following representation of the model for the price formation:

$$p_{t+1} = \alpha + (1-\beta)p_t + \sum_{j=1}^{N_t^{TF}} \omega_j^{TF}(p_t - p_{t-k_j}) + \sum_{j=1}^{N_t^{TT}} \omega_j^{TT}(p_t - c_t^j) + \varepsilon_{p,t}\,,$$

$$\alpha \equiv \theta(\alpha_d - \alpha_s), \quad \beta \equiv \theta(\beta_d + \beta_s), \quad \omega_j^h \equiv \theta \alpha_j^h \beta_j^h, \quad h = TF, TT. \tag{12}$$

Using the convention that $\alpha_t \equiv \sum_{j=1}^{N_t^{TT}} \omega_j^{TT} c_t^j$ and $\beta_t^{TT} \equiv \sum_{j=1}^{N_t^{TT}} \omega_j^{TT}$ Eq. (12) can be rearranged to:

$$p_{t+1} = (\alpha - \alpha_t) + (1 - \beta + \beta_t^{TT})p_t + \sum_{k=0}^{K} \bar{\omega}_{t,k}^{TF} \Delta p_{t-k} + \varepsilon_{p,t}\,, \tag{13}$$

[5]It is worth noting that threshold traders could also be interpreted as "fundamentalists," since the threshold value could also be seen as each agent's subjective estimate of the fundamental value of a certain industrial metal.

where $\bar{\omega}_{t,k}^{TF} \equiv \sum_{i=k+1}^{K} \sum_{j=1}^{N_t^{TF}} \omega_j^{TF} I(k_j = i)$. Finally, it becomes evident that Eq. (13) is notationally equivalent with the sequential ADF test equation given in (Eq. (5)) and this demonstrates that the methodology by Phillips et al. (2011) is also consistent with the heterogeneous agents literature.

4 Data and Empirical Results

In this section we provide a detailed description of our dataset and present the findings of our empirical analysis.

4.1 *The Data*

Our dataset comprises spot[6] prices for several industrial metals and these are taken from the Dow Jones UBS Commodity Index (DJUBSCI) provided by Dow Jones Indexes[7] (http://www.djindexes.com/commodity/), which is composed of commodities traded predominantly on U.S. exchanges with the exception that some of the included industrial metals, viz. aluminum, nickel, and zinc, are traded on the London Metal Exchange (LME). In addition to the latter, we also incorporate copper and an index which aggregates all four of the industrial metals used. The DJ-UBSCI is weighted by the relative amount of trading activity for a particular commodity. Besides the S&P Goldman Sachs Commodity Index (GSCI) the DJ-UBSCI is one of the two largest indices by market share.[8] Our sample period covers each working day from January 2, 1991 to October 19, 2011 and thus exhibits a sufficient sample size that contains the low volatility period up to the early 2000s as well as the high volatility period thereafter, as shown in Fig. 1.[9] As is common practice, each series is taken as natural logarithm. Table 1 reports the descriptive

[6]Alternatively, we have run the whole analysis with futures prices and found qualitatively the same results. These are available upon request.

[7]The Dow Jones-UBS Commodity Indexes[SM] are a joint product of DJI Opco, LLC, a subsidiary of S&P Dow Jones Indices LLC, and UBS Securities LLC ("UBS") and have been licensed for use. S&P® is a registered trademark of Standard & Poor's Financial Services LLC, Dow Jones® is a registered trademark of Dow Jones Trademark Holdings LLC, and UBS® is a registered trademark of UBS AG. All content of the Dow Jones-UBS Commodity Indexes ©S&P Dow Jones Indices LLC and UBS and their respective affiliates 2014. All rights reserved.

[8]Following Tang and Xiong (2010), the correlation between the GS and the DJ-UBS commodity indices is over 0.9. As a result, using GSCI would not significantly change our findings.

[9]Czudaj and Beckmann (2012) show that most spot and futures markets for several commodities including metals were efficient until the turn of the Millennium, but appear to be inefficient thereafter owing to an increase in volatility, which might be attributed to the intense engagement of speculation in commodity markets.

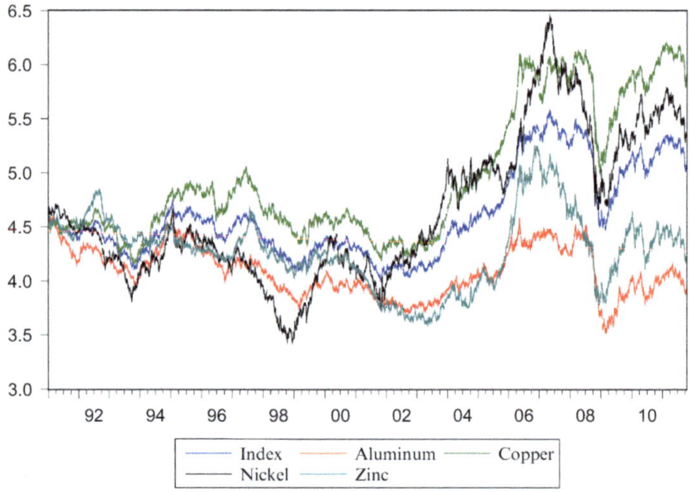

Fig. 1 Natural logarithms of the industrial metals cash prices

Table 1 Descriptive statistics

Ind. metal	Mean	Std. dev.	Skewness	Kurtosis
Index	4.61	0.41	0.76	2.38
Aluminum	4.09	0.23	0.10	2.23
Copper	4.96	0.61	0.78	2.10
Nickel	4.65	0.67	0.60	2.45
Zinc	4.28	0.34	0.16	2.94

statistics of each series and shows that each is subject to excess skewness and a shortage in kurtosis compared to a Gaussian. When splitting the sample period into a pre-2000 and a post-2000 period, it becomes evident that the variance of each series has increased significantly.

4.2 *Empirical Results*

We have used the natural logarithm of the price for each industrial metal (aluminum, copper, nickel, and zinc) and the whole index to estimate Eq. (5) recursively starting with a sample period that includes the first 10 % of the data ($r_0 = 0.1$), which means that the initial sample runs from January 1, 1991 to January 29, 1993 and is incremented by one observation until the entire sample is reached. The adequate lag length has been chosen by minimizing the Schwarz criterion.[10] Table 2 gives the

[10]To achieve robustness, we have also determined the lag length according to the significance of the highest lag as proposed by Campbell and Perron (1991). In general, the corresponding findings confirm ours and are therefore not reported, but are available upon request.

Table 2 Test statistics

Ind. metal	ADF_1	$\sup_{r\in[r_0,1]} ADF_r$
Index	−1.06	1.90**
Aluminum	−2.48	−1.05
Copper	−0.53	2.50***
Nickel	−1.22	2.02**
Zinc	−2.16	0.29

Note: *** indicates significance at a 1 % level, ** at a 5 % level, and * at a 10 % level. The critical values for the (i) ADF_1 statistic and the (ii) $\sup_{r\in[r_0,1]} ADF_r$ statistic are taken from Phillips et al. (2011): (i) 1 % 0.60, 5 % −0.08, 10 % −0.44, (ii) 1 % 2.09, 5 % 1.47, 10 % 1.18, respectively

corresponding ADF_1 and the $\sup_{r\in[r_0,1]} ADF_r$ test statistics. It becomes apparent that according to Evans (1991) explosiveness is a temporary phenomenon and therefore cannot be detected using the standard ADF test, since in this case the unit root null of the prices cannot be rejected for each industrial metal. So, if one has conducted a standard unit root test to check for an explosive bubble, one would conclude that there was no significant evidence of exuberance in metals prices.[11] However, when conducting the $\sup_{r\in[r_0,1]} ADF_r$ test statistic the null is rejected for copper at a 1 %, for nickel at a 5 %, and for the whole index also at a 5 % level. This clearly points in favor of a speculative bubble in copper and nickel prices.

In order to locate the date of the origin and the burst of the bubble, we have plotted the recursively generated $ADF_{r\in[r_0,1]}$ test statistics with their corresponding critical values $cv_\alpha^{ADF}(s) = \ln[\ln(Ts)]/100$ with $s \in [0.1, 1]$ for each industrial metal prices series in Fig. 2. For instance, the entire index exhibits a speculative bubble that started on April 6, 2006 and burst on July 16, 2008. Copper and nickel prices experienced a speculative bubble between January 2006 and September 2008 as well as August 2006 and November 2007, respectively. Nickel prices also show a bubble at the beginning of the nineties. As already indicated by the $\sup_{r\in[r_0,1]} ADF_r$ statistic, the evidence for a bubble in zinc prices is very weak, since the recursively generated $ADF_{r\in[r_0,1]}$ test statistics only slightly crosses the critical value line around 2006 whereas the historical pattern of aluminum prices do not indicate any explosive bubble behavior.[12] When performing a sub-sample analysis that only includes the period after the turn of the Millennium, our findings still hold. The corresponding statistics and graphs are not reported to save space, but are available upon request.

[11]This finding is consistent with other studies that examined other assets or commodities such as, for instance, Gutierrez (2013) in the case of agricultural commodities.

[12]When using futures instead of spot prices, the evidence for a speculative bubble in zinc prices becomes stronger.

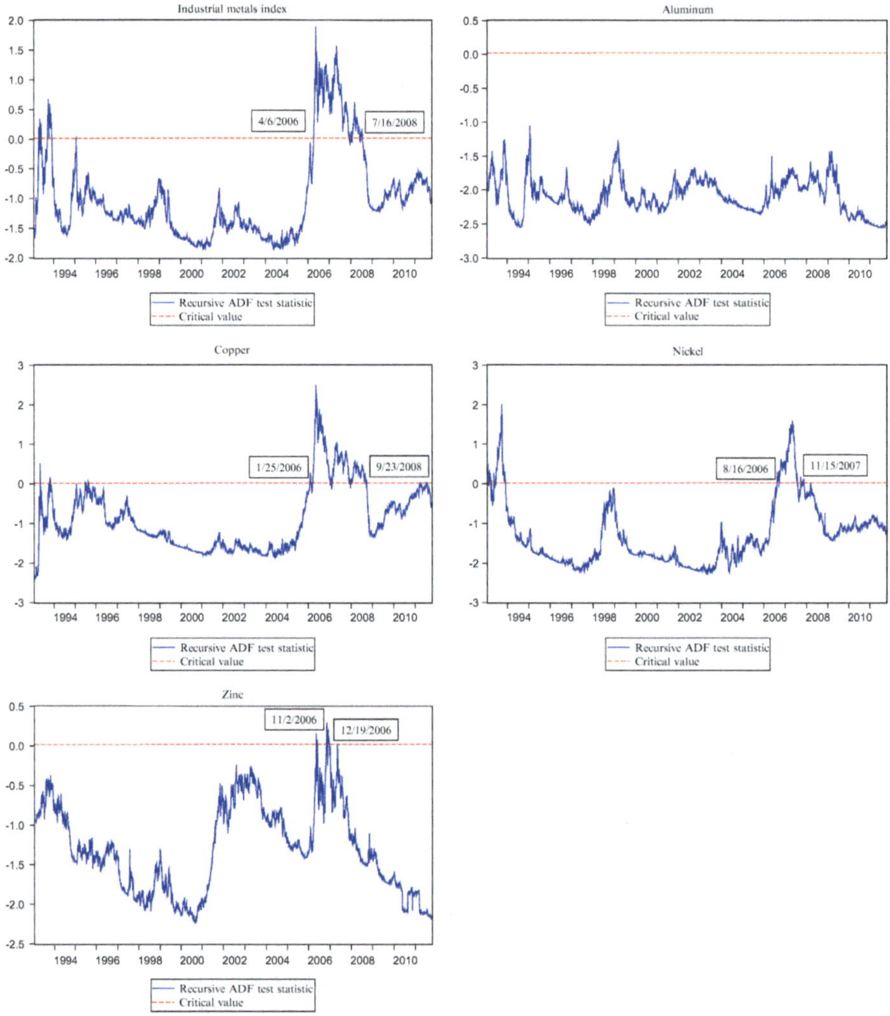

Fig. 2 Recursive ADF_r statistics

Conclusion

In this study we intended to answer the question if prices for industrial metals exhibit a speculative bubble using a novel framework. Seen as a whole, our results indicate that prices of industrial metals have behaved like a bubble for the period between 2006 and 2008. As outlined in Sect. 3, this may be traced back to the dominance of the trading strategies followed by chartists facing

(continued)

certain price thresholds. However, this finding is not clear-cut for each metal price. While prices for copper and nickel have been subject to a speculative bubble around 2006 and 2008, the evidence for a bubble in zinc prices is weak and aluminum prices do not exhibit any indication of a speculative bubble.

Therefore, it is possible that index traders have amplified price movements for industrial metals during that period and that financial activity in their futures markets and/or speculation may be the reason for the explosive behavior of prices around 2006 and 2008. However, given that one may think of Eq. (5) as a reduced form of an unknown structural model, this approach solely allows detecting periods where actual prices deviated from their fundamentals. It remains unclear whether these deviations may be attributed to factors such as financial speculation, hoarding or the actions of positive feedback traders. To examine the causes for the found bubble behavior, structural models are required. The construction of these is left for future research.

Further research should also be concerned about the appropriate policy response if a bubble is detected. Although asset price bubbles exhibit a challenge for both researchers and policymakers over several decades, the abatement and the prevention of such a bubble (and especially an abrupt bursting of a bubble) is still of crucial importance.

References

Baur, D., & Glover, K. (2012). A gold bubble? Working Paper Series, Finance Discipline Group, UTS Business School, University of Technology, Sydney No. 175.

Beckmann, J., & Czudaj, R. (2013). The forward pricing function of industrial metal futures - Evidence from cointegration and smooth transition regression analysis. *International Review of Applied Economics*, *27*(4), 472–490.

Campbell, J. Y., & Perron, P. (1991). Pitfalls and opportunities: What macroeconomists should know about unit roots. In O. J. Blanchard & S. Fisher (Eds.), *NBER macroeconomics annual* (Vol. 6, pp. 141–220). Cambridge: MIT Press.

Campbell, J. Y., & Shiller, R. (1988). Stock prices, earnings and expected dividends. *Journal of Finance*, *43*(3), 661–676

Campbell, J. Y., & Shiller, R. (1989). The dividend-price ratio and expectations of future dividends and discount factors. *Review of Financial Studies*, *1*(3), 195–228.

Chen, M. H. (2010). Understanding world metals prices - Returns, volatility and diversification. *Resources Policy*, *35*(3), 127–140.

Czudaj, R., & Beckmann, J. (2012). Spot and futures commodity markets and the unbiasedness hypothesis - Evidence from a novel panel unit root test. *Economics Bulletin*, *32*(2), 1695–1707.

Diba, B. T., & Grossman, H. I. (1988). Explosive rational bubbles in stock prices. *American Economic Review*, *78*(3), 520–530.

Dickey, D., & Fuller, W. A. (1979). Distribution of the estimates for autoregressive time series with a unit root. *Journal of the American Statistical Association*, *74*(366), 427–431.

Evans, G. W. (1991). Pitfalls in testing for explosive bubbles in asset prices. *American Economic Review*, *81*(4), 922–930.
Gensler, G. (2009). Testimony before the United States Senate Subcommittee on Financial Services and General Government. SEC Congressional Testimony, Washington, 2 June 2009.
Gutierrez, L. (2013). Speculative bubbles in agricultural commodity markets. *European Review of Agricultural Economics*, *40*(2), 217–238.
Homm, U., & Breitung, J. (2012). Testing for speculative bubbles in stock markets: A comparison of alternative methods. *Journal of Financial Econometrics*, *10*(1), 198–231.
Kaldor, N. (1939). Speculation and economic stability. *Review of Economic Studies*, *7*(1), 1–27.
Masters, M. W. (2008) Written Testimony before the Committee on Homeland Security and Governmental Affairs. United States Senate. May 20. http://hsgac.senate.gov/public/_files/052008Masters.pdf. Accessed 31 July 2013.
Masters, M. W., & White, A. K. (2008). The accidental hunt brothers: How institutional investors are driving up food and energy prices. Special Report. http://www.vermontfuel.com/VFDA_News_files/How%20Institutional%20Investors%20Are%20Driving%20Up%20Food%20And%0Energy%20Prices_2.pdf. Accessed 31 July 2013.
Phillips, P. C. B., Wu, Y., & Yu, J. (2011). Explosive behavior in the 1990s Nasdaq: When did exuberance escalate asset values? *International Economic Review*, *52*(1), 201–226.
Stiglitz, J. E. (1990). Symposium on bubbles. *Journal of Economic Perspectives*, *4*(2), 13–18.
Summers, L. H. (1986). Does the stock market rationally reflect fundamental values? *Journal of Finance*, *41*(3), 591–601.
Tang, K., & Xiong, W. (2010) Index Investment and Financialization of Commodities. NBER Working Papers No. 16385.
Tirole, J. (1982). On the possibility of speculation under rational expectations. *Econometrica*, *50*(5), 1163–1181.
Tirole, J. (1985). Asset bubbles and overlapping generations. *Econometrica*, *53*(6), 1071–1100.
Working, H. (1949). The theory of price of storage. *American Economic Review*, *39*(6), 1254–1262.

Forecasting Unpredictable Variables

Helmut Lütkepohl

Abstract Stock market indexes are difficult to predict at longer horizons in efficient markets. Possibilities to improve forecasts of such "unpredictable" variables are considered. In particular, forecasts based on data transformations and multivariate forecasts are compared, using monthly data. Although standard statistical methods indicate that forecast improvements may be possible by using multivariate models, mean squared error gains are not obtained in out-of-sample forecasting. Forecasts based on the log transformation lead to improvements in forecast accuracy, however.

1 Introduction

The recent stock market turbulences have caused many certificates based on major stock market indexes such as the European Euro Stoxx 50, the German DAX, or the American Dow Jones to violate critical thresholds. Thereby their payoff has become a function of the level of their underlying index. In fact, in many cases the payoff is simply a constant multiple of the index level. Hence, it is desirable to have predictions of the levels of the stock indexes to decide on a good time for selling or buying the certificates.

On the other hand, assuming efficient markets, stock returns are often viewed as unpredictable at least at longer horizons such as a month or more. This result would suggest that also the levels of the stock indexes are unpredictable. Although arguments have been put forward, why there may still be some predictability in stock returns, there are also studies that by and large confirm that longer term predictability of stock returns is very limited or absent.

Although in this situation one cannot hope to find a great potential for forecast improvements, it is conceivable that the levels of the stock indexes contain predictable components even if the returns are largely unpredictable. The objective of this study is to explore a number of possibilities for improving predictions of the levels of a range of stock indexes.

H. Lütkepohl (✉)
DIW Berlin and Freie Universität Berlin, Mohrenstr. 58, 10117 Berlin, Germany
e-mail: hluetkepohl@diw.de

J. Beran et al. (eds.), *Empirical Economic and Financial Research*,
Advanced Studies in Theoretical and Applied Econometrics 48,
DOI 10.1007/978-3-319-03122-4_18

Forecasting is a traditional objective of time series analysis (e.g., Heiler, 1980, 1991). A number of models and methods exist that have been developed for that purpose. In this study I explore the potential of some methods that may be promising for improving forecast precision for the variables of interest in the present context.

The first idea is based on a classical result by Granger and Newbold (1976) stating that the unbiased minimum mean squared error (MSE) forecast of the exponential of a variable is not the exponential of the optimal forecast of the variable. Stock returns are typically determined as first differences of natural logarithms (logs) of stock prices. Thus, computing a forecast of a stock index directly from a corresponding forecast of the returns may not be optimal. Also, of course, predicting the stock indexes directly, say, with an autoregressive moving average (ARMA) model may not be optimal. Generally, forecasting nonlinear transformations of a variable may be preferable to forecasting the variable directly. The aforementioned result by Granger and Newbold (1976) tells us that simply inverting the forecast of the transformed series may not result in the best forecasts of the original variable. Indeed, Lütkepohl and Xu (2012) found that forecasts based on logs may have smaller MSEs than forecasts based on the levels directly. Therefore in this study I explore the potential of the more general Box–Cox class of transformations to improve standard predictions of stock indexes. I consider an estimator of the optimal predictor based on such transformations.

A further potentially useful extension of these ideas is to consider multivariate systems. There is in fact some evidence that the major stock indexes are related (e.g., King and Wadhwani, 1990; Hamao et al., 1990; Cheung and Ng, 1996). It is investigated whether combining the additional information available in a set of stock indexes with nonlinear transforms of the variables may improve forecasts.

I use end-of-month values for the period 1990M1 to 2007M12 of nine stock indexes, the Dow Jones Euro Stoxx 50 (Stoxx), FTSE, DAX, CAC 40 (CAC), Dow Jones (DJ), Nasdaq, S&P 500 (SP), Nikkei and HangSeng (HS). Using data up to 2007 only means, of course, that the recent crisis years are largely excluded. In this kind of investigation this may be useful in order to avoid possible distortions that may arise from structural changes caused by the crisis in the generation mechanisms of the stock index series of interest. The indexes cover a good range of different regions and segments of the stock markets in the world. The data are obtained from Datastream. They are also used by Lütkepohl and Xu (2012) in analyzing whether forecast precision can be improved by using logs.

The forecast precision is measured by the MSE. Of course, one could use measures tailored precisely to the payoff function of a specific certificate. In this study I prefer to work with the MSE as a general purpose measure because thereby the results may be of more general interest and use. It is found that using the log transformed series as basis for predictions tends to improve the forecast MSE. Although multivariate methods in-sample indicate a potential for gains in forecast accuracy, such gains are not obtained in out-of-sample forecast comparisons.

The structure of this study is as follows. In the next section I summarize results related to optimal forecasts of time series when forecasts of a transformed variable are of interest. Moreover, an estimator of the optimal predictor is proposed. In Sect. 3

univariate forecasts of the stock indexes based on the Box–Cox transformation are explored and in Sect. 4 forecasts based on multivariate models are considered. Finally, the last section concludes.

2 Minimum MSE Forecasts Based on Nonlinear Transformations

Suppose we are interested in forecasting a variable y_t that is a function of another variable x_t, that is, $y_t = \varphi(x_t)$. If a forecast of x_t is available, it can be used to construct a forecast for y_t. Let $x_{t+h|t}$ denote the optimal (minimum MSE) h-steps ahead predictor of x_{t+h} based on information up to time t. It is well known that $x_{t+h|t}$ is the conditional expectation (e.g., Lütkepohl (2005, Chap. 2)),

$$x_{t+h|t} = E(x_{t+h}|x_t, x_{t-1}, \ldots) \equiv E_t(x_{t+h}).$$

An h-steps ahead forecast of y_t may be obtained as

$$y^{nai}_{t+h|t} = \varphi(x_{t+h|t}).$$

It is known from the work of Granger and Newbold (1976) that this forecast may not be optimal which is why they call it a naïve forecast. In fact, denoting the forecast error associated with $x_{t+h|t}$ by $u_t^{(h)} = x_{t+h} - x_{t+h|t}$, it is clear that

$$E_t(y_{t+h}) = E_t\varphi(x_{t+h}) = E_t\varphi(x_{t+h|t} + u_t^{(h)}) \neq \varphi(x_{t+h|t})$$

in general.

Consider, for instance, the case where $x_t = \log(y_t)$ so that $\varphi(\cdot) = \exp(\cdot)$, i.e., $y_t = \exp(x_t)$. In that case,

$$E_t(y_{t+h}) = E_t[\exp(x_{t+h|t} + u_t^{(h)})] = \exp(x_{t+h|t})E_t(\exp u_t^{(h)}). \tag{1}$$

If $u_t^{(h)} \sim \mathcal{N}(0, \sigma_x^2(h))$, where $\mathcal{N}(\cdot,\cdot)$ signifies a normal distribution and $\sigma_x^2(h)$ denotes the forecast error variance, then $E(\exp u_t^{(h)}) = \exp[\frac{1}{2}\sigma_x^2(h)]$ so that the optimal predictor for y_{t+h} is

$$y^{nopt}_{t+h|t} = \exp[x_{t+h|t} + \tfrac{1}{2}\sigma_x^2(h)]. \tag{2}$$

This result was also established by Granger and Newbold (1976) and the forecast was considered by Lütkepohl and Xu (2012) for the stock indexes of interest in the present study. Clearly, the forecast error $u_t^{(h)}$ will be normally distributed if x_t is a Gaussian (normally distributed) ARMA process. In that case the forecast error variance $\sigma_x^2(h)$ can be estimated straightforwardly and, hence, the same is true for the normal optimal forecast for y_t based on the optimal forecast of x_t. Using the normal optimal predictor based on the normal distribution is plausible if the variable y_t is transformed into x_t with the explicit objective to get a more normally distributed data generation process (DGP). The log transformation is often used for that purpose and, hence, reverting it by the exponential function, the optimal forecast given in (2) is relevant. To distinguish it from the forecast proposed in the following, I call it the *normal optimal forecast*.

In general, assuming a Gaussian DGP for x_t is not suitable and neither is the use of the forecast (2). In particular, such an assumption is problematic for the stock index series of interest in the present study. Even in that case finding an estimator for the optimal forecast may not be difficult. Given that the exponential function is of primary interest in the following, I consider the case $y_t = \exp(x_t)$ now. In fact, the DGP of x_t will typically be an autoregressive process of order p [AR(p)], $x_t = \nu + \alpha_1 x_{t-1} + \cdots + \alpha_p x_{t-p} + u_t$, so that

$$\begin{aligned} x_{t+h} &= \nu + \alpha_1 x_{t+h-1} + \cdots + \alpha_p x_{t+h-p} + u_{t+h} \\ &= \nu^{(h)} + \alpha_1^{(h)} x_t + \cdots + \alpha_p^{(h)} x_{t+1-p} \\ &\quad + u_{t+h} + \phi_1 u_{t+h-1} + \cdots + \phi_{h-1} u_{t+1}, \end{aligned}$$

where $\nu^{(h)}$ and $\alpha_i^{(h)}$, $i = 1, \ldots, p$, are functions of the original AR parameters and

$$\phi_i = \sum_{j=1}^{\min(i,p)} \phi_{i-j} \alpha_j$$

may be computed recursively for $i = 1, 2, \ldots$, using $\phi_0 = 1$ (e.g., Lütkepohl (2005, Chap. 2)). This suggests an estimator

$$\hat{E}_t(\exp u_t^{(h)}) = (T - h + 1)^{-1} \sum_{t=h}^{T} \exp(u_t + \phi_1 u_{t-1} + \cdots + \phi_{h-1} u_{t-h+1}) \qquad (3)$$

of the correction term for adjusting the naïve forecast. Hence, the estimated optimal h-steps ahead forecast of y_t has the form

$$y_{t+h|t}^{opt} = \exp(x_{t+h|t}) \hat{E}_t(\exp u_t^{(h)}). \qquad (4)$$

A standard law of large numbers can be invoked to show consistency of this estimator. For example, if u_t is independent white noise with time invariant, finite variance, standard asymptotic results can be applied.

Notice that, although we have presented the optimal forecast for a single transformed variable, the formulae and arguments carry over to the case where the variable of interest is part of a multivariate system. In that case the forecast, the associated forecast error, and the forecast error variance are computed from the system under consideration. Apart from that, all arguments carry over as long as the nonlinear transformation is applied to the individual variables (see Ariño and Franses (2000) and Bårdsen and Lütkepohl (2011) for discussions of special cases).

Of course, in practice we also have to replace the forecasts and the quantities on the right-hand side of the equality sign in (3) by estimates. The usual parameter estimates and estimation residuals are used for that purpose in the next section.

3 Univariate Forecasts of Stock Indexes

Before a comparison of different predictors for the variables of interest is performed in Sect. 3.3, their unit root properties are discussed in Sect. 3.1 and the Box–Cox class of transformations is considered in Sect. 3.2.

3.1 Unit Root Analysis

I have performed a unit root analysis for the full sample period from 1990M1 to 2007M12 for the original variables and their logs. For that purpose I have applied Dickey–Fuller (DF) tests with linear trend and present the results in Table 1. All tests are based on AR(1) models, that is, no lagged differences are used in the test regression. Assuming efficient markets, the model under the unit root null hypothesis is plausible, that is, the changes of the variables or the returns (first differences of logs) should not be predictable. Also the standard model selection criteria (AIC, HQ, SC) suggest order one for all series when a maximum lag order of five is allowed for.[1] The only exception is the Stoxx series for which the more profligate AIC estimates order two. Thus, overall using the DF rather than an augmented DF test is justified.

With only one exception the unit root null hypothesis cannot be rejected. The Nikkei index is the exception when the original variable is used, whereas even for this series a unit root cannot be rejected at the 10 % level when logs are considered. This result is in line with a finding by Granger and Hallman (1991). They point out that for a random walk x_t, the autocorrelations of $y_t = \exp(x_t)$ may decay more quickly than for a variable integrated of order one ($I(1)$ variable) and a DF test tends to reject a unit root more often than for a standard $I(1)$ variable. Thus, if the log index series are indeed random walks, one would expect occasional rejections of a unit root in the original series. This result for the Nikkei index is still worth

[1]The computations reported in this subsection and in Sect. 4.1 are performed with the software JMulTi, see Lütkepohl and Krätzig (2004), where more details on the criteria and statistical methods can be found.

Table 1 Unit root tests for stock index series, sample period: 1990M1–2007M12

Index	Original variables DF	Original variables KPSS	Logs DF	Logs KPSS
Stoxx	−1.37	0.439	−1.28	0.646
FTSE	−1.47	0.564	−1.49	0.715
DAX	−1.33	0.335	−1.59	0.512
CAC	−1.54	0.293	−1.70	0.379
DJ	−2.07	0.483	−1.45	0.856
Nasdaq	−1.93	0.404	−1.53	0.723
SP	−1.55	0.490	−1.25	0.761
Nikkei	−3.99	0.373	−2.45	0.359
HS	−1.17	0.298	−2.33	0.569

DF tests all based on AR(1) (as recommended by SC and mostly also by AIC) model with trend, critical values: −3.13 (10 %), −3.41 (5 %), −3.96 (1 %). KPSS tests allowing for a linear trend and with four lags, critical values: 0.119 (10 %), 0.146 (5 %), 0.216 (1 %). Computations performed with JMulTi (Lütkepohl and Krätzig 2004)

keeping in mind because it may have an impact in the multivariate cointegration analysis to be carried out in Sect. 4.1.

To confirm the DF test results, I have also performed KPSS tests where the null hypothesis is stationarity. The results are also presented in Table 1. Again a linear trend is allowed for. For all series, both original and in logs, the corresponding test value exceeds the critical value associated with a 1 % significance level. Thus, stationarity for all series is clearly rejected in favor of a unit root. Although this result was to be expected and the return series (first differences of logs) are typically used in economic analyses, these findings are reassuring because they confirm that the statistical properties of the series are indeed in line with those assumed in other studies. They also lend support to the "unpredictability" property of the returns. Whether forecast improvements are still possible is, of course, the issue to be investigated in the following.

3.2 *Box–Cox Transformation*

The original series and the logs are the two extreme ends of the Box–Cox transformed series (Box and Cox, 1964). For a variable y_t and a nonnegative real number λ, the Box–Cox transformation is defined as

$$y_t^{(\lambda)} = \begin{cases} \dfrac{y_t^{\lambda} - 1}{\lambda} & \text{for } \lambda > 0, \\ \log y_t & \text{for } \lambda = 0. \end{cases}$$

Thus, for $\lambda = 1$ this is just the original series shifted by -1, whereas for $\lambda \to 0$ the transformation approaches the log. The transformation is meant to stabilize the variance and more generally to make the distribution of the transformed variable more normal (see also Heiler, 1981, p. 391). Thus, if y_t is such that $y_t^{(\lambda)}$ is normally distributed for $\lambda \in [0, 1]$, the transformation may be useful also from a forecasting point of view because Gaussian variables may be predicted well by linear processes such as ARMA processes.

Although the Box–Cox transformation with $\lambda \neq 0$ and $\lambda \neq 1$ may lead to a variable that is difficult to interpret from an economic point of view, for the present purposes the statistical properties are of central importance and, hence, I consider the Box–Cox transformation for the stock index series. If the transformation actually leads to a normally distributed variable, estimation of λ by minimizing the variance of the transformed variable seems plausible. Denoting the differencing operator by Δ and assuming that $\Delta y_t^{(\lambda)}$ is Gaussian white noise for some $\lambda \in [0, 1]$, the estimator for λ is chosen so as to minimize the sample variance of $\Delta y_t^{(\lambda)}$, that is, the objective function is $T^{-1} \sum_{t=2}^{T} (\Delta y_t^{(\lambda)} - \overline{\Delta y^{(\lambda)}})^2$. Using a grid search over λ, it turns out that the log transformation is indeed optimal for all nine series.[2]

Clearly, for the set of index series under consideration the normality assumption is problematic even after transformation. In fact, the return series have quite nonnormal features such as outliers and volatility clusters. Still using the sample variance as basis for estimating λ seems plausible, given the objective of the transformation. In fact, more sophisticated procedures for estimating λ exist (see Proietti and Lütkepohl, 2013). I do not consider them here but base the following analysis exclusively on the original variables and the logs.

3.3 Estimating the Optimal Predictor Based on Logs

In the forecast comparison I account for the fact that the sample period is characterized by rather special periods for some of the markets. Therefore, using only one sample and one forecast period for comparison purposes may give a misleading picture. Hence, I use two different sample beginnings for estimation and model specification, the first one is 1990M1 and the second one is 1995M1. Moreover, I use three different periods for forecast evaluation, 2001M1–2007M12, 2003M1–2007M12, and 2005M1–2007M12.

I compare four different predictors for the original index series. The first one is the standard linear predictor based on an AR model for the first differences of the original variable. This predictor will be referred to as linear forecast ($y_{t+h|t}^{lin}$). The second predictor is the naïve one presented in Sect. 2 ($y_{t+h|t}^{nai}$) which is based on the exponential transformation of a forecast for the logs. In this case the forecasts

[2]Computations of this and the following subsection are performed with own MATLAB programs.

are based on AR models for the returns. Finally, based on the same models, the optimal forecasts under normality ($y^{nopt}_{t+h|t}$) and the optimal forecasts with estimated correction term ($y^{opt}_{t+h|t}$) are considered.

Models are fitted to increasingly larger samples. For instance, for the longer sample period starting in 1990M1 and a forecast period 2001M1–2007M12, the first model is fitted to data from 1990M1 to 2000M12 and 1- to 6-steps ahead forecasts are produced for 2001M1–2001M6. Then one observation is added to the sample and model fitting is repeated. Thereby the shortest sample for model specification and fitting has $T = 132$ observations and for each forecast horizon eventually 79 out-of-sample forecasts are produced and used for computing MSEs. Whenever the sample is increased by a new observation, a full new specification and estimation is performed. For AR order selection I have used primarily the parsimonious SC with a maximum lag order of 4, although I have also experimented with AIC. The results were qualitatively the same. Using SC for model specification means effectively that all forecasts are based on random walks for the levels or the logs of the series, as appropriate. Thus, the results that are discussed in the following indicate the MSE gains due to the log transformation and not due to differences in the number of AR lags or the like. This point is important to remember when it comes to comparisons with the multivariate forecasts in Sect. 4.2.

In Table 2 I use the linear forecast ($y^{lin}_{t+h|t}$) as a benchmark and report the MSEs of the optimal forecasts ($y^{opt}_{t+h|t}$) relative to those of the linear forecasts. An asterisk indicates that the difference between the forecast MSEs is significant at the 5 % level based on a two-sided Harvey et al. (1997) version of the Diebold and Mariano (1995) (DM) test. Numbers greater than one mean, of course, that the corresponding linear forecast has a smaller MSE than the optimal forecast.

From Table 2 it is apparent that there are some markets for which the linear forecast beats the optimal one in the forecast period 2001M1–2007M12. Clearly this period includes the period of market consolidation in Europe and the USA after the new market bubble bursted in the early years of the new millennium. Note, however, that only in one case the linear forecast is significantly superior to the optimal predictor (see the one-step ahead forecasts of Stoxx for the sample period starting in 1995M1 and the forecast period 2001M1–2007M12). The gains from using the optimal forecast are in some cases quite substantial. For instance, for the HS index there are a number of cases where the optimal forecast produces an MSE that is less than 80 % of that of the linear forecast. The overall conclusion from Table 2 is that the gains from using the optimal forecast can be substantial whereas the losses tend to be small.

Of course, one may wonder about the relative performance of the other two forecasts under consideration. In particular, comparing the optimal to the normal optimal forecast may be of interest. Therefore I present the MSEs of the optimal forecast ($y^{opt}_{t+h|t}$) relative to the normal optimal forecast ($y^{nopt}_{t+h|t}$) in Table 3. The most striking observation from that table is perhaps that all numbers are rather close to one. Thus, the two forecasts do not differ much. Sometimes the normal

Table 2 MSEs of univariate optimal forecasts ($y^{opt}_{t+h|t}$) relative to univariate linear forecasts ($y^{lin}_{t+h|t}$)

		Beginning of sample period: 1990M1			Beginning of sample period: 1995M1		
	Forecast	Forecast period			Forecast period		
Index	horizon	2001–2007	2003–2007	2005–2007	2001–2007	2003–2007	2005–2007
Stoxx	1	1.0463	0.9667	0.9493	1.0720*	0.9749	0.9592
	3	1.1215	0.8940	0.8678	1.1926	0.9138	0.8910
	6	1.2313	0.7003*	0.6603	1.3701	0.7223	0.6870
FTSE	1	1.0256	0.9747	0.9684	1.0270	0.9812	0.9770
	3	1.0750	0.8906	0.8907	1.0719	0.9250	0.9235
	6	1.1327	0.7404*	0.7306	1.1268	0.8402*	0.8258
DAX	1	1.0136	0.9433	0.9211	1.0296	0.9423	0.9187
	3	1.0382	0.8631	0.8329	1.0877	0.8497	0.8147
	6	1.0669	0.7293*	0.6936*	1.1616	0.6899*	0.6452*
CAC	1	1.0286	0.9655	0.9568	1.0590	0.9715	0.9624
	3	1.0762	0.9080	0.9054	1.1610	0.9198	0.9203
	6	1.1373	0.8048	0.8107	1.3109	0.8004	0.8276
DJ	1	1.0360	0.9799	0.9915	1.0473	0.9945	1.0054
	3	1.0952	0.9031	0.8970	1.1197	0.9457	0.9395
	6	1.1965	0.8153	0.7344	1.2308	0.8983	0.8190
Nasdaq	1	1.0426	0.9914	1.0421	1.0479	0.9976	1.0448
	3	1.1414	0.9652	1.0446	1.1501	0.9815	1.0523
	6	1.3095	0.9062	0.9006	1.3385	0.9405	0.9267
SP	1	1.0424	0.9730	1.0034	1.0534	0.9869	1.0168
	3	1.1112	0.8998	0.9399	1.1349	0.9380	0.9809
	6	1.2182	0.7761	0.7721	1.2638	0.8567	0.8691
Nikkei	1	0.9286*	0.8705*	0.9024*	0.9826	0.9580*	0.9713
	3	0.8500	0.7609*	0.8202	0.9594	0.9038*	0.9357
	6	0.7763	0.6838*	0.7678	0.9372	0.8503*	0.9043
HS	1	1.0071	0.8996	0.8702	0.9982	0.9264*	0.9053
	3	0.9889	0.7794	0.7324	0.9758	0.8630	0.8308
	6	0.9164	0.7240	0.6999	0.9404	0.8548	0.8377

AR order selection based on SC with maximum lag order 4
* Significant at 5 % level according to DM test with two-sided alternative

optimal forecast is significantly better than the optimal forecast and in other cases the situation is just the other way round. A clear winner is not apparent in the table.

I have also compared the naïve forecasts to the other three forecasts and found that it is typically quite close to the optimal and normal optimal forecast. This finding is also reported by Lütkepohl and Xu (2012) as far as the normal optimal forecast is concerned. Therefore I do not report detailed results here. The overall conclusion so far is then that using logs for prediction can be quite beneficial in terms of forecast MSE. Whether the naïve, the normal optimal or the optimal

Table 3 MSEs of univariate optimal forecasts ($y^{opt}_{t+h|t}$) relative to univariate normal optimal forecasts ($y^{nopt}_{t+h|t}$)

Index	Forecast horizon	Beginning of sample period: 1990M1 Forecast period 2001–2007	2003–2007	2005–2007	Beginning of sample period: 1995M1 Forecast period 2001–2007	2003–2007	2005–2007
Stoxx	1	0.9998	1.0001	1.0002	0.9996*	1.0001	1.0002
	3	1.0074	0.9949	0.9928	1.0155	0.9945	0.9915
	6	1.0258	0.9719*	0.9777*	1.0479	0.9652*	0.9750
FTSE	1	0.9999	1.0001	1.0001	0.9999	1.0002	1.0002
	3	1.0070	0.9911*	0.9920	1.0010	1.0018	0.9994
	6	1.0212	0.9813*	0.9908*	1.0099	1.0412	1.0445
DAX	1	0.9999	1.0006	1.0008	0.9998	1.0006	1.0008
	3	1.0007	1.0033	1.0029	1.0076	0.9961	0.9942
	6	1.0091	0.9944	0.9962	1.0264	0.9800*	0.9818*
CAC	1	0.9998	1.0002	1.0003	0.9997*	1.0001	1.0002
	3	1.0024	0.9981	0.9967	1.0101	0.9952	0.9933*
	6	1.0076	1.0074	1.0074	1.0388	0.9825*	0.9886
DJ	1	0.9999	1.0000	0.9999	0.9997	0.9999	0.9998
	3	0.9946	0.9983	0.9932	0.9861*	0.9960	0.9866
	6	0.9825	0.9971	0.9906	0.9554	0.9869	0.9727
Nasdaq	1	0.9996	0.9998	0.9993	0.9992	0.9997	0.9989
	3	1.0036	1.0008	1.0015	0.9967	0.9990	0.9926*
	6	1.0219	0.9984	0.9819*	1.0152	0.9919	0.9451
SP	1	0.9999	1.0000	0.9999	0.9997*	1.0000	0.9998
	3	0.9975	0.9986	0.9929	0.9921	0.9984	0.9865
	6	1.0032	0.9968	0.9794	0.9947	0.9963	0.9553
Nikkei	1	1.0001	1.0003*	1.0003	1.0001	1.0003*	1.0002
	3	0.9988	0.9964	0.9965	0.9994	0.9893	0.9911
	6	0.9973	0.9916	0.9921	1.0007	0.9696	0.9766
HS	1	0.9998	1.0002	1.0003	0.9997	1.0006	1.0007
	3	0.9971	1.0081	1.0088	0.9939	1.0298	1.0311
	6	1.0019	1.0294	1.0354	1.0132	1.0767	1.0790

AR order selection based on SC with maximum lag order 4
* Significant at 5% level according to DM test with two-sided alternative

predictor is used to convert forecasts for the logs into forecasts for the original variables is of limited importance.

So far I have not taken into account serial dependence although I have in principle allowed for it. My statistical procedures favor simple random walk models. The different markets underlying the stock indexes are related, however, and that fact may be useful to take into account in forecasting. I will do so in the next section.

4 Multivariate Forecasts of Stock Indexes

It is a straightforward implication of the discussion in Lütkepohl (2005, Sect. 6.6) that a genuine cointegration relation between integrated series implies Granger-causality between them at least in one direction and, thus, improvements in forecasts. Therefore I first check the cointegration relations among the series in Sect. 4.1 and in Sect. 4.2 the multivariate forecasts are compared.

4.1 Cointegration Analysis

In Table 4 cointegration tests for all pairs of series for the full sample period 1990M1–2007M12 are reported. The table shows the VAR orders proposed by AIC when a maximum order of 4 is allowed for as well as the corresponding p-values of the Johansen trace test (Johansen, 1995) for the null hypothesis of no cointegration. The test is based on a model which allows for a linear trend in the variables but not in the cointegration relation, that is, the trend is orthogonal to the cointegration relation. Rejecting the null hypothesis suggests that there is a cointegration relation between the two variables. Indeed in Table 4 there are a number of small p-values, say smaller than 5 %. Thus, there may be a number of cointegration relations in the set of variables under consideration. Evidence for cointegration is found both in the original variables and the logs.

There are 13 p-values in the column associated with the original variables which are smaller than 0.05. Eight of them are associated with pairs involving the Nikkei index. One may be tempted to conclude that the Nikkei index is cointegrated with all the other variables. Recalling, however, that the DF unit root test for the Nikkei has rejected the unit root, qualifies this conclusion. It may well be that those features of the Nikkei index that caused the DF test to reject are now responsible for a significant cointegration test. Note that the cointegration rank of a bivariate system with one $I(1)$ and one stationary variable is one, the cointegration relation being a trivial one that consists of the stationary variable only. Hence, the cointegration findings in pairs involving the Nikkei index may not be genuine cointegration relations. Thus, they may not induce forecast improvements. Ignoring those pairs, there are still five pairs left where genuine cointegration is found: (Stoxx, FTSE), (Stoxx, Nasdaq), (Stoxx, SP), (CAC, Nasdaq), (CAC, SP). Such an outcome in 36 tests is not likely to be purely due to chance, although the properties of the tests may be problematic given that the series have outliers and volatility clustering in the residuals. Still, there may well be strong relations between the series that can be exploited for improving forecasts.

On the other hand, if there is a genuine cointegration relation between (Stoxx, Nasdaq) and (CAC, Nasdaq), say, then there must also be a cointegration relation between Stoxx and CAC. A similar comment applies to Stoxx, SP and CAC. Such a relation is not found, however. Of course, the inability to reject the null hypothesis

Table 4 Bivariate cointegration analysis for stock index series, sample period: 1990M1–2007M12

	Original variables		Logs	
Index pair	VAR order	p-Value	VAR order	p-Value
Stoxx/FTSE	3	0.019	1	0.001
Stoxx/DAX	3	0.975	1	0.878
Stoxx/CAC	4	0.649	1	0.618
Stoxx/DJ	3	0.656	1	0.256
Stoxx/Nasdaq	1	0.000	1	0.000
Stoxx/SP	3	0.009	2	0.002
Stoxx/Nikkei	1	0.002	1	0.084
Stoxx/HS	2	0.849	1	0.186
FTSE/DAX	3	0.114	3	0.004
FTSE/CAC	3	0.084	1	0.046
FTSE/DJ	1	0.911	1	0.717
FTSE/Nasdaq	1	0.339	1	0.185
FTSE/SP	1	0.681	1	0.458
FTSE/Nikkei	1	0.009	1	0.194
FTSE/HS	1	0.991	1	0.536
DAX/CAC	1	0.978	1	0.828
DAX/DJ	3	0.725	1	0.252
DAX/Nasdaq	1	0.151	1	0.010
DAX/SP	3	0.210	1	0.026
DAX/Nikkei	1	0.004	1	0.146
DAX/HS	1	0.439	1	0.084
CAC/DJ	4	0.385	2	0.101
CAC/Nasdaq	1	0.000	1	0.004
CAC/SP	4	0.004	3	0.001
CAC/Nikkei	1	0.004	1	0.148
CAC/HS	1	0.964	1	0.397
DJ/Nasdaq	1	0.699	1	0.530
DJ/SP	1	0.894	1	0.750
DJ/Nikkei	1	0.007	1	0.116
DJ/HS	1	0.994	1	0.626
Nasdaq/SP	1	0.447	1	0.377
Nasdaq/Nikkei	1	0.006	1	0.118
Nasdaq/HS	1	0.961	1	0.698
SP/Nikkei	1	0.007	1	0.117
SP/HS	1	0.996	1	0.714
Nikkei/HS	1	0.017	1	0.116

The null hypothesis is no cointegration, that is, cointegration rank zero. p-Values for Johansen's trace test obtained from JMulTi (Lütkepohl and Krätzig, 2004) with linear trend orthogonal to cointegration relation. VAR order choice by AIC with maximum order 4

of no cointegration relation may be blamed to the lack of power of the test. Given the very large p-value of 0.649 of the test of cointegration between Stoxx and CAC, such an argument has little bite, however. In fact, I have checked for cointegration between these two variables also with the test proposed by Saikkonen and Lütkepohl (2000) that may be more powerful in the present situation and also did not find evidence for a cointegration relation between Stoxx and CAC. This discussion suggests that it is not at all clear that the cointegration relations found for the original variables in Table 4 are in fact real. Hence, it is not at all clear that there will be gains in forecast precision from using systems of stock indexes.

Note, however, that the VAR orders chosen by AIC indicate that there may be short-term dynamics in some of the bivariate models that may again be exploited for prediction. Overall, for the original variables the evidence in Table 4 may lead to the expectation that there are gains in forecast precision from using multivariate models. The evidence is by no means clear, however, and an out-of-sample comparison of forecasts is needed to settle the matter.

The situation is similar for the logs of the series. In this case the VAR orders are one with only four exceptions. A cointegration relation is found in nine of the 36 pairs of variables if a 5 % significance level is used for the cointegration tests. Now none of the indexes cointegrates with the log Nikkei which lends further support to the argument that the cointegration found between the original Nikkei and the other indexes may not reflect a proper cointegration relation. The nine pairs of possibly cointegrated log variables are (Stoxx, FTSE), (Stoxx, Nasdaq), (Stoxx, SP), (FTSE, DAX), (FTSE, CAC), (DAX, Nasdaq), (DAX, SP), (CAC, Nasdaq), (CAC, SP). Thus, I find a cointegration relation in one fourth of the pairs which is difficult to blame to chance if there are no such relations. On the other hand, there are again many inconsistencies in the results. In other words, if the nine pairs of variables are really cointegrated, then there must be many more pairs of cointegrated variables which are not confirmed by the p-values in Table 4.

Thus, the overall conclusion from the cointegration analysis is that the evidence for relations that can be exploited for improving predictions is limited and rather mixed. It is sufficient, however, to justify the ex ante forecast comparison that is conducted in the following.

4.2 Forecast Comparison

Since some of the results in Table 4 are consistent with bivariate systems of two independent random walks, I exclude all pairs of series where such a DGP may be at work. In fact, I focus on those systems where a cointegration relation is found in both the levels and the logs because they should in theory beat the univariate forecasts. This reduces the set of pairs to be considered in the forecast comparison to five: (Stoxx, FTSE), (Stoxx, Nasdaq), (Stoxx, SP), (CAC, Nasdaq), (CAC, SP). For some of these bivariate systems the AIC also detects short-term dynamics that justify higher lag orders than one. Thus, based on standard time series methodology there should be some gain in forecast precision relative to the univariate case. This is the first issue considered.

Relative forecast MSEs of the optimal bivariate forecasts divided by the corresponding univariate linear forecast MSEs are presented in Table 5. The underlying forecasts are based on models chosen by the parsimonious SC. The reason for considering SC forecasts is that a more parsimonious model was found to be better

Table 5 MSEs of bivariate optimal forecasts relative to univariate linear forecasts

		Beginning of sample period: 1990M1			Beginning of sample period: 1995M1		
	Forecast	Forecast period			Forecast period		
Index	horizon	2001–2007	2003–2007	2005–2007	2001–2007	2003–2007	2005–2007
Stoxx	1	0.9512	1.0113	0.9930	0.9984	1.0992	1.0451
	3	0.8960	1.1315	0.9690	1.0368	1.4446	1.1156
	6	0.8392	1.3465	0.8416	1.0997	2.2464	1.1810
FTSE	1	1.0028	1.0097	0.9895	1.0543	1.0788	1.0205
	3	1.0155	1.0563	0.9314	1.1693	1.3794	1.0246
	6	1.0348	1.0776	0.7975	1.3037	1.8453	1.0219
Stoxx	1	0.9232	1.0077	1.0438	0.9471	1.0087	1.0359
	3	0.7879	1.0357	1.0933	0.8623	1.0639	1.0801
	6	0.6351	1.1268	1.0528	0.7554	1.2196	0.9951
Nasdaq	1	1.0425	1.0184	1.0956	1.1210	1.0286	1.0937
	3	1.1363	1.0530	1.1465	1.4065	1.0770	1.1482
	6	1.2676	1.1326	1.0750	1.7120	1.1684	1.0861
Stoxx	1	0.9757	1.0619	0.9242	0.9969	1.2126	0.9896
	3	0.9109	1.1357	0.8113	0.9705	1.6071	0.9774
	6	0.8539	1.2693	0.4567	0.9870	2.4416	0.6931
SP	1	1.0309	1.0662	1.1377	1.0890	1.1927	1.2138
	3	1.0504	1.1227	1.2412	1.2118	1.4734	1.4642
	6	1.1241	1.3551	1.3126	1.4069	2.1527	1.8452
CAC	1	0.9696	1.1209	1.2464	0.9522	1.0715	1.1778
	3	0.8757	1.2652	1.5392	0.8155	1.1976	1.3858
	6	0.7875	1.5522	2.0574	0.6945	1.4557	1.6637
Nasdaq	1	1.0214	0.9989	1.1010	1.1167	1.0120	1.0719
	3	1.0628	1.0193	1.2144	1.3738	1.0448	1.1171
	6	1.1057	1.1082	1.3912	1.6429	1.0925	1.0307
CAC	1	0.9702	1.0699	1.1433	0.9742	1.0170	0.9463
	3	0.8925	1.1266	1.3100	0.9276	1.0831	0.9258
	6	0.8202	1.2571	1.6576	0.9173	1.1572	0.7893
SP	1	0.9963	1.0142	1.1557	1.0621	1.0490	1.1239
	3	0.9695	1.0431	1.4600	1.1571	1.1108	1.2253
	6	0.9637	1.1894	2.0395	1.2899	1.2470	1.3073

VAR order selection based on SC with maximum lag order of 4. None of the MSE differences is significant at the 5 % level according to a DM test suited for multivariate forecasting in previous studies. Thus, overall in Table 5 I give an advantage to the multivariate models. Theoretically the best multivariate predictor is compared to the worst univariate one. Of course, at this point it is not fully clear that the estimated optimal predictor is really superior to its competitors in the multivariate case. I will return to this point later when I discuss the robustness of the results.

A first glimpse at Table 5 shows that there are many numbers greater than one. Hence, the worst univariate predictors seem to outperform the best multivariate ones. A closer examination reveals in fact that none of the MSE differences is significant at the 5 % level according to the DM test. There are some significant differences at the 10 % level which are not indicated, however. Although there are cases where the multivariate forecasts produce a smaller MSE than the univariate ones, it seems fair to conclude that overall no gains in out-of-sample prediction accuracy can be expected from using the multivariate models for the stock indexes. Of course, this is not the first study with that kind of conclusion. In the present case it is striking, however, how clearly the multivariate modelling technology points at potential for forecast improvements due to the enlarged information set. Of course, one may argue that our procedures for multivariate modelling are flawed because the residuals may still contain conditional heteroskedasticity. Vilasuso (2001) indeed finds that tests for Granger-causality, for example, tend to reject noncausality too often in the presence of ARCH in the residuals. Still the methodology is quite standard and can apparently lead to misleading conclusions regarding out-of-sample predictions. In fact, Cheung and Ng (1996) found Granger-causal relations in more frequently observed SP and Nikkei data even when conditional heteroskedasticity is taken into account. Based on the present out-of-sample forecast comparison, it is difficult to find arguments in favor of the multivariate forecasts, however.

I also checked the robustness of these results in different directions. First of all, I used the AIC for specifying the VAR order in the multivariate case and I compared to univariate random walks (AR(0) for the first differences) as before. Many results do not change at all because the AIC often also selects VAR order one. Generally, the same picture emerges as in Table 5. As one would expect, in some cases the multivariate forecasts even get worse when a larger VAR order is used.

It may also be of interest whether the optimal forecast in the multivariate case actually performs better than other forecasts based on logs. Therefore I compared the bivariate linear and optimal forecasts. In the multivariate case the results (not shown) are indeed less clearly in favor of the optimal predictor than for univariate models. Although in some cases the optimal forecast delivers sizeable reductions in the MSE, overall it tends to provide no improvements or makes things worse. Hence, it is perhaps justified to take a closer look at a comparison between multivariate and univariate linear forecasts. Relative MSEs are given in Table 6. They confirm slight improvements for the bivariate forecasts over the situation seen in Table 5. Still the general conclusion remains: A general clear advantage of the bivariate forecasts is not apparent.

Table 6 MSEs of bivariate linear forecasts relative to univariate linear forecasts

		Beginning of sample period: 1990M1			Beginning of sample period: 1995M1		
	Forecast	Forecast period			Forecast period		
Index	horizon	2001–2007	2003–2007	2005–2007	2001–2007	2003–2007	2005–2007
Stoxx	1	0.9500	0.9719	0.9599	0.9816	1.0875	1.0023
	3	0.8854	0.9982	0.8820	0.9768	1.3842	0.9892
	6	0.8072	1.0493	0.6927	0.9697	2.0025	0.8916
FTSE	1	0.9797	1.0087	0.9921	1.0177	1.0498	1.0083
	3	0.9455	1.0545	0.9387	1.0517	1.2147	0.9895
	6	0.9071	1.0965	0.8400	1.0791	1.4060	0.9393
Stoxx	1	0.9169	1.0172	1.1085	0.9068	1.0333	1.1252
	3	0.7932	1.0782	1.2546	0.7739	1.1173	1.3038
	6	0.6336	1.2209	1.4124	0.6059	1.3312	1.5547
Nasdaq	1	1.0554	1.0007	1.0111	1.0767	1.0008	1.0154
	3	1.1793	1.0044	1.0202	1.2566	1.0056	1.0297
	6	1.2822	1.0075	1.0228	1.3591	1.0132	1.0403
Stoxx	1	0.9824	1.0819	0.9246	0.9802	1.1643	0.9891
	3	0.9194	1.1673	0.8130	0.9215	1.4288	0.9778
	6	0.8453	1.2931	0.4531	0.8565	1.8687	0.6997
SP	1	0.9910	1.0194	1.0894	1.0024	1.0459	1.1041
	3	0.9343	1.0135	1.1377	0.9835	1.0950	1.1779
	6	0.8786	1.0867	1.0978	0.9565	1.2045	1.2027
CAC	1	0.9506	1.1226	1.2700	0.9364	1.1179	1.2559
	3	0.8284	1.2921	1.5837	0.8043	1.3171	1.5728
	6	0.6923	1.5568	2.0072	0.6639	1.6755	2.0461
Nasdaq	1	1.0160	1.0029	1.0503	1.0698	1.0020	1.0158
	3	1.0398	1.0247	1.1298	1.2207	1.0144	1.0385
	6	0.9995	1.0663	1.2839	1.2766	1.0242	1.0423
CAC	1	0.9666	0.9937	1.0028	0.9438	0.9860	0.9330
	3	0.8866	0.9491	1.0045	0.8519	1.0028	0.8814
	6	0.8080	0.8660	0.9795	0.7796	1.0051	0.6960
SP	1	0.9826	0.9946	1.1096	0.9923	1.0080	1.0695
	3	0.9296	0.9852	1.2844	0.9727	1.0300	1.1269
	6	0.8746	1.0447	1.5645	0.9447	1.0746	1.1522

VAR order selection based on SC with maximum lag order of 4

Conclusions
In this study I consider a range of methods for improving forecasts of stock market indexes. Such variables should be difficult or impossible to predict at longer horizons of several months in efficient markets. I use a monthly

(continued)

dataset for nine stock price indexes and I compare a range of methods and forecasts using different sample and forecast periods. Varying the sample and forecast periods turns out to be important because the results are to some extent sensitive to these periods.

For univariate forecasts I investigate the potential of nonlinear transformations of the Box–Cox type for improving prediction accuracy as measured by the forecast MSE. It turns out that applying the log transformation which is a boundary case of the Box–Cox transformation can be beneficial in forecasting. For some sample and forecast periods substantial gains in forecast precision are obtained even if a naïve forecast is used that simply reverses the log to get a forecast of the original variable of interest. Improvements from using more sophisticated transformed forecasts are overall limited.

Since there is some spillover between the markets underlying the indexes considered, it seems plausible to use also multivariate methods for prediction. Standard multivariate time series methods indicate that some of the indexes are cointegrated and, hence, taking advantage of that relationship should theoretically result in superior forecasts. Unfortunately, gains in forecast precision are not found in out-of-sample comparisons. Thus, although one may conclude from a standard analysis that there is a potential for gains in forecast precision from using multivariate methods these may be illusionary in practice. On the other hand, using logs for forecasting and transforming the log variables to obtain forecasts of the original variables of interest can be recommended.

References

Ariño, M. A., & Franses, P. H. (2000). Forecasting the levels of vector autoregressive log-transformed time series. *International Journal of Forecasting, 16*, 111–116.

Bårdsen, G., & Lütkepohl, H. (2011). Forecasting levels of log variables in vector autoregressions. *International Journal of Forecasting, 27*, 1108–1115.

Box, G. E. P., & Cox, D. R. (1964). An analysis of transformations. *Journal of the Royal Statistical Society B, 26*, 211–243.

Cheung, Y.-W., & Ng, L. K. (1996). A causality-in-variance test and its application to financial market prices. *Journal of Econometrics, 72*, 33–48.

Diebold, F. X., & Mariano, R. S. (1995). Comparing predictive accuracy. *Journal of Business & Economic Statistics, 13*, 253–263.

Granger, C. W. J., & Hallman, J. (1991). Nonlinear transformations of integrated time series. *Journal of Time Series Analysis, 12*, 207–224.

Granger, C. W. J., & Newbold, P. (1976). Forecasting transformed series. *Journal of the Royal Statistical Society B, 38*, 189–203.

Hamao, Y., Masulis, R. W., & Ng, V. (1990). Correlations in price changes and volatility across international markets. *Review of Financial Studies, 3*, 281–307.

Harvey, D., Leybourne, S., & Newbold, P. (1997). Testing the equality of prediction mean squared errors. *International Journal of Forecasting, 13*, 281–291.

Heiler, S. (1980). Prediction of economic processes with linear regression part. In M. Nerlove, S. Heiler, H.-J. Lenz, B. Schips, & H. Garbers (Eds.), *Problems of time series analysis* (pp. 41–61). Mannheim: Bibliographisches Institut.

Heiler, S. (1981). Zeitreihenanalyse heute. Ein Überblick, *Allgemeines Statistisches Archiv, 65*, 376–402.

Heiler, S. (1991). Zeitreihenanalyse - Ein kurzer Abriß der Entwicklung, *Allgemeines Statistisches Archiv, 75*, 1–8.

Johansen, S. (1995). *Likelihood-based inference in cointegrated vector autoregressive models*. Oxford: Oxford University Press.

King, M. A., & Wadhwani, S. (1990). Transmission of volatility between stock markets. *Review of Financial Studies, 3*, 5–33.

Lütkepohl, H. (2005). *New introduction to multiple time series analysis*. Berlin: Springer.

Lütkepohl, H., & Krätzig, M. (Eds.). (2004). *Applied time series econometrics*. Cambridge: Cambridge University Press.

Lütkepohl, H., & Xu, F. (2012). The role of the log transformation in forecasting economic variables. *Empirical Economics, 42*, 619–638.

Proietti, T., & Lütkepohl, H. (2013). Does the Box-Cox transformation help in forecasting macroeconomic time series? *International Journal of Forecasting, 29*, 88–99.

Saikkonen, P., & Lütkepohl, H. (2000). Testing for the cointegrating rank of a VAR process with an intercept. *Econometric Theory, 16*, 373–406.

Vilasuso, J. (2001). Causality tests and conditional heteroskedasticity: Monte Carlo evidence. *Journal of Econometrics, 101*, 25–35.

Dynamic Modeling of the Correlation Smile

Alfred Hamerle and Christian Scherr

Abstract We discuss the equity-based pricing of CDX tranches within a structural dynamic approach and focus on the valuation impact of general model specifications. Therefore, we examine the influence of market dynamics, idiosyncratic jumps, loss term structures, and portfolio heterogeneity on the pricing of tranches. The resulting spread deviations are quantified through implied correlations because this scales premium payments across all tranches to a comparable level and, in addition, enables reliable inferences on the meaning of the discussed model features.

1 Introduction

The recent debate on the relative pricing of equity and credit risk markets (see Collin-Dufresne et al., 2012; Coval et al., 2009; Hamerle et al., 2012; Li and Zhao, 2011; Luo and Carverhill, 2011) raises the issue of the extent to which the applied models themselves drive the published results. In particular, this emerges all the more with respect to the large variety of proposed models and corresponding findings. An initial way to address this topic seems to be a comparison of different valuation techniques by referring to a homogenous set of input data. However, this in fact fails because even within a certain class of model type the number of parameters and model components turns out to be significantly different. Concerning structural approaches, one might deal, for example, with static models, comprising only a sparse number of parameters (see, e.g., Coval et al., 2009), or adopt fully dynamic techniques with dozens of variables as in Collin-Dufresne et al. (2012).

Because of these differences, we restrict ourselves to a structural dynamic approach and examine the impact of general model specifications on the pricing

A. Hamerle
Faculty of Business and Economics, University of Regensburg, 93040 Regensburg, Germany
e-mail: Alfred.Hamerle@wiwi.uni-regensburg.de

C. Scherr (✉)
Risk Research Prof. Hamerle GmbH & Co. KG, Josef-Engert-Straße 11, 93053 Regensburg, Germany
e-mail: Christian.Scherr@risk-research.de

J. Beran et al. (eds.), *Empirical Economic and Financial Research*, Advanced Studies in Theoretical and Applied Econometrics 48,
DOI 10.1007/978-3-319-03122-4_19

of credit derivatives, such as the inclusion of idiosyncratic jumps. In this sense, we proceed similarly to Agca et al. (2008), who quantify the effects of ignoring empirical regulatories on the valuation of CDO tranches. Their aim, however, is different because they wish to explain the appearance of the so-called correlation smile (see also Andersen and Sidenius, 2004; Kalemanova et al., 2007; Moosbrucker, 2006), which proves the poor reliability of the standard one-factor Gaussian copula model. In addition, all proposed techniques are of static nature, whereas our analysis refers to a basic approach that already captures the most important empirical phenomena and thus serves as a reference for measuring the impact of general model specifications.

To set up the basic approach, we adopt the structural model recently proposed by Hamerle et al. (2013). Using CAPM-like techniques, they introduce a simple dynamic model to overcome the main disadvantages associated with purely diffusion-based techniques. In addition to a component that depicts continuous changes, they also include jumps to capture discontinuous information. Hence, our basic model contains the most important characteristics that, according to Collin-Dufresne et al. (2012), a reliable approach should offer. Firstly, it is intended to be fully dynamic, which is accomplished by definition because we are dealing with a time-continuous stochastic process. Secondly, the model must not be exclusively based on a diffusion motion because this leads to the so-called predictability of default, and thus short-time spreads become vanishingly low (see, e.g., Sepp, 2006). Due to the presence of jumps, our approach is not in danger of exhibiting these disadvantages.

To quantify the impact of different model specifications, we compare the corresponding risk premiums to those of our basic approach. However, the spread rates of different tranches are generally of a different scale, and thus, if measured in absolute values, slight deviations in the equity tranche acquire much more weight than large deviations within the senior tranches. To avoid such effects, we adopt the concept of implied correlations because, as a consequence, quotes are of the same magnitude and spread deviations become comparable. Thus, we evaluate the deviations with respect to our basic model and report the pricing effect of model changes in terms of implied correlations.

The proposed model changes are chosen in such a way as to preserve the analytical tractability of the different approaches. For example, we add idiosyncratic jumps to the asset value process. Analogously to the idiosyncratic diffusion motion, these depict changes in firm value that are not influenced by the macroeconomic dynamics but reflect information causing discontinuous movements. A crucial topic within our analysis is the weight we assign to these idiosyncratic jumps because this directly influences the magnitude of correlation among the assets in the modeled reference pool. Correlation matters, because it affects the terminal loss distribution of the portfolio, which in turn influences tranche prices. For example, if there is a significant number of scenarios in which the portfolio loss is close to zero, the equity tranche can survive, at least in part. Hence, the spread rates of equity tranches decrease. For senior tranches, things are different. Increasing the probability of extreme losses entails the eventuality of subordinated capital being wiped out completely and also senior tranches getting hit. Because spread rates reflect expected losses, premium payments have to increase. A decreasing correlation reduces the incidence of extreme events and the loss distribution becomes more centered. As a consequence, equity tranches often suffer substantial losses and have to offer high spread payments. Conversely, senior tranches are hit sparsely and thus only have to yield low premiums on the notional.

However, if the correlation were the only quantity determining tranche prices, dynamic models would not yield significant advantages in the context of modeling credit derivatives because terminal distributions are also specified by proposing static models. Yet, static models have a tremendous disadvantage: they cannot describe the evolution of portfolio loss dynamics over time. Yet, these are also essential to evaluate the loss dynamics of tranches. The temporal growth of tranche losses affects the spread rate of a tranche because spread payments always refer to the remaining notional. If tranches are likely to suffer early losses, spread rates have to rise in return for missed payments. Senior tranches are expected to have very low losses, and therefore the explicit loss dynamics should not significantly influence the associated premiums. This changes, however, as one moves through the capital structure down to the equity tranche. Due to its position, this exhibits maximum sensitivity to early defaults in the portfolio. This motivates our quantitative analysis, which determines the extent to which loss dynamics in the underlying portfolio influence tranche prices.

Besides idiosyncratic jumps and loss dynamics, there are two more topics we wish to discuss in the course of this paper, namely the meaning of market return dynamics and the homogeneity assumption. Whereas there is no doubt about the influence of equity dynamics, a clear economic theory on the impact of the homogeneity assumption is missing. Therefore, our empirical analysis is also intended to yield new insights into this topic.

Accordingly, the remainder of the paper is organized as follows. In Sect. 2, we provide a brief overview of credit derivatives and some details on the correlation smile. The mathematics of the market and the asset value dynamics are discussed in Sect. 3. In the context of the model analysis presented in Sect. 4, we quantify the impacts of the proposed model changes. A conclusion is given in section “Conclusion”.

2 Credit Derivatives and Correlation Smile

2.1 Credit Derivatives

2.1.1 CDS Indices

Analogous to equity indices, comprising a certain number of stocks, CDS indices represent a portfolio of credit default swap contracts. In the empirical section of this article, we focus on the CDX North American Investment Grade index

(CDX.NA.IG), which aggregates 125 equally weighted CDS contracts, each written on a North American investment grade name. There are several maturities of this index, namely 1, 2, 3, 4, 5, 7, and 10 years, whereby the contract with the 5-year horizon offers the highest degree of liquidity. The CDX.NA.IG is revised every 6 months on March 20 and September 20, the so-called roll dates. On these dates, both defaulted and illiquid names are replaced. Similar to a CDS contract, the issuer (protection buyer) has to pay quarterly spread premiums to the investor (protection seller). In the case of default, the latter is obliged to render compensation for the loss caused by the defaulted company. In general, this loss, also referred to as Loss Given Default (LGD), is a firm-specific, stochastic variable. For reasons of simplicity, here we fix the LGD to the standard value of 0.6. As a further consequence of default, the notional value of the contract is reduced by a factor of $\frac{1}{125}$, disregarding the actual loss. In a risk-neutral environment, the spread rate of this contract is given by

$$s^i := \frac{LGD \cdot \sum_{i=1}^{n} \sum_{j=1}^{m} e^{-rt_j} \cdot \mathbb{P}\left(t_{j-1} < \tau_i \leq t_j\right)}{\sum_{i=1}^{n} \sum_{j=1}^{m} \Delta_j \cdot e^{-rt_j} \cdot \mathbb{P}\left(\tau_i > t_j\right)} \tag{1}$$

Here, $\Delta_j := t_j - t_{j-1}$ denotes the time period between two subsequent payment dates, r the risk-free interest rate, and τ_i the default time of reference name i.

2.1.2 Index Tranches

By dividing their capital structure, CDS indices are also used to create structured finance securities, called index tranches. These tranches induce a vertical capital structure on the index and are specified by the covered loss range. A tranche begins to suffer losses as the portfolio loss L_t exceeds the attachment point α, and its notional is completely wiped out if the portfolio loss increases beyond the detachment point β. For example, the CDX.NA.IG has the tranches 0–3 % (equity), 3–7 % (mezzanine), 7–10 %, 10–15 %, 15–30 % (senior), and 30–100 % (super-senior). The spread rate of a tranche is given by

$$s_{\alpha,\beta} := \frac{\sum_{j=1}^{m} e^{-rt_j} \cdot \left[\mathbb{E}\left(L_{\alpha,\beta}^{t_j}\right) - \mathbb{E}\left(L_{\alpha,\beta}^{t_{j-1}}\right)\right]}{\sum_{j=1}^{m} \Delta_j \cdot e^{-rt_j} \cdot \left[1 - \mathbb{E}\left(L_{\alpha,\beta}^{t_j}\right)\right]} \tag{2}$$

where the loss profile of a tranche follows

$$L_{\alpha,\beta}^{t} := \frac{\min\left(\beta, L_t\right) - \min\left(\alpha, L_t\right)}{\beta - \alpha} \tag{3}$$

2.2 Correlation Smiles

In the context of modeling credit derivatives, the one-factor Gaussian copula model is similar to the Black–Scholes approach for the pricing of options. Hence, it does not come as a surprise that there is also a phenomenon, called the correlation smile, that corresponds to the empirically observed volatility smile.

2.2.1 Volatility Smile

The famous Black–Scholes pricing formula owes its popularity mainly to the fact that, based on the intuitive Brownian motion, Black and Scholes (1973) elaborated an analytical formula for the pricing of European options, including the contemporary stock price S_0, the strike level K, the maturity T, the interest rate r, and the volatility σ of the underlying asset. Whereas S_0, K, T, and r are explicitly observable quantities or parameters characterizing the proposed contract, the volatility can, at best, be estimated. In turn, only the volatility parameter is available to control the results within the Black–Scholes model. Given the market price of a completely specified European option, one can fit the Black–Scholes model to this quote by choosing the (unique) volatility that yields the desired value. If the Black–Scholes model could completely describe market dynamics, all the (implied) volatilities would be identical across different maturities and strike levels. Yet, these volatilities are not generally constant but yield patterns that resemble smiles or skews if plotted against the strike level or maturity. This suggests that the Black–Scholes model is not suited to replicate option prices. However, the general popularity of this model is testified by the fact that it is market convention to quote option prices in terms of implied volatility. This fictive number, placed in the "wrong" Black–Scholes formula, by construction reveals the predefined value and therefore offers an alternative way to report prices of options.

2.2.2 Correlation Smile

Within the Gaussian model, there are only two parameters that can be used to control the model's features, namely the default barrier $\tilde{D}$ and the homogenous asset return correlation ρ. It is a general convention to fix the default barrier such that the model spread matches the empirically observed index spread. As a consequence, ρ is the only parameter affecting tranche prices, and the market spread of a fixed tranche is replicated by evaluating the level of the generic or implied correlation that yields this spread. For a given set of tranche prices on an arbitrary day, this procedure is expected to reveal five different correlations.[1] The resulting confliction

[1] Super-senior tranches of the pre-crisis CDX.NA.IG are commonly assumed to be (almost) riskless and thus omitted from our analysis.

can be resolved simply by realizing that the one-factor Gaussian copula model does not offer a reliable description of the pooled assets (see, e.g., Shreve, 2009). However, analogous to the Black–Scholes model, the Gaussian approach also offers an analytical formula for the valuation of tranches,[2] which in turn explains its popularity and the fact that tranche spreads are also quoted in terms of implied correlations.

3 Asset Value Dynamics

3.1 General Model Features

With respect to our basic asset pool model, we specify the firm value dynamics to satisfy the stochastic differential equation stated by Kou (2002):

$$\frac{dA(t)}{A(t-)} = (r - \lambda_a \zeta_a)\, dt + \sigma_a dB_a(t) + d\left[\sum_{i=1}^{N_a^m(t)} (V_{a,i} - 1)\right] \tag{4}$$

Hence, three basic components control the evolution of a company's asset value return: the drift component, the diffusion motion, and the jump part. The drift rate is specified by $(r - \lambda_a \zeta_a)$, which contains the risk-free interest rate as well as the compensator that accounts for the expected drift caused by the jump process. Continuously occurring changes are depicted by the Brownian diffusion $\sigma_a B_a(t)$. The jump part specifies systematic jumps to which all companies are exposed. The number of these jumps is denoted by $N_a^m(t)$ and follows a Poisson process with the intensity λ_a. The random number $V_{a,i},\ i \in \{1, \ldots, N_a^m(t)\}$, is characterized by the density of its logarithmic version

$$Y_{a,i} := \ln(V_{a,i}) \tag{5}$$

that follows an asymmetric double exponential distribution:

$$f_{Y_{a,i}}(y) = p \cdot \eta_1 e^{-\eta_1 y} \mathbf{1}_{y \geq 0} + q \cdot \eta_2 e^{\eta_2 y} \mathbf{1}_{y<0}, \quad \eta_1 > 1,\ \eta_2 > 0 \tag{6}$$

Therefore, $p, q \geq 0,\ p + q = 1$, define the conditional probabilities of upward and downward jumps. Because $N_a^m(t)$ and $V_{a,i}$ are stochastically independent, the process

[2]For technical details, we refer interested readers to Scherr (2012).

$$C_a^m(t) := \sum_{i=1}^{N_a^m(t)} (V_{a,i} - 1) \tag{7}$$

is a compound Poisson process, with expectation

$$\mathbb{E}\left[C_a^m(t)\right] = \lambda_a t \left(\frac{p\eta_1}{\eta_1 - 1} + \frac{q\eta_2}{\eta_2 + 1} - 1\right) \tag{8}$$

Performing calculations in the context of exponential Lévy models, one generally refers to logarithmic returns because these can be treated more easily. Applying Itô's Lemma to

$$X(t) := \ln\left[A(t)\right] \tag{9}$$

yields

$$X(t) = \left(r - \frac{\sigma_a^2}{2} - \lambda_a \zeta_a\right) t + \sigma_a B_a(t) + \sum_{i=1}^{N_a^m(t)} Y_{a,i} \tag{10}$$

Without loss of generality, we assume $A_0 = 0$, and hence the logarithmic return $X(t)$ is given by a standard Lévy process that comprises continuous as well as discontinuous movements.

3.2 *First Passage Time Distribution*

In modeling credit risk, dynamic approaches are usually specified as first passage time models. This concept was introduced by Black and Cox (1976) and accounts for the fact that a company can default at any time during the credit period. A default is triggered the moment the asset value touches or crosses some predefined default boundary, which represents the company's level of liabilities. The first passage time τ is defined mathematically as follows:

$$\tau := \inf\{t | A_t \leq D\} = \inf\{t | X_t \leq b\} \tag{11}$$

Here, D denotes the default barrier and b its logarithmic version. Because in our model setting the loss dynamics are determined solely by the default dynamics, the distribution of the first passage time, according to (2), is crucial.

There are only a few types of processes that offer an analytically known distribution of τ. For example, this pertains to the standard Brownian motion and spectrally negative Lévy processes. The Kou model applied in this paper also features an analytically known distribution of the first passage time, as formulated by Kou and Wang (2003) and Lipton (2002). For a comprehensive summary of the (technical) details, we refer interested readers to Scherr (2012).

The analytical nature of the proposed first passage time model enables a very fast (numerical) determination of loss dynamics and, based on these, the company's spread rate. In turn, given a quoted spread rate, the calibration of a homogenous pool can be conducted by a numerical optimization algorithm, due to the linearity of the expectation operator. If there were no analytically known distribution, calibration would have to be done by simulation techniques, which, despite the rapid growth of computational power, are still very time-consuming and also may potentially yield biased results. This especially appears over the course of extended time periods as well as processes with jumps (Broadie and Kaya, 2006; Kou and Wang, 2003). Therefore, the analyticity of our modeling approach, enabling unbiased and fast evaluations at firm and portfolio level, constitutes a major advantage of the presented approach.

3.3 *Integration of Market Risk*

3.3.1 Modeling Equity Dynamics

Besides analytical knowledge about the first passage time distribution, there is another important feature of the Kou model, namely the closed-form option-pricing formula. Extending the classical Black–Scholes approach, Kou (2002) calculated an explicit pricing function for European options where the underlying equity dynamics are given by

$$\frac{dS(t)}{S(t-)} = (r - \lambda_s \zeta_s)\, dt + \sigma_s dB_s(t) + d\left[\sum_{i=1}^{N_s(t)} (V_{s,i} - 1)\right] \tag{12}$$

Analogous to the asset value model, the random number $V_{s,i}$, $i \in \{1, \ldots, N_s(t)\}$, is characterized by the density of its logarithmic version

$$Y_{s,i} := \ln(V_{s,i}) \tag{13}$$

that also exhibits an asymmetric double exponential distribution:

$$f_{Y_{s,i}}(y) = p \cdot \xi_1 e^{-\xi_1 y} \mathbf{1}_{y \geq 0} + q \cdot \xi_2 e^{\xi_2 y} \mathbf{1}_{y<0}, \quad \xi_1 > 1,\ \xi_2 > 0 \tag{14}$$

Hence, the price $C\ (K, T)$ of a European call option written on an equity asset that follows (12) can be evaluated as a function of the strike level K and the maturity T[3]:

[3]The explicit functional dependence is stated in Scherr (2012).

$$C(K,T) = \Upsilon\left(r + \frac{1}{2}\sigma_s^2 - \lambda_s\zeta_s, \sigma_s, \tilde{\lambda}_s, \tilde{p}, \tilde{\xi}_1, \tilde{\xi}_2; \ln(K), T\right) \\ - K\exp(-rT)\cdot\Upsilon\left(r - \frac{1}{2}\sigma_s^2 - \lambda_s\zeta_s, \sigma_s, \lambda_s, p, \xi_1, \xi_2; \ln(K), T\right) \tag{15}$$

where

$$\tilde{p} = \frac{p}{1+\zeta_s}\cdot\frac{\xi_1}{\xi_1 - 1}, \quad \tilde{\xi}_1 = \xi_1 - 1, \quad \tilde{\xi}_2 = \xi_2 + 1, \quad \tilde{\lambda}_s = \lambda_s(\zeta_s + 1) \tag{16}$$

If we specify $S(t)$ to reflect the dynamics of an equity index, for example the S&P 500, and use this index as a proxy for the market dynamics, the logarithmic market returns are also given by a double exponential jump-diffusion process. By calibrating these equity dynamics to market data, given a fixed σ_s, we can ascertain the unknown parameter values of the jump part. Following Hamerle et al. (2013), we choose $\sigma_s = 0.1$.

3.3.2 Coupling Equity and Asset Dynamics

In our asset value model, the diffusion parameter σ_a, as well as λ_a, are used to set up the coupling between market and asset dynamics. This coupling reflects the notion that companies are exposed to both market and idiosyncratic risks. Whereas market risk simultaneously influences the evolution of all companies in a portfolio, idiosyncratic risks independently affect firm values. Adopting this basic idea of the CAP-model, we specify the asset value diffusion to follow the market diffusion up to a factor β. Additionally, we introduce an independent Brownian motion B_a^i to depict the continuous evolution of idiosyncratic risk. Thus, the asset value diffusion is given by

$$\sigma_a B_a = \beta\sigma_s B_s + \sigma_a^i B_a^i \sim \mathcal{N}\left(0, \sigma_a^2\right) \tag{17}$$

Here, we made use of the fact that the superposition of independent Brownian motions again turns out to be Brownian.

With respect to the jump part of our firm value model, we apply the parameters λ_s and ξ_s to specify the corresponding asset value dynamics. Due to the fact that jumps in the firm value are caused exclusively by jumps in the equity process, we fix the jump rate λ_a to be equal to λ_s. However, the jump distribution must be different because within our approach the level of debt is assumed to be constant, which in turn reduces the effects of discontinuous movements in the market value. We account for this fact by adopting the β factor introduced above and define

$$Y_{a,i} := \beta \cdot Y_{s,i} \tag{18}$$

Applying the transformation formula, it is easy to show that this way of proceeding preserves the distribution characteristic and thus proves to be consistent with the given firm value dynamics. Furthermore, the distribution parameter of $Y_{a,i}$ can be evaluated as follows:

$$\eta_a = \frac{1}{\beta}\xi_s \tag{19}$$

reflecting, on average, the damped amplitude of jumps. For reasons of simplicity, we restrict ourselves to the limiting case of $q = 1$, concerning both asset and equity dynamics. Thus, we define $\eta_a := \eta_2$ and $\xi_s := \xi_2$.

4 Model Changes and Correlation Smiles

4.1 Data Description

The database for our analysis relies primarily on quotes that were offered in addition to the publication of Coval et al. (2009) and are available at the webpage of the publishing journal. These quotes comprise data on 5-year S&P 500 index options, spread rates of the 5-year CDX.NA.IG and associated tranches as well as time-congruent swap rates. The swap rates are also offered by www.swap-rates.com and used as risk-free interest rates. The time series cover the period from September 22, 2004 to September 19, 2007, which corresponds exactly to the duration period of the CDX.NA.IG Series 3 through Series 8. In addition, the data on S&P 500 index options provide daily information on option prices with respect to 13 different strike levels and also report the time series of the S&P 500 index level.

4.2 Basic Model

For the purpose of calibrating our basic model, we utilize prices of S&P 500 index options and spread rates of the 5-year CDX.NA.IG that were observed on February 6, 2006. We choose this date because within our analysis we wish to analyze the pricing impact of model changes with respect to a common market environment.[4] On average, the pre-crisis spread rate of the 5-year CDX.NA.IG can be calculated to about 45 bps (the exact mean value amounts to 45.87 bps), which, for example, was the market quote on February 6, 2006. In addition, this date is also located in the center of our time series.

[4] According to Collin-Dufresne et al. (2012) and Coval et al. (2009), we specify Series 3 through 8 to represent the pre-crisis period.

To calibrate our market model, we must back out the optimal value of (λ_s, ξ_s). Because all the other input variables required for the pricing of options are known, namely the contemporary index level, strike price, interest rate, and maturity, we perform a numerical optimization procedure that minimizes the sum of in-sample quadratic pricing errors:

$$\mathscr{E}(\lambda_s, \xi_s) := \sum_{i=1}^{13} \left[\tilde{P}_i(\lambda_s, \xi_s) - P_i\right]^2 \tag{20}$$

where $\tilde{P}_i$ denotes the model price and P_i the corresponding empirical value. As a result of this procedure, we obtain

$$(\lambda_s, \xi_s)_{opt} := (0.125, 2.91) \tag{21}$$

which is used to determine the model implied volatility skew shown by the solid line in Fig. 1. This curve, as well as the market-implied volatilities, marked by the crosses, is plotted against the moneyness level m, which we define by

$$m := \frac{K}{S_0} \tag{22}$$

On average, the relative pricing error amounts to 0.30 %, which emphasizes the high fitting quality of the chosen market model, relying only on two degrees of freedom. Concerning the pool model, we choose $\beta = 0.5$ and $\sigma_a = 0.2$ to capture the main results of a corresponding survey performed by Collin-Dufresne et al. (2012). In this regard, the sparse number of parameters constitutes a further advantage of our approach because besides $(\lambda_s, \xi_s)_{opt}$ we only have to determine the

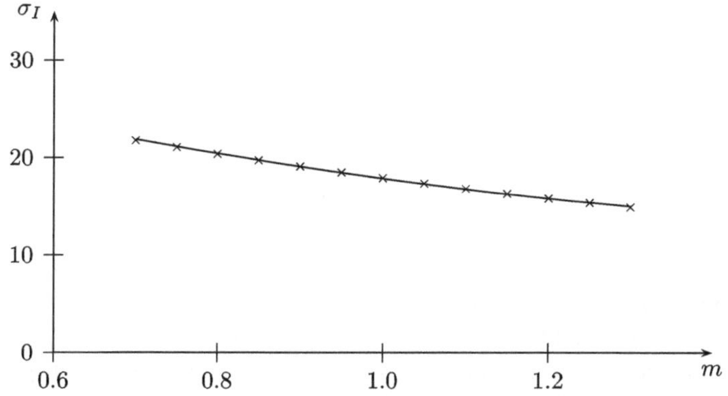

Fig. 1 Implied volatility σ_I of the market model. The *solid line* shows the resulting function extracted from 5-year S&P 500 index option prices (marked by the *crosses*). All values are quoted in percent

logarithmic default boundary b. This can be done by evaluating the (unique) zero of

$$s_i^m(b) - s_i^e \tag{23}$$

where s_i^m denotes the model implied spread rate and s_i^e the empirically observed index spread of the CDX.NA.IG on February 6, 2006. A simple numerical procedure yields $b = -1.141$, which completes our setup.

4.3 Market Dynamics

The basic concept of our pricing model refers to the notion that the common dynamics of asset values are affected only by the temporal evolution of the corresponding equity market. In this context, predefined changes in the market dynamics are intended to have a similar impact on the model implied spread rates. If, for example, the risk neutral probability of negative market states increases, premium payments on senior tranches are supposed to rise. By contrast, if option prices imply a significant incidence of positive market states, equity spreads are expected to fall.

Here, we analyze the pricing impact of market dynamics by adopting the couples of jump parameters that imply the minimum and maximum as well as the 25 %, 50 %, and 75 % quantile of the terminal logarithmic return variance in our time series:

$$\mathbb{V}\left[\ln\left(S_T\right)\right] = \sigma_s^2 T + 2\frac{\lambda T}{\xi_s^2} \tag{24}$$

We use the resulting parameters to specify our asset value model (besides the default boundary, we keep all the other parameters fixed) and perform a recalibration to match the target value of 45 bps. Accordingly, a further advantage of our modeling approach emerges. Given the numerically determined default barrier, we can prove the reliability of simulated tranche spreads because the applied Monte Carlo techniques must also yield the desired index level. Otherwise, computational efforts have to be increased to avoid biased results. We use the modeled spread rates to back out the implied correlations within the Gaussian model and depict the resulting values in Fig. 2.

In addition, Table 1 presents the deviations compared to our basic model. Concerning equity and senior tranches, the extreme specifications of market dynamics impact significantly on the premium payments. In line with the economic mechanism discussed above, the low variance scenario causes equity spreads to rise and senior spreads to fall, whereas the high variance scenario implies reduced payments on equity and heightened payments on senior notionals. These results can be simply explained by the different incidences of both positive and negative market states. Due to its position in the capital structure, the mezzanine tranche exhibits

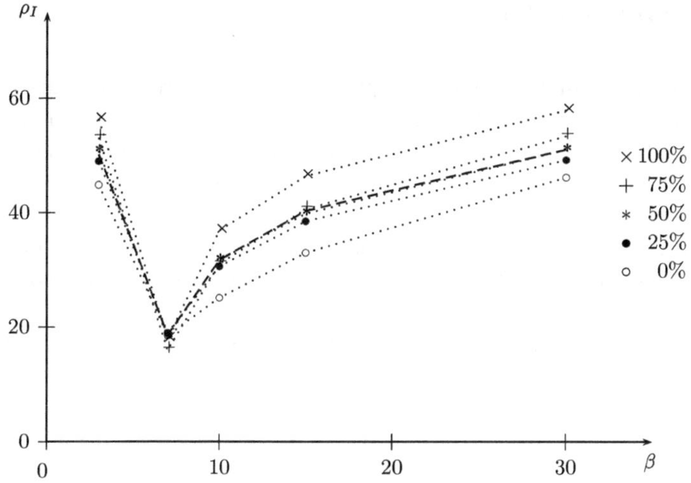

Fig. 2 Implied correlation ρ_I with respect to changes in market dynamics. The *dashed curve* refers to our basic model, whereas the *legend symbols* specify the different equity dynamics. All values are quoted in percent

Table 1 Deviations of implied correlations caused by the use of different market dynamics. z symbolizes the various quantiles of the terminal logarithmic return variance and ϵ_i denotes the deviation of the ith tranche, where $i = 1$ refers to the equity tranche, $i = 2$ to the mezzanine tranche, etc.

z	0%	25%	50%	75%	100%
ϵ_1	5.4	1.2	0.6	2.9	6.1
ϵ_2	0.0	0.4	0.3	2.6	0.6
ϵ_3	6.6	1.1	0.0	0.7	5.1
ϵ_4	7.3	1.8	0.5	0.3	6.1
ϵ_5	4.9	1.8	0.0	2.4	6.9

only a minimum response to the market dynamics, and consequently spread rates also vary only slightly. In addition, if we focus on the range that comprises the scenarios between the 25 % and 75 % quantile of the logarithmic return variance, the pricing impact occurs in the economically expected direction, but, surprisingly, also appears to be limited. This finding may potentially be ascribed to the tempered market environment within the pre-crisis period, which causes the corresponding market dynamics to be at a comparable level. However, given our results, a more detailed analysis of the pricing impact of market dynamics would seem to be a worthwhile objective of future research.

4.4 Idiosyncratic Jumps

The jump part of our basic model captures solely the arrival of "discontinuous" information, such as political power changes, judicial decisions, and so on, which commonly affect the modeled asset values. Hence, a more general approach comprises the embedding of idiosyncratic jumps that depict sudden firm-specific events, for example, an unexpected change in the board of directors. Integrating these jumps, of course, entails the mutual dependencies of the company dynamics to decline. Consequently, equity spread rates are expected to rise, whereas senior rates are supposed to fall.

To examine these suggestions, we include idiosyncratic jumps by adding the compound Poisson process

$$C_a^i(t) = \sum_{i=1}^{N_a^i(t)} (V_{a,i} - 1) \tag{25}$$

with jump intensity λ_a^i and independent jump variables, whose logarithmic values again follow a double exponential distribution.[5] Furthermore, we choose the jump intensities to follow

$$\begin{aligned} \lambda_a^m &= \varrho \cdot \lambda_a \\ \lambda_a^i &= (1-\varrho) \cdot \lambda_a, \quad 0 \leq \varrho \leq 1 \end{aligned} \tag{26}$$

and define

$$\eta_a^m := \eta_a^i := \eta_a \tag{27}$$

Assuming stochastic independence between the systematic and the idiosyncratic jump part, we obtain, in total, a compound process with jump intensity

$$\varrho \cdot \lambda_a + (1-\varrho) \cdot \lambda_a = \lambda_a \tag{28}$$

and jump parameter η_a. Hence, in terms of distribution, the jump part of our basic and the present approach is identical. This can easily be seen from the characteristic function of the compound Poisson process $C(t)$:

$$\Phi_{C_t}(u) = \exp\left[\lambda t \int_{\mathbb{R}} \left(e^{iux} - 1\right) f(x)dx\right] \tag{29}$$

[5] Analogous to our basic model, we restrict ourselves to the limit of almost surely negative jumps.

where λ denotes the jump intensity and $f(x)$ the density of the jump distribution. Due to the distributional equivalence, the present model does not have to be recalibrated, and one can simply adopt the default boundary of the basic model. In addition, the model implied spread rates of indices with shorter maturities also remain unchanged because within this approach the choice of ϱ does not affect the term structure of losses.

In turn, this means that we can calibrate the model to reproduce the quoted index spread, but nevertheless have the flexibility to choose the weighting of jumps. At the limit $\varrho = 1$, the proposed model coincides with the basic one, whereas $\varrho = 0$ implies that there are no systematic jumps.

To analyze the impact of different levels of ϱ, we strobe the interval $[0.8, 0.0]$ by steps of 0.2. The corresponding results are depicted in Fig. 3, which in particular shows that across all tranches the choice of ϱ crucially affects the implied correlations. Due to the numerical decline of extreme events, equity spreads significantly rise, whereas senior spreads almost vanish. As reported in Table 2, especially the impact on the most senior tranche turns out to be very substantial. In the case of $\rho = 0.2$, as well as $\rho = 0.0$, the Gaussian model cannot reproduce the spread rates of the mezzanine tranche implied by the model and, in addition, a degeneration of the smile pattern can be observed.

From a general perspective, these results imply that introducing idiosyncratic jumps does not necessarily yield a significant contribution to the term structure properties of a dynamic model but may dramatically influence the pricing of tranches. This finding constitutes the main contribution of our paper, in particular

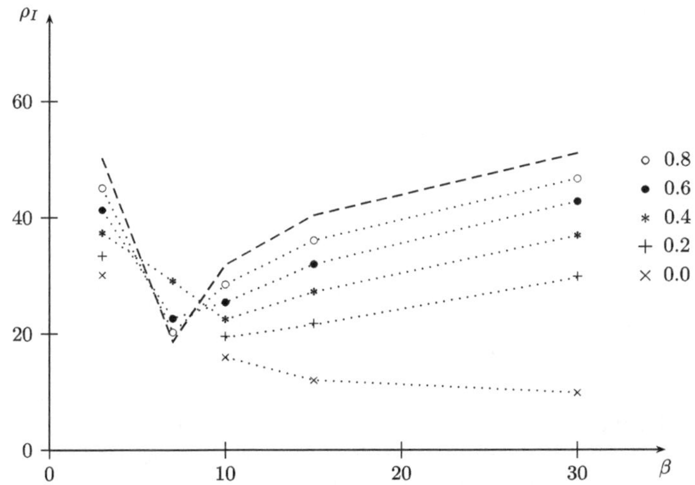

Fig. 3 Implied correlation ρ_I with respect to the inclusion of idiosyncratic jumps. The *dashed curve* refers to the basic model, whereas the *legend symbols* specify the jump weighting ϱ. All values are quoted in percent

Table 2 Deviations of implied correlations caused by the inclusion of idiosyncratic jumps

ϱ	0.0	0.2	0.4	0.6	0.8
ϵ_1	20.1	17.1	13.0	8.9	5.1
ϵ_2	–	–	10.4	4.0	1.7
ϵ_3	15.9	12.5	9.4	6.4	3.3
ϵ_4	28.4	18.8	13.2	8.4	4.3
ϵ_5	41.3	21.5	14.2	8.4	4.4

with respect to the contemporary debate on the relative pricing of equity and credit derivatives.

4.5 Term Structure of Tranche Losses

According to the terms of contract, premium payments of tranches always refer to the remaining notional that has not been exhausted as a consequence of portfolio losses. In that regard, due to the absence of loss enhancement, the equity tranche exhibits maximum sensitivity to defaults in the portfolio. For example, if a company declares insolvency soon after contract release, the equity holder immediately loses $\frac{0.6}{125 \cdot 0.03} = 16\,\%$ of his spread payments. By contrast, senior tranches are expected to suffer very low losses, and thus the explicit loss dynamics should not significantly affect risk premiums. An examination of the impact of loss dynamics is of particular importance with respect to static models because within the modeling process one has to fix generically the corresponding term structures. In the case of the standard Gaussian model, the expected portfolio loss is assumed to grow with a constant hazard rate and thus according to the function

$$\mathbb{E}\left(L_t\right) = 1 - e^{-\lambda t} \tag{30}$$

Here, the hazard rate λ is chosen so that $\mathbb{E}\left(L_T\right)$ meets the desired level of loss at maturity.

A further alternative to fixing generically the temporal evolution of losses can be seen from the source code published by Coval et al. (2009).[6] Evaluating tranche prices, they assume linearly declining notionals. The term structure implied by our dynamic model is based on the assumption that a company defaults as soon as the asset value touches or deceeds a predefined default barrier. Based on this threshold, the portfolio analysis can be conducted by applying Monte Carlo simulation techniques, whereas the results, among others, are used to determine the term structures of expected losses implied by the model.

[6] In the following, we use the abbreviation CJS.

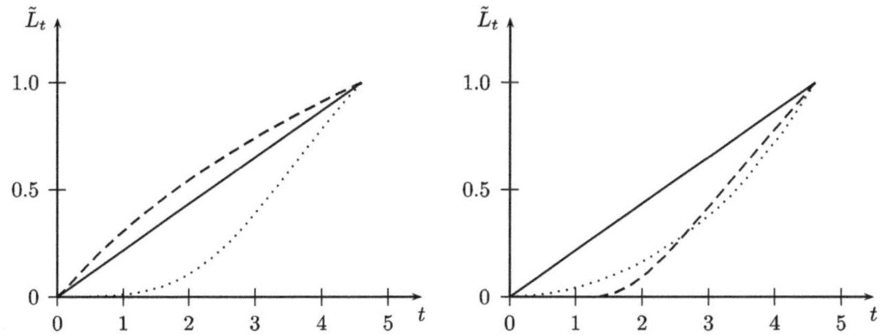

Fig. 4 Comparison of relative loss term structures $\widetilde{L}_t$. The calculations refer to the one-factor Gaussian copula model (*dashed line*), the CJS model (*solid line*), and our basic approach (*dotted line*) and comprise the equity (*left-hand side*) and the most senior tranche (*right-hand side*)

Table 3 Deviations of implied correlations caused by applying various term structures of tranche losses

γ	$\frac{1}{4}$	$\frac{1}{2}$	1	2	4
ϵ_1	17.8	13.1	7.4	2.0	1.9
ϵ_2	19.1	9.7	4.8	1.6	0.3
ϵ_3	6.7	4.9	2.8	1.0	0.3
ϵ_4	5.4	4.1	2.5	1.0	0.1
ϵ_5	4.1	3.2	2.1	1.0	0.2

To compare the temporal evolution of losses across different tranches, we have to take into account that expected tranche losses are of a different scale. Hence, for each tranche, we rescale the dynamics of losses by the expected loss at maturity and obtain modified loss curves that start at zero, increase monotonically and take one as their terminal value. Figure 4 shows the resulting term structures for the equity and the most senior tranche within the Gaussian, the CJS, and our basic approach. Concerning the equity tranche, the one-factor approach shows a "frontloaded" term structure, whereas expected losses of the most senior tranche are "backloaded." By definition, within the CJS-model, tranche exposures decline linearly over time. The term structures of our basic approach have a similar shape, and both exhibit a convex pattern.

To examine the impact of loss dynamics on the tranche spreads in a general setting, we substitute the first passage time dynamics by

$$L^{\gamma}_{\alpha,\beta}(t) = f_{\gamma}(t) \cdot L^{T}_{\alpha,\beta} \tag{31}$$

where

$$f_{\gamma}(t) := \left(\frac{t}{T}\right)^{\gamma}, \quad \gamma \in \left\{\frac{1}{4}, \frac{1}{2}, 1, 2, 4\right\} \tag{32}$$

Based on the chosen scenario, denoted by γ, we adopt the terminal tranche losses offered by our basic model and evaluate the spread rates by applying the polynomial

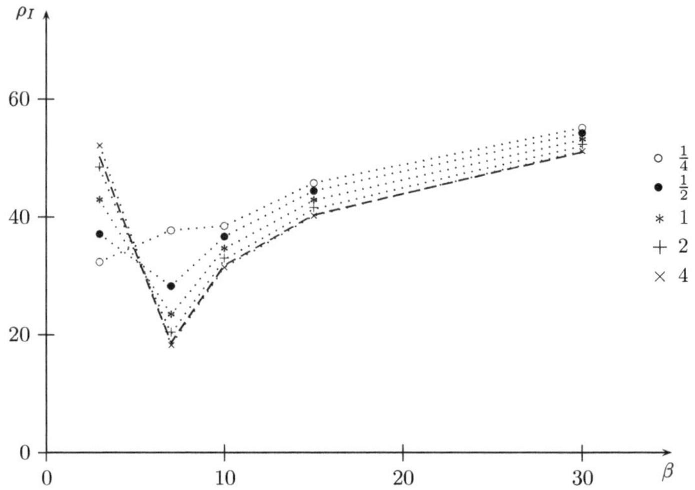

Fig. 5 Implied correlation ρ_I with respect to the use of different loss dynamics. The *dashed curve* refers to the basic model, whereas the *legend symbols* specify the generic loss scenarios. All values are quoted in percent

term structures. Furthermore, we back out implied correlations and calculate the corresponding deviations to measure the effects on our reference scenario.

Moving from $\gamma = \frac{1}{4}$ to $\gamma = 4$, premium payments decline because losses tend to occur later and, on average, the outstanding notionals are higher. According to Table 3, the sensitivity of the single tranches decreases by moving the capital structure upwards. As economically expected and discussed above, the timing of defaults seriously impacts on the spread rates of equity and mezzanine tranches, whereas senior tranches are less sensitive to the term structure pattern. These findings are also displayed in Fig. 5. Hence, the term structures of losses may significantly affect premium payments of tranches, and in particular the generic specification of loss dynamics should be conducted carefully to avoid biased results.

4.6 *Portfolio Heterogeneity*

Our basic model refers to a homogenous pool, which implies that under the risk-neutral measure all companies offer identical default dynamics. On the one hand, this assumption is quite a simplification, but, on the other hand, it also enables an analytical calibration of the portfolio model and thus ensures the approach to be highly applicable. The easiest way to analyze the impact of this assumption is to split the portfolio into two parts that are homogenous by themselves and offer spread rates resembling the observed index spread.

Here, we fix the homogenous spread rates of $n_1 := 63$ companies to a certain level s_1^p and calculate the corresponding value s_2^p of the remaining $n_2 := 62$ companies. In this context, we follow Bluhm and Overbeck (2006, p. 270), who propose a pricing formula of a CDS index, based purely on the properties of the pooled contracts. Rewriting this formula yields

$$\delta_2 \cdot \left(s_i - s_2^p\right) = \frac{n_1}{n_2} \cdot \delta_1 \cdot \left(s_1^p - s_i\right) \tag{33}$$

The risky duration δ_i, $i = 1, 2$, is defined by

$$\delta_i := \sum_{k=1}^{K} e^{-rt_i} \left(1 - p_i^{t_k}\right), \quad t_K = T \tag{34}$$

where

$$p_i^t := \mathbb{P}\left(\tau_i \leq t\right) \tag{35}$$

Given s_1^p, the corresponding default boundary can easily be evaluated. To back out the default boundary of the second part, we use Eq. (33). Again, due to the analytically known first passage time distribution, we can perform computations very quickly and without bias. The calibration procedure thus yields two different default barriers, which are used to specify the temporal evolution of the portfolio as well as the loss dynamics of tranches. Table 4 reports the corresponding numerical results. The correlation smiles displayed in Fig. 6 show a significant impact of portfolio heterogeneity, in particular with respect to the tranches of lower seniority. Figure 6 also shows that an amplification of the portfolio heterogeneity entails a heightened level of implied correlation.

Hence, the homogeneity assumption may imply downward biased spread rates of senior tranches and also cause equity spreads which exceed the actual level. As a consequence, in the context of modeling multi-name derivatives, there should always be a pre-testing of the pooled entities to determine whether or not the homogeneity assumption constitutes a valid simplification.

Table 4 Deviations of implied correlations caused by introducing portfolio heterogeneity

s_1^p	5 bps	15 bps	25 bps	35 bps
ϵ_1	10.3	5.6	2.2	0.3
ϵ_2	–	10.8	5.8	1.9
ϵ_3	10.1	5.3	2.8	1.4
ϵ_4	4.6	2.5	1.9	1.1
ϵ_5	3.5	2.6	1.9	1.1

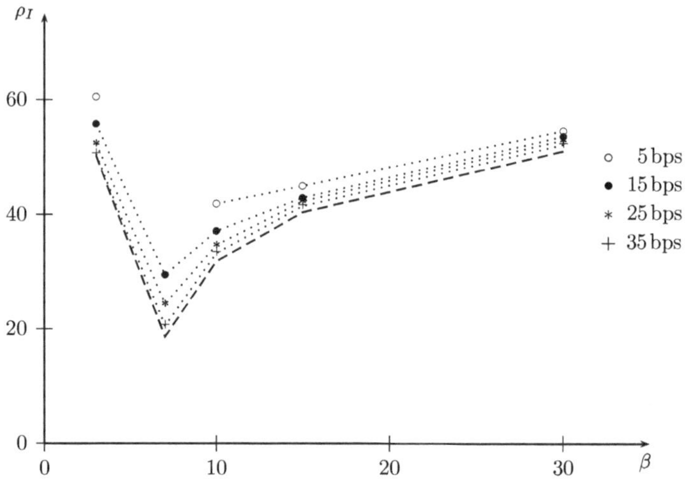

Fig. 6 Implied correlation ρ_I with respect to the integration of portfolio heterogeneity. The *dashed curve* refers to the basic model, whereas the *legend symbols* specify the different heterogeneity scenarios. All values are quoted in percent

Conclusion

In this article, we analyze the pricing of pre-crisis CDX.NA.IG tranches within a structural dynamic approach. As expected, the mutual dependencies of asset value dynamics, controlled by the weighting of idiosyncratic jumps, affect spread rates at most, whereas the choice of the term structure of losses, as well as the homogeneity assumption, particularly drives tranches of lower seniority. Disregarding portfolio heterogeneity also seems to imply systematically biased results. Surprisingly, our analysis additionally demonstrates a comparatively limited impact of market dynamics on the tranche spreads.

Of course, there are many issues left that were not covered by our analysis. This is mainly reasoned by the fact that the proposed alterations are chosen in such a way as to ensure analytical tractability, at least at the single-name level. In this regard, further research might, for example, deal with the impact of generalizing model scalars into random variables, which includes recovery rates as well as interest and dividend rates. In addition, the default boundary could be specified as a function of time and the heterogeneity of the pool might be accounted for at a more fine-grained level. However, increasing model complexity always involves the danger of hidden effects emerging, as clearly demonstrated in this article.

References

Agca, S., Agrawal, D., & Islam, S. (2008). Implied correlations: Smiles or smirks. *Journal of Derivatives, 16*, 7–35.

Andersen, L., & Sidenius, J. (2004). Extensions to the Gaussian copula: Random recovery and random factor loadings. *Journal of Credit Risk, 1*, 29–70.

Black, F., & Cox, J. (1976). Valuing corporate securities: Some effects of bond indenture provisions. *Journal of Finance, 31*, 351–367.

Black, F., & Scholes, M. (1973). The pricing of options and corporate liabilities. *Journal of Political Economy, 87*, 637–659.

Bluhm, C., & Overbeck, L. (2006). Structured credit portfolio analysis, baskets and CDOs. London: Chapman & Hall/CRC.

Broadie, M., & Kaya, O. (2006). Exact simulation of stochastic volatility and other affine jump diffusion processes. *Operations Research, 54*, 217–231.

Collin-Dufresne, P., Goldstein, R., & Yang, F. (2012). On the relative pricing of long maturity index options and collateralized debt obligations. *Journal of Finance, 67*, 1983–2014.

Coval, J., Jurek, J., & Stafford, E. (2009). Economic catastrophe bonds. *American Economic Review, 99*, 628–666.

Hamerle, A., Igl, A., & Plank, K. (2012). Correlation smile, volatility skew, and systematic risk sensitivity of tranches. *Journal of Derivatives, 19*, 8–27.

Hamerle, A., Plank, K., & Scherr, C. (2013). Dynamic modeling of credit derivatives. In D. Rösch & H. Scheule (Eds.), *Credit securitisations and derivatives Challenges for the Global Markets*. Chichester: Wiley.

Kalemanova, A., Schmid, B., & Werner, R. (2007). The normal inverse Gaussian distribution for synthetic CDO pricing. *Journal of Derivatives, 14*, 80–94.

Kou, S. (2002). A jump-diffusion model for option pricing. *Management Science, 48*, 1086–1101.

Kou, S., & Wang, H. (2003). First passage times of a jump diffusion process. *Advances in Applied Probability, 35*, 504–531.

Li, H., & Zhao, F. (2011). Economic catastrophe bonds: Inefficient market or inadequate model? Working Paper, University of Michigan.

Lipton, A. (2002). Assets with jumps. *Risk, 15*, 149–153.

Luo, D., & Carverhill, A. (2011). Pricing and integration of the CDX tranches in the financial market. Working Paper, University of Hong Kong.

Moosbrucker, T. (2006). Explaining the correlation smile using variance gamma distributions. *Journal of Fixed Income, 16*, 71–87.

Scherr, C. (2012). A semi-analytical approach to the dynamic modeling of credit derivatives. Working Paper, University of Regensburg.

Sepp, A. (2006, September). Extended CreditGrades model with stochastic volatility and jumps. *Wilmott Magazine*, 50–62.

Shreve, S. (2009, Spring). Did faulty mathematical models cause the financial fiasco? *Analytics*, 6–7.

Findings of the Signal Approach: A Case Study for Kazakhstan

Klaus Abberger and Wolfgang Nierhaus

Abstract This study concentrates on the signal approach for the monitoring of currency crises risks. It focuses on the properties of individual indicators prior to observed currency crises in Kazakhstan. The indicators are used to build composite indicators. An advanced approach uses principal components analysis for the construction of composite indicators. Furthermore, the common signal approach is improved by robust statistical methods. The estimation period reaches from 1997 to 2007. It is shown that most of the composite indicators are able to flag the reported crises in this time span at an early stage. In a second step it is checked whether the crisis observed in 2009 is signalled in advance.

1 Introduction

Forecasting currency crises is a challenging task. A well-known standard approach is the signal approach developed by Kaminsky, Lizondo and Reinhart (KLR). Following this approach currency crises are identified by means of a foreign exchange market pressure index. This pressure index serves as a reference series for dating currency crises. In a second step KLR propose the monitoring of macroeconomic variables (single indicators) that may tend to show unusual behaviour in periods (1 or 2 years) prior to currency turbulences. An indicator sends a crisis warning signal whenever it moves beyond a given critical threshold. Moreover, composite indicators can be constructed that encompass the signalling behaviour of the selected individual indicators. Finally, crises probabilities can be estimated. This procedure, which can be performed for each single country with reported currency crises, characterizes the signal approach.

K. Abberger (✉)
KOF Swiss Economic Institute, Leonhardstrasse 21, 8092 Zurich, Switzerland
e-mail: abberger@kof.ethz.ch

W. Nierhaus
Ifo Institute - Leibniz Institute for Economic Research at the University of Munich, Poschingerstrasse 5, 81679 Munich, Germany
e-mail: nierhaus@ifo.de

J. Beran et al. (eds.), *Empirical Economic and Financial Research*,
Advanced Studies in Theoretical and Applied Econometrics 48,
DOI 10.1007/978-3-319-03122-4_20

The following case study concentrates on the signal approach for Kazakhstan. It focuses on the signalling properties of individual macroeconomic indicators prior to episodes of foreign exchange market turbulences in Kazakhstan, as indicated by the exchange market pressure index. The individual indicators are used to build composite currency crises indicators by exploiting the signal behaviour of each individual indicator. A refined approach uses principal components analysis of the individual indicators to construct composite indicators. The estimation period of the critical thresholds reaches from January 1997 to December 2007. For this time span it is shown that most of the composite indicators are able to flag the two reported currency crises in this time span at an early stage (in-sample analysis). In a second step it is checked whether the crisis observed in February 2009 is signalled by the composite indicators in advance (out-of-sample analysis). All data were taken from the Agency of Statistics of the Republic of Kazakhstan, the National Bank of Kazakhstan and International Financial Statistics (IFS), published by the International Monetary Fund. An important requirement for an early-warning system to function properly is timeliness. For this reason this study is based on monthly data or on quarterly data, which has been transformed into monthly data by means of temporal disaggregation techniques.

2 The Signal Approach

2.1 Defining Currency Turbulences

Following the signal approach, currency turbulences should be defined using definite criteria. Currency crises are identified by means of a foreign exchange market pressure index relying on the symptoms of such episodes of currency turbulences[1]:

- a sudden and sharp devaluation of a currency,
- a substantial decrease in foreign exchange reserves

It is quite important to focus on both aspects, because currency crises can break out that leads to a sharp devaluation of a currency. But sometimes monetary institutions try to avoid these devaluations. They intervene to avoid or soften the devaluation. Although no sharp devaluation occurred in these cases, they are also currency crises because the authorities were forced to intervene. Such hidden or sometimes avoided crises are visible in the foreign exchange reserves because they are used to intervene. For a method that is used to give early warnings on currency crises it is important that visible and hidden or avoided crises are included in the calculations. Hence an index of pressure in the foreign exchange market IP_t at month t is constructed

[1] See Kaminsky et al. (1998), Schnatz (1998, 1999a,b), Deutsche Bundesbank (1999), and Nierhaus (2000).

by using the monthly rates of change of the foreign exchange reserves and the real exchange rate.

$$IP_t = \gamma_1 \Delta wr_t - \gamma_2 \Delta rer_t \tag{1}$$

Δwr_t is the rate of change of the foreign exchange reserves; Δrer_t is the rate of change of the real exchange rate, which is given by the nominal exchange rate of the domestic currency to the USD, adjusted for consumer prices ($rer_t = er_{CURRENCY|US\$,t} \cdot CPI_{US,t}/CPI_t$).

A rise in the real exchange rate corresponds to a real depreciation of the currency. A real depreciation of the currency follows from a nominal depreciation of the currency and/or a rise in US consumer prices and/or a decline in domestic consumer prices. Since the variances of Δrer_t and Δwr_t are different, they are weighted (γ_1 and γ_2) by using the standard deviation of the variables. The real exchange rate is used to avoid corrections for periods with high inflation differentials between home and abroad.[2]

Tensions in the foreign exchange market are identified for periods when the foreign exchange market index swings deeply into the negative. In the present study, for a currency turbulence, the pressure index IP_t must be below its mean μ more than three times the standard deviation $\sigma = \sqrt{var(IP_t)}$, as proposed by KLR.[3] If a new event occurs within three quarters, then the time in-between is defined as a crisis episode. Otherwise the last point in time of the event is fixed as the end of the episode.[4]

The true σ is unknown and must be estimated from data at hand.[5] Since the analysis of currency crises means searching for extreme events in time series, the question arises as to how to measure scale. Empirical variance and empirical standard deviation are estimators, which are very sensitive against outliers. Data used for the analysis of currency crises contain extreme events or outliers, therefore robust estimation methods might be preferable. With non-robust estimators, outliers could mask themselves. One robust measure of scale is the median of absolute deviations from the median (MAD). This robust scale estimator is used in the study at hand. The MAD is adjusted by a factor for asymptotically normal consistency. It holds

$$E\left[1.4862 \cdot MAD(X_1, X_2, X_3, \ldots)\right] = \sigma \tag{2}$$

for X_j, $j = 1, 2, 3, \ldots, n$, distributed as $N(\mu, \sigma)$ and large n.

[2] See Schnatz (1999b).

[3] See Kaminsky et al. (1998, p. 16).

[4] See Schnatz (1999b).

[5] Also unknown is μ, which is estimated by the arithmetic mean m of IP_t.

2.2 Selecting Indicators

The signal approach uses indicators to detect currency crises in advance. Since currency crises are extreme events, they usually are preceded by extreme developments or imbalances. So they might be detected by leading indicators, showing exceptional high or low values before the crises start. With this conception in mind it is obvious to condense the information contained in leading indicators to a binary variable, which differentiates whether the indicator is in a normal or in an extreme range. This is an important feature of the signal approach. The indicators are transformed to binary variables and are not used in their original form. A leading indicator is said to issue a warning signal if it exceeds (is below) a critical threshold level. This level has to be chosen appropriately to balance the risks of having numerous false signals and the risk of not registering crises.[6]

From the statistical point of view the signal approach can be characterized as a nonparametric approach, since it does not require the assumption of a specific model (in contrast to logit models or Markov-switching models). Indeed the parametric models may be more efficient when the models assumptions hold in reality. The signal approach, on the other hand, should be a quite versatile method.

To fix ideas, let St be a binary signal variable, depending on the value of the individual indicator V_t at time t, the critical cutoff value δ and the expected sign (+/-) before crises:

$$S_t^+ = \begin{cases} 1 \text{ if } V_t > \delta \\ 0 \text{ if } V_t \leq \delta \end{cases} \text{ or } S_t^- = \begin{cases} 1 \text{ if } V_t < \delta \\ 0 \text{ if } V_t \geq \delta \end{cases} \tag{3}$$

In this concept the informative content of an observation at time t is reduced to one of the two possibilities: either the indicator exceeds (is below) the threshold δ and gives a crisis warning signal ($S_t = 1$), or it is below (exceeds) the threshold sending no signal ($S_t = 0$). However, there may be correct signals and false signals. An indicator sends a correct signal if $S_t = 1$ and a crisis happens within 12 months or $S_t = 0$ and no crisis happens within a time-window of 12 months. In the first case the indicator sends a signal and is followed within 12 months by a currency crisis. In the second case the indicator does not send a signal and is not followed by a crisis.

By contrast, the indicator issues a false signal if $S_t = 1$ and no crisis happens within 12 months or $S_t = 0$ and a crisis happens within 12 months. In the third case the indicator sends a signal and is not followed by a crisis. In the last case the indicator does not send a signal and is followed by currency turbulence. Altogether, the performance of an indicator can be measured in terms of Table 1.

Following KLR, a perfect indicator would only produce signals that belong to the north-west and south-east cells of the matrix. It would issue a signal in every month

[6] See Kaminsky et al. (1998).

Table 1 Classification table

	Crisis within 12 months	No crisis within 12 months
Signal is sent: $S_t = 1$	A (=number of signals)	B (=number of signals)
No signal is sent: $S_t = 0$	C (=number of signals)	D (=number of signals)

Table 2 Conditional crisis probabilities

	Crisis within 12 months	No crisis within 12 months
Signal is sent: $S_t = 1$	A /(A+B)	B/(A+B)
No signal is sent: $S_t = 0$	C/(C+D)	D/(C+D)

that is followed by a crisis ($A > 0$), so that the number of missing warning signals C equals zero, and it would not send a signal in every month that is not followed by a crisis ($D > 0$), so that the number of wrong warning signals B equals zero.

On the basis of this concept, the overall performance of an indicator V_t (that is the ability to issue correct signals and to avoid false signals) can be measured by the noise-to-signal ratio ω. This figure is defined as the ratio of the number of false warning signals divided by the number of observations in tranquil periods $B/(B + D)$ and the number of correct warning signals divided by the number observations in the run-up period $A/(A + C)$. Indicators with $\omega > 1$ are excluded from the analysis.

Following KLR, another way of interpreting the results of noisiness of the indicators is by comparing the probability of a crisis conditional on a warning signal from the indicator $P(\text{Crisis}|\text{warning signal}) = A/(A + B)$ with the unconditional probability of a crisis $P(\text{Crisis}) = (A + C)/(A + B + C + D)$. If the indicator has useful information, then the conditional probability of a crisis should be higher than the unconditional one (see Table 2).

Another measure for the quality of an indicator V_t is the odds ratio γ. The odds for a currency crisis within 12 months (or not), given a signal S_t (that is warning signal or not) can be defined in terms of conditional crisis probabilities. The odds for a crisis conditional on a warning signal is $[A/(A + B)]/[B/(A + B)] = A/B$. The odds for a crisis conditional on a missing warning signal is $C/(C + D)]/[D/(C + D) = C/D$. Then the odds ratio γ is defined as

$$\gamma = (A/B)/(C/D) = (A \cdot D)/(B \cdot C) \tag{4}$$

Finally, in order to discriminate between "normal" and "abnormal" behaviour of an individual indicator, the threshold δ has to be defined. If the cutoff value is set at a rather high level, the indicator is likely to miss all but the most severe crises. In contrast, if the threshold is set very low, the indicator is likely to catch all crises but is also likely to send many false warning signals in tranquil periods. A commonly used way is to set the cutoff value δ in relation to specific percentiles of the distribution of indicator observations. Here an α-percentile is calculated corresponding to the maximum possible number of correct signals prior to currency crisis (here generally 12) in relation to the total number of available observations. Subtracting this value from one puts the threshold in the area of the frequency distribution with the high values.[7]

2.3 Composite Indicators

Based on the assumption that the greater the number of leading indicators signalling a crisis, the higher the probability that such a crisis would actually occur, KLR proposed a number of composite leading indices. Composite indicators are constructed by weighting together the signals $S_{r,,t}$ of k individual indicators $V_{r,t}$.[8]

$$S_t = \sum_{r=1,\ldots,k} S_{r,,t} w_r \text{ and } \sum_{r=1,\ldots,k} w_r = 1. \tag{5}$$

Obviously there are two rules for determining the weights of the specific indicator signals. One approach focuses on equal weights; the other would exploit the observed forecasting performance of the individual indicators before past crises. The latter approach is clearly favourable if future crises are driven by the same economic factors as the past crises, whereas the equal weight approach is neutral.

2.4 Calculating Crisis Probabilities

While composite currency crises indicators show changes in the strength or weakness of crisis warning signals, the index levels cannot be directly interpreted. However, it is possible to assign a particular estimated crisis probability to any value of a composite crisis indicator by dividing the entire sample into several groups, each corresponding to a particular range of the composite indicator, and calculating the proportion of months associated with crises for each group, using the formula

$$P\ (\text{ crisis}|a < S_t < b) = \frac{\text{Number of months with } a < S_t < b \text{ and a crisis following within 12 months}}{\text{Number of months with } a < S_t < b} \tag{6}$$

---

[7] $\alpha = 1-$ (Max no. of alarms/Total no. of observations). For indicators with an expected sign $(-)$ this rule has to be modified: $\alpha =$(Max no. of alarms/Total no. of observations). See Schnatz (1999a).

[8] See Kaminsky (1998) for a detailed discussion of combining individual indicators.

where S_t is the value of the composite indicator at time t, a is the lower bound of a particular range of the index, b is the upper bound of the range, and $P(\text{crisis} \mid a < S_t < b)$ is the estimated probability of a crisis occurring within 12 months conditional on S_t lying in the range between the lower and upper bounds a and b.[9] In the present study, the entire sample was divided, ranked by the value of the composite indicator, into five groups. The groups are classified in intervals as follows: 0, 0–30, 30–40, 40–50, 50–100.

3 Results for Kazakhstan

3.1 Observed Currency Crises

Figure 1 illustrates the conduct of an exchange market pressure index calculated for Kazakhstan. As said before, tensions in the foreign exchange market are identified for periods when the pressure index swings sharply into the negative. For dating a currency crisis, the pressure index IP_t must exceed its mean three times the adjusted MAD (see solid line). Following these rules, three crisis periods were detected for Kazakhstan (shaded areas).

The most prominent observation is the 1998/99 turbulence. The exchange rate devalued within 10 months from 79.4 Tenge per USD (September 1998) to 130.4 Tenge per USD (June 1999), and the currency reserves dropped in September 1998 by 12.8 % and in March 1999 by 15.4 %. In August 2007 the Banking Crisis took

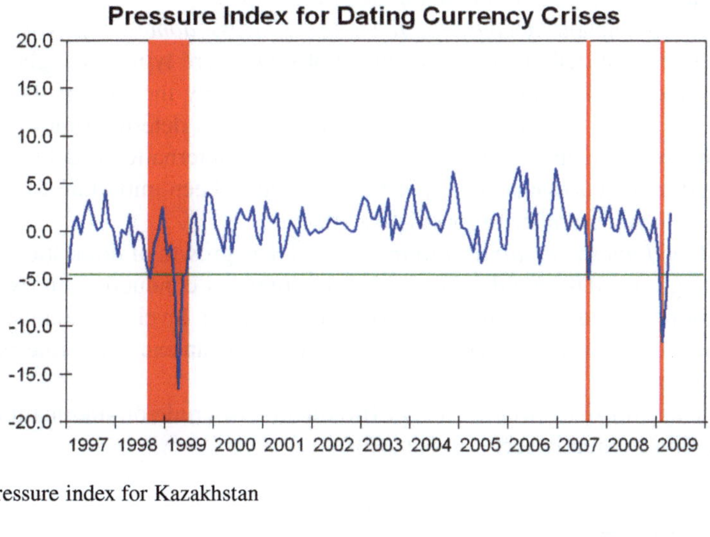

Fig. 1 Pressure index for Kazakhstan

[9] See Zhuang and Dowling (2002) and Knedlik and Scheufele (2007).

place, accompanied by a remarkable decrease in foreign exchange reserves. In February 2009, the National Bank of Kazakhstan (NBK) defined a new level of exchange rate of the national currency, 150 Tenge per USD ±3 % or ±5 Tenge (before: band within 117–123 Tenge per USD or 120 Tenge ±2 %). Starting from the fourth quarter of 2008 until February, the NBK spent US$ 6 billion (including US$ 2.7 billion in January 2009) to maintain stability in the foreign exchange market.[10]

3.2 Identifying Individual Indicators for Kazakhstan

The signal approach proposes the monitoring of a quantity of macroeconomic variables (single indicators) that show unusual patterns in periods prior to currency turbulences. The following list of indicators with noise-to-signal ratios below one displayed a conspicuous behaviour prior to currency turbulences, and will be used in this study for that reason.[11]

- *Deviation of the real exchange rate from its least absolute deviations trend (LAD trend).* The LAD trend minimizes the sum of absolute values of deviations (errors) from the trend line. The least absolute deviations trend is robust in that it is resistant to outliers in the data. A negative difference from the LAD trend indicates an overvaluation. A multi-country comparison of real exchange rates shows that currencies often tend to be overvalued prior to speculative attacks.
- *Export growth.* An overvaluation of a currency should have repercussions on trade flows. Export growth often declines in the run-up to currency crises, including periods prior to the outbreak of the crises.
- *Balance on current account as a share of Gross domestic product (GDP).* Current account deficits as a percentage of GDP were typically higher prior to speculative attacks than in tranquil periods. Not only the loss of international competitiveness, which should show up already in a deterioration of the trade account, but also the funds necessary to service international debts, which is reflected in the current account position, may have been important for assessing a country's vulnerability to speculative attacks.
- *Growth of domestic credit as a share of GDP.* The growth of domestic credit as a percentage of GDP could indicate that a country is conducting an excessively expansionary economic policy. Moreover, a large level of domestic credit growth could indicate excessive lending financed by an exchange-rate-orientated monetary policy.
- *Change of oil price (Brent).* Energy (production of crude oil and natural gas) is the leading economic sector in Kazakhstan.

[10]See National Bank of Kazakhstan, press release No. 3, February 4, 2009.

[11]For a detailed discussion see Schnatz (1998) and Ahec-Šonje and Babić (2003).

- *Real interest rate.* An increase of real interest rates could mean shrinking liquidity in the financial system of a country.
- *Growth of real GDP.* An overvaluation of a currency should dampen economic activity, measured by real gross domestic product.
- *Money Supply.* An increase in M1 means that the monetary policy is expansionary, causing pressure for the domestic currency.
- *Lending/deposit interest rates differential.* A widening lending to deposit rate differential can signal a risk increase and deterioration of bank portfolios, as well as lack of competition and supervisory and regulatory weaknesses.
- *External debt as a share of GDP.* A growing external dept to GDP ratio often signals an increasing external vulnerability.

The individual indicators were analysed according to the methods of KLR. Thresholds were calculated for the time span January 1997 to December 2007.

4 Conduct of Composite Indicators

4.1 Signal Approach

As composite leading indices contain more information and are in general more reliable than single indicators, they are used for predicting currency crises in Kazakhstan. The first approach focuses on the traditional signal method. Under the signal approach, composite indicators are constructed by weighting together the warning signals of single indicators. Indicator $S1$ gives equal weights (=1/10) to all individual signal variables S_r

$$S1_t = \sum_{r=1,\ldots,10} S_{r,t}/10 \tag{7}$$

In any month, we can observe between zero and ten signals, so $0 \leq S1_t \leq 1$.

A second indicator uses the information on the forecasting accuracy of each indicator S_r by exploiting the noise-to-signal ratios $\omega_r = [B_r/(B_r + D_r)]/[A_r/(A_r + C_r)]$:

$$S2_t = \sum_{r=1,\ldots,10} S_{r,t} \cdot \frac{1/\omega_r}{\sum_{r=1,\ldots,10} 1/\omega_r}. \tag{8}$$

Here the signals of the individual indicators are weighted by the inverse of their noise-to-signal ratios, which were divided by the sum of the inverse noise-to-signal ratios to add up to unity. Composite indicator 2 gives more weight to the signalling behaviour of individual indicators with low noise-to-signal ratios.

Composite indicator 3 uses the information coming from the specific odds-ratios $\gamma_r = (A_r \cdot D_r)/(B_r \cdot C_r)$ of the single indicators S_r:

$$S3_t = \sum_{r=1,\ldots,10} S_{r,t} \cdot \frac{\gamma_r}{\sum_{r=1,\ldots,10} \gamma_r}. \tag{9}$$

This indicator gives more weight to the signalling behaviour of individual indicators with high odds-ratios.

Figure 2 shows the conduct of the three composite indicators in Kazakhstan. Crises periods are represented by shaded areas. The dotted line shows the calculated indicator thresholds δ_S. The composite indicator sends a warning signal whenever the indicator moves above δ_S. The estimation period for the thresholds reaches from January 1997 to December 2007, thus allowing an out-of-sample test with the crisis in Kazakhstan, which happened in February 2009. In addition, the estimated crises probabilities are shown in Fig. 2. Here the dotted lines mark the 50 % probability for a currency crisis.

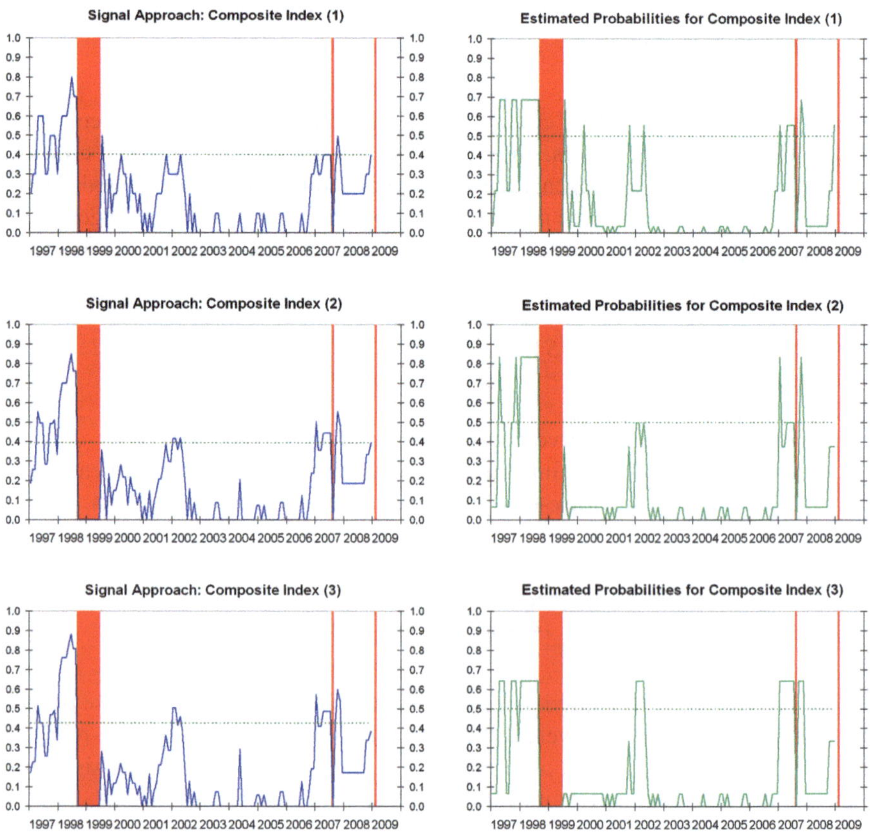

Fig. 2 Currency crises indicators for Kazakhstan

4.2 *Mixed Approach: Principal Components and Single Indicators*

A larger number of indicators can be firstly condensed with the help of principal component analysis (PCA).[12] The first principal component accounts for as much variability (measured by variance) in the data as possible. Each succeeding component accounts for as much of the remaining variability as possible, under the constraint that every principal component is uncorrelated with the preceding ones. Mathematically, PCA leads to an eigenvalue decomposition of the covariance, or as in this analysis of the correlation matrix of the leading indicators. The eigenvectors give the weighting scheme of the indicators, and the corresponding eigenvalues are equal to the variance, explained by the corresponding principal component. To condense the information contained in the whole indicator set, only a few principal components are extracted and used in the signal approach. Here a relative ad hoc procedure is used. Only principal components with eigenvalues greater than one are chosen. This simple procedure is called Kaiser criterion. In a second step the components are examined for plausibility.

Here a mixed approach is pursued. On the one hand, two predominant individual indicators, namely the real exchange rate (deviation from LAD trend)[13] and the change of oil price, are used as input for the composite indicator; on the other hand, the principal components with eigenvalues greater than one of the remaining eight indicators. For the identification of the "expected sign" of the principal components before currency crises, a cross-correlation analysis with the pressure index for the time span January 1997 to December 2000 was carried out. The inverse direction of the observed largest cross-correlation was taken for the expected sign of the principal component.

Indicator $S4$ gives equal weights to the warning signals of the five individual input series. Indicator $S5$ uses the information on the forecasting accuracy of each input series by exploiting the specific noise-to-signal ratios. Once again the warning signals are weighted by the inverse of their noise-to-signal ratios. Finally indicator $S6$ uses the odd-ratios of the input series as a weighting scheme. Figure 3 presents the composite indicators and the estimated crises probabilities.

Obviously, there is no unambiguous composite indicator that shows best results for Kazakhstan (see Table 3). This finding is not very astonishing, taking into account that all time-series are relatively short and that there are only two observed currency turbulences in the in-sample-period 1997–2007. However, the noise-to-signal ratios of all composite crises indicators are well below unity. The estimated conditional probability for a currency crisis $P(\text{Crisis}|\text{signal})$ is in all cases higher than the unconditional probability for a crisis. Furthermore, the odds ratios are

[12]See Jolliffe (2002).

[13]A multi-country comparison of real exchange rates shows that currencies often tend to be overvalued prior to speculative attacks.

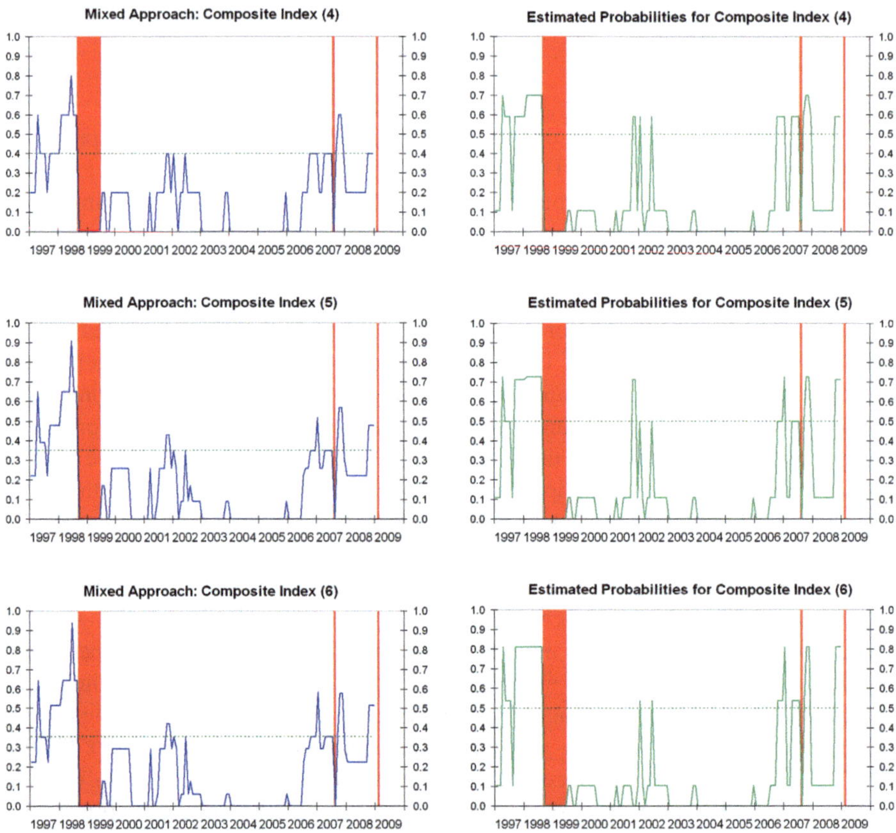

Fig. 3 Currency crises indicators for Kazakhstan, mixed approach

Table 3 Performance of composite currency crises indicators

	Noise-to-signal ratio	Odds-ratio	P(Crisis | signal)	P(Crisis | signal) -P(Crises)
Signal approach				
Composite indicator (1)	0.11	15.57	0.69	0.49
Composite indicator (2)	0.12	22.25	0.67	0.47
Composite indicator (3)	0.11	25.71	0.70	0.50
Mixed approach				
Composite indicator (4)	0.11	12.90	0.70	0.50
Composite indicator (5)	0.15	13.15	0.62	0.42
Composite indicator (6)	0.10	21.75	0.72	0.52

clearly above one. Consequently, all indicators exhibit useful information (see Table 3).

Indicator 1 as well as indicator 4 misses the 2007 crisis, the remaining four indicators signal all crises in the in-sample-period 1997–2007. Concerning the out-of-sample-crisis 2009, only indicators 5 and 6 from the mixed approach gave correct warning signals in the preceding year 2008. Finally, indicators 2 and 3 as well as indicators 5 and 6 showed some false alarms in 2001/2002.

Conclusions

This study concentrates on the signal approach for the monitoring of currency crises risks in Kazakhstan. Currency crises are identified by means of a foreign exchange market pressure index. This pressure index serves as a reference series for dating currency crises. Individual indicators are used to build composite currency crises indicators by exploiting the signal behaviour of each individual indicator. A refined approach uses principal components analysis of the individual indicators to construct composite indicators. A mixed approach is then used in the article: On the one hand, two predominant individual indicators, namely the real exchange rate (deviation from LAD trend) and the change of oil price, are used as input for the composite indicator; on the other hand, the principal components with eigenvalues greater than one of remaining eight indicators.The estimation period of the critical thresholds reaches from January 1997 to December 2007. For this time span it is shown that most of the composite indicators are able to flag the two reported currency crises in this time span at an early stage. However, there is no unambiguous composite indicator that shows best results for Kazakhstan. This finding is not very astonishing, taking into account that all time-series are relatively short and that there are only two observed currency turbulences in the in-sample-period 1997–2007.

The signal approach was developed by Kaminsky, Lizondo and Reinhart (KLR) in 1998. Since then various modification were suggested and alternative approaches developed. For example, the signal approach has been criticized for being a nonparametric approach. Various alternative model based approaches have been discussed. Prominent model based approaches are binary-choice models and the Markov-switching approach.[14] An early warning system based on a multinomial logit model was developed by Bussiere and Fratscher (2006). However their aim was to predict financial crises. Markov-switching models in some studies outperformed binary-choice models.[15] Unlike the other approaches, the Markov-switching approach does not depend on an a priori definition of crises. The crises are estimated by the model. However, this is often seen as a drawback because economic interpretation of the regimes could be arbitrary. Since all approaches have

(continued)

their pros ad cons the nonparametric signal approach has its own value. Some recent developments may help to improve the signal approach further. For example, El Shagi et al. (2012) propose a bootstrap approach to assess significance.

References

Abiad, A. (2003). Early Warning Systems: A Survey and a Regime-Switching Approach. IMF Working Paper, WP/02/32.

Ahec-Šonje, A., & Babić, A. (2003). Measuring and predicting currency disturbances: The 'signals' approach. *Ekonomski Pregled, 54*(1–2), 3–37.

Bussiere, M., & Fratscher, M. (2006). Towards a new early warning system of financial crises. *Journal of International Money and Finance, 25*, 953–973.

Deutsche Bundesbank (1999). The role of economic fundamentals in the emergence of currency crises in emerging markets. *Monthly Reports of the Deutsche Bundesbank*, 15–27.

El Shagi, M., Knedlik, T., & von Schweinitz, G. (2012). Predicting financial crises: The (statistical) significance of the signals approach. IWH Discussion Papers, No. 3/2012.

Jolliffe, I. T. (2002). *Principal component analysis* (2nd ed.). Springer series in statistics. New York, NY: Springer.

Kaminsky, G. (1998). Currency and banking crises: The early warnings of distress, board of governors of the federal reserve system. *International Finance Discussion Papers, 629*, 1–28.

Kaminsky, G., Lizondo, S., & Reinhart, C. M. (1998). Leading indicators of currency crisis. *IMF Staff Papers, 45*(1), 1–49.

Knedlik, T., & Scheufele, R. (2007). Three methods of forecasting currency crises: Which made the run in signaling the South African currency crisis of June 2006? IWH-Discussions Papers, Nr. 17.

Nierhaus, W. (2000). Currency crises indicators - The signal approach. In *25th CIRET Conference*, Paris.

Schnatz, B. (1998). Macroeconomic determinants of currency turbulences in emerging markets. Deutsche Bundesbank Discussion Paper No. 3/98.

Schnatz, B. (1999a). Currency crises in emerging markets - The case of Turkey, mimeo.

Schnatz, B. (1999b). The sudden freeze of the asian miracle: The role of macroeconomic fundamentals. *Asian-Pacific Journal of Finance*, 2(1), 1–19.

Zhuang J., & Dowling J. M. (2002). Causes of the 1997 Asian Financial Crisis: What Can an Early Warning System Model Tell Us? ERD Working Paper series no. 26.

Double Conditional Smoothing of High-Frequency Volatility Surface Under a Spatial Model

Christian Peitz and Yuanhua Feng

Abstract This article investigates a spatial model to analyze high-frequency returns in a nonparametric way. This model allows us to study the slow change of the volatility over a long period of time as well as the daily volatility patterns at the same time. A double conditional kernel regression is introduced to estimate the mean as well as the volatility surface. The idea is to smooth the data over the time of day on a given day in a first step. Those results are then smoothed over all observation days in a second step. It is shown that our proposal is equivalent to a common two-dimensional kernel regression. However, it runs much quicker than the traditional approach. Moreover, the first conditional smoothing also provides useful intermediate results. This idea works both for ultra-high frequency data and for adapted equidistant high frequency data. Asymptotic results for the proposed estimators in the latter case are obtained under suitable conditions. Selected examples show that the proposal works very well in practice. The impact of the 2008 financial crisis on the volatility surface is also discussed briefly.

1 Introduction

The analysis of financial market behavior based on high-frequency data became one of the most important sub-areas of financial econometrics. Especially the analysis of the volatility is an important topic in this area, because it can give valuable information about the risk of an asset, for example. Analyzing time series or return series without considering its volatility over time leads to a huge loss of information and inappropriate investment or trading decisions (French et al., 1987). The volatility is defined as the degree of price or return movement derived from historical time series. Its main property is that it is not constant but that it varies significantly over time (Andersen et al., 2001).

C. Peitz (✉) • Y. Feng
Faculty of Business Administration and Economics, University of Paderborn, Paderborn, Germany
e-mail: christian.peitz@upb.de; yuanhua.feng@wiwi.upb.de

J. Beran et al. (eds.), *Empirical Economic and Financial Research*, Advanced Studies in Theoretical and Applied Econometrics 48,
DOI 10.1007/978-3-319-03122-4_21

The aim of this paper is to analyze high frequency financial data over a relatively long period, in order to discover changes in the daily pattern of the volatility before, during and after the 2008 financial crisis. A widely used model in this context was introduced by Andersen and Bollerslev (1997, 1998) and by Andersen et al. (2000), where the volatility is decomposed into a deterministic intraday and a conditional daily component. This idea is extended in different ways. The focus of this paper is on examining the impact of the financial crisis on the localized average volatility variance. At first, we propose to represent the return data in a three-dimensional form. Under this new model the deterministic volatility component is defined as a volatility surface, which can, e.g., be estimated by a common two-dimensional kernel regression. The problem with this traditional method is that it runs extremely slowly in the current context due to the huge number of observations. A double-conditional smoothing technique is hence introduced to solve this problem, where the data is first smoothed in one dimension and the intermediate smoothing results are smoothed again in the other dimension. It is shown that this approach is equivalent to a common two-dimensional kernel regression, which runs however much faster than the traditional method. Moreover, this approach also helps us to obtain more detailed answers of many questions, which may also open a new research direction.

So far as we know, the spatial model and the double-conditional smoothing technique are original approaches for modelling high-frequency returns. Note that the intraday seasonality considered in Andersen and Bollerslev (1997, 1998) and Engle and Sokalska (2012) can be thought of as the average curve of this volatility surface over all trading days, while the long-term deterministic volatility component in Feng and McNeil (2008) corresponds to the average curve of the volatility surface over all trading time points. Another very important advantage of this new method is that it provides more detailed results. Already after the first smoothing step, we obtained some interesting and important intermediate results, which cannot be provided by the traditional approach. The new method runs therefore not only much faster, but is also more powerful than the common two-dimensional kernel smoothing. Application of the new approaches is illustrated using 1-min returns of two German firms within a period of several years. The model itself is common. However, it is clear that the proposed spatial model and the double-conditional smoothing can also be applied to other kinds of data with suitable structure.

The remaining part of this paper is structured as follows. In Sect. 2 the model is defined and its setup is described. Section 3 discusses the econometric issues. The model is applied to real financial data examples in Sect. 4. Section "Conclusion" concludes the paper.

2 The Model

The method of smoothing in two steps introduced in this section is the main outcome of this work, since it is a new developed model which allows us to discuss high frequency data over a day, but also over a particular time span every day.

Concerning the computing time, this new approach is clearly better than the traditional approach.

With this new method, time series can be transformed into a spatial model. In this (new) direction, there are many open questions which will be addressed at a later point in this paper. The basic definition of the model is that the observations are defined as a two-dimensional variable, the return matrix:

$$r_{x_i,t_j} : \{1,2,\ldots,n_t\} \times \{1,2,\ldots,n_x\} \tag{1}$$

where

x_i is the return series of the trading day i
t_j the return series of the trading time j or point in time
n_t reflects the total number of returns on day i
n_x is the number of trading days

Note:

(1) in a single time series: r_i, $i = 1,\ldots,N$ where N is the total number of returns.
(2) in the two-dimensional form: $r\left(x_i,t_j\right), i = 1,\ldots,n_x,\ j = 1,\ldots,n_t$, where n_x is the number of observed days and n_t the number of returns on day i. Altogether have $n = \sum_{i=1}^{n_x} n_t$

The setup of the two-dimensional lattice spatial model is:

$$r\left(x_i,t_j\right) = m\left(x_i,t_j\right) + \sigma\left(x_i,t_j\right)\varepsilon_{ij} \tag{2}$$

where

$r\left(x_i,t_j\right)$ is the return matrix which includes all time series
$m\left(x_i,t_j\right)$ is a smooth mean function
$\sigma\left(x_i,t_j\right)$ represents the smooth scale function (or volatility trend)
ε_{ij} is the error term

Note:

(1) In our assumption x_i and t_j are equidistantly distributed. But as noted above, t_j can be non-equidistant as well. If t_j is equidistantly distributed, we define our data as high frequency data and if t_j is non-equidistantly distributed, we define it as ultra-high frequency data.
(2) For the sake of simplicity, only equidistant data is used and considered in this work.

This two-dimensional volatility model offers an advantageous approach to capture the volatility change at any time point, such as local volatility at a fixed time interval at all trading days or intraday volatility in various moments within 1 day.

3 Econometric Issues

In this section we will discuss statistical properties of our two-step smoothing estimator and we will estimate the smooth mean function and the smooth scale function. Their asymptotic properties are derived. For more theoretical results, details, and proofs please see the Appendix.

3.1 *Estimation of m*

Consider the estimation of $m(x,t)$ first. Let y_{ij} denote the observations. Assume that the data are arranged in the form of a single time series $\tilde{y}_l$ associated with the coordinates $(\tilde{x}_l, \tilde{t}_l)$, where $l = 1, \ldots, n$ and $n = n_x * n_t$ is the total number of observations. The common bivariate kernel estimator of $m(x,t)$ is defined by

$$\hat{m}(x,t) = \sum_{l=1}^{n} \tilde{w}_l^m \tilde{y}_l, \tag{3}$$

where

$$\tilde{w}_l^m = K_\mu \left(\frac{\tilde{x}_l - x}{h_x^m}, \frac{\tilde{t}_l - t}{h_t^m} \right) \left[\sum_{l=1}^{n} K_m \left(\frac{\tilde{x}_l - x}{h_x^m}, \frac{\tilde{t}_l - t}{h_t^m} \right) \right]^{-1}. \tag{4}$$

$K_m(u_x, u_t)$ is a bivariate kernel function, and h_x^m and h_t^m are the bandwidths for $\tilde{x}$ and $\tilde{t}$, respectively. Under the data structure of Model (2), the above bivariate kernel estimator can be represented as

$$\tilde{m}(x,t) = \sum_{d=1}^{D} \sum_{t=1}^{n_d} w_{dt}^m r_{dt}, \tag{5}$$

where

$$w_{dt}^m = K_m \left(\frac{x_d - x}{h_x^m}, \frac{y_t - y}{h_y^m} \right) \left[\sum_{d=1}^{D} \sum_{t=1}^{n_d} K_m \left(\frac{x_d - x}{h_x^m}, \frac{y_t - y}{h_y^m} \right) \right]^{-1}. \tag{6}$$

Assume that K_m is a product kernel $K_m(u_x, u_t) = K_x^m(u_x) K_t^m(u_t)$, then $\hat{m}(x,t)$ can be rewritten as

$$\hat{m}(x,t) = \sum_{d=1}^{n_x} \sum_{t=1}^{n_t} w_{ix}^m w_{jt}^m y_{ij}, \tag{7}$$

which can be further rewritten as

$$\hat{m}(x,t) = \sum_{d=1}^{n_x} w_{ix}^m \hat{m}_x(x_i, \bullet) \tag{8}$$

or

$$\hat{m}(x,t) = \sum_{t=1}^{n_t} w_{jt}^m \hat{m}_t(\bullet, t_j), \tag{9}$$

where

$$w_{ix}^m = K_x^m \left(\frac{x_i - x}{h_x^m}\right) \left[\sum_{d=1}^{n_x} K_x^m \left(\frac{x_i - x}{h_x^m}\right)\right]^{-1},$$

$$w_{jt}^m = K_t^m \left(\frac{t_j - t}{h_t^m}\right) \left[\sum_{t=1}^{n_t} K_t^m \left(\frac{t_j - t}{h_t^m}\right)\right]^{-1}$$

are common kernel weights of a univariate kernel regression, and

$$\hat{m}_x(x_i, \bullet) = \sum_{t=1}^{n_t} w_{jt}^m y_{ij} \tag{10}$$

and

$$\hat{m}_t(\bullet, t_j) = \sum_{d=1}^{n_x} w_{ix}^m y_{ij} \tag{11}$$

are two univariate kernel estimators over the daytime and all observation days carried out on a given observation day or at a given time point, respectively. In this paper $\hat{m}_x(x_i, \bullet)$ and $\hat{m}_t(\bullet, t_j)$ will be called the first stage conditional kernel estimators of a bivariate kernel regression under Model (2), each of them consists of a panel of smoothed curves obtained by univariate kernel regression over one of the two explanatory variables, conditional on the other. The final estimators defined in (8) or (9) are hence called double-conditional kernel estimators, which provide two equivalent procedures of the double-conditional smoothing approach. It is obvious that all estimators defined in (3), (5), and (7) through (9) are all equivalent to each other. Note however that the first estimator applies to any bivariate kernel regression problem but the others are only defined under Model (2).

3.2 Estimation of σ^2

As mentioned before, our main purpose is to estimate the high-frequency volatility surface $\sigma(x,t)$ by means of an estimator of $\sigma^2(x,t)$. The latter can be estimated from the squared residuals using kernel (see, e.g., Feng and Heiler 1998; Heiler 2001). To this end let $r_{ij} = y_{ij} - m(x_i, t_j)$ be the centralized returns. Following Model (2) we have

$$\begin{aligned} r_{ij}^2 &= \sigma^2(x_i, t_j) + \sigma^2(x_i, t_j)(\varepsilon_{ij}^2 - 1) \\ &= \sigma^2(x_i, t_j) + \sigma^2(x_i, t_j)\nu_{ij}, \end{aligned} \tag{12}$$

where $\nu_{ij} = \varepsilon_{ij}^2 - 1$ with $E[\nu_{ij}] = 0$. In this paper, we will assume that ν_{ij} is again a weakly stationary random field. Corresponding assumptions on its dependence structure will be stated later. We see, the variance surface is itself the mean function of another heteroskedastic nonparametric regression model, where $\sigma^2(x,t)$ is also the volatility surface at the same time. Let $\hat{m}(x,t)$ be as defined above and define $\hat{r}_{ij} = y_{ij} - \hat{m}(x_i, t_j)$. Again, let $K_\sigma(u) = K_\sigma^x(u_x)K_\sigma^t(u_t)$ be a product kernel, and h_x^σ and h_t^σ be the corresponding bandwidths. We propose to estimate the variance surface as follows:

$$\hat{\sigma}^2(x,t) = \sum_{i=1}^{n_x} w_{ix}^\sigma \hat{\sigma}_x(x_i, \bullet) \tag{13}$$

or

$$\hat{\sigma}^2(x,t) = \sum_{j=1}^{n_t} w_{jt}^\sigma \hat{\sigma}_t(\bullet, t_j), \tag{14}$$

where w_{ix}^σ and w_{jt}^σ are defined similarly to w_{ix}^μ and w_{jt}^μ but using $K_\sigma^x(u_x)$ and $K_\sigma^t(u_t)$, respectively,

$$\hat{\sigma}_x^2(x_i, \bullet) = \sum_{j=1}^{n_t} w_{jt}^\sigma \hat{r}_{ij}^2 \tag{15}$$

and

$$\hat{\sigma}_t^2(\bullet, t_j) = \sum_{i=1}^{n_x} w_{ix}^\sigma \hat{r}_{ij}^2. \tag{16}$$

The volatility surface is then estimated by $\hat{\sigma}(x,t) = \sqrt{\hat{\sigma}^2(x,t)}$. Again, $\hat{\sigma}_t^2(x_i, \bullet)$ and $\hat{\sigma}_t^2(\bullet, t_j)$ are valuable intermediate smoothing results.

We see, the double-conditional smoothing approach does not provide new kernel estimators of $m(x,t)$ and $\sigma(x,t)$. The resulting estimators are exactly the same as those obtained by the common bivariate kernel approach. Hence the above is just another algorithm to carry out kernel smoothing under the proposed lattice spatial model with repeat observations in each dimension. However, in this context the double-conditional algorithm runs much faster and it also exhibits some further important advantages compared to the traditional approach. This will be explained in the next subsection.

4 Practical Implementation and Empirical Results

4.1 Data

The data set to which the introduced algorithm was applied consists of two high frequency financial time series, namely the stock of the BMW AG and the Allianz AG. Both companies are listed in the German DAX. The ultra-high frequent data was directly obtained from the Thomson Reuters Tick History Database and processed accordingly in order to obtain 1-min data. Stocks listed in the XETRA are traded from 9:00 to 17:30, thus the number of 1-min observations per day is 511. The examined time period, i.e., the number of observed days starting from January 2006 to September 2011 is 1,442. Thus, the total number of observations is 736,862. The data of the BMW AG and the Allianz AG was chosen as both show the typical characteristics described in the prevailing literature. Concerning the fitting of the spatial model to the selected data, the bandwidths $h_x^\sigma = 200$ and $h_t^\sigma = 100$ were chosen for modelling the number of observed days and the time of day, respectively. The values were selected based on experience as well as trial and error, making a trade-off between the bias and the variance.

4.2 The Results

First of all the base for the carried out calculations is shown graphically in the following in the form of the two-dimensional returns surface. The abscissa represents the observation period (the years). The ordinate represents the trading time and the applicate the dimension of the returns. In the following, the results for BMW are displayed in the left figure and the ones for Allianz in the right one (Fig. 1).

When looking at the figures of the returns the influence of the financial crisis on them becomes directly apparent. The large fluctuations which are highlighted in green show the acute phase of the financial crisis where returns increase abruptly as a consequence. The analysis of the change in the volatility in two directions is of

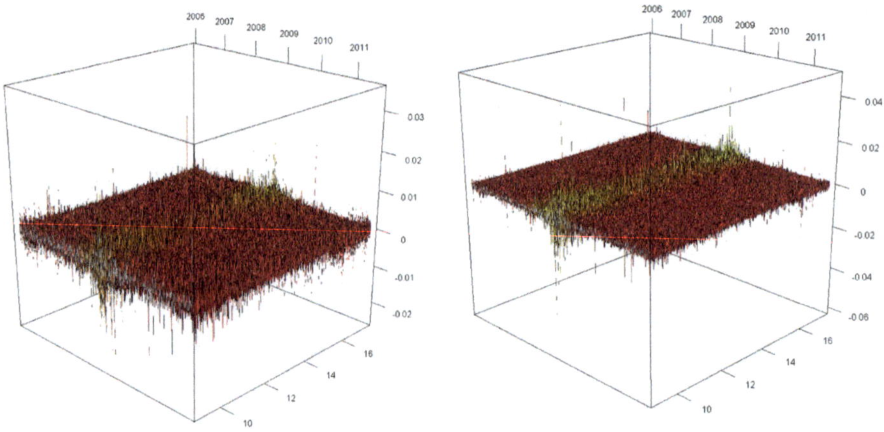

Fig. 1 Returns of BMW and Allianz in a three-dimensional space

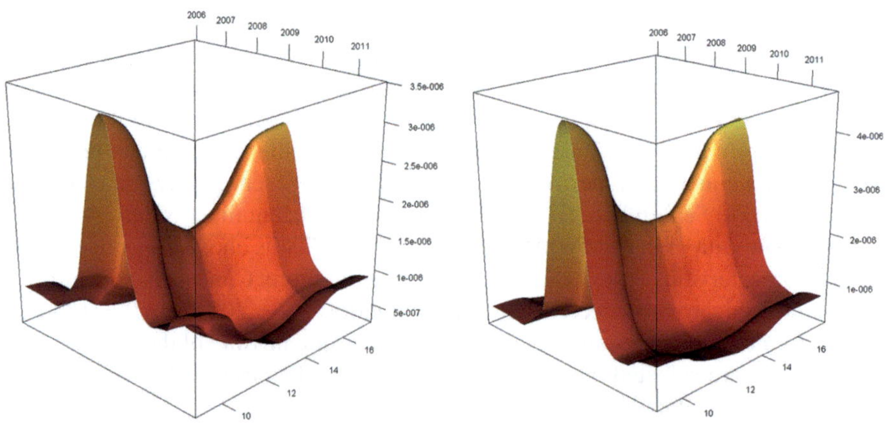

Fig. 2 Surfaces of the volatilities of BMW and the Allianz

great interest, but requires the development of new methods. One was proposed in this paper: The idea of the spatial model based on the double-conditional smoothing approach. With the package "rgl" in R we can obtain the three-dimensional image plots, which show the complete estimated surface of the volatility in high-frequency returns.

Figure 2 shows the surface of the volatility in a three-dimensional space. It is visible directly that the two saddle surfaces show a very similar pattern, on a slightly different level. A minor difference is that the daily U-shape pattern is slightly more pronounced at BMW than at Allianz. The change in color from orange to green indicates that the volatility changes from small to large. That is, the volatility is large in the middle of this observation period and small at the beginning and at the end of it. In the vertical direction the volatility near the open and close of XETRA

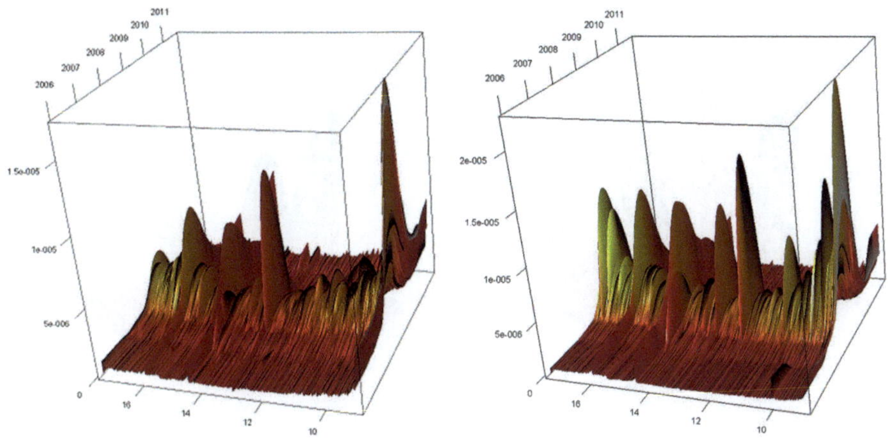

Fig. 3 First smoothing step for the surfaces of the volatilities of BMW and the Allianz

is generally larger than that around noon. Figure 2 further shows that the daily pattern of volatilities is typically U-shaped whereas the pattern of the entire period of analysis is inversely U-shaped.

As described earlier, the practical implementation of this new approach allows for analyzing intermediate results. As can be seen in Fig. 3 the results of the first smoothing step, i.e. each time of a trading day smoothed over the entire observation period can be visualized and thus examined in detail. The same can be done for the second smoothing step, where the individual days of the observation period each are smoothed over the times of day. Thus for the first smoothing step, there are 511 discs representing the time of trading day, which makes the identification of outliers possible. Consequently for the second smoothing step there are 1,442 smoothed day-curves. The data example of BMW shows significantly more outliers than the one of Allianz. Specifically, in this example you can see again very closely the increase in volatility from mid-2008 to end of 2009. In times of the world financial crisis, the volatility increases by a multiple (Fig. 4).

In order to present the results in a more conventional manner, three randomly selected days of both examined stocks were compared individually. The black curve shows the volatility on 14 June 2006, i.e. shortly prior to the financial crisis. The green curve shows the volatility of BMW on 14 June 2010, i.e. shortly after the financial crisis. The influence of the financial crisis can be directly seen when looking at the red curve, which reflects the 14 June 2008. Apparently the volatility during the financial crisis is much higher than before and after it. Please note that this effect is of course also visible for days other than the here selected ones. The examples were chosen to represent a day, before, during, and after the financial crisis each. Therefore similar results are expected when different days of the same periods are chosen (Fig. 5).

Simultaneously to examining 3 days in detail in the following three times of day are discussed for the whole period of observation. The three chosen times of day

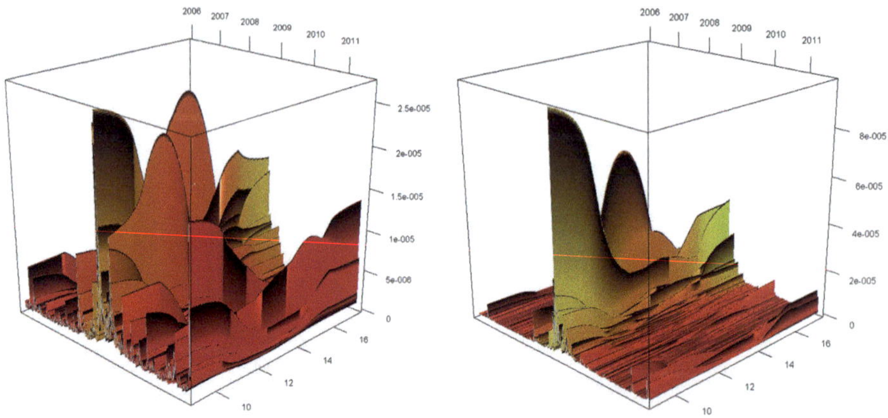

Fig. 4 Second smoothing step for the surfaces of the volatilities of BMW and Allianz

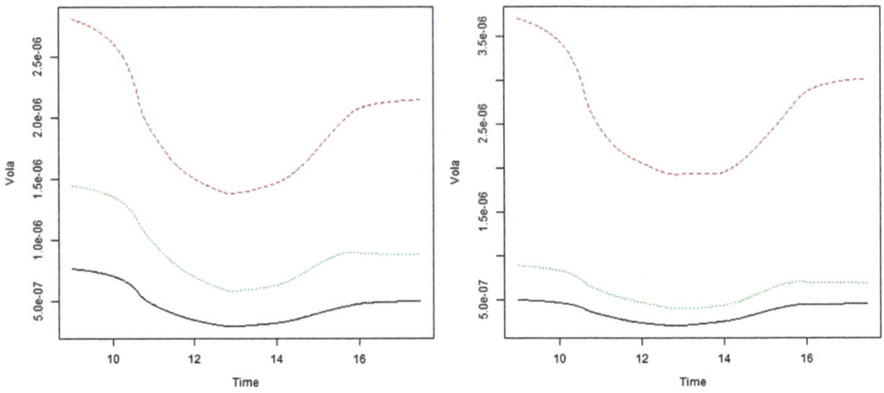

Fig. 5 Volatilities of BMW and Allianz (three times of day over the daytime)

are 9:00, 13:00, and 16:00 as practical examples and literature suggests that those are times of much, little and much trading activity, respectively. What can be seen at first glance is that the volatility at 13:00 is the lowest whereas the volatility at 9:00 is the highest and at 16:00 the volatility is at a middle level. This is in line with the results of the prevailing literature which states that the volatility is low when little is traded and vice versa. In addition the influence of the financial crisis can be seen here as well. Over the course of time the volatility increases notably during the period of the financial crisis. Despite the clearly defaring volatility levels of the examined times of day, their volatilities follow a very similar trend. With the beginning of the financial crisis the volatilities in all three times of day increase at the same slope. The same holds for the decrease after the financial crisis.

The volatility of these return series is a typical example for the fact that the volatility is highest near the opening of the trading days in the period of financial

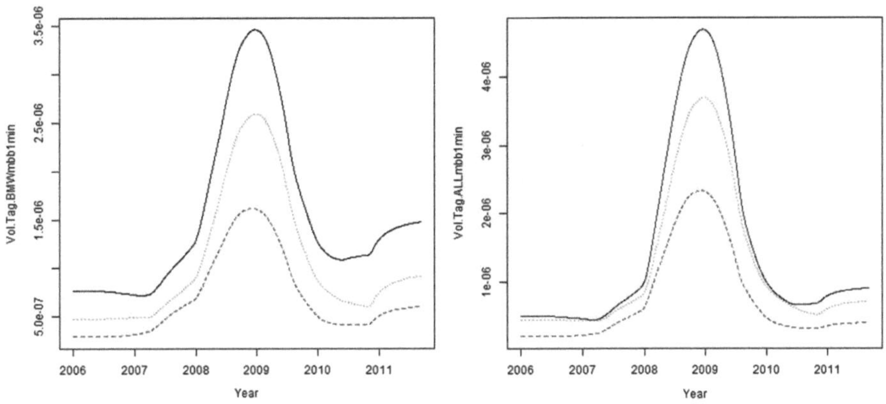

Fig. 6 Volatilities of BMW and Allianz (3 days over a long period)

crisis. When one-dimensional returns on the vertical axis are fixed, there is an obvious change in the local volatility. It means that the volatility takes a higher value in the middle of the observation period (in 2008) than the other years, and the volatility at the end of the observation period is larger than that at the beginning (Fig. 6). When one-dimensional returns on the horizontal axis are fixed, we can obtain the intraday volatility which appears in the vertical direction. The intraday volatility shows that the volatility is highest near the opening of the trading day, lowest at noon, and before the close it is higher than at noon (Fig. 5). The intraday volatility has a higher value in the period of financial crisis. All in all we can see that the volatility is highest at the opening of a trading day in 2008, due to the simultaneous effect of the financial crisis and the intraday effect.

Conclusion

The model of the double-conditional smoothing brings innovations in several ways. First of all with the new method (and the associated algorithm) it is now possible to get a surface of the volatility in two directions very quickly. Especially by the enormous advantage in the computing time, the possibilities of analysis with the new method exceed the ones of the two-dimensional kernel regression by far.

On the other hand, it is possible to obtain valuable intermediate results. So far, there was no way to represent these results. With the gained knowledge it is possible to implement the model in several other economic fields. It is confirmed that the new algorithm not only provides the same results as the traditional algorithm, but moreover, the algorithm is more flexible. The

(continued)

new algorithm is far superior concerning running time, amount of results, flexibility, and usage.

It is clear that there are a few open questions in this new area. One open question is the computing time: How strong is the computing time really reduced? What other advantages does the algorithm have? Also a deeper comparison of the two methods of analyzing examples with additional applications is necessary. A further point is the adaptation of different GARCH models.

Appendix: Some Technical Details

Detailed discussion on the theoretical background, possible extensions, and asymptotic properties of the double-conditional smoothing may be found in Feng (2013). In the following the main findings of that study together with some new results (see Corollary 1 below) are summarized briefly without proof. For more information we refer the reader to the abovementioned paper.

Note that the effect of the error in the estimation of the mean surface $\mu(x,t)$ on the proposed nonparametric estimators of the volatility surface is asymptotically negligible. In the following it is hence assumed that $\mu(x,t) \equiv 0$ for convenience. The asymptotic properties of the proposed estimators of the volatility surface will be established under the following spatial multiplicative component GARCH for intraday returns with random effects:

$$r_{i,j} = n_t^{-1/2}\sigma(x_i, t_j)Y_{i,j}, i = 1, \ldots, n_x, j = 1, \ldots, n_t, \tag{17}$$

where $n_t^{-1/2}$ is a standardizing factor and we will define $\tilde{r}_{i,j} = \sqrt{n_t} r_{i,j}$. The stochastic part of this model is specified as follows:

$$Y_{i,j} = \omega_i^{1/2} h_i^{1/2} \lambda_j^{1/2} q_{i,j}^{1/2} \varepsilon_{i,j}, \tag{18}$$

where h_i is a daily conditional variance component and is governed by a separate exogenous stochastic process, and $q_{i,j}$ stand for unit intraday volatility components. We will denote the intraday GARCH processes by $Z_{i,j} = q_{i,j}^{1/2}\varepsilon_{i,j}$. Models (17) and (18) together extend the multiplicative component GARCH of Engle and Sokalska (2012) in different ways. The latter is again an extension of the general framework for high-frequency returns of Andersen and Bollerslev (1998). In the case without random effects, i.e. when $\omega_i \equiv \lambda_j \equiv 1$, Model (18) reduces to

$$Y_{i,j} = h_i^{1/2} q_{i,j}^{1/2} \varepsilon_{i,j}, \tag{19}$$

which is similar to that defined by Eqs. (6) and (7) in Engle and Sokalska (2012). Models (17) and (19) hence provide an extension of their model with the intraday seasonality there being replaced by the entire nonparametric volatility surface, while keeping the stochastic part to be the same.

For driving the asymptotic properties of the nonparametric estimators of the volatility surface, the following regularity assumptions are required.

A1. Assumed that $Y_{i,j}$ is defined by (18), where $\varepsilon_{i,j}$ are i.i.d. random variables with zero mean, unit variance, and finite fourth moment $m_4^{\varepsilon} < \infty$.
A2. For given i, $Z_{i,j}$ follows a GARCH model, whose coefficients are independent of i, unit variance, and finite fourth moment $m_4^Z = m_2^q m_4^{\varepsilon}$. Furthermore, it is assumed that the intraday GARCH processes on different days are independent of each other.
A3. The daily conditional variance component h_i is independent of $\varepsilon_{i,j}$, stationary with unit mean, finite variance, and exponentially decaying autocovariances.
A4. Furthermore, it is assumed that ω_i, λ_j, $Z_{i,j}$ and h_i are mutually independent.
A5. $\mathscr{K}(u)$ is a product kernel $\mathscr{K}(u) = K_1(u_x)K_2(u_t)$. For simplicity assume that K_1 and K_2 are the same Lipschitz continuous symmetric density on the support $[-1, 1]$.
A6. $\sigma_t^2(x,t)$ is a smooth function with absolutely continuous second derivatives.
A7. b_x and b_t fulfill $b_x \to 0$, $n_x b_x \to \infty$ as $n_x \to \infty$, $b_t \to 0$ and $n_t b_t \to \infty$ as $n_t \to \infty$.

Conditions for the existence of the fourth moments of a GARCH model are well known in the literature (see, e.g., Bollerslev, 1986, and He and Teräsvirta, 1999). For instance, if $Z_{i,j}$ follows a GARCH(1, 1) with i.i.d. standard-normal innovations, this condition reduces to $3\alpha^2 + 2\alpha\beta + \beta^2 < 1$. The assumption that the GARCH coefficients on all days are the same is necessary for the stationarity of the random field $Z_{i,j}$. A3 ensures that the daily volatility h_i can be estimated and eliminated beforehand. The assumption that the autocovariances of h_i decay exponentially is made for convenience but unnecessary. This condition is, e.g., fulfilled, if h_i follows a daily GARCH model with finite fourth moment. A4 is made for simplification. Assumptions A5 through A7 are standard requirements used in bivariate kernel regression.

Now, we will define the *acf response function of a kernel function*, which will simplify the derivation and representation of the asymptotic variance of $\hat{\sigma}^2(x,t)$.

Definition 1 For a univariate kernel function $K(u)$ with support $[-1, 1]$, its *acf response function* $\Gamma_K(u)$ is a nonnegative symmetric function with support $[-2, 2]$:

$$\Gamma_K(u) = \int_{-1}^{u+1} K(v)K(v-u)dv \tag{20}$$

for $u \in [-2, 0]$,

$$\Gamma_K(u) = \int_{u-1}^{1} K(v)K(v-u)dv \tag{21}$$

for $u \in [0, 2]$ and zero otherwise.

The acf response function of a product kernel function $\mathscr{K}(u_1, u_2)$ is defined by $\Gamma_{\mathscr{K}}(u_1, u_2) = \Gamma_K(u_1)\Gamma_K(u_2)$. The acf response function of a kernel function measures the asymptotic contribution of the acf of certain lag to the variance of a kernel estimator and is a useful tool for driving the asymptotic variance of a bivariate kernel regression estimator under dependent errors. In the univariate case, well-known results on the asymptotic variance of a kernel regression estimator with time series errors can be easily proved by means of this concept.

Furthermore, we define $\mu_2(K) = \int u^2 K_1(u)du$, $R(K) = \int K_1^2(u)du$ and $I(\Gamma_K) = \int \Gamma_K(u)du$. Our main findings on the double-conditional kernel estimator $\hat{\sigma}^2(x,t)$ and the two associate intermediate smoothers in the first stage are summarized in the following theorem.

Theorem 1 *Consider the estimation at an interior point* $0 < x, t < 1$. *Under the assumptions A1 through A7 we have*

(i) The mean and variance of conditional smoother $\hat{\sigma}^2(t|x_i)$ *are given by*

$$E[\hat{\sigma}^2(t|x_i)] \approx h_i\omega_i \left\{ \sigma^2(x_i,t) + \frac{\mu_2(K)}{2} b_t^2 [\sigma^2(x,t)]_t'' \right\}, \tag{22}$$

$$var[\hat{\sigma}^2(t|x_i)] \approx h_i^2\omega_i^2 \frac{\sigma^4(x_i,t)V_t}{n_x b_x} R(K). \tag{23}$$

(ii) The mean and variance of conditional smoother $\hat{\sigma}^2(x|t_j)$ *are given by*

$$E[\hat{\sigma}^2(x|t_j)] \approx \lambda_j \left\{ \sigma^2(x,t_j) + \frac{\mu_2(K)}{2} b_x^2 [\sigma^2(x,t)]_x'' \right\}, \tag{24}$$

$$var[\hat{\sigma}^2(x|t_j)] \approx \lambda_j^2 \frac{\sigma^4(x,t_j)V_x}{n_x b_x} R(K). \tag{25}$$

(iii) The bias and variance of $\hat{\sigma}^2(x,t)$ *are given by*

$$B[\hat{\sigma}^2(x,t)] \approx \frac{\mu_2(K)}{2} \{ b_x^2 [\sigma^2(x,t)]_x'' + b_t^2 [\sigma^2(x,t)]_t'' \}, \tag{26}$$

$$var[\hat{\sigma}^2(x,t)] \approx \sigma^4(x,t) \left[\frac{VR^2(K)}{n_x b_x n_t b_t} + \left(\frac{m_2^h \sigma_\omega^2 + V_h}{n_x b_x} + \frac{\sigma_\lambda^2}{n_t b_t} \right) R(K) I(\Gamma_K) \right], \tag{27}$$

where V_x, V_t, V, *and* V_h *are constants as defined in Feng (2013).*

Theorem 1 shows in particular that the intermediate estimators of the volatility surface are inconsistent and the rate of convergence of the final estimator is dominated by the order $\max\{O[(n_x b_x)^{-1/2}], O[(n_t b_t)^{-1/2}]\}$, which is much lower than $O[(n_x b_x n_t b_t)^{-1/2}]$, the rate of convergence in the case with i.i.d. innovations.

If the volatility surface is estimated under the multiplicative component GARCH of Engle and Sokalska (2012) without random effect, as defined in (19), the asymptotic variances of the proposed estimators are simplified. That for the final volatility surface estimator is given in the following corollary.

Corollary 1 *Assume that $Y_{i,j}$ is defined in (19). Under corresponding conditions of Theorem 1, the variance of $\hat{\sigma}^2(x,t)$ is given by*

$$var[\hat{\sigma}^2(x,t)] \approx \sigma^4(x,t)\left[\frac{V^* R^2(K)}{n_x b_x n_t b_t} + \frac{V_h R(K) I(\Gamma_K)}{n_x b_x}\right], \quad (28)$$

where V^* denotes another constant.

We see, if there is no random effect, the asymptotic variance $\hat{\sigma}^2(x,t)$ is dominated by the daily GARCH component. The rate of convergence of $\hat{\sigma}^2(x,t)$ is now of the order $O[(n_x b_x)^{-1/2}]$, which is again much lower than $O[(n_x b_x n_t b_t)^{-1/2}]$.

References

Andersen, T. G., & Bollerslev, T. (1997). Intraday periodicity and volatility persistence in financial markets. *Journal of Empirical Finance, 4*, 115–158.

Andersen, T. G., & Bollerslev, T. (1998). Deutsche Mark-dollar volatility: Intraday activity patterns, macroeconomic announcements, and longer-run dependencies. *The Journal of Finance, 53*, 219–265.

Andersen, T. G., Bollerslev, T., & Cai, J. (2000). Intraday and interday volatility in the Japanese stock market. *Journal of International Financial Markets, Institutions and Money, 10*, 107–130.

Andersen, T. G., Bollerslev, T., Diebold, F. X., & Ebens, H. (2001). The distribution of realized stock return volatility. *Journal of Financial Economics, 61*(1), 43–76.

Bollerslev, T. (1986). Generalized autoregressive conditional heteroskedasticity. *Journal of Econometrics, 31*, 307–327.

Engle, R. F., & Sokalska, M. E. (2012). Forecasting intraday volatility in the US equity market. Multiplicative component GARCH. *Journal of Financial Econometrics, 10*, 54–83.

Feng, Y. (2013). Double-conditional smoothing of the volatility surface under a spatial multiplicative component GARCH for high-frequency returns with random effects. Preprint, University of Paderborn.

Feng, Y., & Heiler, S. (1998). Locally weighted autoregression. In R. Galata & H. Küchenhoff (Eds.), *Econometrics in theory and practice*. Festschrift für Hans Schneeweiß (pp. 101–117). Heidelberg: Physica-Verlag.

Feng, Y., & McNeil, A. J. (2008). Modelling of scale change, periodicity and conditional heteroskedasticity in return volatility. *Economic Modelling, 25*, 850–867.

French, K. R., Schwert, G. W., & Stambaugh, R. F. (1987). Expected stock returns and volatility. *Journal of Financial Economics, 19*(1), 3–29.

He, C., & Teräsvirta, T. (1999). Fourth moment structures of the GARCH(p,q) process. *Econometric Theorie, 15*, 824–846.

Heiler, S. (2001). Nonparametric time series analysis: Nonparametric regression, locally weighted regression, autoregression, and quantile regression. In D. Peña, G. C. Tiao, & R. S. Tsay (Eds.), *A course in time series analysis* (pp. 308–347). New York: Wiley.

Zillmer's Population Model: Theory and Application

Peter Pflaumer

Abstract August Zillmer (1831–1893) was a German life insurance actuary in Berlin. He is credited for one of the first German textbooks on actuarial mathematics. His name is associated with the Zillmer method of calculating life insurance reserves. In this paper, August Zillmer's early contribution to demographic analysis, which is virtually unknown, is described and appreciated. In 1863 he published a discrete population model, and produced several age distributions using a given life table and different population growth rates. He showed that the resulting age distributions will eventually become stable. Although the stable model in demography can be traced back to Euler in 1760, Zillmer's model is the first dynamic analysis of the influence of changes in population growth rates on the age distribution and population parameters such as mean age. His results and conclusions are discussed and compared with modern demographic methods. Finally, Zillmer's model is considered as a tool for special population forecasts, where new inputs (births) do not depend on the population size of other age-groups.

1 Introduction

A stable population is a population in which proportions in all age classes remain fixed if mortality is constant and births increase exponentially over time. The concept of a stable population can be traced to Euler in 1760. Some years later, Thomas Malthus employed the results of stable population theory in collaboration with Joshua Milne, an English actuary (cf. Coale, 1979).

In Germany, Ludwig Moser, a professor of physics in Königsberg, refers in his book to Euler's work (cf. Moser, 1839). Ladislaus von Bortkiewicz formulated a continuous version of the stable model (cf. Bortkiewicz, 1898, 1911).

Alfred Lotka rediscovered independently the fundamentals of the stable Malthusian theory (cf. Lotka, 1907). In an important paper written with Francis R. Sharpe, he showed that a closed population with fixed fertility and mortality

P. Pflaumer (✉)
University of Applied Sciences Kempten, Kempten, Germany
e-mail: peter.pflaumer@tu-dortmund.de

J. Beran et al. (eds.), *Empirical Economic and Financial Research*,
Advanced Studies in Theoretical and Applied Econometrics 48,
DOI 10.1007/978-3-319-03122-4_22

rates acquires a stable age distribution (cf. Sharpe and Lotka 1911). Although he was not the first to discover the age composition of a population with a fixed life table and a constant rate of increase (Lotka himself referred to such a population as Malthusian, not stable), he was the first who proved that the continued prevalence of fixed schedules of fertility and mortality would generate a stable population (cf. Coale, 1979).

Virtually unknown is August Zillmer's contribution to the stable model in demography. In 1863 he published a discrete population model, and produced several age distributions using a given life table and different population growth rates. He showed that the resulting age distributions will eventually become stable (cf. Zillmer, 1863a). August Zillmer (1831–1893) was a German life insurance actuary in Berlin. He is credited for one of the first German textbooks of actuarial mathematics (cf. Zillmer, 1861). His name is associated with the Zillmer method of calculating life insurance reserves (cf. Zillmer, 1863b). Lotka later knew that both Bortkiewicz and Zillmer independently developed the fundamentals of the stable Malthusian theory (cf. Lotka, 1932).

However, neither Bortkiewicz nor Zillmer applied self-renewal models in population analysis (cf. Lotka, 1937; Samuelson, 1976). As a demographer, Zillmer is almost unknown in Germany today. He is not even cited in the biographical lexicon of the history of demography, in which almost 400 biographies of German population scientists are published (cf. Lischke and Michel, 2007).

In this paper, the population model of Zillmer is presented and compared to modern methods of demography. The notation and symbols of today will be used. The model with a geometric increase in births is described in detail. Zillmer's calculations are recalculated using Microsoft Excel. Zillmer's results differ from the recalculated results, which are shown here, only by rounding errors. Zillmer's results, which he obtains using a model with an arithmetic increase in the number of births, are only briefly mentioned.

2 Zillmer's Demographic Model

First, Zillmer derives formulas of the parameters of the stationary model or life table model. He uses the life table of 17 English life insurance companies of the actuary Jones (1843). This life table was expanded through the age classes 1–10 (cf. Heym, 1863).

Under the assumption that births occur simultaneously at the beginning of the year, while deaths in all age classes are distributed uniformly over the year, he obtains the following parameters of the life table or the stationary population,where l_x is the number of persons surviving to exact age x, and d_x is the number of deaths between exact ages x and $x + 1$:

Life expectancy:

$$\overset{o}{e}_o = \frac{\frac{l_0+l_1}{2} + \frac{l_1+l_2}{2} + \frac{l_2+l_3}{2} + \cdots}{l_0} = \frac{\sum_{x=0}^{\omega} l_x - \frac{l_0}{2}}{l_0} = \frac{\sum_{x=0}^{\omega} l_x}{l_0} - \frac{1}{2}$$

Birth rate (reciprocal value):

$$\frac{1}{b} = \overset{o}{e}_o .$$

Death rate (reciprocal value):

$$\frac{1}{d} = \overset{o}{e}_o .$$

Mean age at death:

$$\begin{aligned} \nu &= \frac{1 \cdot d_0 + 2 \cdot d_1 + 3 \cdot d_2 + \cdots}{l_0} - \frac{1}{2} \\ &= \frac{(l_0 - l_1) + 2 \cdot (l_1 - l_2) + 3 \cdot (l_2 - l_3) + \cdots}{l_0} - \frac{1}{2} \\ &= \frac{l_0 + l_1 + l_2 + \cdots}{l_0} - \frac{1}{2} = \overset{o}{e}_o . \end{aligned}$$

Mean age of the stationary population:

$$\mu = \frac{\sum_{x=0}^{\omega} \left(x + \frac{1}{2}\right) \frac{l_x + l_{x+1}}{2}}{\sum_{x=0}^{\omega} l_x - \frac{l_0}{2}} = \frac{\sum_{x=0}^{\omega} (x+1) \cdot l_x - \frac{1}{2} \sum_{x=0}^{\omega} l_x}{\sum_{x=0}^{\omega} l_x - \frac{l_0}{2}} - \frac{1}{2} .$$

Life expectancy and mean age in the continuous case with $l(0) = 1$ are (cf. Keyfitz, 1977):

$$\overset{o}{e}_o = \int_0^{\omega} l(x)\mathrm{d}x = -\int_0^{\omega} x \cdot \frac{\mathrm{d}l(x)}{\mathrm{d}x}\mathrm{d}x$$

and

$$\mu = \frac{\int_0^{\omega} x \cdot l(x)\mathrm{d}x}{\int_0^{\omega} l(x)\mathrm{d}x} .$$

With the assumed life table, one obtains the following parameter values (cf. also Zillmer, 1863a, 74) (Table 1).

Now Zillmer assumes a geometric increase in the number of births, $l_{0t} = l_0 \cdot q^t$, where l_{0t} is the number of births at time 0 and $q > 1$ is the growth factor. It is easy

Table 1 Life table parameters

Life expectancy	41.105
Birth rate (reciprocal value)	41.105
Death rate (reciprocal value)	41.105
Mean age at death	41.105
Mean age of the stationary population	32.433

to show that the population P_n and the number of deaths D_n at time $n < \omega$ are given by

$$P_n = \sum_{x=0}^{n-1} l_x\, q^{n-x} + \sum_{x=n}^{\omega} l_x = q^n \sum_{x=0}^{n-1} l_x\, q^{-x} + \sum_{x=n}^{\omega} l_x$$

$$D_n = \sum_{x=0}^{n-1} d_x\, q^{n-x} + \sum_{x=n}^{\omega} d_x = q^n \sum_{x=0}^{n-1} d_x\, q^{-x} + \sum_{x=n}^{\omega} d_x\,.$$

Zillmer derives the following parameters:

Birth rate (reciprocal value) at time n:

$$\frac{1}{b} = \frac{P_n - \frac{1}{2} D_n}{l_0\, q^n}\,.$$

Death rate (reciprocal value) at time n:

$$\frac{1}{d} = \frac{P_n - \frac{1}{2} D_n}{D_n} = \frac{P_n}{D_n} - \frac{1}{2}\,.$$

Mean age of death at time n:

$$\begin{aligned} \nu &= \frac{\sum_{x=0}^{n-1} (x+1)\, d_x\, q^{n-x} + \sum_{x=n}^{\omega} (x+1)\, d_x}{D_n} - \frac{1}{2} \\ &= \frac{q^n \sum_{x=0}^{n-1} (x+1)\, d_x\, q^{-x} + \sum_{x=n}^{\omega} (x+1)\, d_x}{D_n} - \frac{1}{2}\,. \end{aligned}$$

Mean age of the population at time n:

$$\begin{aligned} \mu = &\frac{\sum_{x=0}^{n-1}(x+1) l_x\, q^{n-x} + \sum_{x=n}^{\omega}(x+1) l_x}{P_n - \frac{1}{2} D_n} \\ &- \frac{\frac{1}{2}\left(\sum_{x=0}^{n-1}(x+1) d_x\, q^{n-x} + \sum_{x=n}^{\omega}(x+1) d_x\right)}{P_n - \frac{1}{2} D_n} - \frac{1}{2} \end{aligned}$$

$$= \frac{q^n \sum_{x=0}^{n-1} (x+1)\, l_x\, q^{-x} + \sum_{x=n}^{\omega} (x+1)\, l_x}{P_n - \frac{1}{2} D_n}$$

$$- \frac{\frac{1}{2} \left(q^n \sum_{x=0}^{n-1} (x+1)\, d_x\, q^{-x} + \sum_{x=n}^{\omega} (x+1)\, d_x \right)}{P_n - \frac{1}{2} D_n} - \frac{1}{2}.$$

The parameters become substantially simpler if $n > \omega$ (cf. Zillmer, 1863a, 78) as follows:

Birth rate (reciprocal value):

$$\frac{1}{b} = \frac{\sum_{x=0}^{\omega} l_x\, q^{-x} - \frac{1}{2} \sum_{x=0}^{\omega} d_x\, q^{-x}}{l_0}.$$

Death rate (reciprocal value):

$$\frac{1}{d} = \frac{\sum_{x=0}^{\omega} l_x\, q^{-x} - \frac{1}{2} \sum_{x=0}^{\omega} d_x\, q^{-x}}{\sum_{x=0}^{\omega} d_x\, q^{-x}}.$$

Vitality index:

$$\frac{d}{b} = \frac{\sum_{x=0}^{\omega} d_x\, q^{-x}}{l_0}.$$

Mean age of death:

$$\nu = \frac{\sum_{x=0}^{\omega} (x+1) d_x\, q^{-x}}{\sum_{x=0}^{\omega} d_x\, q^{-x}} - \frac{1}{2}.$$

Mean age of the stable population:

$$\mu = \frac{\sum_{x=0}^{\omega} (x+1) l_x\, q^{-x} - \frac{1}{2} \sum_{x=0}^{\omega} (x+1) d_x\, q^{-x}}{\sum_{x=0}^{\omega} l_x\, q^{-x} - \frac{1}{2} \sum_{x=0}^{\omega} d_x\, q^{-x}} - \frac{1}{2}.$$

Because n no longer occurs in the parameter definitions, they are independent of the time n. The age structure no longer changes and the population is stable. If $q = 1$, one obtains the parameters of a stationary population. In the continuous case of a stable population the parameters are (cf. Lotka, 1939 or Keyfitz, 1977):

Birth rate (reciprocal value):

$$\frac{1}{b} = \int_0^{\omega} \mathbf{e}^{-rx} l(x) \mathrm{d}x\,.$$

Death rate (reciprocal value):

$$\frac{1}{d} = \frac{\int_0^\omega \mathbf{e}^{-rx} l(x)\mu(x)\mathrm{d}x}{\int_0^\omega \mathbf{e}^{-rx} l(x)\mathrm{d}x},$$

where $\mu(x) = -\frac{\frac{\mathrm{d}l(x)}{\mathrm{d}x}}{l(x)}$ is the force of mortality.
Mean age at death:

$$\nu = \frac{\int_0^\omega x \cdot \mathbf{e}^{-rx} l(x)\mu(x)\mathrm{d}x}{\int_0^\omega \mathbf{e}^{-rx} l(x)\mu(x)\mathrm{d}x}.$$

Mean age of the stable population:

$$\mu = \frac{\int_0^\omega x \cdot \mathbf{e}^{-rx} l(x)\mathrm{d}x}{\int_0^\omega \mathbf{e}^{-rx} l(x)\mathrm{d}x}.$$

With the assumed life table and the derived formulas, Zillmer calculates population parameters at time n, which are presented in the following tables.

In contrast to a comparative static analysis, in which only the condition at time 0 is compared with that at time 100, Zillmer carries out a dynamic analysis, in which the temporal flow between both time points is regarded.

Finally, Zillmer calculates parameters for the stable population assuming different growth factors.

Zillmer was not able to explain the increase of the death rate d (decrease of $1/d$) with the increasing population growth rate. He wrote: "Diese Tabelle zeigt die eigenthümliche Ertscheinung, daß bei mässiger Vermehrung der Geburten die Sterbeziffer höher, also scheinbar günstiger ist, als bei stärkerer Vermehrung der Geburten" (cf. Zillmer, 1863a, 114).

This problem was first formally solved by Bortkiewicz (1898). He concluded that if the force of mortality function is an increasing function of age x, d is a decreasing (or $1/d$ an increasing) function of the growth rate; if the force of mortality function is a falling function of x, then d is an increasing (or $1/d$ a decreasing) function of the growth rate. If the force of mortality is constant, then d or $1/d$ are also constant (Tables 2 and 3).

In a real life table, the force of mortality is first decreasing and then increasing. Current life tables in industrial countries are characterized by a predominantly increasing function of the force of mortality. Therefore, the death rate will decline with an increase in the growth rate. The life table used by Zillmer shows a sharp falling force of mortality up to the age of 10. It reflects the typical mortality pattern of a pre-industrial country: high child and youth mortality. This bath-tub function of the force of mortality explains the death rate pattern. At first, the death rate d will decrease with moderate growth rates due to the younger age structure of the

Table 2 Population parameters with an annual growth rate of 1 %

n	$1/b$	$1/d$	ν	μ	$100\ d/b$
0	41.105	41.105	41.105	32.433	100.00
10	37.617	40.465	40.067	32.145	92.96
20	35.056	40.187	38.754	31.454	87.23
30	33.238	40.331	37.332	30.568	82.41
40	32.012	40.827	35.869	29.678	78.41
50	31.246	41.580	34.440	28.933	75.15
60	30.827	42.435	33.147	28.417	72.64
70	30.645	43.165	32.151	28.146	71.00
80	30.594	43.562	31.617	28.054	70.23
90	30.588	43.655	31.485	28.041	70.07
100	30.588	43.659	31.480	28.041	70.06

Table 3 Population parameters with an annual growth rate of 3.5 %

n	$1/b$	$1/d$	ν	μ	$100\ d/b$
0	41.105	41.105	41.105	32.433	100.00
10	30.340	38.758	37.357	31.372	78.28
20	24.150	37.458	32.511	28.764	64.47
30	20.706	37.391	27.500	25.610	55.38
40	18.884	38.185	22.900	22.866	49.45
50	17.991	39.389	19.108	20.995	45.68
60	17.608	40.569	16.341	19.981	43.40
70	17.477	41.392	14.675	19.567	42.22
80	17.448	41.750	13.988	19.459	41.79
90	17.445	41.818	13.857	19.446	41.72
100	17.445	41.820	13.853	19.446	41.71

population; the proportion of elderly persons with high mortality declines. This favorable effect is reversed into the opposite direction if the growth rate climbs further. The proportion of children and young people with a high mortality risk then becomes so large that the advantage of the younger age structure is lost. Altogether, the high proportion of children and young people with high mortality causes an increase in the death rate d or a decline in the reciprocal value $1/d$ (cf. Table 4).

Finally, let us briefly mention Zillmer's analysis under the assumption of a linear increase in births. He develops corresponding formulas for this case as well (cf. Zillmer, 1863a, S. 114f). In contrast to the geometric increase, the parameters are not independent of time n. The population converges for large n against the original stationary population. The stationarity explains itself simply through the fact that a linear increase in births implies a declining growth rate of births. After a sufficient period of time, the growth rate becomes more or less zero, resulting in the age structure of the stationary population.

Table 4 Parameters of the stable model

q	$1/b$	$1/d$	ν	μ	d/b
1	41.105	41.105	41.105	32.433	1.000
1.01	30.588	43.659	31.480	28.041	0.701
1.025	21.268	43.652	19.449	22.461	0.487
1.03	19.187	42.858	16.409	20.886	0.448
1.035	17.445	41.820	13.853	19.447	0.417
1.04	15.973	40.624	11.738	18.138	0.393

3 Population Forecasting with the Zillmer Model

Population forecasts have received a great deal of attention during recent years. They are widely used for planning and policy purposes. Planners and policy makers need a reliable insight into future developments of size and composition of their populations.

A population projection model that is generally used is based on the well-known cohort-component method and leads to a population projection that is broken down into categories of age and sex. This model is based on a projection of the population through its components, fertility, mortality, and migration. The initial population that is broken down into categories of age and sex is taken as the basis for the model. This population is reduced by the number of deaths for each interval in the projected time frame by means of age- and sex-specific death rates. The number of births will be determined with help from age-specific birth rates for surviving women. The entire birth figure will then become the new birth cohort in the projection model. Finally, the expected figure for immigrants and emigrants has to be estimated. The following representation of the cohort-component method refers back to Leslie (1945). The projection model for the female population is represented by the following recurrence equation:

$$n_{t+1} = L_t \cdot n_t + I_t \quad \text{for} \quad t = 0, 1, 2, \ldots$$

The vector n_t represents the number of women in the different age classes at time t. After one projection interval, the population n_{t+1}, broken down by age, can be obtained by multiplying n_t with the projection matrix L_t and adding a net immigration vector I_t, which is adjusted by the number of births and deaths in the corresponding time interval. The projection or Leslie matrix contains age-specific maternity rates in the first row and age-specific survivor rates in the sub-diagonal. Otherwise it contains only zeros.

$$L_t = \begin{pmatrix} 0 & 0 & m_{1t} & \dots & 0 \\ s_{1t} & 0 & 0 & \dots & 0 \\ 0 & s_{2t} & 0 & \dots & 0 \\ 0 & 0 & s_{3t} & \dots & 0 \\ \vdots & \vdots & & & \vdots \\ 0 & 0 & \dots & s_{n-1t} & 0 \end{pmatrix}.$$

Details of the calculation of the elements of the vector and matrices of the projection model are shown, e.g., in Keyfitz (1977) or Pflaumer (1988a).

An early application of the Leslie model for the Federal Republic of Germany can be found in Heiler (1978). Already at this time, Heiler realized in his long-term population projection the problems for the future of the social security system in countries with low fertility. He proposed solutions long before policy and economics addressed this problem.

Most users of population forecasts now realize that populations are not perfectly predictable. As a result, there has been an increasing interest in questions related to the performance of population projection models. Several ways exist of considering the uncertainty which inevitably arises with population forecasting. One method makes several forecast variants, e.g., high, medium, and low projections are made. Alternative approaches are the formulation of population models, in which the vital rates are either probabilities (cf. Pollard, 1973; Heiler, 1982) or random variables (cf., e.g., Bohk, 2011). The stochastic assumptions imply that the population size at a certain time is also a random variable. Its distribution and its confidence intervals can be deduced either by theoretical methods (e.g., Sykes, 1969) or by means of Monte Carlo simulation methods (e.g., Pflaumer, 1988b).

If the new inputs (births) do not depend on the populations of the other age-groups (e.g., forecasting size and age structure of students at universities, or manpower demand in human resource), then the Leslie matrix has to be modified. In this case, the new exogenous input must be modeled as a time series. An overview of various methods of time series analysis can be found, e.g., in Heiler (1981). A simple assumption is the geometric development of the new input, as has been assumed by Zillmer (1863a) in his population analysis, with q as the growth factor. The transition described by Zillmer from a stationary to a stable population is, in principle, a population projection with a stationary population as an original population. Formally, Zillmer's model can be described by the previous recurrence equation and the following projection matrix, which is a special case of the Leslie matrix:

$$Z = \begin{pmatrix} q & 0 & 0 & \dots & 0 \\ s_1 & 0 & 0 & \dots & 0 \\ 0 & s_2 & 0 & \cdots & 0 \\ 0 & 0 & s_3 & \dots & 0 \\ \vdots & \vdots & & & \vdots \\ 0 & 0 & \dots & s_{n-1} & 0 \end{pmatrix}.$$

The growth factor is represented by q, which is the stable eigenvalue of the matrix Z. If $q > 1$, then the population grows; if $q < 1$, then it decreases; and in the case of a stationary population, the growth factor is given by $q = 1$.

Boes (2004) essentially applies the Zillmer model in order to calculate survivor functions for German university students, i.e., the probabilities that a student will still be enrolled at the end of a given semester.

In Zillmer's investigation, ergodicity is achieved when age-specific death rates have been constant for a long time and births increase at a fixed growth rate. Zillmer did not consider age-specific fertility rates in his analysis. Zillmer's model would imply that the age-specific fertility rates or the net reproduction rate would change over time until the population became stable. Lotka (1939) demonstrated, however, that a population subjected to fixed age-specific mortality and fertility rates will eventually become stable. The number of births will fluctuate with decreasing oscillations and finally grow with a constant rate in the stable situation.

Conclusion

Zillmer is one of the pioneers of quantitative demography. Long before Bortkiewicz (1898) and Lotka (1907), he analyzed the relationship between birth rate and age structure of a population. His approach is dynamic in contrast to the comparative static approach, which is limited to the consideration of the initial and final state of a population. Zillmer's dynamic model aims to trace and study the behavior of the population through time, and to determine whether this population tends to move towards equilibrium.

He showed the relationship between average age of death, birth and death rate, and clearly recognized that the average age of death depends on the growth rate of a population, and is therefore not an appropriate measure of the mortality of a population. These empirically based results were later mathematically proven in a continuous model by Bortkiewicz (1898).

Although these relationships have long been researched and published, these facts do not seem to be known in some applications, for example, when the mean number of years spent at universities are calculated incorrectly. Along with Siegfried Heiler and other professors of the Department of Statistics at the University of Dortmund, Davies (1988) criticized the incorrect

(continued)

method of calculating this average in a commissioned report of the Ministry of Science and Research in North Rhine-Westphalia. However, as an answer to the critics, the Ministry declared the correctness of the numbers by decree.

Appendix

See Table 5.

Table 5 Life table of the 17 English life insurance companies with additions of Zillmer (1863a) and Heym (1863)

x	l_x	x	l_x	x	l_x	x	l_x
0	144,218	26	89,137	51	68,409	76	21,797
1	122,692	27	88,434	52	67,253	77	19,548
2	114,339	28	87,726	53	66,046	78	17,369
3	110,050	29	87,012	54	64,785	79	15,277
4	107,344	30	86,292	55	63,469	80	13,290
5	105,471	31	85,565	56	62,094	81	11,424
6	104,052	32	84,831	57	60,658	82	9,694
7	102,890	33	84,089	58	59,161	83	8,112
8	101,889	34	83,339	59	57,600	84	6,685
9	100,996	35	82,581	60	55,973	85	5,417
10	100,179	36	81,814	61	54,275	86	4,306
11	99,416	37	81,038	62	52,505	87	3,348
12	98,691	38	80,253	63	50,661	88	2,537
13	97,992	39	79,458	64	48,744	89	1,864
14	97,310	40	78,653	65	46,754	90	1,319
15	96,636	41	77,838	66	44,693	91	892
16	95,965	42	77,012	67	42,565	92	570
17	95,293	43	76,173	68	40,374	93	339
18	94,620	44	75,316	69	38,128	94	184
19	93,945	45	74,435	70	35,837	95	89
20	93,268	46	73,526	71	33,510	96	37
21	92,588	47	72,582	72	31,159	97	13
22	91,905	48	71,601	73	28,797	98	4
23	91,219	49	70,580	74	26,439	99	1
24	90,529	50	69,517	75	24,100	100	0
25	89,835						

Source: Zillmer (1861, 1863a) and Heym (1863)

References

Boes, S. (2004). Die Anwendung der Konzepte probabilistischer Bevölkerungsmodelle auf Prognosen für den Hochschulbereich. Diss, Dortmund.

Bohk, C. (2011). Ein probabilistisches Bevölkerungsmodell. Heidelberg.

Bortkiewicz, L. V. (1898). Die mittlere Lebensdauer. Die Methoden ihrer Bestimmung und ihr Verhältnis zur Sterblichkeitsmessung. Staatswissenschaftliche Studien, 4. Band, 6. Heft. Jena.

Bortkiewicz, L. V. (1911). Die Sterbeziffer und der Frauenüberschuß in der stationären und in der progressiven Bevölkerung. *Bulletin de l'Institut International de Statistique, 19*, 63–183.

Coale, A. J. (1979). The use of modern analytical demography by T.R. Malthus. *Population Studies, 33*(2), 329–332.

Davies, L. (1988). Die Aktualität der falschen Zahlen. *Deutsche Universitätszeitung, 4*, 24–25.

Euler, L. (1760). Récherches générales sur la mortalité et la multiplication. *Mémoires de l'Académie Royale des Sciences et Belles Lettres, 16*, 144–164.

Heiler, S. (1978). Der Geburtenrückgang in der Bundesrepublik und seine Auswirkungen. Forschungsbericht des Fachbereichs Statistik, Dortmund.

Heiler, S. (1981). Zeitreihenanalyse heute, ein Überblick. *Allgemeines Statistisches Archiv, 65*, 376–402.

Heiler, S. (1982). Die Verwendung von Zeitreihenverfahren und Verzweigungsprozessen zur Bevölkerungsvorhersage. In W. Piesch & W. Förster (Hrsg.), *Angewandte Statistik und Wirtschaftsforschung heute*, Vandenhoeck & Ruprecht, (pp. 66–75). Göttingen.

Heym, K. (1863). Ueber eine Ergänzung der Tafel der 17 englischen Gesellschaften. Rundschau der Versicherungen von Masius, XIII. Jg., pp. 245–249.

Jones, J. (1843). *A series of tables of annuities and assurances, calculated from a new rate of mortality among assured lives*. Longman, Brown, Green & Longmans, London.

Keyfitz, N. (1977). *Applied mathematical demography*. New York: Wiley.

Leslie, P. H. (1945). On the use of matrices in certain population mathematics. *Biometrika, 33*, 183–212.

Lischke, R.-J., Michel, H. (2007). *Biographisches Lexikon zur Geschichte der Demographie*. Duncker & Humblot, Berlin.

Lotka, A. J. (1907). Relation between birth rates and death rates. *Science N.S., XXVI*(653), 21–22.

Lotka, A. J. (1932). Zur Dynamik der Bevölkerungsentwicklung. *Allgemeines Statistisches Archiv, 22*, 587–588.

Lotka, A. J. (1937). A historical error corrected. *Human Biology, 9*, 104–107.

Lotka, A. J. (1939). Théorie analytique des associations biologiques. Part II, Analyse démographique avec application particulière á l'espèce humaine, Actualités Scientifiques et Indistruelles, No. 780, Paris.

Moser, L. (1839). Die Gesetze der Lebensdauer. Nebst Untersuchungen ueber Dauer, Fruchtbarkeit d. Ehen, ueber Toedtlichkeit d. Krankheiten, Verhaeltnis d. Witterung u.s.w.; und e. Anh. enth. d. Berechnung d. Leibrenten, Lebensversicherungen, Witwenpensionen u. Tontinen; ein Lehrbuch. Berlin.

Pflaumer, P. (1988a). *Methoden der Bevölkerungsvorausschätzung unter besonderer Berücksichtigung der Unsicherheit*. Duncker & Humblot, Berlin.

Pflaumer, P. (1988b). Confidence intervals for population projections based on Monte Carlo methods. *International Journal of Forecasting, 4*, 135–142.

Pollard, H. H. (1973). *Mathematical models for the growth of human population*. Cambridge: Cambridge University Press.

Samuelson, P. A. (1976). Resolving a historical confusion in population analysis. *Human Biology, 48*, 559–580.

Sharpe, F. R., Lotka, A. J. (1911). A problem in age-distribution. *Philosophical Magazine, Series 6, 21*, 435–438.

Sykes, Z. M. (1969). Some stochastic version of the matrix model for population dynamics. *Journal of the American Statistical Association, 44*, 111–130.

Zillmer, A. (1861). *Die mathematischen Rechnungen bei Lebens- und Rentenversicherungen.* Nicolaische Verlagsbuchhandlung, Berlin.
Zillmer, A. (1863a). Ueber die Geburtenziffer, die Sterbeziffer, das durchschnittliche Sterbealter und den Zusammenhang dieser Zahlen mit der mittleren Lebensdauer. Rundschau der Versicherungen von Masius, XIII. Jg., 71–78 und 112–118.
Zillmer, A. (1863b). Beiträge zur Theorie der Prämienreserve bei Lebensversicherungsanstalten. Hahmer, Stettin.

Part III
New Econometric Approaches

Adaptive Estimation of Regression Parameters for the Gaussian Scale Mixture Model

Roger Koenker

Abstract A proposal of Van der Vaart (1996) for an adaptive estimator of a location parameter from a family of normal scale mixtures is explored. Recent developments in convex optimization have dramatically improved the computational feasibility of the Kiefer and Wolfowitz (Ann Math Stat 27:887–906, 1956) nonparametric maximum likelihood estimator for general mixture models and yield an effective strategy for estimating the efficient score function for the location parameter in this setting. The approach is extended to regression and performance is evaluated with a small simulation experiment.

1 Introduction

The Princeton Robustness Study, Andrews et al. (1972), arguably the most influential simulation experiment ever conducted in statistics, compared performance of a 68 distinct location estimators focusing almost exclusively scale mixtures of Gaussian models. While such scale mixtures do not constitute an enormous class, see, for example, Efron and Olshen (1978), they are convenient for several reasons: their symmetry ensures a well-defined location estimand, their unimodality affirms Tukey's dictum that "all distributions are normal in the middle," and probably most significantly, conditional normality facilitates some nice Monte-Carlo tricks that lead to improvements in simulation efficiency.

A prototypical problem is the Tukey contaminated normal location model,

$$Y_i = \alpha + u_i \tag{1}$$

with iid u_i from the contaminated normal distribution, $F_{\epsilon,\sigma}(u) = (1-\epsilon)\Phi(u) + \epsilon\Phi(u/\sigma)$. We would like to estimate the center of symmetry, α, of the distribution of the Y_i's. Yet we do not know ϵ, nor the value of σ; how should we proceed? Of course we could adopt any one of the estimators proposed in the Princeton Study,

R. Koenker (✉)
Department of Economics, University of Illinois, Champaign, IL 61820, USA
e-mail: rkoenker@uiuc.edu

J. Beran et al. (eds.), *Empirical Economic and Financial Research*,
Advanced Studies in Theoretical and Applied Econometrics 48,
DOI 10.1007/978-3-319-03122-4_23

or one of the multitudes of more recent proposals. But we are feeling greedy, and would like to have an estimator that is also asymptotically fully efficient.

The Tukey model is a very special case of a more general Gamma mixture model in which we have (1), and the u_i's are iid with density,

$$g(v) = \int_0^\infty \gamma(v|\theta) dF(\theta)$$

where $\theta = \sigma^2$, and γ is the $\chi^2(1)$ density with free scale parameter θ,

$$\gamma(v|\theta) = \frac{1}{\Gamma(1/2)\sqrt{2\theta}} v^{-1/2} \exp(-v/(2\theta))$$

Our strategy will be to estimate this mixture model *nonparametrically* and employ it to construct an adaptive M-estimator for α. This strategy may be viewed as an example of the general proposal of Van der Vaart (1996) for constructing efficient MLEs for semiparametric models.

2 Empirical Bayes and the Kiefer–Wolfowitz MLE

Given iid observations, $V_1, \cdots, V_n$, from the density,

$$g(v) = \int_0^\infty \gamma(v|\theta) dF(\theta)$$

we can estimate F and hence the density g by maximum likelihood. This was first suggested by Robbins (1951) and then much more explicitly by Kiefer and Wolfowitz (1956). It is an essential piece of the empirical Bayes approach developed by Robbins (1956) and many subsequent authors. The initial approach to computing the Kiefer–Wolfowitz estimator was provided by Laird (1978) employing the EM algorithm, however EM is excruciatingly slow. Fortunately, there is a better approach that exploits recent developments in convex optimization.

The Kiefer–Wolfowitz problem can be reformulated as a convex maximum likelihood problem and solved by standard interior point methods. To accomplish this we define a grid of values, $\{0 < v_1 < \cdots < v_m < \infty\}$, and let $\mathscr{F}$ denote the set of distributions with support contained in the interval, $[v_1, v_m]$. The problem,

$$\max_{f \in \mathscr{F}} \sum_{i=1}^{n} \log\Big(\sum_{j=1}^{m} \gamma(V_i, v_j) f_j\Big),$$

can be rewritten as

$$\min\{-\sum_{i=1}^{n}\log(g_i) \mid Af = g,\ f \in \mathscr{S}\},$$

where $A = (\gamma(V_i, v_j))$ and $\mathscr{S} = \{s \in \mathbb{R}^m | 1^\top s = 1,\ s \geq 0\}$. So f_j denotes the estimated mixing density estimate $\hat{f}$ at the grid point v_j, and g_i denotes the estimated mixture density estimate, $\hat{g}$, evaluated at V_i.

This is easily recognized as a convex optimization problem with an additively separable convex objective function subject to linear equality and inequality constraints, hence amenable to modern interior point methods of solution. For this purpose, we rely on the Mosek system of Andersen (2010) and its R interface, Friberg (2012). Implementations of all the procedures described here are available in the R package REBayes, Koenker (2012). For further details on computational aspects see Koenker and Mizera (2011).

Given a consistent initial estimate of α, for example as provided by the sample median, the Kiefer–Wolfowitz estimate of the mixing distribution can be used to construct an estimate of the optimal influence function, $\hat{\psi}$, that can be used in turn to produce an asymptotically efficient M-estimator of the location parameter. More explicitly, we define our estimator, $\hat{\alpha}_n$, as follows:

(1) Preliminary estimate: $\tilde{\alpha} = \text{median}(Y_1, \cdots, Y_n)$
(2) Mixture estimate: $\hat{f} = \text{argmax}_{f \in \mathscr{F}} \sum_{i=1}^{n} \log(\sum_{j=1}^{m} \gamma(Y_i - \tilde{\alpha}, v_j) f_j)$,
(3) Solve for $\hat{\alpha}$ such that $\hat{\psi}(Y_i - \alpha) = 0$, where $\hat{\psi}(u) = (\log \hat{g}(u))'$, and $\hat{g}(u) = \int \gamma(u, v) d\hat{F}(v)$.

Theorem 1 (Van der Vaart (1996)) *For the Gaussian scale mixture model* (1) *with* F *supported on* $[v_1, v_m]$, *the estimator* $\hat{\alpha}$ *is asymptotically efficient, that is,* $\sqrt{n}(\hat{\alpha}_n - \alpha) \rightsquigarrow \mathbf{N}(0, 1/\mathbb{I}(g))$, *where* $\mathbb{I}(g)$ *is the Fisher information for location of the density,* $g(u) = \int \gamma(u, v) dF(v)$.

This result depends crucially on the orthogonality of the score function for the location parameter with that of the score of the (nuisance) mixing distribution and relies obviously on the symmetry inherent in the scale mixture model. In this way it is closely related to earlier literature on adaptation by Stein (1956), Stone (1975), Bickel (1982), and others. But it is also much more specialized since it covers a much smaller class of models. The restriction on the domain of $\mathscr{F}$ could presumably be relaxed by letting $v_1 \to 0$ and $v_m \to \infty$ (slowly) as $n \to \infty$. From the argument for the foregoing result in van der Vaart it is clear that the location model can be immediately extended to linear regression which will be considered in the next section.

3 Some Simulation Evidence

To explore the practical benefits of such an estimator we consider two simple simulation settings: the first corresponds to our prototypical Tukey model in which the scale mixture is composed of only two mass points, and the other is a smooth mixture in which scale is generated as $\sqrt{\chi^2_3/3}$, so the Y_i's are marginally Student t on three degrees of freedom. We will consider the simple bivariate linear regression model,

$$Y_i = \beta_0 + x_i \beta_1 + u_i$$

where the u_i's are iid from the scale mixture of Gaussian model described in the previous section. The x_i's are generated iidly from the standard Gaussian distribution, so intercept and slope estimators for the model have the same asymptotic variance. The usual median regression (least absolute error) estimator will be used as an initial estimator for our adaptive estimator and we will compare performance of both with the ubiquitous least squares estimator.

3.1 Some Implementation Details

Our implementation of the Kiefer–Wolfowitz estimator requires several decisions about the grid $v_1, \cdots, v_m$. For scale mixtures of the type considered here it is natural to adopt an equally spaced grid on a log scale. I have used $m = 300$ points with $v_1 = \log(\max\{0.1, \min\{r_1, \cdots, r_n\}\})$ and $v_m = \log(\max\{r_1, \cdots, r_n\})$. Bounding the support of the mixing distribution away from zero seems to be important, but a corresponding upper bound on the support has not proven to be necessary.

Given an estimate of the mixing distribution, $\hat{F}$, the score function for the efficient M-estimator is easily calculated to be

$$\hat{\psi}(u) = (-\log \hat{g}(u))' = \frac{\int u\varphi(u/\sigma)/\sigma^3 d\hat{F}(\sigma)}{\int \varphi(u/\sigma)/\sigma d\hat{F}(\sigma)}.$$

We compute this estimate again on a relatively fine grid, and pass a spline representation of the score function to a slightly modified version of the robust regression function, `rlm()` of the R package MASS, Venables and Ripley (2002), where the final M-estimate is computed using iteratively reweighted least squares.

Table 1 MSE scaled by sample size, n, for Tukey scale mixture of normals

n	LAE	LSE	Adaptive
100	1.756	1.726	1.308
200	1.805	1.665	1.279
400	1.823	1.750	1.284
800	1.838	1.753	1.304
∞	1.803	1.800	1.256

Table 2 MSE scaled by sample size, n, for Student t(3) mixture of normals

n	LAE	LSE	Adaptive
100	1.893	2.880	1.684
200	1.845	2.873	1.579
400	1.807	2.915	1.540
800	1.765	2.946	1.524
∞	1.851	3.000	1.500

3.2 Simulation Results

For the Tukey scale mixture model (1) with $\epsilon = 0.1$ and $\sigma = 3$ mean and median regression have essentially the same asymptotic variance of about 1.80, while the efficient (MLE) estimator has asymptotic variance of about 1.25. In Table 1 we see that the simulation performance of the three estimators is in close accord with these theoretical predictions. We report the combined mean squared error for intercept and slope parameters scaled by the sample size so that each row of the table is comparable to the asymptotic variance reported in the last row.

It seems entirely plausible that the proposed procedure, based as it is on the Kiefer–Wolfowitz nonparametric estimate of the mixing distribution, would do better with discrete mixture models for scale like the Tukey model than for continuous mixtures like the Student t(3) model chosen as our second test case. Kiefer–Wolfowitz delivers a discrete mixing distribution usually with only a few mass points. Nevertheless, in Table 2 we see that the proposed adaptive estimator performs quite well for the Student t(3) case achieving close to full asymptotic efficiency for sample sizes 400 and 800.

Conclusions

Various extensions naturally suggest themselves. One could replace the Gaussian mixture model with an alternative; Van der Vaart (1996) suggests the logistic as a possibility. As long as one maintains the symmetry of the base distribution adaptivity is still tenable, but symmetry, while an article of faith in much of the robustness literature, may be hard to justify. Of course, if we are only interested in slope parameters in the regression setting and are

(continued)

willing to maintain the iid error assumption, then symmetry can be relaxed as Bickel (1982) has noted.

The challenge of achieving full asymptotic efficiency while retaining some form of robustness has been a continuing theme of the literature. Various styles of ψ-function carpentry designed to attenuate the influence of outliers may improve performance in small to modest sample sizes. Nothing, so far, has been mentioned about the evil influence of outlying design observations; this too could be considered in further work.

Acknowledgements This research was partially supported by NSF grant SES-11-53548.

References

Andersen, E. D. (2010). *The MOSEK optimization tools manual (Version 6.0)*. Available from http://www.mosek.com.

Andrews, D., Bickel, P., Hampel, F., Huber, P., Rogers, W., & Tukey, J. W. (1972). *Robust estimates of location: Survey and advances*. Princeton: Princeton University Press.

Bickel, P. J. (1982). On adaptive estimation. *The Annals of Statistics, 10*, 647–671.

Efron, B., & Olshen, R. A. (1978). How broad is the class of normal scale mixtures? *The Annals of Statistics, 5*, 1159–1164.

Friberg, H. A. (2012). *Users guide to the R-to-MOSEK interface*. Available from http://rmosek.r-forge.r-project.org.

Kiefer, J., & Wolfowitz, J. (1956). Consistency of the maximum likelihood estimator in the presence of infinitely many incidental parameters. *The Annals of Mathematical Statistics, 27*, 887–906.

Koenker, R. (2012). *REBayes: An R package for empirical Bayes methods*. Available from http://www.econ.uiuc.edu/~roger/research/ebayes/ebayes.html.

Koenker, R., & Mizera, I. (2011). *Shape constraints, compound decisions and empirical Bayes rules*. http://www.econ.uiuc.edu/~roger/research/ebayes/ebayes.html.

Laird, N. (1978). Nonparametric Maximum Likelihood Estimation of a Mixing Distribution,' *Journal of the American Statistical Association, 73*, 805–811.

Robbins, H. (1951). Asymptotically subminimax solutions of compound statistical decision problems. In *Proceedings of the Berkeley Symposium on Mathematical Statistics and Probability*, (Vol. I). Berkeley: University of California Press.

Robbins, H. (1956). An empirical Bayes approach to statistics. In *Proceedings of the Third Berkeley Symposium on Mathematical Statistics and Probability* (Vol. I). Berkeley: University of California Press.

Stein, C. (1956). Efficient nonparametric testing and estimation. In *Proceedings of the Third Berkeley Symposium on Mathematical Statistics and Probability* (Vol. 1, pp. 187–195).

Stone, C. J. (1975). Adaptive maximum likelihood estimators of a location parameter. *The Annals of Statistics, 3*, 267–284.

Van der Vaart, A. (1996). Efficient maximum likelihood estimation in semiparametric mixture models. *The Annals of Statistics, 24*, 862–878.

Venables, W. N., & Ripley, B. D. (2002). *Modern applied statistics with S* (4th ed.). New York: Springer.

The Structure of Generalized Linear Dynamic Factor Models

Manfred Deistler, Wolfgang Scherrer, and Brian D.O. Anderson

Abstract In this contribution we present a structure theory for generalized linear dynamic factor models. Generalized dynamic factor models have been proposed approximately a decade ago for modeling of high dimensional time series where the cross sectional dimension is of the same order of magnitude as the sample size. In these models the classical assumption for factor models, that the noise components are mutually uncorrelated, is relaxed by allowing for weak dependence. Structure theory turns out to be important for estimation and model selection. The results obtained heavily draw from linear system theory.

The contribution consists of two main parts. In the first part we deal with "denoising", i.e. with getting rid of the noise in the observations. In the second part we deal with constructing linear dynamic systems for the latent variables. Here an important result is the generic zerolessness of the transfer function relating the latent variables and the dynamic factors. This allows for modeling the latent variables by (singular) autoregressions which simplifies estimation.

1 Introduction

Analysis and forecasting of high dimensional time series is an important area in the so-called big data revolution. High dimensional time series can be found in many fields such as econometrics, finance, genetics, environmental research and chemometrics.

The main reasons for joint modeling of high dimensional time series are:

- The analysis of dynamic relations between the time series

M. Deistler (✉) • W. Scherrer
Institut für Wirtschaftsmathematik, Technische Universität Wien, Wien, Austria
e-mail: Manfred.Deistler@tuwien.ac.at; Wolfgang.Scherrer@tuwien.ac.at

B.D.O. Anderson
Research School of Information Sciences and Engineering, Australian National University, Canberra, ACT, Australia
e-mail: brian.anderson@anu.edu.au

J. Beran et al. (eds.), *Empirical Economic and Financial Research*,
Advanced Studies in Theoretical and Applied Econometrics 48,
DOI 10.1007/978-3-319-03122-4_24

- Extraction of factors or features common to all time series (construction of indices)
- The improvement of forecasts, by using the past of many time series.

The "traditional" approach to multivariate time series is plagued by the so-called curse of dimensionality. Let T denote the sample size and N denote the cross sectional dimension. If we perform "unstructured" AR modeling, then the dimension of the parameters space is $N^2 p + N(N+1)/2$ (where p is the AR order). Thus this dimension increases with N^2, whereas the number of data points, NT, is linear in N. For this reason, for high dimensional time series, model classes with reduced complexity have been used. There are several approaches for this:

- Traditional structural macro-econometric modeling which uses over-identifying a-priori restrictions
- Hierarchical Bayesian modeling, where the prior distribution of the original parameter depends on a few hyper parameters (Doan et al. 1984).
- "Sparse" AR models. A particular class of such sparse models corresponds to the so-called graphical time series models, where, e.g. the zero coefficients correspond to lack of conditional Granger causality (Flamm et al. 2012).
- Factor models and (dynamical) principal components analysis. Such models allow for dimension reduction in cross section by using co-movements in the time series.

Here we consider a particular class of factor models, the so-called generalized linear dynamic factor models (GDFMs). GDFMs generalize

- Generalized linear static factor models, as introduced in Chamberlain (1983) and Chamberlain and Rothschild (1983). These models generalize static factor models with strictly idiosyncratic noise, i.e. with uncorrelated noise components, by allowing for "weak dependence" between the noise components.
- Linear dynamic factor models with strictly idiosyncratic noise (Engle and Watson 1981; Geweke 1977; Sargent and Sims 1977; Scherrer and Deistler 1998)

The main features of GDFMs are

- They allow for modeling of dynamics (here in a stationary context)
- Uncorrelatedness of the noise components is generalized to weak dependence
- "Co-movement" of the individual single time series has to be assumed.
- Whereas the observations are ordered in time the results are "permutation invariant" in cross section. Of course, here additional structure, e.g. corresponding to spatial distance, might be imposed
- Strictly speaking, for GDFMs, sequences of model classes, indexed by the cross sectional dimension N are considered.

GDFMs have been developed over the last 13 years, say, and have been successfully applied, for instance, in macroeconometrics since. The main early references are Forni et al. (2000), Forni and Lippi (2001), and Stock and Watson (2002) and further important contributions are Bai and Ng (2002), Bai (2003), Deistler et al. (2010), and Doz et al. (2011).

The rest of the paper is organized as follows: In Sect. 2 the model class is described. Section 3 is concerned with denoising. Section 4 deals with the realization of latent variables and static factors by state space and ARMA systems. Section 5 deals with the AR case, which is generic in the "typical" situation considered here. Section 6 treats the Yule–Walker equations for singular AR systems and Sect. 7 outlines the relevance of our results for estimation and model selection.

2 GDFMs: The Model Class

We assume that the N-dimensional observations, y_t^N, are of the form

$$y_t^N = \hat{y}_t^N + u_t^N, \ t \in \mathbb{Z} \tag{1}$$

where $\hat{y}_t^N$ are the *latent variables* and u_t^N is the (weakly dependent) noise.

Throughout we impose the following assumptions:

(A.1) $\mathbf{E}\hat{y}_t^N = \mathbf{E}u_t^N = 0 \in \mathbb{R}^N$ for all $t \in \mathbb{Z}$
(A.2) $(\hat{y}_t^N)$ and (u_t^N) are wide sense stationary[1] with absolutely summable covariances.
(A.3) $\mathbf{E}\hat{y}_t^N (u_s^N)' = 0$ for all $t, s \in \mathbb{Z}$

Thus the spectral densities exist and, using an obvious notation, we obtain for the spectral densities

$$f_y^N(\theta) = f_{\hat{y}}^N(\theta) + f_u^N(\theta), \ \theta \in [-\pi, \pi] \tag{2}$$

For GDFMs the asymptotic analysis is performed for $T \to \infty$ and $N \to \infty$; thus, we consider sequences of GDFMs for $N \to \infty$. In addition we assume throughout that the entries in the vectors are nested, e.g. $\hat{y}_t^{N+1}$ is of the form $((\hat{y}_t^N)', \hat{y}_{N+1,t})'$ where $\hat{y}_{i,t}$ denotes the i-th component of $\hat{y}_t^{N+1}$.

The following assumptions constitute the core of our definition of GDFMs. Here we always assume that N is large enough:

(A.4) (Strong dependence of the latent variables): $f_{\hat{y}}^N$ is a rational spectral density matrix with constant (i.e. for all $\theta \in [-\pi, \pi]$) rank $q < N$; q does not depend on N. The first q eigenvalues of $f_{\hat{y}}^N$ diverge to infinity for all frequencies, as $N \to \infty$.
(A.5) (Weak dependence in the noise): The largest eigenvalue of $f_u^N(\theta)$ is uniformly bounded for all $\theta \in [-\pi, \pi]$ and all N.

[1]It should be noted, however, that recently GDFMs for integrated processes have been proposed.

Since we assume that the spectral density $f_{\hat{y}}^N$ of the latent variables $\hat{y}_t^N$ is rational, it can be realized by a state space or ARMA system. Here our focus is on state space systems

$$x_{t+1}^N = F^N x_t^N + G^N \varepsilon_{t+1}^N \tag{3}$$

$$\hat{y}_t^N = H^N x_t^N \tag{4}$$

where x_t^N is an n-dimensional, say, (minimal) state and $F^N \in \mathbb{R}^{n\times n}$, $G^N \in \mathbb{R}^{n\times q}$, $H^N \in \mathbb{R}^{N\times n}$ are parameter matrices. We assume that the system is minimal, stable and miniphase and accordingly

$$\hat{y}_t^N = w^N(z)\varepsilon_t^N \tag{5}$$

where $w^N(z) = H^N(I - F^N z)^{-1}G^N$ is a rational, causal and miniphase transfer function and where z is used for the backward shift on the integers $\mathbb{Z}$ as well as for a complex variable. This will be discussed in detail in Sect. 4. In (5), ε_t^N is a minimal *dynamic factor* of dimension q.

The above representation (5) shows that the latent variables are driven by the q dimensional factor process ε_t. Typically $q \ll N$ holds. This generates the co-movement of the latent variables and the observed variables. The assumption (A.5) implies that the noise components are only weakly dependent, which means that the noise can be eliminated by suitable (dynamic) cross sectional averages. This property will be used for "denoising", i.e. for getting $\hat{y}_t^N$ from y_t^N (for $N \to \infty$), as will be discussed in Sect. 3.

In a number of applications GDFMs have been quite successfully applied which shows that the above assumptions in many cases at least provide a reasonable approximation of the true data generating mechanism. There exist (testing) procedures which try to assess whether the given data is compatible with the assumptions. In particular estimation routines (see, e.g., Hallin and Liška 2007) for the number of factor q implicitly test this assumption.

In addition we assume:

(A.6) The spectral density $f_{\hat{y}}^N$ corresponds to a state space system (3),(4) with state dimension n, independent of N.

By (A.6) the McMillan degree of the spectral density $f_{\hat{y}}^N$ is smaller than or equal to $2n$, independent of N. (A.6) is an assumption of bounded complexity dynamics. It is justifiable in a number of applications, e.g. when there is a true underlying system (of finite order) and the number N of sensors is increasing (over sensoring). Recently a theory for the case where q is independent of N, but n is allowed to increase with N has been developed in Forni et al. (2011).

As will be shown in Sect. 4, (A.6) implies that the minimal dynamic factor ε_t, the state x_t and F, G in (3), (4) can be chosen independent of N. Furthermore this assumption implies the existence of a *static factor*, z_t say, which may be chosen independent of N and thus

$$\hat{y}_t^N = L^N z_t \tag{6}$$

holds. Note that z_t is called a static factor since the factor loading matrix $L^N \in \mathbb{R}^{N \times r}$ is a constant matrix whereas the corresponding factor loading matrix $w^N(z)$ for ε_t^N in (5) is a transfer function matrix. Let us denote the minimal dimension of such a static factor z_t by r. Then clearly

$$q \leq r$$

holds. In a certain sense the case $q < r$ is of particular interest, since it allows for further complexity reduction.

Given the assumptions, the decomposition (1) of the observed variables into latent variables and noise is unique, asymptotically with N going to infinity. However, the factor loading matrix L^N and the static factor z_t are only unique up to post-respectively pre-multiplication with non-singular matrices. If we assume that the dynamic factors ε_t^N are the innovations of the latent variables, then they are unique up to pre-multiplication by non-singular matrices.

3 Denoising

In this section we consider the problem of estimating the factors and/or the latent variables $\hat{y}_{it}$, i.e. we want to eliminate the noise u_{it} from the observations y_{it}. We will concentrate on the estimation of the static factors z_t and corresponding estimates of the latent variables. The dynamic case will be shortly treated in Sect. 3.2.

3.1 Estimation of the Static Factors z_t

Here we consider the static factor model as defined in (6). Since the spectral density f_u^N of (u_t^N) is uniformly bounded by (A.5) it follows that the covariance matrices $\gamma_u^N(0) = \mathbf{E}u_t^N(u_t^N)'$ are also bounded, i.e. there exists a constant, $\overline{\gamma} < \infty$ say, such that

$$\gamma_u^N(0) \leq \overline{\gamma} I_N \text{ for all } N \in \mathbb{N} \tag{7}$$

holds. For the latent variables $\hat{y}_t^N = L^N z_t$ we assume

(A.7) $\gamma_z(0) = \mathbf{E}z_t z_t'$ is positive definite and the minimum eigenvalue of $(L^N)'L^N$ converges to infinity for $N \to \infty$.

This assumption (together with the assumptions above) implies that

$$y_t^N = \hat{y}_t^N + u_t^N = L^N z_t + u_t^N$$

is a (static) generalized factor model as defined in Chamberlain (1983) and Chamberlain and Rothschild (1983) and the denoising can be performed by a simple static principal component analysis (PCA) as described below.

A sequence of row vectors $(a^N \in \mathbb{R}^{1\times N} \mid N \in \mathbb{N})$ with $a^N(a^N)' \to 0$ is called an *averaging sequence,* since by the property (7) it follows that $a^N u_t^N$ converges to zero in mean squares sense. This key idea has been proposed in Chamberlain (1983), however with a different name, namely "well diversified portfolio". Therefore such sequences may be used for "denoising" purposes. If $a^N y_t^N$ has a (non-zero) limit, then this limit has to be an element of the space spanned by the components of the factors z_{it}, $i = 1, \ldots, r$ in the Hilbert space L_2 of the underlying probability space $(\Omega, \mathscr{A}, P)$. A straightforward generalization is to consider sequences of matrices $(A^N \in \mathbb{R}^{r\times N} \mid N \in \mathbb{N})$ with $A^N(A^N)' \to 0 \in \mathbb{R}^{r\times r}$. Clearly

$$A^N y_t^N = A^N L^N z_t + A^N u_t^N \longrightarrow z_t$$

holds if and only if $(A^N L^N) \to I_r$ and thus averaging sequences with this property yield consistent estimates of the static factors z_t. There are a number of possible ways to construct such a denoising sequence A^N.

First let us assume that we know the factor loadings matrix L^N and the covariance matrices $\gamma_z(0)$ and $\gamma_u^N(0)$. The best (in the mean squares sense) linear estimate of z_t given y_t^N is

$$\begin{aligned}
\hat{z}_t &= \mathbf{E}(z_t(y_t^N)')\left(\mathbf{E}(y_t^N(y_t^N)')\right)^{-1} y_t^N \\
&= \gamma_z(0)(L^N)'(L^N\gamma_z(0)(L^N)' + \gamma_u^N(0))^{-1} y_t^N \\
&= \underbrace{\left(\gamma_z(0)^{-1} + (L^N)'(\gamma_u^N(0))^{-1}L^N\right)^{-1}(L^N)'(\gamma_u^N(0))^{-1}}_{=:A^N} y_t^N
\end{aligned} \tag{8}$$

This estimate is the orthogonal projection of z_t onto the space spanned by the observed variables y_t^N. If we in addition to (7) assume that the noise covariances are bounded from below by

$$\gamma_u^N(0) \geq \underline{\gamma} I_N \text{ for all } N \in \mathbb{N} \text{ with } \underline{\gamma} > 0 \tag{9}$$

then it is easy to prove that the sequence (A^N) defined above is an averaging (matrix) sequence and that $A^N L^N \to I_r$. Thus we get consistent estimates of the factor z_t. In the above formulas one may even replace $\gamma_u^N(0)$ by a rough approximation $\gamma_0 I_N$, $\gamma_0 \geq 0$ and one still gets a consistent estimate

$$\hat{z}_t = \left(\gamma_0\gamma_z(0)^{-1} + (L^N)'L^N\right)^{-1}(L^N)'y_t^N \tag{10}$$

for the factor z_t.

The latent variables are given by $\hat{y}_t^N = L^N z_t$. Therefore an obvious estimate of $\hat{y}_t^N$, for known L^N, is

$$\hat{\hat{y}}_t^N = L^N \hat{z}_t \tag{11}$$

Clearly this estimate is consistent if $\hat{z}_t$ is a consistent estimate of the true factor z_t. To be more precise if $\hat{z}_t \to z_t$ in mean squares sense then $\hat{\hat{y}}_{it} \to \hat{y}_{it}$ in mean squares sense where $\hat{y}_{it}$ and $\hat{\hat{y}}_{it}$ denote the i-th component of $\hat{y}_t^N$ and $\hat{\hat{y}}_t^N$, respectively. If we use the estimate $\hat{z}_t$ defined in (8), then $\hat{\hat{y}}_t^N = L^N \hat{z}_t$ equals the projection of $\hat{y}_t^N$ onto the space spanned by the observed variables y_t^N, i.e. $\hat{\hat{y}}_t^N = L^N \hat{z}_t$ is the best (in a mean squares sense) estimate of $\hat{y}_t^N$.

Of course in practice the above estimates are not operational because the parameters, in particular the loading matrix L^N, are not known. For many (operational) estimates the PCA is a starting point. The PCA is a decomposition of the covariance matrix $\gamma_y^N(0) = \mathbf{E} y_t^N (y_t^N)'$ of the form

$$\gamma_y^N(0) = U_1 \Lambda_1 U_1' + U_2 \Lambda_2 U_2'$$

where $U = (U_1, U_2) \in \mathbb{R}^{N \times N}$ is an orthogonal matrix whose columns are the eigenvectors of $\gamma_y^N(0)$ and $\Lambda_1 \in \mathbb{R}^{r \times r}$, $\Lambda_2 \in \mathbb{R}^{(N-r)\times(N-r)}$ are diagonal matrices with diagonal elements equal to the eigenvalues of $\gamma_y^N(0)$. The eigenvalues (and thus the diagonal entries of Λ_1 and Λ_2) are arranged in decreasing order which in particular implies that the minimal diagonal element of Λ_1 is larger than or equal to the maximum diagonal element of Λ_2. Note that U_i and Λ_i depend on the cross sectional dimension N. However, for simplicity we do not use an explicit notation for this dependence. Our assumptions together with basic properties of eigenvalues of symmetric matrices imply

$$\lambda_r(\Lambda_1) = \lambda_r(\gamma_y^N(0)) \geq \lambda_r(L^N \gamma_z(0)(L^N)') \to \infty$$

$$\lambda_1(\Lambda_2) = \lambda_{r+1}(\gamma_y^N(0)) \leq \lambda_1(\gamma_u^N(0)) \leq \overline{\gamma}$$

Here $\lambda_k(M)$ denotes the k-th eigenvalue of a symmetric matrix $M = M'$ where the eigenvalues are ordered as $\lambda_1(M) \geq \lambda_2(M) \geq \cdots$.

An estimate of z_t now is defined as

$$\hat{z}_t = \underbrace{\Lambda_1^{-1/2} U_1'}_{=:A^N} y_t^N \tag{12}$$

where $\Lambda_1^{-1/2}$ is the diagonal matrix defined by $(\Lambda_1^{-1/2})(\Lambda_1^{-1/2}) = \Lambda_1^{-1}$. This estimate, in general, is not consistent for z_t, but gives a consistent estimate for the space spanned by the components of z_t in the following sense. Let $T^N = A^N L^N$ then

$$((T^N)^{-1}\hat{z}_t - z_t) \to 0 \text{ for } N \to \infty$$

and $T^N(T^N)'$ is bounded from below and from above from a certain N_0 onwards, i.e. there exists constants $0 < \underline{c} \leq \overline{c} < \infty$ such that

$$\underline{c}I_r \leq T^N(T^N)' \leq \overline{c}I_r \text{ for all } N \geq N_0$$

First note that $A^N(A^N)' = \Lambda_1^{-1} \to 0$, i.e. (A^N) is an averaging sequence which implies that $A^N u_t^N \to 0$ and thus

$$(\hat{z}_t - T^N z_t) = A^N y_t^N - A^N L^N z_t = A^N u_t^N \to 0$$

Furthermore this implies

$$\mathbf{E}T^N z_t z_t'(T^N)' - \mathbf{E}\hat{z}_t\hat{z}_t' = T^N \gamma_z(0)(T^N)' - I_r \to 0$$

Together these two statements prove the above claim.

The latent variables then are estimated as follows. Note that $\hat{y}_{it}$ is the projection of y_{it} onto the space spanned by the components of the factor z_t since u_{it} is orthogonal to z_t. Correspondingly one may estimate the latent variables by the projection of the observed variables y_{it} onto the estimated factor $\hat{z}_t$. For the PCA estimate $\hat{z}_t$ defined in (12) we get

$$\hat{\hat{y}}_t^N = \mathbf{E}y_t^N\hat{z}_t'\left(\mathbf{E}\hat{z}_t\hat{z}_t'\right)^{-1}\hat{z}_t = \gamma_y^N(0)(A^N)'\left(A^N\gamma_y^N(0)(A^N)'\right)^{-1}A^N y_t^N = U_1U_1'y_t^N$$

Since the PCA based estimate $\hat{z}_t$ gives a consistent estimate of the space spanned by z_t one can easily show that the above estimate of the latent variables is consistent too, i.e. $\hat{\hat{y}}_{it} \longrightarrow \hat{y}_{it}$ for $N \to \infty$.

Up to now we have assumed that we have given the covariance matrix $\gamma_y^N(0)$. However, given suitable regularity assumptions which guarantee consistency of the sample covariances one can show that PCA gives consistent estimates of the factors and of the latent variables if one replaces in the above formulas the population moments with sample moments. See, e.g., Bai (2003), Bai and Ng (2002), and Stock and Watson (2002).

A slightly different route for the estimation of the factors and the latent variables is taken in Forni et al. (2005). Suppose for the moment that we have given the covariance matrices $\gamma_{\hat{y}}^N(0)$ and $\gamma_u^N(0)$ of the latent variables and the noise, respectively. A linear combination $a^N y_t^N = a^N\hat{y}_t^N + a^N u_t^N$ is close to the factor space if the variance of $a^N\hat{y}_t^N$ is large compared to the variance of $a^N u_t^N$. Therefore it makes sense to determine the weights a^N as the solution of the optimization problem

$$\max_{a\in\mathbb{R}^N} a\gamma_{\hat{y}}^N(0)a' \text{ s.t. } a\gamma_u^N(0)a' = 1$$

Iterating this argument one determines r such weighting vectors a_j, $j = 1, \ldots, r$ recursively by

$$a_j = \arg\max_{a \in \mathbb{R}^N} a\gamma_{\hat{y}}^N(0)a' \ \text{ s.t. } a\gamma_u^N(0)a' = 1 \text{ and } a\gamma_u^N(0)a_i' = 0 \text{ for } 1 \leq i < j$$

The solutions a_j are generalized eigenvectors of the pair $(\gamma_{\hat{y}}^N(0), \gamma_u^N(0))$, i.e. they satisfy

$$a_j\gamma_{\hat{y}}^N(0) = \lambda_j a_j \gamma_u^N(0), \quad j = 1, \ldots, N$$

with the normalization constraints $a_j\gamma_u^N(0)a_j' = 1$ and $a_j\gamma_u^N(0)a_i' = 0$ for $i \neq j$. The λ_j's are the associated generalized eigenvalues. Now let $A^N = ((1+\lambda_1)^{-1/2}a_1', (1+\lambda_2)^{-1/2}a_2', \ldots, (1+\lambda_1)^{-1/2}a_r')'$ and define

$$\hat{z}_t = A^N y_t^N \tag{13}$$

as an estimate for the factors z_t. It is immediate to see that $\mathbf{E}\hat{z}_t\hat{z}_t' = I_r$ and that A^N is an averaging sequence if the noise variances are bounded from below as in (9). One can also show that $\hat{z}_t$ is a consistent estimate for the factor space. The latent variables then are estimated by the projection of the latent variables onto the space spanned by the estimated factors, i.e.

$$\hat{\hat{y}}_t^N = \mathbf{E}\hat{y}_t^N\hat{z}_t' \left(\mathbf{E}\hat{z}_t\hat{z}_t'\right)^{-1} \hat{z}_t = \gamma_{\hat{y}}^N(0)(A^N)'A^N y_t^N \tag{14}$$

This estimation scheme gives the same factor space as the estimate (8) and thus the corresponding estimates for the latent variables coincide, provided that $\gamma_{\hat{y}}^N(0) = L^N\gamma_z(0)(L^N)'$ holds. In order to get a feasible estimate one has first to estimate the covariance matrices $\gamma_{\hat{y}}^N(0)$ and $\gamma_u^N(0)$. The authors Forni et al. (2005) obtain such estimates via the dynamic PCA as will be outlined at the end of Sect. 3.2. Since this procedure incorporates information about the underlying (dynamic) factor model one may hope for an improvement as compared to the (static) PCA scheme.

The above estimates for the factors and the latent variables ignore possible serial correlations which might help to improve the estimates. A possible strategy for doing so was introduced by Doz et al. (2011). Suppose that the factor process (z_t) is an AR(p) process[2] of the form $z_t = a_1 z_{t-1} + \cdots + a_p z_{t-p} + \nu_t$ where (ν_t) is a white noise process and that the noise u_t^N is a (spherical) white noise with $\gamma_u^N(0) = \mathbf{E}u_t^N(u_t^N)' = \gamma_0 I_N$. A state space model for the observed variables y_t^N is as follows:

[2]A motivation for the choice of an AR model for the static factors z_t is given in Sect. 5.

$$\underbrace{\begin{pmatrix} z_t \\ z_{t-1} \\ \vdots \\ z_{t-p+1} \end{pmatrix}}_{x_t} = \begin{pmatrix} a_1 & \cdots & a_{p-1} & a_p \\ I & & & 0 \\ & \ddots & & \\ & & I & 0 \end{pmatrix} \underbrace{\begin{pmatrix} z_{t-1} \\ z_{t-2} \\ \vdots \\ z_{t-p} \end{pmatrix}}_{x_{t-1}} + \begin{pmatrix} I \\ 0 \\ \vdots \\ 0 \end{pmatrix} \nu_t$$

$$y_t^N = (L^N, 0, \ldots, 0)x_t + u_t^N$$

With a Kalman smoother one then may obtain the best linear estimate of z_t (rsp. the state x_t) given a sample $y_1^N, \ldots, y_T^N$, i.e. the linear projection of z_t onto the space spanned by the components of $y_1^N, \ldots, y_T^N$. If the above model is correct, then this dynamic estimate of course improves the "static" estimate (8) since more information is used to construct the estimates for z_t. Furthermore one can show that this estimate is consistent even in the case that the above state space model is (slightly) miss specified, in particular even if the noise u_t^N does not satisfy the very restrictive assumptions above. The drawback of this approach is that the estimates for z_t depend both on future and past values of the observed variables y_t^N and thus this estimate is not suited for prediction purposes. Secondly the quality of the estimate depends on time t, i.e. it makes a difference whether the factors at the start ($t \approx 1$), at the end ($t \approx T$) or in the middle of the sample ($t \approx T/2$) are considered.

In order to obtain a feasible estimation algorithm one first has to estimate the parameters of the above state space model. In Doz et al. (2011) the following procedure is proposed to this end. The PCA procedure gives initial estimates $\hat{z}_t$ for the factors z_t, an estimate $\hat{L}^N = U_1 \Lambda^{1/2}$ for the factor loading matrix and $\hat{\gamma}_0 = \frac{1}{N}\mathrm{tr}(U_2 \Lambda_2 U_2')$ is an estimate for the variance of the errors u_{it}. (Note that here U_i, Λ_i are computed from the sample covariance matrix $\hat{\gamma}_y^N(0)$.) Then an AR model is fitted to the estimated factors $\hat{z}_1, \ldots, \hat{z}_T$ yielding estimates for the AR parameters $a_1, \ldots, a_p$ and the covariance matrix of the noise ν_t. It is shown in Doz et al. (2011) that (given suitable assumptions) this procedure gives consistent estimates for the factors (resp. the factor space).

3.2 *Estimation of the Dynamic Factors*

In order to estimate the dynamic factors ε_t, see Eq. (5), the concept of averaging sequences is generalized to the so-called *dynamic averaging sequences* as follows, see Forni and Lippi (2001). Let $a^N(z)$ denote a sequence of $1 \times N$ dimensional filters for which

$$\int_{-\pi}^{\pi} a^N(e^{-i\theta})(a^N(e^{-i\theta}))^* d\theta \longrightarrow 0 \ \text{ for } N \longrightarrow \infty$$

holds. Then by assumption (A.5) the filtered noise $a^N(z)u_t^N$ converges in mean squares to zero and if $a^N(z)y_t^N$ has a limit then this limit is an element of the space spanned by the factor process (ε_t).

The starting point for the estimation of ε_t and of the latent variables $\hat{y}_{it}$ is the dynamic PCA as described in Brillinger (1981, Chap. 9). Let $\lambda_j(\theta)$ and $u_j(\theta)$ denote the j-largest eigenvalue of $f_y^N(\theta)$ and $u_j(\theta)$ be the corresponding (left) eigenvector. This means we have $f_y^N(\theta) = \sum_{j=1}^N \lambda_j(\theta)u_j^*(\theta)u_j(\theta)$. (Again for simplicity we do not explicitly notate the dependence of the eigenvectors and eigenvalues on N.) Note that by assumption (A.4) $\lambda_j(\theta)$ converges to infinity for $1 \le j \le q$ and $N \to \infty$ and that $\lambda_j(\theta)$ is bounded for $j > q$. Analogously to the static PCA then estimates of the factor ε_t are defined as

$$\hat{\varepsilon}_t = A^N(z)y_t^N$$

where the (dynamic averaging) filter $A^N(z)$ are computed by

$$A^N = \sum_{k=-\infty}^{\infty} a_k^N z^k,\ (a_k^N)^* = [(a_{1k}^N)^*, \ldots, (a_{rk}^N)^*] \text{ and } a_{sk}^N = \int_{-\pi}^{\pi} \lambda_s^{-1/2}(\theta)u_s(\theta)e^{ik\theta}d\theta \tag{15}$$

Furthermore let

$$\hat{y}_t^N = (B^N(z))^* B^N(z)y_t^N \tag{16}$$

where

$$B^N(z) = \sum_{k=-\infty}^{\infty} b_k^N z^k\ ,\ (b_k^N)^* = [(b_{1k}^N)^*, \ldots, (b_{rk}^N)^*] \text{ and } b_{sk}^N = \int_{-\pi}^{\pi} u_s(\theta)e^{ik\theta}d\theta \tag{17}$$

It is proven in Forni and Lippi (2001) that these estimates are consistent for the factors and for the latent variables. In the paper Forni et al. (2000) a feasible estimation scheme is constructed based on the above ideas. First the population spectral density $f_y^N(\theta)$ is replaced by a consistent estimate, $\hat{f}_y^N(\theta)$ say. From the eigenvalue decomposition of this estimated spectral density then estimates for the filter A^N and B^N are computed as in (15) and (17). In order to get operational estimates the infinite filters furthermore are approximated by finite order filters of the form

$$\hat{A}^N = \sum_{k=-M}^{M} \hat{a}_k^N z^k \text{ and } \hat{B}^N = \sum_{k=-M}^{M} \hat{b}_k^N z^k \tag{18}$$

where the order M converges to infinity with increasing sample size. Note that the above filters (and the estimated filters) are in general two sided. This holds in particular for the filters related to the latent variables. Therefore these estimates for the latent variables are not suited for prediction purposes.

At the end of this sub-section we shortly explain the estimation of the covariance matrix of the latent variables and of the noise which is used in one of the denoising schemes explained in Sect. 3.1, see Eqs. (13) and (14). The spectral density of the estimated latent variables, see (16), is equal to $\sum_{j=1}^{r} \lambda_j(\theta) u_j^*(\theta) u_j(\theta)$ and thus the covariance matrices are estimated through

$$\hat{\gamma}_{\hat{y}}^N(0) = \int_{-\pi}^{\pi} \left[\sum_{j=1}^{r} \lambda_j(\theta) u_j^*(\theta) u_j(\theta) \right] d\theta$$

and

$$\hat{\gamma}_u^N(0) = \int_{-\pi}^{\pi} \left[\sum_{j=r+1}^{N} \lambda_j(\theta) u_j^*(\theta) u_j(\theta) \right] d\theta$$

Of course starting from a sample the eigenvalues and eigenvalues are computed from an eigenvalue decomposition of an (consistent) estimate of the spectral density f_y^N.

4 Structure Theory for the Latent Process

In this and the next section we deal with structure theory for the latent process. In this idealized setting we assume that the observations have been completely denoised and we commence from the population spectral density $f_{\hat{y}}^N$ of the latent variables $\hat{y}_t^N$, We proceed in three steps

- Spectral factorization
- Construction of a minimal static factor z_t
- Construction of a model for the dynamics of (z_t) with the dynamic factors ε_t as innovations.

4.1 *The Spectral Factorization and the Wold Representation of the Latent Process*

The following result is well known (Hannan 1970; Rozanov 1967). Here we omit the superscript N if no confusion can arise.

Theorem 1 *Every ($N \times N$-dimensional) rational spectral density $f_{\hat{y}}$ of constant rank q can be factorized as*

$$f_{\hat{y}}(\lambda) = w(e^{-i\lambda}) w(e^{-i\lambda})^* \qquad (19)$$

where

$$w(z) = \sum_{j=0}^{\infty} w_j z^j, \quad w_j \in \mathbb{R}^{N \times q}$$

is rational, analytic in $|z| \leq 1$ and has rank q for all $|z| \leq 1$. Here * denotes the conjugate transpose. In addition such a w is unique up to post multiplication by constant orthogonal matrices.

A transfer function matrix w with the above properties is called a stable, miniphase factor of $f_{\hat{y}}$. There exist q dimensional white noise (ε_t) with $\mathbf{E}\varepsilon_t \varepsilon_t' = 2\pi I_q$ such that

$$\hat{y}_t = w(z)\varepsilon_t = \sum_{j=0}^{\infty} w_j \varepsilon_{t-j} \tag{20}$$

Now let

$$w = ulv \tag{21}$$

where u and v are unimodular polynomial matrices and where l is an $N \times q$-dimensional, quasi diagonal rational matrix whose (i,i)-th element is of the form $n_i(z)/d_i(z)$ where n_i, d_i are coprime and monic polynomials and n_i divides n_{i+1} and d_{i+1} divides d_i. Then (21) is called the Smith McMillan form of $w(z)$ (Hannan and Deistler 1988, Chap. 2). As easily seen a particular left inverse of w is

$$w^- = v^{-1}(l'l)^{-1}l'u^{-1} \tag{22}$$

where w^- is rational and has no poles and zeros for $|z| \leq 1$. This implies that (20) is already a Wold representation and the innovations ε_t in (20) are minimal dynamic factors.

A transfer function matrix w is called *zeroless* if all numerator polynomials of the diagonal elements of l are equal to one. In this case w^- is a polynomial matrix.

4.2 Minimal Static Factor

From (4) it is clear that x_t^N is a static factor, which is not necessarily minimal, as discussed below. Then

$$\operatorname{rk} \underbrace{\mathbf{E}\hat{y}_t^N(\hat{y}_t^N)'}_{=\gamma_{\hat{y}}^N(0)} = \operatorname{rk} H^N \mathbf{E}x_t^N(x_t^N)'(H^N) \leq n$$

and therefore, by (A.6), $\text{rk}\gamma_{\hat{y}}^N(0)$ is bounded by n, independent of N. This implies that the rank of $\gamma_{\hat{y}}^N(0)$ is constant from a certain N_0 onwards. Let r denote this rank, i.e. let $\text{rk}(\gamma_{\hat{y}}^N(0)) = r$ for all $N \geq N_0$. Furthermore, we see that also the minimal static factor z_t can be chosen independent of N. Take, for instance, a z_t consisting of the first basis elements in $\hat{y}_t^N$ spanning the space generated by the components of $\hat{y}_t^N$ in the Hilbert space L_2. Minimal static factors are unique up to premultiplication by constant non-singular matrices. They may be obtained via a factorization

$$\gamma_{\hat{y}}^N(0) = L^N(L^N)', \;\; L^N \in \mathbb{R}^{N \times r}, \;\; \text{rk}(L^N) = r$$

of the covariance matrix $\gamma_{\hat{y}}^N(0)$ as

$$z_t = \underbrace{\left((L^N)'L^N\right)^{-1}(L^N)'}_{L^{N-}} \hat{y}_t^N \tag{23}$$

Clearly z_t has a rational spectral density of the form

$$f_z(\theta) = L^{N-} f_{\hat{y}}^N (L^{N-})'$$

and, for $q < r$, f_z is singular. Note that

$$z_t = \underbrace{L^{N-} w^N(z)}_{=k^N(z)} \varepsilon_t^N = k^N(z)\varepsilon_t^N \tag{24}$$

is a Wold representation of (z_t), because $w^{N-}L^N z_t = \varepsilon_t^N$ and $w^{N-}L^N$ is a causal transfer function. Thus $k^N(z)$ is a causal miniphase spectral factor of f_z. Since such a spectral factor is unique up to post multiplication by non-singular matrices it follows that we may chose ε_t and k independent of N.

Remark A.1 As shown above (A.6) implies that the rank of $\gamma_{\hat{y}}^N(0)$ is bounded. Vice versa it is easy to see that a bound on the rank of $\gamma_{\hat{y}}^N(0)$ implies (A.6) under our assumptions (A.1)–(A.5).

4.3 State Space Realizations for the Latent Process and the Minimal Static Factors

The problem of realization is to find a system for a given transfer function. Here our focus is on state space systems, for instance for a minimal static factor $z_t = k(z)\varepsilon_t$ we have

$$x_{t+1} = Fx_t + G\varepsilon_{t+1} \tag{25}$$

$$z_t = C x_t \tag{26}$$

where x_t is an n-dimensional, say, (minimal) state and $F \in \mathbb{R}^{n \times n}$, $G \in \mathbb{R}^{n \times q}$, $C \in \mathbb{R}^{r \times n}$ are parameter matrices. We assume minimality (i.e. the system (25), (26) is controllable and observable), stability, i.e.

$$|\lambda_{\max}(F)| < 1$$

where $\lambda_{\max}(F)$ is an eigenvalue of F of maximum modulus and the miniphase condition, i.e. that

$$M(z) = \begin{pmatrix} I - Fz & -G \\ C & 0 \end{pmatrix} \tag{27}$$

has rank $n + q$ for $|z| \leq 1$. Note that the zeros of $M(z)$ are the zeros of $k(z) = C(I - Fz)^{-1}G$ as defined via its Smith McMillan form (see Kailath 1980). For given k a unique state space realization may be obtained, e.g. by echelon forms, see Deistler et al. (2010).

From this state space realization we immediately get a state space realization for the latent variables $\hat{y}_t^N = L^N z_t$

$$x_{t+1} = F x_t + G \varepsilon_{t+1} \tag{28}$$

$$\hat{y}_t^N = \underbrace{L^N C}_{H^N} x_t = H^N x_t \tag{29}$$

This state space system is minimal, stable and miniphase. We also see that due to our assumptions the state x_t, the innovations ε_t and the matrices F and G may be chosen independent of N, compare (3) and (4). Only the matrix H^N depends on N, however note that the H^N's are nested, i.e. the first N rows of H^{N+1} coincide with H^N.

The rational transfer function $k(z)$ in (24) may be written as a left matrix fraction $k(z) = a^{-1}(z)b(z)$ (Hannan and Deistler 1988, Chap. 2) giving rise to an ARMA realization

$$a(z)z_t = b(z)\varepsilon_t$$

where we w.r.o.g. assume that $(a(z), b(z))$ are left coprime, stable and miniphase.

Alternatively, we may write a right matrix fraction

$$k(z) = d(z)c^{-1}(z)$$

see Forni et al. (2005). This gives rise to a factor representation of $\hat{y}_t^N$ of the form

$$\hat{y}_t^N = D^N(z)\mu_t, \quad D^N(z) = L^N d(z) \quad \text{and } c(z)\mu_t = \varepsilon_t$$

i.e. with a minimal dynamic factor μ_t which is an AR process and a factor loading matrix $D^N(z) = L^N d(z)$ which is a finite impulse response filter.

5 Zeroless Transfer Functions and Singular AR Systems

In this section we will show that for the case $r > q$, generically, the static factor can be modeled by an AR system. This is important because estimation of AR systems is much easier compared to the ARMA case.

Let us repeat that a transfer function is called zeroless if all numerator polynomials in l in its Smith McMillan form are equal to one.

Lemma 1 *The transfer function $w(z)$ is zeroless if and only if $k(z)$ is zeroless.*

Proof As is shown in Kailath (1980), $w(z)$ is zeroless if and only if the associated $M(z)$ in (27) has rank $n + q$ for all $z \in \mathbb{C}$. An analogous statement holds for $k(z)$ and thus

$$\begin{pmatrix} I - Fz & -G \\ H^N & 0 \end{pmatrix} = \begin{pmatrix} I & 0 \\ 0 & L^N \end{pmatrix} \begin{pmatrix} I - Fz & -G \\ C & 0 \end{pmatrix} \tag{30}$$

together with $\mathrm{rk}(L^N) = r$ yields the desired result. □

The proof of the theorem below is given in Anderson and Deistler (2008b) and Anderson et al. (2013). Note that a property is said to hold generically on a given set, if it holds on an open and dense subset.

Theorem 2 *Consider the set of all minimal state space systems (F, G, C) for given state dimension n, output dimension r and input dimension q, where $r > q$ holds. Then the corresponding transfer functions are zeroless for generic values of $(F, G, C) \in \mathbb{R}^{n\times n} \times \mathbb{R}^{n\times q} \times \mathbb{R}^{r\times n}$.*

The theorem states, that, in a certain setting, tall transfer functions are generically zeroless. For simple special cases this is immediate. Consider, e.g., the MA(1) case for $r = 2$, $q = 1$:

$$\begin{aligned} z_{1t} &= b_{11}\varepsilon_t + b_{12}\varepsilon_{t-1} \\ z_{2t} &= b_{21}\varepsilon_t + b_{22}\varepsilon_{t-1} \end{aligned}$$

then the system is zeroless whenever

$$b_{11}b_{22} - b_{12}b_{21} \neq 0$$

holds.

We have (see Anderson and Deistler 2008a)

Theorem 3 *Let k denote a stable miniphase factor of the spectral density f_z of (z_t). (Remember that such a factor is unique up to post multiplication with non-singular matrices.) The following statements are equivalent*

1) k is zeroless.
2) There exist a polynomial left inverse k^- for k.
3) (z_t) is an AR process, i.e.

$$z_t = a_1 z_{t-1} + \cdots + a_p z_{t-p} + \nu_t \tag{31}$$

where

$$\det(I - a_1 z - \cdots - a_p z^p) \neq 0 \ \ for\ |z| \leq 1 \tag{32}$$

and (ν_t) is white noise with $\gamma_\nu(0) = \mathbf{E}\nu_t\nu_t'$ and $\mathrm{rk}(\gamma_\nu(0)) = q$.

Remark A.2 We call an AR system (31) *regular* if $\mathrm{rk}(\gamma_\nu(0)) = r$ and *singular* if $\mathrm{rk}(\gamma_\nu(0)) < r$ holds. This means that in the case $q < r$ we have to deal with singular AR systems. Clearly we may write (31) as

$$a(z)z_t = b\varepsilon_t \tag{33}$$

where $\gamma_\varepsilon(0) = \mathbf{E}\varepsilon_t\varepsilon_t' = I_q$ and $\mathrm{rk}(b) = q$, and where $\gamma_\nu(0) = bb'$ holds.

Remark A.3 Two AR systems $(a(z), b)$ and $(\bar{a}(z), \bar{b})$ are called *observationally equivalent* if their transfer functions $a^{-1}(z)b$ and $\bar{a}^{-1}(z)\bar{b}$ are the same up to post multiplication by an orthogonal matrix. Let $\delta(a(z))$ denote the degree of $a(z)$. We assume throughout that the specified degree of $a(z)$ is given by p, i.e. $\delta(a(z)) \leq p$, the stability condition (32), and $a(0) = I$. Note that our notion of observational equivalence is based on the stationary solution

$$z_t = a^{-1}(z)b\varepsilon_t$$

and does not take into account other solutions, compare Deistler et al. (2011).

Proof Let

$$k = u \begin{bmatrix} l \\ 0_{r-q\times q} \end{bmatrix} v$$

denote the Smith McMillan form of k, where u, v are two unimodular matrices, l is a $q \times q$ diagonal matrix and $0_{r-q\times q}$ denotes a zero matrix of suitable dimension. The i-th diagonal entry of l is $n_i(z)/d_i(z)$ where n_i, d_i are coprime and monic polynomials. The spectral factor k is zeroless if and only if $n_i = 1$ holds for $i = 1, \ldots, q$.

Clearly

$$k^- = v^{-1} \begin{bmatrix} l^{-1} & 0 \end{bmatrix} u^{-1}$$

is a left inverse of k and k^- is polynomial if and only if k is zeroless. Note that this left inverse corresponds to (22). This proves 1) $\Rightarrow$ 2). Conversely, if there exist a polynomial left inverse, k^- say, then $k^-k = I_q$ implies $k^-u_1 l = v^{-1}$ where $u = [u_1, u_2]$ has been partitioned conformingly. This implies $n_i(z) \neq 0$ for all $z \in \mathbb{C}$ and thus k must be zeroless.

Next we define

$$\bar{k} = u \begin{bmatrix} l & 0_{q \times r-q} \\ 0_{r-q \times q} & I_q \end{bmatrix} \begin{bmatrix} v & 0_{q \times r-q} \\ 0_{r-q \times q} & I_{r-q} \end{bmatrix}$$

which gives

$$z_t = k(z)\varepsilon_t = \bar{k}(z) \begin{bmatrix} \varepsilon_t \\ 0_{r-q} \end{bmatrix}$$

and thus

$$\begin{bmatrix} \varepsilon_t \\ 0_{r-q} \end{bmatrix} = \bar{k}^{-1}(z) z_t = \begin{bmatrix} v^{-1}(z) & 0_{q \times r-q} \\ 0_{r-q \times q} & I_{r-q} \end{bmatrix} \begin{bmatrix} l^{-1}(z) & 0_{q \times r-q} \\ 0_{r-q \times q} & I_q \end{bmatrix} u^{-1}(z) z_t$$

If k is zeroless, then $\bar{k}^{-1}$ is polynomial and premultiplying the above equation with $\bar{k}(0)$ yields a *stable* AR system

$$\underbrace{\bar{k}(0)\bar{k}(z)^{-1}}_{a(z)} z_t = a(z) z_t = \underbrace{\bar{k}(0) \begin{bmatrix} \varepsilon_t \\ 0_{r-q} \end{bmatrix}}_{\nu_t} = \nu_t$$

with $a(0) = I_r$. Thus 1) $\Rightarrow$ 3).

To prove the converse first note that (see, e.g., Anderson and Deistler 2008b) k is zeroless if and only if for every left coprime MFD $\bar{a}^{-1}\bar{b} = k$, the polynomial matrix $\bar{b}$ is zeroless. If we start with an AR system (33), then for $q < r$, the pair $(a(z), b)$ is not necessarily left coprime. By $a(0) = I$, the greatest common divisor $r(z)$ of $(a(z), b)$ may be chosen with $r(0) = I$ and thus extracting such a common divisor (see Hannan and Deistler 1988; Kailath 1980) we obtain a left coprime system $(\tilde{a}(z), b)$ (where b remains the same) and thus, as $\mathrm{rk}(b) = q$, $k = a(z)^{-1}b = \tilde{a}^{-1}(z)b$ is zeroless. □

The next theorem (see Anderson et al. 2012a) states that for $(\bar{a}(z), b)$ non-necessarily left coprime, there is an observationally equivalent left coprime pair $(a(z), b)$ satisfying the same degree restriction p.

Theorem 4 *Every AR system $(\bar{a}(z), b)$ with $\delta(\bar{a}(z)) \leq p$ can be transformed to an observationally equivalent AR system $(a(z), b)$ such that $\delta(a(z)) \leq p$ and $(a(z), b)$ are left coprime.*

6 The Yule–Walker Equations

As is well known and has been stated before, in the usual (regular) case, estimation of AR systems is much easier than estimation of ARMA systems or state space systems, because AR systems can be estimated, e.g., by the Yule–Walker equations, which are linear in the AR parameters, whereas in the ARMA (or state space) case usually numerical optimization procedures are applied. This also holds for the singular case and shows the importance of Theorem 2.

The Yule–Walker equations are of the form

$$(a_1, \ldots, a_p)\Gamma_p = (\gamma_z(1), \ldots, \gamma_z(p)) \tag{34}$$

$$\gamma_\nu(0) = \gamma_z(0) - (a_1, \ldots, a_p)(\gamma_z(1), \ldots, \gamma_z(p))' \tag{35}$$

where $\gamma_z(j) = \mathbf{E}z_{t+j}z_t'$ and

$$\Gamma_m = (\gamma_z(j-i))_{i,j=1,\ldots,m}$$

are the population moments of (z_t). From an estimator $\hat{z}_t$ of z_t, these second moments can be estimated and yield a Yule–Walker estimator of $(a_1, \ldots, a_p)$ and $\gamma_\nu(0)$ via (34) and (35).

As is well known and easy to see, Γ_m for a regular AR process is non-singular for all m. On the other hand for a singular AR process, premultiplying (31) by a vector $a \neq 0$ such that $a\gamma_\nu(0) = 0$ yields a dependence relation between the components in $(z_t', z_{t-1}', \ldots, z_{t-p}')$ and thus Γ_{p+1} is singular. However, the matrix Γ_p may be singular or non-singular. Now (33) may be written in companion form as

$$\underbrace{\begin{pmatrix} z_t \\ z_{t-1} \\ \vdots \\ z_{t-p+1} \end{pmatrix}}_{x_t} = \underbrace{\begin{pmatrix} a_1 & \cdots & a_{p-1} & a_p \\ I & & & 0 \\ & \ddots & & \\ & & I & 0 \end{pmatrix}}_{F} \underbrace{\begin{pmatrix} z_{t-1} \\ z_{t-2} \\ \vdots \\ z_{t-p} \end{pmatrix}}_{x_{t-1}} + \underbrace{\begin{pmatrix} b \\ 0 \\ \vdots \\ 0 \end{pmatrix}}_{G} \varepsilon_t$$

$$z_t = (I, 0, \ldots, 0)x_t$$

As is well known and easy to see,

$$\Gamma_p = \mathbf{E}x_t x_t'$$

is non-singular if and only if (F, G) is controllable. For this case, the Yule–Walker equations (34) and (35) have a unique solution. As shown in Anderson et al. (2012b) (F, G) is generically controllable in the parameter space. However, in this context, the notion of genericity has to be used with care, as it depends on the choice of p.

If Γ_p is singular, of course the solution of (34) are not unique, where $\gamma_\nu(0)$ remains unique. Because of the linearity the solution set of (34) has an affine structure in the sense that every row of $(a_1, \dots, a_p)$ is of the form one particular solution plus the left kernel of Γ_p. Since $\gamma_z(j)$, $j > p$ are uniquely determined by $\gamma_z(k)$, $k = 0, \dots, p$ the solution set of (34) is the set of all observationally equivalent AR systems (without imposing the stability condition (32)). The structure of the solution set has been discussed in Chen et al. (2011). In case of singular Γ_p, uniqueness in (34) may be achieved by taking the minimum norm solution (see Deistler et al. 2010; Filler 2010) or by describing column degrees in a(z) (see Deistler et al. 2011).

7 Estimation and Model Selection

Structure theory as described in the previous sections is important for understanding data driven modeling for GDFMs. In general terms, here, data driven modeling consists of two main parts, parameter estimation and model selection, where the latter is performed by estimation of integers such as r or q. We do not treat estimation (and in particular properties of estimators) in detail here. Let us only mention that the estimation procedure we have in mind (and we had also in mind in Deistler et al. 2010) is of the following form:

1. Estimation of the (minimal) dimension r of the static factors z_t as well as the static factor itself using a PCA on $\gamma_y^N(0)$, as described in Sect. 3.1.
2. Estimate the maximum lag p in the AR system (33) from the given $\hat{z}_t$ using an information criterion and estimate $a_1, \dots, a_p$ from the Yule–Walker equations as described in Sect. 6.
   If the estimate of Γ_p is "close to being singular", a truncation procedure as described in Deistler et al. (2010) and Filler (2010) or a specification of columns degrees in $a(z)$ as in Deistler et al. (2011) may be used.
3. Using the Yule–Walker estimate for the covariance of ν_t in (31) a PCA is performed to estimate the dimension of the minimal dynamic factors, as well as ε_t itself and thus of b in (33).

Remark A.4 Under a number of additional assumptions, for instance assumptions guaranteeing that the sample second moments converge to their population counter parts, the procedure sketched above can be shown to be consistent. There is a number of alternative procedures available (see, e.g., Doz et al. 2012; Stock and Watson 2002) and in addition our procedure may be improved, for instance by iterations.

Remark A.5 Our focus is on data driven modeling of the latent variables. However, sometimes also noise models, e.g. univariate AR systems for the components of u_t, are used.

8 Summary

Forecasting and analysis of high dimensional time series is part of the "big data revolution" and it is important in many areas of application. GDFMs which have been proposed slightly more than a decade ago (Forni et al. 2000; Forni and Lippi 2001; Stock and Watson 2002) are an important tool for this task. In our contribution we present a structure theory for this model class. In particular we consider denoising and realization, the latter in the sense of finding a system representation for the spectral density of the latent variables. The importance of AR modeling is emphasized. Yule–Walker equations and their solutions are discussed. Finally an estimation procedure making use of the structure theory is described.

References

Anderson, B. D. O., & Deistler, M. (2008a). Generalized linear dynamic factor models—a structure theory. In *47th IEEE Conference on Decision and Control, CDC 2008* (pp. 1980–1985).

Anderson, B. D. O., & Deistler, M. (2008b). Properties of zero-free transfer function matrices. *SICE Journal of Control, Measurement, and System Integration, 1*(4), 284–292.

Anderson, B. D. O., Deistler, M., Chen, W., & Filler, A. (2012). Autoregressive models of singular spectral matrices. *Automatica, 48*(11), 2843–2849.

Anderson, B. D. O., Deistler, M., Felsenstein, E., Funovits, B., Zadrozny, P., & Eichler, M., et al. (2012). Identifiability of regular and singular multivariate autoregressive models from mixed frequency data. In *IEEE 51st Annual Conference on Decision and Control (CDC)* (pp. 184–189).

Anderson, B. D. O., Deistler, M., & Filler, A. (2013). *Generic properties of system zeros*. Manuscript, Research Group Econometrics and System Theory, TU Vienna.

Bai, J. (2003) Inferential theory for factor models of large dimension. *Econometrica, 71*(1), 135–171.

Bai, J., & Ng, S. (2002). Determining the number of factors in approximate factor models. *Econometrica, 70*(1), 191–221.

Brillinger, D. R. (1981). *Time series data analysis and theory*. San-Francisco/London: Holden-Day.

Chamberlain, G. (1983). Funds, factors, and diversification in arbitrage pricing models. *Econometrica, 51*(5), 1305–1323.

Chamberlain, G., & Rothschild, M. (1983). Arbitrage, factor structure, and mean-variance analysis on large asset markets. *Econometrica, 51*(5), 1281–1304.

Chen, W., Anderson, B. D., Deistler, M., & Filler, A. (2011). Solutions of Yule-Walker equations for singular AR processes. *Journal of Time Series Analysis, 32*(5), 531–538.

Deistler, M., Anderson, B. D. O., Filler, A., & Chen, W. (2010). Modelling high dimensional time series by generalized factor models. In *Proceedings of the 19th International Symposium on Mathematical Theory of Networks and Systems* (MTNS 2010 - July, 2010, Budapest, Hungary) (pp. 323–329). Piscataway, USA: Institute of Electrical and Electronics Engineers (IEEE Inc.).

Deistler, M., Anderson, B. D. O., Filler, A., Zinner, C., & Chen, W. (2010). Generalized linear dynamic factor models—an approach via singular autoregression. *European Journal of Control, 16*(3), 211–224.

Deistler, M., Filler, A., & Funovits, M. (2011). AR systems and AR processes: The singular case. *Communications in Informatics and Systems, 11*(3), 225–236.

Doan, T., Litterman, R., & Sims, C. (1984). Forecasting and conditional projection using realistic prior distribution. *Econometric Reviews, 3*, 1–100.
Doz, C., Giannone, D., & Reichlin, L. (2011). A two-step estimator for large approximate dynamic factor models based on Kalman filtering. *Journal of Econometrics, 164*(1), 188–205 (Annals Issue on Forecasting).
Doz, C., Giannone, D., & Reichlin, L. (2012). A quasi-maximum likelihood approach for large, approximate dynamic factor models. *The Review of Economics and Statistics, 94*(4), 1014–1024.
Engle, R., & Watson, M. (1981). A one-factor multivariate time series model of metropolitan wage rates. *Journal of the American Statistical Association, 76*(376), 774–781.
Filler, A. (2010). *Generalized dynamic factor models; structure theory and estimation for single frequency and mixed frequency data* (Ph.D. thesis). Technische Universität Wien.
Flamm, C., Kalliauer, U., Deistler, M., Waser, M., & Graef, A. (2012). Graphs for dependence and causality in multivariate time series. In L. Wang & G. Hugues, (Eds.), *System identification, environmental modelling, and control system design*, Chap. 7 (pp. 133–151). London: Springer.
Forni, M., Hallin, M., Lippi, M., & Reichlin, L. (2000). The generalized dynamic-factor model: Identification and estimation. *The Review of Economics and Statistics, 82*(4), 540–554.
Forni, M., Hallin, M., Lippi, M., & Reichlin, L. (2005). The generalized dynamic factor model. *Journal of the American Statistical Association, 100*(471), 830–840.
Forni, M., Hallin, M., Lippi, M., & Zaffaroni, P. (2011). *One-sided representations of generalized dynamic factor models*. Working Papers ECARES 2011-019, ULB - Universite Libre de Bruxelles.
Forni, M., & Lippi, M. (2001). The generalized dynamic factor model: Representation theory. *Econometric Theory, 17*, 1113–114.
Geweke, J. F. (1977). The dynamic factor analysis of economic time series. In D. Aigner & A. Goldberger (Eds.), *Latent variables in socioeconomic models*. Amsterdam: North Holland.
Hallin, M., & Liška, R. (2007). Determining the number of factors in the general dynamic factor model. *Journal of the American Statistical Association, 102*(478), 603–617.
Hannan, E. J. (1970). *Multiple time series*. New York: Wiley.
Hannan, E. J., & Deistler, M. (2012). *The statistical theory of linear systems*. Classics in applied mathematics. Philadelphia: SIAM (Originally published: Wiley, New York, 1988).
Kailath, T. (1980). *Linear systems*. New Jersey: Prentice Hall/Englewood Cliffs.
Rozanov, Y. A. (1967). *Stationary random processes*. San Francisco: Holden-Day.
Sargent, T. J., & Sims, C. A. (1977). Business cycle modeling without pretending to have too much a priori economic theory. In C. A. Sims (Ed.), *New methods in business cycle research: Proceedings from a conference* (pp. 45–109). Minneapolis: Federal Reserve Bank of Minneapolis.
Scherrer, W., & Deistler, M. (1998). A structure theory for linear dynamic errors-in-variables models. *SIAM Journal on Control and Optimization, 36*(6), 2148–2175.
Stock, J. H., & Watson, M. W. (2002). Forecasting using principal components from a large number of predictors. *Journal of the American Statistical Association, 97*(460), 1167–1179.

Forecasting Under Structural Change

Liudas Giraitis, George Kapetanios, Mohaimen Mansur, and Simon Price

Abstract Forecasting strategies that are robust to structural breaks have earned renewed attention in the literature. They are built on weighted averages downweighting past information and include forecasting with rolling window, exponential smoothing or exponentially weighted moving average and forecast pooling. These simple strategies are particularly attractive because they are easy to implement, possibly robust to different types of structural change and can adjust for breaks in real time. This review introduces the dynamic model to be forecast, explains in detail how the data-dependent tuning parameter for discounting the past data is selected and how basic forecasts are constructed and the forecast error estimated. It comments on the forecast error and the impact of weak and strong dependence of noise on the quality of the prediction. It also describes various forecasting methods and evaluates their practical performance in robust forecasting.

1 Introduction

Dealing with structural change has become one of the most crucial challenges in economic and financial time series modelling and forecasting. In econometrics, structural change usually refers to evolution of a parameter of interest of a dynamic model that makes its estimation and/or prediction unstable. The change can be as dramatic as an abrupt shift or permanent break caused, for example, by introduction of a new monetary policy, breakdown of an exchange rate regime or sudden rise in oil price; or the change can be slow, smooth and continuous induced, for example, by gradual progress in technology or production. Empirical evidence of structural change is widespread and well documented. Stock and Watson (1996) investigate

L. Giraitis (✉) • G. Kapetanios • M. Mansur
Queen Mary, University of London, London, UK
e-mail: L.Giraitis@qmul.ac.uk; G.Kapetanios@qmul.ac.uk; M.Mansur@qmul.ac.uk

S. Price
Bank of England, London, UK

City University, London, UK
e-mail: simon.price@bankofengland.gsi.gov.uk

J. Beran et al. (eds.), *Empirical Economic and Financial Research*,
Advanced Studies in Theoretical and Applied Econometrics 48,
DOI 10.1007/978-3-319-03122-4_25

many US macroeconomic time series and find instability in both univariate and bivariate relationships. In finance, structural changes are detected in interest rates (see, e.g., Garcia and Perron 1996; Ang and Bekaert 2002) and stock prices and returns (see, e.g., Timmermann 2001; Pesaran and Timmermann 2002). Such structural change or parameter instability has been identified as one of the main culprits for forecast failures (see Hendry 2000) and, not surprisingly, detection of breaks and forecast strategies in the presence of breaks have earned a lot of attention among researchers. Nonetheless, real time forecasting of time series which are subject to structural change remains to be a critical challenge to date and is often complicated further by presence of other features of time series such as persistence (see Rossi 2012).

A natural strategy for forecasting in an unstable environment would be finding the last change point and using only the post-break data for estimation of a model and forecasting. However, standard tests of structural breaks are hardly suitable for real time forecasting, small breaks are difficult to detect, and the amount of post-break data may be insufficient. Moreover, Pesaran and Timmermann (2007) point out that a trade-off between bias and forecast error variance implies that it is not always optimal to use only post-break data, and generally beneficial to include some pre-break information.

A second line of strategies involves formally modelling the break process itself and estimating its characteristics such as timing, size and duration. A standard model of this kind is the Markov-switching model of Hamilton (1989). Clements and Krolzig (1998), however, demonstrate via a Monte Carlo study that despite the true data generating process being Markov-switching regime, switching models fail to forecast as accurately as a simple linear AR(1) model in many instances.

Research on Bayesian methods learning about change-points from past and exploiting this information as priors in modelling and forecasting continues to evolve rapidly (see, e.g., Pesaran et al. 2006; Koop and Potter 2007; Maheu and Gordon 2008). As an alternative to the dilemma of whether to restrict the number of breaks occurring in-sample to be fixed or to treat it as unknown, a class of the time-varying parameter (TVP) models arises, which assume that a change occurs each point in time (see, e.g., Stock and Watson 2007; D'Agostino et al. 2013).

The difficulty in finding a single best forecasting model leads to the idea of combining forecasts of different models by averaging (see, e.g., Pesaran and Timmermann 2007; Clark and McCracken 2010).

Robust forecasting approaches have earned renewed attention in the literature. This class of methods builds on downweighting past information and includes forecasting with rolling windows, exponential smoothing or exponentially weighted moving averages (EWMA), forecast pooling with window averaging, etc. These simple strategies are particularly attractive because they are easy to implement, possibly robust to different types of structural change and can adjust for breaks without delay, which is particularly helpful for real time forecasting. On the downside, a priori selected fixed rate discounting of the old data may prove costly when the true model is break-free.

A significant contribution in this respect is due to Pesaran and Timmermann (2007). These authors explore two strategies: one is selecting a single window by cross-validation based on pseudo-out-of-sample losses and the other is pooling forecasts from the same model obtained with different window sizes which should perform well in situations where the breaks are mild and hence difficult to detect. The issue of structural change occurring in real time and the challenge it poses for time series forecasting is partly but systematically addressed in Eklund et al. (2010). They exploit data-downweighting break-robust methods. One crucial question they do not answer is how much to downweight older data. The challenge of forecasting under recent and ongoing structural change has been dealt in a generic setting in a recent work of Giraitis et al. (2013). Alongside breaks these authors consider various other types of structural changes including deterministic and stochastic trends and smooth cycles. They exploit the typical data-discounting robust-to-break models such as rolling windows, EWMA, forecast averaging over different windows and various extensions of them. However, they make the selection of the tuning parameter which defines the discounting weights data-dependent by minimising the forecast mean squared error. They provide detailed theoretical and simulation analyses of their proposal and convincing evidence of good performance of methods with data-selected discount rates when applied to a number of US macroeconomic and financial time series.

While Giraitis et al. (2013) consider persistence in time series through short memory autoregressive dependence in noise process, they do not explore the possibility of long memory which is often considered as a common but crucial property of many economic and financial series. Mansur (2013) extends the work of Giraitis et al. (2013) by offering a more complex yet realistic forecasting environment where structural change in a dynamic model is accompanied by noises with long range dependence. This adds a new dimension to the existing challenge of real time forecasting under structural changes. It also contributes to an interesting and ongoing argument in the econometric literature about possible "spurious" relationship between long range dependence and structural change and potential forecasting difficulties this may create. Many researchers argue that presence of long memory in the data can be easily confused with structural change (see, e.g., Diebold and Inoue 2001; Gourieroux and Jasiak 2001; Granger and Hyung 2004; Kapetanios 2006). This aggravates the already difficult problem of forecasting under structural change further. Given that it is often difficult to distinguish between the two, it is desirable to establish forecast methods that are robust to structural change and also appropriately account for long memory persistence.

The rest of the paper is structured as follows. Section 2 introduces the dynamic model to be forecast that was proposed and developed in Giraitis et al. (2013) and Mansur (2013). We discuss in detail how the tuning parameter defining the rate of downweighting is optimally selected from data and how forecasts are constructed. Section 3 contains theoretical results and Sect. 4 reviews the forecast strategies and presents Monte Carlo evidence for evaluation of performance of robust forecast strategies.

2 Adaptive Forecast Strategy

Our adaptive forecast strategy aims at out-of-sample forecasting under minimal structural assumptions. It seeks to adapt to the unknown model and does not involve model fitting and parameter estimation. Such forecasting introduced in Pesaran and Timmermann (2007) and Eklund et al. (2010) was subsequently developed by Giraitis et al. (2013). It considers a simple but general location model given by

$$y_t = \beta_t + u_t, \quad t = 1, 2, \ldots, T \tag{1}$$

where y_t is the variable to be forecast, β_t is a persistent process ("signal") of unknown type and u_t is a dependent noise. Unlike most of the previous works where β_t's mainly describe structural breaks, this framework offers more flexibility and generality in the sense that it does not impose any structure on a deterministic and stochastic trend β_t and adapts to its changes, such as structural breaks in the mean.

While Giraitis et al. (2013) specify the noise u_t to be a stationary short memory process, Mansur (2013) explores the possibility of long range dependence in the noise. Standard definitions in the statistical literature define short memory as the absolute summability of the auto-covariances $\gamma_u(k) = \text{Cov}(u_{j+k}, u_j)$, $\sum_{k=0}^{\infty} |\gamma_u(k)| < \infty$, and long memory as the slow decay of $\gamma_u(k) \sim c_\gamma k^{-1+2d}$, as k increases, for some $0 < d < 1/2$ and $c_\gamma > 0$. Unlike short memory, the autocorrelations of long memory processes are non-summable.

One can expect the long memory noise process u_t to generate substantial amount of persistence itself, which is a common feature of economic and financial time series, to be forecast by our adaptive method, and to feed into y_t diluting the underlying model structure. Forecasting perspectives of such persistent series y_t, undergoing structural change, are of great interest in applications.

The downweighting forecasting method relies simply on a weighted combination of historical data. A forecast of y_t is based on (local) averaging of past values $y_{t-1}, \ldots, y_1$:

$$\hat{y}_{t|t-1,H} = \sum_{j=1}^{t-1} w_{tj,H}\, y_{t-j} = w_{t1,H}\, y_{t-1} + \ldots + w_{t,t-1,H}\, y_1 \tag{2}$$

with weights $w_{tj,H} \geq 0$ such that $w_{t1,H} + \ldots + w_{t,t-1,H} = 1$ and parameterised by a single tuning parameter H. Two types of weighting schemes are particularly popular in practice, namely the rolling window and the EWMA. Such forecasting requires choosing a tuning parameter which determines the rate at which past information will be discounted. Performance of such forecast methods using a priori selected tuning parameter is known to be sensitive to the choice of the tuning parameter, see Pesaran and Pick (2011) and Eklund et al. (2010). Clearly, setting the discounting parameter to a single fixed value is a risky strategy and unlikely to produce accurate forecasts if a series is subject to structural change.

Adaptive Methods Giraitis et al. (2013) advocate a data-dependent selection of the tuning parameter H and provide theoretical justification on how such a selection can be optimal. It does not require any particular modelling and estimation of the structure of β_t. The data based tuning parameter H is chosen on the basis of in-sample forecast performance evaluated over a part of the sample. The structure of the kernel type weights $w_{tj,H}$ is described in what follows.

Their definition requires a kernel function $K(x) \geq 0$, $x \geq 0$ which is continuous and differentiable on its support, such that $\int_0^\infty K(u)du = 1$, $K(0) > 0$, and for some $C > 0, c > 0$,

$$K(x) \leq C\exp(-c|x|), \quad |(d/dx)K(x)| \leq C/(1+x^2), \qquad x > 0.$$

For $t \geq 1$, $H > 0$, we set

$$w_{tj,H} = \frac{K(j/H)}{\sum_{s=1}^{t-1} K(s/H)}, \qquad j = 1, \cdots, t-1.$$

Examples The main classes of commonly used weights, such as rolling window weights, exponential weights, triangular window weights, etc. satisfy this assumption.

(i) *Rolling window* weights $w_{tj,H}$, $j = 1, 2, \ldots.., t-1$, correspond to $K(u) = I(0 \leq u \leq 1)$. They are defined as follows:
for $H < t$, $w_{tj,H} = H^{-1}I(1 \leq j \leq H)$;
for $H \geq t$, $w_{tj,H} = (t-1)^{-1}I(1 \leq j \leq t-1)$, where I is the indicator function.

(ii) *EWMA* weights are defined with $K(x) = e^{-x}$, $x \in [0, \infty)$. Then, with $\rho = \exp(-1/H) \in (0, 1)$,
$K(j/H) = \rho^j$, $w_{tj,H} = \rho^j / \sum_{k=1}^{t-1} \rho^k$, $1 \leq j \leq t-1$.

While the rolling window simply averages the H previous observations, the EWMA forecast uses all observations $y_1, \cdots, y_{t-1}$, smoothly downweighting the more distant past. These classes of weights are parameterised by a single parameter H.

Selection of the Tuning Parameter, *H* Suppose we have a sample of T observations $y_1, \ldots, y_T$. The one-step-ahead forecast $\hat{y}_{T+1|T,H}$ requires to select the tuning parameter H. Data adaptive selection of H is done by a cross-validation method using the evaluation sample of in-sample forecasts $\hat{y}_{t|t-1,H}$, $t = T_0, \cdots, T$ to compute the mean squared forecast error (MSFE),

$$Q_{T,H} := \frac{1}{T_n}\sum_{t=T_0}^{T}(y_t - \hat{y}_{t|t-1,H})^2,$$

and then choosing the tuning parameter H which generates the smallest MSFE:

$$\hat{H} := \arg\min_{H \in I_T} Q_{T,H}.$$

Here $T_n := T - T_0 + 1$ is the length of cross-validation period, T_0 is the starting point and the minimisation interval $I_T = [a, H_{\max}]$ is selected such that $T^{2/3} < H_{\max} < T_0 T^{-\delta}$ with $0 < \delta < 1$ and $a > 0$.

Although the adaptive forecast $\hat{y}_{T+1|T,\hat{H}}$ cannot outperform the best forecast $\hat{y}_{T+1|T,H_{opt}}$ with the unknown fixed value H_{opt} minimising the MSE, $\omega_{T,H} := E(y_{T+1} - \hat{y}_{T+1|T,H})^2$, it is desirable to achieve asymptotic equivalence of their MSFEs. Giraitis et al. (2013) show that the forecast $\hat{y}_{T+1|T,\hat{H}}$ of y_{T+1}, obtained with the data-tuned $\hat{H}$, minimises the asymptotic MSE, $\omega_{T,H}$, in H, hence making the weighted forecast procedure $\hat{y}_{T+1|T,\hat{H}}$ operational. It is also asymptotically optimal:

$$\omega_{T,\hat{H}} = \omega_{T,H_{opt}} + o(1),$$

and the quantity $Q_{T,\hat{H}}$ provides an estimate for the forecast error $\omega_{T,\hat{H}}$:

$$Q_{T,\hat{H}} = \omega_{T,\hat{H}} + o_p(1).$$

Giraitis et al. (2013) show that for a number of models $y_t = \beta_t + u_t$ with deterministic and stochastic trends β_t and short memory u_t's,

$$Q_{T,H} = \hat{\sigma}^2_{T,u} + E[Q_{T,H} - \sigma^2_u](1 + o_p(1)), \quad T \to \infty, \quad H \to \infty, \tag{3}$$

uniformly in H, where $\sigma_u^2 = Eu_1^2$ and $\hat{\sigma}^2_{T,u} := T_n^{-1} \sum_{j=T_0}^{T} u_j^2$. They verify that the deterministic function $E[Q_{T,H} - \sigma_u^2]$ has a unique minimum, which enables selection of the optimal data-tuned parameter H that asymptotically minimises the objective function $Q_{T,H}$.

3 Theoretical Results

We illustrate the theoretical properties of the weighted forecast $\hat{y}_{T+1|T,\hat{H}}$ with data selected tuning parameter $\hat{H}$ by two examples of $y_t = \beta_t + u_t$ where β_t is either a constant or a linear trend and the noise u_t has either short or long memory.

The following assumption describes the class of noise processes u_t. We suppose that u_t is a stationary linear process:

$$u_t = \sum_{j=0}^{\infty} a_j \varepsilon_{t-j}, \quad t \in \mathbb{Z}, \qquad \varepsilon_j \sim \mathrm{IID}(0, \sigma_\varepsilon^2), \qquad E\varepsilon_1^4 < \infty. \tag{4}$$

In addition, we assume that u_t has either short memory (i) or long memory (ii).

(i) u_t has short memory (SM) property $\sum_{k=0}^{\infty} |\gamma_u(k)| < \infty$, and

$$s_u^2 := \sum_{k=-\infty}^{\infty} \gamma_u(k) > 0, \qquad \sum_{k \geq n} |\gamma_u(k)| = o(\log^{-2} n).$$

(ii) u_t has long memory (LM): for some $c_\gamma > 0$ and $0 < d < 1/2$,

$$\gamma_u(k) \sim c_\gamma k^{-1+2d}, \qquad k \to \infty.$$

Cases (i) and (ii) were discussed in Giraitis et al. (2013) and Mansur (2013), respectively.

Define the weights

$$w_{j,H} = K(j/H) / \sum_{s=1}^{\infty} K(s/H), \qquad j \geq 1.$$

In (ii) $a_T \sim b_T$ denotes that $a_T / b_T \to 1$, as T increases. We write $o_{p,H}(1)$ to indicate that

$\sup_{H \in I_T} |o_{p,H}(1)| \to_p 0$, while $o_H(1)$ stands for $\sup_{H \in I_T} |o_H(1)| \to 0$, as $T \to \infty$.

3.1 *Forecasting a Stationary Process y_t*

The case of a stationary process $y_t = \mu + u_t$ provides an additional illustrative evidence of the practical use of weighted averaging forecasting. For i.i.d. random variables y_t, the optimal forecast of y_{T+1} is the sample mean $\bar{y}_T = T^{-1} \sum_{t=1}^{T} y_t$, (rolling window over the period $t = 1, \cdots, T$). However, when persistence increases, for a long memory or near non-stationary process y_t, the sample mean forecast $\bar{y}_T$ will be outperformed by averaging $\hat{y}_{T+1|T,\hat{H}} = H^{-1} \sum_{t=T+1-H}^{T} y_t$ over the last few observations $y_{T+1-H}, \ldots, y_T$.

Data based selection of the tuning parameter H allows the selection of the optimal rolling window width H even if the structure of y_t is not known, providing a simple and efficient forecasting strategy for persistent stationary process y_t. (Such a strategy extends also for unit root processes, see Giraitis et al. 2013.)

We shall use notation

$$q_{u,H} := E\big(u_0 - \sum_{j=1}^{\infty} w_{j,H} u_{-j}\big)^2 - \sigma_u^2.$$

For SM u_t, set $\kappa_2 = \int_0^\infty K^2(x)dx$ and $\kappa_0 = K(0)$ and define

$$\lambda_{SM} = s_u^2(\kappa_2 - \kappa_0) + \sigma_u^2\kappa_0.$$

For LM u_t, define

$$\lambda_{LM} = c_\gamma\Big[\int_0^\infty\int_0^\infty K(x)K(y)|x-y|^{-1+2d}dydx - 2\int_0^\infty K(x)x^{-1+2d}dx\Big].$$

Theorem 1 *Suppose that $y_t = \mu + u_t, t \geq 1$, where u_t is a stationary linear process (4), satisfying either SM assumption (i) or LM assumption (ii).*
Then, as $T \to \infty$, for $H \in I_T$,

$$\begin{aligned} Q_{T,H} &= \hat{\sigma}^2_{T,u} + q_{u,H}\big(1 + o_{p,H}(1)\big), \\ \omega_{T,H} &= \sigma_u^2 + q_{u,H}\big(1 + o_H(1)\big), \end{aligned}$$

where, as
$H \to \infty$,

$$\begin{aligned} q_{u,H} &= \lambda_{SM}H^{-1}(1 + o(1)) \ \ \textit{under (i)}, \\ q_{u,H} &= \lambda_{LM}H^{-1+2d}(1 + o(1)) \ \ \textit{under (ii)}. \end{aligned}$$

Theorem 1 implies that $Q_{T,H}$ is a consistent estimate of $\omega_{T,H}$. The following corollary shows that the forecast $y_{T+1|T,\hat{H}}$ computed with the data-tuned $\hat{H}$ has the same MSE as the forecast $y_{T+1|T,H_{opt}}$ with the tuning parameter H_{opt}.

Corollary 1 *If $q_{u,H}$ reaches its minimum at some finite H_0, then*

$$\begin{aligned} \omega_{T,\hat{H}} &= \omega_{T,H_{opt}} + o_p(1), \\ Q_{T,\hat{H}} &= \omega_{T,\hat{H}} + o_p(1) = \sigma_u^2 + q_{u,H_0} + o_p(1). \end{aligned}$$

Remark 1 Corollary 1 implies that the quality of a forecast with the tuning parameter $\hat{H}$ is the same as with the parameter H_{opt} that minimises the forecast error $\omega_{T,H}$. While $\hat{H}$ can be evaluated from the data, H_{opt} is unknown. Observe that $\lambda_{SM} < 0$ and $\lambda_{LM} < 0$ in view of (5) imply that $\hat{H}$ remains bounded when T increases, so only a few most recent observations will contribute in forecasting. In turn, whether $\lambda_{SM} < 0$ or $\lambda_{LM} < 0$ holds depends on the shape of the kernel function K and the strength of dependence in u_t.

For example, $\lambda_{LM} < 0$ holds for the rolling window weights and LM u_t's. Indeed, then $K(x) = I(0 \leq x \leq 1)$, and

$$\lambda_{LM} = c_\gamma \int_0^\infty \int_0^\infty K(x)K(y)|x-y|^{-1+2d} dxdy - 2c_\gamma \int_0^\infty K(x)x^{-1+2d} dx$$
$$= c_\gamma \Big(\int_0^1 \int_0^1 |x-y|^{-1+2d} dxdy - 2 \int_0^1 x^{-1+2d} dx \Big)$$
$$= 2c_\gamma \Big(\int_0^1 \int_0^x u^{-1+2d} dudx - \frac{1}{2d} \Big) = -\frac{2c_\gamma}{1+2d} < 0.$$

Thus, the width $\hat{H}$ of the rolling window remains finite, as T increases, and the error of the rolling window forecast is smaller than σ_u^2.

On the contrary, under short memory, property $\lambda_{SM} < 0$ cannot be produced by the rolling window weights, because they yield $\kappa_2 = \kappa_0 = 1$, and thus $\lambda_{SM} = \sigma_u^2$ is always positive. However, for the exponential kernel $K(x) = e^{-x}$, $x \geq 0$, $\lambda_{SM} = \sigma_u^2 - s_u^2/2$ becomes negative when the long-run variance of u_t is sufficiently large: $s_u^2 > 2\sigma_u^2$, for example, for an AR(1) model u_t with autoregressive parameter greater than $1/3$.

3.2 Forecasting a Trend Stationary Process

When forecasting a process $y_t = at + u_t$, that combines a deterministic trend and a stationary noise u_t, it is natural to expect the weighted average forecast to be driven by the last few observations which is confirmed by theoretical results.

Denote

$$q_{\beta,H} := \Big(\sum_{j=1}^{\infty} w_{j,H}\, j\Big)^2, \qquad \kappa := \Big(\int_0^\infty K(x)xdx\Big)^2.$$

Notation $q_{u,H}$ is the same as in Theorem 1.

Theorem 2 *Let $y_t = at + u_t, t = 1, \cdots, T$, $a \neq 0$, where u_t is a stationary linear process (4), satisfying either SM assumption (i) or LM assumption (ii).*
Then, as $T \to \infty$, for $H \in I_T$,

$$Q_{T,H} = \hat{\sigma}_{T,u}^2 + q_{\beta,H} + q_{u,H} + o_{p,H}(H^2),$$
$$\omega_{T,H} = \sigma_u^2 + q_{\beta,H} + q_{u,H} + o_H(H^2),$$

where $q_{\beta,H} + q_{u,H} = \kappa H^2 + o(H^2)$, as $H \to \infty$.

Theorem 2 allows us to establish the following basic properties of the forecast $y_{T+1|T,\hat{H}}$ of a trend stationary process y_t.

Corollary 2 *Under assumptions of Theorem 2, $\hat{H}$ stays bounded:*

$$\omega_{T,\hat{H}} = \omega_{T,H_{opt}} + o_p(1),$$
$$Q_{T,\hat{H}} = \omega_{T,\hat{H}} + o_p(1) = \sigma_u^2 + q_{\beta,H_0} + q_{u,H_0} + o_p(1),$$

where H_0 is a minimiser of $q_{\beta,H} + q_{u,H}$.

In the presence of a deterministic trend the optimal $\hat{H}$ will take small values and the averaging forecast will be based on the last few observations.

4 Practical Performance

4.1 Forecast Methods

We resort to the range of parametric forecast methods analysed in Giraitis et al. (2013). Their weights are defined as functions of a tuning parameter. They discount past data and are known to be robust to historical and ongoing structural changes. For comparison, we consider parametric methods with fixed and data-dependent discounting parameters. We compare forecasts against a number of simple benchmark models. In Sect. 2 we have introduced the *Rolling window* and *EWMA* methods.

Rolling Window The weights are flat in the sense that all the observations in the window get equal weights while the older data get zero weights. The one-step-ahead forecast $\hat{y}_{t|t-1}$ is then simply the average of H previous observations. In the tables we refer to this method as *Rolling H*. Besides selecting H optimally from data we use two fixed window methods with $H = 20$ and 30.

Exponential EWMA Weights The closer the parameter ρ is to zero the faster is the rate of discounting and the main weights are concentrated on the last few data points. The closer ρ is to 1 the slower is the rate and significant weights are attached to datum in distant past. In tables this method is denoted as *Exponential* ρ. We consider several fixed value downweighting methods with $\rho = 0.4, 0.6, 0.8, 0.9$. The data-tuned parameter is denoted as $\hat{\rho}$.

Polynomial Method This uses weights

$$w_{tj,H} = (t-j)^{-\alpha} / \left(\sum\nolimits_{k=1}^{t-1} k^{-\alpha} \right), \quad 1 \le j \le t-1, \text{ with } \alpha > 0.$$

The past is downweighted at a slower rate than with exponential weights. This method is referred to as *Polynomial* α. We do not consider any fixed value for α and only report data-dependent downweighting with estimated parameter $\hat{\alpha}$.

Dynamic Weighting Giraitis et al. (2013) proposed a more flexible extension of exponential weighting where the weights attached to the first few lags are not determined by parametric functions, but rather freely chosen along with the tuning parameter, H. Thus, analogously to an AR process, the first p weights, $w_1, w_2, \ldots, w_p$ are estimated as additional parameters, while the remaining weights are functions of H. The weight function is defined as:

$$\tilde{w}_{tj,H} = \begin{cases} w_j, & j = 1, \ldots, p \\ K(j/H), & j = p+1, \ldots, t-1, \quad H \in I_T, \end{cases} \tag{5}$$

and the final weights are standardised as $w_{tj,H} = \tilde{w}_{tj,H} / \left(\sum_{j=1}^{t-1} \tilde{w}_{tj,H}\right)$ to sum to one. Note that Q_T is jointly minimised over $w_1, w_2, \ldots, w_p$ and H. We consider a parsimonious representation by specifying $p = 1$ and choose exponential kernel K. We refer to it as *Dynamic*.

Residual Methods Giraitis et al. (2013) argue that if a time series explicitly allows for modelling the conditional mean of the process and a forecaster has a preferred parametric model for it, then it might be helpful to first fit the model and use the robust methods to forecast the residuals from the model. The original location model (1) is restrictive and not suitable for conditional modelling and a more generic forecasting model is therefore proposed to illustrate the approach:

$$y_t = f(x_t) + y_t', \; t = 1, 2, \ldots.$$

where y_t is the variable of interest, x_t is the vector of predicted variables which may contain lags of y_t, and y_t' is the vector of residuals which are unexplained by $f(x_t)$. In the presence of structural change, y_t' is expected to contain any remaining persistence in y_t such as trends, breaks or other forms of dependence, and the robust methods should perform well in such scenario. Forecasts of $f(x_t)$ and y_t' are then combined to generate improved forecasts of y_t.

We adopt the widely popular AR(1) process to model the conditional mean which gives $f(x_t) = \phi y_{t-1}$. The residuals y_t' are forecasted using the parametric weights discussed above. The forecast of y_{t+1} based on $y_1, y_2, \ldots, y_t$ is computed as $\hat{y}_{t+1} = \hat{\phi} y_t + \hat{y}'_{t+1|t,\hat{H}}$. Two versions of the residual methods are considered.

Exponential AR Method In this method the tuning parameter H and the autoregressive parameter ϕ are jointly estimated by minimising the in-sample MSFE, $Q_{T,H} = Q_{T,H\phi}$ which is computed by defining $y_t' = y_t - \phi y_{t-1}$ and using exponential weights. We refer to this as *Exp. AR*.

Exponential Residual Method This is a two-stage method, where the autoregressive parameter ϕ at y_{t-1} is estimated by OLS separately from the parameters associated with forecasting y_t'. It forecasts residuals $y_t' = y_t - \phi y_{t-1}$ using exponential weights producing $\hat{H}$ and the forecast $\hat{y}'_{t+1|t,\hat{H}}$. We refer to it as *Exp. Residual*.

4.1.1 The Benchmark and Other Competitors

Full Sample Mean This benchmark forecast is the average of all observations in the sample:

$$\hat{y}_{benchmark,T+1} = \frac{1}{T}\sum_{t=1}^{T} y_t.$$

AR(1) Forecast We include forecasts based on an AR(1) dynamics which is often considered as a stable and consistent predictor of time series. The one-step-ahead forecast is given by:

$$\hat{y}_{T+1|T} = \hat{\phi}\, y_T.$$

Last Observation Forecast For unit root process a simple yet competitive forecast is simply 'no change' forecast:

$$\hat{y}_{T+1|T} = y_T.$$

Averaging Method Pesaran and Timmermann (2007) advocate a simple robust method where the one-step-ahead forecast $\overline{y}_{T+1|T}$ is the average of the rolling window forecasts $\hat{y}_{T+1|T,H}$ obtained using all possible window sizes, H, that include the last observation:

$$\overline{y}_{T+1|T} = \frac{1}{T}\sum_{H=1}^{T} \hat{y}_{T+1|T,H}, \quad \hat{y}_{T+1|T,H} = \frac{1}{H}\sum_{t=T-H+1}^{T} y_t.$$

This method does not require selection of any discount parameter but the minimum window size is used for forecasting, which is usually of minor significance. We refer to this as *Averaging*.

4.2 Illustrative Examples, Monte Carlo Experiments

Now we turn to the practical justification of the optimal properties of the selection procedure of H for $y_t = \beta_t + u_t$, where β_t is a persistent process (deterministic or stochastic trend) of unknown type, and u_t is a stationary noise term. Our objective is to verify that the forecast $y_{T+1|T,\hat{H}}$ of y_{T+1} with the optimal tuning parameter $\hat{H}$ produces comparable MSEs to those of the best forecast $y_{T+1|T,H}$ with the fixed H, e.g., we use $H = 20, 30$ for the rolling window and $\rho = 0.4, 0.6, 0.8$ and 0.9 for the exponential weights.

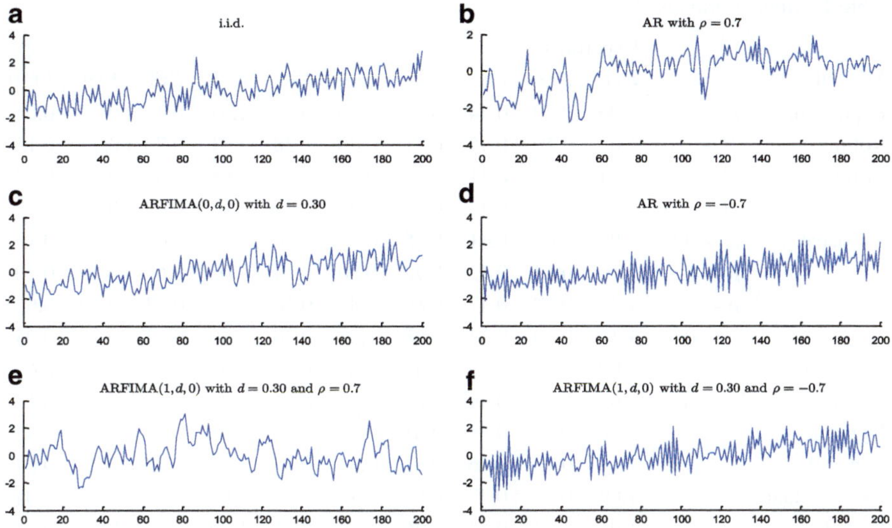

Fig. 1 Plots of generated series $y_t = 0.05t + 3u_t$ in *Ex*3 for different noise u_t: (**a**) i.i.d., (**b**) AR(1) with $\rho = 0.7$, (**c**) *ARFIMA*(0,d,0) with $d = 0.3$, (**d**) AR(1) with $\rho = -0.7$, (**e**) *ARFIMA*(1,d,0) with $d = 0.3$ and $\rho = 0.7$, (**f**) *ARFIMA*(1,d,0) with $d = 0.3$ and $\rho = -0.7$

We consider ten data generating processes as in Giraitis et al. (2013):

$Ex1.\ y_t = u_t.$

$Ex2.\ y_t = 0.05t + 5u_t.$

$Ex3.\ y_t = 0.05t + 3u_t.$

$$Ex4.\ y_t = \begin{cases} u_t, & t \le 0.55T \\ 1 + u_t, & t > 0.55T. \end{cases}$$

$Ex5.\ y_t = 2\sin(2\pi t/T) + 3u_t.$

$Ex6.\ y_t = 2\sin(2\pi t/T) + u_t.$

$Ex7.\ y_t = 2T^{-1/2}\sum_{i=1}^{t} v_i + 3u_t.$

$Ex8.\ y_t = 2T^{-1/2}\sum_{i=1}^{t} v_i + u_t.$

$Ex9.\ y_t = 0.5\sum_{i=1}^{t} v_i + u_t.$

$Ex10.\ y_t = \sum_{i=1}^{t} u_i.$

In order to get a first-hand idea about the dynamic behaviour of the generated series y_t, it is useful to analyse their plots. Figure 1 shows plots of a trend stationary process y_t of *Ex*3, for more plots see Mansur (2013). In *Ex*7 − 9, $v_i \sim IID(0, 1)$.

4.2.1 General Patterns, Observations, Conclusions

In *Ex*1, y_t is determined by the noise process alone and there is no structural change. It is not surprising that forecasting an i.i.d. process requires accounting for a long past and that the benchmark sample mean should perform the best; see Table 1. Similarly, it is expected that a simple *AR*(1) benchmark will be difficult to outperform when forecasting persistent autoregressive processes. Long-term dependence can create a false impression of structural change and make prior

Table 1 Monte Carlo results

Method		Experiments									
		*Ex*1	*Ex*2	*Ex*3	*Ex*4	*Ex*5	*Ex*6	*Ex*7	*Ex*8	*Ex*9	*Ex*10
Exponential	$\rho = \hat{\rho}$	1.09	0.70	0.44	0.79	0.80	0.25	1.03	0.70	0.21	0.04
Rolling	$H = \hat{H}$	1.07	0.69	0.45	0.81	0.80	0.28	1.01	0.70	0.27	0.15
Rolling	$H = 20$	1.04	0.66	0.41	0.76	0.76	0.26	0.98	0.67	0.32	0.27
	$H = 30$	1.03	0.65	0.42	0.77	0.76	0.31	0.97	0.69	0.40	0.37
Exponential	$\rho = 0.9$	1.04	0.66	0.41	0.75	0.76	0.26	0.97	0.65	0.27	0.19
	$\rho = 0.8$	1.10	0.69	0.43	0.78	0.80	0.24	1.02	0.67	0.21	0.10
	$\rho = 0.6$	1.23	0.77	0.47	0.86	0.89	0.26	1.14	0.73	0.20	0.06
	$\rho = 0.4$	1.41	0.89	0.54	0.98	1.03	0.30	1.30	0.83	0.21	0.05
Averaging		1.00	0.75	0.59	0.85	0.84	0.58	0.97	0.78	0.64	0.62
Polynomial	$\alpha = \hat{\alpha}$	1.03	0.73	0.49	0.81	0.82	0.31	0.99	0.70	0.32	0.15
Dynamic		1.16	0.72	0.45	0.81	0.82	0.26	1.08	0.71	0.21	0.05
Exp. AR		1.11	0.73	0.46	0.83	0.83	0.27	1.07	0.72	0.22	0.04
Exp. residual		1.09	0.71	0.47	0.86	0.82	0.32	1.03	0.72	0.25	0.04
Last obs.		1.95	1.23	0.74	1.36	1.44	0.41	1.79	1.14	0.27	0.04
AR(1)		1.00	0.81	0.60	0.83	0.87	0.38	0.98	0.84	0.31	0.05

$T = 200$. $u_t \sim \text{IID}(0, 1)$. Relative MSFEs of one-step-ahead forecasts with respect to the full sample mean benchmark

selection of a forecast model difficult. Additional persistence through autoregressive dependence could make the series closer to unit root. An AR(1) benchmark should still do well, but as persistence increases the "last observation" forecasts should be equally competitive.

Both *Ex*2 and *Ex*3 introduce linear monotonically increasing trends in y_t and differ only in the size of variance of noise process. Giraitis et al. (2013) argue that such linear trends may be unrealistic but they can offer reasonable representations of time series which are detrended through standard techniques such as differencing or filtering. Moreover, Fig. 1 confirms that the effects of such trends are small enough to be dominated and muted by the noise processes. While linear trends are visually detectable for an i.i.d. noise, they become more obscure with increasing persistence. The panel (e) of Fig. 1 confirms that when short and long memory persistence are combined, the trends can vanish completely.

The functional form of y_t in *Ex*4 accommodates structural break in the mean. The break occurs halfway the sample at time $t_0 = 0.55T$. Giraitis et al. (2013) argue that since the post-break period is greater than $\sqrt{T}$, as required by their theory, the robust forecasting methods should take into account of such "not-too-recent" breaks and yield forecasts that are significantly better than the benchmark sample mean. Their Monte Carlo study confirms their claims. Although the shift in mean can be well identified in i.i.d. or weak long memory series, it becomes more concealed with increasing persistence in the noise process. Thus, it is of interest to see how methods with data-dependent discounting cope with these complex situations.

The purpose of $Ex5$ and $Ex6$ is to introduce smooth cyclical bounded trends as observed in standard business cycles. Such trends are less likely to be completely removed from standard detrending and therefore more realistic than a linear trend. The sample mean benchmark should do poorly, particularly for $Ex6$ where oscillation of the trend is wider compared to the variance of the noise process. Realisations of such processes show that higher persistence can distort shapes of smooth cycles to substantial extent.

$Ex7$ and $Ex8$ accommodate the bounded stochastic trend β_t's and represent increasingly popular time-varying coefficients type dynamic models. $Ex9$ considers unbounded random walk (unit root) process, observed under noise u_t. $Ex10$ analyses the standard unit root model.

In general, the time series plots of $Ex1$–10 show that long memory can give false impression of structural change. Moreover, persistence in the noise processes induced by long memory or mixture of short and long memory dependence can confound types of structural changes in a time series. Thus is worth investigating whether typical robust-to-structural-change methods, such as rolling window and EWMA methods, can perform well in forecasting in presence of long memory. We argue that as long as the choice of tuning parameter is data-dependent such methods can generate forecasts that are comparable to the best possible fixed parameter forecasts.

4.2.2 Monte Carlo Results

We discuss Monte Carlo results of small sample performance of the adaptive forecasting techniques in predicting time series $y_t = \beta_t + u_t$ with i.i.d. and long memory noise u_t. In modelling the noise we use the standard normal i.i.d. noise $u_t \sim IID(0,1)$, and we opt to use the long memory $ARFIMA(1,d,0)$ model for u_t defined as:

$$(1-\rho L)(1-L)^d u_t = \varepsilon_t,$$

where $|\rho| < 1$ is the AR(1) parameter, $0 < d < 1/2$ is the long memory parameter that induces long memory property (ii) and L is the lag operator.

After choosing a starting point $\tau = T - 100$, we apply reported methods to construct one-step-ahead forecasts $\hat{y}_{t|t-1,H}$, $t = \tau, \ldots, T$. We compare performance of method j with the forecast error

$$MSFE_j = (T-\tau+1)^{-1} \sum\nolimits_{t=\tau}^{T} (\hat{y}^{(j)}_{t|t-1,H} - y_t)^2$$

with the benchmark forecast by sample mean $\bar{y}_t$ with the forecast error $MSFE_{sm} := (T-\tau+1)^{-1} \sum_{t=\tau}^{T} (\bar{y}_t - y_t)^2$ by computing the relative $RMSFE = \frac{MSFE_j}{MSFE_{sm}}$. Results for different long memory specifications of the noise processes are presented in Tables 2 and 3.

Table 2 Monte Carlo results

Method		Experiments									
		*Ex*1	*Ex*2	*Ex*3	*Ex*4	*Ex*5	*Ex*6	*Ex*7	*Ex*8	*Ex*9	*Ex*10
Exponential	$\rho = \hat{\rho}$	0.90	0.66	0.42	0.68	0.67	0.21	0.85	0.62	0.19	0.01
Rolling	$H = \hat{H}$	0.96	0.75	0.46	0.74	0.73	0.25	0.90	0.69	0.28	0.06
Rolling	$H = 20$	0.97	0.73	0.48	0.79	0.77	0.34	0.92	0.76	0.51	0.30
	$H = 30$	0.98	0.76	0.53	0.83	0.84	0.53	0.94	0.82	0.63	0.45
Exponential	$\rho = 0.9$	0.89	0.65	0.42	0.68	0.67	0.24	0.84	0.63	0.30	0.10
	$\rho = 0.8$	0.87	0.64	0.41	0.66	0.65	0.21	0.82	0.60	0.22	0.04
	$\rho = 0.6$	0.90	0.66	0.45	0.67	0.67	0.21	0.86	0.61	0.19	0.02
	$\rho = 0.4$	0.98	0.71	0.45	0.72	0.72	0.22	0.91	0.66	0.19	0.01
Averaging		0.96	0.79	0.66	0.85	0.84	0.58	0.93	0.82	0.66	0.53
Polynomial	$\alpha = \hat{\alpha}$	0.87	0.65	0.46	0.67	0.66	0.28	0.82	0.63	0.30	0.02
Dynamic		0.89	0.65	0.42	0.67	0.66	0.21	0.83	0.62	0.20	0.01
Exp. AR		0.89	0.66	0.42	0.68	0.67	0.21	0.84	0.62	0.20	0.01
Exp. residual		0.88	0.66	0.43	0.67	0.68	0.25	0.83	0.63	0.22	0.01
Last obs.		1.26	0.90	0.56	0.92	0.93	0.28	1.17	0.83	0.23	0.01
AR(1)		0.85	0.67	0.47	0.67	0.68	0.25	0.81	0.63	0.21	0.01

$T = 200$. $u_t \sim ARFIMA(0, 0.3, 0)$. Relative MSFEs of one-step-ahead forecasts with respect to the full sample mean benchmark

Table 3 Monte Carlo results

Method		Experiments									
		*Ex*1	*Ex*2	*Ex*3	*Ex*4	*Ex*5	*Ex*6	*Ex*7	*Ex*8	*Ex*9	*Ex*10
Exponential	$\rho = \hat{\rho}$	1.01	0.76	0.52	0.76	0.78	0.26	0.95	0.70	0.24	0.02
Rolling	$H = \hat{H}$	1.03	0.78	0.53	0.76	0.79	0.28	0.96	0.71	0.30	0.07
Rolling	$H = 20$	1.01	0.75	0.53	0.77	0.78	0.38	0.94	0.76	0.50	0.33
	$H = 30$	1.00	0.78	0.57	0.81	0.84	0.54	0.95	0.82	0.63	0.49
Exponential	$\rho = 0.9$	1.03	0.76	0.51	0.74	0.77	0.27	0.95	0.69	0.30	0.11
	$\rho = 0.8$	1.17	0.83	0.55	0.78	0.82	0.26	1.03	0.76	0.24	0.05
	$\rho = 0.6$	1.35	0.99	0.66	0.93	0.99	0.30	1.26	0.84	0.24	0.03
	$\rho = 0.4$	1.70	1.26	0.83	1.16	1.24	0.38	1.55	1.05	0.28	0.02
Averaging		1.00	0.81	0.65	0.84	0.85	0.59	0.95	0.83	0.65	0.55
Polynomial	$\alpha = \hat{\alpha}$	1.00	0.84	0.62	0.83	0.85	0.34	0.97	0.76	0.33	0.16
Dynamic		0.76	0.55	0.37	0.54	0.55	0.17	0.70	0.51	0.20	0.02
Exp. AR		0.74	0.56	0.38	0.55	0.55	0.17	0.69	0.52	0.19	0.02
Exp. residual		0.74	0.59	0.47	0.61	0.61	0.38	0.71	0.65	0.36	0.03
Last obs.		2.93	2.14	1.43	1.99	2.13	0.65	2.67	1.79	0.45	0.03
AR(1)		0.75	0.83	0.77	0.83	0.82	0.49	0.81	0.84	0.38	0.03

$T = 200$. $u_t \sim ARFIMA(1, 0.3, 0)$ with $\rho = -0.7$. Relative MSFEs of one-step-ahead forecasts with the full sample mean benchmark

The columns represent data-generating models $Ex1$–10 and the rows represent different forecasting methods. Entries of the tables are *MSFE* of different methods relative to sample average, as defined above.

We begin by discussing the results in Tables 1 and 2 which feature i.i.d and long memory $ARFIMA(0, 0.30, 0)$ noises. Table 1 records sole dominance of the benchmark over the competitors when $y_t = u_t$ which is expected, and gains over the benchmark when y_t has a persistent component β_t.

In Table 2, *RMSFE* values below unity suggest that, in general, all the reported forecasting methods, both with fixed and data-driven discounting, are useful for processes with moderately strong long memory. Even the simplest case of "no structural change", $y_t = u_t$ reported in the first column $Ex1$ of Table 2 shows that forecasts of most of the competing methods, including the rolling-window schemes, outperform the benchmark of the full-sample average. The gains are, however, small. Gains over the benchmark are more pronounced when y_t has a persistent component β_t. Then, even naive "last observation" forecasts are better than the mean forecast in most of the experiments. Persistence entering y_t through long memory u_t requires stronger discounting than for i.i.d. noise u_t and using information contained in the more recent past.

The data-dependent exponential weights do not exactly match the best fixed value forecast method but are reasonably comparable and are never among the worst performing methods.

Methods using data-adjusted rolling-window forecast better than methods with fixed windows of size $H = 20$ and $H = 30$ and also outperform the averaging method of rolling windows advocated by Pesaran and Timmermann (2007). This justifies the use of data-driven choice of downweighting parameter for rolling windows.

Overall, comparison of competing forecasting methods in Tables 1 and 2 show that the full sample AR(1) forecasts are in general very good compared to the benchmark, but are often outperformed by most of the adaptive data-tuned methods. Forecasts based on the residual methods are impressive. Among the adaptive robust forecasting methods the dynamic weighting method, where the weight of the last observation is optimally chosen from data simultaneously with the exponential weighting parameter, consistently provides forecasts that are comparable to the best possible forecasts for all the experiments. The exponential AR method is also equally competitive.

The advantages of data-based adaptive forecasting methods become clearly evident when we consider $ARFIMA(1, 0.3, 0)$ noise u_t with a negative AR coefficient $\rho = -0.7$. Table 3 reports the corresponding *RMSFE*s. Although the full sample AR(1) forecast consistently beats the benchmark sample mean, it is outperformed by most of the adaptive forecasting techniques including the rolling window methods. Notable differences between the results of $ARFIMA(1, 0.3, 0)$ with positive $\rho = 0.7$, which we do not report, and those from models with negative AR coefficient, are that margins of gains over the benchmark are higher in the former and that forecasts using data-tuned exponential and rolling-window methods become more comparable, to AR forecasts, in the latter. For $\rho = -0.7$, the data-based selection of downweighting, particularly, the dynamic weighting and the exponential AR weighting are the most dominant predictors. The residual methods also generate very good forecasts in most of the experiments. Maximum reduction in relative *MSFE* of the fixed parameter EWMA methods comes from methods with very low discounting rates emphasising the necessity of including information of the more distant past. The optimally chosen exponential weights lead to forecasts that are comparable to the forecasts generated by the best performing fixed parameter methods. The "no-change" (Last Observation) forecast is by far the worst reporting *RMSFE*s which are mostly much higher than unity.

The Monte Carlo experiments with i.i.d. and long memory time series noise u_t generated by *ARFIMA* models confirm that accuracy of forecasts varies based on the degree of persistence and consequently depends on appropriate downweighting of past observations. The facts that many of the data-tuned discounting always match, if not outperform, the best forecast with fixed downweighting parameter and that the optimal rate of discounting cannot be observed in advance, prove the superiority of data-tuned adaptive forecasting techniques, particularly when facing structural changes.

References

Ang, A., & Bekaert, G. (2002). Regime switches in interest rates. *Journal of Business & Economic Statistics, 20*(2), 163–182.

Clark, T. E., & McCracken, M. W. (2010). Averaging forecasts from VARs with uncertain instabilities. *Journal of Applied Econometrics, 25*(1), 5–29.

Clements, M. P., & Krolzig, H. M. (1998). A comparison of the forecast performance of Markov-switching and threshold autoregressive models of US GNP. *The Econometrics Journal, 1*(1), 47–75.

D'Agostino, A., Gambetti, L., & Giannone, D. (2013). Macroeconomic forecasting and structural change. *Journal of Applied Econometrics, 28*, 82–101.

Diebold, F. X., & Inoue, A. (2001). Long memory and regime switching. *Journal of Econometrics, 105*(1), 131–159.

Eklund, J., Kapetanios, G., & Price, S. (2010). Forecasting in the Presence of Recent Structural Change. Bank of England Working Paper, 406.

Garcia, R., & Perron, P. (1996). An analysis of the real interest rate under regime shifts. *The Review of Economics and Statistics, 79*, 111–125.

Giraitis, L., Kapetanios, G., & Price, S. (2013). Adaptive forecasting in the presence of recent and ongoing structural change. *Journal of Econometrics, 177*, 153–170.

Gourieroux, C., & Jasiak, J. (2001). Memory and infrequent breaks. *Economics Letters, 70*(1), 29–41.

Granger, C. W., & Hyung, N. (2004). Occasional structural breaks and long memory with an application to the S&P 500 absolute stock returns. *Journal of Empirical Finance, 11*(3), 399–421.

Hamilton, J. D. (1989). A new approach to the economic analysis of nonstationary time series and the business cycle. *Econometrica, 57*(2), 357–384.

Hendry, D. F. (2000). On detectable and non-detectable structural change. *Structural Change and Economic Dynamics, 11*(1), 45–65.

Kapetanios, G. (2006). Nonlinear autoregressive models and long memory. *Economics Letters, 91*(3), 360–368.
Koop, G., & Potter, S. M. (2007). Estimation and forecasting in models with multiple breaks. *The Review of Economic Studies, 74*(3), 763–789.
Maheu, J. M., & Gordon, S. (2008). Learning, forecasting and structural breaks. *Journal of Applied Econometrics, 23*(5), 553–583.
Mansur, M. (2013). Ph.D. thesis. Queen Mary, University of London.
Pesaran, M. H., Pettenuzzo, D., & Timmermann, A. (2006). Forecasting time series subject to multiple structural breaks. *The Review of Economic Studies, 73*(4), 1057–1084.
Pesaran, M. H., & Pick, A. (2011). Forecast combination across estimation windows. *Journal of Business & Economic Statistics, 29*(2), 307–318.
Pesaran, M. H., & Timmermann, A. (2002). Market timing and return prediction under model instability. *Journal of Empirical Finance, 9*(5), 495–510.
Pesaran, M. H., & Timmermann, A. (2007). Selection of estimation window in the presence of breaks. *Journal of Econometrics, 137*(1), 134–161.
Rossi, B. (2012). Advances in forecasting under instability. In G. Elliott & A. Timmermann (Eds.), *Handbook of economic forecasting*. North Holland: Elsevier.
Stock, J. H., & Watson, M. W. (1996). Evidence on structural instability in macroeconomic time series relations. *Journal of Business & Economic Statistics, 14*(1), 11–30.
Stock, J. H., & Watson, M. W. (2007). Why has US inflation become harder to forecast? *Journal of Money, Credit and Banking, 39*(s1), 3–33.
Timmermann, A. (2001). Structural breaks, incomplete information, and stock prices. *Journal of Business & Economic Statistics, 19*(3), 299–314.

Distribution of the Durbin–Watson Statistic in Near Integrated Processes

Uwe Hassler and Mehdi Hosseinkouchack

Abstract This paper analyzes the Durbin–Watson (DW) statistic for near-integrated processes. Using the Fredholm approach the limiting characteristic function of DW is derived, in particular focusing on the effect of a "large initial condition" growing with the sample size. Random and deterministic initial conditions are distinguished. We document the asymptotic local power of DW when testing for integration.

1 Introduction

In a series of papers Durbin and Watson (1950, 1951, 1971) developed a celebrated test to detect serial correlation of order one. The corresponding Durbin–Watson (DW) statistic was proposed by Sargan and Bhargava (1983) in order to test the null hypothesis of a random walk,

$$y_t = \rho y_{t-1} + \varepsilon_t \, , \; t = 1, \ldots, T \, , \quad H_0 : \rho = 1 \, .$$

Bhargava (1986) established that the DW statistic for a random walk is uniformly most powerful against the alternative of a stationary AR(1) process. Local power of DW was investigated by Hisamatsu and Maekawa (1994) following the technique by White (1958). Hisamatsu and Maekawa (1994) worked under the following assumptions: (1) a model without intercept like above, (2) a zero (or at least negligible) starting value y_0, (3) serially independent innovations $\{\varepsilon_t\}$, and (4) homoskedastic innovations. Nabeya and Tanaka (1988, 1990a) and Tanaka (1990, 1996) introduced the so-called Fredholm approach to econometrics. Using this approach, Nabeya and Tanaka (1990b) investigated the local power of DW under a more realistic setup. They allowed for an intercept and also a linear trend in the model and for errors displaying serial correlation and heteroskedasticity of a certain

U. Hassler (✉) • M. Hosseinkouchack
Goethe-Universität Frankfurt, Grueneburgplatz 1, 60323 Frankfurt, Germany
e-mail: hassler@wiwi.uni-frankfurt.de; hosseinkouchack@wiwi.uni-frankfurt.de

J. Beran et al. (eds.), *Empirical Economic and Financial Research*,
Advanced Studies in Theoretical and Applied Econometrics 48,
DOI 10.1007/978-3-319-03122-4_26

degree. Here, we go one step beyond and relax the zero starting value assumption. To this end we adopt the Fredholm approach as well.[1]

In particular, we obtain the limiting characteristic function of the DW statistic for near-integrated processes driven by serially correlated and heteroskedastic processes with the primary focus to reveal the effect of a "large initial condition" growing with $\sqrt{T}$, where T is the sample size. This starting value assumption has been picked out as a central theme by Müller and Elliott (2003), see also Harvey et al. (2009) for a recent discussion.

The rest of the paper is organized as follows. Section 2 becomes precise on the notation and the assumptions. The underlying Fredholm approach is presented and discussed in Sect. 3. Section 4 contains the limiting results. Section 5 illustrates the power function of DW. A summary concludes the paper. Proofs are relegated to the Appendix.

2 Notation and Assumptions

Before becoming precise on our assumptions we fix some standard notation. Let $\mathbb{I}(\cdot)$ denote the usual indicator function, while I_T stands for the identity matrix of size T. All integrals are from 0 to 1 if not indicated otherwise, and $w(\cdot)$ indicates a Wiener process or standard Brownian motion.

We assume that the time series observations $\{y_t\}$ are generated from

$$y_t = x_t + \eta_t \,, \quad \eta_t = \rho\, \eta_{t-1} + u_t \,, \quad t = 1, \ldots, T, \tag{1}$$

where x_t is the deterministic component of y_t which we restrict to be a constant or a linear time trend. We maintain that the following conventional assumption governs the behavior of the stochastic process $\{u_t\}$.

Assumption 1 The sequence $\{u_t\}$ is generated by

$$u_t = \sum_{j=0}^{\infty} \alpha_j \varepsilon_{t-j} \quad \text{with } \alpha_0 = 1 \,, \quad \sum_{j=0}^{\infty} |\alpha_j| < \infty \,, \quad a := \sum_{j=0}^{\infty} \alpha_j \neq 0 \,,$$

while $\{\varepsilon_t\}$ is a sequence of martingale differences with

$$\text{plim}_{T\to\infty} \frac{1}{T} \sum_{t=1}^{T} E\left(\varepsilon_t^2 | F_{t-1}\right) = \sigma^2 \,, \ \text{plim}_{T\to\infty} \frac{1}{T} \sum_{t=1}^{T} E\left(\varepsilon_t^2 \mathbb{I}\left(|\varepsilon_t| > \sqrt{T}\gamma\right) | F_{t-1}\right) = 0,$$

[1] Further applications of this approach in a similar context are by Nabeya (2000) to seasonal unit roots, and by Kurozumi (2002) and Presno and López (2003) to stationarity testing.

for any $\gamma > 0$, $0 < \sigma^2 < \infty$, and that F_t is the σ-algebra generated by the ε_s, $s \leq t$. Also we let $\sigma_u^2 := \lim_{T\to\infty} \frac{1}{T}\sum_{t=1}^{T} E\left(u_t^2\right)$ and $\omega_u^2 := \lim_{T\to\infty} T^{-1} E\left(\sum_{t=1}^{T} u_t\right)^2 = \sigma^2 a^2$.

Assumption 2 In model (1) we allow ρ to be time-dependent and set $\rho_T = 1 - \frac{c}{T}$ with $c > 0$, where the null distribution is covered as limiting case ($c \to 0$).

Assumption 3 For the starting value $\eta_0 = \xi$ we assume: a) $\xi = o_p(\sqrt{T})$ ("small starting value"), where ξ may be random or deterministic; b) $\xi = \delta\sqrt{\omega_u^2/\left(1-\rho_T^2\right)}$ where $\delta \sim N\left[\mu_\delta \mathbb{I}\left(\sigma_\delta^2 = 0\right), \sigma_\delta^2\right]$ and independent from $\{u_t\}$ ("large starting value").

Assumption 1 allows for heteroskedasticity of $\{u_t\}$. If we assume homoskedasticity, $E\left(\varepsilon_t^2 | F_{t-1}\right) = \sigma^2$, then $\{u_t\}$ is stationary. Under Assumption 1 an invariance principle is guaranteed (see, for example, Phillips and Solo 1992). By Assumption 2, the process $\{\eta_t\}$ is near-integrated as defined by Phillips (1987). The initial condition under Assumption 3a) will be negligible as $T \to \infty$. The effect of initial condition under Assumption 3b) will not be negligible and the specification of δ, compactly, covers both random and fixed cases depending on the value of σ_δ.

We distinguish the model with demeaning from that with detrending using μ and τ for the corresponding cases. The test statistics $DW_{j,T}$ ($j = \mu, \tau$) are given by

$$DW_{j,T} = \frac{T}{\hat{\omega}^2} \frac{\sum_{t=2}^{T}\left(\hat{\eta}_t^j - \hat{\eta}_{t-1}^j\right)^2}{\sum_{t=1}^{T}\left(\hat{\eta}_t^j\right)^2}, \tag{2}$$

where $\hat{\eta}_t^j$ are OLS residuals calculated from (1) with $\hat{\omega}^2$ being a consistent estimator of σ_u^2/ω_u^2 (see Hamilton 1994, Sect. 10.5, for further discussions).

$DW_{j,T}$ rejects a null hypothesis of $\rho = 1$ in favor of $\rho < 1$ for too large values. The critical values are typically taken from the limiting distributions, DW_j, which are characterized explicitly further down,

$$DW_{j,T} \xrightarrow{D} DW_j\,, \quad j = \mu, \tau\,,$$

where $\xrightarrow{D}$ denotes convergence in distribution as $T \to \infty$.

3 Fredholm Approach

The Fredholm approach relies on expressing limiting distributions as double Stieltjes integrals over a positive definite kernel $K(s,t)$ that is symmetric and continuous on $[0, 1] \times [0, 1]$.[2] Given a kernel, one defines a type I Fredholm integral equation as

$$f(t) = \lambda \int K(s,t)\, f(s)\, ds\,,$$

with eigenvalue λ and eigenfunction f. The corresponding Fredholm determinant (FD) of the kernel is defined as (see Tanaka 1990, Eq. (24))

$$D(\lambda) = \lim_{T\to\infty} \det \left(I_T - \frac{\lambda}{T}\left[K\left(\frac{j}{T},\frac{k}{T}\right)\right]_{j,k=1,\ldots,T} \right). \tag{3}$$

Further, the so-called resolvent $\Gamma(s,t;\lambda)$ of the kernel (see Tanaka 1990, Eq. (25)) is

$$\Gamma(s,t;\lambda) = K(s,t) + \lambda \int \Gamma(s,u;\lambda)\, K(u,t)\, du\,. \tag{4}$$

Those are the ingredients used to determine limiting characteristic functions following Nabeya and Tanaka (1990a) and more generally Tanaka (1990).[3]

Let DW_j $(j = \mu, \tau)$ represent the limit of $DW_{j,T}$. DW_j^{-1} can be written as $S_X = \int \{X(t) + n(t)\}^2 dt$ for some stochastic process $X(t)$ and an integrable function $n(t)$. Tanaka (1996, Theorem 5.9, p. 164) gives the characteristic function of random variables such as S_X summarized in the following lemma.

Lemma 1 *The characteristic function of*

$$S_X = \int [X(t) + n(t)]^2\, dt \tag{5}$$

for a continuous function $n(t)$ is given by

$$Ee^{i\theta S_X} = [D(2i\theta)]^{-1/2} \exp\left[i\theta \int n^2(t)\, dt - 2\theta^2 \int h(t)\, n(t)\, dt \right], \tag{6}$$

[2] Nabeya (2000, 2001) extend the Fredholm approach to cover a class of discontinuous kernels.

[3] For a more extensive discussion of integral equations of the Fredholm type, we refer to Hochstadt (1973) and Kondo (1991).

where $h(t)$ is the solution of the following type II Fredholm integral equation

$$h(t) = m(t) + \lambda \int K(s,t)\, h(s)\, ds, \tag{7}$$

evaluated at $\lambda = 2i\theta$, $K(s,t)$ is the covariance of $X(t)$, and $m(t) = \int K(s,t)\, n(s)\, ds$.

Remark 1 Although Tanaka (1996, Theorem 5.9) presents this lemma for the covariance $K(s,t)$ of $X(t)$, his exposition generalizes for a more general case. Adopting his arguments one can see that Lemma 1 essentially relies on an orthogonal decomposition of $X(t)$, which does not necessarily have to be based on the covariance of $X(t)$. In particular, if there exists a symmetric and continuous function $C(s,t)$ such that

$$\int X^2(t)\, dt = \int\int C(s,t)\, dw(s)\, dw(t),$$

then we may find $h(t)$ as in (7) by solving $h(t) = \int C(s,t)\, n(s)\, ds + \lambda \int C(s,t)\, h(s)\, ds$. This may in some cases shorten and simplify the derivations. As will be seen in the Appendix, we may find the characteristic function of DW_μ resorting to this remark.

4 Characteristic Functions

In Proposition 2 below, we will give expressions for the characteristic functions of DW_j^{-1} ($j = \mu, \tau$) employing Lemma 1. To that end we use that $DW_j^{-1} = \int \left[X_j(t) + n_j(t)\right]^2 dt$ for some integrable functions $n_j(t)$ and demeaned and detrended Ornstein–Uhlenbeck processes $X_\mu(t)$ and $X_\tau(t)$, respectively, see Lemma 2 in the Appendix. $n_\mu(t)$ and $n_\tau(t)$ capture the effect of the initial condition whose exact forms are given in the Appendix. Hence, we are left with deriving the covariance functions of $X_\mu(t)$ and $X_\tau(t)$. We provide these rather straightforward results in the following proposition.

Proposition 1 *The covariance functions of $X_\mu(t)$ and $X_\tau(t)$ from $DW_j^{-1} = \int \left[X_j(t) + n_j(t)\right]^2 dt$ are*

$$K_\mu(s,t) = K_1(s,t) - g(t) - g(s) + \omega_0,$$

$$K_\tau(s,t) = K_1(s,t) + \sum\nolimits_{k=1}^{8} \phi_k(s)\, \psi_k(t),$$

where $K_1(s,t) = \frac{1}{2c}\left[e^{-c|s-t|} - e^{-c(s+t)}\right]$ and the functions $\phi_k(s)$, $\psi_k(s)$, $k = 1, 2, \ldots, 8$, and $g(s)$ and the constant ω_0 can be found in the Appendix.

The problem dealt with in this paper technically translates into finding $h_j(t)$ as outlined in Lemma 1 for $K_j(s,t)$, $j = \mu, \tau$, i.e. finding $h_j(t)$ that solves a type II Fredholm integral equation of the form (7). Solving a Fredholm integral equation in general requires the knowledge of the FD and the resolvent of the associated kernel. The FD for $K_j(s,t)$ $(j = \mu, \tau)$ are known (Nabeya and Tanaka 1990b),but not the resolvents. Finding the resolvent is in general tedious, let alone the difficulties one might face finding $h_j(t)$ once FD and the resolvent are known. To overcome these difficulties, we suggest a different approach to find $h_j(t)$ which follows.[4] As we see from Proposition 1 kernels of the integral equations considered here are of the following general form

$$K(s,t) = K_1(s,t) + \sum_{k=1}^{n} \phi_k(s)\,\psi_k(t).$$

Thus to solve for $h(t)$ in

$$h(t) = m(t) + \lambda \int K(s,t)\,h(s)\,ds, \tag{8}$$

we let $\upsilon = \sqrt{\lambda - c^2}$ and observe that (8) is equivalent to

$$h''(t) + \upsilon^2 h(t) = m''(t) - c^2 m(t) + \lambda \sum_{k=1}^{n} b_k \left[\psi_k''(t) - c^2 \psi_k(t)\right], \tag{9}$$

with the following boundary conditions

$$h(0) = m(0) + \lambda \sum_{k=1}^{n} b_k \psi_k(0), \tag{10}$$

$$h'(0) = m'(0) + \lambda \sum_{k=1}^{n} b_k \psi_k'(0) + \lambda b_{n+1}, \tag{11}$$

where

$$b_k = \int \phi_k(s)\,h(s)\,ds,\ k = 1, 2, \ldots, n \text{ and } b_{n+1} = \int e^{-cs} h(s)\,ds. \tag{12}$$

The solution to (9) can now be written as

$$h(t) = c_1 \cos \upsilon t + c_2 \sin \upsilon t + g_m(t) + \sum_{k=1}^{n} b_k g_k(t) \tag{13}$$

where $g_k(t)$, $k = 1, 2, \ldots, n$, are special solutions to the following differential equations

[4]Nabeya and Tanaka (1988) use a similar method to find the FD of kernel of the general form $K(s,t) = \min(s,t) + \sum_{k=1}^{n} \phi_k(s)\,\psi_k(t)$. See page 148 of Tanaka (1996) for some examples.

$$g_k''(t) + \upsilon^2 g_k(t) = \lambda \left[\psi_k''(t) - c^2 \psi_k(t)\right], k = 1, 2, \ldots, n,$$

and $g_m(t)$ is a special solution of

$$g_m''(t) + \upsilon^2 g_m(t) = m''(t) - c^2 m(t).$$

Using the boundary conditions (10) and (11) together with equations from (12) the unknowns c_1, c_2, b_1, b_2, ..., b_{n+1} are found giving an explicit form for (13). The solution for $h(t)$ can then be used for the purposes of Lemma 1. It is important to note that if we replace $K_1(s,t)$ with any other nondegenerate kernel, the boundary conditions (10) and (11) need to be modified accordingly.

Using the method described above we establish the following proposition containing our main results for DW_j $(j = \mu, \tau)$.

Proposition 2 *For DW_j $(j = \mu, \tau)$ we have under Assumptions 1, 2, and 3b)*

$$E\left[e^{i\theta DW_j^{-1}}\right] = \left[D_j(2i\theta)\right]^{-1/2} \left\{1 - \frac{\sigma_\delta^2}{c}\left[i\theta\Theta_j - 2\theta^2\Psi_j(\theta;c)\right]\right\}^{-1/2} \times$$

$$\exp\left\{\frac{\mu_\delta^2\left[i\theta\Theta_j - 2\theta^2\Psi_j(\theta;c)\right]}{2c - 2\sigma_\delta^2\left[i\theta\Theta_j - 2\theta^2\Psi_j(\theta;c)\right]}\right\},$$

where $D_j(\lambda)$ is the FD of $K_j(s,t)$ with $\upsilon = \sqrt{\lambda - c^2}$,

$$D_\mu(\lambda) = \frac{e^{-c}}{\upsilon^4}\left[\upsilon\left(\lambda - c^3\right)\sin\upsilon - \left(c^2\upsilon^2 + 2c\lambda\right)\cos\upsilon + 2c\lambda\right],$$

$$D_\tau(\lambda) = e^{-c}\left[\left(\frac{c^5 - 4\lambda c^2}{\upsilon^4} - \frac{12\lambda(c+1)\left(c^2+\lambda\right)}{\upsilon^6}\right)\frac{\sin\upsilon}{\upsilon}\right.$$

$$\left. + \left(\frac{c^4}{\upsilon^4} + \frac{8\lambda c^3}{\upsilon^6} - \frac{48\lambda^2(c+1)}{\upsilon^8}\right)\cos\upsilon + \frac{4\lambda\upsilon^2c^2(c+3) + 48\lambda^2(c+1)}{\upsilon^8}\right],$$

and

$$\Theta_\mu = \frac{e^{-2c}}{2c^2}\left(-1 + e^c\right)\left(c - 2e^c + ce^c + 2\right),$$

$$\Theta_\tau = \frac{e^{-c}}{c^4}\left[-4\left(-6 + c^2\right) - 8\left(3 + c^2\right)\cosh c + c\left(24 + c^2\right)\sinh c\right],$$

where $\Psi_j(\theta;c)$ for $j = \mu, \tau$ are given in the Appendix.

Remark 2 Under Assumption 3a) the limiting distributions of DW_j, $j = \mu$, τ, are the same as the limiting distributions derived under a zero initial condition in Nabeya and Tanaka (1990b). These results are covered here when $\mu_\delta = \sigma_\delta^2 = 0$.

Remark 3 The Fredholm determinants, $D_j(\lambda)$, are taken from Nabeya and Tanaka (1990b).

Remark 4 It is possible to derive the characteristic functions using Girsanov's theorem (see Girsanov 1960) given, for example, in Chap. 4 of Tanaka (1996). Further, note that Girsanov's theorem has been tailored to statistics of the form of DW_j under Lemma 1 in Elliott and Müller (2006).

5 Power Calculation

To calculate the asymptotic power function of $DW_{j,T}$ ($j = \mu, \tau$) we need the quantiles $c_{j,1-\alpha}$ as critical values where ($j = \mu, \tau$)

$$P(DW_j > c_{j,1-\alpha}) = P\left(DW_j^{-1} < c_{j,1-\alpha}^{-1}\right) = \alpha\,.$$

Our graphs rely on the $\alpha = 5\,\%$ level with critical values $c_{\mu,0.95} = 27.35230$ and $c_{\tau,0.95} = 42.71679$ taken, up to an inversion, from Table 1 of Nabeya and Tanaka (1990b). Let $\phi(\theta; c)$ stand for the characteristic functions obtained in Proposition 2 for large initial conditions of both deterministic and random cases in a local neighborhood to the null hypothesis characterized by c. With $x = c_{j,1-\alpha}^{-1}$ we hence can compute the local power by evaluating the distribution function of DW_j^{-1} where we employ the following inversion formula given in Imhof (1961)

$$F(x; c) = \frac{1}{2} - \frac{1}{\pi}\int_0^\infty \frac{1}{\theta}\mathrm{Im}\left[e^{-i\theta x}\phi(\theta; c)\right] d\theta. \tag{14}$$

When it comes to practical computations, Imhof's formula (14) is evaluated using a simple Simpson's rule while correcting for the possible phase shifts which arise due to the square root map over the complex domain (see Tanaka 1996, Chap. 6, for a discussion).[5]

Figure 1 shows the local power functions of DW_j ($j = \mu, \tau$) for a deterministic large initial condition, that is for $\sigma_\delta^2 = 0$ in Assumption 3b). As is clear from Proposition 2, the power function is symmetric around $\mu_\delta = 0$ and decreasing in μ_δ^2 for any level of the local-to-unity parameter c.

For the random case we set $\mu_\delta = 0$. Figure 2 contains graphs for $\sigma_\delta \in \{0, 0.1, \ldots, 3\}$; to keep shape conformity with the case of a large deterministic initial condition the graphs are arranged symmetrically around 0. Figure 2 shows by how much the power decreases in the variance of the initial condition.

[5]The inversion formula (14) is derived in Gurland (1948) and Gil-Pelaez (1951).

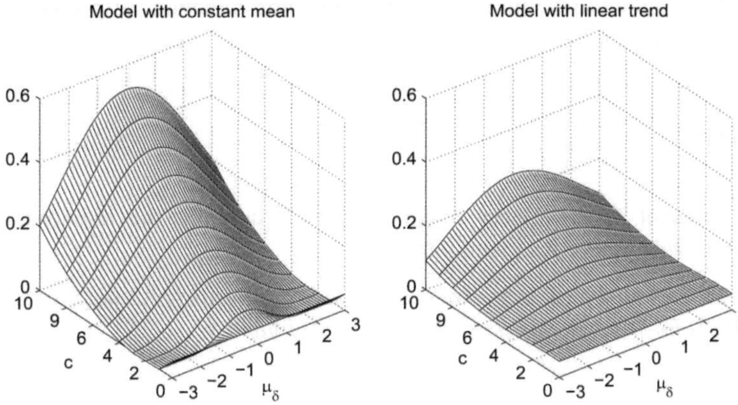

Fig. 1 Power function of DW_j $(j = \mu, \tau)$ for a large deterministic initial condition with $\mu_\delta \in \{-3, -2.9, \ldots, 3\}$, $c \in \{0, 1, \ldots, 10\}$ and $\sigma_\delta = 0$

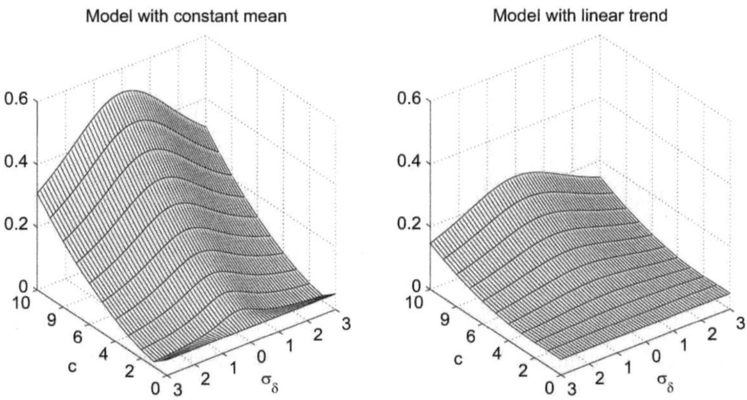

Fig. 2 Power function of DW_j $(j = \mu, \tau)$ for a large random initial condition with $\sigma_\delta \in \{3, 2.9, \ldots, 0, 0.1, \ldots, 3\}$, $c \in \{0, 1, \ldots, 10\}$ and $\mu_\delta = 0$

6 Summary

We analyze the effect of a large initial condition, random or deterministic, on the local-to-unity power of the Durbin–Watson unit root test. Using the Fredholm approach the characteristic function of the limiting distributions are derived. We observe the following findings. First, the local power after detrending is considerably lower than in case of a constant mean. Second, a large initial value has a negative effect on power: the maximum power is achieved for $\mu_\delta = \sigma_\delta = 0$, which corresponds to a "small initial condition." Finally, comparing Figs. 1 and 2 one learns that deterministic and random initials values have a similar effect depending only on the magnitude of the mean or the standard deviation, respectively, of the large initial condition.

Appendix

First we present a preliminary result. Lemma 2 contains the required limiting distributions in terms of Riemann integrals.

Lemma 2 *Let $\{y_t\}$ be generated according to (1) and satisfy Assumptions 1 and 2. It then holds for the test statistics from (2) asymptotically*

$$DW_{j,T} \xrightarrow{D} DW_j = \left(\int \left\{ w_c^j(r) \right\}^2 dr \right)^{-1}, \; j = \mu, \, \tau,$$

where under Assumption 3b)

$$w_c^{\mu}(r) = w_c(r) - \int w_c(s)\, ds,$$

$$w_c^{\tau}(r) = w_c^{\mu}(r) - 12\left(r - \frac{1}{2}\right) \int \left(s - \frac{1}{2}\right) w_c(s)\, ds,$$

with $w_c(r) = w(r)$ for $c = 0$ and

$$w_c(r) = \delta\,(e^{-cr} - 1)(2c)^{-1/2} + J_c(r) \;\; for\; c > 0$$

and the standard Ornstein–Uhlenbeck process $J_c(r) = \int_0^r e^{-c(r-s)} dw(s)$.

Proof The proof is standard by using similar arguments as in Phillips (1987) and Müller and Elliott (2003).

Proof of Proposition 1

We set $\upsilon = \sqrt{\lambda - c^2}$. For DW_{μ} we have $w_c^{\mu}(s) = w_c(r) - \int w_c(s)\, ds$, thus

$$\begin{aligned} Cov\left[w_c^{\mu}(s), w_c^{\mu}(t)\right] &= Cov\left[J_c(s) - \int J_c(s)\, ds, J_c(t) - \int J_c(s)\, ds\right] \\ &= K_1(s,t) - \int Cov\left[J_c(s), J_c(t)\right] ds - \int Cov\left[J_c(s), J_c(t)\right] dt \\ &\quad + \int \int Cov\left[J_c(s), J_c(t)\right] ds \\ &= K_1(s,t) - g(t) - g(s) + \omega_0 \end{aligned}$$

where

$$g(t) = \frac{e^{-c(1+s)}(1-e^{cs})(1-2e^{c}+e^{cs})}{2c^2},$$

$$\omega_0 = -\frac{3-2c+e^{-2c}-4e^{-c}}{2c^3}.$$

For DW_τ we have $w_c^\tau(s) = w_c^\mu(s) - 12\left(s-\frac{1}{2}\right)\int\left(u-\frac{1}{2}\right)w_c(u)\,du$, thus

$$\begin{aligned}
Cov\left[w_c^\tau(s), w_c^\tau(t)\right] &= Cov\left[w_c^\mu(s), w_c^\mu(t)\right] - 12\left(t-\frac{1}{2}\right)\int\left(u-\frac{1}{2}\right) \\
&\quad Cov\left[J_c(s) - \int J_c(v)\,dv, J_c(u)\right]du \\
&\quad -12\left(s-\frac{1}{2}\right)\int\left(u-\frac{1}{2}\right)Cov\left[J_c(u), J_c(t)\right. \\
&\quad \left. -\int J_c(v)\,dv\right]du \\
&\quad +144\left(s-\frac{1}{2}\right)\left(t-\frac{1}{2}\right)\int\int\left(u-\frac{1}{2}\right)\left(v-\frac{1}{2}\right) \\
&\quad \times Cov\left[J_c(u), J_c(v)\right]dudv \\
&= Cov\left[w_c^\mu(s), w_c^\mu(t)\right] \\
&\quad -12\left(t-\frac{1}{2}\right)\int\left(u-\frac{1}{2}\right)Cov\left[J_c(s), J_c(u)\right]du \\
&\quad +12\left(t-\frac{1}{2}\right)\int\int\left(u-\frac{1}{2}\right)Cov\left[J_c(v), J_c(u)\right]dvdu \\
&\quad -12\left(s-\frac{1}{2}\right)\int\left(u-\frac{1}{2}\right)Cov\left[J_c(u), J_c(t)\right]du \\
&\quad +12\left(s-\frac{1}{2}\right)\int\int\left(u-\frac{1}{2}\right)Cov\left[J_c(u), J_c(v)\right]dvdu \\
&\quad +144\left(s-\frac{1}{2}\right)\left(t-\frac{1}{2}\right)\int\int\left(u-\frac{1}{2}\right)\left(v-\frac{1}{2}\right) \\
&\quad \times Cov\left[J_c(u), J_c(v)\right]dudv
\end{aligned}$$

With some calculus the desired result is obtained. In particular we have with $\phi_1(s) = -1$, $\phi_2(s) = -g(s)$, $\phi_3(s) = -3f_1(s)$, $\phi_4(s) = -3(s-1/2)$, $\phi_5(s) = 3\omega_1$, $\phi_6(s) = 3\omega_1(s-1/2)$, $\phi_7(s) = 6\omega_2(s-1/2)$, $\phi_8(s) = \omega_0$, $\psi_1(t) = g(t)$,

$\psi_2(t) = \psi_6(t) = \psi_8(t) = 1$, $\psi_3(t) = \psi_5(t) = \psi_7(t) = t - 1/2$ and $\psi_4(t) = f_1(t)$ while

$$f_1(s) = \frac{e^{-c(1+s)}}{c^3} \times \left[2 + c + 2ce^c - (2+c)e^{2cs} + 2ce^{c+cs}(2s-1)\right],$$

$$\omega_1 = \frac{e^{-2c}(e^c - 1)}{c^4} \times [2 + c + (c-2)e^c],$$
$$\omega_2 = \frac{e^{-2c}}{c^5} \times \left[-3(c+2)^2 - 12c(2+c)e^c + \left(12c - 9c^2 + 2c^3 + 12\right)e^{2c}\right].$$

This completes the proof.

Proof of Proposition 2

Let $\mathcal{L}(X) = \mathcal{L}(Y)$ stand for equality in distribution of X and Y and set $A = \delta(2c)^{-1/2}$. To begin with, we do the proofs conditioning on δ. Consider first DW_μ. To shorten the proofs for DW_μ we work with the following representation for a demeaned Ornstein–Uhlenbeck process given under Theorem 3 of Nabeya and Tanaka (1990b), for their $R_1^{(2)}$ test statistic, i.e. we write

$$\mathcal{L}\left(\int\left\{J_c(r) - \int J_c(s)\,ds\right\}^2 dr\right) = \mathcal{L}\left(\int\int K_0(s,t)\,dw(t)\,dw(s)\right),$$

where $K_0(s,t) = \frac{1}{2c}\left[e^{-c|s-t|} - e^{-c(2-s-t)}\right] - \frac{1}{c^2}p(s)\,p(t)$ with $p(t) = 1 - e^{-c(1-t)}$. Using Lemma 2, we find that

$$n_\mu(t) = A\left(e^{-ct} - 1\right) - A\int\left(e^{-ct} - 1\right)dt.$$

For DW_μ we will be looking for $h_\mu(t)$ in

$$h_\mu(t) = m_\mu(t) + \lambda\int K_0(s,t)\,h_\mu(t)(s)\,ds, \tag{15}$$

where $m_\mu(t) = \int K_0(s,t)\,n_\mu(s)\,ds$. Equation (15) is equivalent to the following boundary condition differential equation

$$h_\mu''(t) + \upsilon^2 h_\mu(t) = m_\mu''(t) - c^2 m_\mu(t) + \lambda b_1, \tag{16}$$

with

$$h_{\mu}(1) = m_{\mu}(1) - \frac{1}{c^2}\lambda b_1 p(1), \tag{17}$$

$$h'_{\mu}(1) = m'_{\mu}(1) - \lambda e^{-c} b_2 - \frac{1}{c^2}\lambda p'(1) b_1, \tag{18}$$

where $b_1 = \int p(s) h_{\mu}(s) ds$ and $b_2 = \int e^{cs} h_{\mu}(s) ds$. Thus have

$$h_{\mu}(t) = c_1^{\mu} \cos \upsilon t + c_2^{\mu} \sin \upsilon t + g_{\mu}(t) + b_1 g_1(t),$$

where $g_{\mu}(t)$ is a special solution to $g''_{\mu}(t) + \upsilon^2 g_{\mu}(t) = m''_{\mu}(t) - c^2 m_{\mu}(t)$ and $g_1(t)$ is a special solution to $g''_1(t) + \upsilon^2 g_1(t) = \lambda$. Boundary conditions (17) and (18) together with $h_{\mu}(t)$ imply

$$c_1^{\mu} \cos \upsilon + c_1^{\mu} \sin \upsilon + \left[g_1(1) + \frac{1}{c^2}\lambda p(1) \right] b_1 = m_{\mu}(1) - g_{\mu}(1),$$

$$-c_1^{\mu} \upsilon \sin \upsilon + c_1^{\mu} \upsilon \cos \upsilon + \left[\frac{1}{c^2}\lambda p'(1) + g'_1(1) \right] b_1 + \lambda e^{-c} b_2 = m'_{\mu}(1) - g'_{\mu}(1),$$

while expressions for b_1 and b_2 imply that

$$c_1^{\mu} \int p(s) \cos \upsilon s ds + c_1^{\mu} \int p(s) \sin \upsilon s ds + b_1 \left(\int p(s) g_1(s) ds - 1 \right)$$
$$= - \int p(s) g_{\mu}(s) ds$$

$$c_1^{\mu} \int e^{cs} \cos \upsilon s ds + c_1^{\mu} \int e^{cs} \sin \upsilon s ds + b_1 \int e^{cs} g_1(s) ds - b_2$$
$$= - \int e^{cs} g_{\mu}(s) ds$$

These form a system of linear equations in c_1^{μ}, c_2^{μ}, b_1, and b_2, which in turn identifies them. With some calculus we write

$$\int n_{\mu}(t) h_{\mu}(t) dt = \frac{A e^{-2c}}{2c^2 \lambda \upsilon} \times$$
$$[-A(-1 + e^c)(2 + c + (-2 + c)e^c)$$
$$+2e^c \left(c c_2^{\mu} \lambda - c e^c \left(c^2 c_2^{\mu} - c^2 c_1^{\mu} - (-1 + c) c_2^{\mu} \upsilon^2 \right) \right)$$
$$+2c e^c \left(c^3 c_2^{\mu} - c c_2^{\mu} \lambda + c_2^{\mu} (-1 + e^c) \lambda - c^2 c_1^{\mu} \upsilon \right) \cos \upsilon$$
$$-2c e^c \left(c^3 c_1^{\mu} - c c_1^{\mu} \lambda + c_1^{\mu} (-1 + e^c) \lambda + c^2 c_2^{\mu} \upsilon \right) \sin \upsilon].$$

Solving for c_1^{μ} and c_2^{μ} we find that they are both a multiple of A, hence

$$\Psi_{\mu}(\theta; c) = \frac{1}{A^2} \int n_{\mu}(t)\, h_{\mu}(t)\, dt,$$

is free of A. Now with $\Theta_{\mu} = \int n_{\mu}^2(t)\, dt$, an application of Lemma 1 results in

$$E\left[e^{i\theta \int \{w_c^{\mu}(r)\}^2 dr} | \delta\right] = \left[D_{\mu}(2i\theta)\right]^{-1/2} \exp\left[i\theta A^2 \Theta_{\mu} - 2\theta^2 A^2 \Psi_{\mu}(\theta; c)\right].$$

As $\sqrt{2c}A = \delta \sim N\left(\mu_{\delta}, \sigma_{\delta}^2\right)$, standard manipulations complete the proof for $j = \mu$.

Next we turn to DW_{τ}. Using Lemma 2 we find that

$$n_{\tau}(t) = A\left[\left(e^{-ct} - 1\right) - \int \left(e^{-ct} - 1\right) dt - 12(t - 1/2) \int (t - 1/2)\left(e^{-ct} - 1\right) dt\right].$$

Here we will be looking for $h_{\tau}(t)$ in the

$$h_{\tau}(t) = m_{\tau}(t) + \lambda \int K_{\tau}(s,t)\, h_{\tau}(t)(s)\, ds, \tag{19}$$

where $m_{\tau}(t) = \int K_{\tau}(s,t)\, n_{\tau}(s)\, ds$ and $K_{\tau}(s,t)$ is from Proposition 1. Equation (19) can be written as

$$h_{\tau}''(t) + \upsilon^2 h_{\tau}(t) = m_{\tau}''(t) - c^2 m_{\tau}(t) + \lambda \sum\nolimits_{k=1}^{8} b_k \left[\psi_k''(t) - c^2 \psi_k(t)\right], \tag{20}$$

with the following boundary conditions

$$h_{\tau}(0) = m_{\tau}(0) + \lambda \sum\nolimits_{k=1}^{8} b_k \psi_k(0), \tag{21}$$

$$h_{\tau}'(0) = m_{\tau}'(0) + \lambda \sum\nolimits_{k=1}^{8} b_k \psi_k'(0) + \lambda b_9, \tag{22}$$

where

$$b_k = \int \phi_k(s)\, h_{\tau}(s)\, ds,\ k = 1, \ldots, 8 \text{ and } b_9 = \int e^{-cs} h(s)\, ds. \tag{23}$$

The solution to (20) is

$$h_{\tau}(t) = c_1^{\tau} \cos \upsilon t + c_2^{\tau} \sin \upsilon t + g_{\tau}(t) + \sum\nolimits_{k=1}^{8} b_k g_k(t) \tag{24}$$

where $g_k(t)$, $k = 1, 2, \ldots, 8$, are special solutions to the following differential equations

$$g_k''(t) + \upsilon^2 g_k(t) = \lambda\left[\psi_k''(t) - c^2\psi_k(t)\right], k = 1, 2, \ldots, 8,$$

and $g_\tau(t)$ is a special solution of $g_\tau''(t) + \upsilon^2 g_\tau(t) = m_\tau''(t) - c^2 m_\tau(t)$. The solution given in (24) can be written as

$$\begin{aligned} h_\tau(t) &= c_1^\tau \cos\upsilon t + c_2^\tau \sin\upsilon t + g_\tau(t) - b_1\frac{\lambda}{\upsilon^2} - \frac{\lambda c^2}{\upsilon^2}(b_2 + b_6 + b_8) \\ &+ (b_3 + b_5 + b_7)\lambda c^2 \frac{1-2t}{2\upsilon^2} + b_4\lambda\frac{1-2t}{2\upsilon^2}. \end{aligned} \tag{25}$$

The boundary conditions in (21) and (22) imply

$$\begin{aligned} m_\tau(0) - g_\tau(0) = c_1^\tau &+ \frac{\lambda}{2\upsilon^2}(-2b_1 + b_4) \\ &+\frac{\lambda}{2}\left(\frac{c^2}{\upsilon^2} + 1\right)(-2b_2 + b_3 + b_5 - 2b_6 + b_7 - 2b_8) \end{aligned}$$

$$\begin{aligned} m_\tau'(0) - g_\tau'(0) = c_2^\tau\mu - \lambda b_1 g'(0) &- \lambda\left(\frac{c^2}{\upsilon^2} + 1\right)(b_3 + b_5 + b_7) \\ &-\left(\frac{1}{\upsilon^2} + f'(0)\right)\lambda b_4 - \lambda b_5, \end{aligned}$$

while expressions given under (23) characterize nine more equations. These equations form a system of linear equations in unknowns c_1^τ, c_2^τ, b_1, ..., b_9, which can be simply solved to fully identify (25). Let $\Theta_\tau = \int n_\tau(t)^2 dt$. Also as for the constant case we set

$$\Psi_\tau(\theta; c) = \frac{1}{A^2}\int n_\tau(t)\, h_\tau(t)\, dt,$$

whose expression is long and we do not report here. When solving this integral we see that $\Psi_\tau(\theta; c)$ is free of A. As before we apply Lemma 1 to establish the following

$$E\left[e^{i\theta\int\{w_c^\tau(r)\}^2 dr}|\delta\right] = \left[D_\tau(2i\theta)\right]^{-1/2}\exp\left[i\theta A^2\Theta_\tau - 2\theta^2 A^2\Psi_\tau(\theta; c)\right].$$

Now, using $E\left[e^{i\theta\int\{w_c^\tau(r)\}^2 dr}\right] = EE\left[e^{i\theta\int\{w_c^\tau(r)\}^2 dr}|\delta\right]$, standard manipulations complete the proof.

References

Bhargava, A. (1986). On the theory of testing for unit roots in observed time series. *Review of Economic Studies*, *53*, 369–384.

Durbin, J., & Watson, G. S. (1950). Testing for serial correlation in least squares regression. *I. Biometrika*, *37*, 409–428.

Durbin, J., & Watson, G. S. (1951). Testing for serial correlation in least squares regression. *II. Biometrika*, *38*, 159–178.

Durbin, J., & Watson, G. S. (1971). Testing for serial correlation in least squares regression. *III. Biometrika*, *58*, 1–19.

Elliott, G., & Müller, U. K. (2006). Minimizing the impact of the initial condition on testing for unit roots. *Journal of Econometrics*, *135*, 285–310.

Gil-Pelaez, J. (1951). Note on the inversion theorem. *Biometrika*, *38*, 481–482.

Girsanov, I. (1960). On transforming a certain class of stochastic processes by absolutely continuous substitution of measures. *Theory of Probability and Its Applications*, *5*, 285–301.

Gurland, J. (1948). Inversion formulae for the distribution of ratios. *Annals of Mathematical Statistics*, *19*, 228–237.

Hamilton, J. D. (1994). *Time series analysis*. Cambridge: Cambridge University Press.

Harvey, D. I., Leybourne, S. J., & Taylor, A. M. R. (2009). Unit root testing in practice: Dealing with uncertainty over the trend and initial condition. *Econometric Theory*, *25*, 587–636.

Hisamatsu, H., & Maekawa, K. (1994). The distribution of the Durbin-Watson statistic in integrated and near-integrated models. *Journal of Econometrics*, *61*, 367–382.

Hochstadt, H. (1973). *Integral equations*. New York: Wiley.

Imhof, J. P. (1961). Computing the distribution of quadratic forms in normal variables. *Biometrika*, *4*, 419–426.

Kondo, J. (1991). *Integral equations*. Oxford: Clarendon Press.

Kurozumi, E. (2002). Testing for stationarity with a break. *Journal of Econometrics*, *108*, 63–99.

Müller, U. K., & Elliott, G. (2003). Tests for unit roots and the initial condition. *Econometrica*, *71*, 1269–1286.

Nabeya, S. (2000). Asymptotic distributions for unit root test statistics in nearly integrated seasonal autoregressive models. *Econometric Theory*, *16*, 200–230.

Nabeya, S. (2001). Approximation to the limiting distribution of t- and F-statistics in testing for seasonal unit roots. *Econometric Theory*, *17*, 711–737.

Nabeya, S., & Tanaka, K. (1988). Asymptotic theory of a test for the constancy of regression coefficients against the random walk alternative. *Annals of Statistics*, *16*, 218–235.

Nabeya, S., & Tanaka, K. (1990a). A general approach to the limiting distribution for estimators in time series regression with nonstable autoregressive errors. *Econometrica*, *58*, 145–163.

Nabeya, S., & Tanaka, K. (1990b). Limiting power of unit-root tests in time-series regression. *Journal of Econometrics*, *46*, 247–271.

Phillips, P. C. B. (1987). Towards a unified asymptotic theory for autoregressions. *Biometrika*, *74*, 535–547.

Phillips, P. C. B., & Solo, V. (1992). Asymptotics for linear processes. *The Annals of Statistics*, *20*, 971–1001.

Presno, M. J., & López, A. J. (2003). Testing for stationarity in series with a shift in the mean. A Fredholm approach. *Test*, *12*, 195–213.

Sargan, J. D., & Bhargava, A. (1983). Testing residuals from least squares regression for being generated by the gaussian random walk. *Econometrica*, *51*, 153–174.

Tanaka, K. (1990). The Fredholm approach to asymptotic inference on nonstationary and noninvertible time series models. *Econometric Theory*, *6*, 411–432.

Tanaka, K. (1996). *Time series analysis: Nonstationary and noninvertible distribution theory*. New York: Wiley.

White, J. S. (1958). The limiting distribution of the serial correlation coefficient in the explosive case. *Annals of Mathematical Statistics*, *29*, 1188–1197.

Testing for Cointegration in a Double-LSTR Framework

Claudia Grote and Philipp Sibbertsen

Abstract This paper investigates the finite-sample properties of the smooth transition-based cointegration test proposed by Kapetanios et al. (Econ Theory 22:279–303, 2006) when the data generating process under the alternative hypothesis is a globally stationary second order LSTR model. The provided procedure describes an application to long-run equilibrium relations involving real exchange rates with symmetric behaviour. We utilise the properties of the double LSTR transition function that features unit root behaviour within the inner regime and symmetric behaviour in the outer regimes. Hence, under the null hypothesis we imply no cointegration and globally stationary D-LSTR cointegration under the alternative. As a result of the identification problem the limiting distribution derived under the null hypothesis is non-standard. The Double LSTR is capable of producing three-regime TAR nonlinearity when the transition parameter tends to infinity as well as generating exponential-type nonlinearity that closely approximates ESTR nonlinearity. Therefore, we find that the Double LSTR error correction model has power against both of these alternatives.

1 Introduction

Ever since the concept of cointegration has been introduced by Granger (1981) and Engle and Granger (1987), research on cointegrated time series has experienced a broad expansion. Yet it is still developing and of great importance for economic applications such as exchange rates and equity indices, cf. Maki (2013) or Zhang (2013). One of the latest research branches is the extension of cointegration to

---

This paper is dedicated to Sigfried Heiler, a most inspiring econometrician. We are indebted to Philip Bertram for helpful comments and remarks.

C. Grote • P. Sibbertsen (✉)
Faculty of Economics and Management, Institute of Statistics, Leibniz University Hannover, 30167 Hannover, Germany
e-mail: grote@statistik.uni-hannover.de; sibbertsen@statistik.uni-hannover.de

J. Beran et al. (eds.), *Empirical Economic and Financial Research*,
Advanced Studies in Theoretical and Applied Econometrics 48,
DOI 10.1007/978-3-319-03122-4_27

nonlinear dynamics and regime-switching error correction mechanisms. With regard to the nonlinear cointegration literature, a distinction is drawn between time-varying cointegration on the one hand, cf. Bierens and Martins (2010) or Shi and Phillips (2012), and nonlinear adjustment processes on the other hand. Recently, the latter has been of major interest implying unsteady and unproportional correction of the disequilibrium error which is why particular attention has been directed towards testing the existence of nonlinearities, cf. Kapetanios et al. (2006) henceforth KSS, or Kiliç (2011). Thus, due to the ability to incorporate smooth dynamic adjustment via smooth transition (STR) functions, STR-models are widely applied for modelling the disequilibrium error.

Regime-switching cointegration can be considered as an approach that deals with the combination of nonlinearities and nonstationarities. It combines cointegration as the global problem and nonlinearity as the local problem, cf. Balke and Fomby (1997). Depending on the specification, the underlying testing problem can be formulated as either unit root *or* linearity against STR cointegration, see also Dufrénot et al. (2006). First approaches suggested a null hypothesis of no nonlinear adjustment in a linear cointegration framework and consequently based inference on a linear error correction model (ECM), cf. Seo (2004) or Nedeljkovic (2011). Among others KSS established appropriate theoretical foundations for inference based on a nonlinear ECM. In accordance with these authors it is reasonable to utilise a test that is designed to have power against the alternative of nonlinear dynamic adjustment.

The reason why research focus has come to allow nonlinear short-run dynamics in the adjustment process to deviations from long-run equilibrium relations is, e.g., contemporaneous price differentials for a certain good. Since it is acknowledged that Jevons's law of one price does not apply intertemporally, researchers have decided to ease conventional restrictions like the assumption of efficient markets. For instance, exchange rates under the purchasing power parity in the presence of transaction costs exemplify the necessity of regime-switching dynamics in econometrics, compare Taylor et al. (2001) or Taylor (2001).

However, first advances in nonlinear cointegration refer to Balke and Fomby (1997) who introduced threshold cointegration. According to them error correction requires the disequilibrium error to exceed a critical threshold, implying that price deviations between two locations are corrected by arbitrage only when deviations were sufficiently large. Subsequent extension can be found in Siklos and Granger (1997) or Chen et al. (2005). For particular contributions with respect to testing see Enders and Granger (1998), Lo and Zivot (2001) or Hansen and Seo (2002). If the switch is rather smooth than discrete, STR ECMs, brought forward by, e.g., Taylor and Peel (2000) or Kiliç (2011), are applied. If the transition between the slowly adjusting inner regime and the quickly adjusting outer regimes are associated with small and large price deviations, respectively, an exponential STR ECM should be employed. If negative and positive deviations are corrected differently, the adjustment process is subject to asymmetric behaviour. In that case a logistic transition function is just appropriate for the adjustment process.

In this paper we propose D-LSTR as an overall generalisation of STR functions. More precisely this work addresses STR-based nonlinear adjustment processes and especially a globally stationary Double-LSTR cointegration process with symmetric behaviour in the outer regimes. The aim is to show that D-LSTR cointegration has better power than other STR functions. We are especially interested in the power results compared to KSS's nonlinear cointegration test based on a globally stationary exponential-STR cointegration alternative.
The rest of the paper is organised as follows. In Sect. 2 the testing framework for the t- and F-type test is set up and in Sect. 3 the cointegration tests are introduced. Section 4 presents the power results and section "Conclusion" concludes.

2 Model Setup

We start with a nonlinear vector error correction model (VECM) as in KSS, derived from an $(n \times 1)$-vector $\mathbf{z}_t = (z_{1t}, \ldots, z_{nt})$, consisting of I(1) stochastic processes being given by

$$\boldsymbol{\Delta}\mathbf{z}_t = \boldsymbol{\alpha}\boldsymbol{\beta}'\mathbf{z}_{t-1} + \mathscr{G}(\boldsymbol{\beta}'z_{t-1}) + \sum_{i=1}^{p} \boldsymbol{\Gamma}_i \boldsymbol{\Delta} z_{t-i} + \boldsymbol{\varepsilon}_t, \qquad \text{with } t = 1, \ldots, T. \tag{1}$$

The first and second terms on the right-hand side represent the linear and nonlinear error correction term. $\alpha_{(n \times r)}$ contains the linear adjustment parameters that describe the percentaged correction in period t, while $\beta_{(n \times r)}$ is the cointegrating vector. The cointegration relation is assumed to be linear which is why the second error correction term simply underlies a nonlinear transformation according to the insinuated nonlinear transition function, $\mathscr{G}(\cdot)$. Concerning the specific transition function $\mathscr{G}(\cdot)$ in our testing approach we will go into detail in the ongoing subsection. For some further explanatory power of the model lagged autocorrelations are included in Γ, depending on the optimal lag order p. The $(n \times n)$ error process $\boldsymbol{\varepsilon}_t$ is $iid\,(\mathbf{0}, \boldsymbol{\Sigma})$ with $\boldsymbol{\Sigma}$ being a positive definite matrix. It is assumed that the initial values $\mathbf{Z_0} \equiv (\mathbf{z}_{-p}, \ldots, \mathbf{z}_0)$ are known and $A(z)$ is given by $(1-z)\mathbf{I}_n - \boldsymbol{\alpha}\boldsymbol{\beta}'z - \sum_{i=1}^{p} \boldsymbol{\Gamma}_i (1-z)z^i$. If $\det A(z) = 0$, then $|z| > 1$ or $z = 1$ which implies that the number of unit roots equals $n - r$ with r being the quantity of cointegration relations.
Since we intent to analyse at most one conditional long-run cointegration relation the vector $\mathbf{z}_t$ is decomposed into $(y_t, \mathbf{x}_t')'$, the dependent and the explanatory variable, respectively. The scalar y_t is hereby conditioned by $\mathbf{x}_t$ given the past values of $\mathbf{z}_t$. Hence we obtain

$$\Delta\mathbf{z}_t = \boldsymbol{\alpha} u_{t-1} + \mathscr{G}(u_{t-1}) + \sum_{i=1}^{p} \boldsymbol{\Gamma} \boldsymbol{\Delta} z_{t-i} + \boldsymbol{\varepsilon}_t, \qquad t = 1, \ldots, T \tag{2}$$

whereby the linear cointegration relation is enclosed in

$$u_t = y_t - \boldsymbol{\beta}'_x \mathbf{x}_t\,, \tag{3}$$

with $\boldsymbol{\beta}_x \sim (k \times 1)$ containing the cointegration parameters and k equal to $(n-1)$.

2.1 Double Logistic STR

In our model setup we presume that the switches between regimes are induced by a second-order logistic STR or double LSTR (D-LSTR) process, originally proposed by Jansen and Teräsvirta (1996), derived from

$$\mathcal{G}(s_t; \gamma, c) = (1 + \exp\{-\gamma(s_t - c_1)(s_t - c_2)\})^{-1}\,, \qquad c_1 \leq c_2, \gamma > 0\,.$$

s_t is the state variable that causes the switch between regimes. Here s_t is replaced by the lagged variable of the cointegration relation's error u_{t-1} where the value of u_{t-1} determines if the threshold is met or not. The threshold values c_1 and c_2 are chosen to be $c_1 = -\sqrt{c}$ and $c_2 = \sqrt{c}$ assuming that $-c_1 = c_2$ holds. Therefore, $\mathcal{G}(\cdot)$ simplifies to

$$\mathcal{G}(s_t; \gamma, c) = \left(1 + \exp\{-\gamma(y_{t-1}^2 - c\}\right)^{-1}, \quad \gamma \geq 0\,, \tag{4}$$

and a symmetric transition function is obtained. The smoothness parameter γ determines the gradual changing strength of adjustment for the changes in regimes. The reason why we propose D-LSTR in contrast to an ESTR function is that the D-LSTR approach features special properties. Firstly D-LSTR can display symmetric and stationary behaviour in the outer regimes once $u_{t-1} < -\sqrt{c}$ or $u_{t-1} > \sqrt{c}$, on the one hand. On the other hand, it can display unit root behaviour at the central regime when $-\sqrt{c} < u_{t-1} < \sqrt{c}$. Secondly, it is capable of generating exponential-type nonlinearity that closely approximates ESTR nonlinearity, when the transition parameter tends to infinity, cf. Sollis (2011), even though the D-LSTR model does actually not nest an ESTR-model. Contingent on the value of γ and due to its special properties the D-LSTR function covers not only exponential-type nonlinearity for small and moderate γ but nests 3-regime TAR nonlinearity for $\gamma \to \infty$. Consequently, a self-exciting TAR model is obtained since the state variable equals the transition variable depending on whether the linear combination of y_t and $\mathbf{x_t}$ is stationary or not. This means that the switching of the model depends on the cointegratedness of y_t and $\mathbf{x_t}$. With respect to the assumptions on c_1 and c_2 the outer regimes of this self-exciting TAR model are restricted to be identical.
Furthermore, D-LSTR offers more flexibility concerning the range of the nonstationary regime due to the scaling parameter c, e.g. Kaufmann et al. (2012). In contrast to D-LSTR a possible drawback of an exponential transition function would

be that for $\gamma \to 0$ and $\gamma \to \infty$, the model becomes linear, cf. van Dijk et al. (2002). It should be mentioned that unlike the logistic function the second order logistic function is not bounded between [0, 1]. For finite γ the D-LSTR function realises a minimum different from zero, see van Dijk and Franses (2000). In fact, when $\gamma = 0$, the D-LSTR function $\mathscr{G}(\cdot)$ reduces to 0.5 and the model becomes linear. For this reason, in our testing approach we propose the transition function

$$\mathscr{G}(u_{t-1};\gamma,c) = \left[\left(1+\exp\{-\gamma(u_{t-1}^2 - c)\}\right)^{-1} - 0.5\right], \qquad \gamma > 0\,, \tag{5}$$

following Teräsvirta (1994), who included –0.5 in order to derive linearity tests. In our case subtracting 0.5 ensures that there is no cointegration at all and therefore enables us to test the problem under consideration, what will be issued in an instant. So far, our partitioned model assembles to

$$\begin{aligned}\Delta y_t &= \phi u_{t-1} + \rho u_{t-1}\left[\left(1+\exp\{-\gamma(u_{t-1}^2 - c)\}\right)^{-1} - 0.5\right] + \boldsymbol{\omega}'\boldsymbol{\Delta}\mathbf{x}_t \\ &\quad + \sum_{i=1}^{p}\boldsymbol{\psi}_i'\boldsymbol{\Delta}\mathbf{z}_{t-i} + \epsilon_t \\ \boldsymbol{\Delta}\mathbf{x}_t &= \sum_{i=1}^{p}\boldsymbol{\Gamma}_{xi}\boldsymbol{\Delta}\mathbf{z}_{t-i} + \boldsymbol{\varepsilon}_{xt}\,.\end{aligned} \tag{6}$$

Under the assumption that $\phi = \xi - \gamma$ with $\xi < 0$ the conditional double logistic STR ECM for Δy_t and a marginal vector autoregression model for $\boldsymbol{\Delta}\mathbf{x}_t$ is obtained. For further assumptions and details on certain parameter constraints see KSS.

2.2 *Testing Problem*

We want to test no cointegration against the alternative of globally stationary D-LSTR cointegration. This implies that under the null hypothesis it has to be assured that there is no cointegration in the process. Nonlinear cointegration is solely embodied via the transition function (5) and (6), which consequently needs to be excluded under H_0. As $\mathscr{G}(\cdot)$ reduces to 0.5, when $\gamma = 0$, subtracting one half establishes a feasible null hypothesis. This enables us straightforwardly to formulate the hypotheses as

$$H_0 : \gamma = 0 \qquad \text{vs.} \qquad H_1 : \gamma > 0$$

for testing against globally stationary D-LSTR cointegration. Obviously, $\gamma = 0$ implies that ρ and c are not identified under the Null, referred to as the Davies (1987) problem. The stationarity properties of u_t are determined by the positiveness of γ.

For solving the cointegration problem and in order to test for the nonlinear cointegration relation we apply the Engle and Granger (1987) residual-based two-step procedure. At the first stage the residuals $\hat{u} = y_t - \hat{\boldsymbol{\beta}}_x \mathbf{x}$ are estimated via OLS. At the second stage we expand a first order Taylor series approximation to the STR function due to the non-identification of ρ (ρ and c) in the case of a t-type test (F-type test). The linearisation leads to

$$T_1(\gamma) = 0.5 + 0.25\gamma(u_{t-1}^2 - c). \tag{7}$$

It might seem more appropriate to use a Taylor expansion of a higher order since it captures the symmetric property far better than the line of the first order. Nevertheless, this implies more terms and, respectively, more restrictions to be tested, which might result in a loss of power.
Substituting (7) into (6) we obtain the following auxiliary regression

$$\Delta y_t = \delta_1 \hat{u}_{t-1} + \delta_2 \hat{u}_{t-1}^3 + \boldsymbol{\omega}' \boldsymbol{\Delta} \mathbf{x}_t + \sum_{i=1}^{p} \boldsymbol{\psi}_i' \boldsymbol{\Delta} \mathbf{z}_{t-i} + e_t\,, \tag{8}$$

where we define $\delta_1 \equiv \phi - 0.25\rho\gamma c$ and $\delta_2 \equiv 0.25\rho\gamma$. In accordance with KSS we assume that $\phi = 0$ so that a unit root behaviour around the equilibrium can occur. Imposing $\phi = 0$ does not influence the F-type test as long as $c \neq 0$. For the case that $c = 0$ the test reduces to a t-type test.

3 Cointegration Tests

Setting the switch point c equal to zero finds theoretical justification in many economic and financial applications. Preferably it is utilised in the context of an ESTR function. However, this leads to the following auxiliary regression for the t-type test, where δ_1 and, respectively, $\hat{u}_{t-1}$ cancel out

$$\Delta y_t = \delta_2 \hat{u}_{t-1}^3 + \boldsymbol{\omega}' \boldsymbol{\Delta} \mathbf{x}_t + \sum_{i=1}^{p} \boldsymbol{\psi}_i' \boldsymbol{\Delta} \mathbf{z}_{t-i} + e_t\,,$$

with the corresponding hypotheses

$$H_0 : \delta_2 = 0 \quad \text{vs.} \quad H_1 : \delta_2 < 0\,.$$

The t-statistic is given by

$$t = \frac{\hat{\mathbf{u}}_{-1}^{3'} \mathbf{Q}_1 \Delta \mathbf{y}}{\sqrt{\hat{\sigma}_{NEC}^2 \, \hat{\mathbf{u}}_{-1}^{3'} \, \mathbf{Q}_1 \, \hat{\mathbf{u}}_{-1}^3}} \tag{9}$$

where $\hat{\mathbf{u}}^3_{-1} = \left(\hat{u}^3_0, \ldots, \hat{u}^3_{T-1}\right)$, $\mathbf{Q}_1 = \mathbf{I}_T - \mathbf{S}(\mathbf{S}'\mathbf{S})^{-1}\mathbf{S}'$, $\mathbf{S} = \big(\Delta\mathbf{X}, \Delta\mathbf{Z}_{-1}, \ldots, \Delta\mathbf{Z}_{-p}\big)$ and $\Delta\mathbf{y} = (\Delta y_1, \ldots, \Delta y_T)'$.

Assuming that $c \neq 0$ the auxiliary regression is given by (8). As we have two restrictions in the F-type test case the corresponding couple of hypotheses for testing for nonlinear cointegration are given by:

$$H_0 : \delta_1 = \delta_2 = 0 \quad \text{vs.} \quad H_1 : \delta_1 \neq 0 \text{ or } \delta_2 < 0\,.$$

The F-type statistic has the form

$$F_{NEC} = \frac{(RSS_0 - RSS_1)/2}{RSS_1/(T-3-p)}\,, \tag{10}$$

where RSS_0 is the residual sum of squares obtained by imposing the two restrictions given under the null hypothesis, $\delta_1 = \delta_2 = 0$ and RSS_1 is the residual sum of squares under the alternative. Since the alternative to a unit root is actually one-sided in the direction of stable roots, like here δ_2 is restricted to be less than zero, it might be beneficial to take the one-sidedness of the alternative into account. For this purpose, an approach that incorporates one-sided alternatives can be found in Abadir and Distaso (2007).

In case of a non-cointegrated relation the series remain nonstationary and hence, the limiting distribution of both the t-type and the F-type test will be non-standard under the null hypothesis. Hence, the limiting distributions converge to some functionals of Brownian motions. By similar arguments as in KSS we derive for the t-type test

$$t_{NEC} = \frac{\int B^3 \mathrm{d}W}{\sqrt{\int B^6 \mathrm{d}\alpha}}\,,$$

and for the F-type test

$$F_{NEC} = \frac{1}{2}\left[\int B\mathrm{d}W\right]\begin{bmatrix} \int B^2\mathrm{d}\alpha & \int B^4\mathrm{d}\alpha \\ \int B^4\mathrm{d}\alpha & \int B^6\mathrm{d}\alpha \end{bmatrix}^{-1}\begin{bmatrix} \int B\mathrm{d}W \\ \int B^3\mathrm{d}W \end{bmatrix}\,,$$

where B and W are shorthand notations for $B(\alpha) = W(\alpha) - \mathbf{W}_x(\alpha)'\left(\int_0^1 \mathbf{W}_x(\alpha)\mathbf{W}_x(\alpha)'\mathrm{d}\alpha\right)^{-1} \times \left(\int_0^1 \mathbf{W}_x(\alpha)W_x(\alpha)\mathrm{d}\alpha\right)$ where $W(\alpha)$ and $\mathbf{W}_x(\alpha)$ defined on $\alpha \in [0, 1]$ are independent scalar and k-vector standard Brownian motions. For a proof hereof see KSS.

4 Finite-Sample Properties

In order to examine the power results in dependence of the two major parameters γ and ρ we conduct a Monte Carlo study. For this purpose, the model is simplified to a bivariate ECM, where β_x is assumed to be equal to one and

$$\begin{aligned} \Delta y_t &= \lambda \Delta x_t + \rho u_{t-1}\left[\left(1+\exp\{-\gamma(u_{t-1}^2-c)\}\right)^{-1} - 0.5\right] + \varepsilon_t \\ \Delta x_t &= \nu_t, \qquad u_t = y_t - \beta_x x_t \\ \begin{bmatrix}\varepsilon_t \\ \nu_t\end{bmatrix} &\sim iid\,\mathcal{N}\left(\mathbf{0}, \begin{bmatrix}\sigma_1^2 & 0 \\ 0 & \sigma_2^2\end{bmatrix}\right). \end{aligned}$$

The parameter constellations under investigation are the following:

$$\lambda = \{0.5, 1\}, \rho = \{-1.0, -0.5, -0.3, -0.1\}, \gamma = \{0.8, 1, 2, 1000\}, \text{ and } \sigma_2 = \{1, 4\}.$$

Because γ does not only determine the smoothness of adjustment but determines also how present the effect of the nonlinear error correction is, we expect the test to have power finding a nonlinear cointegration relation, when γ becomes larger. Therefore, we vary γ as is illustrated below, cf. Fig. 1. In accordance with KSS we investigate the impact of the common factor restriction, $\lambda = 1$, for serial correlation in the disturbances. Therefore, we consider different parameter values for $\lambda = \{0.5, 1\}$ and also we want to investigate the impact of different signal-to-noise ratios and vary $\sigma_2^2 = \{1, 4\}$.

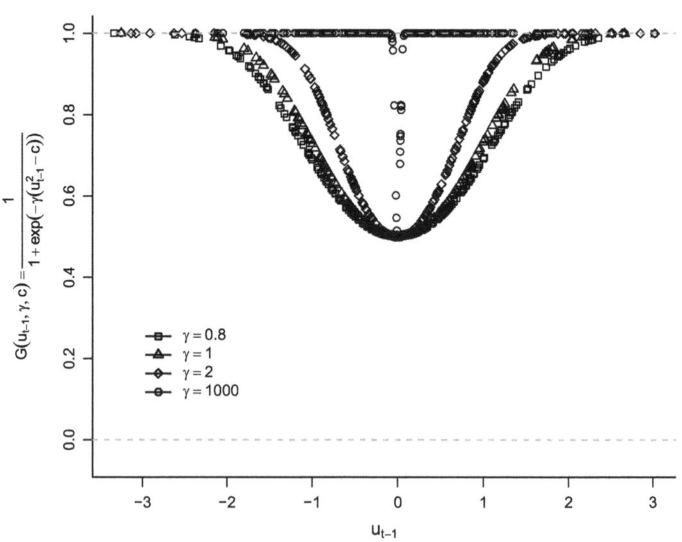

Fig. 1 Transition function depending on a varying γ with a $c = 0$

As mentioned before, the codomain for the transition probabilities has been scaled down to a half and to $[0.5, 1]$, respectively. $\gamma < 1$ are frequently chosen values in the ESTR context, which is why γ is set equal to 0.8, compare the squared line. The triangled and hashed lines show a still very smooth transition whereas the circled line graphs a very fast transition at $\gamma = 1{,}000$. Here the speedy transition results in a 3-regime TAR approximation.
ρ determines how present the nonlinear cointegration is which is why we expect a drop in the power for a sinking ρ. The values for λ are taken from KSS.
In the following table the power results for our t- and F-type test are presented. Additionally we compare these results to a linear cointegration test, wherefore we conducted the Johansen procedure on the globally stationary D-LSTR process, cf. Johansen (1988, 1991) in order to discriminate between a nonlinear and a linear cointegration test. The table provides the power results for all possible combinations of the before mentioned parameter constellations σ_2, ρ, γ, and λ. The results are displayed in Table 1 and Fig. 2.

4.1 Power Results

One can recognise a clear power loss for $\rho > -1$ when $\sigma_2 = 1$. In case that $\sigma_2 = 4$ the power loss begins for $\rho > -0.3$ for raw and demeaned data and for detrended data at $\rho > -0.5$. A power loss for a sinking magnitude of ρ is quite plausible as $\rho < 1$ determines how present cointegration is and thus ensures global stationarity. The power patterns within a particular block of the same kind of data and for the same ρ are however alike. Apparently the transition speed does not make a big difference to the power when γ varies among $\{0.8, 1, 2, 1{,}000\}$. The power gain for a faster transition is marginal. This finding might be due to the possibly low amount of observations in the outer regimes.

It is interesting to observe that the F-type test gains power when the data is demeaned or detrended whereas the t-type test loses power. Regarding the graphs in Fig. 2 it can be seen that the power for $\lambda = 0.5$ dominates the power results for $\lambda = 1$ for both tests and all kinds of data sets and moreover, increases with the variance of the innovations in the regressor x. This finding is analogue to KSS, where the nonlinear tests have superior power when the common factor restriction is violated, which is due to the increased correlation with the regression error, see KSS. As expected Johansen's linear cointegration test is beaten by the nonlinear cointegration tests (t and F) for all different kinds of data sets, see Table 1.

Table 1 Power results for varying parameter constellations of $\{\sigma_2, \lambda, \gamma, \rho\}$

T=100, $\alpha = 0.05$			$\sigma_2 = 1$									$\sigma_2 = 4$								
			Raw data			Demeaned data			Detrended data			Raw data			Demeaned data			Detrended data		
ρ	γ	λ	JOH	t_{NEC}	F_{NEC}	JOH	t_{NEC}	F_{NEC}	JOH	t_{NEC}	F_{NEC}	JOH	t_{NEC}	F_{NEC}	JOH	t_{NEC}	F_{NEC}	JOH	t_{NEC}	F_{NEC}
−1	0.8	0.5	0.9270	0.9984	1.0000	0.9258	0.9902	1.0000	0.8188	0.9712	1.0000	0.9482	1.0000	1.0000	0.9502	1.0000	1.0000	0.8272	0.9998	1.0000
		1	0.8590	0.9968	0.9986	0.8646	0.9744	1.0000	0.7844	0.9424	1.0000	0.8676	0.9976	0.9994	0.8610	0.9764	1.0000	0.7784	0.9408	0.9994
	1	0.5	0.9292	0.9980	1.0000	0.9340	0.9902	1.0000	0.8230	0.9700	0.9998	0.9502	1.0000	1.0000	0.9484	1.0000	1.0000	0.8168	0.9998	1.0000
		1	0.8946	0.9972	1.0000	0.8910	0.9804	0.9996	0.7924	0.9398	1.0000	0.8882	0.9962	1.0000	0.8878	0.9792	1.0000	0.7890	0.9430	1.0000
	2	0.5	0.9410	0.9984	1.0000	0.9460	0.9902	1.0000	0.8040	0.9700	1.0000	0.9488	1.0000	1.0000	0.9478	1.0000	1.0000	0.8280	1.0000	1.0000
		1	0.9162	0.9970	1.0000	0.9162	0.9722	1.0000	0.8068	0.9354	1.0000	0.9214	0.9960	0.9998	0.9158	0.9762	1.0000	0.8140	0.9404	1.0000
	1,000	0.5	0.9438	0.9980	1.0000	0.9416	0.9846	1.0000	0.8244	0.9598	1.0000	0.9450	1.0000	1.0000	0.9464	1.0000	1.0000	0.8212	0.9998	1.0000
		1	0.9392	0.9940	1.0000	0.9342	0.9624	1.0000	0.8146	0.9212	1.0000	0.9374	0.9926	1.0000	0.9336	0.9638	1.0000	0.8236	0.9140	1.0000
−0.5	0.8	0.5	0.5754	0.8962	0.8570	0.5720	0.7268	0.8904	0.5898	0.5682	0.9206	0.9486	0.9984	0.9984	0.9482	0.9922	1.0000	0.8222	0.9516	1.0000
		1	0.3996	0.8606	0.7002	0.4056	0.6256	0.7844	0.4690	0.4724	0.8540	0.4068	0.8452	0.7034	0.4100	0.6350	0.7812	0.4828	0.4632	0.8566
	1	0.5	0.5936	0.9068	0.8658	0.5884	0.7244	0.9106	0.6056	0.5456	0.9298	0.9476	0.9982	0.9982	0.9442	0.9898	1.0000	0.8102	0.9534	0.9998
		1	0.4232	0.8494	0.7210	0.4254	0.6228	0.8064	0.4892	0.4694	0.8744	0.4186	0.8494	0.7344	0.4276	0.6264	0.8146	0.4970	0.4810	0.8756
	2	0.5	0.6392	0.8910	0.8882	0.6476	0.7260	0.9210	0.6348	0.5622	0.9466	0.9480	0.9988	0.9996	0.9462	0.9914	1.0000	0.8264	0.9528	1.0000
		1	0.4818	0.8312	0.7722	0.4936	0.6220	0.8458	0.5490	0.4688	0.9026	0.4850	0.8388	0.7730	0.4898	0.6256	0.8504	0.5260	0.4870	0.8942
	1,000	0.5	0.6858	0.8878	0.9068	0.6710	0.7192	0.9408	0.6564	0.5600	0.9516	0.9446	0.9990	1.0000	0.9388	0.9900	1.0000	0.8198	0.9544	0.9998
		1	0.5318	0.8210	0.8050	0.5332	0.6172	0.8752	0.5696	0.4644	0.9068	0.5388	0.8332	0.8076	0.5284	0.6246	0.8628	0.5626	0.4718	0.9154

−0.3	0.8	0.5	0.2614	0.6226	0.3822	0.2624	0.3746	0.4816	0.3536	0.2566	0.5734	0.9128	0.9586	0.9732	0.9114	0.8652	0.9726	0.7832	0.6612	0.9354
		1	0.1796	0.5484	0.2582	0.1826	0.3076	0.3772	0.2820	0.2100	0.5192	0.1732	0.5592	0.2588	0.1780	0.3176	0.3884	0.2918	0.2108	0.5100
	1	0.5	0.2624	0.6342	0.3954	0.2610	0.3856	0.4920	0.3328	0.2558	0.5766	0.9076	0.9572	0.9762	0.9204	0.8692	0.9716	0.7892	0.6548	0.9378
		1	0.1932	0.5464	0.2662	0.1916	0.3004	0.3932	0.2822	0.2180	0.5190	0.1910	0.5510	0.2632	0.1880	0.3100	0.3888	0.2840	0.2118	0.5152
	2	0.5	0.2876	0.6192	0.4150	0.2842	0.3826	0.5148	0.3774	0.2454	0.5924	0.9188	0.9568	0.9730	0.9086	0.8642	0.9732	0.7760	0.6628	0.9354
		1	0.2134	0.5446	0.2918	0.2022	0.3188	0.4180	0.3052	0.2212	0.5484	0.2080	0.5336	0.2922	0.2014	0.3322	0.4234	0.2976	0.2298	0.5548
	1,000	0.5	0.2868	0.6218	0.4318	0.2990	0.3920	0.5490	0.3802	0.2694	0.6136	0.9126	0.9598	0.9754	0.9244	0.8744	0.9730	0.7888	0.6706	0.9376
		1	0.2178	0.5414	0.3096	0.2100	0.3114	0.4378	0.3042	0.2178	0.5694	0.2140	0.5324	0.3092	0.2208	0.3240	0.4272	0.3186	0.2224	0.5408
−0.1	0.8	0.5	0.0816	0.1816	0.0464	0.0818	0.0992	0.1066	0.1772	0.0726	0.2020	0.2814	0.3822	0.2008	0.2920	0.1998	0.2238	0.2952	0.0764	0.1888
		1	0.0756	0.1628	0.0420	0.0692	0.1014	0.0998	0.1708	0.0774	0.1976	0.0756	0.1620	0.0392	0.0694	0.0926	0.1014	0.1708	0.0768	0.2046
	1	0.5	0.0856	0.1788	0.0430	0.0808	0.0910	0.1092	0.1708	0.0652	0.1900	0.2834	0.3726	0.2012	0.2798	0.2050	0.2306	0.3100	0.0762	0.1990
		1	0.0712	0.1658	0.0380	0.0728	0.0930	0.1046	0.1722	0.0670	0.1846	0.0700	0.1544	0.0420	0.0680	0.0882	0.1036	0.1702	0.0748	0.1958
	2	0.5	0.0774	0.1706	0.0452	0.0776	0.0900	0.1108	0.1710	0.0680	0.1786	0.2872	0.3782	0.1982	0.2916	0.1934	0.2242	0.3150	0.0760	0.1874
		1	0.0696	0.1604	0.0462	0.0688	0.0892	0.0974	0.1762	0.0678	0.2000	0.0748	0.1604	0.0454	0.0670	0.0866	0.0982	0.1688	0.0700	0.2016
	1,000	0.5	0.0760	0.1788	0.0506	0.0732	0.1030	0.1038	0.1768	0.0764	0.1848	0.2850	0.3786	0.1974	0.2890	0.1978	0.2208	0.3012	0.0784	0.1862
		1	0.0750	0.1596	0.0448	0.0688	0.0864	0.1038	0.1672	0.0684	0.2034	0.0688	0.1544	0.0430	0.0782	0.0968	0.1082	0.1668	0.0666	0.1948

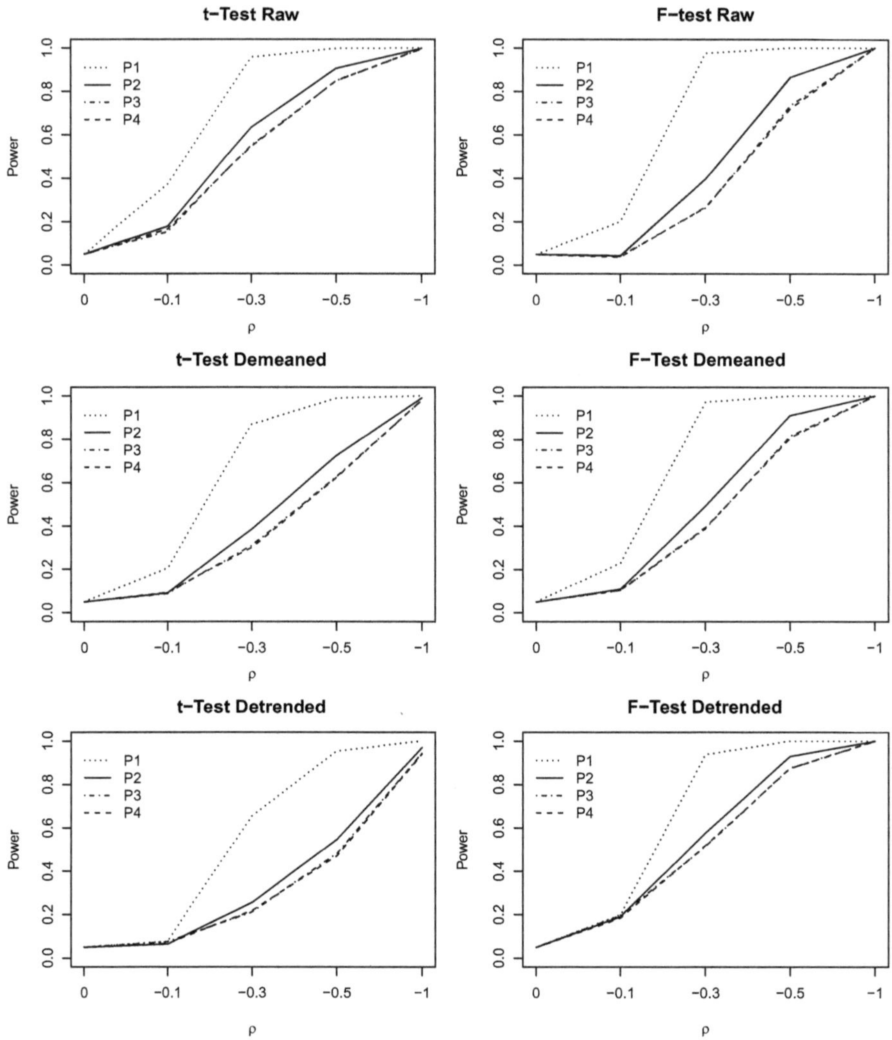

Fig. 2 Power results for the t- and F-type test for $\gamma = 1$

Conclusion

Our proposed D-LSTR function that nests discontinuous adjustment behaviour and is also able to mimic ESTR behaviour has better power than a comparable linear cointegration test. Even though it can be stated for the t- and F-type test that there is a significant power drop for the case when $\rho \geq -0.3$ implying that the cointegration relation is quite weakly present

(continued)

in the process, we can nevertheless conclude that our extension of the KSS testing procedure offers reasonable power results. Compared to the t-type test the F-type test provides even slightly better power results.
In addition to our approach it would be interesting to further discriminate between different cases for $c \neq 0$, what meant a wider inner regime of nonstationarity.

References

Abadir, K., & Distaso, W. (2007). Testing joint hypotheses when one of the alternatives is one-sided. *Journal of Econometrics, 140*, 695–718.

Balke, N., & Fomby, T. (1997). Threshold cointegration. *International Economic Review, 38*, 627–645.

Bierens, H., & Martins, L. (2010). Time-varying cointegration. *Econometric Theory, 26*, 1453–1490.

Chen, L.-H., Finney, M., & Lai, K. (2005). A threshold cointegration analysis of asymmetric price transmission from crude oil to gasoline prices. *Economic Letters, 89*, 233–239.

Davies, R. (1987). Hypothesis testing when a nuisance parameter is present only under the alternative. *Biometrika, 74*, 33–43.

Dufrénot, G., Mathieu, L., Mignon, V., & Péguin-Feissolle, A. (2006). Persistent misalignments of the European exchange rates: Some evidence from non-linear cointegration. *Applied Econometrics, 38*, 203–229.

Enders, W., & Granger, C. (1998). Unit-root tests and asymmetric adjustment with an example using the term structure of interest rates. *Journal of Business & Economic Statistics, 16*, 304–311.

Engle, R., & Granger, C. (1987). Co-integration and error correction: Representation, estimation, and testing. *Econometrica, 55*, 251–276.

Granger, C. (1981). Some properties of time series datat and their use in econometric model specification. *Journal of Econometrics, 16*, 121–130.

Hansen, H., & Seo, B. (2002). Testing for two-regime threshold co-integration in vector error-correction models. *Journal of Econometrics, 110*, 293–318.

Jansen, E., & Teräsvirta, T. (1996). Testing parameter constancy and super exogeneity in econometric equations. *Oxford Bulletin of Economics and Statistics, 58*, 735–763.

Johansen, S. (1988). Statistical analysis of cointegration vectors. *Journal of Economic Dynamics und Control, 12*, 231–254.

Johansen, S. (1991). Estimation and hypothesis testing of cointegration vectors in gaussian vector autoregressive models. *Econometrica, 59*, 1551–1580.

Kapetanios, G., Shin, Y., & Snell, A. (2006). Testing for cointegration in nonlinear smooth transition error correction models. *Econometric Theory, 22*, 279–303.

Kaufmann, H., Kruse, R., & Sibbertsen, P. (2012). A simple specification procedure for the transition function in persistent nonlinear time series models. Discussion Paper, Leibniz University Hannover.

Kiliç, R. (2011). Testing for co-integration and nonlinear adjustment in a smooth transition error correction model. *Journal of Time Series Analysis, 32*, 647–660.

Lo, M., & Zivot, E. (2001). Threshold co-integration and non-linear adjustment to the law of one price. *Macroeconomic Dynamics, 5*, 533–576.

Maki, D. (2013). Detecting cointegration relationships under nonlinear models: Monte carlo analysis and some applications. *Empirical Economics, 45*(1), 605–625.
Nedeljkovic, M. (2011). Testing for smooth transition nonlinearity adjustments of cointegrating systems. Department of Economics, Warwick Economic Research Paper No. 876.
Seo, M. (2004). Cointegration test in the threshold cointegration model. Manuscript, University of Wisconsin-Madison, Department of Economics.
Shi, X., & Phillips, P. (2012). Nonlinear cointegrating regression under weak identification. *Econometric Theory, 28*, 509–547.
Siklos, P., & Granger, C. (1997). Regime sensitive cointegration with an application to interest-rate parity. *Macroeconomic Dynamics, 1*, 640–657.
Sollis, R. (2011). Testing the unit root hypothesis against TAR nonlinearity using STAR-based tests. *Economic Letters, 112*, 19–22.
Taylor, A. (2001). Potential pitfalls for the purchasing power parity puzzle? Sampling and specification biases in mean reversion tests of the law of one price. *Econometrica, 69*, 473–498.
Taylor, A., & Peel, D. (2000). Nonlinear adjustment, long-run equilibrium and exchange rate fundamentals. *Journal of International Money and Finance, 19*, 33–53.
Taylor, M., Peel, D., & Sarno, L. (2001). Nonlinear mean reversion in real exchange rates: Toward a solution to the purchasing power parity puzzles. *International Economic Review, 42*, 1015–1042.
Teräsvirta, T. (1994). Specification, estimation, and evaluation of smooth transition autoregressive models. *Journal of the American Statistical Association, 89*, 208–218.
van Dijk, D., & Franses, P. (2000). Nonlinear error-correction models for interest rates in the Netherlands. In W. Barnett, D. F. Hendry, S. Hylleberg, T. Teräsvirta, D. Tjøstheim, & A. W. Würtz (Eds.), *Non-linear econometric modelling in time series analysis* (pp. 203–227). Cambridge: Cambridge University Press.
van Dijk, D., Teräsvirta, T., & Franses, P. (2002). Smooth transition autoregressive models - A survey of recent developments. *Econometric Reviews, 21*, 1–47.
Zhang, L. (2013). Revisiting the empirics of inflation: A smooth transition error correction approach. *Economics Letters, 119*, 68–71.

Fitting Constrained Vector Autoregression Models

Tucker McElroy and David Findley

Abstract This paper expands the estimation theory for both quasi-maximum likelihood estimates (QMLEs) and Least Squares estimates (LSEs) for potentially misspecified constrained VAR(p) models. Our main result is a linear formula for the QMLE of a constrained VAR(p), which generalizes the Yule–Walker formula for the unconstrained case. We make connections with the known LSE formula and the determinant of the forecast mean square error matrix, showing that the QMLEs for a constrained VAR(p) minimize this determinant but not the component entries of the mean square forecast error matrix, as opposed to the unconstrained case. An application to computing mean square forecast errors from misspecified models is discussed, and numerical comparisons of the different methods are presented and explored.

1 Introduction

An extremely popular vector time series model is the Vector Autoregression of order p, or VAR(p) for short. Constraining a particular coefficient to be zero can affect the estimation of this model considerably, and is an important tool for assessing the impact of related series on short-term forecasting. This paper expands the estimation theory for both quasi-maximum likelihood estimates (QMLEs) and Least Squares estimates (LSEs) for potentially misspecified constrained VAR(p) models. Our main result is a linear formula for the QMLE of a constrained VAR(p), which generalizes the Yule–Walker formula for the unconstrained case; then we connect

---

This article is released to inform interested parties of research and to encourage discussion. The views expressed on statistical issues are those of the authors and not necessarily those of the U.S. Census Bureau.

T. McElroy (✉) • D. Findley
U.S. Census Bureau, Washington, DC, USA
e-mail: tucker.s.mcelroy@census.gov; david.f.findley@census.gov

J. Beran et al. (eds.), *Empirical Economic and Financial Research*,
Advanced Studies in Theoretical and Applied Econometrics 48,
DOI 10.1007/978-3-319-03122-4_28

this with the known LSE formula, concluding that the LSEs and QMLEs retain certain forecasting optimality properties even when the fitted model is misspecified.

The QMLE for a constrained VAR(p) minimizes the Total Innovation Variance (TIV)—i.e., the determinant of the forecast mean square error matrix—and the LSE is asymptotically equivalent to the QMLE. Hence, these estimates provide the best possible parameters—for the given model—with respect to TIV, even when the model is misspecified. TIV has a long history as an overall assessment of predictive capacity (Wilks 1932; Whittle 1953), and is closely connected to the Kullback–Leibler divergence between model and truth; this determinant, once it is properly scaled, provides the data dependent portion of the maximized Gaussian likelihood function. The topic has been treated by many authors (including Akaike 1969, 1974), summarized in Taniguchi and Kakizawa (2000); also see Maïnassara and Francq (2011).

Another feature of the QMLE for unconstrained VAR(p) models is that the resulting fitted model is always stable, whereas this need not be true for LSEs. Opinions vary over the desirability of this trait, as discussed in Lütkepohl (2005). If the true data process is stationary, then ensuring the stability of our fitted model is desirable. But if there may be co-integration or explosive behavior present in the data, then using the QMLEs would be misleading—instead we would prefer to use LSEs.

These results provide some motivation for considering QMLEs for fitting constrained VAR models; given that the formulas are just as simple and fast as the LSEs, and the properties are quite similar, practitioners may be interested in computing them. We also note that the same formulas used to compute QMLEs can be used to determine the pseudo-true values (PTVs) that arise when a misspecified constrained VAR(p) is fitted [via Whittle estimation or maximum likelihood estimation (MLE)] to a data process. A PTV is defined informally as that parameter vector (or vectors, as they may be non-unique) to which estimates converge in probability when the model is misspecified. Having a quick way to compute PTVs is helpful for simulation studies of the impact of model misspecification. For example, if one wanted to gauge the Mean Squared Error (MSE) of forecasting from a misspecified model, the PTVs could be plugged into the forecast filter, and the resulting forecast errors determined from analytical calculations (we discuss this application later in the paper). Since the VAR(p) model is often applied to do forecasting, we also make some connections between the QMLEs for the constrained VAR(p) and the unconstrained case, where the estimates are given by the Yule–Walker (YW) formula. Whereas the YW estimates optimize each entry of the asymptotic one-step ahead forecast MSE matrix, the PTVs in the constrained case only minimize the determinant of this matrix, namely the TIV—which is a weaker property. This suggests that the best we can hope for in the constrained VAR(p) case is to improve forecast MSE in the entangled sense of TIV; while we may minimize TIV, we may not be minimizing the diagonal entries of the forecast MSE matrix! This new and somewhat surprising conclusion is explained in the paper.

Section 2 provides the general theory of the QMLE for constrained VAR models, with connections to the Yule–Walker equations, and the implications to forecasting discussed. These results are compared to known formulas for the LSEs (Lütkepohl 2005), with the outcome that we can make the same conclusions about LSEs asymptotically. Section 3 provides numerical illustrations of the LSE, MLE, and QMLE methods for the bivariate VAR(1), the point being to demonstrate how forecasting performance diverges between the methods when the model is misspecified. In this part of the paper we also discuss an application of PTVs to computing h-step ahead forecast MSE from a misspecified model. A fuller version of this paper is McElroy and Findley (2013), which contains the proofs of results, as well as some additional examples.

2 Theoretical Results

In this section we provide a complete theory of QMLE fitting of constrained VAR models. We begin with some general results about the QMLE method discussed in Taniguchi and Kakizawa (2000), showing that it is sufficient to optimize the TIV. Then we specialize to constrained VAR models, providing an exact solution, and make comparisons to the LSE method.

2.1 General Theory of QMLE

We consider difference stationary processes, and generally follow the treatments of vector time series in Brockwell et al. (1991), Taniguchi and Kakizawa (2000), and Lütkepohl (2005). Included in our framework are the popular co-integrated VAR and VARIMA models used by econometricians, as well as structural VARIMA models. The formulas also cover the case of more unconventional processes that have long-range dependence. For notation we use an underline for every matrix, which for the most part are $m \times m$. The identity matrix is denoted by $\underline{1}_m$. Also in general capital letters refer to composite objects and lowercase letters refer to components (such as coefficients); Latin letters refer to random variables/vectors, and Greek letters refer to deterministic quantities (like parameters). Matrix polynomial and power series functions are defined as $\underline{A}(x) = \sum_{k=0}^{p} \underline{a}_j x^j$ with $p < \infty$ or $p = \infty$ as the case may be. We use B for the backshift operator, which sends a time series back in time: $B\mathbf{X}_t = \mathbf{X}_{t-1}$, working on all components of the vector at once. Then the action of $\underline{A}(B)$ on $\mathbf{X}_t$ is understood by linear extension. Also we introduce the following convenient notation for any matrix power series $\underline{A}(x)$: $[\underline{A}]_\ell^j(x) = \sum_{k=\ell}^{j} \underline{a}_k x^k$.

Let us suppose that the data can be differenced to stationarity by application of a degree d differencing polynomial $\underline{\Delta}(B)$; its application to the observed time series $\{\mathbf{X}_t\}$ yields a covariance stationary time series $\{\mathbf{W}_t\}$, i.e., $\underline{\Delta}(B)\mathbf{X}_t = \mathbf{W}_t$. The operator $\underline{\Delta}(B)$ is referred to as the differencing operator, and in general contains both stable and unstable elements that are not easily separated. As discussed in

Lütkepohl (2005), the zeroes of $\det\underline{\Delta}(z)$ include some on the unit circle of the complex plane, and the rest outside.

The series $\{\mathbf{W}_t\}$ is assumed to be stationary with mean vector $\mathbf{m}$, and we further suppose that it is purely non-deterministic. Its lag h autocovariance matrix will be denoted

$$\Gamma(h) = \mathbb{E}[(\mathbf{W}_{t+h} - \mathbf{m})(\mathbf{W}_t - \mathbf{m})'].$$

The spectral density matrix of $\{\mathbf{W}_t\}$ is denoted by $\underline{F}(\lambda)$, and is defined via $\underline{F}(\lambda) = \sum_{h=-\infty}^{\infty} \Gamma(h) e^{-i\lambda h}$. Hence we have the relation $\Gamma(h) = (2\pi)^{-1} \int_{-\pi}^{\pi} \underline{F}(\lambda)\, e^{i\lambda h}\, d\lambda$. We further assume that $\underline{F}(\lambda)$ has full rank for each λ, which will ensure that the forecast error covariance matrix, defined below, is nontrivial; this condition also implies that $\int_{-\pi}^{\pi} \log\det\underline{F}(\lambda)\, d\lambda > -\infty$.

We will consider any model for $\{\mathbf{W}_t\}$ that is invertible, such that a Wold Decomposition (Brockwell et al. 1991; Reinsel 1996) exists, which means that—when the model is true—we can write

$$\mathbf{W}_t = \mathbf{m} + \underline{\Psi}(B)\mathbf{A}_t, \tag{1}$$

where the series $\{\mathbf{A}_t\}$ is mean zero and uncorrelated (but possibly dependent) over time with positive definite covariance matrix $\underline{\sigma}$. Here $\underline{\Psi}(B)$ is a causal power series with coefficient matrices $\underline{\psi}_k$. By the invertibility assumption, we mean the assumption that $\det\underline{\Psi}(z) \neq 0$ for $|z| \leq 1$ and

$$\int_{-\pi}^{\pi} \log\det\left[\underline{\Psi}\left(e^{-i\lambda}\right) \underline{\Psi}'\left(e^{i\lambda}\right)\right] d\lambda = 0. \tag{2}$$

Thus $\underline{\Psi}^{-1}(z)$ is well defined for $|z| \leq 1$. If our model is correct for the data process, such that (1) holds exactly, then we can write $\mathbf{A}_t = \underline{\Psi}(B)^{-1}[\mathbf{W}_t - \mathbf{m}]$, showing that $\{\mathbf{A}_t\}$ is the linear innovations process of $\{\mathbf{W}_t\}$. The filter $\underline{\Psi}(B)^{-1}$ is called the innovations filter of $\{\mathbf{W}_t\}$.

However, in general any model that we propose is misspecified, so we cannot assume that (1) holds exactly. Let us consider any causal invertible model, i.e., one with a Wold filter representation $\underline{\Psi}_\xi(B)$, such that this Wold filter is parameterized by a vector $\xi \in \Xi$ associated with the model coefficients, while accounting for any coefficient constraints. Invertibility means that $\det\Psi_\xi(z)$ is nonzero for $|z| \leq 1$ for all $\xi \in \Xi$, where Ξ is assumed to be an open convex set. The filter $\underline{\Psi}_\xi(B)$ therefore satisfies (2). In this paper we are principally interested in the so-called separable models, where the parameter ξ does not depend on our parameterization of the innovation variance $\underline{\sigma}$, the covariance of the putative innovations $\{\mathbf{A}_t\}$; for the more general treatment of non-separable models, see Taniguchi and Kakizawa (2000). By specializing to separable models, we can obtain a more focused result.

So assume that ξ is parameterized separately from the distinct entries of the model's innovation covariance matrix. Let ζ denote the vector $\text{vec}\underline{\sigma}$, so that $\underline{\sigma}_\zeta$ refers to our model's innovation covariance matrix. We require this matrix to belong to the set $\mathscr{S}_+$ of all positive definite matrices. Then the full vector of parameters can be written as $\vartheta = [\xi', \zeta']'$, so that the first set of parameters control the Wold filter $\Psi_\xi(B)$, and the second set of parameters parameterize the innovation covariance matrix $\underline{\sigma}_\zeta$. Then the spectral density of this model can be written as

$$\underline{F}_\vartheta(\lambda) = \underline{\Psi}_\xi(e^{-i\lambda})\,\underline{\sigma}_\zeta\,\underline{\Psi}'_\xi(e^{i\lambda}),$$

and furthermore from (2),

$$\frac{1}{2\pi}\int_{-\pi}^{\pi} \log\det\underline{F}_\vartheta(\lambda)\,d\lambda = \log\det\underline{\sigma}_\zeta.$$

This last expression is guaranteed to be positive, since the matrix belongs to $\mathscr{S}_+$.

Now because $\underline{\Psi}_\xi(B)$ is invertible, the one-step ahead forecast filter for the differenced series $\{\mathbf{W}_t\}$ is well defined, and is given by $B^{-1}[\underline{\Psi}_\xi]_1^\infty(B)\,\underline{\Psi}_\xi(B)^{-1}$, as described in McElroy and McCracken (2012). The forecast errors when using such a filter are then given by $\mathbf{E}_t = \underline{\Psi}_\xi(B)^{-1}\,(\mathbf{W}_t - \mathbf{m})$, whose covariance results in the following important matrix:

$$\Omega(\xi) = \mathbb{E}\left[\mathbf{E}_t\mathbf{E}'_t\right] = \frac{1}{2\pi}\int_{-\pi}^{\pi} \underline{\Psi}_\xi(e^{-i\lambda})^{-1}\,\underline{F}(\lambda)\,\underline{\Psi}_\xi(e^{i\lambda})^{\dagger}\,d\lambda. \tag{3}$$

Here $\dagger$ is short for inverse transpose. Note that $\{\mathbf{E}_t\}$ may not be exactly a white noise, because our model is misspecified, or is imperfectly estimated. We label the above matrix as the Forecast Error Variance (FEV) matrix, denoted by $\Omega(\xi)$, the dependence on the parameter ξ being explicit. Note that the FEV is always positive definite, because of our assumption that $\underline{F}(\lambda)$ has full rank for all λ (this can be weakened to having less than full rank for a set of λs of Lebesgue measure zero, which allows us to embrace the possibility of co-integration).

It is reasonable to seek models and parameter values ξ such that the FEV is minimized in an appropriate sense. Because the diagonal entries of the FEV represent forecast MSEs, it is plausible to minimize any of these diagonal entries, or perhaps the trace of $\Omega(\xi)$. Another approach would be to minimize the determinant of the FEV, although this quantity is difficult to interpret in terms of forecast performance. Note that $\det\Omega(\xi)$ is the TIV defined earlier, and is related to the Final Prediction Error (FPE) of Akaike (1969), a scaled version of the determinant of the estimated innovations variance matrix, based upon results of Whittle (1953). Historically, the work of Akaike (1969) forms the basis for using the FEV determinant as a fitting criterion for VAR models. Whittle (1953) refers to $\det\Omega(\xi)$ as the Total Prediction Variance, adopting terminology from Wilks (1932); we utilize the term Total Innovation Variance (TIV) instead, to emphasize its connection to the innovations process. There are many articles that discuss VAR model selection via the FPE criterion of Akaike (1969), and there have been numerous successful applications in industry and econometrics; see Akaike and Kitagawa (1999) for additional applications.

We now provide a treatment of the connection of QMLE and TIV minimization for separable models (they need not be VAR at this point, but rather any separable model with causal invertible Wold representation), which connects Gaussian maximum likelihood estimation to minimization of the TIV. The Kullback–Leibler (KL) discrepancy between a true process' spectrum $\underline{F}$ and a putative model spectrum $\underline{F}_\vartheta$ is defined via

$$D\left(\underline{F}_\vartheta, \underline{F}\right) = \frac{1}{2\pi} \int_{-\pi}^{\pi} \log \det \underline{F}_\vartheta(\lambda) + \operatorname{tr}\left\{\underline{F}_\vartheta\left(\lambda\right)^{-1} \; \underline{F}\left(\lambda\right)\right\} d\lambda.$$

See Taniguchi and Kakizawa (2000) for more exposition. This formula is also valid when the multivariate periodogram $\underline{I}(\lambda) = n^{-1} \sum_{t=1}^{n} \mathbf{W}_t e^{-i\lambda t} \sum_{t=1}^{n} \mathbf{W}_t' e^{i\lambda t}$ is substituted for $\underline{F}$, yielding $D(\underline{F}_\vartheta, \underline{I})$. This quantity is related to -2 times the multivariate Gaussian log likelihood, and is more convenient to work with in empirical applications, since no matrix inversions are required for its calculation. In fact, empirical estimates based on this criterion have similar asymptotic properties to Gaussian maximum likelihood estimates. The definition of a QMLE is a parameter ϑ_I such that $\vartheta \mapsto D(\underline{F}_\vartheta, \underline{I})$ is minimized. The definition of a PTV is a parameter ϑ_F such that $\vartheta \mapsto D(\underline{F}_\vartheta, \underline{F})$ is minimized. The general theory of Taniguchi and Kakizawa (2000) shows that, under suitable conditions on the process and the model (requiring the uniqueness of ϑ_F), that QMLEs are consistent and asymptotically normal for PTVs, and are also efficient when the model is correctly specified. In this case, the PTVs are identical with the true parameters of the process: since $\underline{F} \in \{\underline{F}_\vartheta : \vartheta \in \Xi \times \mathscr{S}_+\}$, there exists some $\tilde{\vartheta}$ such that $\underline{F} = \underline{F}_{\tilde{\vartheta}}$, and the PTVs are identical with this $\tilde{\vartheta}$.

Because QMLEs and MLEs are asymptotically equivalent when the underlying process is Gaussian, PTVs are informative about what parameter estimates are converging to when models are misspecified; this, along with their asymptotic efficiency under correct model specification—and their relative ease of computation—motivates interest in QMLEs (and also PTVs). Now the above formula for KL is general, but in the case of a separable model we have an alternative formula:

$$\begin{aligned} D(\underline{F}_\vartheta, \underline{F}) &= \log \det \underline{\sigma}_\zeta + \frac{1}{2\pi} \int_{-\pi}^{\pi} \operatorname{tr}\left\{\underline{\sigma}_\zeta^{-1}\, \Psi_\xi(e^{-i\lambda})^{-1}\, \underline{F}(\lambda)\, \Psi_\xi'(e^{i\lambda})^{-1}\right\} \\ &= \log \det \underline{\sigma}_\zeta + \operatorname{tr}\left\{\underline{\sigma}_\zeta^{-1}\, \Omega(\xi)\right\}. \end{aligned} \quad (4)$$

This derivation uses (3) and an interchange of integration and trace. In fact, this derivation does not assume any particular model structure for $\underline{F}$, so we can also obtain an alternative formula for $D(\underline{F}_\vartheta, \underline{I})$ as $\log \det \underline{\sigma}_\zeta + \operatorname{tr}\left\{\underline{\sigma}_\zeta^{-1}\, \hat{\Omega}(\xi)\right\}$, where $\hat{\Omega}(\xi)$ is an empirical version of the FEV defined via

$$\hat{\Omega}(\xi) = \frac{1}{2\pi} \int_{-\pi}^{\pi} \underline{\Psi_\xi}(e^{-i\lambda})^{-1} \underline{I}(\lambda) \underline{\Psi_\xi}(e^{i\lambda})^{\dagger} \, d\lambda.$$

We can then determine the PTVs and QMLEs by the same mathematics: by the appropriate simplification of the derivation of Magnus and Neudecker (1999, p. 317), for any fixed $\xi \in \Xi$ the FEV matrix $\Omega(\xi)$ minimizes $\zeta \mapsto D(\underline{F}_{\xi,\zeta}, \underline{F})$ over all parameterizations such that $\underline{\sigma}_\zeta \in \mathscr{S}_+$. This is appropriate for PTVs; for QMLEs, we have $\hat{\Omega}(\xi)$ minimizing $\zeta \mapsto D(\underline{F}_{\xi,\zeta}, \underline{I})$. Recall that the FEV is in $\mathscr{S}_+$ by our full rank assumption on $\underline{F}$; in the case of the QMLEs, the empirical FEV can violate this only in the trivial case that the data equals the zero vector.[1] Then from (4) we obtain

$$D\left(F_{\xi,\mathrm{vec}\Omega(\xi)}, \underline{F}\right) = \log \det \Omega(\xi) + m.$$

This is a concentration of the likelihood, analogously to the procedure with univariate time series, and relates KL to TIV. If we minimize the above expression with respect to ξ, and then compute $\Omega(\xi)$ for that optimal ξ, then we have produced the PTV ϑ. Of course, the dimension m is irrelevant to this problem, as is the presence of the logarithm. Therefore, the PTV ξ_F, which we assume exists uniquely in Ξ, satisfies

$$\xi_F = \arg\min_{\xi \in \Xi} \det \Omega(\xi) \qquad \zeta_F = \mathrm{vec}\, \Omega(\xi_F).$$

Our parameter space should be taken to be a compact convex subset Ω of $\Xi \times \mathrm{vec}\,(\mathscr{S}_+)$ that contains $\vartheta_F = \left[\xi_F', \mathrm{vec}'\Omega(\xi_F)\right]'$. In the next section we will demonstrate the existence and uniqueness of such PTVs for constrained VAR models. The treatment for QMLEs follows identically: the concentrated empirical KL equals m plus the log determinant of the empirical FEV, and hence

$$\xi_I = \arg\min_{\xi \in \Xi} \det \hat{\Omega}(\xi) \qquad \zeta_I = \mathrm{vec}\, \Omega(\xi_I).$$

In summary, we see that the QMLEs and PTVs for ξ are computed by minimizing the empirical and theoretical TIVs, respectively, and then plugging these parameters back into the empirical/theoretical FEV matrix. So whereas the TIV seems to be a non-intuitive quantity in terms of forecast performance, it is actually the right objective function if we wish to obtain statistically efficient parameter estimates in the correct model case. Theorem 3.1.2 of Taniguchi and Kakizawa (2000) gives a

[1]For any vector a, we have $a'\hat{\Omega}(\xi)a = (2\pi n)^{-1} \int_{-\pi}^{\pi} |a' \Psi^{-1}(e^{-i\lambda}) \sum_{t=1}^{n} \mathbf{W}_t e^{-i\lambda t}|^2 \, d\lambda$, so that the expression equals zero iff $a' \Psi^{-1}(e^{-i\lambda}) \cdot \sum_{t=1}^{n} \mathbf{W}_t e^{-i\lambda t} = 0$ almost everywhere with respect to λ; because both terms in this product are polynomials in $e^{-i\lambda}$, the condition is equivalent to one or the other of them being zero. In the one case that $a' \Psi^{-1}(e^{-i\lambda}) = 0$, we at once deduce that a is the zero vector; in the other case, we have that the discrete Fourier Transform $\sum_{t=1}^{n} \mathbf{W}_t e^{-i\lambda t} = 0$ for almost every λ, which can only be true if the data is zero-valued.

central limit theorem for the QMLEs; also see (3.4.25) in Lütkepohl (2005) for the special case of a VAR model, assuming the model is correctly specified.

2.2 Constrained Versus Unconstrained VAR Models

2.2.1 Properties of the Unconstrained Case: Full Optimization

The previous subsection treated general separable models. We now focus on unconstrained VAR models as a further special case. Let $\underline{\phi}$ be an $m \times mp$ dimensional matrix consisting of the concatenation of the coefficient matrices of $\underline{\Phi}(z) = \underline{1}_m - \sum_{j=1}^{p} \underline{\phi}_j z^j$. In terms of the notation of the previous section, $\xi = \text{vec}\,\underline{\phi}$ and $\underline{\Psi}_\xi(B) = \underline{\Phi}(B)^{-1}$. The invertibility assumption given above then dictates that $\underline{\Phi}(z)$ must belong to the set F_p of matrix polynomials such that the zeroes of $\det \underline{\Phi}(z)$ satisfy $|z| > 1$.

It will be convenient to introduce a notation for the transposed autocovariance: let $\underline{R}_{1:p+1,1:p+1}$ denote an $m(p+1)$ dimensional square matrix, which is block-Toeplitz with jkth block matrix given by $\Gamma(k-j) = \Gamma'(j-k)$. We can partition $\underline{R}_{1:p+1,1:p+1}$ into its upper left $p \times p$ block $\Gamma(0)$ and its lower right mp dimensional block $\underline{R}_{2:p+1,2:p+1}$, which is also block-Toeplitz (and equal to $\underline{R}_{1:p,1:p}$). The remaining portions are denoted $\underline{R}_{1,2:p+1}$ and $\underline{R}_{2:p+1,1}$. Then it can be shown that

$$\begin{aligned} \Omega(\xi) &= \Gamma(0) - \sum_{j=1}^{p} \underline{\phi}_j \, \Gamma(-j) - \sum_{k=1}^{p} \Gamma(k)\, \underline{\phi}_k' + \sum_{j,k=1}^{p} \underline{\phi}_j \, \Gamma(k-j)\, \underline{\phi}_k' \\ &= \Gamma(0) - \underline{\phi}\, R_{2:p+1,1} - R_{1,2:p+1}\, \underline{\phi}' + \underline{\phi}\, R_{1:p,1:p}\, \underline{\phi}' \end{aligned} \tag{5}$$

Our treatment looks at PTVs, but if we replace the true autocovariances $\Gamma(h)$ by sample estimates (the inverse Fourier Transforms of the periodogram I) and write $\hat{\Omega}(\xi)$, we can apply the same mathematics as derived below, and obtain an identical treatment of QMLEs.

Let us first examine the case of an unconstrained VAR(p) model: we show that the PTV is the solution to the Yule–Walker (YW) equations (a known result), and also that the PTV minimizes each entry of the FEV matrix, not merely its determinant, the TIV (a new result). Noting that by definition ξ_F is a zero of the derivative of the TIV, we compute it via the chain rule:

$$\frac{\partial}{\partial \xi_\ell} \det\Omega(\xi) = \sum_{r,s} \Omega_{(r,s)}(\xi)\, \frac{\partial \Omega_{rs}(\xi)}{\partial \xi_\ell}.$$

See Mardia et al. (1979). Here $\Omega_{(r,s)}$ is the co-factor of Ω, while Ω_{rs} is just the r,sth entry of the FEV matrix. The chain rule tells us that a *sufficient* condition for the gradient of the FPE to be zero is that the gradients of Ω_{rs} are zero. That is, it is sufficient to find a solution that optimizes all the coefficient functions of the FEV. This is a stronger property than just minimizing detΩ, since there might be solutions that minimize the FPE but do not minimize all of the component functions. In the case of a VAR(p) this stronger property holds, which is remarkable and useful. The following result is a slight elaboration, for the perspective of KL discrepancy minimization, of the results of Whittle (1963) for case of full rank $\{\mathbf{W}_t\}$.

Proposition 1 *Let $\{\mathbf{W}_t\}$ be stationary and invertible, with full rank spectral density matrix. Then the PTV $\underline{\tilde{\phi}}$ for a fitted VAR(p) satisfies the Yule–Walker equations*

$$\sum_{j=1}^{p} \underline{\tilde{\phi}}_j \Gamma(k-j) = \Gamma(k), \; 1 \leq k \leq p, \tag{6}$$

or $\underline{\tilde{\phi}}\,\underline{R}_{1:p,1:p} = \underline{R}_{1,2:p+1}$. Furthermore, the corresponding polynomial $\tilde{\Phi}(z) \in \mathcal{F}_p$ and $\xi_F = vec\underline{\tilde{\phi}}$ uniquely minimizes $\xi \mapsto det\Omega(\xi)$, with the FEV given by (5). The PTV also minimizes $\xi \mapsto \Omega_{rs}(\xi)$ for every $1 \leq r, s \leq m$. The PTV for the FEV is

$$\underline{\sigma}_{\xi_F} = \Omega(\xi_F) = \Gamma(0) - \underline{R}_{1,2:p+1}\,\underline{R}_{1:p,1:p}^{-1}\,\underline{R}_{2:p+1,1}. \tag{7}$$

A parallel result holds for the QMLEs, in the manner described at the beginning of this subsection. That is, the sample autocovariances are defined for $0 \leq h \leq n-1$ by

$$\hat{\Gamma}(h) = n^{-1} \sum_{t=1}^{n-h} \left(\mathbf{W}_{t+h} - \overline{\mathbf{W}}\right)\left(\mathbf{W}_t - \overline{\mathbf{W}}\right)',$$

and $\hat{\Gamma}(-h) = \hat{\Gamma}'(h)$; it is easily seen that these quantities are related to the periodogram via

$$\underline{I}(\lambda) = \sum_{h=-n+1}^{n-1} \hat{\Gamma}(h) e^{-ih\lambda}.$$

We assume that $p \leq n-1$. Then the QMLEs satisfy the empirical YW equations, obtained by replacing $\Gamma(h)$ in (6) by $\hat{\Gamma}(h)$, and so forth. Convergence of QMLEs to PTVs is guaranteed by results in Taniguchi and Kakizawa (2000).

2.2.2 Properties of Optimization for Constrained Models

Now let us consider the case where the VAR model has some constraints. We next provide an explicit solution for the PTV and QMLE when elements of ξ are constrained, which is a novel result.

Note that $\xi = \text{vec}\,\underline{\phi}$ is the full vector of parameters. If some of these are constrained, we can write

$$\text{vec}\,\underline{\phi} = J\,\psi + a \tag{8}$$

for a matrix J that is $m^2 p \times r$, where $r \leq m^2 p$; here, a is an r-vector. The vector ψ consists of all free parameters in $\underline{\phi}$. Unfortunately, there is no guarantee that the PTVs/QMLEs for such a constrained VAR will result in a stable model, and we've found through numerical experiments that this can indeed occur. The structure of J is arbitrary (only that its entries are known quantities, and not parameters), so the case that multiple entries of $\underline{\phi}$ are the same can also be entertained by (8). We next state PTVs and QMLEs for $\underline{\phi}$ together with $\underline{\sigma}_{\xi}$, with each formula being dependent on the other—similarly to the OLS solution discussed in Lütkepohl (2005). The PTV for $\underline{\phi}$ is still denoted by $\tilde{\underline{\phi}}$, but it is computed in terms of the PTV $\tilde{\psi}$, and $\xi_F = \text{vec}\,\tilde{\underline{\phi}} = J\,\tilde{\psi} + a$. Likewise, $\tilde{\underline{\sigma}} = \underline{\sigma}_{\xi_F} = \Omega(\xi_F)$ by the previous subsection's general results. Now we can state our result.

Proposition 2 *Let $\{\mathbf{W}_t\}$ be stationary and invertible, with full rank spectral density matrix. Then the PTV $(\tilde{\psi}, \tilde{\underline{\sigma}})$ for a fitted constrained VAR(p) with constraints of the form (8) satisfies*

$$\tilde{\psi} = \left(J' \left[\underline{R}_{1:p,1:p} \otimes \tilde{\underline{\sigma}}^{-1}\right] J\right)^{-1} J' \left\{\left[\underline{R}'_{1,2:p+1} \otimes \tilde{\underline{\sigma}}^{-1}\right] vec(\underline{1}_m) - \left[\underline{R}_{1:p,1:p} \otimes \tilde{\underline{\sigma}}^{-1}\right] a\right\}$$

$$\tilde{\underline{\sigma}} = \Omega\left(\xi_F\right).$$

Remark 1 The fitted constrained VAR models need not satisfy the Riccati equations, which take the form $\Gamma(0) = \underline{\phi}\,\underline{R}_{1:p,1:p}\,\underline{\phi}' + \underline{\sigma}$, and hence the resulting fitted VAR model need not correspond to a stationary process. This phenomenon arises due to taking unconstrained optimization of the TIV over all $\psi \in \mathbb{R}^r$, whereas only some subset of this space, in general, corresponds to stable VAR processes. It is interesting that enforcing certain kinds of constraints of the type given by (8) essentially forces the PTVs into a region of instability. The broader problem of enforcing stability is not studied in this paper.

Remark 2 In general we cannot substitute the formula for $\tilde{\underline{\sigma}}$ into the formula for $\tilde{\psi}$ and simplify, because the algebra is intractable. In the special case that J is the identity and $a = 0$ (the unconstrained case), the formula for $\tilde{\psi}$ simplifies to

$$\left[\underline{R}^{-1}_{1:p,1:p} \otimes \tilde{\underline{\sigma}}\right] \left[\underline{R}'_{1,2:p+1} \otimes \tilde{\underline{\sigma}}^{-1}\right] \text{vec}(\underline{1}_m) = \text{vec}\left(\underline{R}_{1,2:p+1}\,\underline{R}^{-1}_{1:p,1:p}\right),$$

which is the YW equation. To solve the coupled system, one could propose initial guesses (such as the YW solutions) and iteratively solve the formulas on a computer, hoping for contraction towards the PTV solution pair.

Substituting empirical estimates for the autocovariances, the same mathematics produces formulas for the QMLEs. The empirical counterpart of the asymptotic story is exactly similar. We denote the parameter estimates by

$$\hat{\psi}_{QMLE} = \left(J' \left[\underline{\hat{R}}_{1:p,1:p} \otimes \underline{\hat{\sigma}}_{QMLE}^{-1}\right] J\right)^{-1}$$
$$\cdot J' \left\{\left[\underline{\hat{R}}'_{1,2:p+1} \otimes \underline{\hat{\sigma}}_{QMLE}^{-1}\right] \operatorname{vec}(\underline{1}_m) - \left[\underline{\hat{R}}_{1:p,1:p} \otimes \underline{\hat{\sigma}}_{QMLE}^{-1}\right] a\right\}$$
$$\underline{\hat{\sigma}}_{QMLE} = \Omega\,(\xi_I)\,,$$

and $\xi_I = \operatorname{vec} \underline{\hat{\phi}}_{QMLE} = J\,\hat{\psi}_{QMLE} + a$. These estimates need not result in a stable fitted model (see Sect. 3).

Suppose that the true process is a VAR(p), and we fit a constrained VAR(p) model. Then the QMLEs and PTVs can be computed iteratively via the formulas of Proposition 2. In the special case that the true process is a constrained VAR(p) (i.e., the specified model is correct), then $\mathbf{W}_t = \sum_{j=1}^{p} \underline{\tilde{\phi}}_j \mathbf{W}_{t-j} + \epsilon_t$ and (6) is true. Also, plugging into (5) yields (7), so that Proposition 1 holds for this case. The formula (7) for the FEV is the same as would be obtained using the constrained VAR formula, because the unconstrained model reduces to the constrained model asymptotically. We can use the empirical version of (7) to estimate the FEV consistently, and substitute into the formula for $\hat{\psi}_{QMLE}$; however, these estimates are only consistent for the true parameters under a correct model hypothesis, and need not tend to the PTVs in the case that the model is wrong. Also see the discussion of the estimation of the FEV via LSE methodology in Lütkepohl (2005).

A formula for LSEs for the constrained VAR(p) is given in Lütkepohl (2005), which we translate into our own notation. Omitting mean effects, we let Z be a $pm \times (n-p)$ dimensional matrix, with columns given by $[Z_p, Z_{p+1}, \cdots, Z_{n-1}]$ and $Z_t = [\mathbf{W}'_t, \mathbf{W}'_{t-1}, \cdots, \mathbf{W}'_{t-p+1}]'$. Note that when p is fairly large, some data is being "thrown away." Also let W be $m \times (n-p)$ dimensional, given by $W = [\mathbf{W}_{p+1}, \mathbf{W}_{p+2}, \cdots, \mathbf{W}_n]$.

The method requires some plug-in estimate of the innovation variance, which we generically denote by $\underline{\hat{\sigma}}$; this might be estimated by a separate method, and then plugged in below, as described in Lütkepohl (2005). The LSE formula for ψ is then

$$\hat{\psi}_{LSE} = \left(J' \left[Z\,Z' \otimes \underline{\hat{\sigma}}^{-1}\right] J\right)^{-1} J' \left\{\left[Z W' \otimes \underline{\hat{\sigma}}^{-1}\right] \operatorname{vec}(\underline{1}_m) - \left[Z Z' \otimes \underline{\hat{\sigma}}^{-1}\right] a\right\}.$$

If we were to plug in the QMLE for the innovation covariance matrix, the similarities to the QMLE formula are striking. The above formula can be re-expressed in an equivalent form. Letting $\operatorname{vec}\underline{\hat{\phi}}_{LSE} = J\,\hat{\psi}_{LSE} + a$, we find the equivalent expression

$$J' \operatorname{vec}\left(\underline{\hat{\sigma}}^{-1} \left[\underline{\hat{\phi}}_{LSE}\, Z\,Z' - W\,Z'\right]\right) = 0.$$

Now $n^{-1}\,Z\,Z' \approx \underline{\hat{R}}_{1:p,1:p}$ and $n^{-1}\,W\,Z' \approx \underline{\hat{R}}'_{1,2:p+1}$; the relations would have been exact, except for some missing terms due to the data that gets thrown away by the LSE method. This approximation error is $O_P(1/n)$, and has no impact on the asymptotic behavior. On the other hand, we can re-express the QMLEs as

$$J' \operatorname{vec}\left(\underline{\hat{\sigma}}^{-1}_{QMLE}\left[\underline{\hat{\phi}}_{QMLE}\,\underline{\hat{R}}_{1:p,1:p} - \underline{\hat{R}}_{1,2:p+1}\right]\right) = 0.$$

Notice that the expression in square brackets is identically zero if and only if the QMLE satisfies the Yule–Walker equations [and when J is the identity—i.e., no constraints in play—the above equation reduces to (6)]. So, if we use the QMLE for the innovation variance in the LSE approach—or another estimate that is consistent for the PTV—then the LSEs are approximate solutions to the above QMLE equation. This tells us that their asymptotic behavior is the same, so that LSEs obey the same Central Limit Theorem as the QMLEs, indicated in Taniguchi and Kakizawa (2000), *even when* the VAR model is misspecified.

3 Numerical Illustrations

3.1 Finite-Sample Results

For constrained bivariate VAR(1) models, the chief fitting methods are MLE, QMLE, or LSE. Explicit formulas are given in Sect. 2, which we here implement on four bivariate VAR(1) processes described below. Let Φ denote the first coefficient matrix $\underline{\phi}_1$, with jkth entry denoted Φ_{jk}. The Φ matrices for the four examples are

$$\begin{bmatrix} 1/2 & 1/3 \\ 1/3 & 1/2 \end{bmatrix} \quad \begin{bmatrix} 2/3 & 0 \\ 1 & 1/3 \end{bmatrix} \quad \begin{bmatrix} .95 & 0 \\ 1 & 1/2 \end{bmatrix} \quad \begin{bmatrix} -.25 & .5 \\ -1 & 1.25 \end{bmatrix},$$

and in each case the innovation variance matrix is the identity. All four processes are stable.

We investigate fitting three models—denoted A, B, and C—to each process via QMLE and LSE. Model A is the unconstrained VAR(1), while model B has the constraint that $\Phi_{12} = 0$, and model C has the constraint that $\Phi_{11} = 0$. So model B is a misspecification for the first and fourth processes, while model C is a misspecification for all four processes. For model A the PTVs correspond to the true values, but for models B and C they can be quite different due to misspecification. The PTVs for Φ, for the four processes, respectively, are

$$\begin{bmatrix} .6739 & 0 \\ 1/3 & 1/2 \end{bmatrix} \quad \begin{bmatrix} 2/3 & 0 \\ 1 & 1/3 \end{bmatrix} \quad \begin{bmatrix} .95 & 0 \\ 1 & 1/2 \end{bmatrix} \quad \begin{bmatrix} .4244 & 0 \\ -1 & 1.25 \end{bmatrix},$$

for model B, and for model C are given by

$$\begin{bmatrix} 0 & .5942 \\ 1/3 & 1/2 \end{bmatrix} \quad \begin{bmatrix} 0 & .5373 \\ 0 & .6915 \end{bmatrix} \quad \begin{bmatrix} 0 & .4914 \\ 0 & .9668 \end{bmatrix} \quad \begin{bmatrix} 0 & .1954 \\ .2443 & .7721 \end{bmatrix}.$$

The PTVs for $\underline{\sigma}$ are in all cases equal to $\underline{1}_2$; see additional discussion in McElroy and Findley (2013). These quantities are computed from the formulas of Proposition 2. We see that all the Φ PTVs are stable for the first three processes, but is unstable for model B fitted to the fourth process. However, for model C all PTVs are stable for all four processes; the double zero for the second and third processes with model C is quite interesting.

It is interesting to examine the PTVs in the cases of model B and model C, fitted to the first process. Although these models are misspecified, their misspecification in some sense chiefly pertains to the forecast performance of the first component of the bivariate series; actually, their PTVs for the second component of the bivariate series are correct! That is, utilizing the misspecified models B and C has no impact on the asymptotic forecast performance of the second component series.

The example given by the fourth process begs the question: how often do unstable PTV fits arise in practice? We drew a sample of a million bivariate VAR(1) processes by allowing each entry of Φ to be an independent normal variable, and found that 34 % of these processes were stable; of those, the proportion having stable PTVs arising from fitting model B was only 26 %. This indicates that a high proportion of stable VAR processes may have unstable PTVs when constrained models are utilized. We next proceeded to simulate from these four processes, fitting all three models via both QMLE and LSE methodologies. The results are summarized in Tables 1, 2, 3, and 4. There we present the mean values of the estimates of Φ, computed over 5,000 simulations of the given VAR processes, with sample sizes of 100, 200, and 400. We also present mean values of the maximum and minimum absolute eigenvalues of Φ. Only rarely did unstable estimates arise in practice for the first three processes: this was assessed by computing the proportion of simulations wherein the maximum eigenvalue exceeded one. This only occurred for the LSE estimates in the case of sample size 100; the QMLE method always resulted in stable fits, and the LSE estimates become "increasingly stable" as sample size was increased. For the fourth process, models A and C produced stable fits in finite sample, but virtually all the time model B produced an unstable VAR, as expected.

3.2 Gauging Forecast MSE

We now describe an application of the calculation of PTVs. Suppose that we wished to study the impact of model misspecification on forecast performance, as a function of an underlying process; see Schorfheide (2005) for motivation and discussion. So we suppose that the true $\underline{F}$ is known for the process we are studying, and some misspecified model is fit to the data. McElroy and McCracken (2012) provides

Table 1 Model fitting results for sample sizes 100, 200, 400 from the VAR(1) with $\Phi_{11} = 1/2$, $\Phi_{12} = 1/3$, $\Phi_{21} = 1/3$, $\Phi_{22} = 1/2$, and $\underline{\sigma} = \underline{1}_2$

Parameters	Models					
n = 100	QMLE Model A	QMLE Model B	QMLE Model C	LSE Model A	LSE Model B	LSE Model C
Φ	0.481 0.328	0.649 0	0 0.574	0.487 0.331	0.654 0	0 0.579
	0.329 0.478	0.335 0.471	0.317 0.488	0.332 0.483	0.332 0.483	0.332 0.483
Max $\|\zeta\|$	0.808	0.652	0.734	0.817	0.658	0.742
Min $\|\zeta\|$	0.157	0.467	0.245	0.159	0.481	0.258
Prob unstable	0	0	0	0	0	0
n = 200	QMLE Model A	QMLE Model B	QMLE Model C	LSE Model A	LSE Model B	LSE Model C
Φ	0.490 0.331	0.661 0	0 0.585	0.493 0.333	0.665 0	0 0.587
	0.332 0.489	0.336 0.485	0.326 0.494	0.334 0.492	0.334 0.492	0.334 0.492
Max $\|\zeta\|$	0.821	0.662	0.748	0.826	0.665	0.752
Min $\|\zeta\|$	0.158	0.485	0.253	0.159	0.491	0.260
Prob unstable	0	0	0	0	0	0
n = 400	QMLE Model A	QMLE Model B	QMLE Model C	LSE Model A	LSE Model B	LSE Model C
Φ	0.495 0.332	0.667 0	0 0.588	0.496 0.333	0.668 0	0 0.589
	0.332 0.494	0.334 0.492	0.328 0.497	0.333 0.496	0.333 0.496	0.333 0.496
Max $\|\zeta\|$	0.826	0.667	0.753	0.828	0.668	0.755
Min $\|\zeta\|$	0.163	0.492	0.256	0.163	0.496	0.259
Prob unstable	0	0	0	0	0	0

Models A, B, C are used, corresponding to unconstrained VAR(1), a VAR(1) with $\Phi_{12} = 0$, and a VAR(1) with $\Phi_{11} = 0$, respectively. Mean values for parameter estimates are reported for Φ, as well as the maximal and minimal absolute eigenvalues. Unless both of these are less than one, the fit is unstable, and the proportion of unstable fits is reported

Table 2 Model fitting results for sample sizes 100, 200, 400 from the VAR(1) with $\Phi_{11} = 2/3$, $\Phi_{12} = 0$, $\Phi_{21} = 1$, $\Phi_{22} = 1/3$, and $\underline{\sigma} = \underline{1}_2$

Parameters	Models					
n = 100	QMLE Model A	QMLE Model B	QMLE Model C	LSE Model A	LSE Model B	LSE Model C
Φ	0.647 −.003	0.647 0	0 0.530	0.654 −.003	0.654 0	0 0.230
	0.997 0.324	0.997 0.324	−0.031 0.685	1.007 0.328	1.007 0.328	1.007 0.328
Max $\|\zeta\|$	0.642	0.648	0.646	0.649	0.654	0.665
Min $\|\zeta\|$	0.350	0.324	0.111	0.354	0.328	0.338
Prob unstable	0	0	0	0	0	0
n = 200	QMLE Model A	QMLE Model B	QMLE Model C	LSE Model A	LSE Model B	LSE Model C
Φ	0.658 −0.002	0.657 0	0 0.534	0.661 −0.002	0.661 0	0 0.234
	0.998 0.329	0.998 0.329	−0.015 0.688	1.002 0.331	1.002 0.331	1.002 0.331
Max $\|\zeta\|$	0.643	0.657	0.668	0.646	0.661	0.674
Min $\|\zeta\|$	0.353	0.329	0.071	0.355	0.331	0.343
Prob unstable	0	0	0	0	0	0
n = 400	QMLE Model A	QMLE Model B	QMLE Model C	LSE Model A	LSE Model B	LSE Model C
Φ	0.662 −0.001	0.661 0	0 0.536	0.664 −0.001	0.663 0	0 0.236
	0.999 0.331	0.999 0.331	−0.009 0.689	1.001 0.332	1.001 0.332	1.001 0.332
Max $\|\zeta\|$	0.646	0.661	0.679	0.647	0.663	0.678
Min $\|\zeta\|$	0.351	0.331	0.049	0.352	0.332	0.346
Prob unstable	0	0	0	0	0	0

Models A, B, C are used, corresponding to unconstrained VAR(1), a VAR(1) with $\Phi_{12} = 0$, and a VAR(1) with $\Phi_{11} = 0$, respectively. Mean values for parameter estimates are reported for Φ, as well as the maximal and minimal absolute eigenvalues. Unless both of these are less than one, the fit is unstable, and the proportion of unstable fits is reported

Table 3 Model fitting results for sample sizes 100, 200, 400 from the VAR(1) with $\Phi_{11} = 0.95$, $\Phi_{12} = 0$, $\Phi_{21} = 1$, $\Phi_{22} = 1/2$, and $\underline{\sigma} = \underline{1}_2$

Parameters	Models					
n = 400	QMLE Model A	QMLE Model B	QMLE Model C	LSE Model A	LSE Model B	LSE Model C
Φ	0.925 −0.003	0.922 0	0 0.483	0.934 −0.002	0.932 0	0 0.425
	1.000 0.488	1.000 0.488	−0.260 1.063	1.009 0.495	1.009 0.495	1.009 0.495
Max $\|\zeta\|$	0.913	0.922	0.926	0.923	0.932	0.946
Min $\|\zeta\|$	0.501	0.488	0.149	0.506	0.495	0.451
Prob unstable	0	0	0	0.0030	0.0014	0.0044
n = 200	QMLE Model A	QMLE Model B	QMLE Model C	LSE Model A	LSE Model B	LSE Model C
Φ	0.938 −0.002	0.936 0	0 0.487	0.942 −0.001	0.941 0	0 0.434
	1.000 0.494	0.999 0.495	−0.159 1.029	1.004 0.498	1.004 0.498	1.004 0.498
Max $\|\zeta\|$	0.932	0.936	0.946	0.937	0.941	0.954
Min $\|\zeta\|$	0.501	0.495	0.095	0.503	0.498	0.456
Prob unstable	0	0	0	0	0	0
n = 400	QMLE Model A	QMLE Model B	QMLE Model C	LSE Model A	LSE Model B	LSE Model C
Φ	0.945 −0.001	0.943 0	0 0.490	0.947 −0.001	0.946 0	0 0.439
	1.000 0.497	1.000 0.497	−0.095 1.006	1.002 0.499	1.002 0.499	1.002 0.499
Max $\|\zeta\|$	0.942	0.943	0.957	0.944	0.946	0.958
Min $\|\zeta\|$	0.500	0.497	0.059	0.501	0.499	0.459
Prob unstable	0	0	0	0	0	0

Models A, B, C are used, corresponding to unconstrained VAR(1), a VAR(1) with $\Phi_{12} = 0$, and a VAR(1) with $\Phi_{11} = 0$, respectively. Mean values for parameter estimates are reported for Φ, as well as the maximal and minimal absolute eigenvalues. Unless both of these are less than one, the fit is unstable, and the proportion of unstable fits is reported

Table 4 Model fitting results for sample sizes 100, 200, 400 from the VAR(1) with $\Phi_{11} = -1/4$, $\Phi_{12} = 1/2$, $\Phi_{21} = -1$, $\Phi_{22} = 5/4$, and $\underline{\sigma} = \underline{1}_2$

Parameters	Models					
n = 100	QMLE Model A	QMLE Model B	QMLE Model C	LSE Model A	LSE Model B	LSE Model C
Φ	−0.257 0.504	0.409 0	0 0.183	−0.260 0.509	0.413 0	0 0.408
	−0.989 1.231	−0.947 1.199	0.243 0.753	−0.999 1.243	−.999 1.243	−0.999 1.243
Max $\lvert\zeta\rvert$	0.707	1.199	0.808	0.714	1.243	0.687
Min $\lvert\zeta\rvert$	0.278	0.409	0.055	0.281	0.413	0.598
Prob unstable	0	98.76 %	0	0	100.00 %	0
n = 200	QMLE Model A	QMLE Model B	QMLE Model C	LSE Model A	LSE Model B	LSE Model C
Φ	−0.251 0.501	0.419 0	0 0.189	−0.253 0.504	0.421 0	0 0.406
	−0.994 1.240	−0.973 1.224	0.244 0.763	−0.999 1.247	−0.999 1.247	−0.999 1.247
Max $\lvert\zeta\rvert$	0.722	1.224	0.819	0.726	1.247	0.671
Min $\lvert\zeta\rvert$	0.269	0.418	0.056	0.271	0.421	0.608
Prob unstable	0	100.00 %	0	0	100.00 %	0
n = 400	QMLE Model A	QMLE Model B	QMLE Model C	LSE Model A	LSE Model B	LSE Model C
Φ	−0.251 0.500	0.422 0	0 0.193	−0.251 0.502	0.423 0	0 0.405
	−0.997 1.246	−0.985 1.237	0.243 0.768	−1.000 1.249	−1.000 1.249	−1.000 1.249
Max $\lvert\zeta\rvert$	0.737	1.237	0.825	0.739	1.249	0.659
Min $\lvert\zeta\rvert$	0.258	0.422	0.057	0.259	0.423	0.616
Prob unstable	0	100.00 %	0	0	100.00 %	0

Models A, B, C are used, corresponding to unconstrained VAR(1), a VAR(1) with $\Phi_{12} = 0$, and a VAR(1) with $\Phi_{11} = 0$, respectively. Mean values for parameter estimates are reported for Φ, as well as the maximal and minimal absolute eigenvalues. Unless both of these are less than one, the fit is unstable, and the proportion of unstable fits is reported

expressions for the multi-step forecast error from a misspecified model; the forecast error process is

$$-[\underline{\Delta}^{-1}(B)\underline{\Psi}(B)]_0^{h-1} \underline{\Psi}^{-1}(B) \, \mathbf{W}_{t+h}$$

if we are forecasting h steps ahead. Now the parameter estimates would enter into the coefficients of $\underline{\Psi}$. Asymptotically, these estimates will converge to the PTVs. The variance of the corresponding error process (where parameter estimates have converged to the PTVs) is given by

$$\frac{1}{2\pi}\int_{-\pi}^{\pi} [\underline{\Delta}^{-1}(z)\underline{\Psi}(z)]_0^{h-1} \, \underline{\Psi}^{-1}(z) \, \underline{F}(\lambda) \, \underline{\Psi}^{\dagger}(\overline{z}) \, [\underline{\Psi}'(\overline{z})\underline{\Delta}^{\dagger}(\overline{z})]_0^{h-1} \, d\lambda .$$

This matrix depends on the data process in a double fashion: first through $\underline{F}$ in the center of the integrand, and again through the PTVs involved in $\underline{\Psi}$, which are previously computed as described in Sect. 3. As an example, consider the bivariate VAR(1) models A, B, C of the previous subsection, fitted to any of the first three true processes described above (we ignore the fourth process, because the forecasting formulas do not apply to unstable model fits). The h-step ahead FEV matrix simplifies to

$$\Gamma(0) - \underline{\phi}_1^h \, \Gamma(-h) - \Gamma(h) \, \underline{\phi}_1^{\prime h} + \underline{\phi}_1^h \, \Gamma(0) \, \underline{\phi}_1^{\prime h} .$$

Observe that this is a symmetric matrix, and its minimal value at $h = 1$ is given by the innovation variance matrix $\underline{\sigma}$. Into this formula, we would substitute the appropriate PTVs for $\underline{\phi}_1$ and the true process' autocovariances for $\Gamma(h)$ and $\Gamma(0)$. The resulting entries of the FEV matrix are plotted in Fig. 1 with $1 \leq h \leq 100$, with matrix entries for the first diagonal in red (solid), the second diagonal in green (dotted-dashed), and the off-diagonal in blue (dashed). Some of these plots are identical, which occurs when model B is actually correctly specified.

For the first process, going across the top row of Fig. 1, we note that model A is correctly specified, and both diagonal entries of the forecast variance matrix are the same due to symmetry of Φ. Misspecification, as shown for models B and C of the top row, has no impact on the second diagonal (dotted-dashed), but increases the first diagonal (solid) of the MSE matrix for short horizons. The reason for this behavior is that the PTVs for models B and C are still correct for the second component of the bivariate series, as mentioned above.

For the second process, both models A and B are correctly specified, and hence the MSE plots are identical. Now there is a large discrepancy in forecast performance between the first component series (solid) and the second (dotted-dashed). The final panel for model C shows an interesting feature: forecast performance at low horizons is actually worse than at longer horizons, which can happen for a misspecified model. The third process has a similar story, although model C fares competitively in the long run with the correctly specified models.

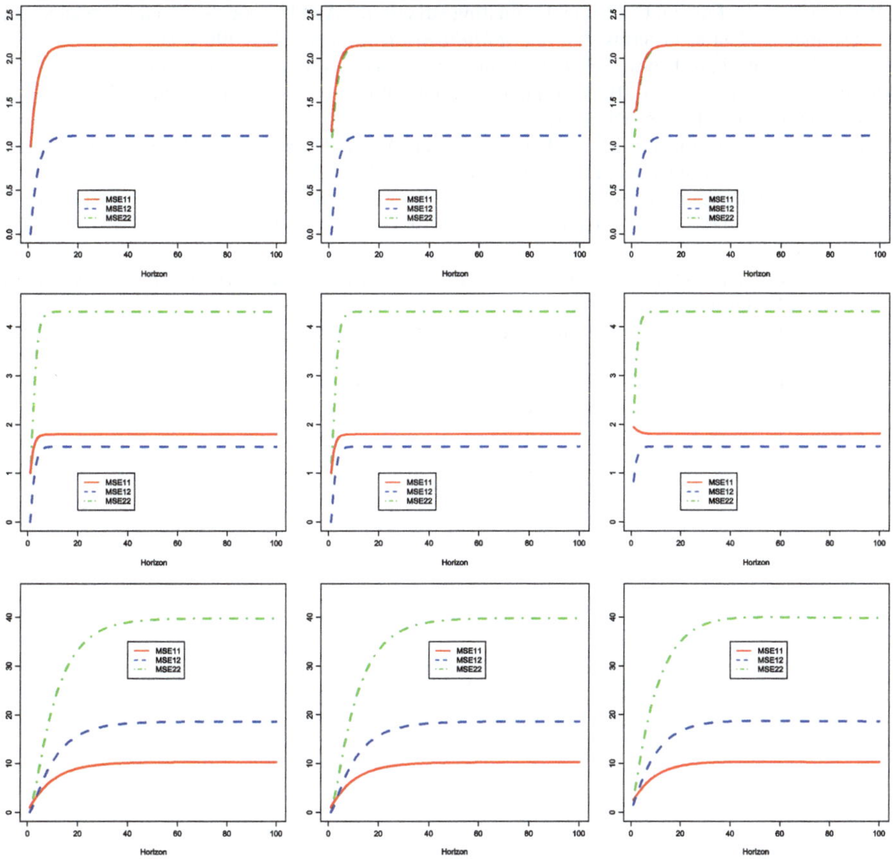

Fig. 1 Asymptotic forecast MSE as a function of forecast horizon. In each panel, the entries of the FEV matrix are plotted, with the first diagonal entry in *red* (*solid*), the second diagonal entry in *green* (*dotted-dashed*), and the off-diagonal in *blue* (*dashed*). The *first row* of panels corresponds to Process 1 of Sect. 3, while the *second row* of panels corresponds to Process 2 and the *third row* to Process 3. The *first column* of panels corresponds to Model A of Sect. 2, while the *second column* of panels corresponds to Model B and the *third column* to Model C

References

Akaike, H. (1969). Fitting autoregressive models for prediction. *Annals of the Institute of Statistical Mathematics, 21*, 243–247.

Akaike, H. (1974). A new look at the statistical model identification. *IEEE Transactions on Automatic Control, 19*, 716–723.

Akaike, H., & Kitagawa, G. (1999) *The practice of time series analysis*. New York: Springer.

Brockwell, P., & Davis, R. (1991). *Time series: Theory and methods* (2nd ed.). New York: Springer.

Lütkepohl, H. (2005). New Introduction to Multiple Time Series Analysis. Berlin: Springer.

Magnus, J., & Neudecker, H. (1999). *Matrix differential calculus with applications in statistics and econometrics*. New York: Wiley.

Maïnassara, B., & Francq, C. (2011). Estimating structural VARMA models with uncorrelated but non-independent error terms. *Journal of Multivariate Analysis, 102*, 496–505
Mardia, K., Kent, J., & Bibby, J. (1979). Multivariate Analysis. London: Academic Press.
McElroy, T., & Findley, F. (2013). Fitting constrained vector autoregression models. U.S. Census Bureau Research Report. RRS 2013/06.
McElroy, T., & McCracken, M. (2012). Multi-Step Ahead Forecasting of Vector Time Series. Federal Reserve Bank of St. Louis, Working Papers, 2012-060A.
Reinsel, G. (1996). *Elements of multivariate time series analysis* (2nd ed.). New York: Springer.
Schorfheide, F. (2005). VAR forecasting under misspecification. *Journal of Econometrics, 128*, 99–136.
Taniguchi, M., & Kakizawa, Y. (2000). *Asymptotic theory of statistical inference for time series*. New York: Springer.
Whittle, P. (1953). The analysis of multiple stationary time series. *Journal of the Royal Statistical Society, Series B, 15*, 125–139.
Whittle, P. (1963). *Prediction and regulation*. London: English Universities Press.
Wilks, S. (1932). Certain generalizations in the analysis of variance. *Biometrika, 24*, 471–494.

Minimax Versions of the Two-Step Two-Sample-Gauß- and t-Test

Wolf Krumbholz and Ingo Starke

Abstract Let Z_G and Z_t be the set of all two-step two-sample (TS) Gauß- and t-tests obeying the classical two-point-condition on the operating characteristic, respectively. Let further $Z_{G,b} \subset Z_G$ and $Z_{t,b} \subset Z_t$ be the subset of the corresponding balanced tests. Starke (Der zweistufige Zwei-Stichproben-t-Test, Logos, Berlin, 2009) developed an algorithm allowing to determine the minimax versions δ_b^* among $Z_{G,b}$ and $Z_{t,b}$ having minimal maximal ASN (=Average Sample Number).

We present for the first time an algorithm allowing to determine the overall minimax version δ^* among Z_G. Furthermore, we investigate the magnitude of the possible reduction of maximal ASN which could be achieved by passing from the balanced to the overall minimax two-step TS-t-test δ^*. These savings on ASN maximum are compared to the enormous additional effort required by determining δ^* instead of Starke's δ_b^* in the t-test case.

1 Introduction

Vangjeli (2009) and Krumbholz et al. (2012) dealt with two-step variants of the classical Gauß- and t-test and determined their minimax versions having minimal maximum of the ASN (=Average Sample Number) among all of these tests obeying the classical two-point-condition on the operating characteristic (OC).

Starke (2009) dealt with two-step variants of the two-sample-t-test (TS-t-test) which became a frequently used tool applied in various disciplines covering econometrics as well as biometrics. He confined himself to investigate only the so-called balanced case in which both samples on each stage have the same size. He developed and implemented an algorithm allowing to determine the minimax version among all balanced two-step TS-t-tests obeying the two-point-condition on their OC. Various examples show ASN maxima of his two-step minimax versions

W. Krumbholz (✉) • I. Starke
Helmut-Schmidt-Universität/Universität der Bundeswehr Hamburg, Postfach 700 822, 22008 Hamburg, Germany
e-mail: wolf.krumbholz@t-online.de; ingo.starke@hsuhh.de

J. Beran et al. (eds.), *Empirical Economic and Financial Research*, Advanced Studies in Theoretical and Applied Econometrics 48,
DOI 10.1007/978-3-319-03122-4_29

remaining always about 14 % below the constant sample sizes of the corresponding one-step TS-t-tests. This considerable saving on sample size and sampling costs yields a strong argument in favour of the two-step testing procedure.

Investigations in Kremer et al. (2009) and Starke (2009) allow to conclude that the minimax version among all two-step TS-t-tests will always coincide with the minimax version among either the balanced or one of the three different close-by balanced two-step TS-t-tests. Thus, in order to determine the minimax version among all TS-t-tests you have to determine Starke's minimax version of the balanced tests as well as the minimax versions of three different close-by balanced tests. The calculation of each of these tests requires the solving of a rather complex optimization problem with two integers (fixing the sample sizes on both stages), three continuous variables (the critical values), and two constraints (the two-point-condition on the OC). Starke's algorithm will also work in the close-by balanced cases. Of course, the OC of the balanced test then has to be substituted by the OC of the different close-by balanced tests. Starke (2009) developed a constructive formula, containing a five-dimensional integral, for the OC of the balanced TS-t-test. We expect seven-dimensional integrals in the corresponding formulas for the OCs of the close-by balanced TS-t-tests. But these formulas are not known at present and would have to be determined at first. Unfortunately, these complex OCs would occur in the most interior loop of the optimization algorithm leading to a considerable increasing of computing time for each minimax close-by balanced test in comparison with the minimax balanced test.

In the present paper, we investigate the magnitude of the reduction of the ASN maximum which may be achieved by passing from the balanced to the overall minimax TS-t-test. In order to reduce the complexity of our investigations we decided to substitute the TS-t-tests by the corresponding TS-Gauß-tests. As a favourable effect the OCs then can be written as one- or three-dimensional integrals and Starke's algorithm still works. Furthermore, all results of our investigation carry over to the TS-t-tests in an obvious manner. At the end of the paper we are able to give a recommendation concerning the question whether it is reasonable to invest the described enormous effort to determine the overall minimax version of the TS-t-test instead of Starke's balanced minimax version in comparison with the magnitude of the achievable saving on ASN maximum.

2 Minimax Versions of the Two-Step TS-t-test

Let X and Y be independent characteristics with

$$X \sim N\,(\mu_x, \sigma_x^2),\;\; Y \sim N\,(\mu_y, \sigma_y^2)$$

and unknown variances $\sigma_x^2,\, \sigma_y^2 > 0$. We assume $\sigma_x = \sigma_y$ and set $\sigma = \sigma_x = \sigma_y$ and

$$\theta = \frac{\mu_x - \mu_y}{\sigma}. \tag{1}$$

We shall deal with one- and two-step versions of the TS-t-test for testing

$$\text{One-sided case:} \quad H_0 : \theta \leq 0 \quad \text{against} \quad H_1 : \theta \geq \theta_0 \tag{2}$$

$$\text{Two-sided case:} \quad H_0 : \theta = 0 \quad \text{against} \quad H_1 : |\theta| \geq \theta_0 \tag{3}$$

for given $\theta_0 > 0$ and levels α, β for the errors of the first and second kind obeying $0 < \beta < 1 - \alpha < 1$. We omit the other one-sided case

$$H_0 : \theta \geq 0 \quad \text{against} \quad H_1 : \theta \leq -\theta_0$$

which is treated completely analogously to (2).

One-step TS-t-test Let $X_1, \ldots, X_{n_x}$ and $Y_1, \ldots, Y_{n_y}$ denote independent iid-samples on X and Y, respectively. Let $\bar{X}, S_x^2$ and $\bar{Y}, S_y^2$ denote the corresponding sample means and sample variances. The *one-step TS t-test* $\delta = (n_x, n_y, k)$ is given by the test statistic

$$T(n_x, n_y) = \frac{\bar{X} - \bar{Y}}{\sqrt{(n_x - 1)\, S_x^2 + (n_y - 1)\, S_y^2}} \sqrt{\frac{n_x\, n_y\, (n_x + n_y - 2)}{n_x + n_y}} \tag{4}$$

and the decision to accept H_0 iff

$$\text{One-sided case:} \quad T\,(n_x, n_y) \leq k \;, \quad k = t_{n_x + n_y - 2;\, 1-\alpha} \tag{5}$$

$$\text{Two-sided case:} \quad |T\,(n_x, n_y)| \leq k \;, \quad k = t_{n_x + n_y - 2;\, 1-\frac{\alpha}{2}} \tag{6}$$

holds (compare Heiler and Rinne, 1971, p. 96). Here $t_{r;\gamma}$ denotes the γ-quantile of the central t distribution with r degrees of freedom. Furthermore, let us denote the cdf of the noncentral t distribution with r degrees of freedom and noncentrality parameter a by $F_{r,a}$. Then the operation characteristic (OC) of $\delta = (n_x, n_y, k)$ is given by:

$$\text{One-sided case:} \quad L(\theta) = P_\theta\left(T(n_x, n_y) \leq k\right) = F_{n_x + n_y - 2\,;\, a(\theta)}\,(k) \tag{7}$$

$$\begin{aligned} \text{Two-sided case:} \quad L(\theta) &= P_\theta\left(|T(n_x, n_y)| \leq k\right) \\ &= F_{n_x + n_y - 2\,;\, a(\theta)}\,(k) - F_{n_x + n_y - 2;\, a(\theta)}\,(-k) \end{aligned} \tag{8}$$

with noncentrality parameter

$$a(\theta) = \sqrt{\frac{n_x\, n_y}{n_x + n_y}}\; \theta \tag{9}$$

The critical value k in (5) and (6) was chosen in order to fulfill the requirement concerning the error of the first kind

$$L(0) \;=\; 1-\alpha. \tag{10}$$

The corresponding requirement, concerning the error of the second kind, is

$$L(\theta_0) \;\leq \beta. \tag{11}$$

Because (n_x, n_y, k) is not uniquely determined by the so-called two-point-condition (10) and (11), it seems reasonable to choose among these tests the one fulfilling

$$n_x + n_y \stackrel{!}{=} \min. \tag{12}$$

It is well known that $L(\theta_0)$, for given $N = n_x + n_y$, takes its minimum if in the case of even N

$$n_x = n_y \tag{13}$$

and in the case of odd N

$$|n_x - n_y| \;=\; 1 \tag{14}$$

hold. Tests $\delta = (n_x, n_y, k)$ with (13) are denoted as *balanced* and those with (14) as *close-by-balanced*. Thus, the test δ obeying (10)–(12) always comes out to be either balanced or close-by balanced.

Two-step TS-t-test The two-step TS-t-test is based on the iid-samples

$$X_1, \ldots, X_{n_{x,1}} \quad \text{and} \quad Y_1, \ldots, Y_{n_{y,1}}$$

on the first stage and on the iid-samples

$$X_{n_{x,1}+1}, \ldots, X_{n_{x,1}+n_{x,2}} \quad \text{and} \quad Y_{n_{y,1}+1}, \ldots, Y_{n_{y,1}+n_{y,2}}$$

on the second stage, being independent of the samples on the first stage. We set

$$\bar{X}_1 \;=\; \frac{1}{n_{x,1}} \sum_{i=1}^{n_{x,1}} X_i \quad , \quad S_{x,1}^2 \;=\; \frac{1}{n_{x,1}-1} \sum_{i=1}^{n_{x,1}} \left(X_i - \bar{X}_1\right)^2$$

$$\bar{Y}_1 \;=\; \frac{1}{n_{y,1}} \sum_{i=1}^{n_{y,1}} Y_i \quad , \quad S_{y,1}^2 \;=\; \frac{1}{n_{y,1}-1} \sum_{i=1}^{n_{y,1}} \left(Y_i - \bar{Y}_1\right)^2$$

$$N_1 \;=\; n_{x,1} \;+\; n_{y,1} \tag{15}$$

$$T_1 = \frac{\bar{X}_1 - \bar{Y}_1}{\sqrt{(n_{x,1}-1)\,S_{x,1}^2 + (n_{y,1}-1)\,S_{y,1}^2}} \sqrt{\frac{n_{x,1}\,n_{y,1}\,(N_1-2)}{N_1}} \tag{16}$$

$$N_2 = n_{x,2} + n_{y,2} \tag{17}$$

$$N_x = n_{x,1} + n_{x,2} \tag{18}$$

$$N_y = n_{y,1} + n_{y,2} \tag{19}$$

$$N = N_1 + N_2 = N_x + N_y \tag{20}$$

$$\bar{\bar{X}} = \frac{1}{N_x} \sum_{i=1}^{N_x} X_i \quad , \quad S_x^2 = \frac{1}{N_x - 1} \sum_{i=1}^{N_x} \left(X_i - \bar{\bar{X}}\right)^2$$

$$\bar{\bar{Y}} = \frac{1}{N_y} \sum_{i=1}^{N_y} Y_i \quad , \quad S_y^2 = \frac{1}{N_y - 1} \sum_{i=1}^{N_y} \left(Y_i - \bar{\bar{Y}}\right)^2$$

$$T = \frac{\bar{\bar{X}} - \bar{\bar{Y}}}{\sqrt{(N_x-1)\,S_x^2 + (N_y-1)\,S_y^2}} \sqrt{\frac{N_x\,N_y\,(N-2)}{N}} \tag{21}$$

The *two-step TS-t-test*

$$\delta = \begin{pmatrix} n_{x,1} \; n_{y,1} \; k_1 \; k_2 \\ n_{x,2} \; n_{y,2} \; k_3 \end{pmatrix}$$

with $n_{x_i}, n_{y_i} \in \mathbb{N}\,(i = 1, 2)$; $k_1, k_2, k_3 \in \mathbb{R}$; $k_1 \le k_2$ is defined by the procedure:

(i) Take the samples on the first stage and determine T_1.

One-sided case	Two-sided case
if $T_1 \le k_1$, then accept H_0	if $\lvert T_1\rvert \le k_1$, then accept H_0
if $T_1 > k_2$, then accept H_1	if $\lvert T_1\rvert > k_2$, then accept H_1
if $k_1 < T_1 \le k_2$, then go to (ii)	if $k_1 < \lvert T_1\rvert \le k_2$, then go to (ii)

(ii) Take the samples on the second stage and determine T.

One-sided case	Two-sided case
if $T \le k_3$, then accept H_0	if $\lvert T\rvert \le k_3$, then accept H_0
if $T > k_3$, then accept H_1	if $\lvert T\rvert > k_3$, then accept H_1

Of course, in the two-sided case the critical values k_i should be nonnegative ($i = 1, 2, 3$). If $k_1 = k_2$, then δ coincides with the one-step test $\delta = (n_{x,1}, n_{y,1}, k_1)$. The OC of the two-step ZS-t-test

$$\delta = \begin{pmatrix} n_{x,1} & n_{y,1} & k_1 & k_2 \\ n_{x,2} & n_{y,2} & k_3 & \end{pmatrix}$$

is defined by:

$$\text{One-sided case: } L(\theta) = P_\theta(T_1 \leq k_1) + P_\theta\left(T \leq k_3,\, k_1 < T_1 \leq k_2\right)$$

$$\text{Two-sided case: } H(\theta) = P_\theta(|T_1| \leq k_1) + P_\theta\left(|T| \leq k_3,\, k_1 < |T_1| \leq k_2\right).$$

The following lemma allows to express the OC H of the two-sided test δ in terms of the OCs of four different one-sided tests.

Lemma 1 *For $k_1, k_2, k_3 \geq 0$ let*

$$\delta_1 = \begin{pmatrix} n_{x,1} & n_{y,1} & k_1 & k_2 \\ n_{x,2} & n_{y,2} & k_3 & \end{pmatrix}, \quad \delta_2 = \begin{pmatrix} n_{x,1} & n_{y,1} & -k_2 & -k_1 \\ n_{x,2} & n_{y,2} & k_3 & \end{pmatrix}$$

$$\delta_3 = \begin{pmatrix} n_{x,1} & n_{y,1} & k_1 & k_2 \\ n_{x,2} & n_{y,2} & -k_3 & \end{pmatrix}, \quad \delta_4 = \begin{pmatrix} n_{x,1} & n_{y,1} & -k_2 & -k_1 \\ n_{x,2} & n_{y,2} & -k_3 & \end{pmatrix}$$

be one-sided TS-t-tests. Let L_i be the OC of δ_i $(1 \leq i \leq 4)$. Then

$$H(\theta) = P_\theta\left(|T_1| \leq k_1\right) + L_1(\theta) + L_2(\theta) - L_3(\theta) - L_4(\theta) \tag{22}$$

holds.

Proof Completely analogously to the proof of Lemma 1 in Krumbholz et al. (2012).

Remark A.1 The calculation of $L(\theta)$ for only one θ is difficult because the noncentral-t-distributed variables T_1 and T are dependent. For the balanced case

$$n_{x,1} = n_{y,1}\ ,\ n_{x,2} = n_{y,2} \tag{23}$$

Starke determined in Sect. 3.2 of Starke (2009) a constructive formula allowing to write the main term

$$P_\theta\left(T \leq k_3,\, k_1 < T_1 \leq k_2\right)$$

of $L(\theta)$ as a five-dimensional integral. He derived this formula by help of the total probability decomposition and the independence of the normal-and χ^2-distributed variables

$$U_i = \sqrt{n_{x,i}}\ \frac{\bar{X}_i - \mu_x}{\sigma} \quad , \quad V_i = \sqrt{n_{y,i}}\ \frac{\bar{Y}_i - \mu_y}{\sigma} \quad (i = 1, 2)$$

and

$$W_i = \frac{n_{x,i} - 1}{\sigma^2}\ S^2_{x,i} \ + \ \frac{n_{y,i} - 1}{\sigma^2}\ S^2_{y,i} \quad (i = 1, 2).$$

Here $\bar{X}_2, \bar{Y}_2,\ S^2_{x,2},\ S^2_{y,2}$ are calculated analogously to $\bar{X}_1, \bar{Y}_1,\ S^2_{x,1},\ S^2_{y,1}$ from the samples on the second stage. A corresponding formula for $L(\theta)$ in the general case is not available so far. Starke's method will lead to a seven-dimensional integral for the main term of $L(\theta)$. The same will hold for the close-by balanced cases

$$n_{x,1} = n_{y,1} \quad , \quad |n_{x,2} - n_{y,2}| \ = \ 1 \tag{24}$$

$$|n_{x,1} - n_{y,1}| \ = \ 1 \quad , \quad n_{x,2} = n_{y,2} \tag{25}$$

and

$$n_{x,1} = n_{y,1} + 1,\ n_{x,2} = n_{y,2} - 1 \quad \vee \quad n_{x,1} = n_{y,1} - 1,\ n_{x,2} = n_{y,2} + 1. \tag{26}$$

In the following we call a balanced TS-t-test with (23) a *test of type 1* and close-by balanced tests with (24),..., (26) *tests of type 2,...,type 4*, respectively. For given parameter θ_0 and error levels α, β, the two-point-condition (10) and (11) of the one-step test is replaced by

$$\text{One-sided case:} \quad L(0) \geq 1 - \alpha\ ,\ L(\theta_0) \leq \beta \tag{27}$$

$$\text{Two-sided case:} \quad H(0) \geq 1 - \alpha\ ,\ H(\theta_0) \leq \beta \tag{28}$$

in the two-step case. Let Z denote the set of all TS-t-tests obeying (27) or (28). The ASN of a TS-t-test

$$\delta = \begin{pmatrix} n_{x,1}\ n_{y,1}\ k_1\ k_2 \\ n_{x,2}\ n_{y,2}\ k_3 \end{pmatrix}$$

is given by:

$$\text{One-sided case:} \quad N_\delta(\theta) \ = \ N_1 + N_2\ P_\theta\left(k_1 < T_1 \leq k_2\right) \tag{29}$$

$$\text{Two-sided case:} \quad N_\delta(\theta) \ = \ N_1 + N_2\ P_\theta\left(k_1 < |T_1| \leq k_2\right). \tag{30}$$

We define

$$N_{\max}(\delta) \ = \ \max_\theta\ N_\delta(\theta) \tag{31}$$

and call the test $\delta^* \in Z$ with

$$N_{\max}(\delta^*) = \min_{\delta \in Z} N_{\max}(\delta) \tag{32}$$

the *minimax version of the two-step TS-t-test.*

Remark A.2 Starke (2009) developed and implemented an algorithm allowing to determine the one-sided as well as the two-sided minimax version δ_1^* of the balanced two-step TS-t-tests. δ_1^* is given by

$$N_{\max}(\delta_1^*) = \min_{\delta \in Z_1} N_{\max}(\delta) \tag{33}$$

with Z_1 denoting the set of all two-step TS-t-tests of type 1 according to (23) fulfilling the two-point-condition (27) or (28).

In the following example for a typical constellation of α, β and θ_0

- the balanced one-step TS-t-test,
- the minimax version δ_1^* of the balanced two-step TS-t-test

are determined. Furthermore, the corresponding Two-Sample-Gauß-Tests (TS-Gaußtests) are determined. These TS-Gaußtests are obtained from the TS-t-tests by replacing all the sample variances occurring in the test statistics (3), (14) and (19) by the now known σ^2. Figure 1 shows the ASN-curves of these tests.

Example 0.1 $\alpha = 0.05 \quad \beta = 0.10 \quad \theta_0 = 0.70$

(i) One-sided case

(a) One-step
Balanced TS-t-test $\quad \eta = (36,\ 36,\ 1.6669)$
Balanced TS-Gaußtest $\quad \eta_G = (35,\ 35,\ 1.6449)$

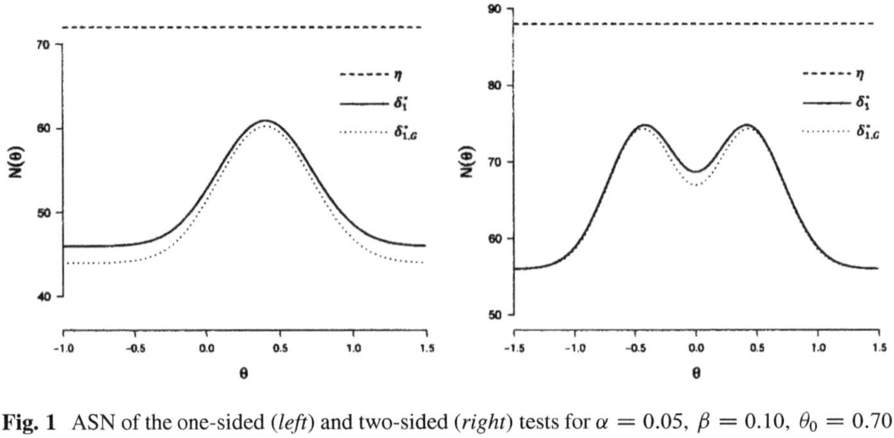

Fig. 1 ASN of the one-sided (*left*) and two-sided (*right*) tests for $\alpha = 0.05,\ \beta = 0.10,\ \theta_0 = 0.70$

(b) Two-step

Balanced TS-t-test $\delta_1^* = \begin{pmatrix} 23\ 23\ 0.7304\ 1.9989 \\ 16\ 16\ 1.7249 \end{pmatrix}$

with $N_{\max}\,(\delta_1^*) = 60.9306$

Balanced TS-Gaußtest $\delta_{1,G}^* = \begin{pmatrix} 22\ 22\ 0.7371\ 1.9374 \\ 18\ 18\ 1.7352 \end{pmatrix}$

with $N_{\max}\,(\delta_{1,G}^*) = 60.2574$

(ii) Two-sided case

(a) One-step

Balanced TS-t-test $\eta = (44,\ 44,\ 1.9879)$

Balanced TS-Gaußtest $\eta_G = (44,\ 44,\ 1.9600)$

(b) Two-step

Balanced TS-t-test $\delta_1^* = \begin{pmatrix} 28\ 28\ 0.8917\ 2.3185 \\ 18\ 18\ 2.0145 \end{pmatrix}$

with $N_{\max}\,(\delta_1^*) = 74.8320$

Balanced TS-Gaußtest $\delta_{1,G}^* = \begin{pmatrix} 28\ 28\ 1.0400\ 2.2511 \\ 20\ 20\ 2.0299 \end{pmatrix}$

with $N_{\max}\,(\delta_{1,G}^*) = 74.3570$

Remark A.3 The $N_{\max}(\delta_1^*)$-value in Example 0.1 remains in the one-sided case 15.37 % and in the two-sided case 14.96 % below the constant sample size $n_x + n_y$ of the corresponding one-step test η. Various examples showed down the line corresponding savings about 14 %. Furthermore, we always observed ASN-maxima taking their values in the one-sided and two-sided case in the interval $(0, \theta_0)$ and $(-\theta_0, \theta_0)$, respectively. This shows that the $N_{\max}$-criterion comes out to be not too pessimistic.

Because of $Z_1 \subset Z$ we get $N_{\max}\,(\delta_1^*) \geq N_{\max}(\delta^*)$. Thus, the two-step balanced minimax test must not coincide with the two-step overall minimax test. For $i = 2, 3, 4$ let Z_i be the set of all two-step close-by balanced TS-t-tests of type i according to (24)–(26) which obey the two-point-condition (27) or (28). The test $\delta_i^* \in Z_i$ with

$$N_{\max}(\delta_i^*) = \min_{\delta \in Z_i} N_{\max}(\delta) \tag{34}$$

is called the *minimax version of the close-by balanced TS-t-test of type i* $(i = 2, 3, 4)$.

Analogously to the one-step case, the two-step overall minimax test δ^* always comes out to be either a balanced or a close-by balanced test, i.e.

$$N_{\max}(\delta^*) = \min_{1 \leq i \leq 4} N_{\max}(\delta_i^*) \tag{35}$$

holds.

In order to determine δ^*, constructive formulas, like Starke's for the OC of the balanced TS-t-test, would have to be derived for the OCs of the three different types of close-by balanced TS-t-tests. If Starke's OC-formula is replaced by the OC-formulas of the close-by balanced tests, Starke's algorithm for δ_1^* would still work and produce the corresponding tests δ_i^* $(2 \leq i \leq 4)$. But the computing time would increase dramatically. The reason for this is that in the most interior loop of Starke's optimization algorithm OC-values would have to be determined in order to check constantly the two-point-condition. The calculation of only one $L(\theta)$-value would require among other things to determine numerically a complex seven-dimensional integral in the one-sided case and, because of Lemma 1, four seven-dimensional integrals in the two-sided case.

In the next sections we shall examine whether the magnitude of the reduction of $N_{\max}(\delta^*)$ in comparison to $N_{\max}(\delta_1^*)$ will justify the enormous additional effort required to determine δ^* instead of Starke's δ_1^*. Therefore, because of (35), we shall calculate for $i = 1, \ldots, 4$ all minimax versions of type i and pick out the overall minimax version.

3 Minimax Versions of the Two-Step TS-Gaußtests

The one-step TS-Gaußtest $\delta = (n_x, n_y, k)$ is defined completely analogously to the one-step TS-t-test. Only the test statistic (3) must be replaced by

$$T(n_x, n_y) = \sqrt{\frac{n_x\, n_y}{n_x + n_y}}\, \frac{\bar{X} - \bar{Y}}{\sigma}. \tag{36}$$

The OC of $\delta = (n_x, n_y, k)$ is now given by:

$$\text{One-sided case:} \quad L(\theta) = P_\theta\left(T(n_x, n_y) \leq k\right) = \Phi\left(k - \sqrt{\frac{n_x\, n_y}{n_x + n_y}}\, \theta\right) \tag{37}$$

$$\begin{aligned}\text{Two-sided case:} \quad L(\theta) &= P_\theta\left(|T(n_x, n_y)| \leq k\right) \\ &= \Phi\left(k - \sqrt{\frac{n_x\, n_y}{n_x + n_y}}\, \theta\right) - \Phi\left(-k - \sqrt{\frac{n_x\, n_y}{n_x + n_y}}\, \theta\right).\end{aligned} \tag{38}$$

Here, Φ denotes the cdf of the $N(0, 1)$ distribution. The two-step TS-Gaußtest

$$\delta = \begin{pmatrix} n_{x,1} & n_{y,1} & k_1 & k_2 \\ n_{x,2} & n_{y,2} & k_3 & \end{pmatrix}$$

is defined completely analogously to the two-step TS-t-test. Only the test statistic on the first stage (13) has now to be replaced by

$$T_1 \;=\; \sqrt{\frac{n_{x,1}\, n_{y,1}}{N_1}}\; \frac{\bar{X}_1 - \bar{Y}_1}{\sigma} \tag{39}$$

and the test statistic on the second stage (19) by

$$T \;=\; \sqrt{\frac{N_x\, N_y}{N}}\; \frac{\bar{\bar{X}} - \bar{\bar{Y}}}{\sigma}. \tag{40}$$

For $v_1, u_1, v_2 \in \mathbb{R}$ we set:

$$a(v_1) = k_1 \sqrt{\frac{N_1}{n_{y,1}}} \;+\; v_1 \sqrt{\frac{n_{x,1}}{n_{y,1}}} \;-\; \theta\, \sqrt{n_{x,1}}$$

$$b(v_1) = k_2 \sqrt{\frac{N_1}{n_{y,1}}} \;+\; v_1 \sqrt{\frac{n_{x,1}}{n_{y,1}}} \;-\; \theta\, \sqrt{n_{x,1}}$$

$$\begin{aligned} H(v_1, u_1, v_2) = {}& k_3 \sqrt{\frac{N_x\, N}{n_{x,2}\, N_y}} \;-\; u_1 \sqrt{\frac{n_{x,1}}{n_{x,2}}} \\ &+ \frac{N_x}{N_y\, \sqrt{n_{x,2}}} \left(v_1 \sqrt{n_{y,1}} \;+\; v_2 \sqrt{n_{y,2}} \right) - \theta\, \frac{N_x}{\sqrt{n_{x,2}}} \end{aligned}$$

$$I\,(v_1, u_1) \;=\; \int_{-\infty}^{\infty} \Phi \left(H\,(v_1, u_1, v_2) \right)\; \Phi'\,(v_2)\, dv_2.$$

In Kremer et al. (2009) the following formula is proved.

Lemma 2 *In the one-sided case the OC of the two-step TS-Gaußtest*

$$\delta = \begin{pmatrix} n_{x,1} & n_{y,1} & k_1 & k_2 \\ n_{x,2} & n_{y,2} & k_3 & \end{pmatrix}$$

is given by

$$\begin{aligned} L(\theta) \;=\; {}& \Phi \left(k_1 - \theta \sqrt{\frac{n_{x,1}\, n_{y,1}}{N_1}} \right) \\ &+ \int_{-\infty}^{\infty} \left(\int_{a(v_1)}^{b(v_1)} I\,(v_1, u_1)\; \Phi'\,(u_1)\, du_1 \right) \Phi'\,(v_1)\, dv_1. \end{aligned} \tag{41}$$

In the balanced case $n_{x,1} = n_{y,1} = n_1$, $n_{x,2} = n_{y,2} = n_2$ the three-dimensional integral (41) simplifies to the one-dimensional integral

$$L(\theta) = \Phi\left(k_1 - \theta\sqrt{\frac{n_1}{2}}\right) + \int_{k_1-\theta\sqrt{\frac{n_1}{2}}}^{k_2-\theta\sqrt{\frac{n_1}{2}}} \Phi(H_1(x))\,\Phi'(x)\,dx \tag{42}$$

with

$$H_1(x) = k_3\sqrt{\frac{n_1+n_2}{n_2}} - x\sqrt{\frac{n_1}{n_2}} - \theta\,\frac{n_1+n_2}{\sqrt{2n_2}}\,. \tag{43}$$

The formulas (41), (42) allow to calculate the OC of arbitrary one-sided two-step TS-Gaußtests and thus especially the OC of the one-sided two-step balanced and close-by balanced TS-Gaußtests.

4 Numerical Examples

In this section we shall determine for some constellations of α, β, θ_0 the minimax versions of the TS-Gaußtest in

- the one-sided one-step
- the one-sided two-step
- the two-sided one-step
- the two-sided two-step

case. Furthermore, the OC of the two-step overall minimax version and the ASN of the one- and two-step minimax versions are plotted. These plots concerning Examples 0.2 and 0.3 are given in Figs. 2 and 3 and Figs. 4 and 5, respectively. In some cases the overall minimax version coincides with that of the balanced tests, in other cases with that of a close-by balanced test.

Example 0.2 $\alpha = 0.05 \quad \beta = 0.10 \quad \theta_0 = 0.75$

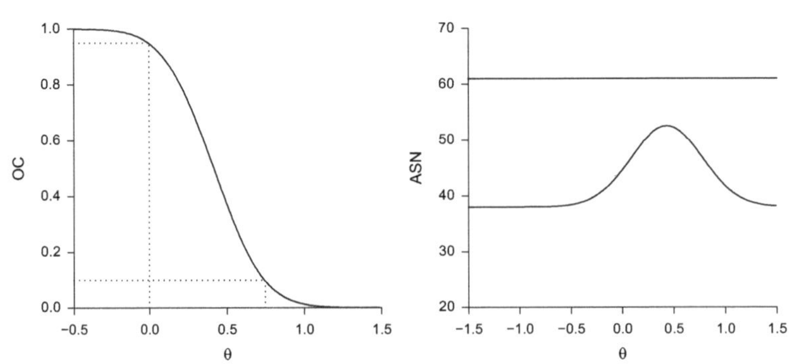

Fig. 2 OC of δ^* (*left*) and ASN of (n_x, n_y, k) and δ^* (*right*) for $\theta_0 = 0.75$, $\alpha = 0.05$, $\beta = 0.10$ (one-sided case)

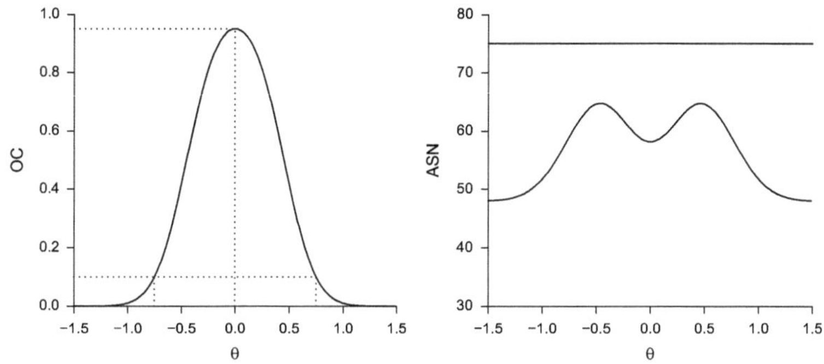

Fig. 3 OC of δ^* (*left*) and ASN of (n_x, n_y, k) and δ^* (*right*) for $\theta_0 = 0.75$, $\alpha = 0.05$, $\beta = 0.10$ (two-sided case)

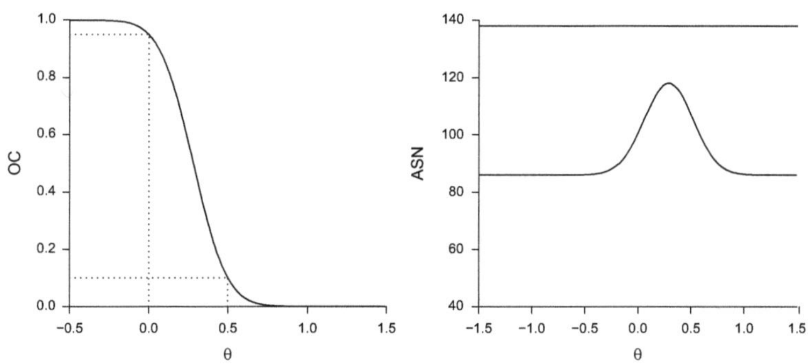

Fig. 4 OC of δ^* (*left*) and ASN of (n_x, n_y, k) and δ^* (*right*) for $\theta_0 = 0.50$, $\alpha = 0.05$, $\beta = 0.10$ (one-sided case)

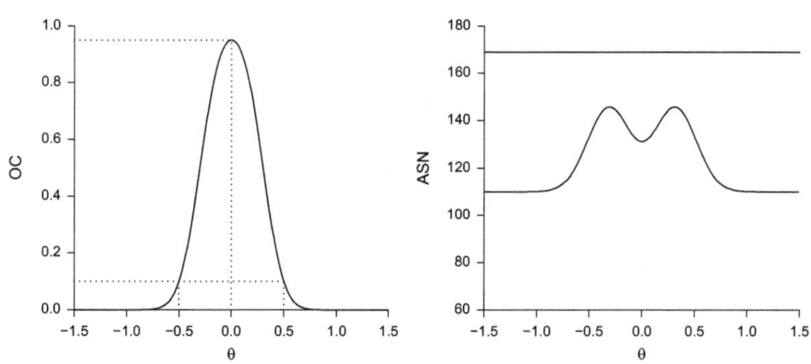

Fig. 5 OC of δ^* (*left*) and ASN of (n_x, n_y, k) and δ^* (*right*) for $\theta_0 = 0.50$, $\alpha = 0.50$, $\beta = 0.10$ (two-sided case)

(i) One-sided case

(a) One-step

$$(n_x, n_y, k) = (31,\ 30,\ 1.6449)$$

(b) Two-step

$$\delta_1^* = \begin{pmatrix} 19\ 19\ 0.7299\ 1.9348 \\ 16\ 16\ 1.7382 \end{pmatrix} \quad \text{with} \quad N_{\max}(\delta_1^*) = 52.5003$$

$$\delta_2^* = \begin{pmatrix} 19\ 19\ 0.7077\ 1.9559 \\ 16\ 15\ 1.7281 \end{pmatrix} \quad \text{with} \quad N_{\max}(\delta_2^*) = 52.4912$$

$$\delta_3^* = \begin{pmatrix} 20\ 19\ 0.7488\ 1.9450 \\ 15\ 15\ 1.7281 \end{pmatrix} \quad \text{with} \quad N_{\max}(\delta_3^*) = 52.5072$$

$$\delta_4^* = \begin{pmatrix} 20\ 19\ 0.7247\ 1.9683 \\ 14\ 15\ 1.7181 \end{pmatrix} \quad \text{with} \quad N_{\max}(\delta_4^*) = 52.5121$$

Minimax test: $\delta^* = \delta_2^*$
Saving of $N_{\max}(\delta^*)$ in comparison to $N_{\max}(\delta_1^*)$: 0.017%.

(ii) Two-sided case

(a) One-step

$$(n_x, n_y, k) = (38,\ 37,\ 1.9600)$$

(b) Two-step

$$\delta_1^* = \begin{pmatrix} 24\ 24\ 1.0196\ 2.2515 \\ 18\ 18\ 2.0324 \end{pmatrix} \quad \text{with} \quad N_{\max}(\delta_1^*) = 64.7823$$

$$\delta_2^* = \begin{pmatrix} 24\ 24\ 1.0376\ 2.2337 \\ 19\ 18\ 2.0406 \end{pmatrix} \quad \text{with} \quad N_{\max}(\delta_2^*) = 64.8007$$

$$\delta_3^* = \begin{pmatrix} 25\ 24\ 1.0338\ 2.2623 \\ 17\ 17\ 2.0248 \end{pmatrix} \quad \text{with} \quad N_{\max}(\delta_3^*) = 64.8006$$

$$\delta_4^* = \begin{pmatrix} 25\ 24\ 1.0543\ 2.2421 \\ 17\ 18\ 2.0332 \end{pmatrix} \quad \text{with} \quad N_{\max}(\delta_4^*) = 64.7835$$

Minimax test: $\delta^* = \delta_1^*$
Saving of $N_{\max}(\delta^*)$ in comparison to $N_{\max}(\delta_1^*)$: 0 %.

Example 0.3 $\alpha = 0.05 \quad \beta = 0.10 \quad \theta_0 = 0.50$

(i) One-sided case

(a) One-step

$$(n_x, n_y, k) = (69,\ 69,\ 1.6449)$$

(b) Two-step

$$\delta_1^* = \begin{pmatrix} 43\ 43\ 0.7249\ 1.9459 \\ 35\ 35\ 1.7316 \end{pmatrix} \quad \text{with} \quad N_{\max}(\delta_1^*) = 118.0914$$

$$\delta_2^* = \begin{pmatrix} 43\ 43\ 0.7147\ 1.9557 \\ 35\ 34\ 1.7271 \end{pmatrix} \quad \text{with} \quad N_{\max}(\delta_2^*) = 118.0889$$

$$\delta_3^* = \begin{pmatrix} 44\ 43\ 0.7331\ 1.9508 \\ 34\ 34\ 1.7271 \end{pmatrix} \quad \text{with} \quad N_{\max}(\delta_3^*) = 118.0957$$

$$\delta_4^* = \begin{pmatrix} 44\ 43\ 0.7435\ 1.9412 \\ 34\ 35\ 1.7315 \end{pmatrix} \quad \text{with} \quad N_{\max}(\delta_4^*) = 118.0997$$

Minimax test: $\delta^* = \delta_2^*$
Saving of $N_{\max}(\delta^*)$ in comparison to $N_{\max}(\delta_1^*)$: 0.002%.

(ii) Two-sided case

(a) One-step

$$(n_x, n_y, k) = (85,\ 84,\ 1.9600)$$

(b) Two-step

$$\delta_1^* = \begin{pmatrix} 55\ 55\ 1.0425\ 2.2516 \\ 39\ 39\ 2.0294 \end{pmatrix} \quad \text{with} \quad N_{\max}(\delta_1^*) = 145.7404$$

$$\delta_2^* = \begin{pmatrix} 55\ 55\ 1.0511\ 2.2516 \\ 40\ 39\ 2.0330 \end{pmatrix} \quad \text{with} \quad N_{\max}(\delta_2^*) = 145.7396$$

$$\delta_3^* = \begin{pmatrix} 55\ 54\ 1.0351\ 2.2473 \\ 40\ 40\ 2.0328 \end{pmatrix} \quad \text{with} \quad N_{\max}(\delta_3^*) = 145.7500$$

$$\delta_4^* = \begin{pmatrix} 56\ 55\ 1.0581\ 2.2472 \\ 38\ 39\ 2.0298 \end{pmatrix} \quad \text{with} \quad N_{\max}(\delta_4^*) = 145.7503$$

Minimax test: $\delta^* = \delta_2^*$
Saving of $N_{\max}(\delta^*)$ in comparison to $N_{\max}(\delta_1^*)$: 0.0005 %.

Concluding Remark

In the last section we presented for the first time overall minimax-versions δ^* of the two-step ZS-Gaußtest. The numerical examples exhibit that savings on minimal maximal ASN can be achieved by adding the close-by balanced tests to the balanced tests. The magnitude of the saving on $N_{\max}(\delta^*)$ in comparison to $N_{\max}(\delta_1^*)$, with δ_1^* being the balanced minimax-version, is very small and remains below 0.02 %.

Similar amounts of saving could be expected for TS-t-tests and would not justify the enormous effort required by passing from Starke's balanced ZS-t-test δ_1^* to the overall minimax test δ^*.

Acknowledgements The authors wish to thank Yvonne Schmitz for technical support.

References

Heiler, S., & Rinne, H. (1971). *Einführung in die Statistik*. Meisenheim: Anton Hain.

Kremer, M., Krumbholz, W., & Starke, I. (2009). *Minimaxversionen des zweistufigen Zwei-Stichproben-Gaußtests*. Discussion Papers in Statistics and Quantitative Economics, Nr. 122, Hamburg.

Krumbholz, W., Rohr, A., & Vangjeli, E. (2012). Minimax versions of the two-stage *t* test. *Statistical Papers*, *53*, 311–321.

Starke, I. (2009). *Der zweistufige Zwei-Stichproben-t-Test mit minimalem ASN-Maximum*. Berlin: Logos.

Vangjeli, E. (2009). *ASN-optimale zweistufige Versionen des Gauß- und t-Tests* (Thesis). Helmut-Schmidt-Universität Hamburg.

Dimensionality Reduction Models in Density Estimation and Classification

Alexander Samarov

Abstract In this paper we consider the problem of multivariate density estimation assuming that the density allows some form of dimensionality reduction. Estimation of high-dimensional densities and dimensionality reduction models are important topics in nonparametric and semi-parametric econometrics.We start with the Independent Component Analysis (ICA) model, which can be considered as a form of dimensionality reduction of a multivariate density. We then consider multiple index model, describing the situations where high-dimensional data has a low-dimensional non-Gaussian component while in all other directions the data are Gaussian, and the independent factor analysis (IFA) model, which generalizes the ordinary factor analysis, principal component analysis, and ICA. For each of these models, we review recent results, obtained in our joint work with Tsybakov, Amato, and Antoniadis, on the accuracy of the corresponding density estimators, which combine model selection with estimation. One of the main applications of multivariate density estimators is in classification, where they can be used to construct plug-in classifiers by estimating the densities of each labeled class. We give a bound to the excess risk of nonparametric plug-in classifiers in terms of the MISE of the density estimators of each class. Combining this bound with the above results on the accuracy of density estimation, we show that the rate of the excess Bayes risk of the corresponding plug-in classifiers does not depend on the dimensionality of the data.

1 Introduction

Complex data sets lying in multidimensional spaces are a commonplace occurrence in many parts of econometrics. The need for analyzing and modeling high-dimensional data often arises in nonparametric and semi-parametric econometrics, quantitative finance, and risk management, among other areas. One of the important

A. Samarov (✉)
Massachusetts Institute of Technology, Cambridge, MA 02139, USA
e-mail: samarov@mit.edu

J. Beran et al. (eds.), *Empirical Economic and Financial Research*,
Advanced Studies in Theoretical and Applied Econometrics 48,
DOI 10.1007/978-3-319-03122-4_30

challenges of the analysis of such data is to reduce its dimensionality in order to identify and visualize its structure.

It is well known that common nonparametric density estimators are quite unreliable even for moderately high-dimensional data. This motivates the use of dimensionality reduction models. The literature on dimensionality reduction is very extensive, and we mention here only some publications that are connected to our context and contain further references (Roweis and Saul 2000; Tenenbaum et al. 2000; Cook and Li 2002; Blanchard et al. 2006; Samarov and Tsybakov 2007).

In this paper we review several dimensionality reduction models analyzed in Samarov and Tsybakov (2004, 2007), and Amato et al. (2010).

In Sect. 2 we consider the ICA model for multivariate density where the distribution of independent sources are not parametrically specified. Following results of Samarov and Tsybakov (2004), we show that the density of this form can be estimated at one-dimensional nonparametric rate, corresponding to the independent component density with the worst smoothness.

In Sect. 3 we discuss multiple index model, describing the situations where high-dimensional data has a low-dimensional non-Gaussian component while in all other directions the data are Gaussian. In Samarov and Tsybakov (2007) we show, using recently developed methods of aggregation of density estimators, that one can estimate the density of this form, without knowing the directions of the non-Gaussian component and its dimension, with the best rate attainable when both non-Gaussian index space and its dimension are known.

In Sect. 4 we consider estimation of a multivariate density in the noisy independent factor analysis (IFA) model with unknown number of latent independent components observed in Gaussian noise. It turns out that the density generated by this model can be estimated with a very fast rate. In Amato et al. (2010) we show that, using recently developed methods of aggregation Juditsky et al. (2005, 2008), we can estimate the density of this form at a parametric root-n rate, up to a logarithmic factor independent of the dimension d.

In Sect. 5 we give a bound to the excess risk of nonparametric plug-in classifiers in terms of the integrated mean square error (MISE) of the density estimators of each class. Combining this bound with the results of previous sections, we show that if the data in each class are generated by one of the models discussed there, the rate of the excess Bayes risk of the corresponding plug-in classifiers does not depend on the dimensionality of the data.

2 Nonparametric Independent Component Analysis

Independent Component Analysis (ICA) is a statistical and computational technique for identifying hidden factors that underlie sets of random variables, measurements, or signals, blind source separation. In the ICA model the observed data variables are assumed to be (linear or nonlinear) mixtures of some unknown latent variables, and the mixing system is also unknown. The latent variables are assumed non-Gaussian and mutually independent; they are called the independent components of the data.

Most of the existing ICA algorithms concentrate on recovering the mixing matrix and either assume the known distribution of sources or allow for their limited, parametric flexibility (Hyvarinen et al. 2001). Most ICA papers either use mixture of Gaussian distributions as source models or assume that the number of independent sources is known, or both. In our work, the ICA serves as a dimensionality reduction model for multivariate nonparametric density estimation; we suppose that the distribution of the sources (factors) and their number are unknown.

The standard (linear, noise-free, full rank) ICA model assumes that d-dimensional observations $\mathbf{X}$ can be represented as

$$\mathbf{X} = A\mathbf{U},$$

where A is an unknown nonsingular $d \times d$-matrix, and $\mathbf{U}$ is an unobserved random d-vector with independent components. The goal of ICA is to estimate the matrix A, or its inverse $B^\top = A^{-1}$, based on a sample $\mathbf{X}_1, \ldots, \mathbf{X}_n$ i.i.d. $p(\mathbf{x})$. When all components of $\mathbf{U}$, with a possible exception of one, are non-Gaussian, the mixing matrix A is identifiable up to the scale and permutation of its columns.

The ICA model can be equivalently written in terms of the probability density of the observed data:

$$p(\mathbf{x}) = |\det(B)| \prod_{j=1}^{d} p_j(\mathbf{x}^\top \beta_j), \quad \mathbf{x} \in \mathbf{R}^d, \tag{1}$$

where $\beta_1, \ldots, \beta_d$ – unknown, linearly independent, unit-length d-vectors, $\det(B)$ is the determinant of the matrix $B = (\beta_1, \ldots, \beta_d)$, $B^\top = A^{-1}$, and $p_j(\cdot)$, $j = 1, \ldots, d$, are probability densities of the independent sources.

Most known ICA methods specify the parametric form of the latent component densities p_j and estimate B together with parameters of p_j using maximum likelihood or minimization of the empirical versions of various divergence criteria between densities, see, e.g., Hyvarinen et al. (2001) and the references therein. In general, densities p_j are unknown, and one can consider ICA as a semiparametric model in which these densities are left unspecified.

In Samarov and Tsybakov (2004) we show that, even without knowing $\beta_1, \ldots, \beta_d$, $p(\mathbf{x})$ can be estimated at one-dimensional nonparametric rate, corresponding to the independent component density with the worst smoothness. Our method of estimating $\beta_1, \ldots, \beta_d$ is based on nonparametric estimation of the average outer product of the density gradient

$$T(p) = \mathbf{E}[\nabla p(X) \nabla^\top p(X)],$$

where ∇p is the gradient of p, and simultaneous diagonalization of this estimated matrix and the sample covariance matrix of the data. After the directions have been estimated at root-n rate, the density (1) can be estimated, e.g. using the kernel estimators for marginal densities, at the usual one-dimensional nonparametric rate.

The method of Samarov and Tsybakov (2004) can be applied to a generalization of ICA where the independent components are multivariate. Our method estimates these statistically independent linear subspaces and reduces the original problem to the fundamental problem of identifying independent subsets of variables.

3 Multi-Index Departure from Normality Model

We consider next another important dimensionality reduction model for density:

$$p(x) = \phi_d(x)g(B^\top x), \qquad x \in \mathbf{R}^d, \tag{2}$$

where B—unknown $d \times m$ matrix with orthonormal columns, $1 \leq m \leq d$, $g : \mathbf{R}^m \to [0, \infty)$ unknown function, and $\phi_d(\cdot)$ is the density of the standard d-variate normal distribution.

A density of this form models the situation where high-dimensional data has a low-dimensional non-Gaussian component ($m << d$) while all other components are Gaussian. Model (2) can be viewed as an extension of the projection pursuit density estimation (PPDE) model, e.g. Huber (1985), and of the ICA model. A model similar to (2) was considered in Blanchard et al. (2006).

Note that the representation (2) is not unique. In particular, if Q_m is an $m \times m$ orthogonal matrix, the density p in (2) can be rewritten as $p(x) = \phi_d(x)g_1(B_1^\top x)$ with $g_1(y) = g(Q_m y)$ and $B_1 = BQ_m$. However, the linear subspace $\mathscr{M}$ spanned by the columns of B is uniquely defined by (2).

By analogy with regression models, e.g. Li (1991), Hristache et al. (2001), we will call $\mathscr{M}$ the *index space*. In particular, if the dimension of $\mathscr{M}$ is 1, model (2) can be viewed as a density analog of the single index model in regression. In general, if the dimension of $\mathscr{M}$ is arbitrary, we call (2) the *multiple index model*.

When the dimension m and an index matrix B (i.e., any of the matrices, equivalent up to an orthogonal transformation, that define the index space $\mathscr{M}$) are specified, the density (2) can be estimated using a kernel estimator

$$\hat{p}_{m,B}(x) = \frac{\phi_d(x)}{\phi_m(B^\top x)} \frac{1}{nh^m} \sum_{i=1}^{n} K\left(\frac{B^\top(X_i - x)}{h}\right),$$

with appropriately chosen bandwidth $h > 0$ and kernel $K : \mathbf{R}^m \to \mathbf{R}^1$. One can show, see Samarov and Tsybakov (2007), that, if the function g is twice differentiable, the mean integrated mean squared error (MISE) of the estimator $\hat{p}_{m,B}$ satisfies:

$$MISE(\hat{p}_{m,B}, p) := \mathbf{E}||\hat{p}_{m,B} - p||^2 = O(n^{-4/(m+4)}), \tag{3}$$

if the bandwidth h is chosen of the order $h \overset{\mathbb{P}}{\sim} n^{-1/(m+4)}$. Using the standard techniques of the minimax lower bounds, it is easy to show that the rate $n^{-4/(m+4)}$ is the optimal MISE rate for this model and thus the estimator $\hat{p}_{m,B}$ with $h \overset{\mathbb{P}}{\sim} n^{-1/(m+4)}$ has the optimal rate for this class of densities.

In Samarov and Tsybakov (2007) we show, using recently developed methods of aggregation of density estimators, that one can estimate this density, without knowing B and m, with the same rate $O(n^{-4/(m+4)})$ as the optimal rate attainable when B and m are known. The aggregate estimator of Samarov and Tsybakov (2007) automatically accomplishes dimension reduction because, if the unknown true dimension m is small, the rate $O(n^{-4/(m+4)})$ is much faster than the best attainable rate $O(n^{-4/(d+4)})$ for a model of full dimension. This estimator can be interpreted as an adaptive estimator, but in contrast to adaptation to unknown smoothness usually considered in nonparametrics, here we deal with adaptation to unknown dimension m and to the index space $\mathscr{M}$ determined by a matrix B.

4 IFA Model

In this section we consider an IFA model with unknown number and distribution of latent factors:

$$\mathbf{X} = A\mathbf{S} + \varepsilon, \tag{4}$$

where A is $d \times m$ unknown deterministic matrix, $m < d$, with orthonormal columns; $\mathbf{S}$ is an m-dimensional random vector of independent components with unknown distributions, and ε is a normal $\mathbf{N}_d(0, \sigma^2 \mathbf{I}_d)$ random vector of noise independent of $\mathbf{S}$.

By independence between the noise and the vector of factors $\mathbf{S}$, the target density $p_{\mathbf{X}}$ can be written as a convolution:

$$p_{\mathbf{X}}(\mathbf{x}) = \int_{\mathbf{R}^m} \phi_{d,\sigma^2}(\mathbf{x} - A\mathbf{s}) F_{\mathbf{S}}(d\mathbf{s}), \tag{5}$$

where ϕ_{d,σ^2} denotes the density of a d-dimensional Gaussian distribution $N_d(0, \sigma^2 \mathbf{I}_d)$ and $F_{\mathbf{S}}$ is the distribution of $\mathbf{S}$.

Note that (5) can be viewed as a variation of the Gaussian mixture model which is widely used in classification, image analysis, mathematical finance, and other areas, cf., e.g., Titterington et al. (1985) and McLachlan and Peel (2000). In Gaussian mixture models, the matrix A is the identity matrix, $F_{\mathbf{S}}$ is typically a discrete distribution with finite support, and variances of the Gaussian terms are usually different.

Since in (5) we have a convolution with a Gaussian distribution, the density $p_{\mathbf{X}}$ has very strong smoothness properties, no matter how irregular the distribution $F_{\mathbf{S}}$

of the factors is, whether or not the factors are independent, and whether or not the mixing matrix A is known. In Amato et al. (2010), we construct a kernel estimator $\hat{p}_n^*$ of $p_{\mathbf{X}}$ such that

$$\mathbf{E}||\hat{p}_n^* - p_{\mathbf{X}}||_2^2 \le C\frac{(\log n)^{d/2}}{n}, \tag{6}$$

where C is a constant and $||\cdot||_2$ is the $L_2(\mathbf{R}^d)$ norm. As in Artiles (2001) and Belitser and Levit (2001), it is not hard to show that the rate given in (6) is optimal for the class of densities $p_{\mathbf{X}}$ defined by (5) with arbitrary probability distribution $F_{\mathbf{S}}$.

Though this rate appears to be very fast asymptotically, it does not guarantee good accuracy for most practical values of n, even if d is moderately large. For example, if $d = 10$, we have $(\log n)^{d/2} > n$ for all $n \le 10^5$.

In order to construct our estimator, we first consider the estimation of $p_{\mathbf{X}}$ when the dimension m, the mixing matrix A, and the level of noise σ^2 are specified. Because of the orthonormality of columns of A, $A^\top$ is the demixing matrix: $A^\top X = S + A^\top \varepsilon$, and the density of X can be written as

$$p_{\mathbf{X}}(\mathbf{x}) = \left(\frac{1}{2\pi\sigma^2}\right)^{(d-m)/2} \exp\left\{-\frac{1}{2\sigma^2}\mathbf{x}^\top(\mathbf{I}_d - AA^\top)\mathbf{x}\right\} \prod_{k=1}^m g_k(\mathbf{a}_k^\top \mathbf{x}),$$

where $\mathbf{a}_k$ denotes the kth column of A and $g_k(u) = (p_{S_k} * \phi_1)(u) = \int_R p_{S_k}(s)\phi_1(u-s)ds$.

In Amato et al. (2010) we show that, using kernel estimators for g_k, one can construct an estimator for the density $p_{\mathbf{X}}$ which has the mean integrated square error (MISE) of the order $(\log n)^{1/2}/n$. Note that neither m nor d affect the rate.

When the index matrix A, its rank m, and the variance of the noise σ^2 are all unknown, we use a model selection type aggregation procedure called the mirror averaging algorithm of Juditsky et al. (2008) to obtain fully adaptive density estimator. We make a few additional assumptions.

Assumption 1 At most one component of the vector of factors $\mathbf{S}$ in (4) has a Gaussian distribution.

Assumption 2 The columns of the matrix A are orthonormal.

Assumption 3 The number of factors m does not exceed an upper bound M, $M < d$.

Assumption 4 The M largest eigenvalues of the covariance matrix $\Sigma_{\mathbf{X}}$ of the observations $\mathbf{X}$ are distinct and the 4th moments of the components of $\mathbf{X}$ are finite.

Assumption 1, needed for the identifiability of A, is standard in the ICA literature, see, e.g., Hyvarinen et al. (2001) Assumption 2 is rather restrictive but, as we show below, together with the assumed independence of the factors, it allows us to eliminate dependence of the rate in (6) on the dimension d. Assumption 3 means that model (4) indeed provides the dimensionality reduction. The assumption

$M < d$ is only needed to estimate the variance σ^2 of the noise; if σ^2 is known, we can allow $M = d$. Assumption 4 is needed to establish root-n consistency of the eigenvectors of the sample covariance matrix of $\mathbf{X}$.

Under these assumptions, in Amato et al. (2010) we construct an estimator for the density of the form (5) that adapts to the unknown m and A, i.e., has the same MISE rate $O((\log n)^{1/2}/n)$, independent of m and d, as in the case when the dimension m, the matrix A, and the variance of the noise σ^2 are known.

5 Application to Nonparametric Classification

One of the main applications of multivariate density estimators is in classification, which is one of the important econometric techniques. These estimators can be used to construct nonparametric classifiers based on estimated densities from labeled data for each class.

The difficulty with such density-based plug-in classifiers is that, even for moderately large dimensions d, standard density estimators have poor accuracy in the tails, i.e., in the region which is important for classification purposes. In this section we consider the nonparametric classification problem and bound the excess misclassification error of a plug-in classifier in terms of the MISE of class-conditional density estimators. This bound implies that, for the class-conditional densities obeying the dimensionality reduction models discussed above, the resulting plug-in classifier has nearly optimal excess error.

Assume that we have J independent training samples $\{X_{j1}, \dots, X_{jN_j}\}$ of sizes N_j, $j = 1, \dots, J$, from J populations with densities $f_1, \dots, f_J$ on $\mathbf{R}^d$. We will denote by $\mathscr{D}$ the union of training samples. Assume that we also have an observation $\mathbf{X} \in \mathbf{R}^d$ independent of these samples and distributed according to one of the f_j. The classification problem consists in predicting the corresponding value of the class label $j \in \{1, \dots, J\}$. We define a classifier or prediction rule as a measurable function $T(\cdot)$ which assigns a class membership based on the explanatory variable, i.e., $T : \mathbf{R}^d \to \{1, \dots, J\}$. The misclassification error associated with a classifier T is usually defined as

$$R(T) = \sum_{j=1}^{J} \pi_j \mathbf{P}_j(T(\mathbf{X}) \neq j) = \sum_{j=1}^{J} \pi_j \int_{\mathbf{R}^d} I(T(\mathbf{x}) \neq j) f_j(\mathbf{x}) d\mathbf{x},$$

where $\mathbf{P}_j$ denotes the class-conditional population probability distribution with density f_j, and π_j is the prior probability of class j. We will consider a slightly more general definition:

$$R_C(T) = \sum_{j=1}^{J} \pi_j \int_C I(T(\mathbf{x}) \neq j) f_j(\mathbf{x}) d\mathbf{x},$$

where C is a Borel subset of $\mathbf{R}^d$. The Bayes classifier T^* is the one with the smallest misclassification error:

$$R_C(T^*) = \min_T R_C(T).$$

In general, the Bayes classifier is not unique. It is easy to see that there exists a Bayes classifier T^* which does not depend on C and which is defined by

$$\pi_{T^*(\mathbf{x})} f_{T^*(\mathbf{x})}(\mathbf{x}) = \min_{1 \le j \le J} \pi_j f_j(\mathbf{x}), \quad \forall\, \mathbf{x} \in \mathbf{R}^d.$$

A classifier trained on the sample $\mathscr{D}$ will be denoted by $T_{\mathscr{D}}(\mathbf{x})$. A key characteristic of such a classifier is the misclassification error $R_C(T_{\mathscr{D}})$. One of the main goals in statistical learning is to construct a classifier with the smallest possible excess risk

$$\mathscr{E}(T_{\mathscr{D}}) = \mathbf{E} R_C(T_{\mathscr{D}}) - R_C(T^*).$$

We consider plug-in classifiers $\hat{T}(\mathbf{x})$ defined by:

$$\pi_{\hat{T}(\mathbf{x})} \hat{f}_{\hat{T}(\mathbf{x})}(\mathbf{x}) = \min_{1 \le j \le J} \pi_j \hat{f}_j(\mathbf{x}), \quad \forall\, \mathbf{x} \in \mathbf{R}^d$$

where $\hat{f}_j$ is an estimator of density f_j based on the training sample $\{X_{j1}, \dots, X_{jN_j}\}$.

The following proposition relates the excess risk $\mathscr{E}(\hat{T})$ of plug-in classifiers to the rate of convergence of the estimators $\hat{f}_j$, see Amato et al. (2010).

Proposition 1

$$\mathscr{E}(\hat{T}) \le \sum_{j=1}^{J} \pi_j \, \mathbf{E} \int_C |\hat{f}_j(\mathbf{x}) - f_j(\mathbf{x})| d\mathbf{x}$$

Assume now that the class-conditional densities follow, for example, the noisy IFA model (5) with different unknown mixing matrices and that $N_j \overset{\mathbb{P}}{\sim} n$ for all j. Let C be a Euclidean ball in $\mathbf{R}^d$ and define each of the estimators $\hat{f}_j$ using the mirror averaging procedure as in the previous section. Then, using results of that section, we have

$$\mathbf{E} \int_C |\hat{f}_j(\mathbf{x}) - f_j(\mathbf{x})| d\mathbf{x} \le \sqrt{|C|}\, \mathbf{E} \|\hat{f}_j - f_j\|_{2,C} = \mathscr{O}\left(\frac{(\log n)^{1/4}}{\sqrt{n}} \right)$$

as $n \to \infty$, where $|C|$ denotes the volume of the ball C and the norm $\|\cdot\|_{2,C}$ is defined as $\|f\|_{2,C}^2 = \int_C f^2(\mathbf{x}) d\mathbf{x}$. Thus, the excess risk $\mathscr{E}(\hat{T})$ converges to 0 at the rate $(\log n)^{1/4}/\sqrt{n}$ independently of the dimension d.

Similarly, we can show, using the above proposition, that, if the class densities follow other dimensionality reduction models considered in this paper, the rate of the excess Bayes risk of the corresponding plug-in classifiers does not depend on the dimensionality of the data.

Acknowledgements Partial support provided by the Singapore-MIT Alliance in Computation and Systems Biology.

References

Amato, U., Antoniadis, A., Samarov, A., & Tsybakov, A. (2010). Noisy independent factor analysis model for density estimation and classification. *Electronic Journal of Statistics*, *4*, 707–736.

Artiles, L. M. (2001). Adaptive Minimax Estimation in Classes of Smooth Functions (Ph.D. thesis). University of Utrecht.

Belitser, E., & Levit, B. (2001). Asymptotically local minimax estimation of infinitely smooth density with censored data. *Annals of the Institute of Statistical Mathematics*, *53*, 289–306.

Blanchard, B., Kawanabe, G. M., Sugiyama, M., Spokoiny, V., & Müller, K. R. (2006). In search of non-gaussian components of a high-dimensional distribution. *Journal of Machine Learning Research*, *7*, 247–282.

Cook, R. D., & Li, B. (2002). Dimension reduction for conditional mean in regression. *Annals of Statistics*, *32*, 455–474.

Hristache, M., Juditsky, A., Polzehl J., & Spokoiny, V. (2001). Structure adaptive approach for dimension reduction. *Annals of Statistics*, *29*, 1537–1566.

Huber, P. (1985). Projection pursuit. *Annals of Statistics*, *13*, 435–475.

Hyvarinen, A., Karhunen, J., & Oja, E. (2001). *Independent component analysis*. New York: Wiley.

Juditsky, A., Rigollet, P., & Tsybakov, A. B. (2008). Learning by mirror averaging. *Annals of Statistics*, *36*, 2183–2206.

Juditsky, A. B., Nazin, A. V., Tsybakov, A. B., & Vayatis, N. (2005). Recursive aggregation of estimators by the mirror descent algorithm with averaging. *Problems of Information Transmission*, *41*, 368–384.

Li, K.-C. (1991). Sliced inverse regression for dimension reduction. *Journal of the American Statistical Association*, *86*, 316–342.

McLachlan, G. J., & Peel, D. (2000). *Finite mixture models*. New York: Wiley.

Roweis, S., & Saul, L. (2000). Nonlinear dimensionality reduction by locally linear embedding. *Science*, *290*, 2323–2326.

Samarov, A., & Tsybakov, A. B. (2004). Nonparametric independent component analysis. *Bernoulli*, *10*, 565–582.

Samarov, A., & Tsybakov, A. B. (2007). Aggregation of density estimators and dimension reduction. In V. Nair (Ed.), *Advances in statistical modeling and inference, essays in honor of K. Doksum*. Series in Biostatistics (Vol. 3, pp. 233–251). London: World Scientific.

Tenenbaum, J. B., de Silva, V., & Langford, J. C. (2000). A global geometric framework for nonlinear dimensionality reduction. *Science*, *290*, 2319–2323.

Titterington, D., Smith, A., & Makov, U. (1985). *Statistical analysis of finite mixture distributions*. New York: Wiley.

On a Craig–Sakamoto Theorem for Orthogonal Projectors

Oskar Maria Baksalary and Götz Trenkler

Abstract The Craig–Sakamoto theorem asserts that real $n \times n$ symmetric matrices $\mathbf{A}$ and $\mathbf{B}$ satisfy $\det(\mathbf{I}_n - a\mathbf{A} - b\mathbf{B}) = \det(\mathbf{I}_n - a\mathbf{A})\det(\mathbf{I}_n - b\mathbf{B})$ for all real numbers a and b if and only if $\mathbf{AB} = \mathbf{0}$. In the present note a counterpart of the theorem for orthogonal projectors is established. The projectors as well as the scalars involved in the result obtained are assumed to be complex.

An essential result known as the Craig–Sakamoto theorem asserts that

$$\mathbf{MN} = \mathbf{0} \Leftrightarrow \det(\mathbf{I}_n - a\mathbf{M} - b\mathbf{N}) = \det(\mathbf{I}_n - a\mathbf{M})\det(\mathbf{I}_n - b\mathbf{N}) \;\; \forall a, b \in \mathbb{R},$$

where $\mathbf{M}$ and $\mathbf{N}$ are $n \times n$ real symmetric matrices and $\mathbf{I}_n$ is the identity matrix of order n. This algebraic result has an important statistical interpretation due to the fact that when $\mathbf{x}$ is an $n \times 1$ real random vector having the multivariate normal distribution $N_n(\mathbf{0}, \mathbf{I}_n)$, then the quadratic forms $\mathbf{x}'\mathbf{Mx}$ and $\mathbf{x}'\mathbf{Nx}$ are distributed independently if and only if $\mathbf{MN} = \mathbf{0}$; cf. Rao and Mitra (1971, Theorem 9.4.1). Actually, in econometrics the Craig–Sakamoto theorem (also called the Craig's theorem) is often formulated on purely statistical basis. For example, Theorem 4.5.5 in Poirier (1995) attributes to the Craig's theorem the following characterization. Let $\mathbf{y}$ be an $n \times 1$ real random vector having the multivariate normal distribution $N_n(\boldsymbol{\mu}, \boldsymbol{\Sigma})$ and let $\mathbf{K}$ and $\mathbf{L}$ be real matrices of dimensions $n \times n$ and $m \times n$, respectively, of which $\mathbf{K}$ is symmetric. Then the linear form $\mathbf{Ly}$ is distributed independently of the quadratic form $\mathbf{y}'\mathbf{Ky}$ if and only if $\mathbf{L\Sigma K} = \mathbf{0}$. Several proofs of the Craig–Sakamoto theorem are available in the literature and history of its development was extensively described; see, e.g., Carrieu (2010), Carrieu and

O.M. Baksalary (✉)
Faculty of Physics, Adam Mickiewicz University, ul. Umultowska 85, 61-614 Poznań, Poland
e-mail: OBaksalary@gmail.com

G. Trenkler
Faculty of Statistics, Dortmund University of Technology, Vogelpothsweg 87, 44221 Dortmund, Germany
e-mail: trenkler@statistik.tu-dortmund.de

J. Beran et al. (eds.), *Empirical Economic and Financial Research*,
Advanced Studies in Theoretical and Applied Econometrics 48,
DOI 10.1007/978-3-319-03122-4_31

Lassère (2009), Driscoll and Gundberg (1986), Driscoll and Krasnicka (1995), Li (2000), Matsuura (2003), Ogawa (1993), Ogawa and Olkin (2008), Olkin (1997), Poirier (1995), Rao and Mitra (1971), Reid and Driscoll (1988), Taussky (1958), and Zhang and Yi (2012).

It is known that a necessary and sufficient condition for the quadratic form $\mathbf{x}'\mathbf{M}\mathbf{x}$ to be distributed as a chi-square variable is that symmetric $\mathbf{M}$ satisfies $\mathbf{M} = \mathbf{M}^2$; cf. Rao and Mitra (1971, Lemma 9.1.2). In the present note a counterpart of the Craig–Sakamoto theorem for orthogonal projectors is established. In other words, we derive necessary and sufficient conditions for two quadratic forms each of which is distributed as a chi-square variable to be distributed independently. The projectors as well as the scalars involved in the result obtained are assumed to be complex.

Let $\mathbb{C}_{m,n}$ denote the set of $m \times n$ complex matrices. The symbols $\mathbf{L}^*$, $\mathscr{R}(\mathbf{L})$, $\mathscr{N}(\mathbf{L})$, and $\text{rk}(\mathbf{L})$ will stand for the conjugate transpose, column space (range), null space, and rank of $\mathbf{L} \in \mathbb{C}_{m,n}$, respectively. Further, for a given $\mathbf{L} \in \mathbb{C}_{n,n}$ we define $\overline{\mathbf{L}} = \mathbf{I}_n - \mathbf{L}$. Another function of a square matrix $\mathbf{L} \in \mathbb{C}_{n,n}$, which will be referred to in what follows, is trace denoted by $\text{tr}(\mathbf{L})$.

A crucial role in the considerations of the present note is played by orthogonal projectors in $\mathbb{C}_{n,1}$ (i.e., Hermitian idempotent matrices of order n). It is known that every such projector is expressible as $\mathbf{L}\mathbf{L}^\dagger$ for some $\mathbf{L} \in \mathbb{C}_{n,m}$, where $\mathbf{L}^\dagger \in \mathbb{C}_{m,n}$ is the Moore–Penrose inverse of $\mathbf{L}$, i.e., the unique solution to the equations

$$\mathbf{L}\mathbf{L}^\dagger\mathbf{L} = \mathbf{L},\ \mathbf{L}^\dagger\mathbf{L}\mathbf{L}^\dagger = \mathbf{L}^\dagger,\ (\mathbf{L}\mathbf{L}^\dagger)^* = \mathbf{L}\mathbf{L}^\dagger,\ (\mathbf{L}^\dagger\mathbf{L})^* = \mathbf{L}^\dagger\mathbf{L}. \tag{1}$$

Then $\mathbf{P}_\mathbf{L} = \mathbf{L}\mathbf{L}^\dagger$ is the orthogonal projector onto $\mathscr{R}(\mathbf{L})$. An important fact is that there is a one-to-one correspondence between an orthogonal projector and the subspace onto which it projects. This means, for example, that if $\mathbf{P}_U$ is the orthogonal projector onto the subspace $U \subseteq \mathbb{C}_{n,1}$, then $\text{rk}(\mathbf{P}_U) = \dim(U)$ and $\mathbf{P}_U = \mathbf{P}_V \Leftrightarrow U = V$.

In what follows we introduce a joint partitioned representation of a pair of orthogonal projectors. Let $\mathbf{P}$ be an $n \times n$ Hermitian idempotent matrix of rank r. By the *spectral theorem*, there exists a unitary $\mathbf{U} \in \mathbb{C}_{n,n}$ such that

$$\mathbf{P} = \mathbf{U}\begin{pmatrix} \mathbf{I}_r & \mathbf{0} \\ \mathbf{0} & \mathbf{0} \end{pmatrix}\mathbf{U}^*. \tag{2}$$

Representation (2) can be used to determine partitioning of any other orthogonal projector in $\mathbb{C}_{n,1}$, say $\mathbf{Q}$. Namely, with the use of the same matrix $\mathbf{U}$, we can write

$$\mathbf{Q} = \mathbf{U}\begin{pmatrix} \mathbf{A} & \mathbf{B} \\ \mathbf{B}^* & \mathbf{D} \end{pmatrix}\mathbf{U}^*, \tag{3}$$

with $\mathbf{B} \in \mathbb{C}_{r,n-r}$ and Hermitian $\mathbf{A} \in \mathbb{C}_{r,r}$, $\mathbf{D} \in \mathbb{C}_{n-r,n-r}$ satisfying

$$\mathbf{A} = \mathbf{A}^2 + \mathbf{B}\mathbf{B}^*, \quad \mathscr{R}(\mathbf{B}) \subseteq \mathscr{R}(\mathbf{A}), \quad \mathbf{A}^\dagger\mathbf{B} = \mathbf{B}\overline{\mathbf{D}}^\dagger, \quad \text{and} \quad \mathscr{R}(\mathbf{B}^*) \subseteq \mathscr{R}(\overline{\mathbf{D}}). \tag{4}$$

Other useful relationships linking the matrices **A**, **B**, and **D** read

$$\text{rk}(\overline{\mathbf{D}}) = n - r + \text{rk}(\mathbf{B}) - \text{rk}(\mathbf{D}) \quad \text{and} \quad \mathbf{P}_{\overline{\mathbf{D}}} = \overline{\mathbf{D}} + \mathbf{B}^*\mathbf{A}^\dagger\mathbf{B}, \tag{5}$$

where $\mathbf{P}_{\overline{\mathbf{D}}}$ is the orthogonal projector onto the column space of $\overline{\mathbf{D}}$. For the derivations of the relationships in (4) and (5), as well as for a collection of further properties of the matrices **A**, **B**, and **D** see, e.g., Baksalary and Trenkler (2009, Sect. 2).

The joint representation based on formulae (2) and (3) proved so far to be very useful in various considerations; see, e.g., Baksalary and Trenkler (2009) where it was used to characterize eigenvalues of various functions of a pair of orthogonal projectors. The key feature of this representation is that it allows to derive formulae for orthogonal projectors onto any subspace determined by the projectors **P** and **Q**, and, in consequence, to characterize dimensions of those subspaces in terms of ranks of matrices **A**, **B**, and **D**. The lemma below provides representations of the orthogonal projectors onto column spaces of $\overline{\mathbf{P}}\,\overline{\mathbf{Q}}$ and $\mathbf{I}_n - \mathbf{P} - \mathbf{Q}$. The symbols $\mathbf{P}_\mathbf{A}$ and $\mathbf{P}_{\overline{\mathbf{D}}}$ used therein denote the orthogonal projectors onto the column spaces of **A** and $\overline{\mathbf{D}}$, respectively.

Lemma 1 *Let* **P** *and* **Q** *be the orthogonal projectors of the forms* (2) *and* (3), *respectively. Then:*

(i) *the orthogonal projector onto* $\mathscr{R}(\overline{\mathbf{P}}\,\overline{\mathbf{Q}})$ *is given by*

$$\mathbf{P}_{\overline{\mathbf{P}}\,\overline{\mathbf{Q}}} = \mathbf{U}\begin{pmatrix} \mathbf{0} & \mathbf{0} \\ \mathbf{0} & \mathbf{P}_{\overline{\mathbf{D}}} \end{pmatrix}\mathbf{U}^*,$$

where $\dim[\mathscr{R}(\overline{\mathbf{P}}\,\overline{\mathbf{Q}})] = n - r + \text{rk}(\mathbf{B}) - \text{rk}(\mathbf{D})$*;*

(ii) *the orthogonal projector onto* $\mathscr{R}(\mathbf{I}_n - \mathbf{P} - \mathbf{Q})$ *is given by*

$$\mathbf{P}_{\mathbf{I}_n - \mathbf{P} - \mathbf{Q}} = \mathbf{U}\begin{pmatrix} \mathbf{P}_\mathbf{A} & \mathbf{0} \\ \mathbf{0} & \mathbf{P}_{\overline{\mathbf{D}}} \end{pmatrix}\mathbf{U}^*,$$

where $\dim[\mathscr{R}(\mathbf{I}_n - \mathbf{P} - \mathbf{Q})] = n - r + \text{rk}(\mathbf{A}) + \text{rk}(\mathbf{B}) - \text{rk}(\mathbf{D})$.

Proof In the light of (4) and (5), it can be verified by exploiting the conditions in (1) that the Moore–Penrose inverse of

$$\overline{\mathbf{P}}\,\overline{\mathbf{Q}} = \mathbf{U}\begin{pmatrix} \mathbf{0} & \mathbf{0} \\ -\mathbf{B}^* & \overline{\mathbf{D}} \end{pmatrix}\mathbf{U}^*$$

is given by

$$(\overline{\mathbf{P}}\,\overline{\mathbf{Q}})^{\dagger} = \mathbf{U}\begin{pmatrix} \mathbf{0} & -\mathbf{A}^{\dagger}\mathbf{B} \\ \mathbf{0} & \mathbf{P}_{\overline{\mathbf{D}}} \end{pmatrix}\mathbf{U}^{*}.$$

Furthermore, it follows that the projector $\mathbf{P}_{\overline{\mathbf{P}}\,\overline{\mathbf{Q}}} = \overline{\mathbf{P}}\,\overline{\mathbf{Q}}(\overline{\mathbf{P}}\,\overline{\mathbf{Q}})^{\dagger}$ takes the form given in point (i) of the lemma. The expression for the dimension of the subspace $\mathscr{R}(\overline{\mathbf{P}}\,\overline{\mathbf{Q}})$ is obtained by combining the fact that $\mathrm{rk}(\mathbf{P}_{\overline{\mathbf{P}}\,\overline{\mathbf{Q}}}) = \mathrm{rk}(\mathbf{P}_{\overline{\mathbf{D}}}) = \mathrm{rk}(\overline{\mathbf{D}})$ with the left-hand side identity in (5).

Point (ii) of the lemma is established in a similar way by utilizing

$$\mathbf{I}_n - \mathbf{P} - \mathbf{Q} = \mathbf{U}\begin{pmatrix} -\mathbf{A} & -\mathbf{B} \\ -\mathbf{B}^{*} & \overline{\mathbf{D}} \end{pmatrix}\mathbf{U}^{*} \quad \text{and} \quad (\mathbf{I}_n - \mathbf{P} - \mathbf{Q})^{\dagger} = \mathbf{U}\begin{pmatrix} -\mathbf{P}_{\mathbf{A}} & -\mathbf{A}^{\dagger}\mathbf{B} \\ -\mathbf{B}^{*}\mathbf{A}^{\dagger} & \mathbf{P}_{\overline{\mathbf{D}}} \end{pmatrix}\mathbf{U}^{*}.$$

Note that the representation of the projector $\mathbf{P}_{\mathbf{I}_n-\mathbf{P}-\mathbf{Q}}$ was derived in Baksalary and Trenkler (2009, Sect. 3). □

The main result of the note is given in what follows.

Theorem 1 *Let* $\mathbf{P}, \mathbf{Q} \in \mathbb{C}_{n,n}$ *be orthogonal projectors. Then the following statements are equivalent:*

(i) $\mathbf{PQ} = \mathbf{0}$,
(ii) $\mathrm{rk}(\mathbf{I}_n - a\mathbf{P} - b\mathbf{Q}) = \mathrm{rk}[(\mathbf{I}_n - a\mathbf{P})(\mathbf{I}_n - b\mathbf{Q})]$ *for all* $a, b \in \mathbb{C}$,
(iii) $\mathscr{R}(\mathbf{I}_n - a\mathbf{P} - b\mathbf{Q}) = \mathscr{R}[(\mathbf{I}_n - a\mathbf{P})(\mathbf{I}_n - b\mathbf{Q})]$ *for all* $a, b \in \mathbb{C}$,
(iv) $\mathrm{tr}(\mathbf{I}_n - a\mathbf{P} - b\mathbf{Q}) = \mathrm{tr}[(\mathbf{I}_n - a\mathbf{P})(\mathbf{I}_n - b\mathbf{Q})]$ *for all* $a, b \in \mathbb{C}$.

Proof Since

$$(\mathbf{I}_n - a\mathbf{P})(\mathbf{I}_n - b\mathbf{Q}) = \mathbf{I}_n - a\mathbf{P} - b\mathbf{Q} + ab\mathbf{PQ},$$

it is clear that point (i) of the theorem yields its points (ii)–(iv).

To show that (ii) ⇒ (i) take $a = 1$ and $b = 1$, in which case the condition in point (ii) of the theorem can be rewritten as $\mathrm{rk}(\mathbf{I}_n - \mathbf{P} - \mathbf{Q}) = \mathrm{rk}(\overline{\mathbf{P}}\,\overline{\mathbf{Q}})$. From Lemma 1 it follows that this equality is satisfied if and only if $\mathrm{rk}(\mathbf{A}) = 0$. Hence, this part of the proof is complete, for straightforward calculations confirm that $\mathbf{A} = \mathbf{0}$ is equivalent to $\mathbf{PQ} = \mathbf{0}$ (note that $\mathbf{A} = \mathbf{0} \Rightarrow \mathbf{B} = \mathbf{0}$).

To demonstrate that also the condition in point (iii) yields (i), we again assume that $a = 1$ and $b = 1$. In such a situation, from the equality in (iii) we obtain $\mathscr{R}(\mathbf{I}_n - \mathbf{P} - \mathbf{Q}) = \mathscr{R}(\overline{\mathbf{P}}\,\overline{\mathbf{Q}})$, which is fulfilled if and only if the projectors $\mathbf{P}_{\overline{\mathbf{P}}\,\overline{\mathbf{Q}}}$ and $\mathbf{P}_{\mathbf{I}_n-\mathbf{P}-\mathbf{Q}}$ coincide. By Lemma 1 we conclude that this happens if and only if $\mathbf{A} = \mathbf{0}$, i.e., $\mathbf{PQ} = \mathbf{0}$.

It remains to prove that also (iv) implies (i). Clearly, when $a = 1$ and $b = 1$, then the condition in (iv) reduces to $\mathrm{tr}(\mathbf{PQ}) = 0$. By exploiting representations (2) and (3) it is seen that this identity is equivalent to $\mathrm{tr}(\mathbf{A}) = 0$. Since $\mathbf{A}$ is Hermitian, it is diagonalizable, which means that its trace equals zero only when $\mathbf{A} = \mathbf{0}$. The proof is thus complete. □

Recall that orthogonal projectors $\mathbf{P}$ and $\mathbf{Q}$ satisfy $\mathbf{PQ} = \mathbf{0}$ if and only if $\mathbf{P} + \mathbf{Q}$ is an orthogonal projector. Further conditions equivalent to $\mathbf{PQ} = \mathbf{0}$ include:

(i) $\mathscr{R}(\mathbf{Q}) \subseteq \mathscr{R}(\overline{\mathbf{P}}\mathbf{Q})$,
(ii) $\mathscr{R}(\mathbf{P}) + \mathscr{R}(\mathbf{Q}) = [\mathscr{R}(\mathbf{P}) \cap \mathscr{N}(\mathbf{Q})] \overset{\perp}{\oplus} [\mathscr{N}(\mathbf{P}) \cap \mathscr{R}(\mathbf{Q})]$,
(iii) $\mathscr{R}(\mathbf{P}) \cap [\mathscr{N}(\mathbf{P}) + \mathscr{R}(\mathbf{Q})] = \{\mathbf{0}\}$,
(iv) $\mathscr{N}(\mathbf{P}) \overset{\perp}{\oplus} [\mathscr{R}(\mathbf{P}) \cap \mathscr{N}(\mathbf{Q})] = \mathbb{C}_{n,1}$,
(v) $\mathscr{N}(\mathbf{P}) = \mathscr{N}(\mathbf{P}) + \mathscr{R}(\mathbf{Q})$.

The inclusion in (i) was asserted in Baksalary and Trenkler (2011), whereas the remaining four identities were established in Baksalary and Trenkler (2013, Theorem 5).

The paper is concluded with the following open problem: are the equivalences claimed in Theorem 1 satisfied only for orthogonal projectors, or are they valid also for other classes of matrices? For example, from the identity

$$\mathscr{R}(\mathbf{I}_n - \mathbf{P} - \mathbf{Q}) = \mathscr{R}(\mathbf{PQ}) \oplus \mathscr{R}(\overline{\mathbf{P}}\,\overline{\mathbf{Q}}),$$

provided in Baksalary and Trenkler (2013, equalities (4.4)), it follows that for $a = 1$ and $b = 1$, conditions (i)–(iii) of Theorem 1 are equivalent also when $\mathbf{P}$ and $\mathbf{Q}$ are not assumed to be Hermitian (i.e., are oblique projectors). On the other hand, when $\mathbf{P}$ and $\mathbf{Q}$ are oblique projectors, then $\mathrm{tr}(\mathbf{PQ}) = 0$ does not imply $\mathbf{PQ} = \mathbf{0}$, which means that point (iv) of Theorem 1 does not yield its point (i). This fact can be verified by exploiting the matrices

$$\mathbf{P} = \begin{pmatrix} 1 & 0 & 1 \\ 0 & 0 & 0 \\ 0 & 0 & 0 \end{pmatrix} \quad \text{and} \quad \mathbf{Q} = \begin{pmatrix} 0 & 0 & 0 \\ 0 & 0 & 0 \\ 0 & 1 & 1 \end{pmatrix}.$$

Acknowledgements The paper was prepared while the first author was visiting the Faculty of Statistics at the Dortmund University of Technology. The financial supports from the German Academic Exchange Service (DAAD) as well as from the project POKL run at the Faculty of Physics of the Adam Mickiewicz University are gratefully acknowledged. The author is also very thankful to the Faculty of Statistics for provision of excellent facilities during the stay.

References

Baksalary, O. M., & Trenkler, G. (2009). Eigenvalues of functions of orthogonal projectors. *Linear Algebra and its Applications*, *431*, 2172–2186.

Baksalary, O. M., & Trenkler, G. (2011). Solution 45–1.1 to Problem 45–1 "Column space counterparts of the known conditions for orthogonal projectors" proposed by OM Baksalary, G Trenkler. *IMAGE – The Bulletin of the International Linear Algebra Society*, *46*, 39–40.

Baksalary, O. M., & Trenkler, G. (2013). On a pair of vector spaces. *Applied Mathematics and Computation*, *219*, 9572–9580.

Baksalary, O. M., & Trenkler, G. (2013). On column and null spaces of functions of a pair of oblique projectors. *Linear and Multilinear Algebra, 61*, 1116–1129.

Carrieu, H. (2010). Close to the Craig–Sakamoto theorem. *Linear Algebra and its Applications, 432*, 777–779.

Carrieu, H., & Lassère, P. (2009). One more simple proof of the Craig–Sakamoto theorem. *Linear Algebra and its Applications, 431*, 1616–1619.

Driscoll, M. F., & Gundberg, W. R. Jr. (1986). A history of the development of Craig's theorem. *The American Statistician, 40*, 65–70.

Driscoll, M. F., & Krasnicka, B. (1995). An accessible proof of Craig's theorem in the general case. *The American Statistician, 49*, 59–62.

Li, C. K. (2000). A simple proof of the Craig–Sakamoto theorem. *Linear Algebra and its Applications, 321*, 281–283.

Matsuura, M. (2003). On the Craig–Sakamoto theorem and Olkin's determinantal result. *Linear Algebra and its Applications, 364*, 321–323.

Ogawa, J. (1993). A history of the development of Craig–Sakamoto's theorem viewed from Japanese standpoint. *Proceedings of the Annals of Institute of Statistical Mathematics, 41*, 47–59.

Ogawa, J., & Olkin, I. (2008). A tale of two countries: The Craig–Sakamoto–Matusita theorem. *Journal of Statistical Planning and Inference, 138*, 3419–3428.

Olkin, I. (1997). A determinantal proof of the Craig–Sakamoto theorem. *Linear Algebra and its Applications, 264*, 217–223.

Poirier, D. J. (1995). *Intermediate statistics and econometrics*. Cambridge, MA: MIT Press.

Rao, C. R., & Mitra, S. K. (1971). *Generalized inverse of matrices and its applications*. New York: Wiley.

Reid, J. G., & Driscoll, M. F. (1988). An accessible proof of Craig's theorem in the noncentral case. *The American Statistician, 42*, 139–142.

Taussky, O. (1958). On a matrix theorem of A.T. Craig and H. Hotelling. *Indagationes Mathematicae, 20*, 139–141.

Zhang, J., & Yi, J. (2012). A simple proof of the generalized Craig–Sakamoto theorem. *Linear Algebra and its Applications, 437*, 781–782.

A Note of Appreciation: High Standards with Heart

Beatrix Dart

This Festschrift honours Siegfried Heiler's distinguished career in statistics on the occasion of his 75th birthday. Since receiving his doctorate from the University of Tübingen in 1967, Siegfried has made outstanding contributions to the field of time series analysis over the past four decades. What impresses is his keen sense of bringing together topics that have empirical relevance, but continue to push the theoretical envelope. One of the stellar examples would be the Berlin Method (Berliner Verfahren), which has been used by the German Federal Statistical Office for their empirical analysis.

Siegfried's students know him to be generous, involved, supportive and demanding. He has an amazing ability to see where ideas, papers, and literatures fit into the big pictures. His career communicates not only his commitment to high standards and relevance but also his commitment to people. Siegfried's generosity and intellect have touched our lives profoundly.

The collection of papers in this volume reflect Siegfried's research interests and openness to new ideas, since they have all been produced by scholars who were either trained by him, or who worked with him on one project or another.

We hope the readership will enjoy the contributions. We are also grateful to the co-editors, Jan Beran, Yuanhua Feng, and Hartmut Hebbel, for making this Festschrift possible.

Happy Birthday, Siegfried!

B. Dart (✉)
Rotman School of Management, University of Toronto, 105 St. George St., Toronto, Canada, M5S 3E1
e-mail: bdart@rotman.utoronto.ca

J. Beran et al. (eds.), *Empirical Economic and Financial Research*,
Advanced Studies in Theoretical and Applied Econometrics 48,
DOI 10.1007/978-3-319-03122-4

MIX
Papier aus verantwortungsvollen Quellen
Paper from responsible sources
FSC® C105338

If you have any concerns about our products,
you can contact us on
ProductSafety@springernature.com

In case Publisher is established outside the EU,
the EU authorized representative is:
Springer Nature Customer Service Center GmbH
Europaplatz 3, 69115 Heidelberg, Germany

Printed by Libri Plureos GmbH
in Hamburg, Germany